Wulf Barsch, "The Balcony," oil on canvas, 72" by 54". Used by permission of the artist.

*Essays in Honor of Hugh W. Nibley
on the Occasion of His Eightieth Birthday
27 March 1990*

BY STUDY AND
ALSO BY FAITH
VOLUME 1

*Edited by
John M. Lundquist
Stephen D. Ricks*

Deseret Book Company
Salt Lake City, Utah
and
Foundation for Ancient Research and Mormon Studies
Provo, Utah

Library of Congress Cataloging-in-Publication Data

By study and also by faith : essays in honor of Hugh W. Nibley on the occasion of his eightieth birthday, 27 March 1990 / edited by John M. Lundquist and Stephen D. Ricks.

    p. cm.

Includes bibliographical references.

ISBN 0-87579-339-8

1. Book of Mormon—Criticism, interpretation, etc. 2. Bible—Criticism, interpretation, etc. 3. Kingdom of God—History of doctrines. 4. Church history—Primitive and early church, ca. 30–600. 5. Mormon Church. 6. Church of Jesus Christ of Latter-day Saints. 7. Nibley, Hugh, 1910–   . I. Nibley, Hugh, 1910–   . II. Lundquist, John M. III. Ricks, Stephen D.

BX8627.B9   1990

291—dc20

89-77960
CIP

Printed in the United States of America

10   9   8   7   6   5   4   3   2

Contents

Religion and Society of Asia

Classics

Key to Abbreviations

CIL	Corpus Inscriptionum Latinorum
CSEL	Corpus Scriptorum Ecclesiasticorum Latinorum
CWHN	*Collected Works of Hugh Nibley*
HC	*History of the Church*
KJV	King James Version of the Bible
JD	*Journal of Discourses*
M	Mishnah
PG	J.-P. Migne, *Patrologiae Cursus Completus . . . Series Graeca* (Paris: Migne, 1857–66), 161 vols.
PL	J.-P. Migne, *Patrologiae Cursus Completus . . . Series Latina* (Paris: Migne, 1844–64), 221 vols.
RSV	Revised Standard Version of the Bible
T	Tosefta
TB	Babylonian Talmud
TY	Talmud Yerushalmi (Jerusalem Talmud)

Foreword

And as all have not faith, seek ye diligently and teach one another words of wisdom; yea, seek ye out of the best books words of wisdom; seek learning, even by study and also by faith. (Doctrine and Covenants 88:118.)

Rabban Gamaliel says: Provide thyself with a teacher, and eschew doubtful matters, and tithe not overmuch by guesswork. (*The Living Talmud,* tr. Judah Goldin [New York: New American Library, 1957], 72.)

Some years ago, I was teaching seminary in the Church Educational System. I had already come under the influence of Hugh Nibley and had largely set my life's course based on his example. Above all else, I considered him to be a great and inspiring teacher, the very best teacher I had ever known. During that period, I would occasionally have good-natured discussions with my seminary coordinator about the characteristics and qualities of a great teacher. At that time, there was a book that was widely used by seminary teachers to improve themselves as teachers. It was a book that emphasized "techniques," including flashy, cute, clever approaches to teaching, many of which seemed to me little more than shallow gimmicks meant to keep young peoples' attention for a few minutes at a time. I presented Nibley as my example of a great teacher, one who by the dynamic and compelling power of his intellect, combined with humility and spiritual greatness, was able to lead people of all ages to deeper understanding and commitment. I remember the supervisor granting that Dr. Nibley was a great scholar, but, he would say, "Nibley's no teacher!" We now have many years of Hugh Nibley's enormous influence on thousands of people at Brigham Young University, throughout the Church, and around the world to demonstrate, if demonstration is still needed, his greatness as a teacher.

This *Festschrift*, or collection of essays, in honor of Hugh Nibley had its genesis in a class in Near Eastern Archaeology that I taught for the Department of Anthropology at Brigham Young University during the Winter Semester of 1984. I brought up the subject one day in class with my students, many of whom were also "Nibleyites." Although I expressed to them my enthusiasm for the project, still I was skeptical about being able to actually bring it off, realizing as I did that such a *Festschrift* would be no ordinary scholarly undertaking and that it would challenge all participants to make it equal to its subject. After class one day, several of my students encouraged me to persist with the plan, and several also offered their assistance.

With this encouragement, I sent a proposal to the directors of the Brigham Young University Religious Studies Center (the most likely publishers) on February 7, 1984. One of the directors, S. Kent Brown, answered my proposal on March 16, stating that the directors had accepted the project and had appointed me its editor. Early in April, I sent Brown a tentative list of contributors, which he circulated among the other directors. In the meantime, I was consulting with colleagues at Brigham Young University and elsewhere as I prepared the first list of potential contributors. This list, consisting of thirty-four names, was completed in May 1984. Of the forty-five authors represented in the present two volumes, twenty-seven were on the first list. An additional seven papers were added to this *Festschrift* from "Tinkling Cymbals, Essays in Honor of Hugh Nibley," which were papers delivered in Provo,

Utah, on the occasion of Nibley's sixty-fifth birthday in 1975, and were issued in typescript. These papers include those by Robert K. Thomas, Richard F. Haglund, Jr., C. Terry Warner and Arthur Henry King, Gordon C. Thomasson, John A. Tvedtnes, "The Melchizedek Material in Alma 13:13–19" by John W. Welch, and the bibliography by Louis Midgley, subsequently expanded and revised. An additional eight papers were brought into the volume as a result of the contacts of my good friend, colleague, and Nibley *Festschrift* coeditor Professor Stephen D. Ricks; and four more were added as a result of my contacts after coming to New York City. The resulting total is forty-seven papers contributed by forty-five authors, as well as a plate contributed by the noted artist Wulf Barsch, resulting in this massive and impressive two-volume work.

The original target date for the receipt of manuscripts was April 4, 1985. The final product will thus have been published very close to five years after that target date, six years after the first potential contributors were contacted. And so my original fears about the monumental nature of this undertaking were justified. And yet, after all of the difficulties, the delays, even the times when it appeared that the project might not be concluded, it is one of the greatest joys of my life to see it appear. During the six years since the inception of the idea, many people have made significant contributions to the success of the final product. There have been two assistant directors of publications of the Religious Studies Center at Brigham Young University, Professors S. Kent Brown and Charles D. Tate, Jr., who gave very considerable time, encouragement, and editorial skill and advice during their respective tenures in that position. The same holds true for their secretary, Charlotte Pollard. And from the very beginning, Professor Robert J. Matthews, dean of religious instruction at Brigham Young University and director of the Religious Studies Center, supported the project and gave his encouragement. Others who have lent invaluable assistance include Johnny Bahbah, Lyle Fletcher, Diane D. Gonzalez, Rebecca Ann Harrison, Cie Mason-Christian, Adam Lamoreaux, Susan Ullman Lamoreaux, Art Pollard, Dennis Ray Thompson, and James V. Tredway. Particular thanks are due to Shirley Smith Ricks, whose timely assistance during the final stages of the production of these volumes has prevented further delays in their completion. Thanks are also due to Deseret Book Company, especially Jack M. Lyon, Patricia J. Parkinson, Patti L. Taylor, Kent Ware, and Emily Watts, for assistance in seeing this project through to completion.

In the spring of 1989, the responsibility for the publication of the *Festschrift* was transferred from the Religious Studies Center to the Foundation for Ancient Research and Mormon Studies (F.A.R.M.S.) and Deseret Book Company. The founder and current member of the board of directors of F.A.R.M.S., Professor John W. Welch, and F.A.R.M.S. president, Professor Stephen D. Ricks, have been the main figures, who, from the spring of 1989 on, ensured and guaranteed that the accumulated papers would be published intact and suggested that they be published in a format conformable to the *Collected Works of Hugh Nibley*. We owe them, as well as F.A.R.M.S., an inestimable debt of gratitude for their support of this project, and indeed for the magnificent publication of the *Collected Works of Hugh Nibley*.

It was in the fall semester of 1959 that I walked into a Brigham Young University history course entitled "Early Oriental History," taught by Hugh Nibley. I wish that every young student could have the experience that I still recall so vividly, of being dazzled, inspired, awestruck, challenged, and stretched to the very limits of my ability and beyond. Each lecture was a fabulous new journey into what was for me uncharted territory. But Nibley himself was leading the way, reading from books and journal articles that he had just discovered the day or the hour before class, sharing with us his unbridled excitement and enthusiasm for the ancient Near Eastern cultures, teaching us the process of scholarship—how theories change, how weak and human scholars are, and instilling in us a love for languages. He always brought us to the very leading edge of current scholarship. He didn't patronize us or pander to us; in his own way he treated us as equals and assumed that we had the same interests, the same enthusiasms, and the same capacity for work that he had. I still have my notes for the class, as well as my exam booklets. Although Nibley will probably be horrified to read this, I still refer to those notes and use them in my own teaching. Although some of the facts and dates in them may be outdated, the underlying ideas are not, and indeed I have been amused to note in recent years that some of Nibley's main ideas from those years, which in the meantime went out of fashion, have now come back into fashion, are again current, and, most important, are being validated by the newest discoveries from archaeological excavation in the Soviet Union and Central Asia!

There were always those who quibbled over Nibley's footnotes, a complaint that I still hear. My experience is that his footnotes, by which I mean the underlying foundation of his scholarship, have withstood the test of time remarkably well. But more important to me, I have always felt that many scholarly careers could be built on his footnotes, by which I mean following his leads, pursuing topics that he touched on briefly, brilliantly pointing the way that he himself did not take at that time but that would be fruitful for someone else to pursue. And it is a tribute to him that many of the papers included in this *Festschrift* are based on his footnotes, so to speak, representing scholarship that the author learned from Nibley, a hint that one might have found in one of his books or articles and followed up on, or a subject that the writer learned at Nibley's feet. We, the editors, feel that every major subject that Dr. Nibley has encompassed in his vast learning and scholarly production is represented here by at least one article, or by an outstanding expert in that field. The table of contents lists papers on subject areas that include the Bible and the ancient Near East, early and Eastern Christianity and formative Judaism, aspects of kingship and the sacred, the religion and society of Asia, the Classics, scriptures of the Latter-day Saints, and modern themes dealing with religion, literature, and society. We are especially proud of the many papers included here by world-renowned scholars, including Drs. Aziz Atiya (now regrettably deceased), James Charlesworth, Cyrus Gordon, Jacob Milgrom, Jacob Neusner, and Raphael Patai, whose papers attest to the wide respect in which Dr. Nibley's work, as well as his personal example, is held. Finally, depending on how one counts these things, we can say that there are represented in the volumes the second or the third generations of Nibley's influence. As editors and publishers, we wish to state that the opinions cited in the various articles are those of the authors and do not necessarily coincide with those of our own.

> Five possessions did the Holy One, blessed be he, set aside for himself in this world, to wit: Torah, one possession; the Heavens and the Earth, another possession; Abraham, another possession; Israel, another possession; the Temple, another possession. (*The Living Talmud*, 238.)

John M. Lundquist
New York City
November 21, 1989

Hugh Winder Nibley:
Bibliography and Register

Compiled by Louis Midgley
Brigham Young University, Provo, Utah

The Collected Works of Hugh Nibley are currently being published by Deseret Book and the Foundation for Ancient Research and Mormon Studies. Nine volumes of this series have been published to date. Its editors have been especially helpful in assembling this bibliography, which remains, however, incomplete and tentative, even though efforts have been made to locate, assemble, and register, as fully and accurately as possible, Nibley's published and unpublished works. The materials to be included in *The Collected Works of Hugh Nibley* are being carefully checked and editorially revised. That process includes exhaustive footnote checking and, where necessary, the correction of both quoted materials and citations. As approved or requested by Nibley, slight adjustments in context are being made. Nibley and his wife Phyllis read and approve the galleys.

In addition to the nine volumes registered in this bibliography, additional volumes are nearing publication, are under preparation, or are projected. These will include at least the following:

(A) a reformatted edition of *The Message of the Joseph Smith Papyri: An Egyptian Endowment* (to be edited by Stephen D. Ricks);

(B) a volume on Joseph Smith, tentatively entitled *Defending the Joseph Smith Story with Scholarship and Satire,* which will contain *No Ma'am, That's Not History; Sounding Brass; The Myth Makers;* and other related items (to be edited by David J. Whittaker);

(C) a new edition of *Abraham in Egypt* (to be edited by Gary P. Gillum);

(D) a volume containing a collection of Nibley's contributions to the discussion of the Pearl of Great Price (to be edited by Gary P. Gillum);

(E) a volume or volumes containing Nibley's work on ancient history, including his treatments of ancient statecraft, rhetoric, religion, and competing claims to wisdom (to be edited by Stephen D. Ricks);

(F) a volume containing Nibley's personal items such as letters, interviews, autobiographical materials, poems, and so forth;

(G) a volume on the hypocephalus [Facsimile No. 2 in the Pearl of Great Price];

(H) a volume containing a transcript of lectures given by Nibley in a class he taught on the Pearl of Great Price, with citations supplied (to be edited by Stephen E. Robinson);

(I) a volume to be titled *"Beyond the Ignorant Present": Temple and Cosmos* (to be edited by Don E. Norton);

(J) a volume to be titled *The Vital Three: Environment, Politics, and Education* (to be edited by Don E. Norton); and

(K) a volume containing a comprehensive, annotated register of his works, as well as a comprehensive index (to be edited by Gary P. Gillum).

Some additional volumes may be necessary to conclude the project. An effort has been made to indicate exactly where it is currently anticipated that the items registered in this bibliography, which are being published or reprinted, are to appear in the collected works.

Anyone possessing or knowing of correspondence by, with, or concerning Hugh Nibley, or other materials such as unpublished manuscripts, transcripts of addresses, or sound recordings of courses, public addresses, lessons, and lectures is invited to contact either Gary P. Gillum, Ancient Studies Archivist handling Nibley materials for the Harold B. Lee Library at Brigham Young University, or the compiler of this bibliography.

Valuable assistance in preparing this bibliography was provided in various ways by John Gee, Gary P. Gillum, Alan Goff, Fran Clark Hafen, Terry Jeffress, Gary F. Novak, Shirley Smith Ricks, Robert F. Smith, James V. Tredway, Melinda Vail, and John W. Welch, though they are, of course, not responsible for any of its deficiencies. The compiler is responsible for the annotations.

ABBREVIATIONS

Professional Periodicals

APSR	*The American Political Science Review*
BYUS	*Brigham Young University Studies*
CJ	*The Classical Journal*
CH	*Church History*
DJMT	*Dialogue: A Journal of Mormon Thought*
JQR	*Jewish Quarterly Review*
RQ	*Revue de Qumran*
TH	*The Historian*
VC	*Vigiliae Christianae*
WS	*Western Speech*
WPQ	*Western Political Quarterly*

Periodicals Published by The Church of Jesus Christ of Latter-day Saints

IE	*The Improvement Era*
MS	*Millennial Star*
NE	*The New Era*
Ens	*Ensign*
Ins	*The Instructor*

Other Abbreviations

BYU	Brigham Young University
CWHN	*The Collected Works of Hugh Nibley*
F.A.R.M.S.	Foundation for Ancient Research and Mormon Studies
RSC	Religious Studies Center, at Brigham Young University
s.s.	single space
d.s.	double space

CATEGORIES OF REGISTERED MATERIALS

Books, monographs, and pamphlets
Articles in professional publications
Articles in nonprofessional publications
Book reviews
Prefaces
Introductions to books
Manuscripts of addresses
Duplicated papers
Open letters (or widely circulated correspondence)
Articles in newspapers
Transcripts of talks or courses
Interviews
Secondary materials concerning Nibley

PUBLICATIONS

1926

• "Of Birthdays." *IE* 29/8 (June 1926): 743.
A poem, written when Nibley was 16, for his grandmother.
To be included in F of the *CWHN*.

• "The Freight Train." *Lyric West* 5/5 (1926): 171.
To be included in the F of the *CWHN*.

1927

• "Two Stars." In *Anthology of Student Verse, for 1925,* edited by Snow Longley. Los Angeles: Los Angeles High School, 1927. 10–12. To be included in F of the *CWHN.*

1939

• "The Roman Games as a Survival of an Archaic Year-Cult." Ph.D. diss., University of California, Berkeley, 1939. 249p.; bibliography: 236–49.

Nibley's dissertation was completed and approved by December 1938. The library at the University of California at Berkeley catalogued the dissertation in early 1939.

1942

• "New Light on Scaliger." *CJ* 37/5 (February 1942): 291–95. To be included in E of the *CWHN.*

1945

• "Basic Arabic Root System." Compiled in Compiegne, France [at the end of World War II] using J. G. Mava, *Arabic-English Dictionary for the Use of Students* (Beirut: Catholic University Press, 1921). 32p., s.s., unpublished handwritten manuscript.

• "Sparsiones." *CJ* 40/9 (June 1945): 515–43. To be included in E of the *CWHN.*

1946

• *No Ma'am, That's Not History: A Brief Review of Mrs. Brodie's Reluctant Vindication of a Prophet She Seeks to Expose.* Salt Lake City: Bookcraft, 1946. 62p. [Subsequently reissued without changes at various times.]

This is a short, witty reply to Fawn M. Brodie's *No Man Knows My History: The Life of Joseph Smith, the Mormon Prophet,* 2d ed., rev. and enlarged (New York: Knopf, 1945; 1971). Nibley's response to Brodie signaled to the Saints that there was still room for a nonnaturalistic account of Joseph Smith's prophetic claims and revelations. Cultural Mormons who celebrated a new enlightenment with the appearance of Brodie's treatment of Joseph Smith and the Book of Mormon were often troubled by what they considered Nibley's flippant response to Brodie. Opposition to his views has also been a common feature of the secular, revisionist element in the so-called New Mormon History, which has tended to see in Brodie's account of Joseph Smith the beginning or basic outline of an acceptable naturalistic account of

Mormon things. Commenting on the reception of Fawn Brodie's biography of Joseph Smith, Thomas G. Alexander claims that "perhaps no book in recent years has evinced more comment." He then contrasted "the scholarly Marvin Hill's" two reviews of Brodie's biography of Joseph Smith (*DJMT* 7/4 [Winter 1972]: 72–85; *CH* 43/1 [March 1974]: 78–96) with "the rather outrageous Hugh Nibley's *No Ma'am That's Not History.* . . . " See Thomas G. Alexander, "The Place of Joseph Smith in the Development of American Religion: A Historiographical Inquiry," *Journal of Mormon History* 5 (1978): 3–17, at 10, n. 9.

The bibliographer-historian Dale L. Morgan, who provided Fawn Brodie with considerable assistance with both the contents and style of her biography of Joseph Smith, described Nibley's pamphlet as "something of a slapstick performance, and the irony of it is, Nibley . . . is much more intoxicated with his own language than you, the 'glib English major,' are." See Morgan's letter to Fawn Brodie, dated June 9, 1946, in *Dale Morgan on Early Mormonism: Correspondence & A New History,* edited by John P. Walker (Salt Lake City: Signature Press, 1986), 125. Tertius Chandler, a dilettantish polymath and friend of Morgan, included a polemic against Nibley's pamphlet in *Chandler's Half-Encyclopedia* ([Dedham, MA]: privately printed, 1956), 662–79. (The entry is entitled "The Controversy over Joseph Smith" and is dated July 14, 1952; it was extended to include other LDS responses to Brodie's biography of Joseph Smith in 'The Controversy over Joseph Smith — Part II," dated September 1, 1952, 675–79). BYU Special Collections has a primitive typescript version of Chandler's "The Controversy over Joseph Smith," dated September 1, 1952, 22p.

To be included in B of the *CWHN.*

1948

• Review of *Our Book of Mormon,* by Sidney B. Sperry. *IE* 51/1 (January 1948): 42.

• "The Book of Mormon as a Mirror of the East." *IE* 51/4 (April 1948): 202–4, 249–51. Reprinted, without illustrations, in the *IE* 73/11 (November 1970): 115–20, 122–25.

The earliest version of Nibley's theory that a portion of the meaning and the historical authenticity of the Book of Mormon can be uncovered and tested by drawing upon the literary remains of the Near East. This essay contains Nibley's initial speculation on possible links between Book of Mormon names and Egyptian etymologies. The series drew the attention of Wesley Walters, who drafted a statement concerning its contents, a statement which was signed by William F.

Albright in 1949. Since that time the Reverend Walters has been an anti-Mormon polemicist.

Essentially included in *Lehi in the Desert; The World of the Jaredites; There Were Jaredites*, vol. 5 of the *CWHN* (Salt Lake City: Deseret Book and F.A.R.M.S., 1988), 25–42.

• "Baptism for the Dead in Ancient Times." A series of articles in the *IE*.

1. "Part I." 51/12 (December 1948): 786–88, 836–38.

1949

• "Baptism for the Dead in Ancient Times." A series of articles in the *IE*, continued.

2. "Part II." 52/1 (January 1949): 24–26, 60.
3. "Part III." 52/2 (February 1949): 90–91, 109–10, 112.
4. "Part IV." 52/3 (March 1949): 146–48, 180–83.
5. "The Dilemma: Part V — Conclusion." 52/4 (April 1949): 212–14.

Reprinted in *Mormonism and Early Christianity*, vol. 4 of the *CWHN* (Salt Lake City: Deseret Book Company and F.A.R.M.S., 1987), 100–167.

Portions of Nibley's position on baptism for the dead were briefly described and then rejected by Bernard M. Foschini, in " 'Those Who Are Baptized for the Dead,' I Cor. 15:29," *Catholic Biblical Quarterly* 13/1 (1951): 52–55, 70–73. Foschini offered a treatment of the language used by Paul and tried to explain away his apparent reference to baptism for the dead in a 96–page series appearing in five numbers of the *Catholic Biblical Quarterly* 12/3, 4 (July, October 1950): 260–76, 379–88; 13/1, 2, 3 (January, April, July 1951): 46–79, 172–98, 278–83.

• "The Arrow, the Hunter, and the State." *WPQ* 2/3 (1949): 328–44.

A study of the role of the marked arrow and related practices, institutions, and beliefs in founding and maintaining ancient regimes.

To be included in E of the *CWHN*.

1950

• "Lehi in the Desert." A series of articles in the *IE*.

1. "Part I." 53/1 (January 1950): 14–16, 66–72.
2. "Part II." 53/2 (February 1950): 102–4, 155–59.
3. "Part III." 53/3 (March 1950): 200–202, 222, 225–26, 229–30.
4. "Part IV." 53/4 (April 1950): 276–77, 320–26.
5. "Part V." 53/5 (May 1950): 382–84, 448–49.
6. "Part VI." 53/6 (June 1950): 486–87, 516–19.
7. "Part VII." 53/7 (July 1950): 566–67, 587–88.

8. "Part VIII." 53/8 (August 1950): 640–42, 670.

9. "Part IX." 53/9 (September 1950): 706–8, 744.

10. "Part X." 53/10 (October 1950): 804–6, 824, 826, 828, 830.

Reprinted, without illustrations, as the first half of *Lehi in the Desert and the World of the Jaredites* (1952); and reprinted, with illustrations, in *Lehi in the Desert; The World of the Jaredites; There Were Jaredites*, vol. 5 of the *CWHN* (Salt Lake City: Deseret Book and F.A.R.M.S., 1988), 1–149.

• "The Christmas Quest." *MS* 112/1 (January 1950): 4–5.

Nibley briefly looked into the question of whether it is possible that the bewildering profusion of Christmas observances might contain, among other things, a latent longing for the gospel of Jesus Christ.

To be included in F of the *CWHN*.

1951

• Review of *The Ancient World*, by Joseph W. Swain. *TH* 13/1 (Spring 1951): 79–81.

To be included in E of the *CWHN*.

• "The Hierocentric State." *WPQ* 4/2 (1951): 226–53.

A study of the role of ritual centers and kingship in ancient regimes. To be included in E of the *CWHN*.

• "The World of the Jaredites." A series of articles in the *IE*.

These articles were written in the form of expository letters to a fictitious "Professor F."

1. "Part I." 54/9 (September 1951): 628–30, 673–75.

2. "Part II." 54/10 (October 1951): 704–6, 752–55.

3. "Part III." 54/11 (November 1951): 786–87, 833–35.

4. "Part IV." 54/12 (December 1951): 862–63, 946–47.

1952

• "The World of the Jaredites." A series of articles in the *IE*, continued.

5. "Part V." 55/1 (January 1952): 22–24.

6. "Part VI." 55/2 (February 1952): 92–94, 98, 100, 102, 104–5.

7. "Part VII." 55/3 (March 1952): 162–65, 167–68.

8. "Part VIII." 55/4 (April 1952): 236–38, 258, 260–65.

9. "Part IX." 55/5 (May 1952): 316–18, 340, 342, 344, 346.

10. "Part X." 55/6 (June 1952): 398–99, 462–64.

11. "Conclusion." 55/7 (July 1952): 510, 550.

Reprinted as the second half of *Lehi in the Desert and the World of the Jaredites* (1952); and reprinted in *Lehi in the Desert; The World of the*

Jaredites; There Were Jaredites, vol. 5 of the *CWHN* (Salt Lake City: Deseret Book and F.A.R.M.S., 1988), 151–282.

• Review of *History of Syria: Including Lebanon and Palestine*, by Philip K. Hitti. *WPQ* 5/2 (June 1952): 312–13.
To be included in E of the *CWHN*.

• Review of *Near Eastern Culture and Society: A Symposium on the Meeting of East and West*, edited by T. Cuyler Young. *WPQ* 5/2 (June 1952): 315–16.
To be included in E of the *CWHN*.

• *Lehi in the Desert and the World of the Jaredites*. Salt Lake City: Bookcraft, 1952. viii, 272p. [The bulk of these materials appeared in the *IE* between 1950 and 1952. The original illustrations and some other materials were not included in the book.]
Contents:
Foreword: by John A. Widtsoe
Lehi in the Desert
    I. The Troubled Orient
    II. Men of the East
    III. Into the Desert
    IV. Desert Ways and Places
    V. The City and the Sand
    VI. Lehi the Winner
The World of the Jaredites
    I. A Twilight World
    II. Departure
    III. Jared on the Steppes
    IV. Jaredite Culture: Splendor and Shame
    V. They Take up the Sword
    VI. A Permanent Heritage
Appendix
    I. East Coast or West Coast?
    II. How Far to Cumorah?
Reprinted in 1980, with an index prepared by Gary P. Gillum, and again in 1987, with corrections, full indexing, and with the original illustrations restored, as the first and second parts of *Lehi in the Desert; The World of the Jaredites; There Were Jaredites*, vol. 5 of the *CWHN* (Salt Lake City: Deseret Book and F.A.R.M.S., 1988), 1–282.

• "Questions on Authority and Passages for Discussion (The Apostasy)." 23p. mimeographed class handout, ca. 1952.
A compendium of passages from the New Testament, from the early fathers of the Church, and from historians of Christian antiquity

on the question of the apostasy. The issues raised in this handout were eventually dealt with systematically in the series that appeared in the *IE* between January and December of 1955 called "The Way of the Church," and also in the essay entitled "The Passing of the Church," *CH* 30/2 (June 1961): 131–54; reprinted in *When the Lights Went Out* (1970), 1–32; and in "The Passing of the Church: Forty Variations on an Unpopular Theme," *BYUS* 16/1 (Autumn 1975): 135–64; and in *Mormonism and Early Christianity*, vol. 4 of the *CWHN* (Salt Lake City: Deseret Book and F.A.R.M.S., 1987), 209–322.

1953

• "The Unsolved Loyalty Problem: Our Western Heritage." *WPQ* 6/4 (1953): 631–57.

An examination of the problem of loyalty in the fourth century, with obvious significance for our own time.

To be included in E of the *CWHN*.

• "The Stick of Judah and the Stick of Joseph." A series of articles in the *IE*.

An examination of the meaning of Ezekiel 37 in relation to the use of tally sticks.

1. "I: The Doctors Disagree." 56/1 (January 1953): 16–17, 38–41.

2. "II: What Were the Sticks?" 56/2 (February 1953): 90–91, 123–27.

3. "Part III." 56/3 (March 1953): 150–52, 191–95.

4. "Part IV." 56/4 (April 1953): 250, 267.

5. "Conclusion." 56/5 (May 1953): 331–32, 334, 336, 338, 341, 343, 345.

[Cf. Lesson (or chapter) XXIV in *An Approach to the Book of Mormon* (1957/1964); and "The Arrow, the Hunter, and the State," *WPQ* 2/3 (1949): 328–44.]

Reprinted in *The Prophetic Book of Mormon*, vol. 8 of the *CWHN* (Salt Lake City: Deseret Book and F.A.R.M.S., 1989), 1–48.

• "Columbus and Revelation," *Ins* 88/10 (October 1953): 319–20.

Reprinted in *The Prophetic Book of Mormon*, vol. 8 of the *CWHN* (Salt Lake City: Deseret Book and F.A.R.M.S., 1989), 49–53.

• "New Approaches to Book of Mormon Study." A series of articles in the *IE*.

1. "Part I: Some Standard Tests." 56/11 (November 1953): 830–31, 859–62.

2. "Part II: Some Standard Tests." 56/12 (December 1953): 919, 1003.

1954

• "New Approaches to Book of Mormon Study." A series of articles in the *IE*, continued.

3. "Part 3." 57/1 (January 1954): 30–32, 41.
4. "Part 4." 57/2 (February 1954): 88–89, 125–26.
5. "Part 5." 57/3 (March 1954): 148–50, 170.
6. "Part 6." 57/4 (April 1954): 232–33, 246, 248–50, 252.
7. "Part 7." 57/5 (May 1954): 308–9, 326, 330.
8. "Part 8." 57/6 (June 1954): 389, 447–48, 450–51.
9. "Conclusion." 57/7 (July 1954): 506–7, 521.

Reprinted in *The Prophetic Book of Mormon*, vol. 8 of the *CWHN* (Salt Lake City: Deseret Book and F.A.R.M.S., 1989), 54–126.

• *Time Vindicates the Prophets*. Salt Lake City: The Church of Jesus Christ of Latter-day Saints, 1954. [Published as 31 separate pamphlets (misnumbered so that no part 20 was presented). These were addresses given over radio station KSL at 9:00 P.M. on the regular Sunday Evening Program of The Church of Jesus Christ of Latter-day Saints.]

1. "How Will It Be When None More Saith 'I Saw'?" March 7, 3p.
2. "A Prophet's Reward." March 14, 4p.
3. "Prophets and Scholars." March 21, 3p.
4. "The Prophets and the Scriptures." March 28, 3p.
5. "Prophecy and Tradition." April 11, 3p.
6. "Easter and the Prophets." April 18, 4p.
7. "Prophecy and Office." April 25, 4p.
8. "Prophets and Crisis." May 2, 4p.
9. "Prophets and Preachers." May 9, 4p.
10. "Prophets and Philosophers." May 16, 4p.
11. "Prophets and Creeds." May 23, 4p.
12. "Two Ways to Remember the Dead." May 30, 4p.
13. "The Prophets and the Plan of Life." June 6, 4p.
14. "The Prophets and the Search for God." June 20, 4p.
15. "Prophets and Martyrs." June 27, 4p.
16. "The Ancient Law of Liberty." July 4, 4p.
17. "Prophets and Gnostics." July 11, 4p.
18. "The Schools and the Prophets." July 18, 4p.
19. "A Prophetic Event." July 25, 4p.
21. "St. Augustine and the Great Transition." August 1, 4p.
22. "A Substitute for Revelation." August 8, 4p.
23. "Prophets and Mystics." August 15, 4p.
24. "Rhetoric and Revelation." August 22, 4p.
25. "Prophets and Miracles." August 29, 4p.
26. "The Book of Mormon as a Witness." September 5, 4p.
27. "Prophets and Reformers." September 12, 4p.
28. "The Prophets and the Open Mind." September 19, 4p.
29. "Prophets and Ritual." September 26, 3p.

30. "The Church of the Prophets." October 10, 4p.

31. "Prophets and Glad Tidings." October 17, 4p.

• *The World and the Prophets*. Salt Lake City: Deseret Book, 1954. 250p. [This is a collection of addresses originally given over station KSL on the Sunday Evening Program at 9:00 P.M. from March to October 1954.]

Contents (the number of the corresponding radio address is given in parentheses):

1. "How Will It Be When None More Saith 'I Saw'?" (1)
2. "A Prophet's Reward" (2)
3. "Prophets and Preachers" (9)
4. "Prophets and Scholars" (3)
5. "Prophets and Philosophers" (10)
6. "Prophets and Creeds" (11)
7. "Prophets and the Search for God" (14)
8. "Prophets and Gnostics" (17)
9. "The Schools and the Prophets" (18)
10. "St. Augustine and the Great Transition" (21)
11. "A Substitute for Revelation" (22)
12. "Prophets and Mystics" (23)
13. "Rhetoric and Revelation" (24)
14. "Prophets and Reformers" (27)
15. "The Prophets and the Open Mind" (28)
16. "Prophets and Miracles" (25)
17. "Prophets and Ritual" (29)
18. "Faster and the Prophets" (6)
19. "Two Ways to Remember the Dead" (12)
20. "Prophets and Martyrs" (15)
21. "The Ancient Law of Liberty" (16)
22. "Prophets and Crisis" (8)
23. "The Prophets and the Scriptures" (4)
24. "The Book of Mormon as a Witness" (26)
25. "Prophecy and Tradition" (5)
26. "The Prophets and the Plan of Life" (13)
27. "A Prophetic Event" (19)
28. "Prophecy and Office" (7)
29. "What Makes a True Church" (30)
30. "Prophets and Glad Tidings" (31)

Index

Reprinted as 2d "enlarged ed." in 1962, and also in a 3d ed., with additions and corrections, as *The World and the Prophets*, vol. 3 of the *CWHN* (Salt Lake City: Deseret Book and F.A.R.M.S., 1987), xii, 333p.

In addition, "Two Ways to Remember the Dead" is reprinted in *Understanding Death*, edited by Brent Barlow (Salt Lake City: Deseret Book, 1979), 189–96.

1955

• "Do Religion and History Conflict?" In *Great Issues Forum*, Series 2: Religion, No. 5 (Salt Lake City: University of Utah, Extension Division, 1955), 22–39.

This is the published version of the first of several exchanges between Nibley and Sterling M. McMurrin. The exchange was held on March 23, 1955, under the sponsorship of the Department of Philosophy at the University of Utah. McMurrin's address, "Religion and the Denial of History," is published on pp. 5–21, although Nibley spoke first.

To be included in I of the *CWHN*.

• "The Way of the Church." A series of articles in three parts in the *IE*. [This series was to have been continued but was actually abandoned. The materials were eventually used in "The Passing of the Church," *CH* 30/2 (June 1961): 131–54; reprinted in *When the Lights Went Out* (1970), 1–32; in *BYUS* 16/1 (Autumn 1975): 139–64; and in *Mormonism and Early Christianity*, vol. 4 of the *CWHN* (Salt Lake City: Deseret Book and F.A.R.M.S., 1987), 209–322.]

"The Way of the Church—I":

1. "Controlling the Past (A Consideration of Methods)." 58/1 (January 1955): 20–22, 44–45.

2. "Controlling the Past." 58/2 (February 1955): 86–87, 104, 106–7.

3. "Controlling the Past: Part III." 58/3 (March 1955): 152–54, 166, 168.

4. "Controlling the Past: Part IV." 58/4 (April 1955): 230–32, 258, 260–61.

5. "Controlling the Past: Part V." 58/5 (May 1955): 306–8, 364–66.

6. "Controlling the Past: Part VI." 58/6 (June 1955): 384–86, 455–56.

"The Way of the Church—II":

7. "Two Views of Church History." 58/7 (July 1955): 502–4, 538.

8. "Two Views of Church History: Part II." 58/8 (August 1955): 570–71, 599–600, 602–6.

9. "Two Views of Church History: Part III." 58/9 (September 1955): 650–53.

10. "Two Views of Church History: Part IV." 58/10 (October 1955): 708–10.

"The Way of the Church—III":

11. "The Apocalyptic Background, I: The Eschatological Dilemma." 58/11 (November 1955): 817, 835–38, 840–41.

12. "The Apocalyptic Background, II: The Eschatological Dilemma." 58/12 (December 1955): 902–3, 968.

1956

• "Victoriosa Loquacitas: The Rise of Rhetoric and the Decline of Everything Else." *WS* 20/2 (Spring 1956): 57–82.

A study of the rhetoric of the second Sophistic movement and its influence on politics and culture generally, with obvious significance for our own time because of the remarkable parallel developments in the current world of politics, business, and education.

To be included in E of the *CWHN*.

• Review of *The Torment of Secrecy: The Background and Consequences of American Security Policies*, by Edward A. Shils. *APSR* 50/3 (September 1956): 887–88.

To be included in E of the *CWHN*.

• "More Voices from the Dust." *Ins* 91/3 (March 1956): 71–72, 74.

Some brief references to the Dead Sea Scrolls.

Reprinted in *Old Testament and Related Studies*, vol. 1 of the *CWHN* (Salt Lake City: Deseret Book and F.A.R.M.S., 1986), 239–44.

• "Historicity and the Bible." Typed transcript of an address given to the seminary and institute faculty at BYU on June 19, 1956.

Reprinted in *Old Testament and Related Studies*, vol. 1 of the *CWHN* (Salt Lake City: Deseret Book and F.A.R.M.S., 1986), 1–19.

• "There Were Jaredites." A series of articles in the *IE*.

1. "There Were Jaredites." 59/1 (January 1956): 30–32, 58–61.

2. "I: Egypt Revisited." 59/2 (February 1956): 88–89, 106, 108.

3. "II: Egypt Revisited." 59/3 (March 1956): 150–52, 185–87.

4. "III: Egypt Revisited." 59/4 (April 1956): 244–45, 252–54, 258.

5. "IV: Egypt Revisited." 59/5 (May 1956): 308–10, 334, 336, 338–40.

6. "V: Egypt Revisited." 59/6 (June 1956): 390–91, 460–61.

7. "The Babylonian Background, I." 59/7 (July 1956): 509–11, 514, 516.

8. "The Babylonian Background, II." 59/8 (August 1956): 566–67, 602.

9. "The Shining Stones—Continued." 59/9 (September 1956): 630–32, 672–75.

10. "Epic Milieu in the Old Testament." 59/10 (October 1956): 710–12, 745–51.

11. " 'Our Own People.' " 59/11 (November 1956): 818–19, 857–58.
12. "Our Own People—Continued." 59/12 (December 1956): 906–7.

1957

• "There Were Jaredites." A series of articles in the *IE*, continued.
13. "Our Own People—Continued." 60/1 (January 1957): 26–7, 41.
14. "Our Own People—Concluded." 60/2 (February 1957): 94–95, 122–24.

Reprinted as part three of *Lehi in the Desert; The World of the Jaredites; There Were Jaredites*, vol. 5 of the *CWHN* (Salt Lake City: Deseret Book and F.A.R.M.S., 1988), 283–454.

• *An Approach to the Book of Mormon.* Salt Lake City: Council of the Twelve Apostles of The Church of Jesus Christ of Latter-day Saints, 1957/Salt Lake City: Deseret Book, 1964. xvi, 416p. (xxii, 416p.).

This book was originally published as the lesson manual for the Melchizedek Priesthood quorums of The Church of Jesus Christ of Latter-day Saints. The 2d ed. contains a new preface by Hugh Nibley and one new chapter (entitled "Strange Ships and Shining Stones"), and it deletes the questions originally appended to each chapter; hence the pagination differs in the two editions. Reprinted as *An Approach to the Book of Mormon*, vol. 6 of the *CWHN*, 3d ed. (Salt Lake City: Deseret Book and F.A.R.M.S., 1988).

Contents:
Preface: Joseph Fielding Smith
Foreword
I. The Changing Scene
    1. Introduction
    2. A Time for Re-examination
II. Lehi's World
    3. An Auspicious Beginning
    4. Lehi as a Representative Man
III. Lehi's Affairs
    5. The Jews and the Caravan Trade
    6. Lehi and the Arabs
    7. Dealings with Egypt
IV. The Doomed City
    8. Politics in Jerusalem
    9. Escapade in Jerusalem
    10. Portrait of Laban
V. The Meaning of the Wilderness
    11. Flight into the Wilderness

An Approach to the Book of Mormon was mentioned by Marvin S. Hill in an essay entitled "The Historiography of Mormonism," *CH* 28/4 (December 1959): 418–26. Hill seems to have preferred to account for the Book of Mormon with what he called "the Smith hypothesis," which is the attempt to understand the Book of Mormon as a product of Joseph's presumably fertile imagination coupled to an unusual responsiveness to his own environment. Hill introduced his comments on Nibley's work by observing that the conflict between Gentiles and the Latter-day Saints is also evident among historians, who are "generally divided into two distinct groups, forging a cleavage of sentiment which is evident in the debates over the origin of the Book of Mormon" (418). According to Hill, the issue "of primary importance is the nature of that unique American scripture, the Book of Mormon. Acclaimed by the faithful as a sacred history of a Christian people in ancient America, the book has been labeled a fraud by non-believers." "The case for the Latter-day Saints," Hill acknowledged, "has been stated often, but with no greater sophistication than that exhibited by Hugh Nibley of Brigham Young University in his *Approach to the Book of*

Mormon (1957). He reviews the culture of the ancient Near East to find that in theme, the details of its narrative, and its use of place and proper names the Book of Mormon is authentic. He states that the marks of genuine antiquity in the record could not have been imitated by anyone in 1830. However intimate his knowledge of ancient history may be, certain difficulties exist in his argument. He cites many phenomena which seem as much American as they do ancient, and exaggerates the significance of details which are hazy or all but lacking. Invariably he handles his topic in an authoritarian fashion, never indicating that some points may be open to question" (418).

Hill's effort to show that "many phenomena," which Nibley thinks are typical of the ancient Near East, "seem as much American as they do ancient" is supported by citing pp. 140, 202–16, 339, and 348 in Nibley's book. Hill did not indicate what on those pages supports his assertions, and those pages seem to have been drawn almost at random from Nibley's book (see 425, n. 3). Hill disagrees with Nibley's having conceived Lehi as a merchant and also about his drawing parallels between the community at Qumran and "the society described in Alma 23" (see 425, n. 4).

1958

• "The Idea of the Temple in History." *MS* 120/8 (August 1958): 228–37, 247–49.

Reprinted as *What Is a Temple? The Idea of the Temple in History* (1963 and 1968); and under the title "What Is a Temple?" in *The Temple in Antiquity: Ancient Records and Modern Perspectives,* edited by Truman G. Madsen (Provo: RSC, 1984), 19–37; and in *Mormonism and Early Christianity,* vol. 4 of the *CWHN* (Salt Lake City: Deseret Book and F.A.R.M.S., 1987), 355–90.

• Review of *Stela 5, Izapa,* by M. Wells Jakeman. Provo, 1958. 7p., s.s., ca. 1958.

A critique of Jakeman's claim to have found and interpreted a stone depicting Lehi's dream of the Tree of Life. This can be compared with Jakeman's response to Nibley's treatment of amateur archaeology, which was circulated in the form of a review of Nibley's *An Approach to the Book of Mormon,* in *UAS Newsletter* 40 (March 30, 1957): 1–11. [This was the newsletter of the University Archaeology Society at BYU.] Jakeman's criticisms of Nibley's remarks about archaeology seem to have led to Nibley's review of Jakeman's claims made about a stone presumably depicting Lehi's dream of the Tree of Life, which are called into question in this review.

1959

• " 'Mixed Voices': A Study in Book of Mormon Criticism." A series of articles in the *IE*:

1. "Kangaroo Court." 62/3 (March 1959): 145–48, 184–87.

2. "Kangaroo Court: Part Two." 62/4 (April 1959): 224–26, 300–301.

3. "Just Another Book? Part One." 62/5 (May 1959): 345–47, 388–91.

4. "Just Another Book? Part Two." 62/6 (June 1959): 412–13, 501–3.

5. "Just Another Book? Part Two, Conclusion." 62/7 (July 1959): 530–31, 565.

6. "The Grab Bag." 62/8 (July 1959): 530–33, 546–48.

7. "What Frontier, What Camp Meeting?" 62/9 (August 1959): 590–92, 610, 612, 614–15.

8. "The Comparative Method." 62/10 (October 1959): 744–47, 759.

9. "The Comparative Method." 62/11 (November 1959): 848, 854, 856.

Reprinted as six chapters in *The Prophetic Book of Mormon,* vol. 8 of the *CWHN* (Salt Lake City: Deseret Book and F.A.R.M.S., 1989), 127–206.

• "Strange Ships and Shining Stones." In *A Book of Mormon Treasury: Selections from the Papers of the Improvement Era.* Salt Lake City: Bookcraft, 1959. 133–51.

See also "There Were Jaredites: Shining Stones," *IE* 59/9 (September 1959): 630–32, 672–75, and cf. *An Approach to the Book of Mormon,* Lesson XXV; and in vol. 6 of the *CWHN* (Salt Lake City: Deseret Book and F.A.R.M.S., 1988), 340–58.

• "Christian Envy of the Temple." A two-part essay in the *JQR*.

A detailed study of the reaction of early Christian writers to the destruction of the temple in Jerusalem.

1. "Christian Envy of the Temple." 50/2 (October 1959): 97–123.

1960

• "Christian Envy of the Temple." Second part of an essay in the *JQR*.

2. "Christian Envy of the Temple." 50/3 (January 1960): 229–40.

Reprinted in *When the Lights Went Out* (1970), 55–58; and in *Mormonism and Early Christianity,* vol. 4 of the *CWHN* (Salt Lake City: Deseret Book and F.A.R.M.S., 1987), 391–434.

• "Nobody to Blame." 8p., s.s., open letter, addressed to "Dear Brother Burgon," dated July 29, 1960, with a cover letter, addressed to "Dear Brother . . . ," 1p., dated August 3, 1960.

To be included in J of the *CWHN*.

1961

• "The Liahona's Cousins." *IE* 64/2 (February 1961): 87–89, 104–6, 108–11.

Reprinted in *Since Cumorah*, vol. 7 of the *CWHN* (Salt Lake City: Deseret Book and F.A.R.M.S., 1988).

• "The Boy, Nephi, in Jerusalem." *Ins* 96/3 (March 1961): 84–85.

Reprinted as "The Boy Nephi in Jerusalem," in *The Prophetic Book of Mormon*, vol. 8 of the *CWHN* (Salt Lake City: Deseret Book and F.A.R.M.S., 1989), 207–11.

• "The Passing of the Church: Forty Variations on an Unpopular Theme." *CH* 30/2 (June 1961): 131–54.

Nibley sets out forty arguments for the apostasy as he examines the expectation of early Christian writers of the fading of the Church. Hans J. Hillerbrand wrote a letter protesting Nibley's thesis because, among other reasons, of the possibility that, if widely accepted, Nibley's view would preclude one such as Hillerbrand from continuing to teach what is traditionally known as "Church history." See Hillerbrand, "The Passing of the Church: Two Comments on a Strange Theme," *CH* 30/3 (December 1961): 481–82; and a response to Hillerbrand by Robert M. Grant, "The Passing of the Church: Comments on Two Comments on a Strange Theme," *CH* 30/3 (December 1961): 482–83.

William A. Clebsch, in his "History and Salvation: An Essay in Distinctions," published in a collection of essays entitled *The Study of Religion in Colleges and Universities*, edited by Paul Ramsey and John F. Wilson (Princeton: Princeton University Press, 1970), 40–72, commented on Nibley's arguments for the apostasy in "The Passing of the Church" as follows:

> During the early 1960s there arose in the pages of *Church History* a brief but in retrospect fascinating argument, which I will trace briefly. The argument not only revolved around the question of the continuity of the Christian church but also involved a more fundamental question about the very survival of the church through its early history. On the basis of his study of patristic writings, Hugh Nibley scored all church historians since Eusebius for describing rather than questioning the survival of the church through the early centuries. That Nibley took a Mormon's viewpoint on the nascent Christian movement does not make any easier the defense of its identity and continuity against his attack. "By its very definition," he wrote, "church history requires unquestioning

acceptance of the basic proposition that the Church did survive. . . . Church history seems to be resolved never to raise
the fundamental question of survival as the only way of avoiding a disastrous answer, and the normal reaction to the question—did the Church remain on earth?—has not been serious
inquiry in a richly documented field, but shocking recoil from
the edge of an abyss into which few can look without a shud-
der" (67; also *CWHN* 4:168–69).

Clebsch continues:

> An incensed retort from Hans J. Hillerbrand, who con-
> fessed that it was to him a "bread and butter" issue, pleaded
> the Reformers' distinction between the church visible and
> invisible as the knife Nibley should have used to cut his knot.
> Further, Hillerbrand proposed the viability of considering
> church history "as the *history of the interpretation of the Sacred
> Scriptures*" (Gerhard Ebeling) or as "the *history of the Gospel
> and its consequences in the world*" (Heinrich Bornkamm). "Or,
> more simply but quite adequately," according to Hillerbrand,
> "one can define church history as the *history of Christianity* or
> the *Christian religion* and avoid thereby the theologically dan-
> gerous term 'church' " (68–69; quoting *CH* 30/3 [December
> 1961]: 481).

According to Clebsch, Robert M. Grant, "at the request of the
journal's editors . . . arose to referee the debate." And he admitted
that only a Catholic understanding of the Church makes any sense.
And he brushed aside Hillerbrand's attempt to slide around the issue
by reducing church history to the "history of interpretation," which
would turn it into merely the history of ideas, or by talking about the
"history of Christianity" or the "history of Christian religion." Albert
Outler then settled the issue by assertion, just as Nibley had said that
it had always been settled. If we cannot tell the story of church history,
Outler held, "then more than the enterprise of church history is at
stake, for the Christian faith itself will not long outlive its major premise: God's real presence in human history—past, present, and future"
(70). "Indeed, the church historian must assume the survival of his
object of investigation." But the assumption of continuity cannot be
settled because the "hard data indicate as much discontinuity as continuity in the church" (70).

The tendency, at least since 1960, has been to turn away from the
doing of "church" history, and to the doing of the history of "religion,"
an even more ambiguous and amorphous term. Among some Mormon
historians there are signs of a shift from "church" to "religious" history.
For example, some effort has been made to place Joseph Smith in the

development of American religion, and even the faithful have been charmed by recent efforts to describe "Mormonism" as "a new religious tradition." "For if it is true that Mormonism represents a new religious tradition, then a narrative of mythic dimensions that relates the origins of that tradition becomes imperative for the true believer," according to Neal E. Lambert and Richard H. Cracroft, in "Literary Form and Historical Understanding: Joseph Smith's First Vision," *Journal of Mormon History* 7 (1980): 40. Jan Shipps later fashioned a book around that bit of speculation. See her *Mormonism: The Story of a New Religious Tradition* (Urbana: University of Illinois Press, 1985).

There has been a tendency, for various reasons, even for Latter-day Saint historians to move away from doing the history of the restoration of the gospel of Jesus Christ and, in that sense, the Church, understood as God's covenant people, toward doing history controlled by questions of a presumed religious development, understood often through sociological and psychological categories. Unwilling to address the issues raised by Nibley, some historians have turned to the study of the Church understood as a political, economic, or cultural institution or artifact, and not as the covenant people of God.

Reprinted in *When the Lights Went Out* (1970), and later in *BYUS* 16/1 (Autumn 1975): 139–64; and in *Mormonism and Early Christianity*, vol. 4 of the *CWHN* (Salt Lake City: Deseret Book and F.A.R.M.S., 1987), 168–208.

• "The Literary Style of the Book of Mormon." *Deseret News*, "Church News," July 29, 1961, 10, 15. Originally a letter addressed to "Dear Mr. ———," dated July 12, 1961.

Circulated under the title "Literary Style of the Book of Mormon Insured Accurate Translation."

Reprinted in *Saints Herald* 108 (October 9, 1961): 968–69, 975; and also in *The Prophetic Book of Mormon*, vol. 8 of the *CWHN* (Salt Lake City: Deseret Book and F.A.R.M.S., 1989), 212–18.

• "Censoring the Joseph Smith Story." A series of articles in the *IE*.

1. "Part I: The Problem." 64/7 (July 1961): 490–92, 522, 524, 526, 528.

2. "Part II: Suppressing the First Vision Story after 1842." 64/8 (August 1961): 577–79, 605–9.

3. "Part III." 64/10 (October 1961): 724–25, 736, 738, 740.

4. "Conclusion." 64/11 (November 1961): 812–13, 865–69.

To be included in B of the *CWHN*.

• *The Myth Makers.* Salt Lake City: Bookcraft, 1961. 293p.

A highly satirical examination of the early criticisms of Joseph Smith.

Contents:
Foreword
Part I. The Crime of Being a Prophet
Part II. Digging in the Dark
Part III. The Greek Psalter Mystery
Bibliography
To be included in B of the *CWHN*.

• "The First Vision." 33p. typed transcript of an address given on February 18, 1961, at a seminar on Joseph Smith held at BYU.

Nibley sets forth various reasons for believing that there had been suppression of the story of the initial vision of Joseph Smith by his enemies between 1820 and 1838. See also the series entitled "Censoring the Joseph Smith Story," published in 1961 in the *IE*.

To be included in B of the *CWHN*.

• "Paul and Moroni." Letter to *Christianity Today* 5/5 (May 22, 1961): 727.

A response to a letter by C. Sumter Logan of the Trinity Presbyterian Church in Ogden, Utah, that had appeared in *Christianity Today* 5/3 (March 27, 1961): 551 (commenting on Moroni 7 and Paul's praise of charity).

To be included in F of the *CWHN*.

1962

• "The Book of Mormon: True or False?" *MS* 124/11 (November 1962): 274–77.

Nibley argues that if Joseph Smith was not telling the truth when he provided the world with the Book of Mormon, then he recklessly exposed his forgery and fraud to public discovery. In the course of his argument, Nibley complains about what is currently being called "parallelomania." Everywhere in Book of Mormon criticism, as well as in the scholarly world generally, various parallels are being noted, and simplistic explanations are made to flow from those supposed parallels. With the Book of Mormon, the end result is that, with those who study nineteenth-century materials and who read English literature, the tendency is to leap to the conclusion that they have discovered the sources upon which Joseph Smith presumably drew in fabricating the Book of Mormon; they are then quick to condemn the book as a forgery, or, when sentimental attachments to the Mormon community remain, they see the fabrication of fiction as a kind of inspiration, or at least as potentially inspiring, thus providing a novel and competing theory of what constitutes divine revelation.

Reprinted in *The Prophetic Book of Mormon*, vol. 8 of the *CWHN* (Salt Lake City: Deseret Book and F.A.R.M.S., 1989), 219–42.

• "How to Write an Anti-Mormon Book." Lecture II, February 17, 1962. In *Seminar on the Prophet Joseph Smith*. Provo: BYU Extension Publications, 1962. 30–41. This was reprinted in 1964, pp. 31–42.

Essentially a preview of *Sounding Brass* (1963). A satirical list of informal rules commonly followed by those anxious to criticize Mormon things.

To be included in B of the *CWHN*.

• *The World and the Prophets*. 2d enl. ed. Salt Lake City: Deseret Book, 1962. 281p., with the addition of "The Doctors' Dilemma" and "The Return of the Prophets?" added in this edition, though they were not part of the original series of radio addresses and have a somewhat different style.

1963

• *Sounding Brass*. Salt Lake City: Bookcraft, 1963. 294p.

This book carries the subtitle "Informal Studies in the Lucrative Art of Telling Stories about Brigham Young and the Mormons" and is a response to Irving Wallace's *The Twenty-Seventh Wife* (New York: Simon & Schuster, 1961). A few historians have been annoyed because Nibley pointed out some of the flaws in anti-Mormon literature. "Hugh Nibley's *Sounding Brass* . . . is a meticulous critique of two anti-Mormon writings. Nibley's book is most useful for the poorly informed who do not have the background to critique sensationalistic or popular works of questionable validity, like those of Ann Eliza Young and Irving Wallace. But it is a pointed and often sarcastic essay that emphasizes in great detail flaws already evident to the knowledgeable reader. The generally uninformed but orthodox Latter-day Saint will find this type of work supportive of his beliefs, but the Mormon who is familiar with critical methodology and with history will prefer a synthesis of the events critiqued. Many scholars find this style of writing to be a sort of intellectual overkill, and it has not been particularly influential among historians." Thomas G. Alexander, "Toward the New Mormon History: An Examination of the Literature on the Latter-day Saints in the Far West," an essay in *Historians and the American West*, edited by Michael P. Malone (Lincoln, NB: University of Nebraska Press, 1983).

Contents:

Introduction

Part I. "In My Mind's Eye Horatio . . . "

Part II. The Two-faced Monster

Part III. How to Write an Anti-Mormon Book (A Handbook for Beginners)

Part IV. It Fairly Sears the Screen—A Romance You Will Never Forget!

Part V. Is There a Danite in the House? You Never Know

Bibliography

To be included in B of the *CWHN*.

• " 'Howlers' in the Book of Mormon." *MS* 125/2 (February 1963): 28–34.

Reprinted in *The Prophetic Book of Mormon*, vol. 8 of the *CWHN* (Salt Lake City: Deseret Book and F.A.R.M.S., 1989), 243–58.

• "Three Shrines: Mantic, Sophic, and Sophistic (The Confrontation of Greek and Christian Religiosity)." Deseret Lectures, Sterling Library Lecture Hall, Yale University, New Haven, Connecticut, under the sponsorship of the LDS Deseret Club at Yale; three typed manuscripts, 20p., d.s. [with extensive citations]; 9p., d.s.; 12p., d.s., given on May 1, 2, 3, 1963.

Combined with "Paths That Stray" and to be included in E of the *CWHN*.

• "Paths That Stray: Some Notes on Sophic and Mantic." 75p., plus an additional 7 lettered pages, and a 14–page bibliography of sources cited, ca. 1963.

To be included in E of the *CWHN*.

• *What Is a Temple? The Idea of the Temple in History*. Provo: BYU Extension Publications, 1963/1968. ii, 18p. (16p.). Reprinted from the *MS* 120/8 (August 1958): 228–37, 247–49. Also appeared as "Die Tempelidee in der Geschichte." *Der Stern* 85/2 (February 1959): 43–60.

Reprinted in *Mormonism and Early Christianity*, vol. 4 of the *CWHN* (Salt Lake City: Deseret Book and F.A.R.M.S., 1988), 355–90.

• *New Discoveries Concerning the Bible and Church History*. Provo: BYU Extension Publications, 1963. 12p.

A series of quotations by various writers on six general topics. Introduces themes taken up more systematically in other essays.

• "The Dead Sea Scrolls: Some Questions and Answers." *Ins* 98/7 (July 1963): 233–35.

An address originally given on July 5, 1962, to the Seminary and Institute faculty assembled at BYU.

Reprinted in *Old Testament and Related Studies*, vol. 1 of the *CWHN* (Salt Lake City: Deseret Book and F.A.R.M.S., 1986), 233–35.

• "Jerusalem's Formula for Peace." 18p. typed transcript of a talk given in 1963.

To be included in J of the *CWHN*.

1964

• *The Early Christian Church in Light of Some Newly Discovered Papyri from Egypt*. Provo: BYU Extension Publications, 1964. 20p.

An address delivered to the BYU Tri-Stake Fireside, March 3, 1964, which draws attention to the contents of some of the Coptic Nag Hammadi materials. Much of this material is included in a more systematic way in *Since Cumorah*.

• "The Philosophical Implications of Automation." 3p., s.s., typed transcript of a lecture given on March 19, 1964.

To be included in J of the *CWHN*.

• *An Approach to the Book of Mormon*. 2d ed. Salt Lake City: Deseret Book, 1964. xxii, 416p.

Originally published in 1957, this edition contains a "Preface to Second Edition" by Hugh Nibley and one new chapter (#25) entitled "Strange Ships and Shining Stones," which is reproduced from a 1959 publication. The questions appended to each chapter in the 1957 edition have been deleted and the pagination of the two editions is different. Reprinted in a 3d ed. as vol. 6 of the *CWHN* (Salt Lake City: Deseret Book and F.A.R.M.S., 1988).

• "Since Cumorah: New Voices from the Dust." A series of articles in the *IE*.

1. "Part I." 67/10 (October 1964): 816–21, 844–47.

2. "Part I (continued)." 67/11 (November 1964): 924–28, 974–75, 977–78, 980–83.

3. "Part I (continued)." 67/12 (December 1964): 1032–35, 1126–28.

1965

• "Since Cumorah: New Voices from the Dust." A series of articles in the *IE*, continued.

4. "Part I (continued)." 68/1 (January 1965): 34–37, 60–64.

5. "Part II: Hidden Treasures: The Search for the Original Scriptures." 68/2 (February 1965): 100–103, 146–47.

6. "Part II: Hidden Treasures: The Search for the Original Scriptures (continued)." 68/3 (March 1965): 210–13, 226, 228, 230, 232, 234.

7. "Part III: Secrecy in the Primitive Church." 68/4 (April 1965): 308–11, 326, 328–32.

8. "Part III: Secrecy in the Primitive Church (continued)." 68/5 (May 1965): 406–7, 444.

9. "Part III: Secrecy in the Primitive Church (concluded)." 68/6 (June 1965): 482–83, 574–76.

10. "The Testament of Lehi: Part I." 68/7 (July 1965): 616–17, 645–48.

11. "The Testament of Lehi: Part I, continued." 68/8 (August 1965): 696–99, 702, 704.

12. "The Story of Zenos." 68/9 (September 1965): 782–83, 792.

13. "The Olive Tree." 68/10 (October 1965): 876–77, 916–17.

14. "The Bible, the Scrolls, and the Book of Mormon — a Problem of Three Bibles." 68/11 (November 1965): 974–77, 1013, 1040.

15. "The Bible, the Scrolls, and the Book of Mormon — a Problem of Three Bibles (continued)." 68/12 (December 1965): 1090–91, 1165–68.

[Continues in 1966.]

• "Qumran and the Companions of the Cave." *RQ* 5/2 (1965): 177–98.

This is a remarkable, complex study of stories that turn up in both Muslim sources and in the Dead Sea Scrolls; these stories and their strange appearances have more significance than appears on the surface.

Reprinted as "The Haunted Wilderness," in *Nibley on the Timely and the Timeless* (Provo: RSC, 1978), 187–212; and again in *Old Testament and Related Studies*, vol. 1 of the *CWHN* (Salt Lake City: Deseret Book and F.A.R.M.S., 1986), 253–84.

• "Early Accounts of Jesus' Childhood." *Ins* 100/1 (January 1965): 35–37.

An assessment of the various infancy materials about the childhood of Jesus.

Reprinted in *Mormonism and Early Christianity*, vol. 4 of the *CWHN* (Salt Lake City: Deseret Book and F.A.R.M.S., 1987), 1–9.

• "The Expanding Gospel." *BYUS* 7/1 (Autumn 1965): 3–27. A talk given as the Second Annual BYU Faculty Lecture on March 17, 1965.

Reprinted in *Nibley on the Timely and the Timeless* (Provo: RSC, 1978), 21–47, and to be included in I of the *CWHN*.

• "Archaeology and Our Religion." 9p. typed paper, 1965.

This is the manuscript of an essay submitted to the *Ins*, rejected, and circulated with two letters, both dated September 16, 1965, one addressed to "Dear Brother," 1p., and the other addressed to "Mr. W," 5p.

The essay has been published in *Old Testament and Related Studies*, vol. 1 of the *CWHN* (Salt Lake City: Deseret Book and F.A.R.M.S., 1986), 21–36. It also appeared in the *Seventh East Press*, January 18, 1982, 4–7, 12.

• "On the Pearl of Great Price." 34p. typed transcript of a lecture given on May 13, 1965.

To be included in D of the *CWHN*.

• "Fact and Fancy in the Interpretation of Ancient Records." 55p. typed transcript of an address given at the third annual Religion Lecture Series at BYU on November 11, 1965. [There is also an outline (1p., s.s.) of the talk that was distributed at the lecture.] The transcript of this address has been circulated under the title "Intre-Ancient Records."

• "Israel's Neighbors." 33p. typed transcript of a talk given on February 24, 1965.

A discussion of the religious and cultural impact of Egypt, Babylon, and other neighbors on events in Israel.

• "Rediscovery of the Apocrypha." 58p., d.s., typed transcript of a lecture given on March 17, 1965.

The imagery and practices found in the Book of Mormon are compared with certain phrases and material concerns found in Jewish and Christian apocryphal writings. Cf. "Unrolling the Scrolls—Some Forgotten Witnesses," in *Old Testament and Related Studies*, vol. 1 of the *CWHN* (Salt Lake City: Deseret Book and F.A.R.M.S., 1986), 115–70.

To be included in I of the *CWHN*.

• BYU Education Week lectures delivered in the summer of 1965 at Oakland, California, 196p. handwritten transcript by Russell Ball.

    I. The Dead Sea Scrolls
        A. Vertical Judaism
        B. Primitive Christianity
        C. The Book of Mormon
    II. New Light from Egypt
        A. Nag Hammadi and the Gnostic Controversy
        B. Early Christian Doctrines According to Coptic Texts
        C. Early Christian Ordinances According to Coptic Texts
    III. Pearl of Great Price Problems
        A. The 1912 Critics Examined
        B. The Present Critics Examined
        C. Some Guesses of Our Own
    IV. Assembly Hour

1966

• "Since Cumorah: New Voices from the Dust." A series of articles in the *IE*, continued.

16. "The Bible, the Scrolls, and the Book of Mormon: A Problem of Three Bibles (continued)." 69/1 (January 1966): 32–34, 44–46.

17. "The Bible, the Scrolls, and the Book of Mormon: A Problem of Three Bibles (continued)." 69/2 (February 1966): 118–22.

18. "The Bible, the Scrolls, and the Book of Mormon: A Problem of Three Bibles (continued)." 69/3 (March 1966): 196–97, 232–34.

19. "The Mysteries of Zenos and Joseph." 69/4 (April 1966): 296–97, 334–36.

20. "Problems, Not Solutions." 69/5 (May 1966): 419–20, 422, 424.

21. ["Problems, Not Solutions (continued)."] 69/6 (June 1966): 582–83.

22. "Epilogue: Since Qumran." 69/7 (July 1966): 636–38.

23. "Since Qumran (continued)." 69/8 (August 1966): 710–12.

24. "(Since Qumran)." 69/9 (September 1966): 794–95, 799–800, 802, 804–5.

25. "(Since Qumran)." 69/10 (October 1966): 884–85.

26. "(Since Qumran)." 69/11 (November 1966): 974–75, 1028–31.

27. "(Since Qumran)." 69/12 (December 1966): 1084–85, 1162–65.

These materials were reprinted in *Since Cumorah* (1967/1970), with two large additions and a deletion; and reprinted again, with corrections and a collation of materials with those published in the book, as vol. 7 of the *CWHN* (Salt Lake City: Deseret Book and F.A.R.M.S., 1988).

• "Evangelium Quadraginta Dierum." *VC* 20/1 (1966): 1–24.

A study of evidences of the teachings of Jesus to his disciples in the forty days after the Resurrection.

Reprinted under the title "The Forty-day Mission of Christ — The Forgotten Heritage," in *When the Lights Went Out* (1970), 33–54; and also reprinted under the original title in *Mormonism and Early Christianity*, vol. 4 of the *CWHN* (Salt Lake City: Deseret Book and F.A.R.M.S., 1987), 10–44.

• "Tenting, Toll, and Taxing." *WPQ* 19/4 (December 1966): 599–630.

An historical study of the roots of taxation, property, and political dominion.

To be included in E of the *CWHN*.

• "Writing and Publication in Graduate School." Provo: Mimeographed by the BYU Graduate School, 1966. 11p.

An address on the rudiments of scholarship given on May 12, 1965, to the BYU History Department Honors Banquet. Presented in the form of a series of answers to hypothetical questions.

To be included in J of the *CWHN*.

1967

• *Since Cumorah: The Book of Mormon in the Modern World.* Salt Lake City: Deseret Book, 1967. xiii, 451p.

This book reprints much of the same material that originally appeared under the same title in the *IE* in 1964–66, but with a somewhat different organization and with some additional materials, specifically on "Military History" (328–70) and "The Prophetic Book of Mormon" (373–444).

Contents:
Preface: Hugh Nibley
Foreword: Richard Lloyd Anderson
Part I. The Book of Mormon as Scripture
    1. " . . . There Can Be No More Bible"
    2. A New Age of Discovery
    3. The Illusive Primitive Church
    4. " . . . But Unto Them It Is Not Given" (Luke 8:10)
    5. The Bible in the Book of Mormon
Part II. Philosophical Notes
    6. Strange Things Strangely Told
    7. Checking on Long-forgotten Lore
Part III. Some Scientific Questions
    8. "Forever Tentative . . . "
Part IV. The Real Background of the Book of Mormon
    9. Some Fairly Foolproof Texts
    10. Prophets in the Wilderness
    11. A Rigorous Test: Military History
Part V. The Prophetic Book of Mormon
    12. Good People and Bad People
    13. Prophecy in the Book of Mormon: The Three Periods
Conclusion
Index

Alexander T. Stecker reviewed *Since Cumorah* in *BYUS* 8/4 (Summer 1968): 465–68. Robert Mesle provided a critical RLDS reaction to it (*Courage* 2/1 [September 1971]: 331–32). At the time he published this review, Mesle was a student at the Graceland College in Lamoni, Iowa, where he now teaches religion and philosophy. Mesle granted that Nibley appeared to be a "very competent scholar in the field of ancient documents and their languages" but observed that Nibley is not "at all objective or critical in the sphere of his own religion." The reason for this observation is that Nibley takes the Book of Mormon seriously as an historically authentic ancient document. Mesle, who claims that in order to be properly objective and sufficiently critical, one must hold that the Book of Mormon and the gospel are fraudulent and spurious rather than authentic and genuine, claimed that Nibley's work is "trite and naive"—it is "both confident scholarship and the tritest of religious defenses," though he neglected to indicate what in *Since Cumorah* was either hackneyed or unsophisticated.

For a sympathetic commentary on the last seventy pages of *Since Cumorah,* the portion of the book that did not appear in the original series in the *IE,* see Louis Midgley, "The Secular Relevance of the Gospel," *DJMT* 4/4 (Winter 1969): 76–85. A complaint was registered against Nibley's position by Duane Stanfield. See the exchange of letters between Stanfield and Midgley, "Letters to the Editor," *DJMT* 5/2 (Summer 1970): 5–7.

Reprinted, with additions and corrections, as *Since Cumorah,* vol. 7 of the *CWHN* (Salt Lake City: Deseret Book and F.A.R.M.S., 1988).

• "The Mormon View of the Book of Mormon." *Concilium: An International Review of Theology* 10 (December 1967): 82–83; also printed in the United States under the same title in *Concilium: Theology in the Age of Renewal* 30 (1968): 170–73, and in other foreign-language editions of this Catholic journal in French, pp. 151–53; Portuguese, pp. 144–47; German, pp. 855–56.

An interesting summary statement of the content and purpose of the Book of Mormon prepared for a volume of *Concilium* devoted to an examination of the Christian scriptures.

Reprinted as "The Book of Mormon: A Minimal Statement," in *Nibley on the Timely and the Timeless* (Provo: RSC, 1978), 149–53; and in *The Prophetic Book of Mormon,* vol. 8 of the *CWHN* (Salt Lake City: Deseret Book and F.A.R.M.S., 1989), 259–64.

• "Brigham Young as a Leader." 21p. typescript of an address delivered on June 6, 1967.

Nibley often drew upon materials he had culled from the writings of Brigham Young to make points on various issues. This and the following three items are in that category.

To be included in J of the *CWHN.*

• "[Brigham Young] The Statesman." 41p. typescript of an address delivered on June 7, 1967.

To be included in J of the *CWHN.*

• "Brigham Young as an Educator." 15p. typescript of an address delivered on June 9[?], 1967.

For a more refined version of Nibley's treatment of Brigham Young's views on education see his "Educating the Saints—A Brigham Young Mosaic," *BYUS* 11/1 (Autumn 1970): 61–87.

• "Brigham Young as a Theologian." 4p. typescript of remarks made in an address delivered on June 9, 1967.

To be included in J of the *CWHN*.

• "Pearl of Great Price Papyri." 15p. transcript of a talk given on March 14, 1967. [Some 10 pages of this item consist of questions and answers.]

• "Dear Sterling." A widely circulated letter to Sterling M. McMurrin. 3p., s.s., August 23, 1967.

Sterling M. McMurrin was at the time working on a book of essays on Mormon things and had apparently invited Nibley to contribute an essay. The book that McMurrin had in mind was never published.

To be included in F of the *CWHN*.

• "Unrolling the Scrolls—Some Forgotten Witnesses." A talk given in Glendale, California, in 1967.

Transcribed and published in *Old Testament and Related Studies*, vol. 1 of the *CWHN* (Salt Lake City: Deseret Book and F.A.R.M.S., 1986), 115–70.

• "Apocryphal Writings." A typed transcript of a talk given at a Long Beach, California, Seminary graduation, late in 1967; 27p., s.s.; 44p., d.s. Also circulated as "Teachings from the Dead Sea Scrolls." Circulated with 11p. of "Sources Cited or Mentioned." A survey of teachings in a large number of apocryphal, pseudepigraphal, and patristic writings. Cf. "Unrolling the Scrolls—Some Forgotten Witnesses," in *Old Testament and Related Studies*, vol. 1 of the *CWHN* (Salt Lake City: Deseret Book and F.A.R.M.S., 1986), 115–70.

To be included in I of the *CWHN*.

1968

• "Phase One." *DJMT* 3/2 (Summer 1968): 99–105.

This essay concerns the debate over the Joseph Smith Papyri and the bulk of the issue contains materials on this issue.

• "Prolegomena to Any Study of the Book of Abraham." *BYUS* 8/2 (Winter 1968): 171–78.

On November 27, 1967, the Metropolitan Museum of Art in New York City made available to the Church certain papyri fragments that had once been in the possession of Joseph Smith. These generated considerable interest and also much controversy over the Book of Abraham and what came to be called the Joseph Smith Papyri.

• "Fragment Found in Salt Lake City." *BYUS* 8/2 (Winter 1968): 191–94.

Reflections on the recovery of the Joseph Smith Papyri from the Metropolitan Museum of Art in New York City.

• "Getting Ready to Begin: An Editorial." *BYUS* 8/3 (Spring 1968): 245–54.

A contribution to the continuing debate over the Joseph Smith Papyri and the historical authenticity of the Book of Abraham.

• "As Things Stand at the Moment." *BYUS* 9/1 (Autumn 1968): 69–102.

More on the continuing debate generated by the recovery of the Joseph Smith Papyri, including a response to Wallace Turner's remarks about the Book of Abraham in the July 15, 1968, *New York Times*.

• "Book of Breathings, P. Louvre 3284." An English translation, 1968. 6p., s.s., typescript, mimeograph, and privately circulated.

This is Nibley's translation of the most famous parallel version of the Egyptian text once in the possession of Joseph Smith. Cf. Richard A. Parker, "The Book of Breathings (Fragment 1, The "Sensen" Text, with Restorations from Louvre Papyrus 3284)," *DJMT* 3/2 (Summer 1968): 98–99; and Klaus Baer, "The Breathing Book of Hôr: A Translation of the Apparent Source of the Book of Abraham," *DJMT* 3/3 (Autumn 1968): 109–34. The hieratic text of P. Louvre 3284 is reproduced in *BYUS* 11/2 (Winter 1971): 154–56.

• *What Is a Temple? The Idea of the Temple in History*. 2d ed. Provo: BYU Press, 1968. ii, 18p. [1st ed., 1963; reprinted from the *MS* 120/8 (August 1958): 228–37, 247–49.]

Reprinted in *Mormonism and Early Christianity*, vol. 4 of the *CWHN* (Salt Lake City: Deseret Book and F.A.R.M.S., 1987), 355–90.

• "A New Look at the Pearl of Great Price." A series of articles in the *IE*.

1. "Part 1, Challenge and Response." 71/1 (January 1968): 18–24.

2. "Part 1, Challenge and Response (continued)." 71/2 (February 1968): 14–18, 20–21.

3. "Part 1, Challenge and Response (continued)." 71/3 (March 1968): 16–18, 20–22.

4. "Part 1, Challenge and Response (continued)." 71/4 (April 1968): 64–69 (includes a long note entitled "We Should Explain," 65–66).

5. "Part 2, May We See Your Credentials?" 71/5 (May 1968): 54–57.

6. "Part 2, May We See Your Credentials? (continued)." 71/6 (June 1968): 18–22.

7. "Part 3, Empaneling the Panel." 71/7 (July 1968): 48–55.

8. "Part 4, Second String." 71/8 (August 1968): 53–64.

9. "Part 5, Facsimile No. 1: A Unique Document." 71/9 (September 1968): 66–80.

10. "Part 5, Facsimile No. 1: A Unique Document (continued)." 71/10 (October 1968): 73–81.

11. "Part 6, Facsimile No. 1: A Unique Document (continued)." 71/11 (November 1968): 36–38, 40, 42, 44.

12. "Part 6, Facsimile No. 1: A Unique Document (continued)." 71/12 (December 1968): 28–33.

1969

• "A New Look at the Pearl of Great Price." A series of articles in the *IE*, continued.

13. "Part 7, The Unknown Abraham." 72/1 (January 1969): 26–33.

14. "Part 7, The Unknown Abraham (continued)." 72/2 (February 1969): 64–67.

15. "Part 8[7], The Unknown Abraham (continued)." 72/3 (March 1969): 76, 79–80, 82, 84.

16. "Part 7, The Unknown Abraham (continued)." 72/4 (April 1969): 66–72.

17. "Part 8[7], The Unknown Abraham (continued)." 72/5 (May 1969): 87–91.

18. "Part 7, The Unknown Abraham (continued)." 72/6 (June 1969): 126–28, 130–32.

19. "Part 7, The Unknown Abraham (continued)." 72/7 (July 1969): 97–101.

20. "Part 8: Facsimile No. 1, By the Figures." 72/7 (July 1969): 101–11.

21. "Part 8: Facsimile No. 1, By the Figures (continued)." 72/8 (August 1969): 75–87.

22. "Part 8, Facsimile No. 1, By the Figures (continued)." 72/9 (September 1969): 85–95.

23. "Part 8, Facsimile No. 1, By the Figures (continued)." 72/10 (October 1969): 85–88.

24. "Part 9, Setting the Stage—The World of Abraham." 72/10 (October 1969): 89–95.

25. "Part 9, Setting the Stage—The World of Abraham (continued)." 72/11 (November 1969): 116–26.

[Continues in 1970.]

• "How to Have a Quiet Campus, Antique Style." *BYUS* 9/4 (Summer 1969): 440–52.

Nibley traces some parallels in educational matters, especially in campus unrest in the decade after 1960, with the medieval world.

To be included in J of the *CWHN*.

• "Secrets of the Scriptures—The Creation." 29p. typed transcript of a talk given in 1969. Cf. "Unrolling the Scrolls," in *Old Testament and Related Studies*, vol. 1 of the *CWHN* (Salt Lake City: Deseret Book and F.A.R.M.S., 1986), 115–70.

• "Science Fiction and the Gospel." 22p., s.s., typed transcript of a talk given on February 13, 1969.

Published, with some changes, in *LDSF 2: Latter-day Science Fiction*, edited by Benjamin Urrutia (Ludlow, MA: Parables, 1985), 5–28. To be included in I of the *CWHN*.

1970

• "A New Look at the Pearl of Great Price." A series of articles in the *IE*, continued.

26. "Part 9, Setting the Stage: The World of Abraham (continued)." 73/1 (January 1970): 56–65.

27. "Part 10, The Sacrifice of Isaac." 73/3 (March 1970): 84–94.

28. "Part 11, The Sacrifice of Sarah." 73/4 (April 1970): 79–95.

29. "Conclusion: Taking Stock." 73/5 (May 1970): 82–89, 91–94

To be included in D of the *CWHN*.

• "Educating the Saints—A Brigham Young Mosaic." *BYUS* 11/1 (Autumn 1970): 61–87.

Comparisons might be made with Nibley's talks on Brigham Young delivered in June 1967.

Reprinted in *Nibley on the Timely and the Timeless* (Provo: RSC, 1978), 229–60; to be included in J of the *CWHN*.

• *Since Cumorah*. Salt Lake City: Deseret Book, 1970. [A reprint of the 1967 edition.]

• *When the Lights Went Out: Three Studies on the Ancient Apostasy*. Salt Lake City: Deseret Book, 1970. 94p.

Three of Nibley's important essays on the fate of the primitive Christian church and its institutions and beliefs previously available only in academic journals in 1959–60, 1961, and 1966 are reprinted and indexed for the Mormon audience.

Contents:

1. The Passing of the Primitive Church (Forty Variations on an Unpopular Theme) [reprinted from *CH* 30/2 (June 1961): 131–54].

2. The Forty-day Mission of Christ—The Forgotten Heritage [reprinted from *VC* 20/1 (1966): 1–24].

3. Christian Envy of the Temple [reprinted from *JQR* 50/2–3 (October 1959; January 1960): 97–123; 229–40].

These essays are all included in *Mormonism and Early Christianity*, vol. 4 of the *CWHN* (Salt Lake City: Deseret Book and F.A.R.M.S., 1987), 10–44, 168–208, 391–434.

• "The Book of Mormon as a Mirror of the East." *IE* 73/11 (November 1970): 115–20, 122–25.

Reprinted from *IE* 51/4 (April 1948): 202–4, 249–51.

• "Brigham Young and the Enemy." In *The Young Democrat*, privately printed leaflets published in two separate parts in 1970. 4p. and 11p.

To be included in J of the *CWHN*.

• "Shalamar." 7p., s.s., typescript used by Nibley for his part on the BYU Women's Program, April 24, 1970. Two slightly different versions of this have been preserved and circulated, both 7p., s.s.

To be included in F of the *CWHN*.

1971

• "The Day of the Amateur." *NE* 1/1 (January 1971): 42–44.

To be included in J of the *CWHN*.

• "Myths and the Scriptures." *NE* 1/10 (October 1971): 34–38.

Reprinted in *Old Testament and Related Studies*, vol. 1 of the *CWHN* (Salt Lake City: Deseret Book and F.A.R.M.S., 1986), 37–47.

• "What Is 'The Book of Breathings'?" *BYUS* 11/2 (Winter 1971): 153–87.

An early version of one part of *The Message of Joseph Smith Papyri* (1975). See also "Book of Breathings, P. Louvre 3284," Nibley's 1968 translation of the text once in the possession of Joseph Smith, and cf. Richard A. Parker, "The Book of Breathings," *DJMT* 3/2 (Summer 1968): 98–99; and Klaus Baer, "Breathing Permit of Hôr," *DJMT* 3/3 (Autumn 1968): 109–34. The hieratic text of P. Louvre 3284 is reproduced in *BYUS* 11/2 (Winter 1971): 154–56.

• "The Meaning of the Kirtland Egyptian Papers." *BYUS* 11/4 (Summer 1971): 350–99.

A detailed study of some materials generated in Kirtland and currently being used by some critics to discredit Joseph Smith.

• "Renounce War" or "A Substitute for Victory." An anti-war letter of March 26, 1971, in *BYU Daily Universe*. See also *Ens* 1/7 (July 1971): 53–55.

To be included in J of the *CWHN*.

• "If There Must Needs Be Offense." *Ens* 1/7 (July 1971): 53–55. See also Nibley's anti-war letter of March 26, 1971, in *BYU Daily Universe*.

To be included in J of the *CWHN*.

• "Brigham Young on the Environment." 6p. typescript of a talk given by Nibley on April 21, 1971, for Earth Week at BYU.

A collection of passages culled from Brigham Young's sermons. See also "Brigham Young on the Environment," in *To the Glory of God* (1972), 3–29.

1972

• "Brigham Young on the Environment." In *To the Glory of God*, the B. West Belnap Memorial volume, edited by Truman G. Madsen and Charles D. Tate. Salt Lake City: Deseret Book, 1972. 3–29.

See also the 6p. mimeograph of quotations from Brigham Young used by Nibley for his Earth Week Lecture, April 21, 1971, on file in the Harold B. Lee Library at BYU.

To be included in J of the *CWHN*.

• "Jerusalem: In Christianity." *Encyclopedia Judaica*, 16 vols. New York: Macmillan/Jerusalem: Keter, 1972. 9:1568–75.

A treatment of the role and symbolic power of Jerusalem for Christians.

This was also circulated in pamphlet form by the Israeli Foreign Ministry; reprinted in *Mormonism and Early Christianity*, vol. 4 of the *CWHN* (Salt Lake City: Deseret Book and F.A.R.M.S., 1987), 323–54.

• "Islam and Mormonism — A Comparison." *Ens* 2/3 (March 1972): 55–64.

Not all of the footnotes containing the citations for the supporting texts and explanations were published with this essay.

• "Ancient Temples: What Do They Signify?" *Ens* 2/9 (September 1972): 46–49.

Reprinted in *The Prophetic Book of Mormon*, vol. 8 of the *CWHN* (Salt Lake City: Deseret Book and F.A.R.M.S., 1989), 265–73.

• "Man's Dominion." *NE* 2/10 (October 1972): 24–31.

Pointed social commentary concerning the state of the natural environment.

Reprinted in *NE* 11/1 (January-February 1981): 46–53, and also available under the title "Subduing the Earth," in *Nibley on the Timely and the Timeless* (Provo: RSC, 1978), 85–99; to be included in J of the *CWHN*.

• *Genesis of the Written Word*. Provo: BYU Press, 1973. This was the Commissioner's Lecture delivered in 1972.

Later reprinted (without the complete footnotes) in *NE* 3/9 (September 1973): 38–50. Also reprinted in *Nibley on the Timely and the Timeless* (Provo: RSC, 1978), 101–27; to be included in E of the *CWHN*.

• "Our Glory and Our Condemnation." In *ASBYU Academics Office Presents: Last Lecture Series, 1971–72*. Provo: BYU, 1972. 1–14. A talk given in 1971 in the Last Lecture series.

Social commentary touching on themes that have become increasingly common in Nibley's various addresses and writings.

Reprinted as "Our Glory or Our Condemnation," in *Approaching Zion*, vol. 9 of the *CWHN* (Salt Lake City: Deseret Book and F.A.R.M.S., 1989), 1–24.

1973

• "The Genesis of the Written Word." *NE* 3/9 (September 1973): 38–50.

Reprinted from the Commissioner's Lecture Series, 1973.

An examination of writing as a gift from God and as a vehicle for the preservation and communication of knowledge of divine things.

To be included in E of the *CWHN*.

• "The Meaning of the Temple." 18p., d.s., typescript, which is a much longer and more accurate version of a transcription of the talk originally delivered at Aspen Grove, September 1, 1973. The talk was given again in 1975 and then circulated in that form. The 1973 version is only about half as long as the 1975 version.

To be included in I of the *CWHN*.

• "What Is Zion? A Distant View." In *What Is Zion? Joseph Smith Lecture Series, 1972–73*. Provo: BYU Press, 1973. 1–21. This talk, originally given in 1973, was circulated prior to publication as "Waiting for Zion," 34p., d.s., typed transcript.

Reprinted in *Sunstone* 13/2 (April 1989): 20–32, and in *Approaching Zion*, vol. 9 of the *CWHN* (Salt Lake City: Deseret Book and F.A.R.M.S., 1989), 25–62.

• "Common Carrier: Author Defends Image of Joseph Smith as Prophet." *Salt Lake Tribune*, Sunday, November 25, 1973, G2.

This was a reply to a "Common Carrier" article by Jerald and Sandra Tanner, in the *Salt Lake Tribune*, November 11, 1973, B6. Nibley focuses on the debate over the book of Abraham and the Joseph Smith Papyri.

To be included in D of the *CWHN*.

• "The Best Possible Test." *DJMT* 8/1 (1973): 73–77.

Nibley's views on revelation and the question of Blacks and the priesthood some five years prior to the June 8, 1978, revelation clarifying the matter for the Saints.

To be included in I of the *CWHN*.

• Review essay of *Bar-Kochba: The Rediscovery of the Legendary Hero of the Second Jewish Revolt against Rome* by Yigael Yadin. *BYUS* 14/1 (Autumn 1973): 115–26.

Nibley points out that Yadin's discoveries seem to show, among other things, that the presumably feminine name Alma was also used by Jews as a masculine name, just as it was in the Book of Mormon. Nibley draws a number of parallels between the Bar Kochba artifacts and the Lehi colony.

Reprinted as "Bar-Kochba and Book of Mormon Backgrounds," in *The Prophetic Book of Mormon*, vol. 8 of the *CWHN* (Salt Lake City: Deseret Book and F.A.R.M.S., 1989), 274–88.

• "Commentary on D&C, Section 1." 2p., s.s., typed notes of a home evening lesson given in October 1973.

A verse-by-verse commentary.

To be included in F of the *CWHN*.

• "What Shall We Do?" 4p., s.s., typed transcript of a home evening lesson given on November 26, 1973.

To be included in F of the *CWHN*.

• "A New Christmas Theme." 3p., s.s., typescript, dated Christmas 1973.

To be included in F of the *CWHN*.

1974

• "The Book of Enoch as a Theodicy." 28p. typed manuscript of a paper read at the regional meeting of the Society for Biblical Literature in Denver, Colorado, in 1974.

Published in *Enoch the Prophet*, vol. 2 of the *CWHN* (Salt Lake City: Deseret Book and F.A.R.M.S., 1986), 66–88.

• "Nibley the Scholar." 13p. typed transcript of a BYU Forum Assembly in which Nibley was interviewed by Louis Midgley on May 21, 1974.

To be included in F of the *CWHN*.

• "Easter and the Prophets." In *Immortality: Famed Discourses on Eternal Progression and Future Existence*, edited by Gordon T. Allred. Salt Lake City: Hawkes, 1974. 211–24. [This essay was reprinted from Nibley's *The World and the Prophets* (Salt Lake City: Deseret Book, 1954).]

• "Two Ways to Remember the Dead." In *Immortality: Famed Discourses on Eternal Progression and Future Existence*, edited by Gordon T. Allred. Salt Lake City: Hawkes, 1974. 199–210. [Also reprinted from Nibley's *The World and the Prophets* (Salt Lake City: Deseret Book, 1954), and reprinted in *Understanding Death*, edited by Brent Barlow (Salt Lake City: Deseret Book, 1979), 189–96.]

• "Treasures in the Heavens: Some Early Christian Insights into the Organizing of Worlds." *DJMT* 8/3–4 (Autumn/Winter 1974): 76–98.

A complex and rich study of the cosmology of the Christian world, which is compared to other similar sources.

Reprinted in *Nibley on the Timely and the Timeless* (Provo: RSC, 1978), 49–84; and in *Old Testament and Related Studies*, vol. 1 of the *CWHN* (Salt Lake City: Deseret Book and F.A.R.M.S., 1986), 171–214.

• "Beyond Politics." *BYUS* 15/1 (Autumn 1974): 3–28. A talk originally given on October 26, 1973, to the Pi Sigma Alpha society in the Political Science Department at BYU.

An argument that political action is desirable, even in an imperfect world, under the condition that it be the pursuit of the common good by reasonable discussion. But such conditions are not often found in the politics of man, which turn out to be instances of force and fraud, fueled by money and the desire for power and gain.

Reprinted in *Nibley on the Timely and the Timeless* (Provo: RSC, 1978), 279–305; to be included in J of the *CWHN*.

• "A Note on F. M. Brodie." 2p., s.s., typescript, ca. 1974.

Brief comments by Nibley on two reviews of Fawn Brodie's *Thomas Jefferson: An Intimate History* (New York: Norton, 1974). He calls attention to similarities between features of his 1946 review of Brodie's *No Man Knows My History* and criticisms of her Jefferson book by David H. Donald in *Commentary* 58/1 (July 1974): 96–98, and Gary Wills in the *New York Review of Books* 21 (April 18, 1974): 26–27.

Nibley's remarks might be compared to the more extensive, though still limited, review of reviews of Brodie's book on Jefferson by Louis Midgley, "The Brodie Connection: Thomas Jefferson and Joseph Smith," *BYUS* 20/1 (Fall 1979): 59–67, and also by Jerry Knudson, "Jefferson the Father of Slave Children? One View of the Book Reviewers," *Journalism History* 3/2 (Summer 1976): 56–58, who examined a somewhat larger sample of the reviews of Brodie's book than did Midgley, though with similar results. Knudson concluded that professional historians had been highly critical of her scholarship.

Brodie responded (*Journalism History* 3/2 [Summer 1977]: 59–60) to Knudson by citing, as examples of historians who had written favorable comments on her book, the advertising blurbs that were provided by her historian friends for W. W. Norton, her publisher. The conclusions found in the Midgley and Knudson essays can be checked against and updated from the more than seventy separate reviews of her Jefferson book, most of which have been assembled in the Brodie

Papers in Special Collections at the Marriott Library, University of Utah.

To be included in B of the *CWHN*.

1975

• "The Passing of the Church: Forty Variations on an Unpopular Theme." *BYUS* 16/1 (Autumn 1975): 139–64.

Reprinted from *CH* 30/2 (1961): 131–54; and included in *Mormonism and Early Christianity*, vol. 4 of the *CWHN* (Salt Lake City: Deseret Book and F.A.R.M.S., 1987), 168–208.

• "Zeal without Knowledge." Academic awareness lecture, 26 June 1975. Original manuscript available in mimeographed form, 22p. and frequently reproduced.

Reprinted in *DJMT* 11/2 (Summer 1978): 101–12, as well as in *Nibley on the Timely and Timeless* (Provo: RSC, 1978), 261–77, and in *Approaching Zion*, vol. 9 of the *CWHN* (Salt Lake City: Deseret Book and F.A.R.M.S., 1989), 63–84.

• *The Message of the Joseph Smith Papyri: An Egyptian Endowment*. Salt Lake City: Deseret Book, 1975. xiii, 305p.

A translation and commentary on the so-called "Book of Breathings" that turned up among the Joseph Smith Papyri, containing parallels with early Christian materials. For reviews, see C. Wilfred Griggs, "A Great Fuss about a Scrap of Papyrus," *Ens* 5/10 (October 1975): 84, and Eric Jay Olson, "A Hint of an Explanation," *DJMT* 9/4 (Winter 1974): 74–75.

Contents:

Explanation

    Chapter I: What Manner of Document?

    Chapter II: Reproduction and Translation of Papyri X and XI

    Chapter III: Translated Correctly?

    Chapter IV: A More Complete Text of the Book of Breathings

Commentary

    Part I: Nature and Purpose of the Book of Breathing(s)

    Part IIa: Purification Rites

    Part IIb: Entering the Temple

    Part III: The Creation of Man

    Part IV: The Garden Story

    Part V: The Long Road Back

    Part VI: The Fearful Passage

    Part VII: Culmination and Conclusion

Appendixes

    I. From the Dead Sea Scrolls (IQS)

II. From the Odes of Solomon
III. The Pearl
IV. From the Pistis Sophia
V. Cyril of Jerusalem's Lectures on the Ordinances
VI. From the Gospel of Philip
Bibliography
Index
To be included in A of the *CWHN*.

• "Some Reasons for the Restored Gospel." 24p., d.s., typed manuscript of the talk given on the occasion of the visit to BYU of Professor Klaus Baer, an eminent Egyptologist and former teacher of Hugh Nibley, then teaching at the University of Chicago.

Nibley provides a listing of various reasons why one should give careful consideration to the restoration of the gospel of Jesus Christ. He deals with Joseph Smith's version of the book of *Enoch,* with the book of Abraham, various compelling elements of the Book of Mormon, and the role of prophetic warnings to the Saints.

• "Sacred Vestments." 32p., d.s., or 19p., s.s, typed transcript of a lecture, which was originally accompanied by slides and given in 1975. This lecture was circulated in two different editions in 1986 and 1987 and is available in a much expanded version, which includes illustrations, in 1988.
To be included in I of the *CWHN*.

• "Enoch the Prophet." In Pearl of Great Price Symposium, held at BYU on November 22, 1975, 76–85, 93–96.
Reprinted in *Enoch the Prophet,* vol. 2 of the *CWHN* (Salt Lake City: Deseret Book and F.A.R.M.S., 1986), 1–18.

• "A Strange Thing in the Land: The Return of the Book of Enoch." A series of articles in the *Ens.*
1. "Part 1." 5/10 (October 1975): 78–84.
2. "Part 2." 5/12 (December 1975): 72–76.

1976

• "A Strange Thing in the Land: The Return of the Book of Enoch." A series of articles in the *Ens,* continued.
3. "Part 3." 6/2 (February 1976): 64–68.
4. "Part 4." 6/3 (March 1976): 62–66.
5. "Part 5." 6/4 (April 1976): 60–64.
6. "Part 6." 6/7 (July 1976): 64–48.
7. "Part 7." 6/10 (October 1976): 76–81.
8. "Part 8." 6/12 (December 1976): 73–78.

[Continues in 1977.]

• "What, Exactly, Is the Purpose and Significance of the Facsimiles in the Book of Abraham?" *Ens* 6/3 (March 1976): 34–36.

This essay was published as part of the section in the *Ens* called "I Have a Question."

To be included in D of the *CWHN*.

• "Nibliography." *Century II* 1/2 (1976): 54–57.

To be included in F of the *CWHN*.

• "In the Party, But Not of the Party." 22p., d.s., typed manuscript for an Academics Lecture given on June 3, 1976, at BYU on politics.

An examination of how the Saints should understand involvement in politics, among other things drawing upon the examples of Paul and Daniel.

To be included in J of the *CWHN*.

• "More Brigham Young on Education." *Sidney B. Sperry Symposium.* Provo: BYU Press, 1976. 2–20. A talk given on March 11, 1976, in the Joseph Smith Auditorium at BYU.

To be included in J of the *CWHN*.

1977

• "A Strange Thing in the Land: The Return of the Book of Enoch." A series of articles in the *Ens,* continued.

9. "Part 9." 7/2 (February 1977): 66–75.

10. "Part 10." 7/3 (March 1977): 86–90.

11. "Part 11." 7/4 (April 1977): 78–89.

12. "Part 12." 7/6 (June 1977): 78–90.

13. "Part 13." 7/8 (August 1977): 66–65.

Reprinted in *Enoch the Prophet,* vol. 2 of the *CWHN* (Salt Lake City: Deseret Book and F.A.R.M.S., 1986), 91–301.

• "The Uses and Abuses of Patriotism." In *American Heritage: A Syllabus for Social Science 100.* Provo: BYU Press, 1977. 188–97. Also circulated as an 18p., d.s., typed manuscript.

This was an essay originally submitted in 1977 for a special issue of the *Ens* as part of the bicentennial celebration of the Declaration of Independence. It was rejected by the editors.

To be included in J of the *CWHN*.

• "Bird Island." *DJMT* 10/4 (Autumn 1977): 120–23. An Academics Awareness Lecture given at BYU on June 26, 1975. This satirical talk was read by Nibley, perhaps as early as 1965.

A version of Nibley's satirical lecture on some of the excesses and weaknesses of archeology and theories of Book of Mormon geography.

To be included in B of the *CWHN*.

• Untitled manuscript in two parts on the book of Abraham: "I. It Takes All Kinds" and "II. Some Warming-up Exercises." 23p. manuscript of a draft of a pamphlet on the book of Abraham. [Part I constitutes the first 8 pages and Part II the remainder of the manuscript.]

These materials were circulated in response to inquiries concerning the debate over the authenticity of the book of Abraham, with a cover letter addressed to "Dear Brother, Sister, Friend," which discussed the charges brought against the book of Abraham by Dee J. Nelson, who advertised himself as a trained Egyptologist and as a Latter-day Saint. Nibley raises questions about Mr. Nelson's credentials, which were later shown to be bogus.

For an exhaustive debunking of Mr. Nelson and his attack on the book of Abraham, see Robert L. and Rosemary Brown, *They Lie in Wait to Deceive*, vol. 1, edited by Barbara Ellsworth, rev. ed. (Mesa, AZ: Brownsworth, 1982). For an example of uncritical use of Mr. Nelson's "work" on the book of Abraham, see Fawn M. Brodie's "Supplement" to *No Man Knows My History*, 2d ed. (New York: Knopf, 1971), where, preliminary to an attack upon Nibley's views on the book of Abraham (424), the reader is urged (on 423) to consult "Mormon scholar Dee Jay Nelson's translation, *The Joseph Smith Papyri*, Parts I and II, and *Joseph Smith's Eye of Ra* (Salt Lake City: Modern Microfilm, 1969)." Brodie and others anxious to find "authorities" who would assert that the book of Abraham was fraudulent and hence that Joseph Smith had been involved in crafting false historical documents, made somewhat uncritical use of both of Nelson's essays.

To be included in D of the *CWHN*.

1978

• "Zeal without Knowledge." *DJMT* 11/2 (Summer 1978): 101–12.

Reprinted in *Approaching Zion*, vol. 9 of the *CWHN* (Salt Lake City: Deseret Book and F.A.R.M.S., 1990), 63–84.

• *Nibley on the Timely and the Timeless: Classic Essays of Hugh Nibley*. Provo: RSC, 1978. xxviii, 323p.

Contents:

Foreword: Truman G. Madsen

An Intellectual Autobiography - HN [reprinted as "Self-Portrait: An Intellectual Autobiography by Hugh Nibley," in *BYU Today* 32/5 (August 1978): 11–13; and to be included in F of the *CWHN*]

1. To Open the Last Dispensation: Moses Chapter 1 [portions of this material first appeared in "A Strange Thing in the Land, Part 7."

Ens 6/10 (October 1976): 76–81; cf. with *Enoch the Prophet*, vol. 2 of the *CWHN* (Salt Lake City: Deseret Book and F.A.R.M.S., 1986), 159–67]

2. The Expanding Gospel [first appeared in *BYUS* 7/1 (Autumn 1965): 3–27; to be included in I of the *CWHN*]

3. Treasures in the Heavens [first appeared in *DJMT* 8/3–4 (Autumn/ Winter 1974): 76–98]

4. Subduing the Earth [first appeared as "Man's Dominion," *NE* 2/10 (October 1972): 24–31; to be included in J of the *CWHN*]

5. Genesis of the Written Word [first appeared in *NE* 3/9 (September 1973): 38–50]

6. The Sacrifice of Isaac [first appeared as "Part 10, The Sacrifice of Isaac," in "A New Look at the Pearl of Great Price," *IE* 73/3 (March 1970): 84–94]

7. The Book of Mormon: A Minimal Statement [first appeared in *Concilium: An International Review of Theology* 10 (December 1967): 82–83; reprinted as "The Mormon View of the Book of Mormon," in *The Prophetic Book of Mormon*, vol. 8 of the *CWHN* (Salt Lake City: Deseret Book and F.A.R.M.S., 1989), 259–64)]

8. Churches in the Wilderness [reprinted in *The Prophetic Book of Mormon*, vol. 8 of the *CWHN* (Salt Lake City: Deseret Book and F.A.R.M.S., 1988), 289–327; this is not the same material that appeared under the same title in *An Approach to the Book of Mormon*, 2d ed. (Salt Lake City: Deseret Book, 1964), 125–34; reprinted as "Qumran and the Companions of the Cave: The Haunted Wilderness," in *Old Testament and Related Studies*, vol. 1 of the *CWHN* (Salt Lake City: Deseret Book and F.A.R.M.S., 1986), 253–84)]

9. The Haunted Wilderness [first appeared in *RQ* 5/2 (1965): 177–98]

10. Their Portrait of a Prophet [first appeared in *The Myth Makers* (Salt Lake City: Bookcraft, 1961)]

11. Educating the Saints [first appeared in *BYUS* 11/1 (Autumn 1970): 61–87; to be included in J of the *CWHN*]

12. Zeal without Knowledge [first appeared in *DJMT* 11/2 (Summer 1978): 101–12; reprinted in *Approaching Zion*, vol. 9 of the *CWHN* (Salt Lake City: Deseret Book and F.A.R.M.S., 1989), 63–84]

13. Beyond Politics [first appeared in *BYUS* 9/1 (Autumn 1974): 3–28; to be included in J of the *CWHN*]

Bibliography (compiled by Louis Midgley)

• "Comments." In *Mormonism, A Faith for All Cultures*, edited by F. LaMond Tullis. Provo: BYU Press, 1978. 22–28.

A response to a paper read by Noel B. Reynolds entitled "Cultural Diversity in the Universal Church," as part of the symposium on the "Expanding Church" held as part of the centennial celebration of BYU.

To be included in I of the *CWHN*.

• "Great Are the Words of Isaiah." In *Proceedings of the Sidney B. Sperry Symposium*. Provo: BYU Press, 1978. 193–207. A lecture delivered on January 28, 1978, at BYU.

Also published in *ASBYU Academics Presents: Outstanding Lectures, 1978–79* (Provo: BYU Press, 1979), 71–88, and reprinted in *Old Testament and Related Studies*, vol. 1 of the *CWHN* (Salt Lake City: Deseret Book and F.A.R.M.S., 1986), 215–37.

• "The Early Christian Prayer Circle." *BYUS* 19/1 (Fall 1978): 41–78.

Draws upon a host of sources and shows certain parallels between an early Christian form of prayer and that of the LDS prayer circle.

Reprinted in *Mormonism and Early Christianity*, vol. 4 of the *CWHN* (Salt Lake City: Deseret Book and F.A.R.M.S., 1987), 45–99.

• "Self-Portrait: An Intellectual Autobiography by Hugh Nibley." *BYU Today* 32/5 (August 1978): 11–13.

Reprinted from *Nibley on the Timely and the Timeless* (Provo: RSC, 1978), xix-xxvii.

When sent a copy of this item, Fawn M. Brodie indicated that she "found the mini-autobiography fascinating in every way. This man surely had a touch of genius, and a great linguistic talent. What a pity that he was emotionally trapped by his allegiance to Joseph Smith and the Book of Mormon. The final paragraph of the 'Self-Portrait' suggests to me that there must be grave deterioration in Nibley at the moment. But it may be that he is not really much changed from what he has been all through the years. What a pity that we never sat down and talked to each other." Letter from Fawn M. Brodie to Everett Cooley, dated August 23, 1978, Brodie Papers, Box 4, Folder 6B, Special Collections, Marriott Library, University of Utah.

To be included in F of the *CWHN*.

• Open letter, September 20, 1978. 16p., s.s., typed. A response to each of the essays in *Tinkling Cymbals* (privately printed, 1978), which was a collection of essays honoring Nibley.

To be included in F of the *CWHN*.

1979

• "A Conversation with Hugh Nibley." *DJMT* 12/4 (Winter 1979): 10–27.

An informal interview conducted by Mary L. Bradford, Gary P. Gillum, and H. Curtis Wright.

To be included in F of the *CWHN*.

• "How Firm a Foundation! What Makes It So." *DJMT* 12/4 (Winter 1979): 29–45. Also published by the Harold B. Lee Library Forum Committee and the Friends of the BYU Library in 1980 as a 15–page leaflet.

The lecture was originally part of the Sesquicentennial Lectures on Mormon Arts. In it the foundations of the kingdom are discussed, ending with a passionate plea for building Zion.

Reprinted in *Approaching Zion*, vol. 9 of the *CWHN* (Salt Lake City: Deseret Book and F.A.R.M.S., 1989), 149–77.

• "Gifts." 20p. typed manuscript for a talk given on March 13, 1979, at BYU in which Nibley interviews himself on the moral advice contained in the Book of Mormon.

Published in *Approaching Zion*, vol. 9 of the *CWHN* (Salt Lake City: Deseret Book and F.A.R.M.S., 1989), 85–117.

• "Judging and Prejudging the Book of Abraham." 8p., s.s., typed manuscript on Joseph Smith and the book of Abraham, 1979.

This essay contains Nibley's views on the book of Abraham presented in the form of questions and answers.

Reprinted as an appendix in Robert L. and Rosemary Brown, *They Lie in Wait to Deceive*, vol. 1, edited by Barbara Ellsworth, rev. ed. (Mesa, AZ: Brownsworth, 1982), 236–45.

To be included in D of the *CWHN*.

• "The Facsimiles of the Book of Abraham." *Sunstone* 4/5–6 (December 1979): 49–51.

A response by Nibley to a criticism of the historicity of the book of Abraham by Edward H. Ashment at the Sunstone Theological Symposium at the University of Utah on August 24–25, 1979.

To be included in D of the *CWHN*.

• "The Word of Wisdom: A Commentary on D&C 89." 6p., s.s., typed transcript of a lesson given in the Manavu Ward Gospel Doctrine Class in 1979.

To be included in I of the *CWHN*.

• "Testing the Book of Mormon." 21p., d.s., typed transcript of a talk given at a Portland Institute Symposium held in Portland, Oregon, in 1979.

Portions of this essay are reprinted as a supplement to the essay entitled "The Book of Mormon: True or False?" in *The Prophetic Book of Mormon*, vol. 8 of the *CWHN* (Salt Lake City: Deseret Book and F.A.R.M.S., 1989), note 29, at 232–42.

• "Two Ways to Remember the Dead." Reprinted in *Understanding*

Death, edited by Brent Barlow. Salt Lake City: Deseret Book, 1979. 189–96.

Reprinted from *The World and the Prophets* (Salt Lake City: Deseret Book, 1954).

1980

• "Patriarchy and Matriarchy." *Blueprints for Living: Perspectives for Latter-day Saint Women,* vol. 1, edited by Maren M. Mouritsen. Provo: BYU Press, 1980. 44–61. An address given at the BYU Women's Conference, February 1, 1980.

Reprinted in *Old Testament and Related Studies,* vol. 1 of the *CWHN* (Salt Lake City: Deseret Book and F.A.R.M.S., 1987), 87–113.

• "Freemen and Kingmen in the Book of Mormon." 20p., s.s., typed typescript of a talk given in 1980, and again on January 18, 1981, at the J. Reuben Clark Law School. [Also circulated as a 30p., d.s., version, dated August 18, 1986.]

Published as "Freemen and King-men in the Book of Mormon," in *The Prophetic Book of Mormon,* vol. 8 of the *CWHN* (Salt Lake City: Deseret Book and F.A.R.M.S., 1989), 328–79.

• "Before Adam." 39p., d.s., typed manuscript for a talk given on April 1, 1980, at BYU.

A controversial examination of evolution and the LDS view on creation and the various roles of Adam.

Published in *Old Testament and Related Studies,* vol. 1 of the *CWHN* (Salt Lake City: Deseret Book and F.A.R.M.S., 1986), 49–85.

• "The Book of Mormon and the Ruins: The Main Issues." 10p. typescript of a lecture on Mesoamerican ruins and pre-Columbian peoples, with two maps, dated July 13, 1980.

See the note provided by the editor to Nibley's "Freemen and King-men in the Book of Mormon," in *The Prophetic Book of Mormon,* vol. 8 of the *CWHN* (Salt Lake City: Deseret Book and F.A.R.M.S., 1989), 378, n. 4.

To be included in F of the *CWHN.*

• "The Three Facsimiles from the Book of Abraham." 92p., d.s., typed transcript of a talk prepared ca. 1980.

To be included in D of the *CWHN.*

• *Lehi in the Desert and the World of the Jaredites.* Salt Lake City: Bookcraft, 1980. Contains a new comprehensive index by Gary P. Gillum.

1981

• *Abraham in Egypt*. Salt Lake City: Deseret Book, 1981. xi, 288. For a critical assessment of this book, see Eric J. Olson's review entitled "The Extremes of Eclecticism," *DJMT* 15/4 (Winter 1982): 123–25.

Comments on this work can be found in Marvin S. Hill, "The 'New Mormon History' Reassessed in Light of Recent Books on Joseph Smith and Mormon Origins," *DJMT* 21/3 (Autumn 1988): 115–27. Hill claims that in 1959, when he first published a review of the historical literature on Mormonism, he "found a group defending the Church on the right, writing faith-promoting history that affirmed the truth of Mormon historical claims. In the center was a group of professionals, some Mormon, some not, who focused on questions other than "Is Mormonism true?" And on the left was a group who insisted that Mormonism was historically untrue, a religious corruption and a fraud" (115). "On the right," in 1988, "is a conservative type of writing which remains largely addressed to Mormon audiences, but is more sophisticated than in the past, faith promoting in purpose, and defends against any negative views expressed by non-Mormons. It is frequently nonprofessional in the sense that defenders often write outside their field of expertise. It tends to proclaim empirical proofs for Mormon claims, and generally ignores contrary scholarly opinion. Those who write in this way are usually motivated by powerful spiritual experiences which they consider to be final evidence of the truth of their claims. Their purpose is often moralistic and didactic, using the historical past to reinforce Mormon religious beliefs and values" (116).

Hill's "conservative right" consists of Nibley, Noel B. Reynolds, Milton V. Backman, Truman G. Madsen, John W. Welch, and Richard L. Bushman. Hill offers Nibley's *Abraham in Egypt* as an example of the literature being produced by a "conservative right" among the Saints who want to "prove" the truth of Mormonism. But he seems unfamiliar with Nibley's views on the question of whether it is possible to "prove" the Book of Mormon. Nibley has summarized his position as follows: "For the past twenty years we have repeated in the pages of *The Improvement Era* and elsewhere that nothing is to be gained by trying to prove or disprove the Book of Mormon, but that a great deal can be gained by reading it and discussing its various aspects" (*Since Cumorah*, 2d ed. [1988], 421; cf. also the material under the heading "Forever Tentative . . . ," 213–27).

What Hill seems to mean by "proof" is an attempt to test the historicity of a purportedly ancient text like the Book of Mormon, or to examine, with historical arguments, the historical foundations of the faith in any manner that might support those texts or defend

Joseph Smith's prophetic claims. Hill now locates himself among those he labels "middle ground historians" who do not think that it is either possible or desirable to defend the prophetic claims of Joseph Smith and the Book of Mormon with historical arguments. His position is naturalistic; hence he finds "other reasons for faith" than information about the past that might support prophetic claims. These other reasons rest on the notion that the "truth" of "a religion" is to be found in its utility in dealing with "ageless human problems" (117, where he is quoting Leonard J. Arrington, *Great Basin Kingdom* [Lincoln: University of Nebraska Press, 1966], viii-ix); that is, "truth" is to be reduced to considerations of social utility and is not to be appropriated by careful examination and testing of the Book of Mormon (or book of Abraham or book of Moses).

Abraham in Egypt, for Hill, "is another conservative work which defends the historicity of the book of Abraham" (118). What he means by "proof" is unclear, but he seems to have in mind anything that can be construed as defending the historicity of texts claimed to be ancient by Joseph Smith. "Nibley addressed the problem created by the discovery . . . of Egyptian papyri which once belonged to Joseph Smith and which one eminent Egyptologist from the Oriental Institute of the University of Chicago contends were the source for the book of Abraham [citing John A. Wilson, *DJMT* 3/2 (Summer 1968): 67–105]. Another Oriental Institute scholar argued that the fragments were Book of the Dead materials and had nothing to do with Abraham [citing Klaus Baer, *DJMT* 3/3 (Autumn 1968): 109–34]. Nibley responded by citing the first description of the book of Abraham in the *Times and Seasons,* which said that the book was a "translation of some ancient Records from [the] [C]atacombs of Egypt, *purporting* to be the writings of Abraham [. . .]" (5 March 1842, 704). Nibley took this to mean that Joseph did not say for certain that they actually were Abraham's writings and argues that "we already know Joseph Smith had power to translate ancient records with or without possession of the original text" [what Nibley actually wrote was that "Joseph Smith had already demonstrated at great length his power to translate ancient records with or without possession of the original text"]. Thus, Nibley contends, "it is the Book of Abraham that is on trial, not Joseph Smith as an Egyptologist[. . .]" (118).

Hill is mistaken when he insists that Professor Wilson, in the essay he cited, said anything about the possible relationship of the Joseph Smith Papyri with the book of Abraham. Wilson said nothing about the book of Abraham, or its possible textual sources. It was, instead, the editor of the journal who had placed in a note preceding Wilson's essay a remark to the effect that "some" of the Joseph Smith Papyri "were apparently used [by Joseph Smith] in preparing the text of . . . the Book of Abraham" (67, headnote to Professor Wilson's essay), which may have been nothing more than a reference to the vignettes that were used to illustrate the book of Abraham. Hill also makes too much of Professor Klaus Baer's remark that "Joseph Smith thought that this papyrus [that is, the so-called 'Breathing Permit' or 'sensen papyrus'] contained the Book of Abraham" (Baer, *DJMT* 3/3 [Autumn 1968]: 111), for he was merely accepting the surmise of Grant S. Heward and Jerald Tanner ("The Source of the Book of Abraham Identified," *DJMT* 3/2 [Summer 1968]: 92–96), both inveterate debunkers of Mormon things.

According to Hill, "Nibley uses several purportedly ancient sources dealing with Abraham which have appeared since Joseph Smith's time to find parallels with the book of Abraham text, and thus to argue for its historicity." It is unclear why Hill labels the texts with which Nibley compares the book of Abraham as "purportedly ancient." And much of the comparative material cited by Nibley could not have been available to Joseph Smith. Hill pounces on the fact that Nibley "admits that these sources date at least hundreds of years after Abraham. One of these, the Apocalypse of Abraham, he indicates dates from the time of Christ. . . . Furthermore, as he says, no one is certain when Abraham lived. Estimates differ as much as two thousand years. . . . Despite this, he contends that to determine the authenticity of the book of Abraham we have only to compare sources from the *same time and place* and weigh the points of conflict and agreement. . . . Just how this can be done when the dates of his new sources are very late and the time of Abraham indeterminate he does not say. Also, he never compares these elements in the book of Abraham and his new sources which do *not* match, thus failing to meet his own essential criteria for proof. It might be better," Hill concludes, "simply to accept the book of Abraham on faith rather than trying to prove it by faulty logic and questionable evidence" (118–19).

Hill has not mastered Nibley's argument. Nibley explains how the book of Abraham can be tested, even though the comparative materials are relatively late and we do not know when Abraham lived. If anything matches between ancient texts and lore associated with the figure of Abraham and the book of Abraham, when those ancient materials were not available to Joseph Smith, then we have some reason to believe that what we have in the book of Abraham might be an authentic ancient record.

Nibley's argument is not difficult to follow. He moves as follows:

first, he sets forth the ideal situation in which historical authenticity may be tested. Then he indicates that, in testing the book of Abraham, we are faced with certain difficulties. Then he argues that the situation is not hopeless because of the difficulties he has described. Since there are available ancient Abrahamic texts that rather closely parallel the book of Abraham, they can function as an auxiliary control. Hence, the book of Abraham can be tested against a remarkable ancient parallel literature, most of which was not known when Joseph Smith lived. That may be a somewhat less rigorous test than the more exacting one that Nibley had set out as the ideal. But the situation is not rendered hopeless, as Hill concludes. At least Hill has not demonstrated that the situation is hopeless or that "faulty logic and questionable evidence" have been employed, as he concludes.

To be published as C in *CWHN*.

• Foreword. *Learn Greek through the New Testament*, by C. Wilfred Griggs and Randall Stewart, edited by Alan F. Keele and Marvin H. Folsom. The Interlinguistica Series in Foreign Languages, 1981.

To be included in E of the *CWHN*.

• "The Lachish Letters: Documents from Lehi's Day." *Ens* 10/12 (December 1981): 48–54.

Reprinted as "The Lachish Letters," in *The Prophetic Book of Mormon*, vol. 8 of the *CWHN* (Salt Lake City: Deseret Book and F.A.R.M.S., 1989), 380–406.

• "The Prophetic Book of Mormon." 17p. typed transcript of a talk given in a BYU Alumni House lecture on September 23, 1981.

This material is not the same as that included in *Since Cumorah* under the same title.

Published in *The Prophetic Book of Mormon*, vol. 8 of the *CWHN* (Salt Lake City: Deseret Book and F.A.R.M.S., 1989), 435–69.

• *Of All Things! A Nibley Quote Book*. Compiled and edited by Gary P. Gillum. Salt Lake City: Signature Books, 1981. xi, 178p.

• "Christ among the Ruins." 37p. typed manuscript dated March 2, 1981. Part 2 of "Souvenirs from Lehi's Jerusalem," which was submitted to the *Ens*.

Light is shed on 3 Nephi by comparisons with the Coptic Gospel of the Twelve Apostles.

Published in *The Prophetic Book of Mormon*, vol. 8 of the *CWHN* (Salt Lake City: Deseret Book and F.A.R.M.S., 1989), 407–34.

1982

• Miscellaneous comments in a panel discussion on the arts. With Eliot Butler, Robert Rees, Dennis Smith, and Eugene England (arbitrator). "BYU Faculty Panel." In *Letters to Smoother, Etc. . . . Proceedings of the 1980 Brigham Young University Symposium on the Humanities,* edited by Joy C. Ross and Steven C. Walker. Provo: BYU Press, 1982. 99–113.

To be included in F of the *CWHN*.

• "Two Shots in the Dark: i. Dark Days in Jerusalem; ii. Christ among the Ruins." In *Book of Mormon Authorship: New Light on Ancient Origins,* edited by Noel B. Reynolds. Provo: RSC, 1982. 103–41.

Reprinted as "Christ among the Ruins," in *The Prophetic Book of Mormon,* vol. 8 of the *CWHN* (Salt Lake City: Deseret Book and F.A.R.M.S., 1989), 380–434.

• "How to Get Rich." 19p., d.s., typed manuscript of an address given in March 1982 in St. George, Utah.

An examination of the blessing and cursing formulas found in the Deuteronomic materials in the Old Testament, with applications for our day.

Reprinted in *Approaching Zion,* vol. 9 of the *CWHN* (Salt Lake City: Deseret Book and F.A.R.M.S., 1989), 178–201.

• "Deny Not the Gifts of God." 21p., d.s., with several pages of insertions, typed manuscript of a talk given in Denver in February or March of 1982.

Social commentary on the order of a number of addresses given in 1982 and thereafter reminding the Saints of the good things God has blessed us with and the law which must govern our use of such gifts.

Published in *Approaching Zion,* vol. 9 of the *CWHN* (Salt Lake City: Deseret Book and F.A.R.M.S., 1989), 118–48.

• "Work We Must, But the Lunch Is Free." 24p., s.s., typed manuscript version of a talk given on April 20, 1982, to the Cannon-Hinckley Club at the Lion House, in Salt Lake City.

A condensed version of this talk was published under the same title in *BYU Today* 36/6 (November 1982): 8–12. The full text was reprinted in *Approaching Zion,* vol. 9 of the *CWHN* (Salt Lake City: Deseret Book and F.A.R.M.S., 1989), 202–51.

• "Funeral Address." 10p., s.s., typed transcript of a talk given at the services for Donald M. Decker on August 11, 1982.

A series of haunting reflections on the stages of life and the meaning of the experiences that each affords an individual as they pass from one stage to another, including death.

Published in *Approaching Zion,* vol. 9 of the *CWHN* (Salt Lake City: Deseret Book and F.A.R.M.S., 1989), 290–307.

• "A New Translation of Isaiah." *BYU Today* 36/7 (December 1982): 23.

A review of Avraham Gileadi's *The Apocalyptic Book of Isaiah, A New Translation and Interpretative Key* (Provo: Hebraeus Press, 1982), 207p.

• "Zion and Babylon Contrasted." Typed transcript of a talk.

• "The Prophetic Book of Mormon." *Seventh East Press*, March 27, 1982, 6–8, 16–17.

A talk given at the BYU Alumni House on September 23, 1981, originally a manuscript of 17p., d.s.

Reprinted in *The Prophetic Book of Mormon*, vol. 8 of the *CWHN* (Salt Lake City: Deseret Book and F.A.R.M.S., 1989), 435–69.

• "Three Degrees of Righteousness from the Old Testament." 17p. typescript of an address, dated November 1982.

Published in *Approaching Zion*, vol. 9 of the *CWHN* (Salt Lake City: Deseret Book and F.A.R.M.S., 1989), 308–40.

• "A Few Notes from 'Where Is the Battle.' " 3p., d.s., dated 1982.

• "Judging and Prejudging the Book of Abraham." An appendix in *They Lie in Wait to Deceive*, vol. 1, by Robert L. and Rosemary Brown. Edited by Barbara Ellsworth, rev. ed. Mesa, AZ: Brownsworth, 1982. 236–45.

To be included in D of the *CWHN*.

1983

• "Acclamatio (Never Cry Mob)." In *Toward a Humanistic Science of Politics: Essays in Honor of Francis Dunham Wormuth*, edited by Dalmas H. Nelson and Richard L. Sklar. Lanham, MD: University Press of America, 1983. 11–22.

In this essay Nibley draws on materials he collected at the beginning of his career on the politics of ancient mobs and draws parallels with contemporary events, including anti-Mormon sentiments. He read a paper with the title "Acclamatio" at the annual meeting of the Southwest Archaeological Foundation in San Diego, California, in 1941.

• "Leaders to Managers: The Fatal Shift." *DJMT* 16/4 (Winter 1983): 12–21. An address delivered at the BYU commencement ceremonies, August 19, 1983, at which Hugh received an honorary doctor of letters degree.

The editors, while correcting an inaccurate citation (18, for example), did not allow Nibley's own translation—"Choke on a gnat and gulp down a camel"—to stand (16).

Also available in *Fireside and Devotional Speeches, 1982–83*, edited by Cynthia M. Gardner (Provo: University Publications Press, 1983), 184–

90; and as "Leadership versus Management," *BYU Today* 38/1 (February 1984): 16–19, 45–47, with photographs of Nibley, at 17, 18, 19; to be included in J of the *CWHN*.

• "Interview: Nibley Talks about Contemporary Issues." *Sunstone Review* 3/11–12 (November-December 1983): 12–14.

To be included in F of the *CWHN*.

• "Dear Friends of the Book of Mormon." An open letter. 2p., ca. 1983, distributed by F.A.R.M.S.

Included as part of the foreword to *The Prophetic Book of Mormon,* vol. 8 of the *CWHN* (Salt Lake City: Deseret Book and F.A.R.M.S., 1989).

• "Christ among the Ruins." *Ens* 13/7 (July 1983): 14, 16–19. Subtitled, "A comparison of the Old World early Christian 'forty-day ministry' story with the New World 3 Nephi accounts."

This is a version of the material published as the second part of "Two Shots in the Dark: i. Dark Days in Jerusalem; ii. Christ among the Ruins," in *Book of Mormon Authorship: New Light on Ancient Origins,* edited by Noel B. Reynolds (Provo: RSC, 1982), 103–41. A version of this essay has been reprinted in *The Prophetic Book of Mormon,* vol. 8 of the *CWHN* (Salt Lake City: Deseret Book and F.A.R.M.S., 1989), 407–34.

1984

• "What Is a Temple?" In *The Temple in Antiquity: Ancient Records and Modern Perspectives,* edited by Truman G. Madsen. Provo: RSC, 1984. 19–37. Reprinted from *What Is a Temple* (1963 and 1968).

Reprinted in *Mormonism and Early Christianity,* vol. 4 of the *CWHN* (Salt Lake City: Deseret Book and F.A.R.M.S., 1987), 355–70.

• "Looking Backward." In *The Temple in Antiquity: Ancient Records and Modern Perspectives,* edited by Truman G. Madsen. Provo: RSC, 1984. 39–51.

Reprinted in *Mormonism and Early Christianity,* vol. 4 of the *CWHN* (Salt Lake City: Deseret Book and F.A.R.M.S., 1987), 370–90.

• "We Will Still Weep for Zion." 21p., s.s., typed manuscript of a talk read in 1984.

Published in *Approaching Zion,* vol. 9 of the *CWHN* (Salt Lake City: Deseret Book and F.A.R.M.S., 1989), 341–77.

• "Breakthroughs I Would Like to See." 15p. typed manuscript for a lecture on the Saints and the Law of Consecration, 1984. This lecture was given on November 8, 1984, at BYU in the Spheres of Influence lecture series entitled "Breakthroughs 84."

Published in *Approaching Zion,* vol. 9 of the *CWHN* (Salt Lake City: Deseret Book and F.A.R.M.S., 1989), 378–406.

1985

• "Scriptural Perspectives on How to Survive the Calamities of the Last Days." *BYUS* 25/1 (Winter 1985): 7–27.
Reprinted in *The Prophetic Book of Mormon,* vol. 8 of the *CWHN* (Salt Lake City: Deseret Book and F.A.R.M.S., 1989), 470–97.

• "Approach to Facsimile II." 35p., d.s., typescript, with an additional 8p. of figures. A Lecture given on May 17, 1985, in Washington, D.C.
To be included in G of the *CWHN.*

• "From the Earth upon Which Thou Standest." In *Looking Toward Home,* edited by Wulf Barsch. Salt Lake City: privately printed, 1985. 10–13.
To be included in I of the *CWHN.*

• "Science Fiction and the Gospel." In *LDSF 2: Latter-day Science Fiction,* edited by Benjamin Urrutia. Ludlow, MA: Parables, 1985. 5–28. The published version of an address given on February 13, 1968, and previously circulated as a typescript.
To be included in I of the *CWHN.*

• "There Is Always Egypt." 29p., d.s., typed transcript of an address delivered on October 25, 1985, on the 26th floor of the Church Office Building, Salt Lake City, UT. This address was delivered during the Ramses II exhibit at BYU to a number of dignitaries from Egypt.

1986

• "Change Out of Control." *Spheres of Influence* 1 (1986): 93–104. A lecture given in the Spheres of Influence lecture series on November 7, 1985, at BYU.
Reprinted in *Approaching Zion,* vol. 9 of the *CWHN* (Salt Lake City: Deseret Book and F.A.R.M.S., 1989), 407–21.

• "The Greatness of Egypt." 44p., d.s., typed transcript of an address delivered on March 12, 1986, as part of the Ramses II International Lecture Series.

• "The Utopians." 36p., d.s., 21p., s.s., typed transcript of a Spheres of Influence lecture given at BYU on November 6, 1986.
Published in *Approaching Zion,* vol. 9 of the *CWHN* (Salt Lake City: Deseret Book and F.A.R.M.S., 1989), 487–523.

• Foreword to *Why the Church Is as True as the Gospel,* by Eugene England. Salt Lake City: Bookcraft, 1986. vii-viii.

To be included in I of the *CWHN*.

• *Old Testament and Related Studies*. Vol. 1 of the *CWHN*. Edited by John W. Welch, Gary P. Gillum, and Don E. Norton. Salt Lake City: Deseret Book and F.A.R.M.S., 1986. xiv, 290p.

This is a collection of studies that are tangentially related to the Old Testament, though some of them are essentially social commentary; for example, "Great Are the Words of Isaiah" is not primarily a study of Isaiah as such.

Contents:

Foreword

Sources and Acknowledgments

Introduction

1. Historicity of the Bible [address given to the seminary and institute faculty at BYU on June 19, 1956]

2. Archaeology and Our Religion [originally privately circulated, with two letters, both dated September 16, 1965, this essay was submitted to the *Ins* but was rejected by the editor for ideological reasons]

3. Myths and the Scriptures [first appeared in *NE* 1/10 (October 1971): 34–38]

4. Before Adam [talk originally read on April 1, 1980, to the Phi Kappa Phi Society at BYU and thereafter privately circulated]

5. Patriarchy and Matriarchy [first appeared in *Blueprints for Living* (1980), 44–61]

6. Unrolling the Scrolls — Some Forgotten Witnesses [a transcription of a talk originally given in Glendale, California, in 1967]

7. Treasures in the Heavens [first appeared in *DJMT* 8/3–4 (Autumn-Winter, 1974): 76–98; reprinted in *Nibley on the Timely and the Timeless* (Provo: RSC, 1978), 49–84]

8. Great Are the Words of Isaiah [an address given at the sixth annual Sidney B. Sperry Symposium on January 28, 1978; first appeared in *Proceedings of the Sidney B. Sperry Symposium* (1978), 193–207]

9. More Voices from the Dust [first appeared in *Ins* 91/3 (March 1956): 71–72, 74]

10. The Dead Sea Scrolls: Some Questions and Answers [originally an address given to the seminary and institute faculty assembled at BYU on July 5, 1962; first appeared in *Ins* 98/7 (July 1963): 233–35]

11. Qumran and the Companions of the Cave: The Haunted Wilderness [first published in *RQ* 5/2 (April 1965): 177–98; reprinted in *Nibley on the Timely and the Timeless* (Provo: RSC, 1978), 187–212]

Scripture References

Index

Old Testament and Related Studies was reviewed by Keith E. Norman under the title "Zeal in Quest of Knowledge," *Sunstone* 11/2 (March 1987): 33–35. Norman appears to appreciate the social criticism found in certain of Nibley's essays—he pictures him as a kind of Old Testament prophet figure striking out at the foibles of contemporary culture, and especially of Latter-day Saints. From Norman's perspective, such elements are presumably acceptable, but he believes that Nibley's "very brilliance, which so dazzles his avid readers, . . . is the source of his weakness as a scholar" (33). Norman then charges Nibley with "notorious selective proof-texting and tendentious disregard of the evidence, or his sarcastic dismissal of arguments which do not support his position" (34). Unfortunately, none of these conclusions is supported by concrete illustrations from the book Norman is reviewing or from other essays by Nibley.

Norman refers to Nibley's "recurring lapses" into what he labels "scriptural literalism" (34), which seems to have some connections with Protestant fundamentalism in Norman's eyes. That seems odd, since Nibley went to some effort in the material Norman was reviewing to distance himself and the restored gospel from biblical fundamentalists, as well as the agnostic stance of so-called liberal scholars. It seems that what Norman objects to in Nibley's stance is his unwillingness to settle for the either-or thinking common to liberal seminary biblical studies in which one must reject literal understandings of the biblical texts in order to avoid being lumped with the fundamentalists.

Norman also feels that in dealing with the Dead Sea Scrolls and the Nag Hammadi manuscripts, which "Nibley invariably manages to read as proto-Mormon documents," that his "selective distortions and creative paraphrases run rampant" (35), though his examples from the *Gospel of Truth* are far from convincing. His effort to convict Nibley of creative paraphrasing in a reference to Ignatius' letter to the Trallians turns out to illustrate rather well Norman's unfamiliarity with the text Nibley was translating. On this and related matters, see the detailed memorandum by Robert F. Smith on Norman's review, 6p., s.s., dated July 18, 1987, in possession of compiler.

Kent P. Jackson (*BYUS* 28/4 [Fall 1988]: 114–19) assumes that the reason for publishing a collected works is to honor a writer "for his many accomplishments," which might be the purpose of a series containing selected works. The editors of the *CWHN* have "not done Nibley a service, nor have they served his readers" (118) by publishing some of the essays in *Old Testament and Related Studies*. Though stressing Nibley's role as defender of Latter-day Saint beliefs (114), positions (115), faith (115), "as the Church's chief apologist" (115), or "as a faithful apologist (in the most positive sense of the word) for the

Church" (119), which he finds praiseworthy, and crediting Nibley with having generated much of the serious scriptural research being done by Latter-day Saints, Jackson claims that Nibley's approach to the past amounts to "distortion." He characterizes Nibley's work as dishonest, even though he praises his "refreshing, imaginative view of things" (118), and "imaginative and iconoclastic way of looking at things" (119).

Jackson expresses "serious misgivings about [Nibley's] methodology" (115) because he assumes that it is not appropriate to fashion an account by gathering "sources from a variety of cultures all over the ancient world" (115). For Jackson, each community was culturally isolated, and threads do not link cultures in the ancient world. Hence, Nibley's comparisons are unseemly. But Jackson's view strikes at the heart of scholarship by denying the possibility of comparative studies or the formation of syntheses. He holds that Nibley begins with presuppositions and hence merely "picks and chooses the bits and pieces he wants" (115), while ignoring what does not fit, in an effort "to manufacture an ancient system of religion that is remarkably similar in many ways to our own" (115). Jackson is annoyed because Nibley looks for things that others have neglected or overlooked.

Jackson claims that Nibley begins with a theory and is incorrigible in the way he reads texts. "Nibley creates an artificial synthesis that never in reality existed" by working "from the conclusions to the evidence—instead of the other way around" (116). Nibley presumably "sees things in the sources that simply don't seem to be there," according to Jackson's reading of the texts. "This is what inevitably happens when scholars let their predetermined conclusions set the agenda for the evidence" (116). Jackson accepts the myth of a neutral observer somehow allowing "the evidence" to speak its truth through the historian without theory, presuppositions, or bias getting in the way. The fact is that all historical scholarship involves selection among alternatives, and presuppositions brought to texts. Jackson's quarrel with Nibley's "method" is both naive and badly conceived. The claim that Nibley assembles texts, choosing "the bits and pieces he wants" as he includes "what suits his presuppositions," while ignoring what does not (115), if it has any substance, is true of every attempt to draw from texts a picture of a world that is made accessible by puzzling over the meaning of what has been written and often overignored or neglected elements of texts. Assumptions, presuppositions, and theories define what will count as "evidence" by making something evident that otherwise would not be understandable or would be neglected. A presuppositionless exegesis is neither necessary nor possible. In the sophisticated literature on method, what constitutes "evidence" is now held to be theory-related and even theory-determined. When one puzzles over the past by reading texts, without preunderstandings consisting of the linguistic horizon brought to a text and also the formal and informal theories and explanations, nothing would be evident. On this and related issues, see Peter Novick, *That Noble Dream: The "Objectivity Question" and the American Historical Profession* (Cambridge: Cambridge University Press, 1988).

While granting that Nibley expresses his views "in refreshing imaginative ways" (118), Jackson is troubled by Nibley's style (117–18). The use of satire or traces of sarcasm, even when directed at the gross follies of powerful and corrupt interests, has "no place in serious scholarship" (117). For example: "A frequent vehicle for this [alleged sacrcasm and name-calling] is the straw-man approach. Nibley frequently misrepresents his opponents' views (through overstatement, oversimplification, or removal from context) to the point that they are ludicrous, after which he has ample cause to criticize them" (117). What is to be made of such a charge in the absence of a single example? While Jackson complains about Nibley's use of satire (117–18), in the passages that he praises, though there is no lessening of irony, no such complaint is forthcoming. Hence he finds Nibley's discussion of the Creation and Creation accounts (64, 69–74) to be "very insightful — and enjoyable reading as well" (118), even though Nibley forcefully satirizes historians, philosophers, and Moslems (64). It seems that when Jackson finds himself in agreement with Nibley, he overlooks what in other places he sees as distortions, methodological pitfalls, and faults both stylistic and scholarly.

Finally, it seems puzzling for Jackson to note on the one hand that "several of the articles lack sufficient documentation" (117), while on the other hand to fault other articles for being too heavily documented.

• *Enoch the Prophet.* Vol. 2 of the *CWHN.* Edited by Stephen D. Ricks. Salt Lake City: Deseret Book and F.A.R.M.S., 1986. viii, 309p.

This book contains a collection of various comparisons of the Enoch materials in the book of Moses with the Slavonic and Ethiopic Enoch texts and other related materials and lore from antiquity, showing the possibility that Joseph Smith's book of *Enoch* could be authentic ancient text.

Contents:

Foreword: Stephen D. Ricks

Part 1: Enoch the Prophet and His World

1. Enoch the Prophet [a version first appeared in *Pearl of Great Price Symposium: Brigham Young University November 22, 1975* (1976), 76–85]

• Open letter. Dated May 7, 1986, 1p., s.s, typed. A letter read by Zina Nibley Petersen at the Bureau of Land Management hearings on wilderness proposals held on May 7, 1986.

To be included in F of the *CWHN*.

1987

• *Lehi in the Desert and the World of the Jaredites*. Salt Lake City: Bookcraft, 1987. viii, 272p. An unedited reprinting of the original version.

• *The World and the Prophets*. Vol. 3 of the *CWHN*. Edited by John W. Welch, Gary P. Gillum, and Don E. Norton. 3d ed. Salt Lake City: Deseret Book and F.A.R.M.S., 1987. xii, 333p. A republication of a corrected version of what were originally a series of talks given over KSL under the title "Time Vindicates the Prophets" and then published under that title in pamphlet form, as well as in book form, as *The World and the Prophets*, both in 1954. A second expanded edition of the book was published in 1962.

Contents:

Foreword: R. Douglas Phillips

1 "How Will It Be When None More Saith 'I Saw'?"

2. A Prophet's Reward

3. Prophets and Preachers

4. Prophets and Scholars

5. Prophets and Philosophers

6. Prophets and Creeds

7. The Prophets and the Search for God

8. Prophets and Gnostics

9. The Schools and the Prophets

10. St. Augustine and the Great Tradition

11. A Substitute for Revelation

12. Prophets and Mystics

• *Mormonism and Early Christianity*. Vol. 4 of the *CWHN*. Edited by Todd M. Compton and Stephen D. Ricks. Salt Lake City: Deseret Book and F.A.R.M.S., 1987. xiii, 446p.

Contents:

Foreword: Todd M. Compton

1. Early Accounts of Jesus' Childhood [first appeared in *Ins* 100/1 (January 1965): 35–37]

2. *Evangelium Quadraginta Dierum*: the Forty-day Mission of Christ — The Forgotten Heritage [first published in *VC* 20/1 (1966): 1–24; reprinted in *When the Lights Went Out* (1970): 33–54]

3. The Early Christian Prayer Circle [first appeared in *BYUS* 19/1(Fall 1978): 41–78]

4. Baptism for the Dead in Ancient Times [first appeared in a series in the *IE* in 1948–49]

5. The Passing of the Primitive Church [first appeared in *CH* 20/2 (June 1961): 131–54]

6. The Way of the Church [first appeared in a series in the *IE* in 1955]

7. Jerusalem in Early Christianity [first appeared in the *Encyclopedia Judaica* (1972), 9:1568–75]

8. What Is a Temple? [first appeared in *MS* 120/8 (August 1958): 228–37; 247–49; reprinted as *What Is a Temple* (1963 and 1968); the concluding section entitled "Looking Backward" was taken from the version published in *The Temple in Antiquity* (1983), 39–51]

9. Christian Envy of the Temple [first appeared in *JQR* 50/2–3 (October 1959; January 1960): 97–123; 229–40; reprinted in *When the Lights Went Out* (1970), 55–88]

Key to Abbreviations

Scripture References

Index

Keith E. Norman has reviewed this volume (see *The John Whitmer Historical Association Journal* 9 [1989]: 108–12). His remarks are generally favorable. He pictures Nibley as "the preeminent Mormon scholar of ancient studies and unofficial apologist for the LDS Church" (108). He notes that Nibley's "biases are never in doubt." This offends Norman, and he complains of "Nibley's apparent lack of a sense of fair play or balance—dare we say Christian charity?" (109). And he also refers to what he calls Nibley's "operative methodology: he is proof-texting—compiling isolated passages to support predetermined conclusions—with little regard for the context of those citations" (109–10). Norman claims that Nibley's faults are thus in ample evidence in the essays found in this volume. "The most obvious [fault] is his tendentiousness, which is perhaps inevitable when one sets out to be a defender of the faith" (111). Norman feels that "the conclusion of each of these essays has been predetermined according to Nibley's Mormonism" (111). But Norman neglects to explain why tendentiousness is a weakness, or why it should be overcome, or how it can be overcome. What is implied in Norman's view is that for one to be tendentious, that is, marked by a tendency to favor a particular point of view—especially Mormonism—is wrong. But why is that necessarily so? Though Norman does not explicitly take up this issue, he provides some clues indicating why he feels that tendentiousness is wrong: he apparently believes that it is a mistake to manifest bias because one ought, instead, to strive for objectivity, balance, or detachment. From the point of view of the commonly held methodological mythology Nibley must be faulted because he lacks the necessary objectivity. But Peter Novick has shown that the American history profession has been made to rest upon an incoherent and vacuous objectivist mythology, which he identifies as the myth of presumably objective historians giving us an objective history (*That Noble Dream* [Cambridge: Cambridge University Press, 1988]). According to the objectivist mythology, biases, inclinations, or propensities favoring a point of view (including especially faith) are corrupting and prevent the historian from discovering what really happened. Obviously such an objectivist ideology works against believers, since they obviously have a point of view. But ironically, Norman is tendentious about the need for detachment, balance, or objectivity, which he clearly endorses. His understanding of historical method is not defended with arguments and is recommended for unexplained and unexamined reasons. Ironically, Norman is biased against the defense of the faith and would presumably feel more comfortable if Nibley had hidden his premises and made an effort to dissemble by making it appear to his readers that he had merely happened to discover some things while wandering around in the literature of antiquity as a dispassionate, disinterested, detached observer interested only in having the facts speak their truth through him. The demand for objectivity turns out to be more a matter of scholarly pretence, style, or tone and therefore has little to do with the substance of reasoning and argumentation and nothing to do with the historical understanding or the business of working out historical explanations. Nibley clearly rejects the affectation of scholarly neutrality, and rightly so. One wonders whether Norman follows what Nibley labels "the Baconian gospel, that one has simply to collect the facts and let them speak for themselves" (375). If so, he has appropriated an outmoded, incoherent view of science which he has unwittingly applied to historical scholarship.

Norman, though respectful of Nibley's learning and command of languages, feels that the documentation in some of the essays in this volume goes too far and was intended to "dazzle" the reader with an "esoteric level of erudition. One essay contains twelve pages of text followed by twenty-two of footnotes, set in smaller type. So much paper and ink are squandered when the editing is sloppy or overly lenient" (111). Without argumentation, Norman hints that the editing for the essay to which he alludes was either shoddy or permissive. But apparently the editors of *Vigiliae Christianae*, a distinguished European journal, who originally published Nibley's essay on the forty-day ministry of Christ, did not feel that they were wasting either paper or ink by publishing the citations appended to that essay. If one were to look for a squandering of ink and paper, would it not be easier to make a case by pointing to advertising copy, newspapers, pornography or a host of other such publications, rather than the endnotes for a serious piece of scholarship?

• "Leaders to Managers: The Fatal Shift." In *Personal Voices: A Celebration of Dialogue*, edited by Mary L. Bradford. Salt Lake City: Signature Books, 1987. 179–91.

Reprinted from *DJMT* 16/4 (Winter 1983): 12–21.

• "The Faith of an Observer: Conversations with Hugh Nibley." 63–minute VHS video, and 32p. annotated typed transcript.
To be included in F of the *CWHN*.

• "Law of Consecration." 50p., d.s, 37p., s.s., typed manuscript of a talk originally given in Church Office Building Auditorium on February 6, 1987.
Published in *Approaching Zion*, vol. 9 of the *CWHN* (Salt Lake City: Deseret Book and F.A.R.M.S., 1989), 422–86.

• "But What Kind of Work." 24p., d.s., typed manuscript for a talk originally given as a talk to the Cannon-Hinckley Club on May 19, 1987, and then delivered at various other places in 1987.
A sequel to Nibley's lecture entitled "Work We Must, But the Lunch Is Free," originally given on April 20, 1982.
Published in *Approaching Zion*, vol. 9 of the *CWHN* (Salt Lake City: Deseret Book and F.A.R.M.S., 1989), 252–89.

• "Brigham Young: Pioneer Conservationist." 14p., s.s, typed transcript, of an address to the Southern Utah Wilderness Alliance, at a rendezvous held in September 1987.
To be included in J of the *CWHN*.

• "Chattanooga." 23p., d.s., typed transcript of an address given in Chattanooga, Tennessee, in August 1987.
The talk is essentially a commentary on certain portions of the Gospel of Matthew.

• "Goods of First and Second Intent." 35p., d.s., typed transcript, of a talk given on October 9, 1987, to the UEA retired teachers association at the Salt Palace in Salt Lake City, Utah.
Reprinted in *Approaching Zion*, vol. 9 of the *CWHN* (Salt Lake City: Deseret Book and F.A.R.M.S., 1989), 524–53.

1988

• *Lehi in the Desert; The World of the Jaredites; There Were Jaredites.* Vol. 5 of the *CWHN*. Edited by John W. Welch, Darrell L. Matthews, and Stephen R. Callister. Salt Lake City: Deseret Book and F.A.R.M.S., 1988. xviii, 464p.
Contents:
Foreword to the 1952 Edition: John A. Widtsoe
Introduction to the 1988 Edition: John W. Welch
Part I: Lehi in the Desert [first appeared in a series in the *IE* in 1950]
Part II: The World of the Jaredites [first appeared in a series in the *IE* in 1951]

Part III: There Were Jaredites [first appeared in a series in the *IE* in 1956–57]
Appendix I: East Coast or West Coast?
Appendix II: How Far to Cumorah?
Scripture References
Index

• "Last Call: An Apocalyptic Warning from the Book of Mormon." *Sunstone* 12/1 (January 1988): 14–25.
Reprinted in *The Prophetic Book of Mormon*, vol. 8 of the *CWHN* (Salt Lake City: Deseret Book and F.A.R.M.S., 1989), 498–532.

• *An Approach to the Book of Mormon*. Vol. 6 of the *CWHN*. Edited by John W. Welch. 3d ed. Salt Lake City: Deseret Book and F.A.R.M.S., 1988. xvii, 541p. A revised edition of the book published under the same title by The Council of the Twelve Apostles of The Church of Jesus Christ of Latter-day Saints in 1957; and in a second edition by Deseret Book in 1964; reprinted in 1976 in the Classics of Mormon Literature series. [This book was originally published as the lesson manual for the Melchizedek Priesthood quorums of The Church of Jesus Christ of Latter-day Saints.]
Contents:
Foreword to the First Edition
Preface to the First Edition: Joseph Fielding Smith
Preface to the 1964 Edition: Hugh Nibley
Part 1: The Changing Scene
    1. Introduction to an Unknown Book
    2. A Time for Reexamination
Part 2: Lehi's World
    3. An Auspicious Beginning
    4. Lehi as a Representative Man
Part 3: Lehi's Affairs
    5. The Jews and the Caravan Trade
    6. Lehi and the Arabs
    7. Dealings with Egypt
Part 4: The Doomed City
    8. Politics in Jerusalem
    9. Escapade in Jerusalem
    10. Portrait of Laban
Part 5: The Meaning of the Wilderness
    11. Flight into the Wilderness
    12. The Pioneer Tradition and the True Church
    13. Church in the Wilderness
Part 6: The Dead Sea Scrolls and the Book of Mormon

• *Since Cumorah: The Book of Mormon in the Modern World.* Vol. 7 of the *CWHN.* Edited by John W. Welch. 2d ed. Salt Lake City: Deseret Book and F.A.R.M.S., 1988. xv, 512p. This is a revised and corrected edition of the book published under the same title by Deseret Book in 1967, with many changes taken from a series in the *IE* that appeared in 1964–66.

Contents:

7. Checking on Long-forgotten Lore
Part III. Some Scientific Questions
    8. "Forever Tentative . . . "
Part IV. The Real Background of the Book of Mormon
    9. Some Fairly Foolproof Texts
    10. Prophets in the Wilderness
    11. A Rigorous Test: Military History
Part V. The Prophetic Book of Mormon
    12. Good People and Bad People
    13. Prophecy in the Book of Mormon: The Three Periods
Momentary Conclusion
Appendix: Comparison of Editions
Scriptural References
Index

• "The Book of Mormon: Forty Years After." A talk given at the Sunstone 1988 Book of Mormon Lecture Series, May 10, 1988, at the Fine Arts Auditorium, University of Utah.

Published in *The Prophetic Book of Mormon*, vol. 8 of the *CWHN* (Salt Lake City: Deseret Book and F.A.R.M.S., 1989), 533–69.

• "The Terrible Questions." 52p., d.s., transcript of a talk given on September 8, 1988, as part of the Deseret Book/F.A.R.M.S. Nibley lecture series.

To be included in I of the *CWHN*.

• "The Meaning of the Atonement." 75p., d.s., transcript of a talk given on November 11, 1988, as part of the Deseret Book/F.A.R.M.S. Nibley lecture series.

Published in *Approaching Zion*, vol. 9 of the *CWHN* (Salt Lake City: Deseret Book and F.A.R.M.S., 1989), 554–614. An abbreviated version was published in the *Student Review*, December 20, 1989, 3.

• "Decorative Hardware with Intricate Meanings." In *The Manti Temple*, edited by Victor J. Rasmussen. Provo: Community Press, 1988. 33–36.

In a portion of a chapter of a book put out by the Manti Temple Centennial Committee in celebrating the hundredth anniversary of that edifice, Nibley interprets the decorations found on six numbered "artifacts" in the Manti Temple, for example, door hinges and handles.

To be included in I of the *CWHN*.

1989

• "One Eternal Round: A Hermetic Version." 59p., d.s., transcript of a talk given on January 12, 1989, as part of the Deseret Book/ F.A.R.M.S. Nibley lecture series.

To be included in I of the *CWHN*.

• "Stewardship of the Air." 22 p., d.s., transcript of a talk given on February 16, 1989, at BYU.

To be included in J of the *CWHN*.

• *The Prophetic Book of Mormon*. Vol. 8 of the *CWHN*. Edited by John W. Welch. Salt Lake City: Deseret Book and F.A.R.M.S., 1989. xi, 595p. A collection of miscellaneous essays on the Book of Mormon.

Contents:

Foreword: John W. Welch

1. Stick of Judah [first appeared as "The Stick of Judah and the Stick of Joseph," a series of articles in *IE* 56/1 (January 1953): 16–17, 38–41; 56/2 (February 1953): 90–91, 123–27; 56/3 (March 1953): 150–52, 191–95; 56/4 (April 1953): 250, 267; 56/5 (May 1953): 331–32, 334, 336, 338, 341, 343, 345]

2. Columbus and Revelation [first published in *Ins* 88/10 (October 1953): 319–20]

3. New Approaches to Book of Mormon Study [first appeared in a series in *IE* 56/11 (November 1953): 830–31, 859–62; 56/12 (December 1953): 919, 1003; 57/1 (January 1954): 30–32, 41; 57/2 (February 1954): 88–89, 125–26; 57/3 (March 1954): 148–50, 170; 57/4 (April 1954): 232–33, 246, 248–50; 57/5 (May 1954): 308–9, 326, 330; 57/6 (June 1954): 389, 447–48, 450–51; 57/7 (July 1954): 506–7, 521]

4. Kangaroo Court [first appeared in *IE* 62/3 (March 1959): 145–48, 184–87; and 62/4 (April 1959): 224–26, 300–301]

5. Just Another Book? [first appeared in *IE* 62/5 (May 1959): 345–47, 388–91; 62/6 (June 1959): 412–13, 501–53; 62/7 (July 1959): 530–31, 565]

6. The Grab Bag [first appeared in *IE* 62/8 (July 1959): 530–33, 546–48]

7. What Frontier, What Camp Meeting? [first appeared in *IE* 62/9 (August 1959): 590–92, 610, 612, 614–15]

8. The Comparative Method [first appeared in *IE* 62/10 (October 1959): 744–47, 759; 62/11 (November 1959): 848, 854, 856]

9. The Boy Nephi in Jerusalem [first appeared in *Ins* 96/3 (March 1961): 84–85]

10. Literary Style Used in the Book of Mormon Insured Accurate Translation [first published in *Deseret News*, "Church News," July 29, 1961, 10, 15]

11. The Book of Mormon: True or False? [first appeared in *MS* 124/11 (November 1962): 274–77, supplemented in note 29 by material taken from a talk given at the Portland Institute Symposium in 1979]

12. Howlers in the Book of Mormon [first appeared in *MS* 125/2 (February 1963): 28–34]

13. The Mormon View of the Book of Mormon [first appeared in *Concilium: An International Review of Theology* 10 (December 1967): 82–83]

14. Ancient Temples: What Do They Signify? [first appeared in *Ens* 2/9 (September 1972): 46–49]

15. Bar Kochba and Book of Mormon Backgrounds [first appeared as a review of Yigael Yadin"s *Bar-Kochba: The Rediscovery of the Legendary Hero of the Second Jewish Revolt Against Rome*, in *BYUS* 14/1 (Autumn 1973): 115–26]

16. Churches in the Wilderness [first appeared in *Nibley on the Timely and the Timeless* (Provo: RSC, 1978), 155–86; not to be confused with the material that appeared under the same title in *An Approach to the Book of Mormon*, 2d ed. (Salt Lake City: Deseret Book, 1964), 125–34]

17. Freemen and King-men in the Book of Mormon [originally a talk given in 1980, and again on January 18, 1981, at the J. Reuben Clark Law School at BYU]

18. The Lachish Letters [first appeared in *Book of Mormon Authorship: New Light on Ancient Origins*, edited by Noel B. Reynolds (Provo: RSC, 1982), 104–21]

19. Christ among the Ruins [first appeared in *Book of Mormon Authorship: New Light on Ancient Origins*, edited by Noel B. Reynolds (Provo: RSC, 1982), 121–41]

20. The Prophetic Book of Mormon [first appeared in *Seventh East Press*, March 27, 1982, 6–8, 16–17; this was originally a talk given at the BYU Alumni House on September 23, 1981]

21. Scriptural Perspectives on How to Survive the Calamities of the Last Days [first appeared in *BYUS* 25/1 (Winter 1985): 7–27]

22. Last Call: An Apocalyptic Warning from the Book of Mormon [first appeared in *Sunstone* 12/1 (January 1988): 14–25]

23. The Book of Mormon: Forty Years After [first given as a talk at the Sunstone 1988 Book of Mormon Lecture Series, May 10, 1988, at the Fine Arts Auditorium, University of Utah]

Scriptural References

Index

• "Reflections on War in the Book of Mormon." A talk given on March 24, 1989, at the F.A.R.M.S. Symposium on Warfare in the Book of Mormon.

To be included as "Warfare and the Book of Mormon" in *Warfare in the Book of Mormon* (Salt Lake City: Deseret Book and F.A.R.M.S., forthcoming in 1990); to be included in J of the *CWHN*.

• "Criticizing the Brethren." 36p., d.s., typed transcript of a talk given on August 18, 1989, at the CES conference held at BYU as well as on August 26, 1989, at the Sunstone Symposium in Salt Lake City. Published as a F.A.R.M.S. paper, 1990.

• *Approaching Zion.* Vol. 9 of the *CWHN.* Edited by Don E. Norton. Salt Lake City: Deseret Book and F.A.R.M.S., 1989. xviii, 631. A collection of miscellaneous essays on Zion and related topics.

Contents

Foreword: Don Norton

1. Our Glory or Our Condemnation [originally published in *ASBYU Academics Office Presents: Last Lecture Series, 1971–72* (Provo: BYU, 1972), 1–14]

2. What Is Zion? A Distant View [originally published as "What Is Zion? A Distant View," in *What Is Zion? Joseph Smith Lecture Series, 1972–73* (Provo: BYU Press, 1973), 1–21; reprinted in *Sunstone* 13/2 (April 1989): 20–32)]

3. Zeal Without Knowledge [first appeared in *DJMT* 11/2 (Summer 1978): 101–12; reprinted in *Nibley On the Timely and the Timeless* (Provo: RSC, 1978), 261–77]

4. Gifts [a talk given on March 13, 1979, at BYU]

5. Deny Not the Gifts [a talk given in February or March 1982]

6. How Firm a Foundation! What Makes It So [originally published as "How Firm a Foundation! What Makes It So," *DJMT* 12/4 (Winter 1979): 29–45; also published by the Harold B. Lee Library Forum Committee and the Friends of the BYU Library in 1980 as a 15–page leaflet]

7. How to Get Rich [a previously unpublished address given in March 1982 in St. George, Utah]

8. Work We Must, but the Lunch Is Free [originally an address given on April 20, 1982, to the Cannon-Hinckley Club at the Lion House, in Salt Lake City, from which a condensed version was published under the same title in *BYU Today* 36/6 (November 1982): 8–12]

9. But What Kind of Work? [a previously unpublished address given on May 19, 1987, to the Cannon-Hinckley Club in Salt Lake City]

10. Funeral Address [an address given at the services for Donald M. Decker on August 11, 1982, in Rexburg, Idaho]

11. Three Degrees of Righteousness from the Old Testament [a previously unpublished address given in November 1982]

12. We Will Still Weep for Zion [a previously unpublished address given in 1984]

13. Breakthroughs I Would Like to See [a previously unpublished lecture given on November 8, 1984, at BYU in the Spheres of Influence lecture series entitled "Breakthroughs 84"]

14. Change Out of Control [originally published in *Spheres of Influence* 1 (1986): 93–104 from a lecture given in the Spheres of Influence lecture series at BYU on November 7, 1985]

15. Law of Consecration [a talk originally given in the Church Office Building in Salt Lake City, Utah, on February 6, 1987]

16. Utopians [a previously unpublished lecture given in the Spheres of Influence lecture series at BYU on November 6, 1986]

17. Goods of First and Second Intent [an address given to the UEA Retired Teachers Association at the Salt Palace in Salt Lake City, Utah, on October 9, 1987]

18. The Meaning of the Atonement [the second address in the "Hugh Nibley Lecture Series" sponsored by Deseret Book and F.A.R.M.S., given on November 10, 1988]

UNDATED ITEMS

• "The Lesson of the Sixth Century B.C." 14p., d.s., transcript of a lecture, n.d.
To be included in E of the *CWHN*.

• "The Jerusalem Scene." 16p. transcript of a lecture, n.d.
Cf. the various versions of Nibley's talk on the Lachish letters.

• "Irenaeus, Lecture #2." 24p., d.s., rough transcription of a talk, n.d.

• "Humanism and the Gospel." 4p. s.s., rough draft of lecture notes, n.d.

• "Peter." 30p. rough transcript of a lecture. [Note: p. 12 is missing.]

• "Plato's Athens." 10p., d.s., typed transcript of a lecture, n.d.
The views of Aristophanes are set forth on corruption in the commercial world of the time. This is then linked to certain themes in the Platonic dialogues (Phaedrus, Gorgius, Sophist, Meno, Apology) in which language can be found in which Socrates quarrels with the Sophists over such matters.

• "Prayer." 1p., d.s., transcript of a prayer given at a BYU graduation ceremony, n.d.

• "Some Significant Statements by Leading Scientists on the Scope of Scientific Authority," 17p., s.s., but pagination is not continuous, n.d.
A class handout which consists of a medley of quotations from

various people, for example, Karl Popper, arranged under headings. The materials were collected after 1965.

• "Ancient Ordinances." 3p. typescript of notes on a talk, n.d.
To be included in I of the *CWHN*.

• "As Far as the Utmost Heavens." 23p. typed transcript of a talk given in 1987 or 1988 somewhere in Alaska.
A talk in which the accomplishments of Joseph Smith are set forth and defended.
To be included in B of the *CWHN*.

• "It Takes All Kinds." 22p., d.s., typed manuscript, with an additional page numbered 22a.

• "Temple." 27p., d.s., typed manuscript, with 9p. of notations by Nibley.
To be included in I of the *CWHN*.

• "Circle and Square." A 30p., d.s., undated and unpublished manuscript.
To be included in I of the *CWHN*.

G-2 Reports—a series of handouts prepared in the fifties and early sixties for distribution to various audiences.

• "G-2 Report, No. 1." 5p., s.s., n.d.
Changes in the religious world and in scholarship concerning religion are illustrated by numerous quotations from various writers.

• "G-2 Report, No. 2." 5p., s.s., n.d.
Changes in religious scholarship further illustrated. Quotations are arranged under headings such as " 'Revelation' No Longer a Dirty Word," "Neo-orthodoxy," "Science."

• "G-2 Report, No. 3." 8p., s.s., n.d.
"Evolution," "Eschatology," etc.

• "G-2 Report, No. 4." 7p., s.s., n.d.
"Eduard Meyer's Comparison of Mohammed and Joseph Smith."

• "G-2 Report, No. 5." 4p., s.s., n.d.
"The God of the Christian Doctors."

• "G-2 Report, No. 6." 5p., s.s., n.d.
"Conflict in the Churches between the God of the Bible and the God of the Philosophers."

• "G-2 Report, No. 7." 7p., s.s., n.d.
"New Testament."

• "G-2 Report, No. 8." 7p., s.s., n.d.
"Introduction: 'An Age of Discovery' and 'Old Testament'."

• "G-2 Report, No. 9." 8p., s.s., n.d.
"Church History."

SECONDARY MATERIALS

• Louis Midgley. "Hugh Nibley: A Short Bibliographical Note." *DJMT* 2/1 (Spring 1967): 119–21.

• Louis Midgley. "Hugh Nibley: The Portrait of a Leader." *IE* 73/5 (May 1970): 79–81.

• Lori Schlinker. "Kitsch in the Visual Arts and Advertisements of The Church of Jesus Christ of Latter-day Saints." Interview #6, in Lori Schlinker's *Kitsch in the Visual Arts* (Provo: BYU, 1971), 60–64.
To be included in J of the *CWHN*.

• "Hugh Nibley: If He's Got It All Together, Why Does He Stand All Alone?" *BYU Today* 28/4 (May 1974): 12–13.

• Truman G. Madsen. Foreword to *Nibley on the Timely and the Timeless*. Provo: RSC, 1978. ix–xvii.

• Hal Williams. "Hugh Nibley and Kimball Hansen: Candidates for the 'Search Society.'" *BYU Today* 34/5 (August 1980): 12–13. An interview in which cosmological issues are discussed.
To be included in F of the *CWHN*.

• Jerry Johnston. "A Legendary Passion for Books and Languages," *Deseret News*, Friday, October 31, 1980, C1. One of a series of interviews concerning the reading habits of prominent Utahns. This was the eighth in the series.
Nibley listed, as his favorite books, the following: (1) Shakespeare, *Complete Works*; (2) Book of Mormon; (3) Homer, *Odyssey*; (4) Goethe, *Faust*; (5) Gaius Petronius, *Satyricon*; (6) Jean Froissart, *Chronicles*. Nibley also said that by age thirteen he knew *Macbeth* by heart and tried to learn *Hamlet*, but found it too long.
To be included in F of the *CWHN*.

• Arnold J. Irvine. "Hugh Nibley: Profile of a Scholar." *Utah Magazine*, Sunday, April 15, 1984, 4–6.

• John W. Welch. "Hugh Nibley and the Book of Mormon." *Ens* 15/4 (April 1985): 50–56.

• John W. Welch. "The Timelessness of Hugh Nibley." *This People* 8/2 (April 1987): 38–39, 42.

• Mark Burns, "Late Night: Starring Hugh Nibley," *Student Review*, September 27, 1989, 4.

• Kevin Stoker. "Truth Stimulates Gospel Scholar." Deseret News, "Church News," October 28, 1989, 6.

1

The Influence of Hugh Nibley: His Presence in the University

Robert K. Thomas
Brigham Young University, Provo, Utah

The verbal bookkeeping that is often useful in presenting complex people is hopelessly ineffective in giving a balanced account of Hugh Nibley. To begin with, on which side of the ledger do we post his glorious absentmindedness? Dental appointments missed may be a liability, but a mind unfettered by circumstance is an asset most of us envy. What appear to be contradictions in others turn out to be complements in him. He is *sui generis* and therefore not subject to a normal audit.

If analysis of Hugh as a person is unfruitful, consideration of him as a *presence* is an overwhelming experience. In the first place, a presence may take on a mythic aura appropriately, and there is little doubt but that the friends and students who have been part of the penumbra that has surrounded his intense scholarly activity during the last quarter-century have been stimulated beyond expectation and have never really lost the glow they first felt in attending him.

Yet he has never been a model to be followed, and he has not stopped long enough for disciples to line up in back of him. The enduring fact of his presence at BYU has been threat, comfort, goad, and—especially—conscience

Presented in honor of Hugh Nibley on his sixty-fifth birthday in the Varsity Theater, Brigham Young University, in connection with the 1975 Annual Welch Lecture Series by Klaus Baer and others in tribute to Dr. Nibley.

to his colleagues. The unembodied, internal conscience that whispers to each would-be scholar that his effort is imperfect may be lulled by rationalization—who has not cooled his intellectual ardor in the present by promises of massive exertion in the future?—but there is something so impelling about those note cards, rubber-banded, boxed, or simply splayed on the lectern in front of Hugh Nibley, that makes the dullest of us flush with scholarly resolve.

Usual academic research is attended by some risks. One may choose to analyze and interpret areas that are so large or complex that early evidence of success is not possible, and one may know years of lonely, silent eloquence while research comes to fruition. Another may know the frustration of having his best efforts nullified by the work of those who bring to successful conclusion the experiments he is still engaged in.

But no research is so difficult as that undertaken to investigate religious positions. While no researcher begins without bias—whatever the object of his exploration—the temptation to emphasize evidence that supports his theological belief may be irresistible for the religious scholar. The deep emotional reinforcement that commitment to particular doctrines provides will usually seep through the chinks in the most objective prose. The problem is not that this occurs—as indicated above, anyone with a hypothesis experiences the same difficulty. The peculiar temptation of the religious researcher is coming to believe that the theological tenets he accepted on faith are, after he has written about them, the result of his work. When this happens, what began, modestly, as investigation becomes justification, and discussion degenerates into contention. A position may be controversial without being contentious. The controversial scholar is not uncommon, but the contentious scholar is a contradiction in terms. There is presumption in contentious assertion that is simply incompatible with honest inquiry.

While acknowledging his religious beliefs, Hugh Nibley has avoided theological stances that go beyond the fundamental position of his Church. He enjoys the give and take of doctrinal debate, and in his hands the familiar, personal letter becomes an unusually effective instrument by which to comment on opposing views. However brisk some of these letters have become—for Hugh can't resist exploiting an obvious opening—his sense of proportion never fails him. He is always the classical satirist.

As often happens when one person exhibits the qualities that many would have, there has been a tendency on the part of some to equate presence with resource. Hugh has been expected to silence opposition with continuing, stunning discoveries and insights—even though the positions he is expected to support may be no more than the personal whim of those who attempt to use him as crutch, club, or mantle. A lesser man might have retreated into cynicism, or into the completely esoteric where the foolish could not follow, but Hugh has patiently corrected, carefully restated—and smiled when his simplest explanation has still been distorted.

An insistence on the significance of patterns keeps Nibley scholarship tentative when the key piece to a historical or scriptural puzzle seems to be found. Wry comments about his own fallibility are never simply the graceful disclaimers of arrogance. His most persistent critics are not so skillful as Hugh himself in identifying and pricking the pretensions that could develop during the course of his work. The reach of his mind is such that the synthesis the Book of Mormon calls "a compound in one"—which is so difficult for most of us to pull together—is his natural mode. He follows implications that a less discriminating mind would lose in the limbo of fragmentary source and dubious translation that are the materials he must use. What Coleridge called the *esemplastic* process, the ability to project new entities that combine evidence in different and persuasive ways, distinguishes a Nibley reading and is the bane of those who prefer to echo traditional interpretations.

The confidence with which Hugh presents a point of view is his compliment to an idea that deserves the most convincing context he can supply for it. No perceptive hearer mistakes this for the assurance with which the earnest amateur often chooses to speak. Failure to fit necessary patterns will check overstatement; other scholars will refute, refine, or extend, but that most fragile of human creations—a synthesizing concept—will get its chance to survive under optimal conditions.

The full influence of Hugh Nibley on other members of the faculty over the years is not easy to gauge. The affectionate respect with which his colleagues viewed him allowed the singular role he chose to play. We were always proud of him but not anxious to pull him away from "the glory that was Greece and the grandeur that was Rome" to the modesty that was Provo. Yet his was never a repudiating isolation; his single-mindedness was not achieved at the cost of rejecting the interests of his friends. Whatever one's academic concern, it took on freshness and stature under the quickening impulse of a conversation with Hugh. Even the malaise of general faculty meetings was routed by his trenchant—and always sprightly—comment.

To fellow faculty members who feared lest humble resources and heavy teaching loads fatally compromise significant research at BYU, Hugh was answer and inspiration. His relentless demand for documents gave impetus to the building of collections that could approximate his expectations—and in so doing raised the aspirations of the entire library.

Few students can talk coherently about their first class from Brother Nibley. For some it was simply a rite of passage, the academic equivalent of a social-unit initiation.

For many it was, at best, a brisk blur edged with random flashes of insight. For a few it was an intellectual implosion, from which they will never recover. For after one has stood in the presence of his first true scholar the world loses a bit of its apparent symmetry, reveals the forces that determined its form and invites an infinite recasting. Never does one's agency seem so unlimited — yet the scholarly life is curiously impersonal, almost abstract. It isn't really possible to know the person who inspires our scholarly activity. One can hardly send a thank-you note to Prometheus. But one can acknowledge the electric force that is generated when a potentially good mind rubs against a great one.

Hugh has assumed the ultimate hazard of scholarly research — the popularization of technical material — without obvious discomposure, and he is equally serene under the critical review of his peers. He has won, and kept, the confidence of General Authorities of the Church, and he holds the titles of husband and father with distinction. In the easy parlance of the day, he has "put it all together." For as Thomas DeQuincey observed: "A great scholar, in the highest sense of the term, is not one who depends simply on an infinite memory, but also on an infinite . . . power of combination; bringing together from the four winds, like the Angel of the Resurrection, what else were dust from dead men's bones, into the unity of breathing life."

2

A Doorkeeper in
the House of the Lord

John W. Welch
Brigham Young University, Provo, Utah

The last person in the world who is interested in celebrating Hugh Nibley's seventy-fifth birthday is Hugh Nibley. He has never asked for such a thing; he avoids recognition like the plague. In complete candor, he faithfully describes himself as follows: "I have always been furiously active in the Church, but I have also been a nonconformist and have never held any office of rank in anything. I have undertaken many assignments given me by the leaders, and much of the work has been anonymous: no rank, no recognition, no anything. While I have been commended for some things, they were never the things which I considered most important. That was entirely a little understanding between me and my Heavenly Father which I have thoroughly enjoyed, though no one else knows anything about it. . . . I would rather be a doorkeeper in the House of the Lord than mingle with the top brass in the tents of the wicked."

Many similar words come to mind as others try to describe him. His life is a rare combination of faith and scholarship, of teaching and research, of orthodoxy and eccentricity, of rigor and homily, of spontaneity and te-

---

A tribute to Hugh Nibley on his seventy-fifth birthday, presented in the Wilkinson Center, Brigham Young University, preceding the premier screening of the motion picture The Faith of an Observer: Conversations with Hugh Nibley.

dium, of anonymity and legend, of an intimidating genius with a genuine humility. "Who is Nibley?" many visiting scholars have asked.

He is sincerely comfortable thinking of himself as a doorkeeper in the House of the Lord. He loves the temple and the gatherings of the Saints and would rather be there than anywhere else. His scholarly and religious endeavors over the past four decades have posted him at important portals through which Mormon generations will pass for years to come. His prolific writings have distilled the comings and goings of millennia of human traffic. With a watchman's panoramic vision, he sees the span of social and intellectual developments from Enoch and Abraham, to Peter and Paul, to Joseph and Brigham. He paces the halls of human knowledge, sometimes charting the territory with great detail, other times simply unlocking doors that lead down passageways others will be exploring for years to come.

Hugh Nibley was born March 27, 1910, in Portland, Oregon. He was perceptive and preceptive from the beginning. His experiences in the natural environment of pristine Oregon awakened in him an enduring sensitivity to mankind's stewardship over the earth. Memorizing much of Shakespeare led him inexorably to the study of Old English, then Latin, then Greek, then Arabic, and on and on. For Hugh Nibley, one profound thing has always led to another.

After serving in the Swiss-German Mission and carrying out a special assignment in Greece, he completed his A.B. in history at UCLA, graduating summa cum laude in 1934. Although he was born into wealth, the family fortune evaporated in the Great Depression, leaving Hugh to struggle for books and graduate-school tuition. He was a university fellow at the University of California at Berkeley (1936-1937), where he earned his doctorate in 1938, studying with such luminaries as the great Semitist William

Popper. His dissertation, entitled *The Roman Games as the Survival of an Archaic Year-Cult*, was composed in three weeks.

Following an appointment as lecturer in social philosophy at the Claremont Colleges in Pomona, California, and after several intense years of service as an army intelligence noncommissioned officer in World War II, he dedicated his promising academic career to the service of The Church of Jesus Christ of Latter-day Saints. At the behest of John A. Widtsoe, Hugh Nibley joined the history faculty at Brigham Young University in 1946, leaving—as Robert Thomas has put it—the " 'glory that was Greece and the grandeur that was Rome' [for] the modesty that was Provo."

He and his wife, Phyllis, became the goodly parents of eight fine children. Their home has been a haven. Its doors have always been open to numerous students and family friends. Their family life has been filled with music, lively discussions about drama and literature, archaeological excursions, the arts and sciences.

He was promoted to the rank of professor of history and religion in 1953. His academic career has been punctuated with a visiting professorship at Berkeley (1959-1960), where he lectured on ancient rhetoric and studied Coptic; with a trip to Jordan in 1964, where he examined the Dead Sea Scrolls; and with advanced studies in Egyptian at the Oriental Institute in Chicago in 1966.

His publications over the past forty years cover a wide range of topics, including ancient history, politics, classics, education, science, Egyptology, early Israel, the Apocrypha and Pseudepigrapha, Christian origins, Book of Mormon, Pearl of Great Price, temples and temple worship, Church history, society, and the gospel. Though he considers it spiritually irrelevant, most of his nearly two hundred titles are classics. A good synopsis of his academic interests can be gleaned by scanning a few of these titles, which include *No Ma'am, That's Not History* (1946); "The Arrow, the Hunter and the State" (1949); *Lehi in the Desert and the World of the Jaredites* (1952); *The World and the Prophets* (1954); *An Approach to the Book of Mormon* (1957); "Christian Envy of the Temple" (1959-1960); "How to Write an Anti-Mormon Book" (1962); "The Expanding Gospel" (1965); *Since Cumorah* (1967); "Brigham Young on the Environment" (1972); "What Is Zion?" (1973); "Beyond Politics" (1974); *The Message of the Joseph Smith Papyri: An Egyptian Endowment* (1975); "The Early Christian Prayer Circle" (1978); "Patriarchy and Matriarchy" (1980); *Abraham in Egypt* (1981); and "Work We Must, but the Lunch Is Free" (1982). All the while, he has carried on voluminous correspondence, magnified his distinctive calling in life as Church teacher and speaker, and has been a major contributor to Church magazines over the years — often on short notice and under considerable pressure from publication deadlines.

His works are characterized by several unmistakable traits. He harbors an urgent sense of placing immediate priority on eternal values. He knows that the door is about to close, that time is running out, that money is not worth it, that the extreme situations involving total extermination of nations in the Book of Mormon are relevant for our day — and for him all these realizations trivialize many pedantic projects and issues. He is relentless in his examination of documents and in providing abundant documentation. His curiosity is inexhaustible. He still feeds his memory a steady diet of vocabulary cards. Discoveries constantly amaze him. His writings often draw parallels or offer new characterizations that others have failed to perceive. His interests are usually ahead of their time. He incisively exposes the shortcomings of scientific absolutism and the fundamental flaws of gospel detractors and zealots. His works are typically bold and daring, challenging but reassuring, resourceful and creative, innovative if not revolutionary, sensitive and insightful.

Still, he does not take himself at all seriously. Repenting and giving thanks are the things he thinks he does best. He sees his learning as forever tentative, incomplete, and accumulating. Once discovered, his innovative insights are so painfully obvious that it is hard for him to see why he had not noticed them before. He willingly describes himself as a buffoon, and from time to time as a frustrated fiction writer, waiting for the real scholarship to begin.

As a university community and as a people, we owe an immeasurable debt to Hugh Nibley for his unique contributions to our lives. His work has changed us all. "Few students can talk coherently about their first class from Hugh Nibley," observed his former academic vice-president. For many, it has been viewed as a necessary "rite of passage," while for others it was an electrifying baptism in the waters of ideas and ideals. Hugh Nibley's manner of speech — tempered hyperbole — instills an extraordinary sense of vitality. His unfailing encouragement to students to satisfy their own curiosity — not his — is the kind of faith that has moved many inert cerebral mountains.

In a word, Hugh Nibley is no ordinary doorman. But then, as far as that goes, he doesn't stand by ordinary doorways either.

3

The Copts and the Bible
Aziz S. Atiya†

I approach the topic of the Copts and the Bible in all
humility as a historian, rather than as a theologian or biblical scholar. Even dealing with the bare bones of the historical aspect of this monumental enterprise must necessarily be a curtailed attempt, for all the facts of our theme
are not yet uncovered. The Copts, whose heritage—and
even whose very existence—was either ignored or forgotten for centuries, have emerged in recent years as a remarkable community in the Christian world, and their role
in the development of early organized Christianity has
become a subject widely studied by modern theologians
and archaeologists. In fact, it has been revealed that Coptic
contributions in the formative years of institutionalized
Christianity were enormous. In the domain of biblical studies, it appears beyond doubt that their literary remains
from the first three centuries of our era stand at the base
of the Bible itself.

Historically speaking, the first attempt at a scientific
compilation of the Bible text must be ascribed to one of
the greatest biblical exegetes of all time, namely Origen
(ca. 185-254), a Coptic scholar born in Alexandria. During
the first half of the third century, when Christianity and
paganism still mingled in Egypt and persecutions were still
rife in every province of the Roman Empire, Origen seems
to have succeeded his mentor, Clement of Alexandria, as
head of a catechetical school of Alexandria. During his
tenure in that office, the school came of age as the world

seat of theological studies, and its literary activities grew
in abundance around the indefatigable personality of that
intellectual giant. Epiphanius, bishop of Salamis, ascribed
to him the authorship of six thousand books, tracts, and
treatises, some of which were colossal in size and magnificent in quality. Of course, we assume that in those days
men of faith pooled their intellectual and spiritual resources; and thus Origen's pupils must have collaborated
in his unusual literary productivity.

One of Origen's principal contributions appeared under the title of Hexapla (Greek "sixfold"). The Hexapla
comprised the complete text of the Old Testament in both
Hebrew and Greek. Origen gathered together the famous
four Greek versions of Aquila of Pontus, Symmachus of
Samaria, and the Septuagint in both the original and the
revised version of Theodotion. Origen was thoroughly acquainted with all of these second-century works. He arranged them in six parallel columns, probably on papyrus,
a perishable organic material, as neither parchment nor
paper was yet in use, which accounts for the work's disappearance. Begun at Alexandria in the early decades of
the third century, the unfinished collation of the Hexapla
was taken by Origen in one of his exiles to Caesarea, where
he completed his monumental undertaking before the middle of that century. Fragments of it were gleaned by F.
Field in his work *Origenis Hexaplorum Quae Supersunt* (2
vols., 1867-1875); but the fifth column of the Septuagint
survived in toto in a Syriac translation by Paul, Jacobite
bishop of Tella in Mesopotamia, in 616-617.

We assumed, however, that Origen's biblical efforts
outside the Hexapla also extended to the books of the New
Testament, where his vast exegetic labors in the Gospels,
Acts, the epistles, and Revelation must of necessity have
included every text with its special commentary.

Contemporary with Origen's biblical endeavor (or
slightly later, but still in or about the third century), is the

stupendous Chester Beatty Papyri, consisting of twelve codices and spreading over the areas of both the Old and New Testaments. Minor sections of that remarkable collection were acquired by the University of Michigan, and some folios escaped to private hands. But the bulk of the treasure has remained in the Chester Beatty collection, now in Dublin; as such it was published in facsimiles and textual transcriptions, with introductions by Sir Frederic G. Kenyon, under the title *The Chester Beatty Biblical Papyri: Description and Texts of Twelve Manuscripts on Papyrus of the Greek Bible*. This series appeared in eight fascicules, each consisting of several brochures. The Old Testament books represented in the collection include Genesis, Numbers, Deuteronomy, Isaiah, Jeremiah, Ecclesiastes, Ezekiel, Daniel, and Esther. Others are the books of Enoch and Melito. Of the books of the New Testament, we have the four canonical Gospels, the Acts, the Pauline epistles, and Revelation. The codices also contain noncanonical writings, such as the *Epistle of Enoch,* which was succeeded by a Christian homily in some eight leaves acquired by the University of Michigan but reproduced with the Chester Beatty texts. The provenance of these manuscripts is tentatively placed in the Fayum, and Coptic glosses by the Coptic scribes who executed them appear in some of them. Many noted scholars participated in examining these codices, including W. E. Crum in relation to the Coptic glosses; Professor H. A. Sanders, the eminent papyrologist of Michigan; Ulrich Wilcken, who dated the papyri at about A.D. 200; Ibscher of Berlin, known as the greatest technician in mending papyrus; and others. A general survey of these manuscripts presents no major variants from the accepted canonical versions, and these manuscripts may have been a natural bridge between the oldest original texts, which had disappeared, and the later codices, with which we will deal separately in our present inquiry.

It would be a grave error to assume that that rich harvest was unique in Egyptian or Coptic antiquity. Other collections must have perished in Alexandria because of the seashore humidity; but in Upper Egypt, samples of various papyri from early Coptic history were saved in the dry sands of the desert. For instance, the Oxyrhynchus Papyri, an archival collection of thousands of papyrus fragments discovered in Middle Egypt in 1897, included documents on every branch of the humanities. Perhaps one of its most significant religious contents is "The Sayings of Jesus." This, of course, is an apocryphal fourth-century text that reminds us of another more recent discovery of equal magnitude—the Nag Hammadi Library.

The Nag Hammadi Library is a fourth-century Gnostic series in the Coptic language, essentially translated from earlier original Greek texts. It consists of thirteen papyrus codices with fifty-two tractates, of which thirty-one were hitherto unknown. It also comprises a number of apocryphal gospels that can hardly be overlooked by biblical scholars. Among these gospels are the *Gospel of Truth* (*Evangelium Veritatis*), the *Gospel of Thomas,* the *Gospel of Philip,* the *Gospel of the Egyptians,* and the *Gospel of Mary.* In addition to the gospels are such works as the *Acts of Peter and the Twelve Apostles* and other acts and epistles. Here, from the heart of the Coptic Upper Egypt, we have five apocryphal gospels and some additional acts and epistles that, whether Gnostic, apocryphal, or technically heretical, will surely give biblical divines fresh materials to consider. These documents should throw additional light on facets of the formative years of the Holy Scriptures.

Another collection of formidable dimensions is the Bodmer Papyri, discovered in the neighborhood of Dishna in Upper Egypt, not far from Nag Hammadi. Although these thirty codices still await critical study, it has been estimated that they are from the second century. If so, this collection is probably the earliest biblical treasure on record.

At this point, we are approaching identification of the definitive moment when the canonical Bible text was formed in Coptic or Egyptian territory. Where do the Copts stand at this important juncture in the long story of the genesis of the Bible's accepted recension? This must in great measure be ascribed to the cumulative work among the Coptic community of scholars in the tradition of Origen. The result of their labor has been described in modern biblical scholarship as the Egyptian Bible text, or perhaps more specifically as the Hesychian Bible Recension cited by St. Jerome. Hesychius was an Egyptian bishop who earned the crown of martyrdom under Galerius, the son-in-law of Diocletian, probably between 303 and 307, that is, only a few years before Emperor Constantine declared Christianity the state religion of the Roman Empire by issuing the Edict of Milan in 313. The Hesychian recension of the Gospels in particular must have been used by subsequent biblical scholars and scribes.

After the triumph of Christianity, Constantine ordered fifty copies of the Bible prepared and distributed among the churches of Christendom. These copies were made at Alexandria or Caesarea, though Alexandria, having the seat of theological and religious studies associated with its unique catechetical school, remains the stronger possibility. These fifty copies must have been executed largely, if not wholly, during the long reign of Athanasius the Apostolic, bishop of Alexandria from 328 to 373. Undoubtedly that great champion of orthodoxy must have participated in the final selection of what was regarded as the canonical Gospels. By no means should this minimize the preceding multitude of earlier apocryphal Gospels cited in the Nag Hammadi Library and elsewhere, though they were condemned as heretical in some letters issued by Athanasius.

(Here it is appropriate to interject a note of the definition of heresy in those early centuries. Heretics and saints in those days were holy men, and sometimes a heretic was a greater ascetic than many saints. In reality, a heretic became heretic when he was defeated by his antagonist; his heresy could have prevailed as orthodoxy if only he had won the day. We must therefore not dismiss heretics indiscriminately as the heralds of Satan.)

However, the present canonical texts of the Gospels are surely the direct descendants of the fifty versions collated by order of Emperor Constantine I. Of these fifty, four copies have survived on the vellum that began to replace Egyptian papyrus. These four are the Codex Vaticanus, the Codex Sinaiticus, the Codex Alexandrinus, and the Codex Ephraemi Syri Rescriptus. Together with the earlier Chester Beatty Papyri, these Egyptian products constitute the source of the text of our current Bible.

We note here that the Copts handled the Greek versions as deftly as they did any Coptic translations. An educated fourth-century Copt was as proficient in Greek as in Coptic, but a Greek knew only Greek. He neither knew Coptic nor had any need to know it. Consequently, we must assume that all texts in either Greek or Coptic that came to us from Alexandria are under the Egyptian umbrella and tied to Coptic biblical scholarship. If rigorously applied, this rule would revolutionize the whole science of patrology, wherein all writers in Greek are now indiscriminately termed Greek Fathers. Looking closely at such names as Demetrius, Athanasius, Cyril, Didymus, and others who wrote Coptic as well as Greek, we must revise the existing description of those giants as Greek simply because their major works are in Greek. The fact that they also wrote in Coptic suggests that we should regard them as Coptic rather than Greek Fathers.

I suppose we must apply this rule in the reverse to biblical studies in Greek and look upon the aforementioned codices as Egyptian products. It is conceivable that all the Bibles ordered by Constantine were based on the Hesychian recension already mentioned as the consummation of Egyptian efforts to present the most authoritative text in Alexandria.

Owing to the singular importance of these four codices in the framework of a Bible symposium, it behooves us to offer a brief description of each. I shall begin with the Codex Vaticanus, which may be considered the oldest complete Bible in that set. It was probably written in Alexandria on fine vellum around the middle of the fourth century. The dating is defined on grounds of Greek paleography characterized by the absence of calligraphic ornamentation of later times. The surviving parts, which are considerable, consist of 759 folios, of which 142 are New Testament texts. Its leaves average 26-1/4 cm by 25 cm, and each page has three columns of forty-two lines each. Its simple uncials are continuous, and the words are not spaced; nor do the sentences have any punctuation. Few majestic initials occur in the manuscript, and a blank space separates each book from the one that follows. Sacred names are abbreviated throughout. Apparently two scribes wrote the manuscript, one the Old Testament and the other the New. Moreover, two readers, one contemporary with the manuscript and a second of much later date, in the tenth or eleventh century, revised the work and made corrections. Pale words were retraced, probably by the latter reader, who chose to overlook incorrect words without tracing on the assumption that they might be effaced by age. The same writer added breathings and accents.

The Codex must have been in the Vatican Library before 1475 because it appeared in the first catalog, which was printed in that year. Then Napoleon carried it with him to Paris during his Italian campaign of 1809. It remained in the French capital until Napoleon's defeat at Waterloo in 1815, when the precious book was returned to Rome. While in Paris, the Codex was examined by J. Leonhard Hug, a German professor from Tübingen, who, for the first time, assessed its age and value. After its return to the Vatican in 1815, it was again scrutinized, this time in 1843 by Constantine Tischendorf, discoverer of the Codex Sinaiticus. But its intrinsic value and unusual importance could be judged only after the text was made accessible to all biblical scholars and classicists through the publication of the whole text in photographic facsimiles at Rome in 1889-1890. Examination of that edition also revealed that sixty-one leaves of the text had been lost.

Second in this Egyptian family of biblical manuscripts is the Codex Sinaiticus, discovered in 1844 in the Monastery of Saint Catherine on Mount Sinai (Jebel Musa) by Constantine Tischendorf. This manuscript consists of 390 leaves of very fine vellum, the remains of what could have originally been at least 730 folios. The extant parts of this work include 242 folios of the Old Testament. The size of the folios averages approximately 37-1/2 cm by 33-1/2 cm, and each page has four columns of forty-eight lines. The lines are written continuously, with no spaces between the words. It has no accents or breathings, though it includes some punctuation.

As in the Codex Vaticanus, sacred names are abbreviated in the Sinaiticus. Three different scribal hands have been identified by their peculiarities, especially in spelling. The New Testament was written almost wholly by the same scribe. Numerous corrections were made in the text, both by its original writers and by others from the fourth to the twelfth century.

The manuscript has the dignified simplicity of the Vaticanus in its calligraphy, and both codices could have originated in Alexandria. Like the Vaticanus, it is probably one of the fifty copies ordered by Constantine.

Since the Codex predates the sixth-century foundation of the Monastery of Saint Catherine, we must assume that it was taken to Mount Sinai by the monks when they went to live there. From an early date, however, Sinai had attracted hermits who resided in caves around the holy mountain beyond the oasis of Pharan, near Jebel Serbal, where a cathedral with a bishopric is known to have existed. That area was associated with the prophet Moses, being the supposed site where the Lord gave him the tablets of the Ten Commandments, and where he received God's initial revelation to him in the burning bush. Consequently, it had been a center for pilgrimage by pious adventurers since the early Middle Ages. Among those early pilgrims was the renowned Spanish nun Etheria, who left an account of that terrain and its holy inhabitants around the year 460. Furthermore, Saint Helena, mother of Constantine, visited the Holy Land in the fourth century and was instrumental in building a church around the traditional site of the burning bush. This church is preserved behind the sanctuary of the present cathedral, which Justinian erected in 525 as part of the monastery complex. He built it both to commemorate Theodora, his queen, and as a pious act to protect the monks and ascetics of Sinai from wild nomadic tribes. That fortified refuge at the foot of Sinai, the Holy Mountain, originally called the Monastery of the Transfiguration, was later renamed in honor of Saint Catherine.

The story of its renaming is interesting. Saint Catherine, a highly literate native of Alexandria living at the end of the third century and the beginning of the fourth, was martyred during the reign of Emperor Maximinus (305-313), and legend has it that angels transported her body to Sinai and deposited it on the mountain that bears her name to this day (Jebel Katrina). Sometime in the ninth century, a monk of Sinai had a vision of her resting place; consequently, the holy men followed that dreamer in a procession to Jebel Katrina, found her body intact, and transferred it to their monastery, which has borne her name ever since.

Throughout the Middle Ages, monks of many nations are known to have flocked to Saint Catherine's monastery with their sacred treasures. This is how the Codex Sinaiticus reached the monastery, although we do not know when that happened.

The discovery of the codex occurred in May 1844 in the monastery library, which is renowned among biblical scholars, classicists, and theologians for its accumulation of Christian manuscripts in numerous languages, especially Greek.[1] Constantine Tischendorf was one of these scholars, and during his exploration he was attracted by a basket full of parchments, of which some moldering specimens had been destroyed by fire. On closer examination, Tischendorf found, in his own words, "a considerable number of sheets of a copy of the Old Testament in Greek, which seemed to me to be one of the most ancient that I have ever seen."[2] He prevailed upon the monastery authorities to let him select forty-three folios that, according to his story, were otherwise destined for the flames, and took them with him to Leipzig, where he edited them in 1846 under the title of Codex Frederico Augustanus in honor of his patron, the king of Saxony.

He returned to Sinai in 1853 and searched again, without results; but in 1859 he came a third time, now armed with a letter of recommendation from Alexander II, the emperor of Russia. Nevertheless, systematic searching yielded no results, and Tischendorf was preparing for departure when the steward of the convent invited him to his cell and put before him a bulky mass wrapped in red cloth. On opening it, to his amazement, Tischendorf found the rest of the parchments he had saved from the basket in 1844. He found Old Testament folios, segments of the Epistle of Barnabas and the Pastor of Hermes, and a complete New Testament. He was allowed to take that unwieldy mass of leaves to a branch monastery in Cairo for further study, since his time in the monastery was coming to a close; and he finally took the folios to Saint Petersburg, where he presented the loose leaves of the manuscript to the Russian czar on behalf of the monastery. In return, the Russian ruler paid the equivalent of $6,750. The valuable codex was retained in the imperial library at the Russian capital until 1933, when the Soviet authorities sold it to the British Museum for the enormous sum of one hundred thousand pounds sterling, the equivalent of half a million dollars. Thus the codex found a permanent home and was delivered on December 27, 1933, as a disorganized pile of loose quires and folios without apparent beginning or end. Here its vellum leaves were treated with the utmost care, organized, and bound in two separate volumes comprising the Old and the New Testament.

The third of the Egyptian family of biblical texts in Greek is another work on vellum known as the Codex Alexandrinus, which is also deposited in the British Museum. Like the other codices, it is written in simple but exquisite uncials; but unlike them it is slightly ornamented with rubrications at the outset of every book, and its paragraphs are defined by larger capital initials in the margins. Its lines, however, are continuous, without spaces between the words, and its marginal initials are placed mostly at the beginning of the line when they follow a verse ending in the middle of the line. The text has few breathings and no accents. Quotations from the Old Testament are marked and sacred names are abbreviated. Each book has a colophon at its termination. Apparently the manuscript is the work of three scribes, with numerous corrections in the same style from the same period. It could date from the early part of the fifth century, a little later than both the Sinaiticus and the Vaticanus.

The Alexandrinus is relatively large, consisting of 773 folios, though the original has been calculated to have been at least 820 folios. The Old Testament occupies 630 folios and the New Testament 143. The dimensions of each folio are approximately 32 cm by 25 cm. The manuscript is composed of quires of eight leaves, and its pagination appears in three sets of numbers: one contemporary in original Greek at the top of each folio, a second from the fourteenth century in Arabic numerals at the outer lower corner of the verso side of the folios, and a third in a relatively modern ink by Patrick Young, librarian of King Charles I.

The strange story of how this codex wandered from Alexandria to the Royal Library in Britain is quite interesting. First, Cyril Lucar, the Melkite Patriarch of Alexandria, in whose library that Codex was deposited, took it with him to Constantinople after his preferment to the Ecumenical Greek Patriarchate in the Turkish capital. There he presented it on January 30, 1625, to Sir Thomas Roe, then ambassador to Turkey, who brought it with him to London in 1628, where he placed it in the Royal Library. It passed to the British Museum in 1757.

On the title page of the book of Genesis, an inscription in Arabic is made by Athanasius the Humble, who lived at the beginning of the fourteenth century. He dedicated the book to the Patriarchal Cell in the city of Alexandria, coupled with a curse against anyone who might succumb to the temptation of moving it from its place. The curse did not, however, alter the course of events.

The fourth of the famous Egyptian family of codices is known as Codex Ephraemi Syri Rescriptus, so called because a twelfth-century scribe, short of vellum, decided to erase the original biblical text by rubbing the leaves with pumice stone or soaking them in lime juice. He rescued the vellum for a new Greek version of the homilies of Mar Ephraem the Syrian, a great fourth-century divine theologian. Thus the manuscript became a palimpsest, the older defaced text still perceptible under a later text on the same vellum by a later scribe. With the help of modern technology and the use of ultraviolet rays, the whole of the original fifth-century text could be construed. It consists of biblical text in full page rather than the numerous columns of the first three codices mentioned. It is written in

similar uncials without accents or breathings, and its words
are continuous without spacing. It is possibly the work of
a single scribe with two occasional marginal inscriptions.
Since it is relatively small, consisting of only 209 folios, the
original must have been much more extensive. The New
Testament section occupies 145 folios and lacks 2 Thessalonians and 2 John.

The provenance of this fourth codex can be traced to
the days of the Medici dynasty in Italy, when it was owned
by Cardinal Ridolfi of Florence. Later it was passed to
another member of the family, Catherine de' Medici, who
married Henry II of France. She took it with her to Paris,
and it was finally deposited in the Bibliothèque Nationale,
where it still remains.

It is not difficult to deduce from this brief survey of
our scripture's ancient manuscripts that we owe a considerable debt to Egyptian or Coptic source material for our
existing Bible recension. In reality, the whole field of Coptic
studies is still in its infancy; and the future may still hold
masses of valuable information on the place of the Copts,
not merely in relation to the Bible but also in the wider
framework of Christian civilization. The whole world is
just beginning to learn more about Coptic faith and culture
after the sect's centuries of persistent struggle under very
adverse circumstances.

Like a great and solitary Egyptian temple sorrowfully
standing on the edge of the desert and suffering repeated
sandstorms until it became almost submerged, so the ancient Coptic church led its lonesome life unnoticed on the
fringe of Christian civilization and was buried in the sands
of oblivion. Like the same massive temple, however, it has
proved itself indestructible, though battered by the winds
of change and obscured by accumulated rubble. In the past
few decades, with increasing security and liberty within
and support and sympathy without, its children have begun, with the tools of scholarship, to recover its original

dimensions and glory from beneath the sands of time. It even shows modest signs of shining again.

The task of reconstructing Coptic contributions through archaeology, papyrology, theology, art, and architecture now belongs to the world of scholarship at large; and the rising centers of Coptic studies in institutions of higher learning are gradually throwing increasing light on a valuable phase of a most ancient Christianity. It is hoped that the Coptic Encyclopaedia now being prepared will be an instrument of great enlightenment as it assembles the scattered facts about this little-known facet of our heritage that stands at the root of almost every segment of Christian civilization.

Notes

1. Constantine Tischendorf, *Codex Sinaiticus: The Ancient Biblical Manuscript Now in the British Museum* (London: Lutterworth Press, 1934), 7–32, recounts the discovery of this codex.

2. Ibid., 24.

4

The Seventy in Scripture

S. Kent Brown
Brigham Young University, Provo, Utah

We know at least two things about the priesthood office of the seventy. Jesus called seventy disciples to serve alongside the twelve (Luke 10:1, 17), and the mission of the seventies in our day is to minister principally to Gentiles (D&C 107:25). When we have said this much, two questions arise: why the number seventy and why to Gentiles? I suggest that the key to both questions lies in a largely neglected corner of the Old Testament—the catalog of the descendants of Noah in Genesis 10. But before examining this "table of the nations," it will be necessary for us to demonstrate that our contemporary office of the seventy had its counterpart within the tribal system of ancient Israel.

One of the earliest notations of the number seventy appears in the summarizing observation that "all the persons of the house of Jacob, that came into Egypt, were seventy" (Genesis 46:27, RSV). Here the number seventy represents the sum of the number of names listed in the preceding verses (Genesis 46:8-25).[1] Interestingly, this figure is repeated a few chapters later, where we read, "And all the souls that came out of the loins of Jacob were seventy souls" (Exodus 1:5).[2] But there is a problem here that requires explanation. For English readers of the scriptures, the problem passage occurs in Stephen's famous speech before his martyrdom when he said, "And Joseph sent and called to him Jacob his father and all his kindred, seventy-five souls" (Acts 7:14, RSV). Why does this number differ from those in the Pentateuch? At first glance, the answer is rather straightforward. Both Stephen who gave the speech and Luke who recorded it were reared in the Greek world, the former possibly a Hellenistic Jew[3] like Paul and the latter possibly a Gentile.[4] Consequently, each of them had become acquainted with the Old Testament in its Greek translation, the Septuagint. We can further observe that for the passages already cited from Genesis chapter 46 and Exodus chapter 1, the Greek version reads seventy-five while the Hebrew text says seventy. Thus, quite naturally, both Stephen and Luke repeated the number seventy-five, a sum with which they were familiar from the Septuagint's account of Jacob's removal to Egypt. The question next arises as to which number was primary and which was secondary. Although the evidence is not everywhere unequivocal and is rather complex, in my view the answer is that the original number was seventy, not seventy-five.

Almost every commentator agrees both that the earliest number in Genesis 46 was seventy and that it tallied the names in the list here of Jacob's male descendants, thus offering a patriarchal roster.[5] The figure seventy was arrived at by including Er and Onan, Judah's sons who died before the Egyptian migration (Genesis 46:12; cf. Genesis 38:6-10) and by excluding Jacob himself (Genesis 46:8) as well as his daughter Dinah (Genesis 46:15).[6] That this list of seventy had been fixed in formulaic terms and was thus regarded with great respect can be seen in the regularly repeated plural "sons of" applied to the one son of Dan (Genesis 46:23).[7] The masculine patriarchal cast of this catalog is underscored when one notes that before or during its inclusion in the narrative of Genesis 46, it was modified to serve a different purpose, namely, to show the number of descendants — whether male or female — who accompanied Jacob into Egypt. This new total was sixty-six (Genesis 46:26) because it excluded, naturally, Joseph and his two sons who were already living in Egypt (Genesis 46:20)[8] and the deceased Er and Onan, which left a total of sixty-five. But it reckoned Dinah, making a total of sixty-six. Thus the modified register of sixty-six became mixed in its gender by including Dinah and consequently diminished the distinctively patriarchal flavor associated with the original number seventy.

Turning to Exodus 1:1-5, I wish to make three points. First, we notice immediately that Joseph's name is omitted from the list of Jacob's sons in verses 2-4. Why? Whereas Genesis 46:8-25 includes Joseph already in Egypt, the table of Reuben and his brothers — omitting Joseph — represents the actual extended family of Jacob that "came into Egypt" (Exodus 1:1). According to Genesis 46:26, the total number of persons reckoned in this migration was sixty-six. But the figure that appears in Exodus 1:5 is seventy. Why? Because, first, the numeral seventy was both older and more important, observations that we have already made. But to make up the tally of seventy, one must count Jacob, Joseph, and Joseph's sons. Interestingly, this is exactly what we find in Exodus 1:5, where Joseph's name is written almost as an afterthought.[9]

Second, there is no question that the first eight verses of Exodus form a major transition in the biblical story. These lines look both forward and backward[10] with the number seventy standing out as the only quantity noted. In a sense, this figure represents the one measurable bridge between the Lord's prophetic covenant with the one man Abraham — who then had no posterity but was to have them as "the sand of the seashore" (Genesis 22:17)[11] — and the fulfillment of that covenantal promise when "the children of Israel were fruitful, and increased abundantly, and multiplied, and waxed exceeding mighty" (Exodus 1:7), a situation that moved Pharaoh against them (Exodus 1:9-10, 15-16).

The third observation is that the first verses of Exodus, while clearly pointing back to Genesis 46, changed the order of the names of Jacob's sons. It is worth noting that in all such lists the names were grouped according to Jacob's wives.[12] In our passage in Exodus, the grouping is according to wives, then concubines, that is, first Leah and Rachel, then Zilpah and Bilhah. All of Leah's sons are listed, then Benjamin. But this order is modified in the arrangement of Genesis 46. There the grouping first inventories descendants of Leah, next those of her handmaid Zilpah, then the children of Rachel, and lastly those of her handmaid Bilhah. We must ask whether this slight alteration matters. In my view, the answer is yes. I suggest that the alteration reflects a movement toward priesthood concerns. Let me explain. All are aware that Reuben was Jacob's firstborn child, through Leah (Genesis 29:32; 49:3), and that he was therefore entitled to the birthright. Moreover, we know that when Reuben forfeited the birthright by transgressing (Genesis 35:22; 49:4), it passed to Joseph and, through him, to his son Ephraim, who was formally adopted — along with Manasseh — by Jacob as his own child (Genesis 48:5-6). Such adjustment in granting the birthright shows that it was not to be passed to Leah's second son Simeon but to Rachel's firstborn Joseph.[13] Bearing in mind that the birthright brought to its recipient the right of officiating as priest for the family or clan, we note that had Joseph died — as his father had been led to believe — then Benjamin would have stood in his place as Rachel's "firstborn."[14] In this light, we note that Exodus 1:2-4 reproduces a list of Jacob's sons that reflects a time when Joseph was still thought to be dead. The six sons of Leah, beginning with Reuben, are mentioned just before Benjamin. If Benjamin was next in line for the birthright after Reuben, why is he not listed immediately after Reuben? Because no editor or author of an ancient Israelite text ever listed Jacob's descendants by writing, say, a register that featured the firstborn sons of his wives, followed by the second children of each, followed by the third, and so forth.[15] Therefore, one can safely conclude that the listing in Exodus 1:2-3 came as close as any editor would ever come to placing Benjamin's name next to Reuben's in a list of all of Jacob's sons. Remembering that none of the sons of the two hand-maids would be eligible for the birthright—at least as long as any sons of Leah and Rachel still lived—and noting that Rachel's "firstborn" Benjamin has been moved closer to Leah's eldest in our list, we conclude that the list in Exodus 1:1-5 exhibits an interest in the grouping of the sons most eligible for the birthright. If we wish to seek other motives that might have influenced the shift in the arrangement of the names from its version in Genesis 46 to its order in Exodus 1, we can observe that no editorial interests appear in the list of Genesis 46 that were decidedly on behalf of Judah or Ephraim, the two later dominant tribes. So, one could argue for an interest in bringing together Leah and Rachel. Leah and Rachel bore the only children eligible for the birthright, the preeminent possession in any ancient clan with its attendant double portion in inheritance and priesthood rights. In a document like the Pentateuch, which focused so clearly on inheritance matters, what else could be meant? This inheritance-priesthood arrangement is also found in Numbers 26, which gives further support to our argument.

Thus we conclude that significant elements have appeared in the early verses of the book of Exodus. First, the concern for the number seventy was so strong that the initial list of Jacob's sons (Exodus 1:2-4)—sixty-six in Genesis 46:26—was modified to include Jacob, Joseph, and Joseph's sons, to increase the figure to seventy. Thus, whereas in Genesis 46:26-27, the number seventy was not the only number present (sixty-six was the number of Jacob's posterity moving into Egypt), in Exodus 1:1-5 seventy is the only number. Second, the number seventy in Exodus represents the quantity which demonstrated that the Lord's prophetic promises to Abraham were being fulfilled even though they were to see yet greater fulfillment.[16] Third, the specific manner in which Exodus 1:2-4 has modified the order of the children of Jacob's wives from Genesis 46 illustrates a particular interest in the two full wives and their children, who, before the discovery that Joseph was still alive in Egypt, were the only sons eligible for the birthright.

Now that we have underscored the strength of the number seventy in the history and custom of at least the patriarchal narrative, we must now turn to the issue brought forward by the Septuagint's readings, the number seventy-five. We noted earlier that Stephen mentioned seventy-five descendants of Jacob who came to live in Egypt (Acts 7:14). That figure was based on the variant readings in the Greek text of both Genesis 46:27 and Exodus 1:5, as well as the Alexandrinus[17] manuscript of Deuteronomy 10:22. It has often been argued that because the third-century translator of the Pentateuch from Hebrew into Greek knew of the expanded list of Jacob's descendants in Numbers 26, he added the additional five names in Genesis 46:20, three grandsons of Joseph and two great-grandsons, "obviously with the intention of including here the ancestors of all the families mentioned" in Numbers 26;[18] the Hebrew text of Genesis 46 had included only those who had surely "been born at the time of the migration into Egypt."[19] While this view need not be modified significantly for our discussion here, we should note that the translator of the Pentateuch into Greek was not responsible for altering the number from seventy to seventy-five in Genesis 46:27, Exodus 1:5, and the Alexandrinus Deuteronomy 10:22. It was already written in the Hebrew copy before him, a fact proven by the Dead Sea Scrolls.[20] Once again, however, the evidence allows us to conclude that even here the figure seventy came before the number seventy-five. Let me explain.

The existence of the number seventy-five, representing

an adjusted total of Jacob's descendants who reached Egypt and now appearing in an independent Hebrew recension of the Old Testament attested at Qumran,[21] would seem to weaken the case for the primacy of the numeral seventy. But the figure seventy-five can be handled rather easily. First, we note two key passages: the table of the gentile nations in Genesis 10 and these fascinating lines in the Song of Moses: "When the most High divided to the nations their inheritance, when he separated the sons of Adam, he set the bounds of the people according to the number of the children of Israel" (Deuteronomy 32:8).

One must understand that the word *nations* refers to the Gentiles (Heb. *goyyîm*). One must notice further that the scriptural account of the division and spreading of the gentile nations occurs in Genesis 10, where names of Noah's male descendants are recorded and, significantly, total seventy in the Hebrew text. Thus, the meaning of Deuteronomy 32:8 is that there was seen to exist a clear correlation between the number of gentile nations descended from Noah and "the number of the children of Israel," or Jacob, which was computed to be seventy.

Having said this much, we must now deal with the variant number seventy-five by examining differences among textual readings of the last line of Deuteronomy 32:8. In the Masoretic text, the phrase is as it appears in the King James Version, "according to the number of the children of Israel," that is, seventy. In the Septuagint, however, the last phrase reads, "according to the number of the angels of God."[22] Moreover, a Hebrew fragment of this passage recovered from Qumran Cave 4 reads still differently, "according to the number of the sons of God."[23] As Geza Vermes points out, "angels of God" and "sons of God" are here "synonyms [and therefore] it is reasonable to conclude that the Septuagint [reading] represents the Qumran type of Hebrew [text]."[24] Vermes states the solution succinctly by responding thus to his own question:

Why do the two differ from the Masoretic reading? The number itself, arrived at by counting the names appearing in Genesis 10, is seventy, and both traditions accept this implicitly. But whereas the Masoretic explanation of this figure is Israel-centered, that of Qumran is not. The thought underlying the former text is that the total number of Gentile countries reflects the "seventy souls" journeying with Jacob from Canaan to Egypt, i.e., the "seventy sons of Israel" according to Exodus 1:5. The Septuagint, and its Hebrew basis attested by a fragment from Cave 4 (4QEx^a), cannot reproduce this simile in Deuteronomy 32:8 because in their version of Exodus 1:5 the retinue of Jacob amounts to seventy-five, not seventy. Their reasoning therefore runs: the guardian angels of the various people were created before man, so when God divided the human race into nations, he ensured that each of the seventy pre-existent angels should have his own special client. Thus the Masoretic "sons of Israel" and the Septuagint-Qumran "angels/ sons of God" cannot be explained as stylistic variations: they derive from autonomous traditions.[25]

Thus while the number seventy still was primary (deriving from the division of gentile nations according to the sons of Noah in Genesis 10) and dominated even the variant readings of Deuteronomy 32:8, we apparently possess evidence here of a harmonizing attempt by a Hebrew scribe to include within the number of Jacob's offspring Joseph's later posterity known from Numbers 26:28-37.[26] This would account for the variant numeral seventy-five appearing in Genesis 46:27, Exodus 1:5, and the Alexandrinus reading of Deuteronomy 10:22. As a result, we can be assured that the figure seventy-five is secondary and can thus be omitted from further consideration.

By bringing the table of the gentile nations of Genesis 10 into the picture, we have opened ourselves to another problem that arises between the Masoretic text and the Septuagint. Simply stated, the Hebrew Masoretic text lists seventy descendants of Noah, the Septuagint seventy-two.[27] Unfortunately, no help in solving this question is forthcoming from the discoveries at the Dead Sea. Instead, the strength of one's argument must rest on three other Old Testament passages where the textual tradition unequivocally supports the number seventy.

The first incident is in Exodus 24. All will recall that a special covenant ceremony is recounted there in which Moses, Aaron, two[28] sons of Aaron, and seventy elders of Israel[29] were invited to the sacred mountain to worship the Lord (Exodus 24:1-11). Unlike earlier passages, here the textual support for the numeral seventy is unanimous. Without doubt, the seventy elders should not be reckoned with the other four invitees — making a total of seventy-four — since the seventy are so plainly singled out in verses 1 and 9. In suggesting further significance of this incident for our purposes, let us examine Numbers 11, which offers additional light. It concerns the Lord's directions to Moses after the prophet had complained about the unrelieved pressures of caring for the Israelites:

> And the Lord said unto Moses, Gather unto me seventy men of the elders of Israel, whom thou knowest to be the elders of the people, and officers over them; and bring them unto the tabernacle of the congregation . . . and I will take of the spirit which is upon thee, and will put it upon them; and they shall bear the burden of the people with thee, that thou bear it not thyself alone (Numbers 11:16-17).

After Moses had gathered "the seventy men of the elders of the people, and set them round about the tabernacle" (Numbers 11:24), the Lord shared Moses' spirit among them. The proof of the reality of the Lord's act was borne out when "they prophesied, and did not cease" (Numbers 11:25). In light of our previous discussion, we must note that the Lord's activities also affected two more men, Eldad and Medad, upon whom the prophetic spirit was allowed to rest (Numbers 11:26). While the number thus affected by the spirit of prophecy totals seventy-two, we should not think that these extra two were *numerically* significant. The correct interpretation came from the lips of Moses: "Would God that all the Lord's people were prophets and that the Lord would put his spirit upon them" (Numbers 11:29). The extra two men who prophesied served clearly as indicators that God wills all his people to enjoy his gift. Beyond this, there is little more to be understood from the inclusion of Eldad and Medad.

The third passage is in Ezekiel 8. In this account, Ezekiel has been transported in vision[30] back to Jerusalem from his home near the river of Chebar (Ezekiel 1:1; 3:15) to witness the destructive cleansing of the polluted city and land. While being escorted through the area of the temple, he was shown a secret ceremony taking place in a decorated subterranean room beneath its courtyard (Ezekiel 8:7-10). Then Ezekiel observed:

> And before them stood seventy men of the elders[31] of the house of Israel, with Jaazaniah the son of Shaphan standing among them. Each had his censer in his hand, and the smoke of the cloud of incense went up. Then he said to me, "Son of man, have you seen what the elders of the house of Israel are doing in the dark, every man in his room of pictures?" (Ezekiel 8:11-12, RSV).

While the nature of the worship service described here remains unclear,[32] we notice immediately that it was seventy elders who had joined together for a special rite whose importance is underscored by its connection with the temple area. In this account, too, the textual support for the number seventy is without exception.

We must ask finally what these three passages have to do with our earlier discussion and, specifically, with Genesis 10 and the question of seventy versus seventy-two. In my view, a good deal. They confirm that, in addition to the twelve-tribe constitution, the numeral seventy represented a specific office within the tribal structure of ancient Israel[33] that was seen to be modeled on the number of both Noah's descendants and Jacob's posterity. Moreover, this inner governing body of seventy was at the same time official and spiritual, functions that in the ancient world were really inseparable. Let us examine the evidence for such conclusions.

In the matter of official activities, the evidence is clear. The event that led to the call of the seventy in the desert was Moses' complaint of "the burden of all this people" (Numbers 11:11) that had been placed upon him: "I am not able to bear all this people alone, because it is too heavy for me" (Numbers 11:14). The Lord's promise to Moses was that the seventy would "bear the burden of the people with thee, that thou bear it not thyself alone" (Numbers 11:17). Consequently, the Lord directed that these seventy were to have official positions among the Israelites: "Gather unto me seventy men of the elders of Israel, whom thou knowest to be the elders of the people, and officers over them" (Numbers 11:16). One notices readily that they were to be of "the elders," already a position of status among Israel's families and clans.[34] Additionally, the Lord used the term *officers*.[35] This designation was used earlier of the Israelite foremen who, under Egyptian supervision, oversaw their fellow slaves while still in Egypt (Exodus 5:6, 10, 14-15, 19). In later times they were given judicial (Deuteronomy 1:15-16) and military responsibilities (Deuteronomy 20:5, 8-9; cf. Deuteronomy 29:10; 2 Chronicles 26:11, "Maaseiah the ruler"), including that of organizing the people for marching (Joshua 1:10; 3:2). As late as the period of the divided kingdom, we have record that such officials were still being chosen from the Levites (2 Chronicles 19:11; 34:13). To be sure, we cannot determine whether every reference to an "officer" in the biblical text points to someone associated with an organization of seventy. We can, however, see that the seventy selected by Moses indeed enjoyed an official position among their fellow Israelites.

The religious involvement of the seventy is even more impressively documented. One must recall initially that the gathering of the seventy on the mountain with Moses and Aaron was specifically done to ratify the covenant made by Israel at Mt. Sinai, this in response to God's invitation (see Exodus 19:5-6).[36] In this extremely important ceremony, the seventy—plus Moses and others—served not only as agents acting on behalf of the larger Israelite nation but also as the guarantors of the covenant by acting as witnesses of the Lord's ratifying presence.[37] In the passage that concerns the appointment of the seventy to assist Moses with the affairs of the camp, the spiritual dimensions were highlighted when the Lord both said to Moses, "I will take of the spirit which is upon thee, and will put it upon them [the seventy]" (Numbers 11:17) and then instructed the people to sanctify themselves in preparation for receiving this special spiritual endowment (Numbers 11:18). The entire event, of course, was set in its proper spiritual perspective when the spirit of prophecy fell upon them all "and did not cease" (Numbers 11:25). In the case of Ezekiel's vision, moreover, the religious trappings cannot be missed. For even though the ceremonial assembly was an abomination, as the Lord declared (Ezekiel 8:6, 9), it is clear that the seventy men (Ezekiel 8:11) in the decorated chamber were participating in a religious rite. Thus, the seventy, wherever mentioned in scripture, are understood to have served as religious or spiritual functionaries as well as in more "secular" capacities.

What can we now say about the issue of seventy versus seventy-two in Genesis 10? We have seen clear evidence of an institution of seventy elders who filled various roles within the larger community and functioned within the twelve-tribe structure. That they played a particularly religious, even cosmic, role can be seen in their spiritual activities at crucial moments during Israel's stay in the desert. It is therefore not amiss to observe that the seventy had special importance for ancient Israelites. The significance is summed up in Deuteronomy 32:8, which, as we noted, made a conceptual link between the inheritances assigned by God to the gentile nations of the earth (Genesis 10) and the seventy descendants of Jacob from whom the tribes were sprung.[38] Both the structural constitution and the consciousness of ancient Israel retained the seventy as an organizational entity, a notion supported by Exodus 24:1, Numbers 11:16, and Ezekiel 8:11. Furthermore, because of the absence of textual variants for this figure in these three passages and because of the persistently strong recollection of the involvement of the seventy at key events, I have concluded that this figure represents the most secure key to the original concept of the number of the gentile nations. Admittedly, this may appear to be a weak link in our thinking since we are engaging in somewhat circular reasoning here. For we say that an Israelite institution of seventy elders mirrors the original belief that there were seventy gentile nations, which numeral itself may provide some basis for this number of officers within the Israelite institution, linked as it was to the number of Jacob's male descendants. One may ask, of course, why the office of the seventy among Israelites would be viewed of as having connection to the seventy descendants of Noah. Except for Deuteronomy 32:8, we possess no clues of direct ties in the Bible.[39] It is only in modern scripture that the seventy's link to the Gentiles is made absolutely clear. From this source we learn that "the Seventy are also called to preach the gospel, and to be especial witnesses unto the gentiles and in all the world" (D&C 107:25). Thus the tie is made and makes plain that the seventy's modern mission is directed primarily toward the gentile nations, which were seventy in number according to the Hebrew manuscripts of Genesis 10.

When we turn to Jesus' call of the seventy disciples in Luke's gospel (Luke 10:1-20), we encounter a familiar ambiguity in the manuscripts: seventy versus seventy-two. Interestingly, this very equivocation demonstrates that Jesus' act of appointing these disciples was understood to be linked to Genesis 10, the passage where this particular difference in numbers originally arose. How do we explain this divergence in the manuscripts of Luke's account? The most natural explanation comes if we maintain that it was seventy whom Jesus called. This figure was then altered in some Lukan manuscripts to read seventy-two by scribes who were familiar with the Septuagint's version of Genesis 10 and, knowing the connection between the two accounts, sought to harmonize the figures in Luke 10:1, 17, with the seventy-two names in the table of Noah's posterity. To argue the other way around requires adopting the untenable point of view that the numeral seventy-two was original. One then must postulate that the manuscripts of Luke—written in Greek—were corrected to seventy by Greek-reading scribes to harmonize with the number of names in the Hebrew version of Genesis 10, a version that could be read by few such scribes in the late first and early second centuries when manuscripts of this gospel were enjoying wider circulation.[40] Consequently, I feel secure in concluding that Jesus called seventy disciples, not seventy-two. Further, these representatives were to be understood as called to serve the Gentiles—if not during Jesus' ministry, at least at a later date[41]—a notion supported by the clear connection both to Genesis 10 and to the duties of the seventy outlined in D&C 107:25.

In conclusion, it now becomes clear why Jesus chose two sets of disciples, the twelve and the seventy. The twelve bore an obvious relation to the tribes of Israel, the seventy to the gentile nations of the earth as well as to an inner structural entity that existed within the tribal system of preexilic Israel. Because of its numerical link to Genesis 10, the figure seventy itself, when applied to Jesus' disciples, anticipated that the gospel message would be taken to the gentile nations after his ministry.[42] In our own time, the seventies have been given by the Lord the monumental, yet distinctive, task of bearing the gospel to the gentile nations of the world, "thus differing from other officers in the church in the duties of their calling" (D&C 107:25).[43]

Notes

1. Discussion has focused on whether the names of Jacob, the father of the others listed (46:6, 8, 26-27), and Dinah (46:15) were to be reckoned so that the number totals seventy. See S. R. Driver, *The Book of Genesis*, 5th ed. (London: Methuen, 1906), 365-66, 368; Gerhard von Rad, *Genesis: A Commentary*, rev. ed. (Philadelphia: Westminster Press, 1972), 402-3.

2. While Exodus 1:2-5 does not really say exactly what we find in Genesis 46 (see the discussion below), it is clear that the list of Exodus 1 refers back to that in Genesis. See Brevard S. Childs, *The Book of Exodus* (Philadelphia: Westminster Press, 1974), 1-2; S. R. Driver, *The Book of Exodus* (Cambridge: Cambridge University Press, 1911), 1; and Moshe Greenberg, *Understanding Exodus*, part 1 (New York: Behrman House, 1969), 18-19.

3. For the continuing discussion regarding Stephen's background, as well as that of his associates who had Greek names, see Johannes Munck, *The Acts of the Apostles*, Anchor Bible (Garden City, NY: Doubleday, 1967), 56-57; Ernst Haenchen, *Die Apostelgeschichte*, 15th ed. (Göttingen: Vandenhoeck & Ruprecht, 1968), 218-22.

4. Among recent discussions of Luke's identity and ethnic origins, see those of Leon Morris, *The Gospel According to St. Luke* (Grand Rapids, MI: Eerdmans, 1974), 14-21; Joseph A. Fitzmyer, *The Gospel According to Luke (I-IX)*, Anchor Bible (Garden City, NY: Doubleday, 1981), 35-47; and Frederick F. Bruce, *The Acts of the Apostles* (London: Tyndale Press, 1962), 1-8.

5. So, for example, von Rad, *Genesis: A Commentary*, 402-3; and John Skinner, *Genesis*, International Critical Commentary Series (Edinburgh: T. and T. Clark, 1910), 492-93.

6. Interestingly, no one has ever made anything of the fact that Serah, the daughter of Asher (Genesis 46:17), was clearly reckoned within the total of Jacob's male posterity.

7. Both the Hebrew and Greek texts employ the expected "sons of" in Genesis 46:23. See the comment of Skinner, *Genesis*, 494: "one of Dan. . . . in spite of *bǝnê*," i.e., "sons." The formulaic quality is further emphasized in "the proportions between the number of children assigned to each wife: Leah 32, Zilpah 16, Rachel 14, Bilhah 7, " ibid., 493. E. A. Speiser, *Genesis*, Anchor Bible (Garden City, NY: Doubleday, 1964), 345, says that "the figure 66 would seem to be a later correction."

8. Both sons and daughters are mentioned in Genesis 46:7. The new total sixty-six (Genesis 46:26) had to exclude Joseph and his sons even though they were listed both before (Genesis 46:20) and after (Genesis 46:27) this number. Since the original catalog was formed according to the wives of Jacob, Joseph naturally had to be included as a son through Rachel. Genesis 46:27 seems to represent an attempt to harmonize the figures seventy and sixty-six.

9. Frank M. Cross, Jr., *The Ancient Library of Qumran and Modern Biblical Studies*, rev. ed. (Garden City, NY: Doubleday, 1961), 184-85, argues that, on the basis of a textual variant of Exodus 1:1-5 found in Cave 4 at Qumran (4QEx[a]) in which Joseph's name appears in the list just before Benjamin, the omission of Joseph's name from Exodus 1:3 in the Masoretic text represents the inferior reading. But it is more reasonable to postulate that because Joseph was so important, a scribe would *insert* Joseph's missing name into a list rather than omit it, whether mistakenly or by design.

10. Both the list of those who came into Egypt and the notice of Jacob's burgeoning posterity point backwards to Genesis 46 and to Genesis 1:28 and 9:1 respectively. The mention of Joseph's death (Exodus 1:6), of Israel's "increased abundance" (Exodus 1:7), and of the "new king over Egypt" (Exodus 1:8) point to the troubles lying ahead for the Israelites.

11. Cf. Genesis 12:2; 13:16; 15:5; 16:10 (promise to Hagar); 17:6; also Genesis 26:4 and 28:14.

12. In Genesis 35:23-26 and Exodus 1:2-4, the sons are arranged by the following order of Jacob's wives: Leah, Rachel, Bilhah, and Zilpah; in Genesis 46:8-25: Leah, Zilpah, Rachel, and Bilhah; in Numbers 26:5-49: Leah and Rachel with the concubines' sons interspersed (Gad [from Zilpah] in 26:15-18; Dan [Bilhah] in 26:42-43; Asher [Zilpah] in 26:44-47; Naphtali [Bilhah] in 26:48-50). Even the order of marching in the wilderness followed an interspersed pattern (Numbers 10:14-28): Leah's sons, Zilpah's son Gad (Numbers 10:20), Rachel's sons, and Bilhah's sons interspersed with Zilpah's (Numbers 10:25-28).

13. 1 Chronicles 5:1; Genesis 48:5-6; 49:4; see also O. J. Babb's article "Birthright" in *The Interpreter's Dictionary of the Bible*, 5 vols. (Nashville: Abingdon, 1962), 1:440-41.

14. This is certainly implied by Benjamin's position in the list of Jacob's sons in Exodus 1:2-4, where his name stands in Joseph's place (according to the Masoretic text).

15. None of the references cited in note 12 exhibits this characteristic. It was even the custom when a family ate together that it was seated "the firstborn according to his birthright, and the youngest according to his youth" (Genesis 43:33).

16. Deuteronomy 10:22 in RSV: "Your fathers went down to Egypt seventy persons; and now the Lord your God has made you as the stars of heaven for multitude." The question has arisen among commentators whether the figure seventy simply means a large number. I take the number to mean what it says. An opposite conclusion is that of von Rad, *Genesis: A Commentary*, 403: "Originally this number was intended, of course, as a round figure, as an approximate, large number of men." He then cites Exodus 24:9 and Numbers 11:16, passages which reflect an institutional entity and thus do not support his observation. A third passage, Judges 8:30, might uphold von Rad's view. I have noted that 2 Kings 10:1, 6-7 may also sustain it. But these latter two passages have a very different character from those in Exodus 24 and Numbers 11.

17. There is a discrepancy among various Septuagint manuscripts for Deuteronomy 10:22. The Alexandrinus reads seventy-five. See *Septuaginta*, Alfred Rahlfs, ed., 2 vols. (Stuttgart: Wüttembergische Biblelanstalt, 1935), 1:306.

18. The Septuagint, after naming Manasseh and Ephraim, also gives the son and grandson of Manasseh, Machir and Gilead, and two sons and a grandson of Ephraim, Shuthelah, Tahan, and Shuthelah's son Eran. The King James Version does not reflect this in Genesis 46:20, but only in Numbers 26:29, 35-36.

19. Driver, *The Book of Genesis*, 368.

20. Published by Patrick W. Skehan in "A Fragment of the 'Song of Moses' (Deuteronomy 32) from Qumran," *Bulletin of the American Schools of Oriental Research* 136 (December 1954): 12. Interestingly, Skehan maintains that the Dead Sea fragment of Deuteronomy 32:8 exhibits the "surely original" reading. See further discussions by Cross, *The Ancient Library of Qumran*, 184-85, and Geza Vermes, *The Dead Sea Scrolls*, rev. ed. (London: Colliers, 1977), 204-5.

21. The question concerning the origin of various recensions of the biblical text naturally arises. Differences in the readings among

texts are usually accounted for by a theory of geographical distribution. For instance, F. M. Cross, Jr., *The Ancient Library of Qumran*, 188-94, suggests the existence of (1) an ancient Palestinian type of text with certain characteristic readings, (2) an Egyptian text borrowed from no. 1 and preserved among Egyptian Jews, and (3) a "conservative" type which was the forerunner of the Masoretic textual tradition. See Vermes's summary and critique of this view (*The Dead Sea Scrolls*, 206-9, 222-23).

22. The Septuagint reads: *kata arithmon aggelōn theou*.

23. The Masoretic text reads: *ləmispar bənê yiśrā'ēl*. The last phrase of the fragment from Qumran (4QDt) reads: *bənê 'ēl*; as Skehan points out, the state of preservation of the manuscript does not allow us to know whether *'ēl* is the spelling of God's name or whether it was more fully written ("A Fragment of the 'Song of Moses'," 12).

24. Vermes, *The Dead Sea Scrolls*, 205.

25. Ibid.

26. Driver, *The Book of Genesis*, 367, points to other passages that deal with Joseph's posterity (1 Chronicles 5:24 and 7:14-27) as well as noting the differences between various accounts of Benjamin's descendants, ascribing them to a "corrupt text," which, however, he does not identify.

27. The two names added in the Septuagint version are "Elisha" in verse 2 after Javan and "Cainan" after Aram in verse 22.

28. Childs, *The Book of Exodus*, 498, notes that the Samaritan version of Exodus 24:1 and 9 adds the names of Eleazar and Ithamar, "completing the list of Aaron's sons" from Exodus 28:1. While Martin Noth, *Exodus: A Commentary* (Philadelphia: SCM/Westminster Press, 1962), 195, tries to convince us that the names of Aaron's sons, Nadab and Abihu, along with Aaron and Moses, were probably glosses in the text, Robert A. Cole, *Exodus: An Introduction and Commentary* (London: Tyndale Press, 1973), 184, tells us that because these two sons of Aaron died under God's judgment (Numbers 3:4), we are assured "of the authenticity of the tradition, for no one would have inserted their names here in the account of such an important event."

29. For the seventy elders as representatives of all Israel in the covenant ceremony, see J. Coert Rylaarsdam and J. Edgar Park, "The Book of Exodus," in *Interpreter's Bible*, 12 vols. (Nashville, TN: Abingdon, 1952), 1:1016, and Ronald E. Clements, *Exodus*, The Cambridge Bible Commentary (Cambridge: University Press, 1972), 158.

30. Some scholars have challenged the notion that the account

in Ezekiel 8:1–11:25 recounted a true visionary experience. See the brief refutation by Walther Eichrodt, *Ezekiel: A Commentary* (London: SCM Press, 1970), 120.

31. The King James Version reads "ancients" for "elders" even though the Hebrew term is used more than 100 times in the Old Testament with the meaning "elders."

32. Both Babylonian and Egyptian rites have been suggested, although most scholars favor the latter. Cf. Eichrodt, *Ezekiel: A Commentary*, 124, and Walther Zimmerli, *Ezekiel 1* (Philadelphia: Fortress Press, 1979), 240-41.

33. Ibid., 240: "It appears probable, from Exodus 24:1, 9, where seventy of the elders of Israel were summoned, as the distinguished men of the people, to see God and to eat the covenant meal before him on the mountain of God, and from Numbers 11:16 (24-25), where seventy elders share something of the spirit of Moses, that there was an institution, sanctified by ancient tradition, of seventy elders as the representatives of Israel. What Ezekiel sees therefore [in 8:11] is not a chance group, but the representatives of Israel, as they had once stood before Yahweh at the making of the covenant."

34. Cf. Exodus 3:16, 18; 4:29.

35. The Hebrew term is *šōṭār*, usually translated in the Septuagint by the Greek *grammateus*, although in two instances it is rendered *grammatoeisagōgeus* (Deuteronomy 1:15; 29:10) and once it is translated by *kritēs* (2 Chronicles 26:11). According to Francis Brown, S. R. Driver, and Charles A. Briggs, *A Hebrew and English Lexicon of the Old Testament* (Oxford: Clarendon Press, 1974), 1009b, the term may have properly meant scribes or organizers although in practical terms it regularly refers to subordinate officers.

36. See the discussion in Noth, *Exodus*, 196, 198, and Childs, *The Book of Exodus*, 502-6.

37. The spoken pledges (Exodus 24:3, 7), the offering of both burnt offerings and peace offerings (Exodus 24:5), the blood rite (Exodus 24:6, 8), the reading of the terms of the covenant (Exodus 24:7), and the sacred meal (Exodus 24:11) all bespeak a solemn covenantal ceremony. See Cole, *Exodus: An Introduction and Commentary*, 184-86.

38. The numeral seventy simply works most easily since the variants eliminate each other: in the instance of Genesis 10, the variant sum is seventy-two, which does not sustain the variant figure seventy-five supported in fragmentary texts of Exodus 1 and Deuteronomy 32 found at Qumran and in the Septuagint's Genesis 46.

39. Although conjectural because we can show no biblical ties,

it is possible that the concerns in the Abrahamic covenant that focus on "all families of the earth" (Genesis 12:3, which likely refers back to "the families of the sons of Noah" in 10:32; cf. 18:18; 22:18; 26:4; Abraham 2:11) may have solidified the number seventy in Israelite institutions as a reminder of their obligation toward the gentile nations of the earth.

40. The Christian sources from which we know how widely the Gospel of Luke and the book of Acts, along with other New Testament texts, were known and venerated within the early church are brought together by Henry Cadbury, "The Tradition," in F. J. Foakes Jackson and Kirsopp Lake, eds., *The Beginnings of Christianity*, 5 vols. part 1, vol. 2 (London: Macmillan, 1922), 209-64; by Bruce, *The Acts of the Apostles*, 1-10; and by Wilhelm Schneemelcher, "The History of the New Testament Canon," in Edgar Hennecke and W. Schneemelcher, eds., *New Testament Apocrypha*, 2 vols. (Philadelphia: Westminster, 1963), 1:28-52.

41. The likelihood that some of the seventy disciples actually went into gentile cities and villages is strongly supported by Jesus' instructions to eat and drink "such things as are set before you" (Luke 10:7-8), especially in light of Jewish food concerns (cf. Morris, *The Gospel According to St. Luke*, 182-83).

42. Evidence exists, of course, that Jesus ministered to Gentiles; see Matthew 8:28-34 (Mark 5:1-10; Luke 8:26-40); Matthew 15:21-28 (Mark 7:24-31); and Luke 7:2-10.

43. Our investigation has been confined to scripture. Tradition, too, reveals a rich tapestry of accounts dealing with the figure seventy (or seventy-two). One thinks, for example, of the legendary seventy-two translators of the Jewish Law from Hebrew to Greek (*Letter of Aristeas*) in James H. Charlesworth, ed., *The Old Testament Pseudepigrapha*, 2 vols. (Garden City, NY: Doubleday, 1983-85), 2:7; the seventy-two angels and princes in heaven corresponding to the seventy-two nations of the world (*3 Enoch* 17:6, 8) in ibid., 1:270; the seventy-two heavens (*First Apocalypse of James* 26:16) in James M. Robinson, ed., *Nag Hammadi Library* (San Francisco: Harper and Row, 1977), 243; and the seventy-two ministering angels who have charge of the seventy-two nations of the earth (*On the Origin of the World* 104:19-20, 105:10-16) in ibid., 165-66. In Judaism, the number of members of the Great Sanhedrin has ranged from seventy-two, to seventy, to seventy-one (the seventy plus one leader), as discussed by Sidney B. Hoenig, *The Great Sanhedrin* (Philadelphia: Dropsie College, 1953), 62-73. In the Semitic tradition, generally, the numbers "seventy to seventy-three are often interchanged" and

"usually designate great diversity," in Mircea Eliade, ed., *The Encyclopedia of Religion*, 12 vols. (New York: Macmillan, 1987), 11:18. For example, in the Talmud, "seventy languages" represent the total diversity of mankind, further supporting the linkage between the seventy called by Jesus and their mission to proclaim the gospel to every nation, kindred, tongue, and people. See, e.g., TB *Sotah* 36a ("The words of the Torah [were inscribed] in seventy languages"), and 36b ("Gabriel came and taught [Joseph in Egypt] the seventy languages"). In addition, we have not explored the natural connection between the number seven and seventy; see Johannes Hehn, *Siebenzahl und Sabbat bei den Babyloniern und im Alten Testament* (Leipzig: J. C. Hinrichs, 1907; reprinted 1968 by Zentralantiquariat der DDR), 89-90.

5

From the Philopedia of Jesus to the Misopedia of the *Acts of Thomas*

James H. Charlesworth
Princeton Theological Seminary, Princeton, New Jersey

The purpose of this little essay is to reveal that Jesus' philopedia was so altered by some second-century Christian groups that it became misopedia. Jesus' own teachings were sometimes changed or even abandoned by those who called him "Lord." My thoughts and research are now presented in honor of Hugh Nibley, that philological genius who has the habit of searing one's consciousness and memory in ways somewhat reminiscent of a welder whom I saw in my youth in Florida.

For the cultural context, we will first look at some Hellenistic attitudes toward children and contrast those with Jewish attitudes, both ancient and contemporaneous.

Children in Hellenistic Culture

According to Iamblichus, children are beloved of the gods (*theophilestatous*).[1] In the cults *hieroi paides*, "sacred children," sang, as the following excerpt illustrates:

> Dianae sumus in fide
> puellae et pueri integri:
> Dianam pueri integri
> puellaeque canamus.
>   (Catullus, *Carmina* 34, 1-4)[2]
>
> We are in truth
> The sacred girls and boys of Diana.

> As sacred boys and girls
> We sing to Diana.

Children were beloved, even cherished, in some segments of Hellenistic culture.[3] The Greeks coined a word, *philopais*, to articulate the love of children.[4]

Another view of children is also evidenced in antiquity. Slave children, *deliciae*, amused and sexually served the decadent rich, especially at banquets. Sometimes they were raped by men or beasts, or devoured by animals during debauched orgies. Undesired offspring—especially girls—were killed or exposed to the elements.[5] Cynics advised against marriage and children.[6] Hellenistic views of the blessed life or the abode of the blessed ones are customarily depicted without children; this perspective is found in Greek (Homer, Hesiod, Pindar, Herodotus, Plato), Roman (Vergil, Lucian), Persian (Yima's golden reign, Mithra's abode, Yima's subterranean hideaway [*vara*]), Egyptian (the Shipwrecked Sailor, Chaeremon), and Jewish (the history of the Rechabites) sources. Hellenistic poetry often focuses on the erotic side of sex to the detriment of the conception of children. Unfortunately, the Greeks created a word for the "hating of one's children," *misopais*.[7]

Children in Israelite and Jewish Traditions

In Israelite and Jewish traditions the child, especially the son, was honored. The celebration of children, offspring, is essential because of two seminal ideas in the Genesis account of creation. God had ordered the creation of "man in our image" (*bəṣalmēnû*), "after our likeness" (*kidmûṯēnû*; Genesis 1:26). This concept, *imago dei*, undergirded much of early Jewish thought, although it is seldom articulated explicitly until the first century A.D.[8] The import of this word of God is paradigmatic; children are to be loved because they are in the image of God. The second pregnant passage is the one in which the Creator commanded Adam and Eve to "be fruitful and multiply" (Genesis 1:28). To bear children is to obey God's first commandment in history. A trifold love is implicitly embodied in one's offspring: the expression of love for the other (the sexual act), the love of God (*imago dei*), and the love of self (one's descendants and name). Teaching children the Torah was also an obligation of Jewish parents: "make them known to your children and your children's children" (Deuteronomy 4:9), and "you shall teach them diligently unto your children" (Deuteronomy 6:7).

The love of children is also regnant in depictions of the paradisiacal future. Isaiah views the blessed future in the following terms:

> The wolf shall dwell with the lamb,
> and the leopard shall lie down with the kid,
> and the calf and the lion and the fatling together,
> and a little child (*wə-naʿar qāṭōn*) shall lead them
> (Isaiah 11:6).

Ancient Israelite tradition emphasized that grandchildren are "the crown of the aged" (Proverbs 17:6), and blessed is the man whose "quiver" is full of children (Psalm 127:5). As is well known, sterility was abhorrent (cf. esp. Genesis 16:2; 20:18; 30:2) and pride of place goes to the gift of a son.[9] Children were evidence of honor, even divine favor; the future of humanity is possible only because of male and female children.[10] Female children are not unimportant; Job rejoices in his daughters (Job 42:15).[11] As R. de Vaux stated, "Dans l'ancien Israël, avoir des enfants, beaucoup d'enfants, était également un honneur envié, et des souhaits étaient formulés au moment du mariage (In ancient Israel, to have many children was a coveted honour, and the wedding guests often expressed the wish that the couple would be blessed with a large family)."[12]

During the period of Early Judaism, from about 250 B.C. to A.D. 200, the trend continued to be toward philopedia within the acknowledged importance of the family.

Ascetic movements began around the middle of the second century B.C., perhaps with the exodus of the followers of the Righteous Teacher from Jerusalem to the western shores of the Dead Sea. While "non-marriage" is found in Judaism it is on the basis of devotion to Torah; it is never linked with misopedia.

In early Jewish literature there are two passages that may be construed to denote a hatred of children. The first is in *1 Enoch* 99:5, which has been translated by E. Isaac as follows:

> In those days, they (the women) shall become pregnant, but they (the sinners) shall come out and abort their infants and cast them out from their midst; they shall (also) abandon their (other) children, casting their infants out while they are still suckling. They shall neither return to them (their babes) nor have compassion upon their beloved ones.[13]

The passage should not be categorized, without qualifications, as indicative of misopedia. The main reference is to unwanted infants, and — most importantly — these two sentences refer to the final woes of the sinners. Such exhortations are descriptions of the eschatological horrors to be confronted by the wicked and must not be confused with misopedia.

The second passage is in Josephus' *Jewish War*. An extremely wealthy woman named Mary, the daughter of Eleazar of the village of Bethezuba, fled to Jerusalem to escape the southward movement of the conquering Roman army. While in the city she treated her son in the most horrifying manner:

> *kai tauth' hama legousa kteinei ton huion, epeit' optēsasa to men hēmisu katesthiei, to de loipon katakalupsasa ephulatten.*

> she slew her son, and then, having roasted the body and devoured half of it, she covered up and stored the remainder.[14]

The social situation is the key to understanding her actions. This passage does not denote misopedia; it reflects insanity due to the hatred of marauding Jewish youths[15] and the debilitations from the famine.

Without any doubt the emphasis in Early Judaism was on the love of family and children. Education in the home was centered on the Torah; religious services conducted every Sabbath in the home and the sacred prayer offered before and after meals solidified the importance of the family as the most important group in Jewish society.[16] The special history of each family was retold in light of the first humans, who formed a family, and the subsequent histories, which centered almost always around the family; and children had their own significant roles, highlighted by the stories about Adam's sons and daughters, Noah's sons, Job's daughters, Abraham's son Isaac, Jacob's twelve sons, Jephtha's daughter, and David during his youth. Telling and retelling such stories not only defined the person and clarified the will of God but also brought the child psychologically, spiritually, and physically close to the parent.

According to Josephus, "sexual intercourse was only for the procreation of children" (*kai tautēn ei melloi teknōn heneka ginesthai*).[17] According to the Mishnah, the world (*hā-ᶜôlām*) was "only created for fruition (*ləp̱iryāh*) and increase (*wə-riḇyāh*)"; then Isaiah 45:18 is quoted: "He created it not a waste: he formed it to be inhabited."[18] The chief blessing of the family, as S. Safrai states, was "the number and survival of children."[19]

A brilliant Jew, sometime between 50 B.C. and A.D. 100, affirmed the importance of children; note the following excerpt from Pseudo-Phocylides:

> Do not remain unmarried, lest you die nameless.
> Give nature her due, you also, beget in your turn
>   as you were begotten.

> Do not prostitute your wife, defiling your children.
> (lines 175-77).[20]

Obviously, more than children are the concerns of this thinker; but his acknowledgment of children and their place in the home is reaffirmed in line 207, in which he exhorts gentleness in training a child. Such traditions are well entrenched in Early Judaism. M. Cohn correctly concludes, "Anerkennung und Pflege des engen geistigen und seelischen Zusammenhanges zwischen Eltern und Kindern charakterisiert die jüd. Familie" (recognition and cultivation of the close spiritual and mental bonds between parents and children characterized the Jewish family).[21]

Jesus' Philopedia

Even those who only read the New Testament cursorily know that Jesus affirmed the sanctity of marriage, the home, and the need to honor both parents and children. He is reputed to have said, "Let the children (ta paidia) come to me, do not hinder them; for to such belongs the kingdom of God" (Mark 10:13-16; cf. also Matthew 19:13-15; Luke 18:15-17). According to Mark, at Capernaum Jesus attempted to instruct the twelve regarding the meaning of greatness. Mark records that Jesus took a child (paidion) and said, "Whoever receives one such child in my name receives me" (Mark 9:37; Matthew 18:5; Luke 9:48). Those doing exegesis must be careful not to confuse a reference to a child with love of children. The pericope in Mark 9:36-37, as Hugh Anderson states, is not about children per se, but about discipleship.[22] The child is chosen to illustrate not philopedia but lowliness, littleness, dependence, and humility. The disciples had quarreled over greatness, each probably seeking to elevate himself. Again the setting, the context, is the source of insightful exegesis.

If Jesus' love of children had been addressed to the Romans in persuasive language to convince them that he was a loving, nonmilitant, peaceful person, then we might suspect this of being a creation of the early Church. But the pericopes mentioned are not apologetic or polemic; they are not shaped, or created, by the kerygmatic and christological concerns of the Church. Their didactic function is derivative from the probability that Jesus loved children.

The acids of critical scholarship, which have been essential in removing the encrusted eisegesis that has obscured the original intent of the Evangelists, and of Jesus himself, have not marred the solid evidence of Jesus' philopedia. The first great critic in the history of the quest for the historical Jesus, D. F. Strauss, affirmed the love of Jesus for children. The Jesus sayings related to children are almost always preserved in contexts that show Jesus being forced "to suppress disputes among" his disciples. Yet the scene with the child in Mark 9 (and parallels), Strauss concludes, "is in itself too specific and remarkable to be a mere background to the ensuing discourse."[23] In addition, the logion about children in Mark 10 is not a creation by the Church; "the saying of Jesus, *Suffer little children, etc.,* . . . bears the stamp of genuineness."[24]

Mark 10:13-16 (and parallels) could be used to teach about discipleship, but behind it lies reliable evidence that Jesus loved children. That presupposition, indeed probable fact, made the analogical teaching "like a child" possible. Jesus identified himself with the humble child and against the proud disciples.

The authenticity of these Jesus traditions is widely and rightly affirmed today.[25] I have no reason to doubt that Jesus' philopedia was represented in his actions and words, even though almost all of these are lost forever and those that have been preserved were recorded for reasons other than to argue for his love of and for children.

An additional proof of Jesus' love of children is reflected perhaps in the peculiar name he habitually uses for God. Over 170 times in the canonical Gospels and twenty times in the *Gospel of Thomas* Jesus calls God "Father."[26] Jesus' name for God (Elohim) is Abba, which is not only translated but also transliterated in the Greek New Testament: *Abba ho patēr* (Mark 14:36; cf. Galatians 4:6 and Romans 8:15). Jesus is related to a loving Father. Jesus also encourages his disciples to share in this relationship, teaching them to say, when they pray, "Father" (Matthew 6:9-13; Luke 11:2-4). Abba is childlike talk and may be rendered colloquially as "Daddy," "dear Father," or even "my Daddy." This is intimate discourse. Jesus tends to eschew the jargon of sophisticated liturgy, which had in his own lifetime moved from spontaneous to statutory prayer; he prefers the language of humble children dependent upon a loving father. Jesus must have seen on innumerable occasions what I have seen only occasionally in Jerusalem: a little child pulling on the garment of a towering father and calling to him with an upward look: "Abba." Jesus probably was not so much appealing to the child's innocence as to his or her utter dependence upon a father, and the humble indwelling of the sphere controlled by the loving father. The conclusion to our reflections and research is palpable: Jesus loved children and felt close to them.[27]

In the context of this Jewish tradition and environment, it is pertinent to ask if Jesus in any way altered the Jewish concept of children. He obviously inherited from the Tanach, early Jewish writings, and oral traditions the love of children. The result of altering the traditions was to elevate the children with their humility over the authorities with their pride. As J. Jeremias pointed out, the status of the child in Judaism was elevated by Jesus' "new view of children."[28] Jeremias rightly emphasized that sayings like Mark 10:14 and Matthew 18:3, "cannot be derived either from contemporary literature or from the community, which shared the patriarchal attitude of its milieu; rather, they belong at the heart of Jesus' message."[29]

Braun stresses another discontinuity between Jesus and his Jewish contemporaries. He alone accorded to children the ability to teach by word and example. In *Jesus of Nazareth: The Man and His Time*, Braun wrote the following: "Children are fitting teachers — a thoroughly unjewish view — not because of their naive view of the world but because of their capacity, innocently and without calculation and guile, to accept a gift."[30] Braun was commenting on the new ideas brought by Jesus and reflected in Mark 10:15 ("Truly, I say to you, whoever does not receive the kingdom of God like a child shall not enter it").

Recently, scholarly research has affirmed Jesus' significant contribution to the history of ideas on the role and status of children. In *God the Father*, for example, R. Hamerton-Kelly attempts to show that Jesus "broke the forms of the patriarchal family in the name of God the Father."[31] Although Hamerton-Kelly is primarily concerned with the place accorded by Jesus to women, he correctly contends that Jesus noticed children as well; he "paid special attention to mothers and children, over the characteristic objections of his disciples."[32]

In *The Practice of Jesus*, H. Echegaray wisely embraces the necessity of basing exegesis on a careful assessment of the social setting confronted by Jesus. In following this methodology he perceives Jesus' unique understanding of children. He wrote:

> Jesus takes the offensive and declares that the kingdom of God belongs to those whom the society of the day regarded as inferiors. This was the case with children who in that period of history were given the "unpleasant" tasks of the household. If men and women are to enter the kingdom, they must become like children, identify with the social condition of inferiority in which children found themselves, and cultivate an attitude of obedience and openness toward the kingdom.[33]

Obviously some Jews in the first century A.D. had a

very high regard for and love of children. Jesus certainly shared this attitude, but he alone elevated children and used them as examples of the proper attitude to the kingdom. Children cannot inaugurate God's rule; they cannot help bring it any closer to the present: no one can. Children know their smallness and utter dependence, so they can graciously and humbly receive an unmerited gift: so must the disciple. Here we are very close to the heart of Jesus' authentic message.

Jesus' creativity and new perspectives often were missed by those who followed him. In fact, one century after his death some of his followers had completely reversed his position on children. His own thesis was perverted into its antithesis: philopedia became misopedia.

Misopedia in the *Acts of Thomas*

By the second century A.D. ascetic strains are evident in Christianity. Encratism (second-century extreme asceticism) probably predates Tatian; it is clearly reflected in his alteration of gospel traditions in the so-called Diatessaron. For example, the famous reference to Anna, the daughter of Phanuel, is rewritten. The statement that she "lived with her husband seven years from her virginity" (Luke 2:36) becomes "she was with (her) husband seven days."

34 ܪܟܝܬܐ ܥܡ ܗܘܬ ܢܒܪܢ ܠܐ ܪܫܒܥܐ.

G. Quispel has drawn attention to the distinction between Encratism and Gnosticism, and the early influence of the former.[35]

Asceticism clearly helped shape the *Acts of Paul;* the husbands of his converts attack him because the women now refuse to cohabit with them. By the middle of the second century A.D. asceticism was pronounced in Syria; and Arthur Vööbus may well be correct in concluding that it was influenced by the ascetic ideas contained in the

Qumran scrolls.[36] As Robert Murray writes, "The enthusiasm for sexual asceticism is all but universal in the Syriac world, Bardaiṣan and perhaps Quq (both Edessenes) being practically the only exceptions."[37]

Even though asceticism is not misopedia, some gnostic documents show that a clear strain of misopedia does grow out of certain ascetic tendencies. The *Acts of Thomas,* for example, was composed in Syriac sometime in the early third century A.D. or (more probably) the latter half of the second century, probably in or near Edessa.[38] In this, the most ascetic document in the Apocrypha and Pseudepigrapha of the New Testament, ascetic ideology reaches its ultimate limit and includes misopedia. Observe how children are portrayed in the *Acts of Thomas,* chapter 12, where the Lord sits down the young people and says:[39]

ܒܗܕܘ ܒ̈ܢܝ ܕܐܚܝ

ܡܠܠ ܥܡܟܘܢ ܘܠܡܢܘ ܐܫܠܡܟܘܢ. ܘܕܥܘ ܕܡܚܕܐ
ܕܡܬܦܨܝܢ ܐܢܬܘܢ ܡܢ ܗܕܐ ܫܘܬܦܘܬܐ ܛܢܦܬܐ.
ܗܘܝܢ ܐܢܬܘܢ ܗܝ̈ܟܠܐ ܕܟܝ̈ܐ. ܘܡܬܦܨܝܢ ܐܢܬܘܢ ܡܢ
ܫ̈ܥܝܐ ܚܫܘܟܐ ܘܓܠ̈ܝܐ. ܘܡܢ ܝܨܦܬܐ ܝܩܝܪܬܐ ܕܒ̈ܢܝܐ.
ܗ̇ܢܘܢ ܕܚܪܬܗܘܢ ܒܟܝܬܐ ܗܝ ܡܪ̈ܝܪܬܐ. ܘܐܢ
ܢܗܘܘܢ ܠܟܘܢ ܫ̈ܥܝܐ. ܡܛܠܬܗܘܢ ܗܘܝܢ ܐܢܬܘܢ
ܓܠܘܙܝܢ ܘܛܠܘܡܝܢ ܠܝܬܡ̈ܐ. ܘܥܠܘܡܝܢ ܠܐܪ̈ܡܠܬܐ.
ܘܡܫܬܢܩܝܢ ܐܢܬܘܢ ܛܒ ܒܥܘܠܝܗܘܢ. ܘܟܠܗܐ
ܚܢܢ ܕܒ̈ܢܝܐ ܥܒ̈ܕܐ ܫܟܝܚܐ ܗܘܝܢ ܠܗܘܢ. ܐܘ
ܕܫ̈ܐܕܐ ܢܦܠ ܥܠܝܗܘܢ. ܐܘ ܕܒܪ ܐܓܪܐ (fol. 4 *a*)
ܐܚܝܕ ܠܗܘܢ. ܐܘ ܕܦܠܓܐ ܢܦܠ ܥܠܝܗܘܢ. ܘܐܢ ܚܠܝܡܝܢ
ܢܗܘܘܢ ܣܪܝܚܝܢ.. ܐܘ ܒܙܢܝܐ ܐܘ ܒܓܢܒܘܬܐ. ܐܘ
ܒܓܘܪܬܐ ܐܘ ܒܢܟܠܘܬܐ. ܐܘ ܒܥܒܕܐ ܣܪܝܩܐ. ܘܡܥܠܝܢ
ܦܘܪ̈ܥܢܐ ܡܬܬܒܥܝܢ ܐܢܬܘܢ ܡܢܗܘܢ. ܐܠܐ ܐܢ

ܬܬܛܦܝܣܘܢ ܠܝ ܘܬܬܢܛܪܘܢ ܢܟܦܐܝܬ ܠܐܠܗܐ.
ܢܗܘܘܢ ܠܟܘܢ ܒ̈ܢܝܐ ܚ̈ܝܐ. ܗ̇ܢܘܢ ܕܚܕ ܡܢ ܟܘܪ̈ܗܢܐ
ܘܚ̈ܒܠܐ ܠܐ ܩܪܒ ܠܗܘܢ. ܘܬܗܘܘܢ ܕܠܐ ܝܨܦܬܐ
ܘܕܠܐ ܥܩܬܐ ܘܕܠܐ ܒܝܫܘܬܐ. ܘܡܣܬܟܠܝܢ ܐܢܬܘܢ
ܕܐܡܬܝ ܬܚܙܘܢ ܡܫܬܘܬܐ ܗ̇ܝ ܕܫܪ̈ܪܐ. ܘܬܗܘܘܢ
ܒܗ̇ ܡܫ̈ܒܚܢܐ. ܘܬܬܡܢܘܢ ܥܡ ܥ̈ܐܠܝ ܠܓܢܘܢܐ ⁘ ⁘

Remember, my children, what my brother (=Thomas) said to you, and know to whom he entrusted you; and know that the moment you extricate yourselves from this defiling intercourse you will become pure temples. Then you are saved from hidden and manifest sufferings, and from the great anxiety of children, whose end is bitter sadness. And if you should have children,[40] because of them you will become deceivers, thieves, beaters of the fatherless, and defrauders of widows; and you will be tormented greatly by their losses. For the greater part of children entails many pains; either the king will attack them,[41] a demon[42] will seize them, or, partial (paralysis)[43] will attack them. And if (they are) healthy they will become defilers, either by adultery, theft, fornication, avarice, or by empty pomposity;[44] and through these defilements you will be tormented by them. But if[45] you will be formed[46] by me, and keep yourselves[47] purely unto God you will have living children, (and) not one of these infirmities and injuries shall touch them. And you will be without anxiety, sadness, and distress. And you will consider[48] (the time) when you will see the true wedding feast; then you will be in it singers, and be numbered with those who enter the bridal feast.[49]

Employing a device known now to be deeply entrenched in Early Judaism, thanks to the discovery of the *Temple Scroll,* the author attributes his own ideas to God. The words seem authoritative and invaluable because they appear to belong to Christ himself. This linguistic phenomenon is also well known from the *Odes of Solomon*.[50]

In an absurd explosion of logic the author confuses children with the origin of all sins: because of children "you will become deceivers, thieves," and all embodiments of evil. On the same level of thought the reasoning is at once irrefutable and absurd: without children there would be no sin because there would be no more humans to commit evils. (The author, however, admits belief in demons, so evil could continue without humans.) The vision is also confused by a false equation between sexual lust and procreation, and between anxiety for children and concern for their welfare. Misogamy has moved precariously close to misogyny and into misopedia.

Our disenchantment with this passage is due to our ideological distance from early Syriac asceticism. The author had begun with a beautiful thought: the embodiment of the supreme importance of one thing and the promised harmony and transcendence of problems through this devotion; the devotee will become a singer who sees and enters into the bridal feast. For him (or her), marriage is to be with Christ. Children are promised; but the thought is not philoprogenitive: that is, children are not "begotten"; they are "adopted" from already begotten children.

Conclusion

We have witnessed more than a diminution of Jesus traditions. In some Syriac communities, by the second century, or the third at the latest, Jesus' original actions and teachings were so significantly misconstrued that they became the antithesis of what they had been. Philopedia lapsed into misopedia. Fortunately, the Church was led away from the path advocated by the author of the *Acts of Thomas* 12. It does not follow, however, that it has understood the perspicacity behind Jesus' philopedia.

Addendum

It can also be noted that these insights into the message of Jesus render the teachings of the Book of Mormon on children that much more meaningful to Latter-day Saints. In one of the most moving accounts in 3 Nephi, the resurrected Jesus blessed the children who were encircled about by angels and fire (3 Nephi 17:11-24), epitomizing a spirit of philopedia evident throughout the Book of Mormon. The words of Lehi state that bearing children was one of the desired purposes of the Fall, for Adam and Eve "would have had no children" had they remained in a state of innocence (2 Nephi 2:22-25). Benjamin exhorts everyone to "become as little children, . . . submissive, meek, humble, patient, full of love, willing to submit to all things which the Lord seeth fit to inflict upon him, even as a child doth submit to his father" (Mosiah 3:18-19) and commands them to teach their children "to walk in the ways of truth and soberness, . . . to love one another, and to serve one another" (Mosiah 4:15). Mormon even matches the love of all children with the perfect love of God: "I am filled with charity, which is everlasting love; wherefore, all children are alike unto me; wherefore, I love little children with a perfect love; and they are all alike and partakers of salvation" (Moroni 8:17) — The Editors, with permission of the author.

[completed in 1985]

Notes

1. Iamblichus, *De Vita Pythagorica* X, 51, in Ludovicus Deubner, ed. (Leipzig: Teubner, 1937), 28.

2. See the excellent discussion of *"pais,"* by Albrecht Oepke in *Theological Dictionary of the New Testament*, 9 vols. (Grand Rapids, MI: Eerdmans, 1964-75), 5:636-54. I am indebted to him for his research.

3. *Hellenistic* is not a term that indicates geographical areas distinct from Palestine; unfortunately some scholars still use it incorrectly. It denotes the world culture of the Hellenistic period that

dates from approximately after the time of Alexander the Great until the decline of the Romans, or roughly from the middle of the third century B.C. until the middle of the fourth century A.D. It is a world and not a Greek culture, because Greek, Roman, Egyptian, Iranian, and Syrian traditions flowed into the first shared culture. One could also include elements from other nations, namely all those from the Irish Celts to the Chinese. I have tried to demonstrate this insight in my contribution to the Valentin Nikiprowetzky Festschrift, "A Study of the History of the Rechabites," *Hellenica et Judaica: Hommage à Valentin Nikiprowetzky,* ed. A. Caquot, M. Hadas-Lebel, and J. Riaud (Leuven: Peeters, 1986), 219–43, and in *The Old Testament Pseudepigrapha and the New Testament,* Society for New Testament Studies Monograph Series 54 (Cambridge: Cambridge University Press, 1985).

4. Cf. Aristaenetus, *Epistolographi* I, 13; *Inscriptiones Graecae,* vol. 12, fasc. 5, 292.7; Julian, *Epistulae* 896. These sources are derived from Liddell, Scott, Jones, and McKenzie's *A Greek-English Lexicon* (Oxford: Clarendon Press, 1973).

5. See H. Herter, "Das Kind im Zeitalter des Hellenismus," *Bonner Jahrbücher des Vereins von Altertumsfreunden im Rheinlande* 132 (1927): 256; and the excellent bibliography supplied by Oepke, *Theological Dictionary,* 5:636-37.

6. Cf. Epictetus, *Discourses* III, 22, 67-82.

7. Cf. Lucian, *Abdicatus* 18.

8. Especially in "The Life of Adam and Eve," in James H. Charlesworth, ed., *The Old Testament Pseudepigrapha,* 2 vols. (Garden City, NY: Doubleday, 1983, 1985), 2:249-95. See the following publications: Jacob Jervell, "Imagines und Imago Dei: Aus der Genesis Exegese des Josephus," in *Josephus Studien: Untersuchungen zu Josephus, dem antiken Judentum und dem Neuen Testament* (Göttingen: Vandenhoeck & Ruprecht, 1974), 197-204; J. Jervell, *Imago Dei: Gen 1.26f. im Spätjudentum, in der Gnosis und in den paulinischen Briefen,* Forschungen zur Religion und Literatur des Alten und Neuen Testaments 58 (Göttingen: Vandenhoeck & Ruprecht, 1960); and John R. Levison, *Portraits of Adam in Early Judaism: From Sirach to 2 Baruch* (Sheffield: Sheffield Academic Press, 1988). Also see the erudite discussion of the *imago dei* by Ephraim E. Urbach in *The Sages: Their Concepts and Beliefs,* tr. Israel Abrahams, 2 vols. (Jerusalem: Magnes, 1975/Cambridge: Harvard University Press, 1987), 1:227-33.

9. Wisdom of Sirach (*Ben Sira*) 30:4-6.

10. TB *Baba Bathra* 16b.

11. Cf. *Testament of Job* 46-52 in Charlesworth, *The Old Testament Pseudepigrapha,* 1:864-68.

12. Roland de Vaux, "Les Enfants," *Les institutions de l'ancien testament*, 2 vols. (Paris: Éditions du Cerf, 1967), 1:71-87 (quotation on p. 71). Also consult the revised English translation: *Ancient Israel: Its Life and Institutions*, tr. John McHugh (London: McGraw-Hill, 1965; repr. 1968), 41-52 (quotation on p. 41).

13. E. Isaac, *1 Enoch*, in Charlesworth, *The Old Testament Pseudepigrapha*, 1:80. For a similar translation with supporting philological notes, see Matthew Black, *The Book of Enoch or I Enoch: A New English Edition*, with James C. VanderKam, Studia in Veteris Testamenti Pseudepigrapha 7 (Leiden: Brill, 1985), 92, and notes.

This passage in *1 Enoch* must not be construed to denote that in some wayward Jewish communities of the third or second centuries B.C. Jewish children were exposed. As J. Duncan M. Derrett, "Law and Society in Jesus's World," in *Aufstieg und Niedergang der römischen Welt* (Berlin: de Gruyter, 1982), II.25.1:477-564, succinctly states with regard to Jewish communities, "Children were not exposed" (p. 516).

14. Josephus, *Jewish War* VI, 208; the Greek is from *Josephus: The Jewish War*, tr. H. St. J. Thackeray, 9 vols. (Cambridge: Harvard University Press, 1928; repr. 1967-68), 3:436-37.

15. Cf. Josephus, *Jewish War* VI, 205.

16. As Philip Birnbaum, *Encyclopedia of Jewish Concepts* (New York: Hebrew, 1979), 9, clarifies, "Religious observances, particularly those connected with the Sabbath and the festivals, strengthened Jewish family life and developed its solidarity to an extent unusual among non-Jews."

17. Josephus, *Against Apion* II, 199; cf. H. St. J. Thackeray, *Josephus: The Life against Apion*, 9 vols. (Cambridge: Harvard University Press, 1926; repr. 1968), 1:372-73.

18. M *Eduyoth* 1:13. The Hebrew is from Chanoch Albeck and Henoch Yalon, eds., *Shishah Sidre Mishnah*, 6 vols. (Jerusalem: Mosed Bialek, 1951-58). The English translation is by Herbert Danby, *The Mishnah* (London: Oxford University Press, 1933; repr. 1964), 424.

19. See Shemuel Safrai's informative "Home and Family," in S. Safrai and M. Stern, eds., *The Jewish People in the First Century*, 2 vols., Compendia Rerum Iudaicarum ad Novum Testamentum 1 (Assen: Van Gorcum, 1974-76), 2:728-92; see esp. 748-52 (quotation on p. 750).

20. Translated by P. W. van der Horst in Charlesworth, *The Old Testament Pseudepigrapha*, 2:580-81.

21. Marcus Cohn, "Kinder und Eltern," in Georg Herlitz et al., *Jüdisches Lexikon: Ein enzyklopädisches Handbuch des jüdischen Wissens*,

4 vols. (Berlin: Jüdischer Verlag, 1927-30), 3:697-99 (quotation from col. 697).

22. Hugh Anderson, *The Gospel of Mark*, New Century Bible (London: Oliphants, 1976), 234.

23. David F. Strauss, *The Life of Jesus Critically Examined*, tr. George Eliot, ed. Peter C. Hodgson, Lives of Jesus Series (London: SCM Press/Philadelphia: Fortress 1972), 397. The original was published in 1835.

24. Ibid., 398 (italics in original).

25. The most influential New Testament scholar of this century, and a severe critic of the reliability of the Jesus tradition, Rudolf Bultmann, *History of the Synoptic Tradition*, tr. John Marsh (New York: Harper & Row, 1963), tended to conclude that Mark 10:13-16 was not formed in a non-Palestinian setting, but within the Palestinian Church (p. 60). For Bultmann, verses 13 through 16 are "a complete apophthegm without v. 15, and its point is stated in v. 14" (p. 32). He continues by contending that the "original unit" is verses 13, 14, and 16 and has "its basis in the Jewish practice of blessing" (p. 32). These insights reveal that Bultmann did not attribute all of Mark 10:13-16 to the later Church, but they do not prove that they are *ipsissma verba Jesu*, which was, of course, not Bultmann's *Tendenz*.

Among numerous recent publications that assume or contend that the tradition of Jesus' love for children is reliable, see especially the following: Eduard Schweizer, *The Good News According to Matthew*, tr. David E. Green (Atlanta: John Knox Press, 1975), 363; John D. Crossan, *In Fragments: The Aphorisms of Jesus* (New York: Harper & Row, 1983), 109; and Ben Witherington III, *Women in the Ministry of Jesus: A Study of Jesus' Attitudes to Women and Their Roles as Reflected in His Earthly Life*, Society for New Testament Studies Monograph Series 51 (Cambridge: Cambridge University Press, 1984), 14. As Ben F. Meyer, *The Aims of Jesus* (London: SCM Press, 1979), contends, Jesus "affirmed the root structures of social existence (Mark 10.2-9 par.; 10.14 parr.; Matt. 7.11 par.; Mark 12.17 parr.)" (p. 249).

26. The pioneering and definitive research was conducted by Joachim Jeremias. See the following publications by him: *Abba: Studien zur neutestamentlichen Theologie und Zeitgeschichte* (Göttingen: Vandenhoeck & Ruprecht, 1966), and *Das Vater-Unser im Lichte der neueren Forschung*, Calwer Hefte 50 (Stuttgart: Calwer, 1962). Each of these has seen subsequent editions. The English translations of the major sections have been published: Jeremias, *The Prayers of Jesus*, tr. John Bowden, Christoph Burchard, and John Reumann, Studies in Biblical Theology, Second Series 6 (Philadelphia: Fortress, 1979).

27. John Reumann brings out an important dimension of the concept of a child. God's kingdom is given freely; it is not a reward nor a result of some action by an individual or group. According to Reumann, *Jesus in the Church's Gospels: Modern Scholarship and the Earliest Sources* (Philadelphia: Fortress, 1973), 151, the gift is to be received as a child; "Man simply receives it, as a child receives a gift" (Mark 10:15). Herbert Braun, *Jesus of Nazareth: The Man and His Time,* tr. Everett R. Kalin (Philadelphia: Fortress, 1979), 50, also stresses this dimension; children are chosen as examples by Jesus, "Because of their capacity, innocently and without calculation and guile, to accept a gift."

28. Joachim Jeremias, *New Testament Theology: The Proclamation of Jesus,* tr. J. Bowden (New York: Scribner, 1971), 227. Jeremias tends to denigrate the place of children in Judaism. He wrote, "In the world of Jesus, children, like women, were counted as things of little value" (ibid.). This statement is simply inaccurate. Perhaps Jeremias meant that in legal terms children were not accorded significant rank, because they "are not in full possession of their intellectual powers" (ibid.). Children, as we have seen, were highly prized in almost all sectors of Early Judaism. Jeremias also erred when he claimed that Jesus "brings children nearer to God than adults" (ibid.). Perhaps he meant to emphasize that children are closer to God than proud adults.

29. Jeremias, *New Testament Theology,* 227-28.

30. Braun, *Jesus of Nazareth,* 50.

31. Robert Hamerton-Kelly, *God the Father: Theology and Patriarchy in the Teaching of Jesus,* Overtures to Biblical Theology Series (Philadelphia: Fortress, 1979), 60.

32. Ibid.

33. Hugo Echegaray, *The Practice of Jesus,* tr. Matthew J. O'Connell (Maryknoll, NY: Orbis Books, 1984), 84.

34. This is not the place to list the publications on the Syriac evidence of the "Diatessaron." Sufficient for the present are the following: Louis Leloir, *Doctrines et méthodes de S. Éphrem d'après son commentaire de l'évangile concordant* (original syriaque et version arménienne = CSCO 220) (Louvain: Secrétariat du Corpus Scriptorum Christianorum Orientalium, 1961); Leloir, *Saint Éphrem, commentaire de l'évangile concordant, texte syriaque, manuscrit Chester Beatty 709,* *edition, traduction,* Chester Beatty Monographs 8 (Dublin: Hodges Figgis, 1963); Leloir, *Éphrem de Nisibe, Commentaire de l'évangile concordant ou Diatessaron traduit du syriaque et de arménienne,* Sources Chrétiennes series 121 (Paris: Éditions du Cerf, 1966); Tj. Baarda,

"A Syriac Fragment of Mar Ephraem's Commentary on the Diates-saron," *New Testament Studies* 8 (1961/62): 287-300; and Pedro O. Valiviesco, "Un nuevo fragmento siríaco del comentario de San Éfren al Diatésaron," *Studia Papyrologica* 5 (1966): 7-17.

35. His numerous publications are cited in James H. Charles-worth, *The New Testament Apocrypha and Pseudepigrapha: A Guide to Publications, with Excursuses on Apocalypses*, ATLA Bibliography Se-ries, 17 (Metuchen, NJ: American Theological Library Association and Scarecrow Press, 1987). Also, see Yves Tissot, "Encratisme et actes apocryphes," in François Bovon et al., eds., *Les actes apocryphes des apôtres: Christianisme et monde païen*, Publications de la faculté de théologie de l'Université de Genève 4 (Geneva: Editions Labor et Fides, 1981), 109-19; and Giulia S. Gasparro, "Gli atti apocrifi degli apostoli e la tradizione dell'enkrateia. Discussione di una recente formula interpretativa," *Augustinianum* 22 (1983): 287-307; and Ugo Bianchi, "Encratismo, acosmismo, diteismo come criteri di analisi storico-religiosa delgi apocrifi," *Augustinianum* 22 (1983): 309-17.

36. Arthur Vööbus, *History of Asceticism in the Syrian Orient*, 2 vols., Corpus Scriptorum Christianorum Orientalium 184, Subs. 14 and 197, Subs. 17 (Louvain: Secretariat du Corpus Scriptorum Chris-tianorum Orientalium, 1958, 1960).

37. Robert Murray, *Symbols of Church and Kingdom: A Study in Early Syriac Tradition* (London: Cambridge University Press, 1975), 11. See the important work by H. J. W. Drivers entitled *Bardaiṣan of Edessa* (Assen: Van Gorcum, 1966).

38. A full bibliography on the *Acts of Thomas* is published in Charlesworth, *The New Testament Apocrypha and Pseudepigrapha*.

39. This section is not preserved in the oldest Syriac manuscript of the *Acts of Thomas*, the fifth- or sixth-century palimpsest, Codex Sinaiticus Syriacus 30, edited by Agnes S. Lewis, *Acta Mythologica Apostolorum*, Horae Semiticae 3 (London: Clay, 1904). The text is from the tenth-century Syriac manuscript, B. M. Add. 14,645, and was edited by William Wright, *Apocryphal Acts of the Apostles*, 2 vols. (London, 1871; repr. Amsterdam: Philo Press, 1968). The Greek cited below is according to Constantinus Tischendorf, "Acta Thomae," in *Acta Apostolorum Apocrypha* (Leipzig: Avenarius et Mendelssohn, 1851), 200.

40. Abbreviations to be used in these notes: Syr. = Syriac; Gk. = Greek; Wright = Wright's *Apocryphal Acts*; James = Montague R. James, *The Aprocryphal New Testament* (Oxford: Clarendon, 1924; 1972); Klijn = Albertus F. Johannes Klijn, *The Acts of Thomas: Intro-duction − Text − Commentary*, Supplements to *Novum Testamentum* 5

(Leiden: Brill, 1962); Bornkamm = Gunther Bornkamm, "The Acts of Thomas," in *New Testament Apocrypha*, ed. Edgar Hennecke and Wilhelm Schneemelcher, tr. R. McL. Wilson, 2 vols. (Philadelphia: Westminster, 1976), 2:425-531, esp. 449; Bovon = Bovon, *Les actes apocryphes des apôtres*; Festugière = Andre-Jean Festugière, *Les actes apocryphes de Jean et de Thomas: Traduction Française et notes critiques*, Cahiers d'orientalisme 6 (Geneva: Cramer, 1983).

My translation is intended to be neither woodenly literal nor freely idiomatic. The Syriac at this place in the text has *ḥsh'*, which means "pain, suffering, disease." Gk.: *ean de ktēsēthe paidas pollous*, "but if you acquire many children . . . " Wright emended the Syr. to *bny'*, "children." Klijn follows Wright, but without discussion or note; the others — James, Bornkamm, and Festugière — translate from the Greek text, which is inferior to the Syriac text, because it derives from the original Syriac; as Festugière states, "tout le monde s'accorde pour dire que l'original est en syriaque" (43). It is possible either that the consonants became confused (but they are quite distinct), or that "pains" may be an intentional euphemism for children; they are defined as those who cause pain. It is the custom today to be hesitant to emend a text. The Greek may indicate either a Syr. *byn'* or an interpretation by a translator. The strongest case for an emendation is the following *mtlthwn*, "on account of them," which seems to presuppose *byn'*, "children."

41. Syr. *npl* with *ʿl* means "attack" not "falls upon" as in the translations by Wright and Klijn. This clause is not found in the Greek, hence the translations by James, Bornkamm, and Festugière do not contain it.

42. Or "a lunatic."

43. Literally "a part"; *plg'* with *k'b* means "partial paralysis," but *k'b* does not occur here. Perhaps *k'b'* (pains) is the *nomen regens* in this long sentence; it appears at the beginning of the sentence. The Gk. is different, but it has a parallel noun here, *hemizēpoi*, "half-dry," or "half-withered"; also four nouns later it has *paralutikoi*, "paralytics." Klijn: "or paralysis befalls them."

44. Or "vainglory" (so Wright and Klijn). Perhaps the author thought that pride, or pomposity, was not intrinsically evil, and so breaking with his style he added the adjective *sryg'*, "empty."

45. Klijn inadvertently omitted the "if"; the error is probably typographical. Wright's version corrects the error.

46. The form *tttpyswn* is interesting and unattested. I parse it to be the second person masculine plural imperfect Ethpaiʿal of *ṭps*, "to typify," and would mean "to be formed," or "be persuaded"

(Wright, Klijn). It could be from the denominative verb *tps*, which comes from *twps'*, "figure, likeness, model, example." The Gk. has *peisthēsesthe*, "you be persuaded" ("Mais, si vous laissez persuader": Festugière) or "obey" (Bornkamm).

47. Or "souls." Gk.: *tas psuchas humōn*, "your souls."

48. Or "hoping"; Klijn: "and you shall be hoping (for the time) . . . "

49. Or "heaven, resting place," which is a metaphor for "bridal chamber."

50. See James H. Charlesworth, ed., *The Odes of Solomon: The Syriac Texts*, SBL Texts and Translations Series 13; Pseudepigrapha Series 7 (Missoula, MT: Scholars Press, 1977).

6

A Hebrew Inscription Authenticated

Cyrus H. Gordon
Brookline, Massachusetts

In dedicating this article to Professor Hugh W. Nibley, I am expressing an admiration I have long felt. Ever since visiting the campus of Brigham Young University two decades ago, I saw in Dr. Nibley a savant who was inspiring a generation of disciples with a love of learning and with the dedication to devote their lives to it. May he, like Moses, live to be a hundred and twenty, with undiminished vision and vigor!

In 1889 a Smithsonian Institution expedition, under the direction of Dr. Cyrus Thomas, unearthed a hitherto undisturbed[1] burial at Bat Creek (Mound #3), Loudon County, Tennessee. In it were nine skeletons, laid out in orderly fashion (as shown in fig. 1). Under the skull and jawbone of the only one with the head pointed south (#1) was found a number of objects, including an inscribed stone (figs. 2 and 3). The text is in Old Hebrew letters (*kĕtāv ʿivrî*) closely akin to those on Jewish coins of the two rebellions against Rome, and therefore to be dated ca. A.D. 100.

The stone is broken at both ends. The two vertical strokes above the line of writing were made with a sharp tool after the discovery of the tomb. The word that ends in two letters after the initial break on the right may be [H]ZQ "strong, strength."[2] But the sequence LYHWD[ ] after the word-divider can be read and translated "for Ju-

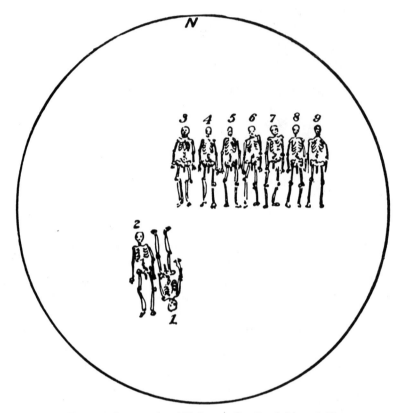

Figure 1: Disposition of Skeletons, Bat Creek Mound #3

dea."[3] The "pearls" (little drilled dots, as at the top of the L and Y) are familiar from coins of both rebellions, especially the Second (Bar Kokhba) Rebellion. The L, Y, and H could appear in several periods. The W, however, is found on coins of Roman date showing that the fifth letter is D (as attested on coins of Roman date) and not an improperly formed aleph. The sole letter on the last line, which approximates an aleph on coins of either rebellion, occurs more commonly on Bar Kokhba coins. It might pos-

Figure 2: Photograph of Bat Creek Inscription

Figure 3: Facsimile of Bat Creek Inscription

sibly serve as the numeral "1" to designate the First Year of the Rebellion.

For epigraphic details and a general discussion, the reader is referred to my article "The Bat Creek Inscription."[4] As noted there,[5] I had already asked the Smithsonian to run a carbon-14 test on the wood fragments and bone implement found with the inscription and other objects under the skull and jawbone of skeleton #1. For various reasons the test was not made then. It remained for Professor J. Huston McCulloch of Ohio State University to reopen the problem of Bat Creek Mound #3 and devote himself to it indefatigably since 1979. He has succeeded in having the wood fragments put through a "state-of-the-art" carbon-14 test which establishes a date not earlier than A.D. 32 and not later than 769.[6]

I stand by the scenario I proposed in 1972: During and after the rebellions, the Jews incurred such intense hostility from the Romans that the more desperate and adventuresome Jews with navigational expertise or contacts[7] tried to get as far away from the long arm of Rome as possible.

The stone was carved either ca. A.D. 100 in the Old World, or aboard ship, or in America by someone trained in the tradition of that script, some time after the refugees landed in what is now the eastern United States. By the time of its interment in Bat Creek Mound #3, it might have been passed down as an heirloom for several generations. But the carbon-14 test proves that the burial took place over seven centuries prior to Columbus' discovery in 1492. The letter-forms imply cultural contact between America and Palestine ca. A.D.100. The inscription cannot be a modern forgery, on the one hand, nor can it be pre-Christian, on the other.

Cyrus Thomas had an ax to grind. His theory was that the Mound Indians (including everybody buried at sites like Bat Creek) were the same people as the local Indians (notably the Cherokees) of modern times. He published the inscription upside-down and called it Cherokee (in the script invented by Sequoyah around 1821). Neither Thomas nor those who have agreed with him have attempted to translate any of the text.

A few amateurs, in the midtwentieth century, matched up two or three of the letters correctly by comparing them with published Phoenician alphabet charts. My friend, Dr. Joseph B. Mahan, Jr., consulted me on the Bat Creek Inscription in 1970. He was convinced that the letters were

Phoenician, after he had compared them with an alphabet chart in the *Cambridge Ancient History*. No one had been able to make any sense of the text either as Phoenician/ Hebrew or as Cherokee. I was the first Semitist to study the text and read the sequence LYHWD[ ] "for Judea."[8] I favored attributing the migration to the Bar Kokhba Rebellion, partly because three different Bar Kokhba coins had been found at three widely separated sites, at quite different times,[9] in the neighboring state of Kentucky. One of the coins might possibly be a modern copy, but the other two cannot easily be accounted for that way.[10]

There are traces of Jewish influence in pre-Columbian America. We may single out the Tepatlaxco (Veracruz) Stele (ca. A.D. 100-300) showing a Mayan wearing phylacteries; the arm windings are seven in number and are followed by finger windings. This monument is noteworthy because no scholar, in any field, has ever questioned its authenticity or pre-Columbian date. To be sure, the Amerindian experts did not detect the Old World origin of the ritual depicted and very few are even now aware of it.[11]

The Bat Creek Inscription is important because it is the first scientifically authenticated pre-Columbian text in an Old World script or language found in America; and, at that, in a flawless archaeological context. It proves that some Old World people not only could, but actually did, cross the Atlantic to America before the Vikings and Columbus.

While the Northwest Semitic (including Jewish) contribution to pre-Columbian America is a fact, we must state unequivocally that Columbus' achievement remains unique and undiminished. It was he who united the Eastern and Western hemispheres so that from 1492 their histories became indissolubly intertwined. His feat was the culmination of trans-Atlantic crossings since remote antiquity. Like all great discoveries, his was not a primitive beginning but the climax of a long development.

We must also state clearly that the boat which carried the Bat Creek Inscription — or its carver — to America in Roman times was not the first to bring immigrants or visitors to the western shores of the Atlantic. Various sea-lanes had brought different Old World peoples to America via both the Pacific and Atlantic. The Hebrews who came to America before the Vikings and Columbus were not the first to come, and no claim that "the Jews discovered America" is justified.[12]

General background on pre-Columbian crossings of the Atlantic and Pacific is available in my *Before Columbus*. Here we need only single out the circumnavigation of Africa by Phoenician mariners commissioned by Pharaoh Necho II around 600 B.C. Herodotus[13] relates that as they sailed westward around what we call the Cape of Good Hope, the sun was on their right. Herodotus confesses that he did not understand how that could be. (After all, he was acquainted only with the Northern Hemisphere where, if we head westward, the sun is always on our left.) Yet, as an honest reporter, he passes on the information to his readers. Modern scholars have long realized that the narrative proves the historicity of the Phoenician circumnavigation of Africa precisely because Herodotus did not understand the solar observation. What is just as significant is that Near East mariners were not only exploring seas in the Southern Hemisphere but also adding to the store of navigational science available in the Near East center of Western civilization, for the celestial observation made by the Phoenicians off the Cape of Good Hope did reach Herodotus on the shores of the eastern Mediterranean.

Two brass bracelets were among the artifacts found with skeleton #1 in Bat Creek Mound #3. Their composition (with lead as well as zinc alloyed with the copper)[14] was used by the Romans from about 45 B.C. to about A.D. 200, thus covering the dates of both Jewish rebellions. Brass of this approximate composition has been used in modern times since at least the fourteenth century. But the carbon-14 test of the wood fragment shows that all the contents of the burial were interred over half a millennium before the first "modern brass" and that therefore the bracelets were fashioned in Roman times.

The authentication of the Bat Creek Inscription raises the theme of global diffusion. However distinctive a high culture may be, it never arises *ex nihilo*. Egypt, for geographical reasons, favored the development of its own very distinctive civilization. Sealed off by mountains and deserts on both sides of the long Nile Valley, it was open to the outside world only at the north and south ends; to wit, the Delta and Black Africa. In between, along the narrow fertile valley, the Egyptians in relative isolation developed as unique a high civilization as ever existed. And yet we know of fundamental factors borrowed by Egypt in early formative periods. The seal cylinder is an obvious loan from Mesopotamia in the fourth to third millennia B.C.[15] The recessed facades of early Egyptian architecture are rightly compared with the same type of recessing in Sumer. It is no accident that the earliest pyramid in Egypt (designed by Imhotep for Joser at Saqqara) is stepped like a ziggurat.[16] The political chief *insi*[17] in Egypt invites comparison with Sumerian *ensí* "ruler (of a city-state)" though both may be of Syro-Palestinian origin.[18] Such borrowings are always modified in the process, and it is the business of the perceptive scholar to detect real (primary) identity in apparent (secondary) difference.[19]

Anyone who works on both Indo-European and Semitic languages knows the great gaps that separate them. That they share vocabulary imbedded at different levels is often enough due to borrowing at various stages. But how are we to explain the same duals they share? We cannot dissociate — or attribute to ordinary borrowing — the Greek dual suffix -$\bar{a}$/-ayn from Arabic -$\bar{a}$/-ayn; nor Homeric Greek *nôï* "we two" from the Old Egyptian and Ugaritic suffix -NY "we two." Since the dual is on the way out in all these languages,[20] this feature shared by Egypto-Semitic and Indo-European is deeply imbedded.[21] Indeed there are so many widespread comparable phenomena that a vigorous school of Afro-Asiatic studies has grown up since World War II, devoted to investigating the relationships among many languages—spanning whole linguistic families—throughout the Old World. Some avant-garde comparativists see detailed connections between Amerindian and Old World families of languages. There is something to this, even though the high margin of error renders the subject too hazardous for cautious linguists.

To clarify the technical side of prehistoric migration, it is to be noted that the simpler the mode of travel, the easier it is to reach difficult places. One can reach rough terrain by jeep where an airplane cannot land; or forested hills by mule, where a jeep would be useless; or mountain peaks (and caverns) on foot, where riding animals would be futile. The same holds, *mutatis mutandis*, for sea travel. A small vessel may survive on stormy high seas when a larger ship might break asunder with the prow atop one high wave and the stern atop another. Moreover, large ships require special harbors; small craft may be beached or find safety in little coves.

When I first became involved in the study of early transoceanic navigation, most prominent authorities considered it impossible. But now that every year daredevils cross the oceans solo (often in tiny primitive craft), relying on winds, currents, and luck, no one can say it is, or ever was, impossible. Yet the person most responsible for changing the intellectual climate regarding early, and even prehistoric, oceanic crossings, was not an authority on navigation and naval architecture (like the late Admiral and Harvard Professor Samuel Eliot Morison), but the maverick anthropologist and showman, Thor Heyerdahl, who had no conventional training in sailing or ship-building.

Heyerdahl and I were on a television program in 1973 in Paris. After the show, we had some time to stroll and talk privately. He explained that although he is Norwegian, he grew up with no experience in seamanship or boat construction. To the contrary, it was his bizarre contraptions like the raft *Kon-Tiki* and his oversized "Egyptian laundry basket" *Ra II* that captured the public's imagination and showed that if vast expanses of ocean could be traversed in such "Rube Goldberg" vessels, we can no longer say that pre-Columbian crossings were impossible. If it can be done by a motley crew aboard *Ra II*, how much more so by the great sailors of antiquity such as the Phoenicians, whose oceangoing vessels ("ships of Tarshish") were infinitely more seaworthy than Heyerdahl's extravaganzas.

Vast expanses of the Pacific (from olden times to the present) have been repeatedly crossed by Polynesian navigators in simple craft such as outrigger canoes. For Polynesians to sail and row a thousand miles to some far-off point like Easter Island might be attributed to "dumb luck," but to return again to their exact point of embarkation cannot be a repeat performance of "dumb luck." The Polynesian science of navigation is quite different from ours, but it is a science nonetheless. When they see a cloud with a green tinge, they know it is reflecting the verdure of a shore where they might land. They know that various specific kinds of birds have rookeries on specific islands, and by observing which birds are in flight, they find specific islands in their seas. They know that waves roll toward, not away from, the coast. By proceeding with, and not against, the waves, they reach the nearest haven by night as well as by day. The Polynesians discovered that when a radiance under the surface (called "underwater lightning"; it is not phosphorescence) is seen darting, the motion is always away from the dry land. When it appears, they can find the shore in darkest night. Those navigators have, of course, also extensive knowledge concerning celestial navigation, winds, and currents.

Virtually every major landmass, plus countless smaller islands, have yielded Pre-Modern skeletal remains of people, often accompanied by artifacts. To get there people had to migrate by land and sea. To reach distant isolated islands, they had to resort to boats or rafts.

It is instructive to outline the changes in "authoritative" opinion during the last half century. In the 1930s, leading anthropologists and historians were insisting that the earliest remains of man in the Western Hemisphere were less than two thousand years old. Now the evidence is pushing mankind in America further and further back into remote pre-Christian millennia. Between 1935 and 1938, when I was stationed at Johns Hopkins University in Baltimore, I often visited the Smithsonian Institution in nearby Washington, where I met the elderly and influential dean of American archaeology, Aleš Hrdlička. His dogma was that Old World man entered pre-Columbian America by only one route: across the Bering Strait. Unless a young anthropologist subscribed to that view, it was virtually impossible for him to get a museum or university job in American anthropology or archaeology. This explains some of the inflexibility in that field down to the present. Gradually the evidence for Pacific crossings found its way into respectable circles, but until now the denial of Atlantic crossings before Columbus and the Vikings is still common in academia.

McCulloch has demonstrated that as long as the Bat Creek Inscription was considered Cherokee, no one questioned its authenticity. It was only after I found it to be Hebrew that the pundits began to brand it as a forgery. But the laboratory tests in 1988 show that all the contents of the undisturbed tomb were interred long before the

Vikings and Columbus reached America, while the letter-forms establish the Imperial Roman date of the script. Similarly, the lead content of the brass bracelets supports the Roman date, once the modern date is ruled out.

In the light of the general mobility of mankind, especially since the Neolithic revolution, all high civilizations owe so much to their predecessors and contemporaries that none of them can have arisen independently. Indeed the *sine qua non* of any high civilization is the creative combination of several stimuli by a talented population that is ready for it.

There are isolated cases of the survival of human babies reared by animals, so we are not declaring individual cases of independent cultural invention a logical impossibility, but only that the regular development of human societies is through the transmission and mingling of cultures. When there is a minimum of mingling, a culture tends to be relatively static.[22] When there is migration or symbiosis, new combinations arise. Some combinations produce brilliant innovation (e.g., classical Greece); others are disastrous.[23]

Greek epic stood on the shoulders of its predecessors. But however much the *Iliad* and *Odyssey* owe to the Gilgamesh and Ugaritic epics, Homer is incomparably greater than the poets of the cuneiform world. Hymns were composed and sung in Sumer and Egypt long before Israel appeared on the stage of history. Yet the Psalms of David eclipsed all that went before and remain the finest in their category to this very day. In the light of ancient trans-Pacific and trans-Atlantic crossings, the effects of borrowings from both directions mingled in Mexico and Central America where the shores of the two oceans come closest together so that gifted people had a maximum of stimuli for developing creative civilizations such as the Mayan.

Not long ago, New World civilization was regarded as quite independent of developments in the Old World. The fact that no pre-Columbian inscription in an Old World script or language was regarded as authentic in respectable academic circles enabled the independent inventionists to maintain that pre-Columbian civilizations in America had arisen in isolation from the rest of the world. The carbon-14 dating of the Bat Creek wood fragments ushers in a new era in which anyone who is not an obscurantist will have to accept not just the possibility but also the actuality of a specific contact between the Eastern and Western hemispheres long before Columbus and the Vikings. The full story may take a long time to unfold, but the fact of global diffusion is here to stay. Moreover, interrelations are two-way streets. Apparent pre-Columbian influences of the Western Hemisphere on the Eastern have been pointed out (mainly, but far from exclusively, by amateurish enthusiasts) and disregarded, if not discredited. The historic facts of West-to-East as well as East-to-West diffusion across both oceans will force blind denial to give way to open-mindedness.[24]

The authentication of the Bat Creek Inscription is a milestone in the process of formulating a credible unified global history.[25]

Notes

1. The latest and best documented account has been written by J. Huston McCulloch, "The Bat Creek Inscription: Cherokee or Hebrew?" *Tennessee Anthropologist* 13/2 (Fall 1988): 79-123. It provides detailed data on the excavation and the artifacts, as well as the inscription, plus the laboratory tests that authenticate the antiquity of the grave and all its contents.

2. To insist on the reading (though it is carved clearly), let alone its meaning, would be unjustified at this time. Professor Robert Stieglitz of Rutgers University makes the interesting suggestion that ZQ (zîq) means "comet" and refers to Bar Kokhba (the Hero's title which means "son of the star").

3. The traces of a final letter, which are compatible with the letter M (but not with H), make it conceivable to read "for the Judeans." YHWD, without final -H, already designates "Judea" in the Achaemenian Age; e.g., Daniel 2:25; 5:13; 6:14; Ezra 5:1, 8; 7:14.

4. Cyrus H. Gordon, "The Bat Creek Inscription," in *The Book of the Descendants of Dr. Benjamin Lee and Dorothy Gordon* (Ventnor, NJ: Ventnor, 1972), 5-18.

5. Ibid., 8.

6. The test (made in Zurich through Beta Analytic, Inc., of Coral Gables, Florida) was reported on 2 May 1988. McCulloch, "The Bat Creek Inscription," describes the technical refinements in the new methods used for the carbon test.

7. See Gordon, "The Bat Creek Inscription," 14-15, on ancient Jewish seamanship.

8. In the postscript to my *Before Columbus* (New York: Crown, 1971), 175-78.

9. The first was found at Louisville in 1932, the second at Clay City in 1952, and the third at Hopkinsville in 1967. Since they are all surface finds, without archaeological context, they cannot by themselves be used as proof of ancient contacts with Roman Judea.

10. For example, Clay City is a small unsophisticated community (population under five hundred) where no one was interested in collecting exotic antiquities such as Bar Kokhba coins.

11. A photographic close-up of "The Phylactery Stele" is reproduced (with an explanation) in my *Riddles in History* (New York: Crown, 1974), 151.

12. Such claims have been attributed to me although I have never said, written, or thought any such thing.

13. Herodotus IV, 42.

14. See Table 4 in McCulloch, "The Bat Creek Inscription," for the composition of the two brass bracelets; one has 68.2% copper, 27.5% zinc, and 3.29% lead; the other has 66.5% copper, 26.5% zinc, and 3.3% lead.

15. Egyptian seal cylinders are different from their Mesopotamian prototypes in several ways. They may bear hieroglyphic inscriptions, have sides without vertical curvature, be made of materials not used in Mesopotamia, etc. Borrowings regularly undergo modification. The obelisk in Washington, D.C., is easily distinguished from its prototypes in Egypt.

16. One of Imhotep's innovations is especially important. It is the first recorded monumental free-standing architecture in stone — and still extant!

17. The Egyptian royal title transliterated *nsw bity*, "King of Upper and Lower Egypt," is rendered phonetically in cuneiform as *insibiya*, showing that the first element was pronounced *insi*.

18. Since neither the Egyptian *insi* nor the Sumerian *ensí* has a

recognizable etymology in those languages, both may be derived from *nāśî'* "prince, king, (and nowadays) president" (lit., "raised up, exalted") in Canaan, which connects Mesopotamia and Egypt.

19. An illustration from another field may highlight this point. A whale looks like a fish, but is in fact an air-breathing mammal. The wings of a bird do not look like the hands of a man, but they share the same origin. This is why only in art do angels have hands as well as wings; in nature, if a creature has the one, it cannot have the other.

20. There are survivals of duals. Arabic even uses duals down to the present day for all nouns even in colloquial speech, and not just for natural pairs (like "hands," "eyes," etc.). But, in modern Greek, and in ancient or modern Hebrew, "two dogs" (etc.) would be in the plural, not dual.

21. For the dual of the first person to survive in Old Egyptian, Ugaritic, and Greek implies very deep roots in an ancient shared stratum.

22. For example, the cultures of the Arabs in remote areas of Arabia (until the nineteenth century) and of the Eskimos (until the relatively modern encroachment of the Europeans and now the Americans) both remained rather static.

23. Cf., for example, the combination of the traditional American way of life with the drug culture of Asia, resulting from the stationing of troops in the Orient. Alcohol is also toxic, but that was a part of the European culture brought by the settlers to America. Opium and other hard drugs were alien to American culture, and its effects on U.S. troops were—and still are—devastating. In Iran, on the other hand, I knew some highly cultivated and respected citizens who were not ruined by smoking opium daily.

24. These generalities have hard facts to back them up. But we should not keep repeating the same facts. I am now preparing studies with *new* detailed hard evidence on ancient Near East contacts with the Far East, India, and America. For the extensive published literature down to 1988, see John L. Sorenson and Martin H. Raish, "Transoceanic Culture Contacts between the Old and New Worlds in Pre-Columbian Times: A Comprehensive Annotated Bibliography," rev. and enl. ed., F.A.R.M.S., May 1988.

25. The discredited pre-Columbian American inscriptions in Old World scripts or languages will have to be reexamined and reevaluated, each on the merits of the evidence, case by case.

7

"Watch and Remember": The New Testament and the Great Apostasy

Kent P. Jackson
Brigham Young University, Provo, Utah

Since its beginning, The Church of Jesus Christ of Latter-day Saints has proclaimed to the world that there was an apostasy of the church which had been founded by Jesus during his earthly ministry and led by his apostles following his ascension.[1] This is a fundamental belief of the restored church. In fact, it is the apostasy of early Christianity which creates the very need for the restored Latter-day Saint faith: if there had not been an apostasy, there would have been no need for a restoration.[2]

Latter-day Saint theology asserts that the church of Jesus and his apostles came to an end not long after its formation; the doctrines which its inspired leaders taught were corrupted and changed by others not of similar inspiration (1 Nephi 13:26-27), the authority to act in God's name was taken from the earth, and the Christian systems that existed in the world after those developments did not enjoy divine endorsement. It was precisely the question of divine endorsement—in Joseph Smith's words, "which of all the sects was right" (Joseph Smith-History 1:18)—that led to the glorious event that ushered in the restoration of the gospel: the appearance of the Father and the Son to the young prophet. In response to Joseph Smith's search for a true church, he was told to join none of them, "for they were all wrong," and all their creeds were "an abomination" in the sight of God (Joseph Smith-History 1:19).[3] The message of the Latter-day Saints is that following seventeen centuries of darkness since the days of the apostles, the heavens were again opened, divinely authored doctrines were revealed anew, the authority to speak and act in God's name was brought back to earth, and the church of Jesus Christ was established again by divine command.

In this paper the apostasy will be discussed on two fronts. First I will examine statements of Jesus and his apostles that foretell the passing of the early church. Then I will consider the evidence in the New Testament that shows apostasy taking place as the New Testament documents were being written.

1. THE APOSTASY FORETOLD

The writings of the New Testament contain several statements made by Jesus and his apostles about the future of their work. Though they labored with great zeal to bring souls to the Lord and to establish the church throughout the world, still their prophetic utterances concerning the end result of their efforts foretold tragedy. In short, they knew that the church would fall into apostasy shortly after their time, and they bore candid testimony of that fact. The following prophetic passages demonstrate that Jesus and his apostles foreknew and foretold the falling of the church.

Matthew 24:5, 9-11

One of the Savior's most significant sermons, the Olivet Discourse, is recorded in Matthew 24-25. In response to questions of the Twelve with regard to the destruction of the temple at Jerusalem and the destruction of the world (see Joseph Smith-Matthew 1:4, 21), Jesus prophesied of events which would transpire in the near and distant future, especially regarding the Jews (Joseph Smith-Matthew 1:21). In this connection, Matthew 24:9-11 records a prophecy of great importance concerning the future of the apostles:

> Then shall they deliver you up to be afflicted, and shall kill you: and ye shall be hated of all nations for my name's sake. And then shall many be offended, and shall betray one another, and shall hate one another. And many false prophets shall rise, and shall deceive many.[4]

The Joseph Smith-Matthew rendering of this passage places it clearly in the context of the first century A.D. (Joseph Smith-Matthew 1:4-21). A number of important statements are contained in these verses. Matthew 24:9 foretells the fate of the apostles themselves: affliction, hatred, and death for Christ's sake (cf. also John 16:1-4). The only scripturally attested fulfillment of the martyrdom prophecy is the death of James at the hands of Herod Agrippa I (Acts 12:1-2), but early Christian tradition tells of similar fates for other apostles. Yet the killing of the apostles was not the cause of the apostasy. Other references clearly teach that Christianity died from an internal wound, the rejection of true doctrine by the members of the church.

Matthew 24:10 provides a valuable prophecy of the rejection of truth by many of the saints. Unfortunately, the King James translation obscures its intended meaning beyond modern recognition with the phrase "then shall many be offended." In the New International Version (NIV), an excellent recent translation, we read: "At that time many will turn away from the faith." From the Phillips Modern English Version: "Then comes the time when many will lose their faith." The Greek verb *skandalízō* in the passive voice (here a third person plural, future tense), means, in a theological sense, "to give up one's faith." "Many," the Savior foretold, will do it at that day. Only those who remain steadfast and are not overcome will be saved (Joseph Smith-Matthew 1:11).

Matthew 24:11 records the additional prophecy that many false prophets would arise and would "deceive *many*" (emphasis added). Recall that the historical context here is the last days of the apostolic era, when the apostles would be afflicted, hated, and killed (Matthew 24:9). Attempting to take their places would be what the Savior calls "many false prophets." The related passage in Matthew 24:5 is also significant: "For many shall come in my name, saying, I am Christ; and shall deceive many." Notice that there would be *many* false Christs, and, like the false prophets, they would deceive *many*. One can only lament the fact that the available sources, scriptural and nonscriptural, give us little history of the fulfillment of these words.

Acts 20:29-31

On his way from Greece to Jerusalem at the end of his third missionary journey, the apostle Paul stopped at the city of Miletus and called for the elders of nearby Ephesus. On their arrival he gave an important address (Acts 20:18-35). The prophecy relevant to the future of the flock over which these elders were "overseers" (Acts 20:28) reads as follows:

> For I know this, that after my departing shall grievous wolves enter in among you, not sparing the flock. Also of your own selves shall men arise, speaking perverse things, to draw away disciples after them. Therefore watch, and remember, that by the space of three years I ceased not to warn every one night and day with tears (Acts 20:29-31).

Paul warned the elders of Asia that following his departure evil forces would damage the church there greatly. "Grievous wolves" would invade and would not spare the flock. At this point in Paul's career, he had experienced years of trouble with Judaizers trying to gain influence among his converts. Perhaps it was similar infiltration of apostate forces that Paul foresaw. It should be recalled that the Judaizers, who had already had great success opposing Paul (e.g., Galatians 1:6), were members of the church. What is being alluded to with the wolf metaphor is undoubtedly not physical attack or external persecution. Instead, Paul was describing the entering of evil forces *into* the church and their gaining power over the saints. That this is the meaning of Paul's words is borne out by verse 30, referring to those in the Asian church—some of whom may have been in Paul's audience as he spoke—who would, in an effort to draw away disciples to themselves, "distort the truth" (Acts 20:30, NIV, REB). Paul ended his prophecy by testifying that for three years he had warned the Asian saints constantly, "with tears," to "watch and remember" (Acts 20:31). Similarly, in his great prophecy of apostasy in 2 Thessalonians, which will be examined next, he also bore witness to the saints that he had warned them well of the coming fall (2 Thessalonians 2:5).

2 Thessalonians 2:1-12

In his first Thessalonian letter Paul cleared up a doctrinal misunderstanding concerning the status of those who would die prior to the Second Coming of Jesus. In the second he warned them of a much greater doctrinal problem—the belief that the "day of Christ" was "at hand" (2 Thessalonians 2:2). We do not know the details of Paul's concern here.[5] Whatever the exact misunderstanding of the Thessalonians may have been, Paul explained that the day of Christ's coming would not take place until after a "falling away" and the revelation of the "man of sin," "the son of perdition" (2 Thessalonians 2:3).

The King James words "falling away" are translated from the Greek noun *apostasía,* from which we get our word "apostasy," which is equal to it in meaning. Whereas the term "falling away" may give the incorrect impression of a process of drifting or gradually losing ground, the original term means something much more drastic. Some modern translations use the terms "the rebellion" (NIV, RSV), "rejection of God" (Phillips), or "the Great Revolt" (JB). The two Greek elements combined in *apostasía* are the verb *hístēmi*, "to stand," and *apó*, "away from"; the basic meaning of the word is "revolution." Ancient sources used the term to describe political rebellion and revolution.[6] What Paul was describing was a revolution against God and his position in the church. And, as he wrote in the following verses, the revolution would succeed.

The chief feature of this revolution would be the triumph of the "man of sin." Paul wrote:

> Let no man deceive you by any means: for that day shall not come, except there come a falling away first, and that man of sin be revealed, the son of perdition; Who opposeth and exalteth himself above all that is called God, or that is worshipped; so that he as God sitteth in the temple of God, shewing himself that he is God (2 Thessalonians 2:3-4).

Latter-day Saint commentators generally equate the "man of sin" mentioned in these verses with Satan, an interpretation with which I concur.[7] As part of the rebellion, Paul noted, Satan would be made manifest. He would exalt himself over all that is called divine in order to assume the place of God and supplant him from his position. The metaphorical term "temple" probably refers to the church, as also in 1 Corinthians 3:16 and Ephesians 2:21.[8] If Paul did have the church in mind here, it is of historical and theological significance that the church survives. But God is not at its head, making that church—following the appearance in it of Satan—no longer the church of God.

Paul's words correspond well with evidence that we have from other scriptures. When the Lord appeared to Joseph Smith in the spring of 1820, he told the young prophet that all of the Christian churches of his day were "wrong" (Joseph Smith-History 1:19). The Book of Mormon prophet Nephi envisioned in the latter days following the Restoration only *two* churches: "the church of the Lamb of God" and "the church of the devil" (1 Nephi 14:10). Since whoever does not belong to "the church of the Lamb of God" belongs to "the church of the devil," as Nephi announced, then all systems of worship outside of The Church of Jesus Christ of Latter-day Saints would be classified as "the church of the devil" by Nephi's definition.[9] It appears that Paul was making the same point as he foretold the "man of sin" supplanting God in the era of the revolution.

To suggest that fallen Christianity has Satan at its head in the place of God is certainly not to say that all that is in it is satanic. Indeed, Latter-day Saints should rejoice — as the heavens undoubtedly do — at the great works of righteousness and faith, and the leavening influence on the world, of those whose lives are touched in any degree by him whose gospel the Saints enjoy in its fulness. But it is only in The Church of Jesus Christ of Latter-day Saints — which the Lord himself has proclaimed to be "the only true and living church upon the face of the whole earth with which I the Lord am well pleased" (D&C 1:30) — that "the power of God unto salvation" (Romans 1:16) is found. The restoration of the fulness of the gospel, with its priesthood and other blessings, took place because it is only in *its* light that salvation in its true sense is possible to humankind. While these features are absent as Satan sits enthroned in what was once the Lord's church, Satan's goal of hindering God's children from returning to their Father's glory is realized. How appropriate therefore is Paul's description of him sitting in the place of God in the church of the *apostasía*.[10]

In the next verse, Paul punctuated his prophecy by reminding the saints that when he had been with them personally, he had taught them of the apostasy and the coming of Satan: "Remember ye not, that, when I was yet with you, I told you these things?" (2 Thessalonians 2:5). But his message did not stop there. Even at that time, said Paul, the "man of sin" was being restrained "from appearing before his appointed time" (2 Thessalonians 2:6, JB). "For the mystery of lawlessness [KJV: 'mystery of iniquity'] is already at work; only he who now restrains it will do so until he is out of the way. And then the lawless one will be revealed" (2 Thessalonians 2:7, RSV). In these verses Paul stated that the overt manifestation of Satan was still in the future. Yet even then the "mystery of iniquity" was operating, waiting in the wings, as it were, for its chance to come to the fore. Paul wrote of some force which restrained the "man of sin" from making his appearance before his time. It is not altogether clear whether he was referring to the Lord, the collective power of the apostleship, or something or someone else as the obstacle to the dominance of the "man of sin." In any case, the message comes through clearly that Satan and his works were at that time already operational but were being held back until the divine power that restrained them would be removed. "And then shall that wicked one be revealed" (2 Thessalonians 2:8, JST).[11]

In 2 Thessalonians 2:9-12 Paul told of the deceptive power of Satan and his apostate priesthood. They would come with "power and signs and lying wonders, and with all deceivableness of unrighteousness" (2 Thessalonians 2:9-10). Those who would follow them are they who "received not the love of the truth," who "believe a lie," and who "believed not the truth, but had pleasure in unrighteousness" (2 Thessalonians 2:10-12). In short, Satan's work, accompanied by signs and miracles meant to counterfeit those of the Lord's true servants, would prosper because many would reject the truth and believe falsehood. Paul, therefore, exhorted his converts to "stand fast" unto "the obtaining of the glory" to which they were called (2 Thessalonians 2:13-15).

2 Thessalonians 2:1-12 constitutes perhaps the most important prophecy in the New Testament concerning the apostasy. Scholars of all perspectives generally agree that Paul was, in fact, expressing his belief in a rebellion of some sort against God that would precede the anticipated second advent of Jesus Christ.[12] Through the light of the restored gospel, Latter-day Saints can understand the full implications of this rebellion.[13]

1 Timothy 4:1-3

In Paul's first letter to Timothy, he prophesied concerning the departure of some of the saints from the faith:

> Now the Spirit speaketh expressly, that in the latter times some shall depart from the faith, giving heed to seducing spirits, and doctrines of devils; speaking lies in hypocrisy; having their conscience seared with a hot iron; forbidding to marry, and commanding to abstain from meats, which God hath created to be received with thanksgiving to them which believe and know the truth (1 Timothy 4:1-3).

This prophecy has a number of features that make it of considerable interest. First of all, Paul specifically stated that his belief in the future defection was the result of revelation. In fact, not only did the Spirit speak these words to Paul, but it did so "expressly." The chronological note is also important. Paul used the term "latter times" (*hústeroi kairoí*) to denote the period in which the developments that he foretold would take place. In the ultimate sense, the period of time in which we now live can be called "the latter times" better than any other. As we learn through modern revelation, our day is the dispensation of the fulness of times—the preparatory era that precedes the Second Coming of the Savior. Yet Paul spoke using a different definition for "latter times." His focus was on the last days of the Christianity of his era, the "latter times" of the early church.

A few decades after Paul foretold the departure of some from the faith in the "latter times," Jude announced to his readers that they were then in "the last time" (*éschatos chrónos*, Jude 1:17-19). Similarly, John expressed to the readers of his first letter the certainty of the fact that they themselves were in "the last hour" (*eschátē hōrā*, 1 John 2:18-19). With the revealed knowledge of important future events, John and Jude knew that they were not in the final era of the world. But their words reveal the fact that they knew that they were in the final days of the Christian church. That was the period of time concerning which the spirit spoke "expressly" (1 Timothy 4:1) to Paul.

As we have seen in other prophecies examined so far, the departure from the faith would be a rebellion against true principles of doctrine. Paul wrote that those who would depart would give heed to what he calls "seducing spirits" and "doctrines of devils." It must be emphasized that what Paul saw was not an abandonment of religion but a shifting of loyalties from "the faith" to a false faith. Accompanying this defection would be the manifestation of the negative character traits cited in 1 Timothy 4:2.

1 Timothy 4:3 is interesting because it mentions two examples of the false ideas that the counterfeit religious system would foster: a prohibition against marriage and a prohibition against certain foods. Beyond that the Apostle gave no further details.

In his prophecy in 1 Timothy, Paul did not express any of the feelings of doom or urgency that are so obvious in the letters of his fellow apostle John, written about thirty-five years later. Yet for Paul the present danger was real enough that he admonished Timothy personally to reject strange ideas (1 Timothy 4:7) and to remind "the brethren" of his warnings (1 Timothy 4:6).

2 Timothy 4:3-4

Paul's final prophecy of the abandonment of true religion is found in the last chapter of 2 Timothy. After exhorting Timothy to "continue in the things" which he had learned (2 Timothy 3:14), Paul spoke of those who would pervert the truth:

> For the time will come when men will not put up with sound doctrine. Instead, to suit their own desires, they will gather around them a great number of teachers to say what their itching ears want to hear. They will turn their ears away from the truth and turn aside to myths (2 Timothy 4:3-4, NIV).

This passage paints a picture of rejection of the truth that is consistent in every detail with the other prophecies examined so far. In the verses that precede it, Paul charged Timothy strongly to "preach," "correct, rebuke and encourage" (NIV) the saints. Verse 3 reveals that the reason for his urgency is the fact that he knew that a time was coming in which men would no longer accept the truth. Paul's desire in this, his last preserved letter, was to hold off the onslaught of the inevitable revolution. As has been noted already, what he foresaw was not an abandonment of religion. Much more serious than that, it was a willful rejection of true doctrine and its replacement by doctrines which were untrue but more to the liking of those who would hear them. Notice that the people involved, although unwilling to put up with correct teachings, desired teachings nonetheless. Having "itching ears," i.e., a desire to hear religion, they would acquire teachers whose doctrines were acceptable to them. The final outcome of their actions would be the abandonment of truth and the acceptance of "fables" (2 Timothy 4:4).

2 Peter 2:1-3

Paul was not alone among the apostles in prophesying doom for early Christianity. In 2 Peter, the chief apostle foretold the introduction of false teachers into the church:

> But there were false prophets also among the people, even as there shall be false teachers among you, who privily shall bring in damnable heresies, even denying the Lord that bought them, and bring upon themselves swift destruction. And many shall follow their pernicious ways; by reason of whom the way of truth shall be evil spoken of (2 Peter 2:1-2).

These false teachers, according to Peter, would "secretly introduce" (NIV) "damnable heresies." So successful would they be that as a result of their efforts, "the way of truth" would be blasphemed (future passive from *blasphēméō*).[14] 2 Peter 2:3 tells us more: "In their greed these teachers will exploit you with stories they have made up" (NIV). This tells us something concerning their purpose: to exploit the members of the church ("make merchandise of you," 2 Peter 2:3, KJV), and their method of doing so: by making up doctrine — "sheer fabrications" (REB).

1 John 2:18; Jude 1:4, 17-18

There are a few passages in the New Testament that give evidence *indirectly* that an apostasy had been foretold. Of these the most informative are found in 1 John 2:18 and Jude 1:4, 17-18. These verses actually speak of apostasy already present in the church. While doing so they make mention of the fact that the saints knew that it should come and had been warned appropriately. John wrote: "Little children, it is the last time: and as *ye have heard that antichrist shall come,* even now are there many antichrists; whereby we know that it is the last time" (1 John 2:18, emphasis added). This passage will be discussed more fully below. What is important at this point is the fact that John reminded the saints to whom he wrote that they had heard earlier that a time would come — called the "last time" (*eschátē hōrā*) — in which "antichrist" would come among the church. They had been warned. Similarly, Jude wrote:

> Certain people have infiltrated among you, *and they*

are the ones you had a warning about, in writing, long ago, when they were condemned for denying all religion, turning the grace of our God into immorality, and rejecting our only Master and Lord, Jesus Christ (Jude 1:4, JB, emphasis added).

This passage, which is much less clear in the King James Version, tells that the readers had received written warning in the past of the coming of "godless men" (NIV) who would pervert the gospel and reject the Lord. After writing more about those predicted apostates and likening them to some of more ancient times, Jude continued:

But, dear friends, *remember what the apostles of our Lord Jesus Christ foretold. They said to you, "In the last times there will be scoffers who will follow their own ungodly desires."* These are the men who divide you, who follow mere natural instincts and do not have the Spirit (Jude 1:17-19, NIV, emphasis added).

The coming in the "last times" (*éschatos chrónos*) of those who would scoff at the true faith had been foretold, according to Jude, by "the apostles."

Revelation 13:1-9

The final prophecy to be examined is found in Revelation 13. Here we read John's vision of the victory of the forces of Satan over the saints of the Lord. In chapter 12 John characterized the continual conflict between Satan and the works of God as the efforts of a red dragon — Satan — to destroy a woman and her children. In Revelation 12:17 we read, "And the dragon was wroth with the woman, and went to make war with the remnant of her seed, which keep the commandments of God, and have the testimony of Jesus Christ." This is part of an ongoing conflict that has existed since before humankind was placed on the earth, and it will continue until Satan suffers final defeat following the Millennium (Revelation 20:10).

The episode from that conflict which is recorded in Revelation 13 is directly relevant to the end of the early Christian church. As the vision continued, John saw the appearance of a beast, "having seven heads and ten horns, and upon his horns ten crowns, and upon his heads the name of blasphemy" (Revelation 13:1). This beast was the agent of the dragon, Satan, from whom he had received "his power and his throne and great authority" (Revelation 13:2, NIV). In John's narrative we find the beast blaspheming God, God's name, his dwelling place, and those who live in heaven (cf. *blasphēméō* in 2 Peter 2:2). John continued: "And it was given unto him to make war with the saints, *and to overcome them*: and power was given him over all kindreds, and tongues, and nations" (Revelation 13:7, emphasis added). Without yielding to the temptation to attach rigid interpretations to John's metaphors, I feel that the information provided is sufficient to enable us to draw two conclusions about the beast, its identity, and its work.

First of all, it is a deputy of Satan; it derives its power from him and does his work (Revelation 13:2, 4). As God's work is "to bring to pass the immortality and eternal life of man" (Moses 1:39), Satan's and that of his beast is to do the opposite. In the Joseph Smith Translation the beast is "in the likeness of the kingdoms of the earth" (Revelation 13:1, JST). "Kingdom" in a scriptural context can mean, of course, any kind of institution, movement, force, or power—religious, political, or otherwise.[15]

The second statement that we can make concerning the beast is that it accomplished what it was sent to do. Verse 7 records the tragic fact that it succeeded: it overcame the saints. In viewing John's beast in the light of its context in Revelation 13 and other prophetic statements concerning the fall of the church, we can identify it as the institutions or forces of Satan that prevailed over early Christianity during and following the time of the apostles. As for the nature of those forces, it should be remembered that the scriptures that we have examined so far present in clear focus the prophetic vision of the apostles: the cause of the apostasy would be the rejection of the truth by the members of the church. In this light, the beast seen by John that overcame the saints might be interpreted best as being Christianity itself—not the Christianity of Jesus, Peter, John, and Paul, but the Christianity that overcame the saints and apostles and survived into the next generation, "in the likeness of the kingdoms of the earth" (Revelation 13:1, JST).[16]

The scriptural passages examined above demonstrate that Jesus and his apostles knew that the church which they headed would come to an end shortly after their generation.[17] They bore a somber witness to that knowledge in the record that they left behind in the New Testament. All Christians who take seriously the apostolic testimony must reckon with the prophetic word of the inspired witnesses that the forces of false religion would prevail over those of the truth; the church which was guided by the power of the apostleship in the first century would no longer exist in the second.

2. THE NEW TESTAMENT WITNESS

One of the strongest witnesses of the Latter-day Saint view of the apostasy of New Testament Christianity is the New Testament itself. Not only does it prophesy that apostasy would take place in the church, but just as significantly it actually records apostasy happening as its books were being written. Its pages record the continuing struggle of the apostles to keep the church free of false ideas and practices. As the first century A.D. progressed, the heresies against which the apostles contended became increasingly virulent and increasingly successful, as the record attests. Near the end of the first century, the apostolic record came to a sudden close.

In order to demonstrate the extent to which the apostasy developed and grew in the first century A.D., I will examine in chronological order several issues from the New Testament epistles and from Revelation. It will become apparent that during the course of the first century, the doctrinal and behavioral problems against which the apostles struggled increased until the apostles could no longer reverse the trend of false religion and save the church from itself. In the earliest letters, written midway through the first century, the apostles had to contend with relatively harmless issues of doctrinal misunderstanding. By the time of the last-written letters at the end of the century, the heresies mentioned are of such a malignant nature that they clearly would destroy the original faith if they were not corrected. The evidence tells us that they were not.

1 and 2 Thessalonians (ca. A.D. 50-51)

In the Thessalonian letters the doctrinal problems to which Paul had to address himself were such that they could, presumably, be corrected fairly easily. In both letters, misunderstandings concerning Jesus' Second Coming are evident. In 1 Thessalonians the problem was the belief that those who were alive when the Second Coming took place would have an advantage over those who had died previously (1 Thessalonians 4:13-17). Paul comforted the saints concerning their faithful dead by telling them that those "who are left alive until the Lord's coming will not have any advantage over those who have died" (1 Thessalonians 4:15, JB). In the second letter, Paul responded to the belief that the "day of Christ" was "at hand" (2 Thessalonians 2:2). He refuted the idea by prophesying of the apostasy that would precede that day (2 Thessalonians 2:3-4).

We can assume that a belief such as that to which Paul responded in 2 Thessalonians could have grave implications for the Church. We should conclude, perhaps, that without Paul's corrective letter the Thessalonian saints may have developed greater problems. The church was fortunate to have an apostle like Paul, who by virtue of his apostolic priesthood authority and divinely endowed spiritual gifts could speak the Lord's word to insure the integrity of the church. One might ask, what happens to the church when such men are no longer in it?

James (ca. mid-50s A.D.)

In the letter of James it is clear that the apostle-writer was contending against incorrect ideas concerning the nature of faith vis-à-vis Christian works. His corrective words include, "For as the body without the spirit is dead, so faith without works is dead also" (James 2:26). An underemphasis of the works of the gospel is perhaps not the kind of problem that would bring all of Christianity to ruin, and James gave us no hint that he expected wholesale apostasy because of it. Yet those who were guilty of disregarding the importance of works had a "dead" religion, to use James's word, and a "dead" religion certainly has no power to save. Perhaps without James's letter more serious problems could have developed.

1 Corinthians (ca. A.D. 56)

As indicated by 1 Corinthians, the church at Corinth had serious problems both in doctrine and in behavior soon after it was founded. Paul wrote this letter, in which he dealt with several unrelated matters, in an effort to correct problems that had come to his attention. I will focus only on a few of them.

In 1 Corinthians 1-4 Paul wrote concerning factions or divisions that had developed in the Corinthian church around various authorities. The mere thought that some may have been focusing their allegiance on him rather than on Christ was so offensive to Paul that he considered himself fortunate that he had not baptized more into the church

(1 Corinthians 1:14-16). He showed his alarm by asking, "Is Christ divided? Was Paul crucified for you? Or were ye baptized in the name of Paul?" (1 Corinthians 1:13). And he told the saints that they were carnal, rather than spiritual, because of their misguided allegiance to individuals (1 Corinthians 3:3-7). It can be argued that this problem in lesser degrees is not the stuff from which apostasy develops. It is clear, however, that if left uncorrected it could result in factions that could bring more serious problems and heretical ideas into the church.

In chapter 5 Paul reprimanded the Corinthian saints in strong terms for allowing a case of incest to go uncorrected. He commanded in the name of the Lord that the guilty party be excommunicated. Paul said, "Know ye not that a little leaven leaveneth the whole lump?" (1 Corinthians 5:6), speaking of the damaging potential of allowing a moral problem as serious as incest to remain unpurged. It should be recalled that a few years later Paul prophesied that the abandonment of true religion would be accompanied by the acceptance of degenerate standards of moral behavior (2 Timothy 3:1-4). The Corinthians were blessed to have Paul's letter to warn them of the danger.

1 Corinthians deals with *doctrinal* heresies as well; Paul felt a need to explain the correct use of the Lord's supper (chap. 11) and spiritual gifts (chaps. 12-14). Yet perhaps the most revealing doctrinal problem at Corinth was the belief of some that there was no resurrection. In chapter 15 Paul gave a series of arguments to establish the validity of the doctrine that Jesus rose from the dead and that all people would do likewise. It is clear that there were some at Corinth who disbelieved this doctrine, and Paul wrote with passion to correct their error, pointing out that Christianity is meaningless if there is no resurrection (1 Corinthians 15:14, 17-19). Christianity is, almost by definition, the belief that Jesus rose from the dead. Paul had been chosen to bear witness to that fact (Acts 1:22; 26:16). He

recognized that denial of that truth was in fact denial of the faith, and he wrote with the power of the apostleship to prevent it.

To deal with each of these issues at Corinth, Paul wrote decisively and firmly. We have no way of knowing to what degree his letter solved the problems by motivating the Corinthian congregation to reject the false ideas that were circulating among them. But the issues involved were serious and potentially very damaging. One can only wonder what would have happened without the corrective efforts of an inspired leader like Paul.

2 Corinthians (ca. A.D. 57)

For the purposes of this study, one particular aspect of 2 Corinthians is significant. This is the letter in which Paul was most revealing of himself, his problems, and his actions. Among the Corinthians were some who had attacked Paul's doctrine and his dedication to the work of the Lord. Paul felt that the situation was serious enough that he needed to defend himself by speaking frankly in his own behalf. Against his own better judgment he boasted of his sacrifices in behalf of the gospel. He told of his beatings, imprisonments, stonings, shipwrecks, pain, hunger, and thirst, and of his visions and revelations (2 Corinthians 11:23-27; 12:1-12). Paul chastised himself for mentioning those things, stating that he was speaking foolishly in doing so (2 Corinthians 11:21, 23). Yet as a representative of the Lord and as the one who had brought the gospel to the readers of the letter, Paul knew that he had an obligation to defend his own integrity and that of his message. If the Corinthian saints rejected Paul, the messenger who brought them the gospel, what would prevent them from rejecting the message as well? His fears appear to have been well-founded. Already they were being taught "another Jesus, whom we have not preached" (2 Corinthians 11:4), and among them were "false apostles, deceitful workers, transforming themselves into the apostles of Christ" (2 Corinthians 11:13).

Galatians (ca. A.D. 58)

In the letter to the Galatians, Paul responded to the problem of a movement within the church that countered his teachings with a Judaized Christianity and attacked him personally. It appears from the letter that the success rate of the anti-Pauline Judaizers was high, which caused Paul a great deal of concern. The false ideas that the Galatians were entertaining were of such a nature that without correction the gospel as taught by him would have been changed drastically. Paul accused the saints of turning to what he called "another gospel" under the influence of those who would "pervert the gospel of Christ" (Galatians 1:6-7). Among other things, he accused them of looking back to the Law of Moses for salvation (Galatians 3:1-5), observing Jewish holidays (Galatians 4:10), and accepting circumcision again (Galatians 5:2-4). So emphatic was he with regard to the apostolic authority of his message and its divine origin that he punctuated his rebuke by saying that even if an angel came from heaven teaching doctrine different than what he had taught, it should be rejected (Galatians 1:6-12)!

Paul clearly viewed the Galatian heresy with alarm. In his concerned effort to save the Galatians from even greater problems, he wrote the letter. We know nothing concerning its results. If during Paul's lifetime the Galatian churches had turned to "another gospel," to use his words, it is likely that they would have turned even farther afield without guidance and correction from men in the church such as Paul who could proclaim: "The gospel which was preached of me is not after man. For I neither received it of man, neither was I taught it, but by the revelation of Jesus Christ" (Galatians 1:11-12).

Colossians (ca. A.D. 61)

Colossians is the only one of the prison epistles in which Paul appears to be contending with a serious doctrinal problem. The nature of the problem, which is often called the "Colossian heresy," is not known precisely. Paul gave us only a few hints concerning it, and rather than dealing directly with the problem, he taught proper doctrine in an affirmative way—presumably in an effort to counterbalance falsehood with increased emphasis on truth. In the letter he wrote at great length concerning the role of Christ as the preeminent being in the universe, giving us one of the greatest statements found anywhere in sacred writings concerning the nature and mission of Jesus (Colossians 1:12-23; cf. 2:9-10). Paul's emphasis suggests that the so-called "Colossian heresy" included incorrect ideas concerning Jesus' standing among the powers of the heavens. In fact, Paul denounced the worship of others who had begun to be revered: "Do not be taken in by people who like groveling to angels and worshiping them; people like that are always going on about some vision they have had, inflating themselves to a false importance with their worldly outlook" (Colossians 2:18, JB).

Some commentators believe that Paul's reference to the worship of angels is evidence of elements of Gnosticism or something similar at Colossae. Gnosticism was a philosophy that may have had its roots outside of Christianity but which became part of various strands of the Christian faith early in its history.[18] It had at its focus a belief that spirit was perfect and holy but that matter, and all that was created of it, was entirely evil. God, who was a being of pure spirit, could have nothing to do with man, a creature of matter (and therefore evil), so instead of worshiping God, Gnostics revered an extensive hierarchy of intermediary deities called aeons. It is not unlikely that Paul's prohibition against the worship of angels, something quite unexpected otherwise in Christianity, was a reference to an aberrant belief akin to the worship of aeons.

One problem that Christian Gnostics faced was that of the nature of Jesus Christ. As Christ was believed to have been both God and man, having had a material body, his position in the heavenly hierarchies was problematic. Perhaps when Paul emphasized Christ's position in a cosmic perspective that was unprecedented in any other letter, the apostle was responding to this kind of ambivalence regarding the role of Jesus. Paul pointed out:

> For in him all things were created, in heaven and on earth, visible and invisible, whether thrones or dominions or principalities or authorities—all things were created through him and for him. He is before all things, and in him all things hold together (Colossians 1:16-17, RSV).

He stated further, "For in him dwelleth all the fulness of the Godhead bodily," and Jesus "is the head of all principality and power" (Colossians 2:9-10). Paul's emphasis on Jesus' preeminence makes good sense in light of the Gnostic hierarchy of intermediary subdeities and the impossibility of fitting Jesus into the system.

The letter to the Colossians is a letter of urgent warning, and rightly so considering the perversion of doctrine to which the saints at Colossae had been exposed. Paul wrote that the blessings of Christ's atonement were available only if the saints were to "continue in the faith grounded and settled, and be not moved away from the hope of the gospel" (Colossians 1:23). Further, "As ye have therefore received Christ Jesus the Lord, so walk ye in him: rooted and built up in him, and stablished in the faith, as ye have been taught" (Colossians 2:6-7). Notice all of the vocabulary of permanence and stability that Paul used to admonish the saints to stay on the course of true doctrine: "grounded," "settled," "rooted," "built up," and "stablished." Paul continued, "Beware lest any man spoil you through philosophy and vain deceit, after the tradition of men, after the rudiments of the world, and not after Christ" (Colossians 2:8).

If Gnosticism in some primitive form was indeed the heresy that was making inroads into the church at Colossae, then the church there was in a dangerous position. Gnostic beliefs were so antithetical to the doctrines of Jesus and the apostles that any attempt to merge or reconcile them could only lead to the ruin of the original faith. Extrabiblical sources tell us that Gnosticism played an important role in the first centuries of Christian history.[19] Whereas the religion of the apostles did not continue, its gnosticized counterpart did.

1 Timothy and Titus (ca. A.D. 63)[20]

The pastoral epistles give additional evidence that apostate doctrines were widespread in Christianity while Paul was still alive. Once again the main source of heretical teaching appears to have been Gnosticism. In 1 Timothy and Titus the evidence for a Gnostic perversion of Christianity is compelling.

The term "gnosticism" comes from the Greek noun *gnōsis*, which means "knowledge." Gnostics were characterized by a belief that they had secret knowledge that had been passed on to them by Jesus or the apostles. They believed that it was through this *gnōsis* that one was saved, by becoming able to rise above the evil physical world. That Paul was aware of Gnosticism and recognized it as a threat is evident in the final words of 1 Timothy: "O Timothy, guard what has been entrusted to you. Avoid the godless chatter and contradictions of what is falsely called *knowledge,* for by professing it some have missed the mark as regards the faith" (1 Timothy 6:20-21, RSV, emphasis added).[21]

In 1 Timothy 1:3-4 Paul counseled Timothy to teach others to avoid "fables and endless genealogies." Similarly, he admonished Titus to speak out against "foolish questions, and genealogies" (Titus 3:9). We know that genealogy for worthy purposes was known among early Christians (see Matthew 1:1-16; Luke 3:23-28; Acts 4:36; Philippians 3:5). What Paul was referring to here was quite different, as he denounced it in the context of speculative doctrinal contention that was "unprofitable and vain" (1 Timothy 1:4; Titus 3:8-9). As stated previously, the Gnostic dualism of pure spirit on one extreme and evil matter on the other gave rise to an extensive hierarchy of subordinate deities. In a descending series beginning with the ultimate god, lower gods were begotten or created in turn until finally the lowest committed the ultimate evil act by creating the material world and man in it. In some second-century Gnostic systems, as contemporary accounts reveal, there were as many as 365 levels in this chain of heavens and divine beings.[22] Paul's prohibition against "endless genealogies" seems to refer to this type of structure. Such diverting speculations do not edify in faith, he said, but "minister questions" (1 Timothy 1:4).[23]

The pastoral epistles show other signs of the popularity of false doctrine in the church, not only of gentile origin but of Jewish origin as well. Paul warned Timothy of those who teach ideas other than the divine doctrine of the word of Jesus Christ. Those who do so are obsessed with "questions and strifes of words," out of which come "perverse disputings of men of corrupt minds" (1 Timothy 6:3-5; cf. 2 Timothy 2:23). He told Titus:

> For there are many unruly and vain talkers and deceivers, specially they of the circumcision: Whose mouths must be stopped, who subvert whole houses, teaching things which they ought not. . . . Wherefore rebuke them sharply, that they may be sound in the faith; Not giving heed to Jewish fables, and command-

ments of men, that turn from the truth (Titus 1:10-11, 13-14).

2 Timothy (ca. A.D. 67)

Paul's final letter, written to his beloved associate Timothy, is the product of the aged apostle as he awaited his execution in Rome. It was in this letter that Paul told of the good fight which he had fought and of the "crown of righteousness" which had been prepared for him (2 Timothy 4:7-8). Paul was an old man when the letter was written, at least by ancient standards, and he was concluding a career of service in the church that had lasted over thirty years. Now he was in chains, knowing that the time of his departure was near (2 Timothy 4:6).

In this pathetic setting Paul spoke of apostasy both future and present. In the future the saints would no longer "endure sound doctrine" (2 Timothy 4:3). But Paul knew that as he wrote, the process was already underway. He warned Timothy against "profane and vain babblings: for they will increase unto more ungodliness. And their word will eat as doth a canker" (2 Timothy 2:16-17). He mentioned two men guilty of spreading cankerous false doctrine, who had ruined the faith of some by teaching that the resurrection had already taken place.

Perhaps Paul's most sorrow-filled words are those found in 2 Timothy 1:15: "This thou knowest, that all they which are in Asia be turned away from me." His choice of words is grim evidence that his work to establish the gospel of Christ in the hearts of his Asian converts was coming to naught. Paul had taught the gospel in Asia thirteen years earlier. The people had accepted it in large numbers (Acts 19:8-22). But now they were turning from him and from his message as well (see 2 Timothy 2:16-18, 23-26). Yet they were turning not back to their ancestral paganism, but to a new Christian paganism — one that had "a form of godliness" but denied "the power thereof" (2 Timothy 3:5; cf. also 4:3-4).

Jude (ca. A.D. 80)

By the time of the writing of Jude, the apostasy that had been prophesied was well underway. Jude tells us as much.

As he began his letter, Jude mentioned that it was necessary for him to write and exhort his readers that they "should earnestly contend for the faith which was once delivered unto the saints" (Jude 1:3). The impression one gets from Jude's urgent words is that "the faith which was once delivered unto the saints" was facing substantial opposition. Jude explained why:

> *Certain people have infiltrated among you,* and they are the ones you had a warning about, in writing, long ago, when they were condemned for denying all religion, turning the grace of our God into immorality, and rejecting our only Master and Lord, Jesus Christ (Jude 1:4, JB, emphasis added).

This passage tells us both of the prophecy of the infiltration of godless men into the church and of its fulfillment. By this point in history the saints had received numerous prophecies that this kind of trouble would come in the last days of the church. Jude's words demonstrate that they knew it and that the time had arrived. His statement does not describe persecution or opposition from without, but apostasy from within, as "certain men crept in unawares" and gained influence to promote their false ideas.

Jude continued by likening the apostates of his day with several from more ancient times. Among other charges with which he condemned them was the fact that they "reject authority, and defame dignitaries" (Jude 1:8, Reicke), an overt act of rebellion similar to that described in 3 John.

Near the end of the letter Jude reminded the readers

again that they had been warned and that the day had arrived:

> But, dear friends, remember what the apostles of our Lord Jesus Christ foretold. They said to you, "In the last times there will be scoffers who will follow their own ungodly desires." These are the men who divide you, who follow mere natural instincts and do not have the Spirit (Jude 1:17-19, NIV).

Revelation (ca. A.D. 96)

In John's apocalypse we find additional convincing evidence that apostasy was ruining the church. As had Jude before him, John told of the forces of rebellion already at work in Christianity. And, as he reported, they were succeeding.

The evidence of apostasy in progress is found in the messages to seven churches of Asia in Revelation 2 and 3. In those communications we can evaluate the spiritual stability of the churches based on the words addressed to each one. It is often suggested that the seven are representative of the church as a whole, given John's propensity for the use of numbers — particularly the number seven — in symbolic ways.[24] We have every reason to believe that the messages were actual communications to the seven churches, yet it is also possible that their words characterize all of Christianity and give us a reasonable evaluation of the faith as a whole near the end of the first century.

To Ephesus the message contained both congratulation and condemnation (Revelation 2:1-7). The Ephesians had been successful in rejecting false apostles and other apostate influences, yet they had fallen and succumbed to other evils to the extent that without immediate repentance they would be cast off by the Lord. Similarly the saints at Pergamos were instructed that if they did not repent the Lord would come against them (Revelation 2:12-17). They were guilty of false religion, characterized as "the doctrine of

Balaam," the Old Testament prophet who led Israel into apostate worship. To Thyatira the condemnation was of the same sort (Revelation 2:18-29). Though worthy of congratulation for good works, the saints there were guilty of allowing a heretical movement referred to by the name Jezebel to "seduce" the Lord's servants among them into apostate practice. Jezebel was proverbial of Old Testament fame for guiding Israel into the worship of false gods. Though challenged to repent before, those who had been seduced by the heresy had refused, leaving the Lord only the option of casting them off. Those who had not been tainted by the doctrine, who had "not known the depths of Satan," were commanded to "hold fast" to what they had. To Sardis the communication was somber: the church there was "ready to die" (Revelation 3:1-6). Only a few had not defiled themselves. If the rest did not repent, their names would be blotted out of "the book of life." Philadelphia received a more promising message (Revelation 3:7-13). It had a "little strength" left, and if it held fast, no one would take its crown.

The two remaining messages are those to Smyrna (Revelation 2:8-11) and Laodicea (Revelation 3:14-22). The saints in Smyrna were praised, and no faults were mentioned concerning the church. But a tragic fate awaited them. They would be imprisoned and suffer martyrdom. They were admonished not to fear what was coming and to be "faithful unto death." In so doing they would receive a "crown of life" and would "not be hurt of the second death." In contrast, the Lord's word to Laodicea was that the church there was spiritually "wretched," "miserable," "poor," "blind," and "naked." Because of its indifference to the things of God, he would spit it out of his mouth.

If the messages to the seven churches of Asia paint a fair picture of the overall status of early Christianity, one cannot avoid the conclusion that the prophecies of apostasy were then being fulfilled. Of the seven churches, only two

were not condemned, and one of those was to suffer martyrdom. One church was ready to die because of its sins;
another was to be spit out of God's mouth. Of the rest,
all were guilty of serious error, and each was told in strong
terms that if it did not repent, it would be rejected.

1 and 2 John (ca. A.D. 98)

John's letters are probably the latest writings of the
New Testament. As such they are the most informative
source for the final days of the Christianity of the apostles.
Predictably, the view that they provide of the church at
the end of the century is a tragic one. John, who at this
point certainly was the senior apostle of the church, told
his readers that the last hours of the church had come, as
prophesied, and that the powers of apostasy were among
them in force. He stated:

> Little children, *it is the last time:* and as ye have heard
> that antichrist shall come, even now are there many
> antichrists; *whereby we know that it is the last time* (1 John
> 2:18, emphasis added).[25]

John and his readers knew that they were in the "last
time" (*eschátē hōrā*, more literally "last hour") because they
knew of prophecies that in the final days of the church
"antichrist" would be found among them. Since "many
antichrists" were then within the church, John knew with
certainty that the final days had arrived.[26]

In Paul's great prophecy in 2 Thessalonians 2:3-4, he
foretold the manifestation of the "man of sin," Satan, in
the period of apostasy. Paul's "man of sin" is the equivalent
of John's "antichrist." Yet the fact that John mentioned
many antichrists among the saints shows that it refers here
not only to Satan singularly, but also to his followers, those
who were inspired of him, and his entire movement. Continuing, John stated that the antichrists had come from
among the saints: "They went out from us, but they were

not of us; for if they had been of us, they would no doubt have continued with us" (1 John 2:19).

Later in his letter, John warned his readers further about apostate influences among them: "Beloved, believe not every spirit, but try the spirits whether they are of God: because many false prophets are gone out into the world" (1 John 4:1). This passage contains three messages of importance to early Christians: (1) Do not believe every "spirit." John used the term "spirit" in a broad sense, possibly to mean something like "idea," "movement," "teacher," or "prophet." (2) Test those influences to see if they are from God. (3) "Many false prophets" were in the world. John clearly was writing about false prophets within Christianity. Recall that in his letter from Patmos to the Ephesians he made mention of false apostles who had been discovered and repelled (Revelation 2:2).

Next, John gave the means by which his readers could test the "spirits" to see if they were of God:

> Hereby know ye the Spirit of God: every spirit that confesseth that Jesus Christ is come in the flesh is of God: and every spirit that confesseth not that Jesus Christ is come in the flesh is not of God: and this is that spirit of antichrist, whereof ye have heard that it should come; and even now already is it in the world (1 John 4:2-3).

The test was simple: if the spirit testified that Jesus had not come in the flesh, that was the anticipated spirit of antichrist.

Apparently John's readers had been influenced by *docetism,* a doctrine that denied that Christ had come in the flesh.[27] Docetism, from the Greek verb *dokéō,* "to seem," held that Christ had not really come in the flesh, but only appeared to do so. This belief was based on the Gnostic view that matter was evil, and that it would be impossible for a divine being such as Christ to be associated with it.

Docetism denied, therefore, the humanity of Christ, his physical suffering, his physical death, and his physical resurrection; he only *seemed* to have a physical body.

John's concern over this doctrinal development is understandable, considering the fact that he had been one of the closest individuals to Jesus during his mortality. To him such a belief was antichrist. In both 1 and 2 John he denounced it strongly (see 1 John 2:26; 2 John 1:7) and pleaded with the saints to hold fast to true doctrine: "Let that therefore abide in you, which ye have heard from the beginning. If that which ye have heard from the beginning shall remain in you, ye also shall continue in the Son, and in the Father" (1 John 2:24).

3 John (ca. A.D. 98)

John's third letter is a letter of apostasy. In it he made reference to one Diotrephes, a local church leader who had refused to receive John. Diotrephes, according to John, "loveth to have the preeminence" among the saints (3 John 1:9). John—the presiding authority of the church—had written to him; but Diotrephes would not receive John. Neither would he receive "the brethren," and he would not let his congregation do so either. In fact, he excommunicated those who would (3 John 1:10).

This was apostasy by any definition. It was rebellion against divinely instituted authority. John promised to deal with the offending leader when he could, but if Diotrephes did not recognize John's authority, no doubt he would not have responded to his discipline either.

We have no way of knowing to what extent this type of rebellion characterized the Christian church at that time. Yet if, as we learn from John's other letters, rebellion against true doctrine was commonplace, undoubtedly the struggle against those who opposed that rebellion was equally widespread. The Diotrephes incident may have been one of many such events, as people of the rising third generation of Christian history had no loyalty to John, the last remaining witness of the first. For those who rejected John, the final legitimate link of doctrinal and priesthood authority between Christ and the church that bore his name in that day was broken.

3. THE END OF THE APOSTOLIC ERA

The New Testament does not preserve for us a complete history of the Christian church of the first century A.D. We possess in addition to the gospels only the twenty-eight chapters of the book of Acts — much of which is not a history of the church but a history of the career of one apostle — and less than two dozen letters. These documents give us only a faint view of the seventy-year period which they span.[28] There are major gaps in our knowledge of the activities of the apostles, their lives, their teachings, and their deaths. We do know that in the early years following the resurrection of Jesus the apostles added additional members to their number as vacancies required. A good case for the fact that there had to be twelve apostles during the early period can be made on the basis of the choosing of Matthias to fill the position vacated by Judas Iscariot. It is significant to note that among the first things that the apostles did following the ascension of Jesus was to choose another to join them. As Peter explained, to fill Judas's place one had to "be ordained to be a witness with us of his resurrection" (Acts 1:22). Others are mentioned as well, who appear to have been added to the group of apostles in the following years. Although we lack the details of their choosing, ordination, or whom they replaced, we know that James (see Acts 12:17 and Acts 15; Galatians 1:19), Paul (Acts 14:14; Romans 1:1), and Barnabas (Acts 14:14; Romans 1:1) were added as time progressed. There may have been others concerning whom we have no information.

It is evident that James, Paul, and Barnabas were made apostles prior to A.D. 50. At least up until that point in history it appears that the Lord perpetuated his system of apostolic succession in accordance with the precedent of the choosing of Matthias: when there was a vacancy in the Twelve, one was chosen to fill it. Later, however, it seems that the succession was ended. By A.D. 95 only John remained, as far as we know. The scriptural record is silent concerning others, but early Christian sources outside of the Bible show John as the only living apostle by the end of the century. When John left his public ministry, apostleship ceased in the church. Had it been God's will, others certainly could have been chosen. But clearly it was not. The Lord allowed the apostleship to die out.[29]

When Jesus sent forth his special witnesses, he commanded them to bear testimony of him to all the world (e.g., Acts 1:8). They did this in two significant ways. First, they traveled far, preaching the gospel and bearing witness of Jesus and his work wherever they went. Second, and perhaps even more importantly, they left their testimony in the form of the records that we call collectively the New Testament. It is the written testimony of the apostles, preserved for all generations as the witness of those who were commissioned to be "witnesses unto [Christ] . . . unto the uttermost part of the earth" (Acts 1:8). The apostles were kept on earth long enough to fulfill the divine command. They did not fail.

The Lord knew, and he gave his apostles to know, that many saints would turn away from the true faith that had been taught to them. We have seen that it happened — slowly at first, but with increasing speed and irreversibility in each succeeding decade. And, as we have seen, with the rejection of true religion came the rejection of true authority as well. There must have come a time at some point near the year A.D. 100 when, had the apostolic succession continued, there would have been twelve apostles on earth and a church that rejected both their doctrine and their authority. This was not allowed to happen. It was fortunate, in fact, that the system of succession was not perpetuated further. By the time of 3 John, ca. A.D. 98, even John, the senior apostle of the church, was being rejected. The Great Apostasy had come.

Notes

1. E.g., Dean C. Jessee, ed., *The Personal Writings of Joseph Smith* (Salt Lake City: Deseret Book, 1984), 5, 200 (Joseph Smith-History 1:18-19), 213; Oliver Cowdery, "Address," *Latter Day Saints' Messenger and Advocate* 1 (October 1834): 2; Orson Pratt, *A Interesting Account of Several Remarkable Visions* (Edinburgh, 1840), 29; James E. Talmage, *The Great Apostasy* (Salt Lake City: Deseret News, 1909), and *The Articles of Faith* (Salt Lake City: The Church of Jesus Christ of Latter-day Saints, 1960), 198-204.

2. It is an honor for me to include a discussion of the apostasy in a volume that celebrates the contributions of Hugh W. Nibley, whose writings contain numerous references to the fall of the Early Christian Church. Over the years he has demonstrated that the Latter-day Saint position on this matter is defensible by an appeal to the earliest Christian documents, including the New Testament itself. In his studies in early Christian history he has pointed out convincingly that the Christian church of the second century was not the same as that of the first. His major works specifically dealing with the apostasy include "The Passing of the Primitive Church: Forty Variations on an Unpopular Theme," and "The Way of the Church," in *Mormonism and Early Christianity*, vol. 4, *The Collected Works of Hugh Nibley* (Salt Lake City: Deseret Book and F.A.R.M.S., 1987), 168-208 and 209-322. The first of these is among Nibley's finest works. Additional discussion of the apostasy is found throughout his other writings, particularly in *Mormonism and Early Christianity* and in *The World and the Prophets*, vol. 3, *The Collected Works of Hugh Nibley* (Salt Lake City: Deseret Book and F.A.R.M.S., 1987).

3. For insights into the phrase, "they were all wrong," see Larry E. Dahl, "The Theological Significance of the First Vision," in Robert L. Millet and Kent P. Jackson, eds., *Studies in Scripture, Vol. 2: The Pearl of Great Price* (Salt Lake City: Randall Book, 1985), 326-27, 331-32.

4. All biblical quotations are from the King James Version unless indicated otherwise by the following abbreviations: JB—Jerusalem Bible; JST—Joseph Smith Translation; NIV—New International Version; Phillips—Phillips Modern English Version; REB—Revised Eng-

lish Bible; Reicke—Bo Reicke, *The Epistles of James, Peter, and Jude,* Anchor Bible (Garden City, NY: Doubleday, 1964); RSV—Revised Standard Version.

5. The Greek verbal conjugation *enéstēken,* translated "at hand" in the King James Bible, has been rendered in a variety of ways in other translations. The basic meaning of the word is "is present," so perhaps the reading "has come" (RSV), or something similar to it as found in the majority of the versions, is more accurate than the ambiguous "at hand." Albrecht Oepke, "Enístēmi," in Gerhard Kittel, ed., *Theological Dictionary of the New Testament,* 10 vols. (Grand Rapids, MI: Eerdmans, 1964), 2:543-44.

6. Heinrich Schlier, "Apostasía," in Kittel, *Theological Dictionary of the New Testament,* 1:513-14; F. F. Bruce, *1 and 2 Thessalonians,* Word Biblical Commentary (Waco, TX: Word Books, 1982), 166. Richard D. Draper pointed out to me why he prefers to use the word "revolution" over "rebellion." In a rebellion the rulers are challenged (and sometimes overthrown) but the state remains intact. In a successful revolution, not only are the leaders overthrown but the constitution is thrown out as well. The basic framework and objectives of the state are discarded in favor of new ones cast in the image of the new leaders. Stephen Robinson's term "mutiny" carries the same connotation. When the captain of the ship is thrown overboard the new men at the helm steer a new course; see Stephen E. Robinson, "Early Christianity and 1 Nephi 13-14," in Monte S. Nyman and Charles D. Tate, Jr., eds., *First Nephi, the Doctrinal Foundation* (Provo, UT: Religious Studies Center, Brigham Young University, 1988), 178. These scenarios describe accurately the ultimate result of the fall of early Christianity.

7. E.g., Bruce R. McConkie, *Doctrinal New Testament Commentary,* 3 vols. (Salt Lake City: Bookcraft, 1966-73), 3:63; Sidney B. Sperry, *Paul's Life and Letters* (Salt Lake City: Bookcraft, 1955; repr. 1987), 103.

8. See Richard Lloyd Anderson, *Understanding Paul* (Salt Lake City: Deseret Book, 1983), 86. See also William F. Orr and James Arthur Walther, *1 Corinthians,* Anchor Bible (Garden City, NY: Doubleday, 1976), 172-74.

9. See Robert E. Parsons, "The Great and Abominable Church," in Kent P. Jackson, ed., *Studies in Scripture, Vol. 7: 1 Nephi to Alma 29* (Salt Lake City: Deseret Book, 1987), 54-59; Robinson, "Early Christianity and 1 Nephi 13-14," 177-91.

10. See Dahl, "The Theological Significance of the First Vision," 326-27, 331-32.

11. Bruce, *1 and 2 Thessalonians*, 170-71; John W. Bailey, "2 Thessalonians, Exegesis," in George A. Buttrick et al., eds., *The Interpreter's Bible*, 12 vols. (Nashville/New York: Abingdon, 1953-57), 11:328.

12. E.g., Bailey, "2 Thessalonians," 11:327.

13. For other insights, see Anderson, *Understanding Paul*, 85-87.

14. See Hermann W. Beyer, "Blasphēméō," in Kittel, *Theological Dictionary of the New Testament*, 1:621-25.

15. Cf. McConkie, *Doctrinal New Testament Commentary*, 3:520-22.

16. See Robinson, "Early Christianity and 1 Nephi 13-14," 188-90.

17. For additional New Testament evidence, see Nibley, "The Passing of the Primitive Church," 194-95, nn. 1-25.

18. An argument for Gnosticism in first-century (New Testament) Christianity is found in R. McL. Wilson, *Gnosis and the New Testament* (Philadelphia: Fortress Press, 1968), 31-84. For a popular introduction to Gnosticism in early Christianity, see Elaine Pagels, *The Gnostic Gospels* (New York: Random House, 1979); see also F. F. Bruce, *New Testament History* (Garden City, NY: Anchor/Doubleday, 1972), 415-18.

19. E.g., Irenaeus, *Against Heresies*; Clement of Alexandria, *The Stromata, or Miscellanies*; Tertullian, *Against Marcion* 1-5, *Against the Valentinians, Prescription against Heretics, Scorpiace*. All of these are available in A. Roberts and J. Donaldson, eds., *The Ante-Nicene Fathers* (Grand Rapids, MI: Eerdmans, 1979-81), vols. 1-3.

20. For excellent discussions concerning the dates of the Pastoral Epistles, see Anderson, *Understanding Paul*, 310-14; D. Edmond Hiebert, *An Introduction to the Pauline Epistles* (Chicago: Moody Press, 1954), 308-24. The dates accepted here necessarily presuppose both Pauline authorship and an early development of Gnosticism in first-century Christianity. Though most definitions or descriptions of Gnosticism reflect its second-century (and later) characteristics, it is not inaccurate to use the term with regard to the movements manifest in Colossians, the Pastoral Letters, and 1-2 John.

21. See Anderson, *Understanding Paul*, 318-20.

22. Irenaeus, *Against Heresies* I, 24, 3-4.

23. See Anderson, *Understanding Paul*, 320-21.

24. Richard Lloyd Anderson, "Ramsay, The Seven Churches, and Early Christian Apostasy," *Newsletter and Proceedings of the Society for Early Historic Archaeology*, 108 (1968): 1-4; J. Massyngberde Ford, *Revelation*, Anchor Bible (Garden City, NY: Doubleday, 1975), 376.

25. Raymond E. Brown's translation reads as follows: "Children, it is the last hour. You heard that Antichrist is to come: well, now many Antichrists have made their appearance, and this makes us certain that it really is the last hour," *The Epistles of John*, Anchor Bible (Garden City, NY: Doubleday, 1982), 329.

26. Scholars generally believe that John had in mind the "last hour" (of whatever duration) before the return of Jesus. See Brown, *The Epistles of John*, 330-32; Stephen S. Smalley, *1, 2, 3 John*, Word Biblical Commentary (Waco, TX: Word Books, 1984), 94-101. While it is not altogether clear how long the apostles anticipated the apostasy to last, this verse and those disucssed above (particularly 2 Thessalonians 2:1-12) demonstrate that the coming of "antichrist" (or the "man of sin") was inevitable before Jesus' return. Assuming, as we must, that John realized that there would be a restoration before the Second Coming, the "last hour" can only point to the end of the church, not the end of the world (see Joseph Smith-Matthew 1:4). Thus Brown's suggestion that John "was wrong" misses the point; *The Epistles of John*, 330.

27. See F. F. Bruce, *The Epistles of John* (Grand Rapids, MI: Eerdmans, 1970), 15-18, 104-5. For a brief survey of interpretations, see I. Howard Marshall, *The Epistles of John*, The New International Commentary on the New Testament (Grand Rapids, MI: Eerdmans, 1978), 14-22.

28. Nibley suggests that censorship and "the silent treatment" are two reasons why so little has survived from the earliest Christianity, showing examples from antiquity; "The Way of the Church," 223-31.

29. Note Nibley's insightful comment: "The failure of the apostles to leave behind them written instructions for the future guidance of the church has often been noted and sadly regretted. It is hard to conceive of such a colossal oversight if the founders had actually envisaged a long future for the church," Nibley, "The Passing of the Primitive Church," 176.

8

Two Letters to the Dead

Sharon R. Keller
Baruch College, New York, New York

The Egyptian Letters to the Dead are a small though significant corpus of epistolary texts whose dates span the centuries of Pharaonic Egypt, ranging from the Old through the New Kingdoms. Alan H. Gardiner and Kurt Sethe were the first to identify these texts as a genre when they published in 1928 the seven Letters known at that time.[1] To date, thirteen Letters have been identified, two of which will be treated here—the Cairo Bowl and the Berlin Bowl.[2]

The genesis of this form of text derives from the Egyptian conception of the afterlife. The Egyptian netherworld was populated by the spirits of the dead, who were able to travel back and forth between their realm and the world of the living and were thus privy to the goings-on in both realms. The dead not only possessed this great knowledge, but they also had the power to harm or assist those whom they left behind.[3]

Generally, the dead were thought to use their power for their own protection; they were envisioned as being able to harm anyone who dared to desecrate their tombs, as well as to look favorably upon those who recited the appropriate utterances and left funerary offerings for their benefit.[4] The power of the deceased transcended the bounds of the netherworld; their potency was capable of reaching into the world of the living.[5] It was in the context of these beliefs that the Egyptian practice of composing Letters to the Dead arose. The Letters were written in the hope that they would sway the deceased to use their influence on behalf of the living.

Although the corpus is relatively small, the contents of these texts are sufficiently similar to constitute a genre. The Letters to the Dead were never written with sentimentality; their authors assumed that the addressees were securely ensconced in the netherworld, so that any inquiry as to their well-being would be unnecessary. Since the dead were cognizant of occurrences in the mortal sphere, there was no need to write to them to keep them informed of day-to-day matters. The Letters to the Dead are thus not mere attempts by the living to communicate with spirits in the netherworld; rather, they are all missives with a practical intent, written specifically in order to rectify distressing situations on earth that could not be dealt with through available mortal channels.

All of the Letters to the Dead were sent by close relatives of the deceased: six of the letters were addressed to a parent, six to a spouse, one to a child, and one to a sibling.[6] These Letters were written only to family members because they were the ones who were obligated to care for their deceased; they were responsible for providing offerings for the spirits, who were dependent upon their living descendants for their perpetual sustenance and continued well-being.[7] Thus the authors of the majority of these texts joined their desire to send a message to the netherworld with their responsibilities to the deceased, and therefore accompanied their pleas with funerary gifts.[8]

Six of the Letters to the Dead were written on pottery bowls that could have held actual food offerings,[9] and one Letter was written on a clay stand that was made to be used as a base to hold an offering bowl. The connection between these seven texts and the actual offerings that may have accompanied them is straightforward; a funerary gift could have been left inside the bowl for the spirit to take. Although there is no evidence to indicate that palpable offerings were left for the spirit in the inscribed bowls, the presence in the tomb of the offering bowls themselves may well have served symbolically as the offering.[10] The remaining three Letters to the Dead that can be linked with gifts to the spirits can be associated only with symbolic offerings.

These gifts, when offered in conjunction with the Letters to the Dead, served multiple functions. These offerings were not considered as guarantees to the outcome of the Letters' pleas; rather, they were combined with the petitions for purely practical purposes. Since the dead visited their tombs to receive the offerings that were brought to them, they could not help but notice the Letters that were left for them in conjunction with these offerings.[11] In this regard, the offerings may be seen as gifts that facilitate the sending of the Letters. In other respects, these offerings may have been intended as unsolicited gifts, or even as bribes to the spirits, brought either in order to placate them, or to entice them to look favorably upon the petition and the petitioner. Some may even have been intended as subtle threats to the spirit: if the plea was not favorably addressed, and the problem presented in the Letter not rectified to the author's satisfaction, then the author (or the person on whose behalf the Letter was written) would have no choice but to abandon the spirit by not bringing funerary offerings in the future.[12]

The situations that occasioned the Letters to the Dead were always family oriented, and their authors wrote either at their own behest, or on behalf of a close family member. Not written by members of the royal class, these documents afford us a glimpse into the workings of family life outside the royal sphere. Since these Letters were written only when problems arose, some of the information that may be gleaned from them relates to extraordinary, although acceptable, cultural practices of ancient Egypt. Five of the Letters deal with inheritance disputes, three of which are cases revolving around fratriarchal versus patriarchal rights. From these three texts we see that a pattern of fratrilineal inheritance existed in Pharaonic Egypt even though it was not the norm.[13]

In addition to illuminating aspects of earthly life, these Letters shed some light on the Egyptian conception of the netherworld. The court in the netherworld, which judged the dead upon their demise so as to grant them entrance into the realm of the dead, is depicted throughout Egyptian literature and art.[14] The Letters to the Dead show that this court had jurisdiction even after the deceased was allowed to enter the netherworld, that cases could be brought before it by members of the community of the dead, that the parties to the case need not all be dead, and that the verdicts handed down by the tribunal could reach beyond the netherworld and affect the living.[15]

Letters to the Dead, as such, are confined to the borders of Egypt. However, many aspects of these Egyptian Letters appear to anticipate elements of Semitic magical bowls. The greatest similarities may be seen between the Letters to the Dead that were written on pottery bowls and the Aramaic Incantation bowls of a later period.[16] There are many points of contact between these bowls, the most obvious of which is the usage of bowls for communication. The Aramaic bowls were not designed to contact deceased relatives, nor were they intended to symbolize an offering, but since they were used as amulets and exorcising texts, they sought to invoke or coopt with the spiritual or demonic world. The choice medium for this contact, obviously, appears to have been pottery bowls, yet the Aramaic bowls sometimes refer to themselves as "letters,"[17] showing that these bowls, just as the Egyptian bowls, were thought of as letters and that the physical bowls were secondary to the text themselves.[18] The texts on the Semitic bowls are often written in a spiral, and both circular and spiral writing is found on the Letters to the Dead. One of the Letters to the Dead has a figure inked on the bottom of the bowl; although this is unique among the extant Egyptian Letters, images are regularly found on the Semitic bowls.[19] None of this is to say that the Egyptian Letters to the Dead are the same as the Semitic Incantation bowls; indeed, there are areas where these two genres do not overlap at all. But what is important to remember is that cultural practices never arise in a vacuum. Just as the Semitic bowls should be analyzed in light of their antecedents, so the Egyptian Letters to the Dead must be viewed in relation to the larger ancient Near Eastern world. As cultural practices transcend geographical boundaries, so too must one's study of them.

THE CAIRO BOWL

Description

This Twelfth Dynasty Letter was written on both the interior and the exterior of a nondescript red pottery bowl.[20] The first nine lines of the text are inscribed vertically on the inside of the bowl, and the text continues with two additional vertical columns on the outside. This is the only extant Letter to the Dead where the text of one Letter is started on the interior of the bowl and completed on its exterior.[21]

Translation

(1) Given by Dedí to the Ḥm-nṯr priest, Intef born of Iw(2)nakht: As for this maid-servant, Imᶜw who (3) is ill, you do not fight for her day and night with all (men)[22] who are doers of evil (4) to her, (and) with all (women)[23] who are doers of evil to her. You wish your threshold destroyed (5) on account of what? Fight for her today like a new thing. Establish (6) her household (so that) water may be poured out for you. If there is nothing from your hand, then your house (7) will be destroyed! Can it be that you

do not know this? Doesn't this maid-servant (8) maintain your house among men? You (must) fight for [her]! (9) Watch over her! (10) Save her from everyone[24] (who is) doing evil to her. (11) Then your house and your children will be established. Good be your hearing.

Analysis

The general framework of this Letter follows the characteristics of the genre: there is a problem on earth that can be rectified only by the intercession of the dead. Yet this Letter cannot be understood completely at first reading, for it neither states the precise nature of the problem nor gives any direct clue as to the position of the main characters within the household. The text does reveal that a woman is sick but remains reticent about the specific details of the illness. Only by a careful analysis of the plea can we deduce the familial station of the sick woman and thereby clarify some of the inherent ambiguities of this Letter.

The text mentions three names—Dedí, Intef, and Imᶜw—but it makes no explicit statements to indicate the roles of or the relationships between these people. Two plausible approaches to resolving the question of roles are initially apparent, and each reading results in a vastly different understanding of the circumstances that fostered the Letter's petition.

The first line, "Given by Dedí to the Ḥm-nṯr priest, Intef born of Iwnakht," might only aim at introducing the characters. In that case, the simplest understanding would make Dedí, as sender of the Letter, the widowed wife whose house is in a state of upheaval, and who petitions her deceased husband to rectify the family's trouble.[25] Imᶜw, "this maid-servant," would then be a highly valued retainer (a female majordomo), who is suffering from a malaise severe enough to jeopardize the stability of the household. Gardiner and Sethe's translation of this text supports this view: they assume that Dedí is the widow, Intef the deceased, and Im^cw their prized servant.[26] Of course, this interpretation presupposes that a staff member's illness could and would destroy both a household and a family.

Even if an incapacitated servant could upset the balance of a family structure, the difficulty with this delegation of roles becomes obvious when one analyzes the key sentence in line six: "Establish her household so that water may be poured out for you." Here, the speaker explains to Intef, if indirectly, that the water offerings for the dead will cease if he does not intercede on behalf of the living. Given this context (the suggestion that if the household is destroyed the funerary offerings will stop), it must be assumed that Im^cw is in some way responsible for pouring out the water. In ancient Egypt, family members were primarily responsible for providing for the dead.[27] If, as implied in the text, Im^cw is responsible for pouring the water, she then must be related to the deceased. It therefore seems that Im^cw cannot be a servant in the conventional sense and that, as a relative of Intef, she may in fact be his widow. If so, her sickness would naturally upset the household's functioning and might even compromise the future lives of the family members.

If Im^cw is the widow, why does she refer to herself as "this maid-servant" when she might simply say, more personally, "me," or "your wife"?[28] This difficulty is a purely modern one. Whereas for a modern reader "this maid-servant" designates an occupation, for a contemporary reader of the Letter the phrase could be understood as a fictive title, employed as a means of humble self-reference.[29]

The use of fictive titles was common throughout the Egypto-Semitic ecumene. A prime example may be found in the Bible, in the first book of Samuel, when the barren woman Hannah prays for a male child:

ותדר נדר ותאמר יהוה צבאות אם־ראה תראה ן
בעני אמתך וזכרתני ולא־תשכח את־אמתך
ונתתה לאמתך זרע אנשים ונתתיו ליהוה כל־
ימי חייו ומורה לא־יעלה על־ראשו:

> So she vowed a vow and said: "Lord of Hosts, if
> You will see the suffering of Your maid-servant and will
> remember me and not forget Your maid-servant, so that
> You will give a male child to Your maid-servant, then I
> will give him to the Lord all the days of his life, and no
> razor will come upon his head" (1 Samuel 1:11).

There can be no doubt that Hannah's petition, although
different from Im^{c}w's, is also a personal plea; the three
biblical references to "Your maid-servant," as well as the
Cairo bowl reference, "As for this maid-servant" (line two),
indicate nothing more than polite subservience. These two
petitions are directed to forces beyond the mortal sphere —
Hannah's to God, and Im^{c}w's to her deceased husband.
Since both women are addressing superiors, the use of
"servant," although not literal, is easily understood.

According to Egypto-Semitic epistolary custom,
expressions of mock-servitude were also used, especially
when a letter was addressed to a superior, but often when
written to an equal. The writers of many of the Hekanakhte
letters use b3k (servant) when referring to themselves in
formal correspondence.[30] Similarly, the Amarna letters are
rife with examples in which (w)ardu (slave) is used for self-
reference. One illustration will suffice here:

li-ma-ad a-wa-te^{mes} ardi-ka an-nu-ti

Verily, understand these words of thy servant.[31]

There is no doubt that this practice was cross-cultural
and widespread. When a term of humility is used in reference to oneself, as it is in Im^{c}w's case, other evidence is
needed to determine whether it is a fact of status or just
a self-deprecating expression.[32]

Now the message on the Cairo Bowl is crystal clear.

The widow Im‘w is quite ill,[33] and she is worried about the future of her home and family. She is convinced that her sickness is caused by malevolent beings (whether in this world or the next).[34] She threatens to cease funerary offerings in the hope of enticing the aid of the spirit of her dead husband. Intervention from the netherworld is needed to arrest the progress of the evil-doers and, thus, to protect her home and her family.

Line Notes

1. *dí Ddí n.* The fact that Dedí "gives" the Letter, rather than "speaking" it, or even "writing" it substantiates the argument that she is not the author of this text but only a secondary messenger or letter-carrier.[35]

Ḥm-nṯr. The common Egyptian title (*Ḥm* = servant, and *nṯr* = god) has semantic parallels in the Bible where "servant of God" or "servant of the Lord," is a recurrent appellative.[36] Whereas "God/the Lord" in these biblical expressions refers specifically to the God of Israel, in the Egyptian term *Ḥm-nṯr,* "*nṯr* is clearly the most general abstract concept, which covers the multiplicity of divine manifestations."[37]

1/2. *Intf ms n Iwnḫt.* The use of the matronymic is unusual although easily explainable. Sympathetic and propitiatory magic tends to identify people with matronymics rather than patronymics; a person is referred to as the son or daughter of their mother. The texts of the Aramaic Incantation bowls regularly identify the clients as the child of the mother, not the child of the father. To this day, when a prayer is uttered for the recovery of a sick person, the standard Jewish custom is to identify that individual as the child of his mother.[38]

2. *b3kt.* See T. G. H. James, *The Ḥekanakhte Papers and Other Middle Kingdom Documents* (New York: Metropolitan Museum of Art Egyptian Expedition, 1962), 128, for a discussion of *b3k* in introductory phrases of letters.

3. *mrt*. This word (*mr* + feminine ending *t*) is related to the Ugaritic *mrr*,[39] and to the Hebrew root *mrr*, from which derive the meanings "bitter" or "bitter distress." In Hebrew the root never refers to a physical illness, but it may indicate psychological distress. A clear illustration is found in Ruth 1:13 when Naomi is speaking to her two widowed daughters-in-law. She attempts to convince them to return to their maternal homes rather than remain with her in the hope that she would bear sons for Levirate marriages.[40]

הלהן | תשברנה עד אשר יגדלו הלהן תעגנה
לבלתי היות לאיש אל בנתי כי־מר־לי מאד מכם
כי־יצאה בי יד־יהוה:

> Should you wait for them to grow up? Should you, for their sakes, be without husbands? No, my daughters, for it embitters me greatly for you that the Lord has gone out (against) me (Ruth 1:13).

Naomi is psychologically distressed on account of the plight of her daughters-in-law.

grḥ rᶜ. This is a merism meaning "all of the time."

irrí. The person who "does" can do either good or evil (*ir* = doer [of good], and *irr* = [doer of evil]). The opposing nuances of "do" are not restricted to the Egyptian language. These same expanded meanings for deed/doer are also found in biblical Hebrew as well as in Akkadian. The Hebrew root ᶜ*ll*, "deed or practice," can indicate a generic deed, a good deed, or an evil deed.

אני יהוה חקר לב בחן כליות ולתת לאיש כדרכו
כפרי מעלליו:

> I, the Lord, search the heart, examine the mind, so that (I may) give to (every) man according to his way with the fruit of his deeds (Jeremiah 17:10).

Here ᶜ*ll* has a clearly generic meaning, that a man's deeds are judged on their individual merit; the text does not support an interpretation of a specific view of the deeds.

גם במעלליו יתנכר־נער אם־זך ואם־ישר פעלו:

O youth is known by his deeds, if they are blameless and they are proper (Proverbs 20:11).

In this verse, ʿll parallels the child's "blameless and proper" actions, and therefore connotes good deeds.

יהוה אלהינו אתה עניתם אל נשא היית להם ונקם על־עלילותם:

O Lord our God, You have answered them; You were a forgiving God to them; yet You took vengeance for their misdeeds (Psalms 99:8).

Here the translation speaks for itself; ʿll is simply "misdeeds."

4. ʿryt. For a discussion of this word in relation to Late Egyptian ʿrt, see William A. Ward, "Late Egyptian ʿr.t: The So-called Upper Room," *Journal of Near Eastern Studies* 44/4 (1985): 329-32.

5. grg. See Hans J. Polotsky, "The Stela of Ḥeḳa-yeb," *Journal of Egyptian Archaeology* 16 (1930): 198, for a discussion of grg "to establish" as the object of pr.

THE BERLIN BOWL

Description

Two physical characteristics of the red pottery Berlin Bowl make it unique among the extant Letters to the Dead—the format of the inscription and the presence of a central figure.[41] Unlike any of the other texts, its plea is inscribed in two concentric circles, the first comprising a complete circle, and the second three-quarters of a circle.[42] Even more interesting than the circular arrangement of the text is the introduction of a portrait in its center.[43] Though crude, this line figure is true to the Egyptian style of drawing, in which the face is portrayed in profile, and the shoulders by a full frontal view.[44] Gardiner identifies the form as female, representing the addressee.[45] Since the letter is addressed to a woman, it follows that the picture on the bowl should in some way represent her, perhaps in order to appease her spirit. However, the image is totally asexual — there is no indication (in the text or in the picture itself) that the image represents a woman. The only possibly telling feature is the headdress, but because it is rough and ambiguous, a case could be made just as easily for its being a man's wig as for its being a woman's. Therefore, it is not certain that the image is that of the deceased wife; the figure could reasonably represent the bereaved husband, the author of the Letter who is beseeching his wife for assistance and includes a picture of himself as a remembrance to his wife. Nonetheless, the presence of a central figure is noteworthy.[46]

Translation

(1) May the King be gracious and grant (your desires),[47] Osiris and Anubis upon his mountain,[48] offerings to venerated [. . .]tet.[49] You were brought there to the city of eternity[50] without any of your spell(s) against me. If evil has been done, or if these blows (occurred) with your knowledge, behold the house of your children[51] is in a fresh misery!

(2) Could it be that evil is being done by your error? Great is your father ⟨in⟩ the necropolis. If there is a complaint in your body, forget it for the sake of your children! Be gracious! Be gracious! May the gods of this place be gracious to you.

Analysis

Though there is a lacuna at the beginning of the Berlin Bowl that is impossible and unnecessary to fill, it is certain that the plea was addressed to a deceased woman. All that is missing from the text is the full spelling of her name; the designation of her being deceased (*ím3ḫ*), here translated as "venerated," and the female determinative remain intact. It is logical to assume that this Letter was sent by her husband.[52] The widower is apparently concerned about the current suffering of his household, but he cannot fathom its cause. He is certain only that the evils facing him are neither of his making, nor of this world: something or someone in the netherworld must be the root of this misfortune. He therefore makes the standard plea of the Letters to the Dead, beseeching his wife for aid.

This short text lends itself to be broken into concise, yet meaningful segments. The formulaic beginning (*Ḥtp dí nsw*) at first appears awkward for a letter of this type because it was generally used for funerary offerings, and not for Letters to the Dead. But this unusual beginning is a key to understanding part of the widower's strategy in presenting the letter to enlist his wife's assistance.

Because the letter was written on a bowl (which is more difficult to inscribe than a flat surface), the medium must have served a function. Coupled with the *Ḥtp dí nsw* formula, the bowl probably was intended to hold a food offering, either real or representative. The presence of this formula in the text, therefore, shows that an offering was intended to accompany the letter, and that the husband sought either to appease his wife with the offering, or to entice her to read the letter and act on his request.

The next sentence, "You were brought here . . . against me," is the center of the petitioner's confusion. He implies that when his wife died everything was just as it should have been—that she was brought "to the city of eternity/to the necropolis" indicates that she was given a proper burial; that she died without any of her spells against her husband shows that the author felt that his wife bore no grudge against him at the time of her death. The author's working assumption is that if there had been enmity between him and his wife before her death he would have become aware of it, for she would have set her "spells" against him. Indeed, he apparently felt that she was content when she died, and, at that time, he assumed that his home and his family were secure. The widower is convinced of his innocence and in the first line of the text he does not even consider the possibility that he may have had some responsibility for his current woes. Up to this point the implied question the author is asking is "How could you do this to me?" Short of actually accusing his wife, he is hinting that she might be ruining his earthly existence without cause.

The strongest argument the widower presents in this sentence of his petition is that his wife received a proper burial. It was very important to the Egyptians, as well as to many ancient people, that a corpse be properly interred. At the end of the Middle Egyptian tale of the Shipwrecked Sailor, the giant serpent reassures the sailor that:

> You (the sailor) will arrive home in two months, you will hug your children, you will be vigorous, at home you will be buried.[53]

The emphasis is placed not only upon the return home, but also on the assurance of a proper burial in the land of Egypt—anything less would be a disgrace.

In the Bible, God condemns the corpses of the people associated with the rebel Jeroboam to remain unburied, and therefore to be devoured by animals:

המת לירבעם בעיר יאכלו הכלבים והמת בשדה
יאכלו עוף השמים כי יהוה דבר:

> The dead of Jeroboam who are in the city, they shall be eaten by dogs, and the dead who are in the field, they shall be eaten by the birds of the sky, so says the Lord (1 Kings 14:11).[54]

In the classical sphere, the story of Antigone is a prime

example of the importance placed upon a dignified burial to ensure the repose of the deceased. Antigone, the model of sororal fidelity, gives up her own life in the attempt to bury the body of her slain brother Polynices, which has been left, by royal edict, to be preyed upon by dogs and vultures.

In the Roman epic *The Aeneid*, Aeneas, during his journey to the underworld (Book VI), met "the resourceless, who had no burial."[55] These souls were doomed to wander for a hundred years without crossing the river Styx because they had been left unburied. Aeneas encounters his former helmsman Palinurus who begs him to "rescue me from my plight. . . . Cast soil upon me yourself . . . that at least in death I may rest at a place of calm."[56] Aeneas is moved by the fate of his former colleague and desires to bury him, but he cannot because he must continue on his mission.

Conversely, in the Apocrypha, Tobit, while listing his righteous deeds, states proudly that he took the task of locating and burying abandoned bodies. He declares:

> I performed many acts of charity to my brethren. I would give my bread to the hungry and my clothing to the naked; and if I saw any one of my people dead and thrown out behind the wall of Nineveh, I would bury him. And if Senacherib the king put to death any who came fleeing from Judea, I buried them secretly. For in his anger he put many to death. When the bodies were sought by the king, they were not found. Then one of the men of Nineveh went and informed the king about me, that I was burying them; so I hid myself. When I learned that I was being searched for to be put to death, I left home in fear.[57]

The setting of this apocryphal work is a literary device, its date being centuries later than the situation described, yet it attests to the continuity of the value placed upon respect for the corpse, a societal value which spanned borders.[58] Attending to the dead by giving them a proper burial was essential, for the dead to remain untended (and, for the Egyptians to be buried outside the confines of Egypt), threatened a terrible fate for the soul.

In the last sentence of the first line of the text, "If evil has been done . . . ," the author changes his plan of action by appealing to his wife's maternal instincts. He subtly informs her that if she does not put an end to these machinations, indeed if she even has the vaguest knowledge of what is going on, she herself is responsible for the destruction of her former home and for the ruination of her family. He does not mention here that he himself is in some sort of trouble; he relies instead upon her concern for her children to awaken her to his plight.[59]

Line two begins by once again changing the strategy of the letter: "Could it be that evil is being done by your error?" Here the husband appears incredulous—he is still the innocent one, but he does not accuse her of malice aforethought as he did above. In the first line of the text he all but states that his wife is guilty, but now he indicates his disbelief in her evil intentions by giving his wife the benefit of the doubt. After all she might not be aware of her role in what has been happening on earth. Whether or not she is aware of her family's misfortunes, his question is most likely a subtle way of telling her to discover the cause of his misfortune and to try to rectify his plight.

Once he has placated her by recognizing the possibility of her innocence, the husband continues his plea and includes the shrewdly worded compliment, "Great is your father ⟨in⟩ the necropolis," which sends a twofold message to the deceased. On the one hand the statement reminds her that she has access to higher powers in the netherworld who might be able to assist, but on the other hand it indirectly threatens her that if she does not come to the aid of her family, other ancestors might be appealed to.

Finally, the husband admits that his wife might indeed bear him a grudge for some conceivable grievance: "If there is a complaint . . . for the sake of your children." Reluctantly he acknowledges that she may have a grievance against him — for everyone may transgress unwittingly. He argues, however, that she should forget her displeasure not for his sake, but for the sake of their children. This is the second time in this short letter where maternal protection is sought. The author is not relying upon his wife's beneficent feelings toward him; rather, he stresses the fact that their children are being threatened. By this point three possibilities for the family's troubles have been covered by the author: the deceased wife is purposefully meddling in the earthly goings-on; she is an innocent who does not know what and why things are happening; or finally, almost as an afterthought, the husband acknowledges that he may have done something to have brought about his current predicament.

The conclusion of the letter indicates just how confident the petitioner is that everything will be rectified in the end. The parting phrases are his last attempt to influence his dead wife, where he entreats her to be gracious. Then the husband indicates his good will and shows his faith in a favorable outcome by invoking blessings on her spirit.

Line Notes

1. *Wsir Inpw*. These two gods, as well as the king, give boons. Therefore, this should be understood as a shorthand for *Ḥtp di Wsir, Ḥtp di Inpw*. "May Osiris be gracious and grant (your desires), and may Anubis be gracious and grant (your desires)."[60]

im3ḫ. "Blessed state of the dead"[61] indicates that the lady whose name follows in the lacuna is the deceased.

ꜥ3. Context demands the translation "there" for this adverb whose usual translation is "here."[62] ꜥ3 is employed six times in the corpus of the Ḥekanakhte letters, three times ꜥ3 "certainly means 'there' where the recipient is."[63]

So, at least in letters, this one adverb may refer either to "there, where you are," or "here, where I am."

r nỉwt nt nḥḥ. "To the city of eternity" is the same phrase as, and is used in a similar way as, the Hebrew phrase *bêt ᶜôlāmô*, "house of eternity/grave" which is found in the Bible:

גם מגבה יראו וחתחתים בדרך וינאץ השקד
ויסתבל החגב ותפר האביונה כי־הלך האדם
אל־בית עולמו וסבבו בשוק הספדים:

> Also when one is afraid of heights, and terrors are on the road, and the almond tree is in blossom, and the grasshopper is burdened, and the caper bush buds anew; but a man goes to the house of his eternity,[64] and the mourners go about in the market place (Ecclesiastes 12:5).

špt. Here translated as "spell" may be cognate to *šíptu*, Akkadian for "incantation."[65]

ḫrdw.t = Ugaritic *ḫrd*, "child/youth."[66] Both of these words may be related to *hardatu*, which is the Eblaite term for "female slaves"; see Dietz O. Edzard, *Hymnen, Beschwörungen und Verwandtes*, Archivi reali di Ebla, Testi V (Rome: Missione archeologica italiana in Siria, 1984), #3 (5:5). Although used at Ebla specifically for "slaves," it may be a cognate to the generic Egypto-Semitic term for children.

m3. See Adolf Erman and Hermann Grapow, *Wörterbuch der aegyptischen Sprache* (Berlin: Akademie-Verlag, 1982), 2:43.

2. *m msḏḏ.t.* This is a perfect correlation to the Hebrew *bišgāgāh*, "a sin of inadvertence."[67]

sp sn. This is parallel in usage to Sumerian *KI MIN* for "read twice" (commonly used as a Sumerogram in Akkadian).

Conclusion

Even though the Letters to the Dead are a genre of literature unique to Egypt, the ancient Egyptians were not unique in their desire to communicate with the dead. The mythology of the ancient Mediterranean world lauds both heroes and gods who travel to and from the netherworld and make contact with the dead.[68] The Bible has no records of anyone who actually traveled to the realm of the dead, but it does recount the successful attempt by Saul to speak with the spirit of the deceased prophet Samuel (1 Samuel 28:5-19).[69] In the mythology, as well as in the Bible, the living inquire of the dead to get a glimpse of the future or to clarify aspects of the past. The dead spirits usually address these inquiries by participating in some form of dialogue with the living.

The Egyptian Letters to the Dead are distinct from these attempts at communication with the dead insofar as the Egyptians did not expect any reciprocal communication from the netherworld. The authors of the Letters to the Dead neither present questions to, nor expect to receive verbal answers from, the deceased. The Letters to the Dead do not seek insight into the future, nor do they attempt to understand the past; the sole aim of these Letters is to convince the addressed spirits to use their acknowledged powers to assist the living so as to rectify distressing situations on earth. The authors of the Letters to the Dead want action, not discussion.[70]

This paper has stressed the areas of contact exhibited between these texts and the larger Egypto-Semitic ecumene. Cultural practices that were prevalent in other areas of the ancient Near East illuminate many of the situations presented in the Letters to the Dead, such as the importance of the proper interment of a corpse in a specific location, and the practice of praying for the birth of a child.

Just as there are similarities between the Egyptian and the ancient Near Eastern spheres, so too are there areas of divergence. When things are borrowed from one culture into another, certain aspects remain the same and others change. The antecedents of the Semitic magic bowls, for example, are most certainly in ancient Egypt, yet these two sets of bowl communications are not identical. Only one of the Egyptian Letters to the Dead was written in a spiral, and only one of the Egyptian bowls has a figure inked on the bottom. In contrast, many of the Semitic magic bowls and both of the inscribed bowls from Minoan Crete exhibit these features. This paper has indicated that Egyptian texts offer insight into the cultures of people beyond the strict confines of Egypt without diminishing the importance of acknowledging points of divergence; it is in elucidating the often overlooked areas of agreement that the broader aspects of both the Egyptian and the Semitic worlds will be better understood.

APPENDIX:
THE CAIRO BOWL

Inside

(1) dí Ddí n ḥm-nṯr Intf ms n Iw
(2) nḫt ín[71] ír t3 b3kt Imíw ntt
(3) mrt nn ʿḥ3.n.k ḥr.s grḥ rʿ ḥnʿ írrí nb
(4) r.s ḥnʿ írrt nbt r.s mrr.k wšt ʿrryt.
(5) k ḥr íḫ ʿḥ3.tw ḥr.s mín mí m3t grg
(6) pr.s stí n.k mw ír nfr.n mk k3 pr.k
(7) ḫb3 ín[72] wn nn rḫ.n.k ntt ín t3 b3kt
(8) ír pr.k m rmṯ ʿḥ3.tw ḥr.[s]
(9) rst ḥr.s

Outside

(10) nḥm.s ḥnʿ[73] írrí nb / írrt nbt
(11) íḫ grg pr.k ẖrdw.k nfr sḏm.k

THE BERLIN BOWL

(1) ḥtp dí nsw h Wsír Inpw tp ḏw.f prt-ẖrw n ím3ẖ [. . .]tt ; íní.ṯ ʿ3 r níwt nt nḥḥ nn špt.ṯ nb r.í ír wn írr.t nn skrw m rḫ.ṯ mṯ pr m-ʿ ẖrdw.ṯ wgg m3

(2) ír wn írr.t m msḏd.t ᶜ3 ít.ṯ ⟨m⟩ ḫr-nṯr ír wn srḫ m ḫt.ṯ smḫ sw n-íb-n ḫrdw.ṯ ḥtp sp sn (= ḥtp ḥtp) ḥtp.n.ṯ nṯrw t3w-wr

Notes

1. Alan H. Gardiner and Kurt Sethe, *Egyptian Letters to the Dead Mainly from the Old and Middle Kingdoms* (London: Egypt Exploration Society, 1928).

2. The K̟aw bowl and the Misplaced Letter to the Dead each have two Letters to the Dead inscribed upon them. There are thus eleven extant objects which contain the thirteen Letters to the Dead.

3. For a general discussion, see Alan H. Gardiner, *The Attitude of the Ancient Egyptians to Death and the Dead* (London: Cambridge University Press, 1935).

4. Gardiner and Sethe, *Egyptian Letters*, 10. See also William K. Simpson, "A Hatnub Stelae of Abydos," *Mitteilungen des deutschen archäologischen Instituts-Abteilung Kairo* 16 (1958): 298-309, and J. Zandee, *Death as an Enemy According to Ancient Egyptian Conceptions* (Leiden: Brill, 1960), 197-200.

5. See Dows Dunham, "The Biographical Inscriptions of Nekhebu in Boston and Cairo," *Journal of Egyptian Archaeology* 24 (1938): 1-8, for a discussion of a funerary stele in which the deceased reminds the living that they will want him to intercede for them in the necropolis, and therefore they should remember to make appropriate funerary offerings to his spirit.

6. The Cairo Text on Linen has two authors; a wife and a son write jointly to their deceased husband/father respectively. There are thus fourteen authors for thirteen Letters.

7. For a discussion of the food-offerings that were brought to the dead, see A. J. Spencer, *Death in Ancient Egypt* (Middlesex: Penguin, 1982), 54-61.

8. Only three of the texts, the Cairo Text on Linen, the Letter to the Dead from the Tomb of Meru, and the Letter to the Dead from Nag ed-Deir N3500, cannot, at this time, be connected in some manner with funerary offerings.

9. There are six Letters that were written on five bowls, the K̟aw bowl is inscribed with two Letters, one on its interior and the other on its exterior.

10. The mere presence of the offering bowl would indicate an offering in perpetuity.

11. Gardiner and Sethe, *Egyptian Letters*, 10.

12. Threatening the spirit with the cessation of funerary offerings is a common ploy mentioned in the Letters.

13. Other issues that these Letters address are more commonplace: one is a simple prayer for a male child, another is designed to ward off a specific nightmare, and three deal with sickness (either physical or psychological). The remaining three Letters rely totally on the prior knowledge of the deceased addressee and do not divulge the nature of the pleas.

14. For a general discussion, see S. G. F. Brandon, *The Judgment of the Dead* (London: Weidenfeld and Nicolson, 1967), chap. 1. Many of the Coffin Text spells were intended to assist the deceased when he went before the tribunal of the god(s). The standard artistic representation of the Egyptian nethercourt is the scene of the "weighing of the heart" regularly found in the Book of the Dead.

15. This is distinct from the phenomena of the dead participating in earthly court proceedings from their place in the netherworld. The prime example of that in Egypt is the trial after the murder of Ramses III in which the testimony of the dead king himself was used in the court; see Battiscombe Gunn, "Notes on Ammenemes I," *Journal of Egyptian Archaeology* 27 (1941): 2-6. The dead could also participate in judicial proceedings through oracles. The deified Amenophis I was approached with a case involving an inheritance dispute which he was to help adjudicate and deliver his decision via an oracle; see J. J. Janssen and P. W. Pestman, "Burial and Inheritance in the Community of the Necropolis Workmen at Thebes," *Journal of the Economic and Social History of the Orient* 11 (1968): 146.

16. In addition, the two Minoan Linear A bowls found at Knossos also have striking resemblances to the Letters to the Dead as well as to the Semitic Incantation bowls.

17. William Rossell, *A Handbook of Aramaic Magical Texts* (Ringwood, NJ: Shelton College, 1953), 122.

18. The primary element was the text, not the medium upon which it was written. The three Letters to the Dead which cannot be connected with offerings to the spirits still must have been considered efficacious by their authors, or they would not have been written in that manner.

19. Both of the bowls from Knossos have figures inked on the bottom of the bowls which cannot be part of the text and are most likely images of some sort.

20. Gardiner and Sethe, *Egyptian Letters*, 8. Until now this text was most recently treated by Cyrus H. Gordon, *Forgotten Scripts:*

Their Ongoing Discovery and Decipherment (New York: Basic Books, 1982), 182-83.

21. The Kaw Bowl consists of two distinct Letters, one written on the inside of the bowl, and the other on the outside.

22. A male determinative is used here.

23. A female determinative is used here.

24. Determined with both a male and a female sign.

25. Intef may or may not be the addressee: all that is evident from the text is that he is a Hm-ntr priest. It makes no practical difference, however, whether he is the husband to whom the letter is addressed, or whether he is simply a priest who is acting as intermediary, that is, as the deliverer of this petition. In this commentary, however, it will be assumed that the deceased is Intef. The difficulty inherent in understanding this text revolves around the identify of Imꜥw, not that of the other characters.

26. Gardiner and Sethe, *Egyptian Letters*, 7.

27. Mortuary priests could be hired to provide for the dead, but the major responsibility remained within the family. See Spencer, *Death in Ancient Egypt*, 54.

28. Or she might even employ the common device of "your sister."

29. Although it sounds contrite to the modern ear, epistolary style still encourages such usages, for example, "your humble servant."

30. T. G. H. James, *The Hekanakhte Papers and Other Middle Kingdom Documents* (New York: Metropolitan Museum of Art Egyptian Expedition, 1962), 128.

31. S. A. B. Mercer, *The Tell El-Amarna Tablets* (Toronto: Macmillan Company of Canada, 1939), 728-29. For further examples see *The Assyrian Dictionary*, Ignace J. Gelb et al., eds. (Chicago: Oriental Institute, 1960-), vol. 1, pt. 2, 251, s.v. *ardu*.

32. Another expression of personal humility employed in the Bible and the cuneiform world is "dog." See 2 Samuel 7:21 and 1 Chronicles 17:19; in both of these examples the Masoretes have pointed the word to read "your heart," but they should read "your dog" as a parallel to "your servant." For Akkadian examples, see *The Assyrian Dictionary* 8:72, s.v. *kalbu*.

33. Whether her illness is physical or psychological is undetermined.

34. Gardiner and Sethe, *Egyptian Letters*, 8.

35. See 'Abd el-Mohsen Bakir, *Egyptian Epistolography from the Eighteenth to the Twenty-first Dynasty* (Cairo: Institut Français d'ar-

cheologie orientale du Caire, 1970), 29-32, for a discussion of delivering letters, and the name of the deliverer as part of the address.

36. ᶜebed-YHWH (Deuteronomy 34:5 ad passim), ᶜebed 'Ādōnāi (Daniel 10:17), and ᶜebed ha-'Ĕlōhîm (Daniel 9:11, Nehemiah 10:30, 1 Chronicles 6:34, and 2 Chronicles 24:9) are all biblical terms for servant of God/the Lord.

37. Erik Hornung, *Conceptions of God in Ancient Egypt: The One and the Many* (Oxford: Griffith Institute at the University Press, 1976), 27.

38. In most other instances Jewish custom dictates using the patronymic.

39. William A. Ward, "Comparative Studies in Egyptian and Ugaritic," *Journal of Near Eastern Studies* 20 (1961): 36.

40. For a discussion of Levirate marriage, see Clair Gottlieb, "Varieties of Marriage in the Old Testament," Ph.D. diss., New York University, 1989.

41. For the physical description of and the rationale for dating this bowl to the Eleventh Dynasty, see Gardiner and Sethe, *Egyptian Letters*, 5.

42. The Letter to the Dead which most closely approximates this pattern of inscription is the Letter to the Dead on a Bowl in the Louvre which combines both circular and spiral writing. The first line of the text is a complete circle, and the second line spirals down to the center of the bowl.

43. For Gardiner's rendition of the portrait, see Gardiner and Sethe, *Egyptian Letters*, pl. 5.

44. There is also an indication of the beginning of one arm.

45. Gardiner and Sethe, *Egyptian Letters*, 7. Battiscombe Gunn, "Notices of Recent Publications," *Journal of Egyptian Archaeology* 16 (1938): 152, feels that the picture of the deceased is a "symbolic way of addressing the communication."

46. Stylistically, the Berlin Bowl has many parallels with the Aramaic Incantation bowls. The circular inscription is akin to the spiral writing commonly found on the Incantation bowls as well as on the two Minoan Linear A bowls found at Knossos. The central figure is also an element familiar from these bowls. It should be noted, however, that the figures on the Incantation bowls are usually demonic.

47. Reading with Gardiner and Sethe, *Egyptian Letters*, 7.

48. The wish is for these two gods also to grant the desires of the deceased. See line notes below.

49. Only the last two elements of the name of the addressee and the feminine determinative are visible after the lacuna.

50. The necropolis.

51. Reading with Gunn, "Notices of Recent Publications," 152.

52. A case could be made for the author of the letter being the son of the deceased. After all, the evil appears to affect the children, "behold the house of your children" (line 1), "for the sake of your children" (line 2). The first person pronominal suffix is used only once in the text (line 1), which could be understood as a reference to the one who fulfilled the obligation of burial: "You were buried (by me) without any of your spells against me." But this reading, making the sender the son, would, of course, raise many unanswerable questions—What happened to the father/husband? Why isn't the letter addressed to "Mother"? and so forth. Since the letter does not cite the relationships of the individuals to each other, any one rendering would only be speculative. Therefore, we must go along with an interpretation that appears to make the most logical sense: the sender is the widower, and the addressee is his deceased wife.

53. Translated from A. de Buck, *Egyptian Readingbook* (Chicago: Ares, 1977), 105.

54. See also 1 Kings 16:4.

55. Vergil, *The Aeneid*, tr. W. F. Jackson Knight (Middlesex: Penguin, 1956), 157.

56. Ibid., 158.

57. Tobit 1:16-20. Bruce Metzger, tr., *The Apocrypha of the Old Testament* (New York: Oxford University Press, 1965), 64.

58. Tobit reflects Zoroastrian religious institutions in the Persian Empire.

59. The phrase "against me" in sentence 2 indicates that the troubles are not just affecting their children.

60. Alan H. Gardiner, *Egyptian Grammar*, 3rd ed. (Oxford: Griffith Institute, 1957), 170-71.

61. Raymond O. Faulkner, *A Concise Dictionary of Middle Egyptian* (Oxford: Griffith Institute, 1976), 20.

62. Gardiner, *Egyptian Grammar*, 155.

63. James, *Hekanakhte Papers*, 110-11.

64. To his "grave."

65. For a discussion of this reading, see Cyrus H. Gordon, "Hby, Possessor of Horns and Tail," *Ugarit-Forschungen* 18 (1986): 131.

66. UT 19.1002.

67. As observed by Constance Wallace in a private communication.

68. Gilgamesh, Odysseus, and Aeneas are but three legendary mortals whose travels took them to the realm of the dead where they actually spoke with the spirits whom they encountered.

69. The fact that necromancy was outlawed indicates that it was a widespread practice. The professionals, like the Witch of Endor, must have had a following, for there is no need to prohibit something which is rare or nonexistent.

70. The Egyptians felt that their Letters were answered when the situations they were complaining about were rectified.

71. Gunn, "Notices of Recent Publications," 152.

72. Ibid.

73. Read *mᶜ* with Gardiner and Sethe, *Egyptian Letters*, 22.

9

Milk and Meat: Unlikely Bedfellows

Jacob Milgrom
University of California, Berkeley, California

The prohibition *lō'-təḇaššel gəḏî beḥalēḇ 'immô*, "you shall not boil a kid in its mother's milk," appears thrice in the Old Testament (Exodus 23:19; 34:26; Deuteronomy 14:21). In Exodus it concludes an appendage to the cultic calendar of sacrificial offerings, but in Deuteronomy it is part of the dietary prohibitions. The change that has occurred between the time of Exodus and Deuteronomy bears investigation, as does the absence of this prohibition from Leviticus. But first, what does this prohibition mean? The rabbis claim that it mandates an absolute ban on mixing dairy and meat dishes, and they interpret its threefold occurrence as prohibiting the eating, cooking, or profiting from such a mixture.[1] The rabbinic solution seems so removed from the plain meaning of the text that we shall, for the present, pass it by without further comment.

Scanning the legion of interpretations put forth through the ages, there are four that merit consideration. One firmly established view is that this prohibition is directed against Canaanite cultic practice. It was first proposed by Maimonides:

> As for the prohibition against eating meat [boiled] in milk, it is in my opinion not improbable that—in addition to this being undoubtedly very gross food and very filling—*idolatry* had something to do with it. Perhaps such food was eaten at one of the ceremonies of

144

their cult or at one of their festivals. A confirmation of this may, in my opinion, be found in the fact that the prohibition against eating "meat [boiled] in milk," when it is mentioned for the first two times, occurs near the commandment concerning pilgrimage: "Three times in the year," and so on (Exodus 23:17; 34:23). It is as if it said: When you go on pilgrimage and enter "the house of the Lord your God" (Exodus 23:19; 34:26), do not cook there in the way they used to do. According to me this is the most probable (lit., the strongest) view regarding the reason for this prohibition; but I have not seen this set down in any of the books of the Sabians (idolaters) that I have read.[2]

Maimonides' opinion that eating a kid boiled in its mother's milk was an idolatrous rite has been championed by commentators down to the present day who, however, have glossed over[3] Maimonides' admission that he had no evidence for it.

Nonetheless, a powerful impetus was given the view, some fifty years ago, with the unearthing of the second millennium Ugaritic texts at Ras Shamra, a site on the Mediterranean coast of Syria. In one of its mythological tablets, the following line appears: *ṭb[ḫg]d bḥlb annḫ bḥmat*,[4] which was translated as "Coo[k a ki]d in milk, a lamb (?) in butter."[5] This text, it should be noted, being broken, requires reconstruction. The reconstruction is, at best, an educated guess — undoubtedly influenced by our biblical prohibition. However, this reconstruction was accepted at once by virtually every interpreter,[6] and it became a dogma of scholarship that Maimonides' intuition concerning the practice as a pagan rite was correct. A notable early skeptic was Gordon,[7] who suggested that "*ṭb[ḫ]*" could mean "slaughter." Other objections posed by Loewenstamm[8] and reinforced by Haran[9] have once and for all vitiated the reconstruction. The objections are as follows:

(1) The broken passage must now be read differently:

ṭb.(?)[*g*]*d*,[10] which indicates that the dividing mark between the two words follows *ṭb*, thereby leaving no room for adding the letter *ḥ*. Thus the reconstruction *ṭb*[*ḥ*]," must be rejected.

(2) Moreover, even were the reconstruction correct, *ṭbḥ* does not mean "cook," but "slaughter."[11]

(3) The probability is that the term *annḥ*, contained in the next clause, corresponding to Akkadian *ananiḥu*, which means "garden" or "plant,"[12] does not refer to an animal but to an herb.[13]

(4) It therefore follows that [*g*]*d* — presuming the correctness of the reconstruction — cannot mean "kid" but, since it must correspond in meaning to the parallel word *annḥ*, also connotes a plant. Hence, *ṭb*[*ḥ*] — keeping in mind that the reading is speculative — cannot mean "slaughter," a term hardly appropriate for a plant.

(5) Finally, there is nothing in the text which states that the kid (?) was cooked (?) in the milk of *its mother*, in which case it has absolutely nothing to do with our biblical prohibition!

In sum, the Ugaritic text in question is a broken one, its suggested reconstruction is palpably wrong, its clearer portion has been misconstrued, and a key word of the biblical prohibition, "mother," is not there. In recent memory, nothing matches this example of the hazards in interpreting broken texts on the basis of a purported biblical echo. Thus, the cultic theory cannot be grounded in Ugaritic practice and, without any support, biblical or extrabiblical, it must be abandoned.

The second theory, also a respected one, espouses a humanitarian interpretation. It originates with Philo of Alexandria who writes as follows:

> He has forbidden any lamb or kid or other like kind of livestock to be snatched away from its mother before it is weaned [cf. Exodus 22:29; Leviticus 22:27]. . . . If indeed anyone thinks [it] good to boil flesh in milk, let

him do so without cruelty and keeping clear of im-
piety. . . . The person who boils the flesh of lambs or
kids or any other young animal in their mother's milk,
shows himself cruelly brutal in character and gelded of
compassion.[14]

Philo's focus on cruelty as the basis for the prohibition
is echoed by Clement of Alexandria[15] and, independently,
by Ibn Ezra[16] and Rashbam (who surely were unaware of
both Philo and Clement).[17] Among moderns, this view is
championed by Haran[18] and Ginsberg[19] who, in agreement
with Philo, argue that the kid law is cut of the same cloth
as the prohibition against slaughtering the dam and its
offspring on the same day (Leviticus 22:28), sacrificing the
newborn during the first week of its life (Leviticus 22:27;
Exodus 22:29), or taking the mother bird together with its
young (Deuteronomy 22:6-7).

Haran builds on the arguments of Ginsberg and Dalman to support his humanitarian theory. Ginsberg suggests, citing Dalman,[20] that he-goats, unlike rams, are ex-
pendable since they provide neither wool nor palatable
meat, and therefore it must have been a common practice
to dispose of one's superfluous male kids during the Sukkot festival.[21] The attribution of this prohibition to Sukkot
would appear to be justified both from its position in the
biblical text when it occurs after injunctions concerning the
other two pilgrimage festivals, Pesach and Shavuot (Exodus 23:18-19; 34:25-26), and from its zoological basis, since
goats give birth to their young in the rainy season which
begins in autumn. "Therefore," argues Haran, "the Israelite is warned that during the feast of ingathering, the
most exuberant and joyful of the annual pilgrim-feasts,
celebrated with much food and drink and the choicest
delicacies—he must remember not to seethe a kid in its
mother's milk, . . . a deliberate reminder of humane behavior even in the midst of general jollity."[22]

If, however, humanitarianism is the motivation, should

not our prohibition embrace all animals instead of being restricted to a kid? Look at the other cited animal prohibitions. It may be true that one may not slaughter the dam and its young on the same day (Leviticus 22:28), but surely it was permitted on successive days. The newborn must be permitted to suckle for seven days (Leviticus 22:27; Exodus 22:29), but on the eighth day it may be brought to the altar—even though it is still suckling. The mother bird and her fledglings or eggs may not be taken together (Deuteronomy 22:6), but surely they may be taken separately (Deuteronomy 22:7). By the same token, the mother goat can in no way be aware that her kid is boiling in her milk. Incidentally, there is genuine doubt whether this prohibition can be tied to the Sukkot festival. Weaning time for goats begins in December[23]—at least two months after Sukkot! Thus, it is more likely that this prohibition was intended to be enforced at all the pilgrimage festivals or, for that matter, whenever a sacrifice was offered at the sanctuary. In any event, the humanitarian theory must give way to another.

Recently, under the influence of the French school of structural anthropology, which has proven so helpful in understanding Leviticus 11,[24] a third theory has been propounded. Starting with the Durkheimian hypothesis that a customary or legal prohibition reflects some societal taboo, J. Soler interprets the kid law as meaning: "You shall not put a mother and her son into the same pot any more than into the same bed."[25] That is to say, it is an injunction against incest.[26] This theory is fascinating but it is undermined by one glaring fault: the word $g\partial\underline{d}\hat{\imath}$, "kid," is asexual. Indeed, in biblical Hebrew, animal names that are masculine in form and have no female counterpart denote both sexes. Thus, in Isaiah's vision of messianic bliss (Isaiah 11:6), the $z\partial'\underline{e}\underline{b}$, "wolf"; $ke\underline{b}e\acute{s}$, "lamb"; $n\bar{a}m\bar{e}r$, "leopard"; and—to cite our case—$g\partial\underline{d}\hat{\imath}$, "kid" are generic names, applying to both male and female of each species. A more instructive proof text is the one cited above: "You shall not slaughter a cow (*šôr*) or ewe (*śeh*) and its young (*bƏnô*) on the same day" (Leviticus 22:28). Despite the use of the masculine forms *šôr* and *śeh* for the parent and *bēn* for the child, the mother and her offspring of either sex are clearly intended. To be sure, as indicated above, the economically unviable male kids were slaughtered for their meat. However, the prohibition as its stands applies to the female as well. Had it been restricted to the male it would have been so worded, e.g., *gƏdî zākār*, "a male kid" (cf. *śeh zākār*, "a male sheep," Exodus 12:5) or *zākār bāizzîm*, "male of the goats" (cf. *zākār babbāqār*, "male of the herd," Leviticus 22:19). Just as it is forbidden to slaughter the mother on the same day as her young — of either sex — so it is forbidden to cook the young — of either sex — in its mother's milk. The social anthropologists, I believe, are correct: society's values are mirrored in its laws and mores, especially in its food taboos. However, in this case, they picked the wrong one.

A fourth, and more fruitful, approach has recently been broached by O. Keel.[27] His iconographic studies in ancient Near Eastern art have led him to the plethora of seals and ceramic and rock tomb-paintings which feature the motif of a mother animal suckling her young. The symbolism takes on cosmic dimensions as soon as it is realized that the portrayed animals can stand for divinities. For example, in Egypt, the human (or animal) nursing at the udders of the cow-goddess Hathor (or another animal divinity) is the young Pharaoh himself. The suckling mother, according to Keel, is thus the symbol of the love and tenderness that are sustained by the divine order of the universe.[28] Since this image, as it appears in the art of Syro-Palestine, is not attributable to any particular deity, it would have encountered no difficulty being incorporated into the monotheism of ancient Israel. There, it would have resulted in a taboo against cooking a kid in its mother's milk, a culinary practice which in effect would have opposed and vitiated the life-sustaining and divinely ordained nurture inherent in all living beings.

Keel, I submit, is on the right track. His explanation, more so than the humanitarian theory, throws clearer light on the prohibition to slay the mother and its young simultaneously (Leviticus 22:28). Here he is in accord with Philo, whom he quotes, that "it is the height of savagery to slay on the same day the generating cause and the living creature generated."[29] Yet when applied to the kid prohibition, Keel's theory does not fully satisfy. The mother has been separated from her young. Thus the image of the suckling mother, which represents the transmission of the life-sustaining force proceeding from generation to generation, is not present. More to the point is another of Philo's comments: "[It is] grossly improper that the substance which fed the living animal should be used to season and flavor the same after its death . . . [and that] the license of man should rise to such a height as to misuse what has sustained its life to destroy also the body which remains in existence."[30] This citation is used by C. M. Carmichael[31] to propose that the root rationale behind the kid prohibition is in opposing the commingling of life and death.[32] A substance which sustains the life of a creature (milk) should not be fused or confused with a process associated with its death (cooking). This would be but another instance of the binary opposition characteristic of biblical ritual and praxis: to separate life from death, holy from common, pure from impure, Israel from the nations.

Both ideas inhering in the kid prohibition—the reverence for life and Israel's separation from the nations—are also present in the dietary laws, the former in the blood prohibition and the latter in the animal prohibitions.[33] Thus the kid prohibition was automatically locked into Israel's dietary system. Therefore, it should occasion no surprise that the kid prohibition, which in Exodus is related to the cult and sacrifices, is transformed in Deuteronomy into a dietary law. Deuteronomy, it should be recalled, has transferred the act of slaughtering an animal for its flesh from the sanctuary to the home. With the centralization of worship at the Temple, Deuteronomy had to enact a concomitant law permitting common slaughter in order to obviate the necessity of journeying to the Temple each time a family desired meat for the table.[34] The result is that the taboo of cooking a kid in its mother's milk, which needed but to be observed within the sanctuary compound while under priestly supervision, henceforth had to be heeded by every Israelite family, without outside supervision, in every kitchen.

The life versus death theory, I submit, completely and neatly elucidates the other prohibitions which, heretofore, have been explained as humane. The common denominator of all these prohibitions is the fusion and confusion of life and death *simultaneously*. Thus, the life-giving process of the mother bird hatching or feeding her young (Deuteronomy 22:6) should not be the occasion of their joint death. The sacrifice of the newborn may be inevitable, but not for the first week while it is constantly at its mother's breast (Leviticus 22:27), and never should both the mother and its young be slain at the same time (Leviticus 22:28). By the same token, the mother's milk, the life-sustaining food for her kid, should never become associated with its death.

Is it then so far-fetched for the rabbis to have deduced that all meat (not just that of the kid) and all milk (not only that of the mother) may not be served together? Their interpretation is clearly an old one. It is already adumbrated in the third-century B.C.E. Septuagint which translates the word *gǝdî* in all three occurrences of the prohibition — but only there — not as "kid" but as "sheep." By the first century C.E. the tradition is recorded by Philo that the prohibition applies to "the flesh of lambs or kids or any other young animal."[35] One cannot say that Philo is dependent upon the Palestinian rabbis for his teaching since he holds, contrary to their view, that the prohibited milk is only that of the animal's mother (a view also held subsequently by the Karaites).[36] Alexandria, then, the home of the Septuagint and Philo, must have harbored a tradition which had extended the biblical prohibition to embrace all animals. It is, therefore, not too difficult to foresee that the next logical step would have been to forbid the use of any milk with any meat. For milk, the life-sustaining force of the animal, should not commingle with meat, the animal that has met its death.

The binary opposition of life and death is also at the root of the severe impurities that are the subject of Leviticus 12-15.[37] It is therefore fitting and logical that Leviticus 11, the chapter that ensconces the life-death principle in the laws dealing with animal impurities, be the prelude to the same principle in the laws dealing with human impurities.

Is it, therefore, not puzzling that the kid prohibition which also embodies this principle does not occur in Leviticus 11? Only one answer, I submit, is possible. The deuteronomic transformation has not yet taken place. Leviticus still breathes the atmosphere of Exodus. Cooking a kid in its mother's milk is still a cultic act, a sacrifice that takes place in the sanctuary under the control of the priests. It is still not the concern of the home, a radical change which only Deuteronomy engineered. Here, once more, is another indication of the preexilic and predeuteronomic origin of the priestly laws in the book of Leviticus.[38]

[Completed March 1985]

Notes

1. M *Ḥullin* 8:4; *Mekhilta Mishpatim*, par. 20; M *Ḥullin* 115b (bar.).

2. Moses Maimonides, *The Guide of the Perplexed*, tr. Shlomo Pines, 2 vols. (Chicago: University of Chicago Press, 1963), part 3:48.

3. Although Umberto Cassuto, *A Commentary on the Book of Ex-*

odus, tr. Israel Abrahams (Jerusalem: Hebrew University, 1951, 1983), 305, does acknowledge that Maimonides was conjecturing.

4. UT 62:14 in G. R. Driver and J. C. L. Gibson, eds., *Canaanite Myths and Legends*, 2nd ed. (Edinburgh: T&T Clark, 1978), 123.

5. Louis Ginsberg, "Notes on 'The Birth of the Gracious and Beautiful Gods,' " *Journal of the Royal Asiatic Society of Great Britain and Ireland* (1935): 65; cf. Charles Virolleaud, "La naissance des dieux gracieux et beaux," *Syria* 14 (1933): 140.

6. For example, Cassuto, *A Commentary on the Book of Exodus*, 305; Driver and Gibson, *Canaanite Myths and Legends*, 123; Theodore M. Gaster, *Thespis* (New York: Gordon Press, 1961, 1975), 407-9, 422-23; Hans Kosmala, "The So-Called Ritual Decalogue," *Annual of the Swedish Theological Institute* 1 (1962): 52-53; Loren R. Fisher, *Ras Shamra Parallels*, 3 vols. (Rome: Pontificium Institutum Biblicum, 1972-81), 29.

7. Cyrus M. Gordon, *Ugaritic Handbook* (Rome: Pontificium Institutum Biblicum, 1947), 232.

8. Samuel E. Loewenstamm, "Lexicographical Notes on 1. ṭbḥ; 2. ḥnny/ḥlny," *Ugarit-Forschungen* 5 (1973): 209.

9. Menahem Haran, "Seething a Kid in Its Mother's Milk," *Journal of Jewish Studies* 20 (1979): 25.

10. Andrée Herdner, *Corpus des Tablettes en Cuneiformes Alphabétiques*, 2 vols. (Paris: Imprimerie Nationale, 1963), 98.

11. Jacob Milgrom, "Profane Slaughter and a Formulaic Key to the Composition of Deuteronomy," *Hebrew Union College Annual* 47 (1976): 1-17.

12. *The Assyrian Dictionary*, Ignace J. Gelb et al., eds. (Chicago: Oriental Institute, 1956–), part 2, 1:111, s.v. ananiḫu.

13. Joseph Aistleitner, *Untersuchungen zur Grammatik des Ugaritischen* (Berlin: Akademie Verlag, 1954), 41; Driver and Gibson, *Canaanite Myths and Legends*, 123, who translate it as "coriander"; André Caquot, Maurice Sznycer, and Andrée Herdner, *Textes Ougaritiques I* (Paris: Éditions du Cerf, 1974), 371, n.q.

14. Philo, *De Virtutibus* 142-44. The English translation here used is F. H. Colson's in the Loeb classics series (Cambridge: Harvard University Press, 1968), 8:250-51.

15. Clement, *Stromata* II, 18 (cited by Haran, "Seething a Kid in Its Mother's Milk," 29).

16. Abraham Ibn Ezra, *Commentary on the Pentateuch*.

17. Ibid.

18. Haran, "Seething a Kid in Its Mother's Milk," 29.

19. Harold L. Ginsberg, *The Jewish Israelian Heritage of Judaism in America* (New York: Jewish Theological Seminary, 1982), 52, n. 69.

20. Gustaf Dalman, *Arbeit und Sitte in Palästina*, 6 vols. (Gütersloh: Bertelsmann, 1928-39), 6:189.

21. Ginsberg, *The Jewish Israelian Heritage*, 53; cf. also Isaac Abravanel, *Exordium Commentariorum in Leviticum* (London: Flesher, 1683).

22. Haran, "Seething a Kid in Its Mother's Milk," 35.

23. Y. Ahituv, "*Šō'n*," in Umberto Cassuto et al., eds., *Encyclopaedia Miqrait*, 8 vols. (Jerusalem: Bialik Institute, 1954-76), 6:648.

24. Jacob Milgrom, *Leviticus*, Anchor Bible (Garden City, NY: Doubleday, forthcoming), vol 1.

25. Jean Soler, "Sémiotique de la nourriture dans la Bible," *Annales Economies Sociétés Civilisations* 28 (1973): 943-55. "The Dietary Prohibitions of the Hebrews," tr. Elborg Forster, *New York Review* 26/10 (June 1979): 24, cf. 30.

26. Fully developed by Francis Martens, "Diététhique ou la cuisine de Dieu," *Communications* 26 (1977): 16-45.

27. Othmar Keel, *Das Böcklein in der Milch seiner Mutter und Verwandtes* (Göttingen: Vandenhoeck and Ruprecht, 1980).

28. Ibid., 51.

29. Philo, *De Virtutibus* 134.

30. Ibid., 143.

31. Calum M. Carmichael, "On Separating Life and Death: An Explanation of Some Biblical Laws," *Harvard Theological Review* 69 (1976): 1-7.

32. Compare Arthur Weyne, "Why We Do Not Mix Meat and Milk," *American Examiner*, Thursday, 31 March 1960, 13.

33. Milgrom, *Leviticus*, vol. 1.

34. Milgrom, "Profane Slaughter."

35. Philo, *De Virtutibus* 144.

36. Leon Nemoy, *Karaite Anthology* (New Haven, CT: Yale University Press, 1952), 267.

37. Milgrom, *Leviticus*, vol. 1.

38. See Jacob Milgrom, *Studies in Cultic Theology and Terminology* (Leiden: Brill, 1983), 104-18.

10

The Book of Daniel in Early Mormon Thought

David J. Whittaker
Brigham Young University, Provo, Utah

Responding to a revelation that he and select associates "journey to the land of Missouri," Joseph Smith visited the state for the first time in July and August 1831. Traveling from his newly established home in Ohio, he concentrated his visit in western Missouri, south of the Missouri River, where several of his followers had arrived earlier. On 20 July 1831 he identified Missouri as the land God had "appointed and consecrated for the gathering of the saints. Wherefore, this is the land of promise, and the place for the city of Zion" (D&C 57:1-2).[1] Two days later ground was dedicated for the construction of a temple.

After returning to Kirtland, Joseph delivered a revelatory summary of his work in Missouri to those followers who had remained in Ohio:

> The keys of the kingdom of God are committed unto man on the earth, and from thence shall the gospel roll forth unto the ends of the earth, as the stone which is cut out of the mountain without hands shall roll forth, until it has filled the whole earth. . . . Call upon the Lord, that his kingdom may go forth upon the earth, that the inhabitants thereof may receive it, and be prepared for the days to come, in the which the Son of Man

Versions of this essay were presented at the American Academy of Religion Annual Meeting, Boston, Massachusetts, December 1987, and at the Mormon History Association Annual Meeting, Logan, Utah, May 1988.

shall come down in heaven, clothed in the brightness of his glory, to meet the kingdom of God which is set up on the earth (D&C 65:2, 5).[2]

Thus, as early as 1831, the image of the "stone cut out of the mountain without hands" (Daniel 2:44) was tied to the Mormon kingdom of God, particularly in Missouri. It is clear from a variety of sources that the book of Daniel was used by early Mormons to predict and justify the triumph of the kingdom they felt sure would be the outcome of their missionary work. This paper examines in more detail the role of the book of Daniel in early Mormonism by focusing on the 1830s, and more particularly on its place in the religious and political culture of the early Mormon Church.[3] What is attempted here is an invitation to further study on this subject.

The Book of Daniel in Western Culture

The book of Daniel reports the events in the life of a Judean exile at the court of Babylon beginning about 605 B.C. The first six chapters describe certain events that occurred to Daniel and three of his companions in this captivity over about a seventy-year period. The remaining six chapters, written in the first person, record a series of visions of future events. The original texts are in two languages: Daniel 2:4-7:28 are in Aramaic; the rest, in Hebrew.

As Joseph had been in Egypt at the beginning of Israel's history, Daniel is in Babylon at the beginning of the critical period of the Exile. Like Joseph, Daniel is tempted, but remains faithful to Israel's God. And, like Joseph, Daniel interpreted dreams and was used by God to influence the political events of his world.

The significant stories of the book include the blessings of abstinence from wine (chap. 1); the delivery of the three persons from the fiery furnace (chap. 3); Daniel's interpreting the handwriting on the wall (chap. 5); and Daniel in the lion's den (chap. 6). Perhaps the most influential part of the volume was Daniel's interpretation of the king's dream (chap. 2) in which the kingdoms of the world in the last days are described as being finally destroyed by a stone cut out of the mountain without hands which rolled forth until it filled the earth. The final chapters (7-12) seem to provide more detail on these events of the last days during which the "Ancient of Days" would play a significant role, as will the "saints of the most high."

Regardless of the arguments relating to the origin of the book of Daniel, whether the Cycle of Daniel stories really date to the sixth century B.C. or, as is more commonly believed by scholars, to the events of the second century B.C., where its apocalyptic messages provided inspiration for the Jews during the Maccabean Revolt, it is clear that the volume was heavily influenced by the author of 1 Enoch and that Daniel's book in turn helped shape the early Christian book of Revelation.[4] Its prophetic timetable and its vision of the collapse of the four world kingdoms before the triumph of the fifth and final kingdom has provided grist for the mills of millennial movements ever since.[5]

Interestingly, it was while writing commentaries on the book of Daniel that the first Christian histories were produced in the third century A.D.[6] Utopian groups throughout European history have also found inspiration in Daniel. Even the English Reformation and later the Puritan Revolution made effective use of its themes.[7] For all of these groups the book of Daniel reminded and reinforced in true believers (1) that God's purposes are greater than the plans of men; (2) that God is the sovereign Lord over the whole history of mankind; and (3) that God will at last vindicate his people, Israel. Daniel's prophecies also assured the faithful that the end was near when God's kingdom would triumph over all others.[8]

The American Puritan search for self-identity was heavily influenced by biblical metaphors. As Sacvan Bercovich and others have shown, Puritan typology drew on the book of Daniel, as is evidenced particularly in many early American sermons, histories, and biographies. Thus the ideological roots of the American identity were early worked out in biblical terms. As a biblically conceptualized nation, America's colonial founders combined providence and patriotism in ways that used biblical metaphors (such as Daniel) that "Americanized" the Millennium.[9] John Berens has argued that this Puritan heritage included (1) the early identification of America as God's New Israel; (2) the jeremiad tradition, particularly the election and fast-day sermons; (3) the blending of national and millennial expectations; and (4) providential history and historiography.[10] Together, these presupposed and thus assured the faithful of God's involvement in history as he led and protected his people. Combined, they helped shape American political culture at the same time they grounded it solidly in biblical images. While they looked back to ancient scripture, they also looked forward to the Millennium.[11]

America's founding fathers obviously drew on this heritage. From its start, but especially during its Revolutionary years, American political ideology drew on the Bible to justify the emerging nation's special place and divine mission in world history. Thus our Revolutionary forefathers found in the book of Daniel an apocalyptic rationale for their own work.[12]

Book of Daniel in Early Mormon Thought, 1823-37

One of the few Smith family documents that has been preserved from the eighteenth century was a letter of Asael Smith, Joseph Smith's grandfather. Written to Jacob Town in January 1796, it clearly reflects the Revolutionary rhetoric which incorporated views taken from Daniel chapter 2:

> He [speaking of the "supreme ruler"] has conducted us through a glorious Revolution and has brought us into the promised land of peace and liberty, and I believe that He is about to bring all the world into the same

beatitude in His own time and way; which, altho' His way may appear never so inconsistent to our blind reason, yet may be perfectly consistent with His designs. And I believe that the stone is now cut out of the mountain without hands, and has smitten the image upon his feet, by which the iron, the clay, the brass, the silver and the gold, *viz.*, all the monarchial and ecclesiastical tyranny will be broken to pieces and become as the chaff of the summer thrashing floor, the wind shall carry them all away, that there shall be no place found for them.[13]

Throughout his life, Joseph Smith was exposed to and influenced by the themes and images of the book of Daniel. Wilford Woodruff, a close associate and careful record keeper, reported that one of the scriptures cited by the angel Moroni to the young Joseph Smith in September 1823 was Daniel 2.[14] Toward the end of his life, the Mormon prophet taught, "I calculate to be one of the instruments in setting up the kingdom of Daniel."[15] Clearly, the book of Daniel gave focus and meaning to his mission. Just how important it was becomes apparent when we examine more closely the early years of the Mormon movement.

In spite of critics' statements to the contrary, Mormonism is a biblical religion. Its founding prophet and his followers grew up with, respected, and regularly used the biblical text in their quest for self-understanding as well as in rationalizing and defending the restored Church. Joseph Smith never taught that the Book of Mormon was a replacement for the Bible, and his own "new translation" of the Bible was, from our perspective today, a very conservative work which modified or enlarged (in targumic fashion) barely 10 percent of the total verses in the KJV, and the bulk of these were found in only five books (Genesis and the four Gospels).[16] He loved and believed in the Bible, and no serious study of his life and thought can ignore this fact. The book of Daniel and its use in the early Church provides further evidence for this view.

As shown above, the book of Daniel (esp. chap. 2) was early tied into the Mormon experience in Missouri, and specifically into their quest for Zion and the kingdom of God. Other revelations given by Joseph Smith to the Church contain phrases and concepts from the book of Daniel. In August 1830, a revelation identified the "Ancient of Days" in Daniel 7 as Adam (D&C 27:11).[17] In March 1831, another revelation spoke of the New Jerusalem, which was to be built in Jackson County, as a "place of safety for the saints of the Most High God" (D&C 45:66).[18] In December 1832, another revelation used the phrase "desolation of abomination" of Daniel 9:27 (D&C 88:85).[19] Also the Mormon health code, the Word of Wisdom, promises wisdom and health to those who obey its counsel in a manner possibly reminiscent of Daniel 1.[20] In February 1834, after Parley P. Pratt and Lyman Wight had arrived in Ohio from Missouri to seek counsel regarding the Mormon expulsion from Jackson County, Daniel 2 may be alluded to in a revelation explaining why the Saints had been persecuted.[21] It was in this context that an "army of Israel" [Zion's Camp] was to be organized to "lift up an ensign of peace."[22] In March 1835, additional revelation spoke for the first time of the Valley of Adam-ondi-Ahman where Adam, "the Ancient of Days," had blessed his own family anciently (D&C 107:53-54).[23] In May 1838 its exact location in northern Missouri was identified.[24]

When the Kirtland Temple was dedicated in March 1836, the dedicatory prayer petitioned the Lord to remember "that the kingdom, which thou hast set up without hands, may become a great mountain and fill the whole earth. That thy church may come forth out of the wilderness of darkness, and shine forth fair as the moon, clear as the sun, and terrible as an army with banners."[25] And when the commandment to build a temple at Far West, Missouri, came in April 1838, it was justified in terms of Daniel's visions.[26]

This emphasis on Daniel in the early revelations was also reflected in early Mormon newspapers. As early as September 1832, *The Evening and the Morning Star* (Independence, Missouri) cited Daniel 2 in its discussion of the future of the Church.[27] In the February 1833 issue it printed a letter from a missionary who enthusiastically reported his work in these terms: "Thus you see brethren that the cause of truth is prospering, and thanks be to our God . . . and as good old Daniel said, his kingdom shall break in pieces all other kingdoms, so it shall be done."[28] In May 1833, the same periodical declared, "There are great things near, and while one nation rises to rejoice, behold another sits down to weep. Verily the fountains of the nations will soon be broken up, for the Lord hath decreed a consumption, and none can stay his hand; yea, as Daniel said: unto the end of the war desolations are determined."[29]

Such emphasis continued in the Mormon press. By 1835 Mormon elders were thoroughly immersed in Daniel typology. The extant records of several early missionaries confirm this.[30] Writing to Oliver Cowdery in November 1835, William W. Phelps wrote that the stone of Daniel 2 started rolling out of the mountain with the coming forth of the Book of Mormon: "There began the church of Christ in 1830; yea, there the stone cut out of the mountain without hands, as foretold by Daniel, commenced rolling to fill the earth, and may it continue, in a moral sense, in dreadful splendor, till it fills the whole, and wickedness is ended. So much for the Hill Cumorah."[31] By 1836 the same periodical, the *LDS Messenger and Advocate* (Kirtland, Ohio) was equating the "Saints of the Most High" in Daniel with members of the Church.[32] And in September 1837, this periodical carried a letter from the Kirtland bishopric in which members there were admonished to endure their troubles so that "the foundation of the kingdom of God might be laid on a sure and certain basis, so that the prophetic vision of Daniel might most certainly be fulfilled.

That this kingdom might break in pieces all other king-doms, and stand forever."[33]

Early Mormon hymnals were another outlet for poetic sentiments that took seriously the visions of Daniel. In the first such collection (1835), at least four hymns incorporated such imagery. Consider these examples:

> The prophecies must be fulfill'd
> Though earth and hell should dare oppose;
> The stone out of the mountain cut,
> Though unobserved, a Kingdom grows.[34]

> As Clouds see them fly to their glorious home—
> As doves to their windows in flocks see them come,
> While empires shall tremble and kingdoms shall rend
> And thrones be cast down as wise Daniel proclaimed.

> And Israel shall flourish and spread far abroad,
> Till earth shall be full of the knowledge of God:
> And thus shall the stone of the mountain roll forth—
> Extend its dominion, and fill the whole earth.[35]

Other hymn texts relating to Daniel could be cited,[36] but these examples illustrate how saturated early Mormon thought was in Daniel typology.

It seems apparent, then, that the kingdom of God in early Mormon thought was identified with the fifth king-dom of Daniel 2, the "stone cut out without hands."[37] Even the United States Constitution, while honored and re-spected by early leaders as a hallowed document, was viewed as but a prelude to the ultimate government by God and his chosen servants.[38] While American protestants saw and encouraged a secularization of the Puritan vision, early Mormons carried it to its logical conclusion.

This vision had serious implications. For Church mem-bers it inspired a powerful belief that motivated a zealous missionary program as well as a firm individual commit-ment to play a part in building Zion in the last days. But non-Mormons saw this Mormon quest as a threat to the established order and took action against it. Even some members revolted at developments that seemed to threaten their own views of what America should be. In some ways, Laurence Moore is right when he argues that as "outsiders" in American society, early Mormons helped their neighbors define for themselves what it meant to be an American by defining what one was not.[39] For this reason Mormon inclusiveness and communitarian outlook were attacked as "un-American" wherever Mormons gathered to build their Zion. These same developments also help us understand the internal dissent that emerged after 1834 in the Church and reached its peak in 1837 in Kirtland and 1838 in northern Missouri. Both experiences were connected to each other and both grew out of the real and imagined consequences of the Mormon quest for Daniel's kingdom.

Marvin Hill has argued that the dissension in Kirtland began after the return of Zion's Camp in 1834, and that this growing dissatisfaction was as much cultural as it was economic when the problems relating to the Kirtland economy erupted in 1837; these became more an excuse than a reason for dissent.[40] What really bothered the dissenters were changes in Church doctrine and organization and their own consequent conclusions that Joseph was getting too powerful and too involved with the "temporal." Much of the growing opposition came, therefore, to center on key aspects of the kingdom of God. These included the "redeeming" of Zion, the consecration of personal property, and the subsequent threats (so they argued) to their personal freedoms. There was here a conflict basic to American political and religious culture.[41]

At least two related aspects need further analysis. The first was articulated in Nathan Hatch's essay, which looked at seekers and primitive Christians in the early Republic who were insistent that the promise of freedom of the American Revolution must be carried out in the churches also.[42] Many early Mormon converts came out of this milieu. Second, and this attitude was related to the first, was a kind of antifederalism that distrusted centralized authority and emphasized individual and states' rights.[43]

One application of this thesis to Mormonism argues that the earliest associates of Joseph Smith came from pockets of antifederalism in New York and Pennsylvania. While more demographic study is needed, surely the political attitudes of those who got involved in the money-digging companies in the 1810s and 1820s shared these anticentralist views. Each seems to have had a seer stone (or closely followed someone who did) for direct communication with Deity, and each participated in the kind of extended limited partnerships these groups created while they engaged in their treasure-hunting activities. These treasure-seeking companies were essentially democracies in which each person shared, according to their contributions, everything they found in their common quest.[44]

Those who formed the first congregations in Mormonism, whether they had been money-diggers or not, shared these views. The early principles of common consent, of group nominating and voting, reveal the democratic tendencies of the movement. But as the Church grew and as new converts required greater organization, it was not possible to maintain a simple democracy where each member had equal access either to power or to revelation for the group as a whole. Thus the Hiram Page episode was an important step toward a more centralized leadership structure.[45] The organization of the First Presidency in 1831 and the calling of the first Quorum of Twelve Apostles in 1835 were similar developments in this direction.[46] The publishing by 1835 of a volume of formal revelations was also viewed by many of the earliest converts as a corruption of "primitive" Mormonism.[47] One important theme in the subsequent writings of those individuals who left the Church in the 1830s was that the Church had changed since they first joined.[48]

There was, then, a definite movement toward centralization, or a kind of federalism, within Mormonism between 1830 and 1840, and this development was linked to both internal and external perceptions and was, in large measure, justified by the use of Daniel's vision of the kingdom of God, a stone cut out without hands and rolling forth to consume the world.[49]

The role of the book of Daniel was particularly noticeable in the events of 1837-38 when both internal dissent and external persecution came to a head. In Kirtland the dissension finally manifested itself in the organization of an opposition church which expressed a longing for the simpler, more "primitive" days of the movement. Calling themselves the "Church of Christ," they reemphasized seer stones, attacked the "authoritarianism" of Joseph Smith, and stressed a democratic approach to church government.[50] The movement was denounced in a speech by Sidney Rigdon, a member of the First Presidency, in July 1837 in the Kirtland temple. In his speech he cited Daniel 2 in his emphasis on the "Saints" taking the kingdom. Mary Fielding wrote from Kirtland on 8 July 1837 to her sister in Canada:

> We had a quiet comfortable waiting upon God in his House. President Rigdon delivered a very striking discourse from Daniel Chap[ter] 2nd Vrs 44. . . . He told us with great warmth indeed, that the Kingdom which was set up should never be destroyed, nor left to other people. No, said he, nor yet change Governours. I really thought from what he said that all opposers from that time rest satisfyed that their exertions would be fruitless, but I do not expect in the least that Satan will give up the contest.[51]

Here Daniel's prophecies were used as a proof text against the dissenters who wanted the kingdom for themselves.

But things got worse, and in January 1838 Joseph Smith abandoned Kirtland and headed for Far West, Missouri.

But before departing, he gave another series of revelations, one of which further spelled out the subordinate role of stake organizations to the First Presidency — a development that led to immediate consequences in Missouri as David Whitmer, a sympathizer with the dissenters in Kirtland, was released as the Missouri stake president.[52]

But dissent followed Church leaders to Missouri. The Whitmer faction and those who shared the views of the dissenters in Kirtland were tried for their membership and expelled from the Church and therefore the community.[53] All of this has seemed sinister to subsequent commentators, but if it is put into the larger perspective of the Mormon quest for a covenant community (a quest that can be followed in Western culture from Acts 2 to the Puritans) and the kingdom of God, then it can be seen as part of a consistent development going back to at least 1831. It also prepares us for a closer look at the events and ideas of the last months of Mormonism in Missouri.

The "Danites" in Mormon History

The student of Mormon history discovers that there are very few primary sources available or extant that deal with the last months of 1838 in Missouri. Because the vast majority of texts relating to these critical months were written *after* December 1838, the importance of the Albert Perry Rockwood letters becomes apparent. They are significant contemporary records of the inner history of the Latter-day Saint community at Far West during this period.[54]

Besides their detail for the events during the final months of 1838, revealing, as it were, a closeness that puts the reader in the eye of the storm, these letters also offer an alternative solution to the old debate over the existence and function of Danites in Mormon society. The existence of groups of armed Mormons called "Danites" during 1838 in Missouri has both plagued faithful Mormons and has also seemingly provided almost unlimited "historical" license to their critics ever since. The presence of the word "Danites" in early sources dealing with the Mormon War in Missouri and the fact that some in the Latter-day Saint community, apparently reacting to the clamor about Danites, crossed out or attempted to delete references to Danites, including the Rockwood material in the Church Archives, have unfortunately further suggested the worst interpretation to critics of the Church as well as to more well-meaning defenders of the faith.

The conceptual framework of Stephen LeSueur's recent book, *The 1838 Mormon War in Missouri,* is based on the assumption that Joseph Smith knew about and even led marauding Danite bands on offensive raids on non-Mormon Missouri farms and villages in 1838. LeSueur's volume consistently maintains an interpretation of the Danites which places major blame on Mormon leaders for their problems in northern Missouri. Thus he concludes that the Court of Inquiry in November 1838 correctly bound Joseph Smith over for trial based on the evidence presented against him, particularly by Sampson Avard. On this matter LeSueur's volume follows directly an old interpretation.[55]

The only other major interpretation has been advanced by Leland Gentry, first in his 1965 dissertation and later as an article in *Brigham Young University Studies.*[56] Basically, Gentry argued that the Danites were real, but that they went through three stages of development: (1) in June at Far West and in July at Adam-ondi-Ahman, groups were organized to aid specifically in the expulsion of dissenters from the Mormon communities; (2) from June to mid-October 1838, Danites provided protection for Mormons against mob violence, primarily a defensive movement; and (3) in October 1838, during the so-called "Mormon War," the Danites began to steal from non-Mormons, a stage and activity justified and led by Sampson Avard. The value of Gentry's thesis has been that it admits to the existence of Danites and even that Joseph Smith could have known about the first two stages, but it dissociates the Mormon prophet from its most militant and illegal manifestations. The irony, argues Gentry, was that Avard, in providing the testimony against Joseph Smith in November 1838 as a witness for the State, successfully shifted all blame for his own activity onto the Mormon prophet.

Historiographically, one finds that the farther removed from 1838 a source is, and the more critical the author is of the Church, the greater the detail the account will contain of illegal activity of such a group. Thus, accounts written by either apostates or other enemies of the Church appearing by 1840 tend to support a more secretive, militaristic, extralegal interpretation of Danite activity. And generally, accounts by faithful Mormons after 1840 tend to be very defensive as they reacted to these written attacks. The main difficulty with most of the critical evidence is that it comes from individuals who were clearly prejudiced against Joseph Smith. In fact, nearly all of the most negative accounts can be traced to two main sources—either the highly questionable and surely self-serving testimony of Sampson Avard at the November 1838 Missouri Court of Inquiry, or to individuals who had or did come to question the whole concept of the kingdom of God in early Mormon thought.

Basically, Avard testified that Joseph Smith was "the prime mover and organizer of this Danite Band," that its purpose was to bring forth "the millenial [sic] kingdom," and that the band was bound together by covenants of secrecy and oaths of death. He revealed the details of a purported secret Danite oath and constitution and described in some detail the night raids this band was to have undertaken against their enemies in northern Missouri. In his testimony Avard referred to the "little stone" spoken of by the prophet Daniel, which he claimed Mormon leaders taught was to go forth and destroy all that was "rotten," first in the state of Missouri and then, presumably, in the United States.[57]

Rockwood's own narrative, if examined closely, suggests that both Mormons and non-Mormons have fundamentally misunderstood what the Danites were, and this misunderstanding is perpetuated in the continued use of the term only in ways that critics of the Church early attached to it. Rockwood's record for 22 October 1838 reads:

> Far West is the head quarters of the Mormon war. the armies of Isreal that were established by revelation from God are seen from my door evry day with their Captains of 10.s 50.s & 100. A portion of each Day is set apart for drill. after which they go to their several stations (VIZ.) 2 Companies of 10.s are to provide the famalies with meal, 2 provide wood, 2 or 3 Build cabbins, 1 Company of 10.s collect & prepare armes, 1 company provide me[a]t, 1 Company are spies, one Company are for express, 1 for guard, 2 Companies are to gather in the famalies that are scattered over the counties in the vicinity, 1 company is to see to & provide for the sick, and the famalies of those that are off on duty, Others are employed in gathering provisions into the city &c &c.
>
> Those companies are called Danites because the Prophet Daniel has said they shall take the kingdom and possess it for-ever.

Rockwood's record does several things for our understanding of the Danites. First, the origin of the "armies of Israel" predates 1838; in fact, it went back to Zion's Camp in 1834 (D&C 105:30-32).[58] There, militia operations within and by the Church in 1834 were tied to divine injunctions to redeem Zion, a central part in Joseph Smith's goal of establishing the latter-day kingdom of God in Missouri. And it has been firmly established that Zion's Camp was a defensive operation, depending solely on the invitation and promises of support of the governor of Missouri.[59]

Second, Rockwood's account of the organization of

Danites speaks of the involvement of the whole Mormon community, and he describes its structure in the biblical terms of companies of tens, fifties, and hundreds (cf. Exodus 18:13-26). He clearly says the various groupings provided all kinds of community service, not just bearing arms. Some groups of Danites were to build houses, others were to gather food, or care for the sick, while others were to help gather the scattered Saints into the community. There can be no doubt that Rockwood is describing the *total* activities of a covenant community that viewed itself in the same terms as ancient Israel. Working in groups, these Danites served the interests of the whole. It was hardly a secret organization working under the cover of darkness. In fact, Rockwood is more explicit about Danite activity in the letters he sends than in the accounts he copies into his own letter-book journal. This would hardly be a proper course to take if the whole thing were to be kept in absolute secrecy as Avard argued. Rockwood thus presents a fundamentally different view than Avard, a view which allows for an interpretation of these developments in much broader perspective, both historically and doctrinally.

Finally, Rockwood reveals that the name "Dan" came not from the warrior tribe of Dan (Genesis 49:16-17; Deuteronomy 33:22; 1 Chronicles 12:35) or from the militant references to the "daughters of Zion" (Isaiah 3:16) as critical sources have alleged, but rather, and more consistently, from the book of Daniel, "because the Prophet Daniel has said they [the Saints] shall take the kingdom and possess it for-ever" (see Daniel 7:22). To the student of Mormon history this brings the whole notion into clear focus: early Mormons consistently used the book of Daniel in their own self-understanding of the mission of the Church. The "stone cut out without hands" was to fill the whole earth. It was, in their minds, the kingdom of God, and it was directly related to their millennial expectations. It was not to be established by bloodshed or law-breaking (cf. D&C 58:19-22; 63:28-31; 98:4-7; 105:5). The righteous were to be gathered out of the world to a central location and, as Rockwood's journal notes, what really bothered their Missouri neighbors (in addition to a number of tactless Mormon comments) was the growing concentration of Mormons in the northern counties and the subsequent implications in a democratic society for economic and political power there. General Clark's counsel, which Rockwood also recorded in his letterbook, to those who remained at Far West after the surrender of Mormon leaders was *not* to gather again.[60]

Throughout Rockwood's letters Mormon millennial expectations are obvious; but nowhere is there the cutthroat secrecy that Avard later succeeded in convincing Judge Austin King and the non-Mormon public that there was. In the other known contemporaneous Mormon references to Danites, the illegal activities that Avard testified about are missing. John Smith's diary speaks of the Danite activity at Adam-ondi-Ahman in very matter-of-fact terms; and the reference in the "Scriptory Book" of Joseph Smith, kept by his scribe George W. Robinson, also confirms the essentials suggested by Rockwood:

> Some time past the brethren or Saints have come up day after day to consecrate, and to bring their offerings into the store house of the lord, to prove him now herewith and se[e] if he will not pour us out a blessing that there will not be room enough to contain it. They have come up hither Thus far, according to the order Revel[. . .] of the Danites we have a company of Danites in these times, to put right physically that which is not right and to cleanse the Church of verry great evils which hath hitherto existed among us inasmuch as they cannot be put right by teachings & persuasyons. This company or part of them exhibited on the fourth day of July. . . . They come up to consecrate by companies of tens, commanded by their captain over ten.[61]

All of this is not to suggest that every member or company of the Mormon militia obeyed all the laws, nor is it to deny that a segment of them was misled by Avard. But as Richard Anderson has recently shown, even the burning of Gallatin and the raid on Millport can be understood as defensive in nature and came only after years of patient suffering.[62] Thus to argue that these were simply the more public side of the very dark Danite activities is not historically accurate. It might be suggested that either Sidney Rigdon's speeches or private counsel could have encouraged Avard's activities, but it is inaccurate to continue to use the term "Danite" to cover only an aberration. Rockwood's record would lead us to conclude that the original intention of Danites was to organize modern Israel more completely into a fully integrated community with each person contributing to the benefit of the whole.

Avard's testimony in November 1838 seems to have laid the foundation for all subsequent interpretations. Surely the accounts of individuals like Reed Peck, John Corrill, William Swartzell, James Hunt, Ebenezer Robinson, and even John D. Lee were framed not by what was happening in the Mormon community but by the interpretative framework that Avard managed to provide for anyone who needed a rationale for rejecting either the leadership of Joseph Smith or the centralizing tendencies of a covenant community intent on establishing Zion.[63]

Students must also consider the various contemporary histories by individuals who remained faithful to the movement as well as other sources, usually autobiographical recollections like those of Mosiah Hancock, William Huntington, or Luman Shurtliff, which are best understood in the same sense as Albert Rockwood used the term Danites.[64]

If this argument has merit, and the Rockwood letters strongly support this interpretation, then the "Danites" in early Mormon history must be completely reevaluated.

When Parley P. Pratt wrote to his wife's family just at the end of the Court of Inquiry, he could, in honesty, tell them that "they accuse us of things that never entered into our hearts."[65] Joseph Smith, from Liberty Jail on 16 December 1838, could add:

> We have learned also since we have been in prison that many false and pernicious things which were calculated to lead the saints far astray and to do great injury have been taught by Dr. Avard as coming from the Presidency . . . which the presidency never knew of being taught in the church by any body until after they were made prisoners. . . . The presidency were ignorant as well as innocent of these things.[66]

We might even consider the influence the Missouri organization had, not on the host of dime novels of nineteenth-century America,[67] but on the Nauvoo "council of fifty," or on the organization Brigham Young gave to the "Camp of Israel" at Winter Quarters in 1847,[68] and on his continued stress on consecration and community building in the Great Basin.[69]

There are other indications of the role of the book of Daniel in 1838 in Missouri. Consider the "Ancient of Days" (Daniel 7:9, 13-14, 22), identified in Mormon thought as Adam,[70] that was tied to various Missouri Mormon sites (D&C 107:53-54; 116).[71] It is also possible that when the official name of the Church was formalized in April 1838, that "latter-day saints" was included because of Daniel's emphasis on the "saints of the Most High" taking and possessing the kingdom in the last days, as well as to counter the organization of the dissenters in Kirtland.[72] Joseph Smith continued to emphasize the central notions of the kingdom of God in northern Missouri, including consecration and united firms,[73] and the "gathering."[74]

It would also seem that an emphasis on Daniel could, in part, explain the shift in tone and content of Joseph Smith's 1838 history. Where his earlier accounts had stressed a personal quest for salvation and forgiveness of sins, his 1838 history now seems to place his early religious experiences into institutional and cosmic focus.[75] Then, too, the fact that the November 1838 Court of Inquiry placed emphasis on the Mormon preaching of Daniel 2:44-45 should confirm for us its perceived place in Latter-day Saint thought.[76]

Finally, Joseph Smith's Liberty Jail letter (March 1839) to the Church, in which he worked through what his Missouri experiences meant, commanded the exiled saints to write histories of their own experiences (thus inviting them to record their part in the history of the kingdom). It also contained several quotes from the book of Daniel.[77] From all that has been said, this should come as no surprise.

The Book of Daniel in Early Mormon Exegesis

If the book of Daniel was as important in early Mormonism as here suggested, we would expect it to surface in early Mormon pamphlets and books after they began to appear in 1837. Space constraints force us to summarize. The most prolific of the early Mormon pamphleteers, Parley P. Pratt, gave the book of Daniel an important place in a number of his works. The first two chapters of his *A Voice of Warning* (1837) cited Daniel 2;[78] his very popular British pamphlet, *A Letter to the Queen* (1841), was essentially an extended commentary on Daniel 2;[79] and Parley authored the 1845 *Proclamation of the Twelve*, which again summarized the teachings of his 1841 tract.[80]

His brother Orson added to the Latter-day Saint literature on Daniel. His early journals (1833-37) document at least ten separate uses of Daniel 2 as a text for his sermons; as early as April 1841 he was discoursing on the topic to his fellow Apostles in England;[81] his own later pamphlets contain commentaries on Daniel.[82] He maintained this emphasis throughout his life.[83]

Other early Mormons also stressed Daniel. For example, Benjamin Winchester, an early church leader in Philadelphia, wrote of Daniel's prophesied kingdom,[84] as did William I. Appleby in his 1844 tract, *A Dissertation on Nebuchadnezzar's Dream*.[85]

Joseph Smith continued to emphasize the book of Daniel during the last years of his life, and this undoubtedly influenced those writers mentioned above. In 1839 he taught that his followers ought to have the building up of Zion as their greatest objective and that great destruction was coming before the Ancient of Days would come.[86] He repeated these sentiments in 1841, adding these words of comfort for his people:

> The kingdom will not be broken up but we shall be scattered and driven gathered again & then dispersed reestablished & driven abroad and so on until the Ancient of days shall sit and the kingdom and power thereof shall the[n] be given to the Saints and they shall possess it forever and ever.[87]

In 1842 he used Daniel 7 for a text and told his audience that Daniel prophesied that "the God of heaven would set up a kingdom in the last days."[88] In 1843 he spoke on Daniel 7 and made some comparisons with the book of Revelation.[89] In 1844 he reflected in some detail on Daniel 2:44, tying it into his early Missouri experiences.[90] A close associate who was with Joseph Smith the night before he was killed wrote, "I heard his testimony in the depths of the prison, within its solid doors where he was thrown on the accusation of treason against the government for preaching from Dan. 2:44."[91]

Even some individuals who rejected Joseph Smith or claimed to be his successor emphasized Daniel's volume in their own claims. For example, Oliver Olney claimed in 1842 that, based on personal visitations from the "Ancient of Days," he was commissioned to set up a temporal kingdom.[92] James J. Strang taught of Daniel's kingdom in his *Book of the Law of the Lord*.[93]

We would even go so far as to suggest that the early Mormon attitudes about the book of Daniel provide not only the background but the rationale for the Council of Fifty in Nauvoo. No one has doubted that Daniel 2 was central to the Mormon political kingdom of God. But while it has been shown how flawed Klaus Hansen's pioneering work is on this topic,[94] it has been less apparent how clearly related developments in Kirtland and Nauvoo were; that the kingdom they spoke of in Nauvoo had been taught earlier in Kirtland, and that events in Missouri are better understood within this larger context.[95]

Just over a month before he was killed, Joseph Smith told an audience:

> The Ancient Prophets declared in the last days the God of heaven shall set up a Kingdom which should never be destroyed nor left to other people; & the very time that was calculated on; *this people* was struggling to bring it out—he that arms himself with Gun, sword, or Pistol except in the defense of truth, will be sorry for it—I never carry any weapon with me bigger than my Pen Knife—when I was dragged before the Cannon and muskets in Missouri, I was unarmed. God will always protect me until my mission is fulfilled. I calculate to be one of the Instruments of setting up the Kingdom of Daniel, by the word of the Lord, and I intend to lay a foundation that will revolutionize the world—I once offered my life to the Missouri Mob as a sacrifice for my people—and here I am—it will not be by Sword or Gun that this kingdom will roll on—the power of truth is such that all nations will be under the necessity of obeying the Gospel.[96]

Conclusion: Early Mormonism and American Political Culture

In many ways Mormon political thought and action embodied and then carried to its logical conclusion the Puritan notion of the religious state or kingdom of God.

The word "kingdom" has always implied a socioeconomic political community. As in early Christianity, this led to misunderstanding and persecution in early Mormon history.[97] Early Mormons did not need the book of Daniel to justify their seeking an earthly kingdom, as the Book of Mormon both prophesied of apocalyptic events and gave ample models of religious societies presided over by prophet-kings. That volume also spoke many times of Christ's second coming. But Daniel provided a biblical text familiar to most Americans and seemed to suggest a discernible timetable for the events of the last days.[98]

The millennial rhetoric that was so central to early Mormonism could easily speak of "armies of God" and use military metaphors. It is both ironic and paradoxical that to understand the early history of Mormonism it is essential that we see, on the one hand, that it was the most American of religions, which fully embraced the goals and visions of her biblical and colonial heritage; and, on the other hand, that for precisely these beliefs Church members were persecuted by those who were sure they were neither biblical nor American. But in using the book of Daniel, early Mormons proved they were both, more so perhaps than any other group.

Notes

1. Doctrine and Covenants (Kirtland, OH: F. G. Williams, 1835), section 27, p. 154.

2. Ibid., section 24, p. 151. This revelation was designated a prayer by Joseph Smith in *Times and Seasons* 5 (1 April 1844): 482.

3. This essay uses the following definition of political culture: "The system of empirical beliefs, expressive symbols and values which defines the situation in which political action takes place." Lucien Pye and Sidney Verba, *Political Culture and Political Development* (Princeton: Princeton University Press, 1965), 513, as cited in Jean H. Baker, "The Ceremonies of Politics, Nineteenth-Century Rituals of National Affirmation," in William J. Cooper, Jr., et al., eds., *A Master's Due: Essays in Honor of David Herbert Donald* (Baton Rouge: Louisiana State University Press, 1985), 165. As Baker sug-

gests, political culture assumes that "societies produce civic arrangements that represent coherent patterns of public life and that [they] are not random happenings." See also John Howe, "Gordon S. Wood and the Analysis of Political Culture in the American Revolutionary Era," *William and Mary Quarterly*, 3rd Series, 44 (July 1987): 569-75, esp. 571.

4. Useful introductions include R. K. Harrison, "The Book of Daniel" in *Introduction to the Old Testament* (Grand Rapids, MI: Eerdmans, 1969), 1105-34; and Louis F. Hartman and Alexander A. Di Lella, *The Book of Daniel*, Anchor Bible (Garden City, NY: Doubleday, 1978). For studies of the book of Daniel which emphasize the apocalyptic themes, see D. S. Russell, *Between the Testaments*, rev. ed. (Philadelphia: Fortress, 1965); Russell, *The Method and Message of Jewish Apocalyptic* (London: SCM, 1964); Russell, *Apocalyptic: Ancient and Modern* (Philadelphia: Fortress, 1968); and G. K. Beale, *The Use of Daniel in Jewish Apocalyptic Literature and in the Revelation of St. John* (Lanham, MD: University Press of America, 1984). A detailed study which emphasizes the volume's structure of tales and visions is John J. Collins, *Daniel: With an Introduction to Apocalyptic Literature* (Grand Rapids, MI: Eerdmans, 1984). Klaus Koch has noted the recent "Apocalyptic Renaissance" in biblical studies which has seen the shifting of the study of apocalyptic writings (like Daniel and Revelation) from the sidelines of the theological and historical discourse to center stage. *The Rediscovery of Apocalyptic* (London: SCM, 1972).

No attempt is made in this paper to treat either the obvious relationship between Daniel and the book of Revelation or the use of the book of Revelation in early Mormon thought. Both aspects would strengthen what is argued herein. Ford has suggested, "it has been computed that in the 404 verses of Revelation, 518 Old Testament citations and allusions are found, 88 of which are from Daniel." J. Massyngberde Ford, *Revelation*, Anchor Bible (Garden City, NY: Doubleday, 1975), 37. It has also been suggested that the book of Daniel could be a commentary on the book of Enoch, a topic that demands more work as Enoch is increasingly found in early Christian literature as well. See Martin Hengel, *Judaism and Hellenism*, tr. John Bowden, 2 vols. (Philadelphia: Fortress, 1974), 1:186-92.

For the student of early Mormon thought, this aspect also invites more work; for example, before Daniel citations began to appear in Joseph Smith's revelations, he had revealed to the Church (June-December 1830) what came to be known as the book of Moses, a significant part of which contains the writings of Enoch (see Moses

6:23-8:3). Thus we must ask if there is a similarity between the use or function of Daniel in early Christianity and early Mormonism. The early Christian connection to Daniel is studied in Reinhard Bodenmann, *Naissance d'une Exegese: Daniel dans l'Eglise ancienne des trois premiers siecles* (Tübingen: Mohr, 1986). This study was called to my attention by Gordon Thomasson. Some scholars suggest that the Olivet Discourse (Mark 13) is based on a midrashic interpretation of Daniel and that the "stone" of Israel in Mark 12:10 refers to the stone of Daniel 2:45. See David E. Aune, *Prophecy in Early Christianity and the Ancient Mediterranean World* (Grand Rapids, MI: Eerdmans, 1983), 184-87; and Donald Juel, *Messianic Exegesis: Christological Interpretation of the Old Testament in Early Christianity* (Philadelphia: Fortress, 1988), chap. 7 on "The Risen Christ and the Son of Man: Christian Use of Daniel 7," 151-70.

Two manuscripts of Daniel were found at Qumran, and it is clear that the volume was revered and cited as scripture by the second century B.C., an argument against it having been written in the second century B.C. For a list of Enoch quotes in Daniel, see the special index in Hartman and Di Lella, *The Book of Daniel*.

5. On the influence of the book of Daniel in Western culture generally, see Norman Cohn, *The Pursuit of the Millennium*, rev. ed. (New York: Oxford University Press, 1970); and Frank E. Manuel and Fritzie P. Manuel, *Utopian Thought in the Western World* (Cambridge: Belknap Press of Harvard University Press, 1979). See also John E. Groh, "The Kingdom of God in the History of Christianity: A Bibliographical Survey," *Church History* 43 (June 1974): 257-67; and Dietrich G. Buss, "Meeting of Heaven and Earth: A Survey and Analysis of the Literature on Millennialism in America, 1965-1985," *Fides et Historia* 20/1 (1988): 5-28.

6. See, for example, the comments of W. H. C. Frend, *The Rise of Christianity* (Philadelphia: Fortress, 1984), 417-18, also 149, 442-43; Ernst Breisach, *Historiography: Ancient, Medieval, and Modern* (Chicago: University of Chicago Press, 1983), 83-84; and, by implication, the comments of Brian Croke, "The Origins of the Christian World Chronicle," in Croke and Alanna M. Emmette, eds., *History and the Historians in Late Antiquity* (Sydney: Pergamon, 1983), 121. The first systematic and official Christian history of the world, which was also a vindication of Christianity, was written by Augustine's student Orosius (*Seven Books of History against the Pagans*) between A.D. 415-418, and it made use of Daniel's images and prophecies.

7. See Ernest L. Tuveson, *Redeemer Nation: The Idea of America's Millennial Role* (Chicago: University of Chicago Press, 1968), 31-32;

B. S. Capp, *The Fifth Monarchy Men: A Study in Seventeenth-Century English Millenarianism* (London: Faber and Faber, 1972); and Leo F. Solt, "The Fifth Monarchy Men: Politics and the Millennium," *Church History* 30 (1961): 314-24. The place of Daniel in the thought of the great English scientist Isaac Newton is treated in Richard S. Westfall, *Never at Rest: A Biography of Isaac Newton* (Cambridge: Cambridge University Press, 1980), 319, 349-50, 804, 816-17, 825-26. See also Newton, *Observations on the Prophecies of Daniel* (London: n.p., 1733).

8. Russell, *The Method and Message of Jewish Apocalyptic*, 50-51.

9. The literature on this is quite large. Bercovitch has written and edited a number of studies, including *The Puritan Origins of the American Self* (New Haven: Yale University Press, 1975); *The American Jeremiad* (Madison: University of Wisconsin Press, 1978); and ed., *Typology and Early American Literature* (Amherst: University of Massachusetts Press, 1972), which has an extensive annotated bibliography, 249-337. See also Tuveson, *Redeemer Nation*, 29-30; Harry S. Stout, "Word and Order in Colonial New England," in Nathan O. Hatch and Mark A. Noll, eds., *The Bible in America: Essays in Cultural History* (New York: Oxford University Press, 1982), 19-38; Harry S. Stout, *The New England Soul: Preaching and Religious Culture in Colonial New England* (New York: Oxford University Press, 1987); Perry Miller, "The End of the World," *William and Mary Quarterly*, 3rd Series, 8 (April 1951): 171-91; J. F. Maclear, "New England and the Fifth Monarchy: The Quest for the Millennium in Early American Puritanism," ibid. 32 (April 1975): 223-60; Mason I. Lowance, Jr., *The Language of Canaan: Metaphor and Symbol in New England from the Puritans to the Transcendentalists* (Cambridge: Harvard University Press, 1980), 36, 41-42, 119-24, 179-81, 211-12; and LeRoy E. Froom, *The Prophetic Faith of Our Fathers: The Historical Development of Prophetic Interpretation*, vols. 3 and 4 (Washington, D.C.: Review and Herald Publishing Association, 1954). Froom's volumes, while very polemical, are valuable compilations of colonial and American literature containing apocalyptic material and themes.

10. *Providence and Patriotism in Early America, 1640-1815* (Charlottesville: University Press of Virginia, 1978), 2-13. More specifically, for the colonial literature on Daniel, see Ephraim Huit, *The Whole Prophecie of Daniel Explained by a Paraphrase* (London: Overton, 1644) [considered to be the first colonial exposition of Daniel]; Thomas Parker, *The Visions and Prophecies of Daniel Expounded* (London: Paxton, 1646); William Aspinwall, *A Brief Description of the Fifth Monarchy, or Kingdome That Is to Come into the World* (London: Sim-

mons, 1653); Cotton Mather, *Things to Be Look'd For* (Cambridge, MA: S. and B. Green, 1691); Cotton Mather, *Things for a Distress'd People to Think Upon* (Boston: B. Green and J. Allen, 1696); Nicholas Noyes, *New-Englands Duty and Interest, to Be an Habitation of Justice, and Mountain of Holiness* (Boston: B. Green and J. Allen, 1698); Increase Mather, *Discourse Concerning Faith and Fervency in Prayer* (Boston: B. Green, 1710); Richard Steere, *The Daniel Catcher, The Life of the Prophet Daniel* (Boston: J. Allen, 1713); William Burnett, *An Essay on Scripture-Prophecy* (Boston: n.p., 1724); and Richard Clarke, *The Prophetic Numbers of Daniel and John Calculated; In Order to Shew the Time, When the Day of Judgment . . . Is to Be Expected* (Boston: Edes and Gill, Green and Russell, 1759).

11. Recent studies include Richard T. Hughes and C. Leonard Allen, *Illusions of Innocence: Protestant Primitivism in America, 1630-1875* (Chicago: University of Chicago Press, 1988); and Richard T. Hughes, ed., *The American Quest for the Primitive Church* (Chicago: University of Chicago Press, 1988).

12. Nathan O. Hatch, *The Sacred Cause of Liberty* (New Haven, CT: Yale University Press, 1977), 148-49, 152-53, 163. See also Stephen Stein, "An Apocalyptic Rationale for the American Revolution," *Early American Literature* 9 (Winter 1975): 211-25; and Ruth Bloch, *Visionary Republic: Millennial Themes in American Thought, 1756-1800* (Cambridge: Cambridge University Press, 1985). The use of Daniel 2:44-45, the stone cut out of the mountain, to interpret the American Revolution or justify its meaning, is illustrated in various pamphlets of the period: Benjamin Gale, *A Brief Essay, or, An Attempt to Prove, from the Prophetic Writings of the Old and New Testament, What Period of Prophecy the Church of God Is Now Under* (New Haven, CT: Th. and S. Green, 1788); Samuel Osgood, *Remarks on the Book of Daniel and on the Revelations* (New York: Greenleaf, 1794); David Austin, *The Downfall of Mystical Babylon; or A Key to the Providence of God, in the Political Operations of 1793-94* (Elizabethtown, NJ: n.p., 1794); and John Mellen, *A Sermon Delivered before His Excellency the Governor* (Boston: Young and Minns, 1797).

Elias Smith, *A Discourse Delivered at Jefferson Hall, Thanksgiving Day, November 25, 1802* (Portsmouth: N. S. and W. Peirce, 1803), suggested that the American Revolution fulfilled Daniel's prediction (Daniel 2:31-45) and that all human institutions were to be destroyed. Jedediah Morse, in a sermon in November 1810 to the Society for Propagating the Gospel among Indians and Others in North America, used Daniel 12:4, 10, as a test for proving that the Napoleonic Wars were destroying the Antichrists of the Turkish Empire and the Papacy in preparation for the end of the world. Elias Smith also used Daniel's images and prophecies in *A Sermon on Nebuchadnezzar's Dream* (Boston: n.p., 1820), and *The Whole World Governed by a Jew; or, The Government of the Second Adam, as King and Priest* (Exeter, NH: Henry Ranlet, 1805).

Perry Miller argued several years ago that "the Old Testament is truly so omnipresent in the American culture of 1800 or 1820 that historians have as much difficulty taking cognizance of it as of the air the people breathed." See his "The Garden of Eden and the Deacon's Meadows," *American Heritage* 7 (December 1955): 55.

13. The letter is reprinted in Brigham H. Roberts, *A Comprehensive History of the Church of Jesus Christ of Latter-day Saints*, 6 vols. (Salt Lake City: Deseret News Press, 1930), 1:7-8, and in Richard Lloyd Anderson, *Joseph Smith's New England Heritage* (Salt Lake City: Deseret Book, 1971), 121-23. Marvin S. Hill has noted that a cousin of Joseph Smith, Joseph Lathrop, in a sermon delivered in May 1797, interpreted events in France at the time as having been foretold in Daniel. See Hill, "The Role of Christian Primitivism in the Origin and Development of the Mormon Kingdom, 1830-1844," Ph.D. diss., University of Chicago, 1968, 17-18. Cf. Froom, *The Prophetic Faith of Our Fathers*, 3:236.

14. See sermon of 20 July 1883, *JD* 24:241. While this is a much later reminiscence, Joseph Smith's 1838 recollection (JS-H 1:41) states that the messenger "quoted many other passages of scripture, and offered many explanations which cannot be mentioned here." Oliver Cowdery, a close associate in the early years of the movement, himself added several scriptural citations to the list Joseph Smith gave; see *LDS Messenger and Advocate* 1 (February and October 1835). Additionally, there are allusions or direct references to Daniel in this 1838 account by Joseph Smith: compare Daniel 8:27 with JS-H 1:46; Daniel 10:12 with JS-H 1:32; Daniel 10:9 with JS-H 1:20; and Daniel 12:9 with JS-H 1:65. The comments of Sidney Rigdon in 1844 probably grew out of these early teachings. See *HC* 6:288-89.

15. Andrew F. Ehat and Lyndon W. Cook, compilers and editors, *The Words of Joseph Smith: The Contemporary Accounts of the Nauvoo Discourses of the Prophet Joseph* (Provo, UT: Religious Studies Center, Brigham Young University, 1980), 367. George A. Smith, another cousin, later spoke of Asael Smith's belief "that something would turn up in his family that would revolutionize the world." *JD* 5:102 (sermon of 2 August 1857).

16. See Robert J. Matthews, *"A Plainer Translation": Joseph Smith's Translation of the Bible* (Provo, UT: Brigham Young University Press,

1975), and the extensive bibliography (3 vols.) compiled by Thomas E. Sherry, *Joseph Smith's Translation of the Bible: A Bibliography of Publication, 1847–1987,* copy in Special Collections, Harold B. Lee Library, Brigham Young University. A larger perspective on the use of the Bible in early Mormonism is provided by Gordon Irving, "The Mormons and the Bible in the 1830s," *BYU Studies* 13 (Summer 1973): 473-88.

17. Doctrine and Covenants (1835), section 50, p. 180. These verses were not in chap. 28 of the *Book of Commandments* (1833). Cf. Daniel 7:13, 22. In a 1 January 1834 letter to John Whitmer, Oliver Cowdery identified Adam as the Angel Michael; Oliver Cowdery Letterbook, Henry E. Huntington Library, San Marino, California, 15.

18. *Book of Commandments* (1833), chap. 48, p. 110; Doctrine and Covenants (1835), section 15, p. 13. Cf. Daniel 7:18.

19. Doctrine and Covenants (1835), section 7, p. 104. See also 1 Maccabees 1:54; Matthew 24:15.

20. Cf. Daniel 1:17 ("knowledge and skill in all learning and wisdom") with D&C 89:18-19 ("wisdom and great treasures of knowledge, even hidden treasures").

21. Doctrine and Covenants (Nauvoo ed., 1844), section 101, pp. 386-87, "until the kingdoms of the world are subdued" (D&C 103:7 in current ed.). Cf. Daniel 2:44 and 7:27.

22. Doctrine and Covenants (1844), June 1834, section 102, pp. 391-94 (D&C 105:16-32, 39-40 in current ed.).

23. Doctrine and Covenants (1835), section 3, p. 86. Cf. Daniel 7:13 ("Ancient of days").

24. Again, Enoch is the "heavenly scribe" recording even events relating to Adam in the book of Moses. See Hugh Nibley, *Enoch the Prophet,* vol. 2, *The Collected Works of Hugh Nibley* (Salt Lake City: Deseret Book and F.A.R.M.S., 1986), 83, 126-37. "The Scriptory Book of Joseph Smith, kept by George W. Robinson," MS in Library-Archives, Historical Department, The Church of Jesus Christ of Latter-day Saints, Salt Lake City (hereafter HDC), 43-44. Known today as D&C 116, it was first published in the *Deseret News,* 2 April 1853, and was added to the 1876 edition of the Doctrine and Covenants. "Adam-ondi-Ahman" had earlier appeared in the D&C (1835), section 75, p. 205 (D&C 78:15 in current ed.). See also William W. Phelps's poem with the same title in *LDS Messenger and Advocate* 1 (June 1835): 144. A contemporary description of Adam-ondi-Ahman is by A. Ripley in *Elder's Journal* 1 (August 1838): 52. Other relevant studies include Leland H. Gentry, "Adam-ondi-Ahman: A

Brief Historical Survey," *BYU Studies* 13 (Summer 1973): 553-76; and Rollin J. Britton, "Adam-ondi-Ahman: A Missouri Contribution to the World-famed Spots of Earth," *Missouri Historical Review* 20 (January 1926): 236-46. Early Mormons were taught that this was the area where Adam and Eve dwelt after they were cast out of the Garden of Eden, a teaching that truly made America special in God's divine plans. This teaching, combined with others that were linked to it, such as the location of Adam's altar and that it was this place where the final scenes of the earth's temporal history would occur, surely help us understand why Daniel's prophecies relating to the Ancient of Days would be so important to early Mormons. Other relevant sources include Oliver B. Huntington, "Adam's Altar and Tower," *Juvenile Instructor* 30 (15 November 1895): 700-701; Leland H. Gentry, "The Land Question at Adam-ondi-Ahman," *BYU Studies* 26 (Spring 1986): 45-56; and John H. Wittorf, "An Historical Investigation of the Ruined 'Altars' at Adam-ondi-Ahman, Missouri," *Newsletter and Proceedings of the Society for Early Historic Archaeology*, M. Wells Jakeman, ed., no. 113 (15 April 1969): 1-8. A related matter is the identity of Gabriel, an angel whose appearance to Daniel is first mentioned in the KJV in Daniel 8:16; 9:21. Joseph Smith was equating Noah with Gabriel publicly by 1839; see Ehat and Cook, *The Words of Joseph Smith*, 8-9, 13. This identification seems first to have been made in 1834; see the letter of Oliver Cowdery to John Whitmer, 1 January 1834, n. 17 above. Cf. D&C 128:21. Here again, Gabriel is a prominent figure in the pseudepigraphic literature, primarily in the Enoch literature, including Joseph Smith's Enoch text.

25. *LDS Messenger and Advocate* 2 (March 1836): 277-80. Known today as section 109, it was added to the Doctrine and Covenants in 1876. See esp. vss. 72-73. As contemporaneous sources indicate, this prayer was composed by a committee prior to the dedication. The committee consisted of Joseph Smith, Jr., Sidney Rigdon, Warren A. Cowdery, Warren Parrish, and Oliver Cowdery. See Leonard J. Arrington, "Oliver Cowdery's Kirtland, Ohio, 'Sketch Book'," *BYU Studies* 12 (Summer 1972): 426.

26. *Elder's Journal* 1 (August 1838): 52-53. Known today as section 115, it was added to the 1876 edition of the Doctrine and Covenants. Cf. D&C 115:6 with Daniel 9:24-27. It is interesting to note that D&C 115 also gave the official name of the Church, a change that was possibly influenced by the book of Daniel. See further n. 72 below. See also the letter of Thomas B. Marsh to Wilford Woodruff, 30 April 1838, MS in HDC, which summarized the contents of D&C

115 in the context of the growing opposition to Joseph Smith in Kirtland.

27. *The Evening and the Morning Star* 1 (September 1832): 6.

28. Ibid., 1 (February 1833): 6. Responding to anti-Mormon literature in England, Joseph Fielding wrote: "The arrows and spears only serve to keep the little stone clear as it rolls along." Letter of 20 June 1841, in *Millennial Star* 2 (August 1841): 53. Lorenzo Snow spoke of his mission in England: "The 'Stone of the Mountain', which you sent to rolling in London . . . has not yet ceased moving, but is daily becoming more rapid and powerful in its revolutions." Letter to Heber C. Kimball, 10 November 1841, in *Times and Seasons* 3 (15 March 1842): 712-13; see also the letter of Lorenzo Snow to Don Carlos Smith, 14 April 1841, in ibid., 2 (1 September 1841): 530.

29. *The Evening and the Morning Star* 1 (May 1833): 7.

30. See, for example, Moses Martin Journal, 28 September 1834, 21. MS in HDC. See also his poem dated about 1834 on "The Church of Christ" which concludes with lines equating the Church with the stone of Daniel 2:44. Parley P. Pratt used Daniel 2 in Canada in 1836. *Autobiography of Parley P. Pratt* (Salt Lake City: Deseret Book, 1980), 143-50. An elder in Oakland, Michigan, preached on Daniel 2 at a local conference, see "Journal History," 26 January 1845, 3. See also the comments of Polly W. Jones and William W. Spencer in letters to Ira Jones Willes about October 1835 where they mention Daniel and the Saints of the Most High possessing the kingdom. Correspondence file, Typescripts in HDC, 16, 19. These last items were called to my attention by Ian Barber.

Nowhere is this emphasis clearer than in the Orson Pratt journals where he consistently used Daniel 2 as a sermon text. See the following dates: 18 July 1833, 1 March 1835, 13 March 1835, 1 April 1835, 5 April 1835, 2 June 1835, 17 October 1835, April 1836, 27 May 1836, and October 1837. MS in HDC.

31. *LDS Messenger and Advocate* 2 (November 1835): 221.

32. Ibid., 2 (May 1836): 307-9.

33. Ibid., 3 (September 1837): 561. This is a letter of Newell K. Whitney, Reynolds Cahoon, and Vinson Knight, 18 September 1837.

34. Emma Smith, compiler, *A Collection of Sacred Hymns, for the Church of the Latter Day Saints* (Kirtland, OH: F. G. Williams, 1835), 11 (#5, vs. 2). This hymn was reprinted in David Rogers, *A Collection of Sacred Hymns for the Church of the Latter Day Saints* (New York: C. Vinten, 1838), 20-21 (#11). A Church conference in October 1839 condemned Rogers's hymnal, not because its contents were unorthodox, but because it was being sold as "the one compiled and

published by Emma Smith." See the discussion in Peter Crawley, "A Bibliography of the Church of Jesus Christ of Latter-day Saints in New York, Ohio, and Missouri," *BYU Studies* 12 (Summer 1972): 524-26 (item 43).

35. Emma Smith hymnal, 108-9 (#80, vss. 6-7); David Rogers's hymnal, 81-83 (#61); and Brigham Young, Parley P. Pratt, and John Taylor, eds., *A Collection of Sacred Hymns, for the Church of Jesus Christ of Latter-day Saints in Europe* (Manchester: W. R. Thomas, 1840), 238 (#213).

36. For other examples see 9 (#3) and 109 (#80) in the 1835 volume; in the Rogers's 1838 collection, 21 (#12), 33 (#21), 42-43 (#28), 55-57 (#40), 94 (#70), and 102-3 (#79); in Christopher Merkley, *A Small Selection of Choice Hymns for the Church of Jesus Christ of Latter Day Saints* (n.p.: Printed for the publisher, 1841), 17-18 (#9), 20-22 (#10), and 23-24 (#13); and in the 1841 Manchester Hymnal, 274 (#239), 277 (#240), 280 (#242), and 288 (#248). An interesting study would be to compare this kind of material in Mormon hymnals with those in contemporary Protestant hymnals.

37. Other early references to the book of Daniel include *The Evening and the Morning Star* 1 (March 1833): 3; 1 (April 1833): 168, Kirtland ed.; 1 (May 1833): 7; 2 (June 1833): 100, 101; 2 (April 1834): 294-95; 2 (May 1834): 306, 310; 2 (June 1834): 323-24; *LDS Messenger and Advocate* 1 (March 1835): 95; 1 (May 1835): 114-15, 126-28; 1 (June 1835): 129-31; 1 (August 1835): 168-70; *Elder's Journal* 1 (July 1838): 36-37. Sidney Rigdon preached in 1836 from Daniel; see the letter of Charles Olcott, April 1836, in *LDS Messenger and Advocate* 2 (May 1836): 315-16, quoting from *Ohio Free Press*. Of course Mormons used other biblical texts. For example, see the studies of Gordon Irving, esp. "The Mormons and the Bible in the 1830s," *BYU Studies* 13 (Summer 1973): 473-88.

38. See Noel B. Reynolds, "The Doctrine of an Inspired Constitution," *BYU Studies* 16 (Spring 1976): 315-40. See also n. 49 below.

39. R. Laurence Moore, *Religious Outsiders and the Making of Americans* (New York: Oxford University Press, 1986), 25-47. Moore tends to blame the victim in his approach to early Mormon history.

40. See Marvin S. Hill, "Quest for Refuge: An Hypothesis as to the Social Origins and Nature of the Mormon Political Kingdom," *Journal of Mormon History* 2 (1975): 3-20; and esp. Hill, "Cultural Crisis in the Mormon Kingdom: A Reconsideration of the Causes of Kirtland Dissent," *Church History* 49 (September 1980): 286-97.

41. See particularly, Nathan O. Hatch, "The Christian Movement and the Demand for a Theology of the People," *Journal of American*

History 67 (December 1980): 545-67. See also Robert H. Wiebe, *The Opening of American Society* (New York: Knopf, 1984), 152-60; and Gordon S. Wood, "Evangelical America and Early Mormonism," *New York History* 61 (October 1980): 359-86.

42. Hatch, "The Christian Movement," 545-67. As Hatch shows, the followers of Alexander Campbell, many of whom were among the first converts to Mormonism, shared these views. See also Richard T. Hughes, "From Primitive Church to Civil Religion: The Millennial Odyssey of Alexander Campbell," *Journal of the American Academy of Religion* 44 (March 1976): 87-103.

43. From a reading of Mormon sources in the 1830s it seems that many of the earliest converts had assimilated a radical whig ideology that included (1) a fear of concentrated power, (2) a concern for personal liberty, (3) a fear of conspiracies which were seen as natural products of too concentrated power in the hands of a few, and (4) a belief that rulers will tend to use corrupt measures to acquire dominion over their subjects. See the discussion in Bernard Bailyn, *The Ideological Origins of the American Revolution* (Cambridge: Belknap Press of Harvard University Press, 1967), 32-54. It is clear that these attitudes survived well into early American history.

It is very difficult to generalize about the political ideology of Jacksonian America. The 1828 election began a two-party system coalescing around Whigs and Democrats. But from the beginning each party drew upon a variety of interest groups, and this movement was shattered by the sectional conflicts polarized through the slavery issue by the 1840s. Recent scholarship has revealed how complex the situation was, and that the era was an uncomfortable compromise between various groups that is best seen in relation to the most prominent public issues of Jackson's presidency, especially the nullification crisis and the fight over the national bank. But even here, the politics do not reveal a simple split over economic interests. A good survey of the era's politics, including the various third parties, is Edward Pessen, *Jacksonian America: Society, Personality, and Politics*, rev. ed. (Homewood, IL: Dorsey, 1978), 149-323, plus an extensive bibliographical essay. See also Daniel W. Howe, *The Political Culture of the American Whigs* (Chicago: University of Chicago Press, 1979); Richard L. McCormick, *The Second American Party System: Party Formation in the Jacksonian Era* (New York: Norton, 1973); and McCormick, *The Party Period and Public Policy* (New York: Oxford University Press, 1986), esp. chaps. 4-5.

The Whig party seems to have appealed, in part, to those who, like their colonial counterparts, feared a concentration of power.

Thus, in the North especially, anti-Masonic party members were drawn to the Whigs, and increasingly came to oppose Jackson. Here is an explanation of the behavior of William W. Phelps: he had been very active in the anti-Masonic movement, even publishing anti-Masonic newspapers where his strong dislike of aristocratic exclusiveness and political monopolization were voiced. Phelps's 1838 rejection of the centralizing tendencies of the Mormon kingdom of God surely reflected these same concerns, even though he had earlier seen Mormonism as political anti-Masonry. One suspects the same rationale in other Mormons' attitudes by 1838: compare Orson Hyde's letter to Brigham Young, 30 March 1839, MS in HDC; the comments of John Corrill, "I had rather enjoy liberty in hell than suffer bondage in heaven!" in his 1839 History (p. 48 in MS), but deleted from the published version, per Stephen C. LeSueur, *The 1838 Mormon War in Missouri* (Columbia: University of Missouri Press, 1987), 260; and Ebenezer Robinson's account of the strong Latter-day Saint reaction to Joseph Smith's request for a fixed salary in 1838, *The Return* 1 (September 1889): 136-38, cf. Hill, "The Role of Christian Primitivism," 132, n. 3, 191-92.

Much work has yet to be done before we can fully understand Joseph Smith's relationship to the political culture of his time. Another fruitful avenue would be to examine more closely the political thought of Oliver Cowdery. From his coauthoring the "Articles and Covenants" (*The Evening and the Morning Star* 2 [June 1833]: 1-2; D&C 20) in 1829 (see the earliest draft in HDC, Revelations Collection); his possible coauthorship of the "Political Motto" of the Church (*HC* 3:9); his authorship of a major statement on government (D&C 134); and his editorship of the *Northern Times* (Kirtland, OH), all suggest an anticentralist, prodemocratic philosophy which sought to *limit* church government by carefully defining what its bounds were. See Max Parkin, "Mormon Political Involvement in Ohio," *BYU Studies* 9 (Summer 1969): 484-502, for a closer look at the *Northern Times*. Unfortunately, few copies of the newspaper are extant. Cowdery's communication to the Missouri High Council (the group that finally excommunicated him from the Church in April 1838), was suggestive of his political attitudes; see his comments in Donald Q. Cannon and Lyndon W. Cook, eds., *Far West Record* (Salt Lake City: Deseret Book, 1983), 165; also his letter dated 4 February 1838 at Far West to Warren and Lyman Cowdery, MS in Cowdery Letterbook, Huntington Library, 84. Thus, while some Mormons opposed rank and privilege by supporting the Whig party in the early 1830s, many of these same leaders came to see this very situation emerging within the Church by 1837-38.

44. For a sample of one such agreement involving members of the Smith family, see *Salt Lake Tribune*, 23 April 1880, cited in Francis W. Kirkham, *A New Witness for Christ in America*, 2 vols. (Salt Lake City: Utah Printing, 1960), 1:492-94. See also Ronald W. Walker, "The Persisting Idea of Treasure Hunting in America," *BYU Studies* 24 (Fall 1984): 429-59. The idea of a possible relationship between antifederalism and early Mormonism was first suggested to me by Gordon Thomasson.

45. *Book of Commandments* (1833), chap. 30, pp. 67-68. Fawn Brodie noted the key role that the Hiram Page episode played in the growth of the Church hierarchy in *No Man Knows My History: The Life of Joseph Smith, The Mormon Prophet* (New York: Knopf, 1945), 92. See also the more extended study by Bruce G. Stewart, "Hiram Page: An Historical and Sociological Analysis of an Early Mormon Prototype," master's thesis, Brigham Young University, 1986, esp. chaps. 4-5. Many of those individuals who were drawn to Page were later critics of Joseph Smith.

46. See D. Michael Quinn, "The Evolution of the Presiding Quorums of the LDS Church," *Journal of Mormon History* 1 (1974): 21-39; and Quinn, "From Sacred Grove to Sacral Power Structure," *Dialogue, A Journal of Mormon Thought* 17 (Summer 1984): 9-34.

47. See the "Preface" to the 1835 edition of the Doctrine and Covenants, iv.

48. Consider, for example, the later comments and writings of such individuals as David Whitmer, *An Address to All Believers in Christ*; John Whitmer, "History"; Benjamin Winchester, "Primitive Mormonism," *Salt Lake Tribune*, 22 September 1889, 2; and Ebenezer Robinson, throughout *The Return*. Warren Cowdery spoke for many in this group when he editorialized in 1837: "If we gave our privilege to one man, we virtually give him our money and our liberties, and make him a monarch, absolute and despotic, and ourselves abject slaves or fawning sycophants. If we grant privileges and monopolies to a few, they always continue to undermine the fundamental principles of freedom, and, sooner or later, convert the purest and most liberal form of Government into the rankest aristocracy." *LDS Messenger and Advocate* 3 (July 1837): 538.

49. Joseph Smith's strongest and most specific statements about the Constitution came after 1838; and by 1844 he was suggesting that the leaders of the Church were to be a "living Constitution." See the comments of Joseph F. Smith, Minutes of the Council of Fifty, 21 April 1880, typescript in Archives, Harold B. Lee Library, Brigham Young University. More contemporary perspectives are in Dean C. Jessee, ed., "Joseph Smith's 19 July 1840 Discourse," *BYU*

Studies 19 (Spring 1979): 390-94; and the letter of Orson Pratt to George A. Smith, 21 January 1841, MS in HDC.

50. For more detailed information on this movement, see Max H. Parkin, "Conflict at Kirtland: The Nature and Causes of Internal and External Conflict of the Mormons in Ohio between 1830 and 1838," master's thesis, Brigham Young University, 1966, 308-25; Milton V. Backman, Jr., *The Heavens Resound: A History of the Latter-day Saints in Ohio, 1830-1838* (Salt Lake City: Deseret Book, 1983), 323-29; HC 2:528; and George A. Smith, *JD* 7:115 (10 January 1858).

51. MS in Mary Fielding Smith Collection, HDC. Also in Kenneth W. Godfrey, Audrey M. Godfrey, and Jill Mulvay Derr, eds., *Women's Voices: An Untold History of the Latter-day Saints, 1830-1900* (Salt Lake City: Deseret Book, 1985), 60. Rigdon's powerful oratory, particularly in Missouri, has not been placed into the context of American patriotic rhetoric that had its origins in the colonial jeremiad. For example, compare "Reflections for the Fourth of July, 1834," *The Evening and the Morning Star* 2 (July 1834), which suggests that all earthly governments will crumble, and Rigdon's *Oration Delivered by Mr. S. Rigdon on the 4th of July 1838 at Far West* (Far West, MO: Printed at the Journal Office, 1838), with other American patriotic discourses. See, for example, Cedric Larson, "Patriotism in Carmine: 162 Years of July 4th Oratory," *Quarterly Journal of Speech* 26 (February 1940): 12-25; Robert P. Hay, "Freedom's Jubilee: One Hundred Years of the Fourth of July, 1776-1876," Ph.D. diss., University of Kentucky, 1967; and Barnet Baskerville, *The People's Voice: The Orator in American Society* (Lexington: University of Kentucky Press, 1979). Even Rigdon's "Salt Sermon" (17 June 1838), directed at dissenters at Far West, is less ominous if seen within the larger tradition of American jeremiads and more particularly so when compared with the anti-Tory sermons of the American Revolution and the War of 1812. It was also probably anchored in D&C 101:39-40 rather than Matthew 5:13, although these two texts are obviously related.

52. The text of this 12 January 1838 revelation, one of three given the same day, is in "The Scriptory Book of Joseph Smith," MS in HDC. Another revelation on the same day addressed the question of procedural matters for bringing the president of the Church before a Church court.

53. Basic accounts of these events are in Leland H. Gentry, "A History of the Latter-day Saints in Northern Missouri from 1836 to 1839," Ph.D. diss., Brigham Young University, 1965, 68-114. See also Cannon and Cook, *Far West Record*, 162-80. Cf. D&C 64:35.

54. For detailed information, both textual and historical, see Dean

C. Jessee and David J. Whittaker, eds., "The Last Months of Mormonism in Missouri: The Albert Perry Rockwood Journal," *BYU Studies* 28 (Winter 1988): 5-41. Rockwood's letterbook is at Yale University; handwritten copies of the original letters he sent to friends and relatives in Massachusetts are in HDC. Some of the following material is taken from the introduction to the published Rockwood Journal.

55. LeSueur, *The 1838 Mormon War in Missouri*, esp. 37-47, 195-204, 207-11. Earlier histories that followed Avard's testimony include John C. Bennett, *History of the Saints, or an Exposé of Joe Smith and the Mormons* (Boston: Leland and Whiting, 1842), 265-72; Henry Caswall, *The Prophet of the Nineteenth Century; or, the Rise, Progress, and Present State of the Mormons* (London: Printed for J. G. F. and J. Rivington, 1843), 155-73; John Hyde, Jr., *Mormonism, Its Leaders and Designs* (New York: Fetridge, 1857), 104-5; Charles Mackay, *The Mormons or, Latter-day Saints: A Contemporary History* (London: Office of the National Illustrated Library, 1851), 89-91; T. B. H. Stenhouse, *The Rocky Mountain Saints; A Full and Complete History of the Mormons* (New York: D. Appleton, 1873), 91-94; William A. Linn, *The Story of the Mormons* (New York: Macmillan, 1902), 189-93; M. R. Werner, *Brigham Young* (New York: Harcourt, Brace, 1925), 102-3; Fawn M. Brodie, *No Man Knows My History* (New York: Knopf, 1945), 214-16, 219, 228, 244, 314-15; and Jerald and Sandra Tanner, *Mormonism: Shadow or Reality*, enlarged ed. (Salt Lake City: Modern Microfilm, 1972), 428-50.

56. See Gentry, "A History of the Latter-day Saints," 213-87; and Leland H. Gentry, "The Danite Band of 1838," *BYU Studies* 14 (Summer 1974): 421-50.

57. For Avard's testimony see *Documents Containing the Correspondence, Orders, Etc. in Relation to the Disturbances with the Mormons; And Evidence Given before the Hon. Austin A. King* (Fayette, MO: Office of the Boon's Lick Democrat, 1841), 97-108.

58. See Doctrine and Covenants (1844), section 102, pp. 390-94.

59. See Peter Crawley and Richard Lloyd Anderson, "The Social and Political Realities of Zion's Camp," *BYU Studies* 14 (Summer 1974): 406-20.

60. See the 4 July 1836 letter of Anderson Wilson and Emelia Wilson to Samuel Turrentine, which suggests the logic of non-Mormon resistance to Mormon bloc-voting and rule by a new majority: "They intend to emigrate here 'til they outnumber us. Then they would rule the country at pleasure. . . . We thought of fighting. This was cruel to fight a people who had not broke the law, and in

this way we became excited. . . . Not that I boast of ourselves, but the spirit that possessed every breast plainly showed that they would either possess their country or the tomb. . . . We defend these principles at all hazards, although we are trampling on our law and Constitution. But we can't help it in no way while we possessed the spirit of 76." See Durward T. Stokes, ed., "The Wilson Letters, 1835-1849," *Missouri Historical Review* 60 (July 1966): 504-8, as cited in Richard Lloyd Anderson, *BYU Studies* 26 (Summer 1986): 12. Clearly both Mormons and their Missouri neighbors claimed a higher law for their behavior. In his study of the Jackson County problems, Richard Bushman pointed out years ago, "The Saints' vision of an earthly kingdom compelled them to seek a measure of political power. After their expulsion from Jackson County, the Mormons knew they must find a sanctuary where they could build their holy city; and only the state could assure them asylum. But Americans could not tolerate social control in Mormon hands. From the beginning until the last decade of the century, the fear of religious aliens in power lay at the heart of gentile hatreds and fears." See Richard L. Bushman, "Mormon Persecution in Missouri, 1833," *BYU Studies* 3 (Autumn 1960): 20.

61. "The Scriptory Book of Joseph Smith," 61, 27 July 1838. MS in HDC.

62. See Richard Lloyd Anderson, "Atchison's Letters and the Causes of Mormon Expulsion from Missouri," *BYU Studies* 26 (Summer 1986): 3-47.

63. Avard was the key to the investigation; see LeSueur, *The 1838 Mormon War in Missouri*, 198; *Documents Containing the Correspondence, Orders, Etc.*, 90. Yet everyone knew what an unreliable person he was, including General Clark. Nancy Rigdon testified (*Documents Containing the Correspondence, Orders, Etc.*, 147), "I have heard Sampson Avard say that he would swear to a lie to accomplish his object." Sidney Rigdon was even more to the point; see his *An Appeal to the American People* (Cincinnati: Glezen and Shepard, 1840), 66. Reed Peck, whose discussion of Danite activity shows his own prejudice against what he saw as the authoritarian leadership of the Church, reveals his dislike for Avard. See Reed Peck Manuscript, dated 18 September 1839, MS in Henry E. Huntington Library, and first published in Lu B. Cake, *Peepstone Joe and the Peck Manuscript* (New York: Published by L. B. Cake, 1899). John P. Greene wrote that "Doctor Avard also swore false concerning a constitution, as he said, was introduced among the Danites." Greene does not deny the existence of Danites, only Avard's version and accounts. See *Facts Relative to*

the Expulsion of the Mormons, or Latter-day Saints from the State of Missouri (Cincinnati: Brooks, 1839), 33. See also the statement of Lorenzo Young on the Danites in James A. Little, "Biography of Lorenzo Dow Young," *Utah Historical Quarterly* 14 (January-October 1946): 52-53. Even Mosiah Hancock's "Autobiography," MS in HDC, sought to distance the Danites, presumably those of Avard's testimony, from the Mormons; he wrote that these Danites were "of a different stripe" (15). Avard was born about 1800 in St. Peter's, Isle of Guernsey, England. Prior to his conversion to Mormonism, Avard had been a Campbellite preacher. See letter of Orson Pratt, 18 November 1835, in *LDS Messenger and Advocate* 2 (November 1835): 223-24; also Pratt's Journal, November 1835, MS in HDC.

Other early sources that reveal confusion, anger, or rejection of the centralizing tendencies of the Mormon kingdom include James H. Hunt, *Mormonism* (St. Louis: Ustick and Davies, 1844), 165-66, 195-96; statement of Thomas B. Marsh, 24 October 1838 (cf. *HC* 3:167), but compare his comments in *JD* 5:206-7 (6 September 1857); John Corrill, *A Brief History of the Church* (St. Louis: Printed for the Author, 1839), 32, 33, 38, 45-48; David Whitmer, *An Address to All Believers in Christ* (Richmond, MO: David Whitmer, 1887), 27-29, 35, who argued that Sidney Rigdon instigated the Danites even though Avard was the leader; and John Whitmer, "History" (MS in Archives, Reorganized Church of Jesus Christ of Latter Day Saints, Independence, MO), esp. chap. 2. William Swartzell, *Mormonism Exposed, Being a Journal of a Residence in Missouri from the 28th of May to the 20th of August, 1838* (Pekin, OH: Published by the author, 1840), claims to be a published diary and as such contains many detailed references to Danite activity. The absence of an original manuscript of the diary and a close look at internal evidence suggest that he is too knowledgeable about future events and that this source ought not be taken at face value. Swartzell refers to the group as "darnites," a strange title for the group by a work that claims to be a contemporary journal. Much of this record seems to reflect Avard's allegations projected back onto Mormon history, yet this source has been constantly used as an independent source to provide proof for Avard's testimony. And even if it is based on an original journal, it ends in August 1838, before the more critical events of 1838 occurred. Thomas Sharp, the publisher of the anti-Mormon *Warsaw Signal*, first summarized Avard's testimony in the issue of 16 June 1841. It clearly confirmed Sharp's perceptions of the Mormons.

64. John Smith's diary, MS in HDC, refers to Danite meetings at Adam-ondi-Ahman, including 4 August (the third meeting since

22 July); 18 August (hears a lecture on consecration and voted to conform); and 15 October (attended conference, "whole church appointed our officers and every man went to work in respective occupations"). John E. Thompson, "A Chronology of Danite Meetings in Adam-ondi-Ahman, Missouri, July to September 1838," *Restoration* 4 (January 1985): 11-14, provides a useful overview, but he only sees in these references the traditional, sinister meanings. Lyman Wight's diary for this period was destroyed in a fire at the RLDS library early in this century (1907); it would, no doubt, further clarify his involvement, particularly since he was a leader in the Adam-ondi-Ahman area. But quotes from it, used by Rollin J. Britton, who seems to have cited the original as quoted in Joseph Smith III and Heman C. Smith, eds., *The History of the Church of Jesus Christ of Latter Day Saints*, 4 vols. (Lamoni, IA: Reorganized Church of Jesus Christ of Latter Day Saints, 1897), 2:295-98, would support the interpretation given herein. See the entry for 12 November 1838 when he reacts to Avard's testimony before the Court of Inquiry: "Court opened this morning and Sampson Avard was sworn. He was a man whose character was perfectly run down in all classes of society, and he being a perfect stranger, palmed himself upon the Mormon Church, invented schemes and plans to go against mobocracy, which were perfectly derogatory to the laws of this State and of the United States, and frequently endeavored to enforce them upon members of the Church, and when repulsed by Joseph Smith, he would frequently become chagrined. At one time he told me that the Presidency of the Church feared he would have too much influence and gain the honor which the First Presidency desired for themselves. At one time he said to me that he would 'be damned' if he did not carry his plans through. More than once did he raise a conspiracy against them [the Presidency] in order to take their lives, thinking that he might then rule the Church. Now when he was brought before the court, he swore that all these treasonable purposes (which he had sworn in his heart to perform) originated with us." Quoted in Rollin J. Britton, *Early Days on Grand River and the Mormon War* (Columbia, MO: State Historical Society of Missouri, 1920), 86.

The Reminiscences of Morris Phelps, MS in HDC, 5-6, probably written after 1852, provide the basis for the material in *HC* 3:178-82, as well as for the statement of John Taylor in the Bancroft Library (1884) who lays the blame on Avard; the *Autobiography of Luman Andros Shurtliff*, MS in HDC, 120, written after 1850, states the "Danite society" was got up "for our personal defense also of our families,

Property and our Religion." He joined in August 1838, considering the Danites a good institution and a blessing for his people. Nowhere does he imply the illegalities Avard did, even though he speaks of signs and passwords and uses military metaphors. In 1885 Anson Call gave a statement to B. H. Roberts and John M. Whitaker which referred to the Danites as a military order "according to the Mosaic Order" (MS in HDC, 5; or typescript, dated 30 December 1885, 2). He remembered Avard as the head of the organization, yet says the facts of the matter agree with Joseph Smith's record, suggesting either confusion or only a peripheral involvement or knowledge.

Even Ebenezer Robinson, *The Return* 2 (June 1890): 287, seems to have equated the "Order of Enoch" and the "Danites" and placed all the blame for "secret societies" on John C. Bennett later in 1842! Like many others, Robinson revealed a strong reaction to the temporal power of Joseph Smith that colors his account. No doubt he used the theme of the Danites to attack this more central concern.

Hosea Stout spoke in 1846 of the "Danite evolutions of horsemanship as practiced in the War in Davis[s] County Missouri in the fall of 1838." *On the Mormon Frontier: The Diary of Hosea Stout*, ed. Juanita Brooks, 2 vols. (Salt Lake City: University of Utah Press for the Utah State Historical Society, 1964), 1:141 (21 March 1846). This is hardly a sinister reference, and clearly in line with the formations mentioned in the Rockwood letters. Dimick B. Huntington's Reminiscences (MS in HDC, 13-15, written about 1845) indicate that he was appointed in May 1838 a "Captain of the Guard in the Da. . . . s[Danites]." This was hardly another sinister appointment; he had been appointed a Constable in Far West and in June he was appointed deputy sheriff—all, it would seem, positions of public trust. One even suspects that, following Rockwood, regular civic positions were just incorporated into the Mormon kingdom, much like what happened later in Nauvoo and the Salt Lake Valley.

Finally, much has been made of the election-day battle at Gallatin on 6 August 1838, at which a violent confrontation occurred between Mormons and non-Mormons. It seems that when Mormons were prevented from voting, a fight broke out. Then a Danite distress signal was called out, a number of Mormons came to the rescue of those being accosted. Students of this period forget that most fraternal organizations in early America had elements of "secret" rites, code names, and distress calls. But most accounts, including that of LeSueur (*The 1838 Mormon War in Missouri*, 59-64) see the action as additional proof that a select group of Danites showed their violent nature by responding to their special distress call. But this presupposes that only Avard-type Danites voted, which is absurd; doesn't it make more sense to understand the situation in the same way as Rockwood did, that the whole community of men had been organized into "Danites"? A useful overview of this episode is Reed C. Durham, Jr., "The Election Day Battle at Gallatin," *BYU Studies* 13 (Autumn 1972): 36-61.

65. See "Journal History," 1 December 1838, MS in HDC.

66. Dean C. Jessee, ed., *The Personal Writings of Joseph Smith* (Salt Lake City: Deseret Book, 1984), 380.

67. See Rebecca Foster Cornwall and Leonard J. Arrington, "Perpetuation of a Myth: Mormon Danites in Five Western Novels, 1840-1890," *BYU Studies* 23 (Spring 1983): 147-65. This study indicates (p. 149) that by 1900 at least fifty-six novels had been published in English which used the Danite theme as part of their story line. Years ago Hugh Nibley correctly observed that "The Danites thus supply the anti-Mormon fraternity with a blank check backed by unlimited horror," *Sounding Brass* (Salt Lake City: Bookcraft, 1963), 217.

68. *Millennial Star* 14 (1 May 1852): 150-51. Known today as D&C 136, it was first added to the Doctrine and Covenants in 1876; see esp. vss. 2-11. This same organization was used in the evacuation of Nauvoo in 1846. It was also used in organizing the militia in the Salt Lake Valley; see the letter of the Quorum of the Twelve Apostles to the Saints in the Salt Lake Valley, 9 September 1847, MS in HDC. See also the comments of Parley Pratt regarding the establishment of the Nauvoo Legion in *Millennial Star* 3 (August 1842): 69.

69. See Leonard J. Arrington, Feramorz Y. Fox, and Dean L. May, *Building the City of God: Community and Cooperation among the Mormons* (Salt Lake City: Deseret Book, 1976). It also seems probable that Brigham Young's later emphasis on the key role of Adam in Latter-day Saint thought had its genesis in this early milieu; for an introduction to his later thought, see David J. Buerger, "The Adam-God Doctrine," *Dialogue* 15 (Spring 1982): 14-58. Unfortunately Buerger fails to see the earlier roots of Young's thought.

70. See n. 23 above. See also Orson Pratt, "The Ancient of Days," *Times and Seasons* 4 (15 May 1843): 204; reprinted in *Millennial Star* 4 (December 1843): 123-24. When the temple endowment was established in Nauvoo, it was justified as "setting forth the order pertaining to the Ancient of Days." See *HC* 5:1-2.

71. See also "Adam-ondi-Ahman" in D&C 78:15; 107:53-57; 116:1. See also n. 24 above.

72. Cf. D&C 115:4 with Daniel 7:22. A useful overview of the

changes to the name of the Church is Richard Lloyd Anderson, "What Changes Have Been Made in the Name of the Church?" *Ensign* 9 (January 1979): 13-14. Particularly revealing is the 19 October 1834 letter of John Smith to Elias Smith, who had raised questions about changes in the name of the Church: "Now I come to the great question that seems to burden you so much — what business anyone has to call the Church of Christ the Church of the Latter Day Saints or call the children of God saints. I answer the Church of Christ is the Church of Saints and always was. . . . Search the ancient prophecies, you will find that they say considerable about Saints. See Daniel 7ch 18, 22, 27th verses evidently meaning the Church of the Latter Day Saints or the Chr. of Christ. . . . Tell Amos that the work of the Lord prospers, the church increases in numbers very fast, prejudice is giving away in this region [Kirtland,] a spirit of inquiry prevails almost universally, finally the work rools [*sic*] on and will until the saints of the Latter Day takes the kingdom and possess the kingdom & yea I repeat it the church of the Latter Day Saints will prosper in spite of wicked men and Devils until it fills the whole earth." MS in HDC. This letter was called to my attention by Steve Sorensen.

73. See Lyndon W. Cook, *Joseph Smith and the Law of Consecration* (Provo: Grandin, 1985), 71-83. The revelation on tithing, D&C 118, ought not to be interpreted as meaning just 10 percent, as the term was used in a broad sense to describe general offerings to the Church.

74. For example, members of the Quorum of the Twelve Apostles were to leave for their mission to Great Britain from Far West. See D&C 118:4-5 and Ronald K. Esplin, "The Emergence of Brigham Young and the Twelve to Mormon Leadership, 1830-1841," Ph.D. diss., Brigham Young University, 1981, 363-72. Little emphasis has been given to the early Mormon sense of sacred space/place. Surely the sites identified with Adam could be understood in the context discussed in Steven L. Olsen, "Community Celebrations and Mormon Ideology of Place," *Sunstone* 5 (May-June 1980): 41-45. See also Roger Henrie, "The Perception of Sacred Space: The Case of Utah and Other Sacred Places in Mormondom," master's thesis, Brigham Young University, 1972.

75. It is possible to overstate the issues here, but if a narrow look is given to just the accounts of Joseph's first vision, it is possible to agree with Marvin Hill, who first pointed out this shift in emphasis. See "The First Vision Controversy: A Critique and Reconciliation," *Dialogue* 15 (Summer 1982): 31-64.

76. See *Documents Containing the Correspondence, Orders, Etc.*, 111 (John Corrill), 128 (George M. Hinkle), 135 (Burr Riggs), 139 (John Whitmer), and 139 (Alanson Ripley).

77. Compare D&C 121:12 with Daniel 2:21; D&C 121:26 with Daniel 2:28; D&C 121:32 with Daniel 11:36; D&C 121:33 with Daniel 4:35 and 12:4; and D&C 121:46 with Daniel 7:14. The whole letter was not used when D&C 121-23 was prepared for the 1876 edition. For the entire Liberty Jail letter see *HC* 3:289-305. Here, no attention has been paid to the deleted sections, some of which also have allusions to the book of Daniel.

78. *A Voice of Warning and Instruction to All People, Containing a Declaration of the Faith and Doctrine of the Church of the Latter-day Saints, Commonly Called Mormons* (New York: W. Sandford, 1837), chaps. 1-2. Outside the standard works of the Church, this was probably the most important and widely distributed Latter-day Saint work in the nineteenth century. Jan Shipps has recognized the importance of the themes of the book of Daniel in the early Mormon attempts to establish a Hebraic kingdom in America, see *Mormonism: The Story of a New Religious Tradition* (Urbana: University of Illinois Press, 1985), 121, and 186-87, n. 21.

79. *A Letter to the Queen, Touching the Signs of the Times, and the Political Destiny of the World* (Manchester: Printed and published by P. P. Pratt, 1841). See also Parley P. Pratt, "The Kingdom of God, or the Stone Cut Out of the Mountain without Hands," *Millennial Star* 3 (September 1842): 92-94; and his discourse of 20 January 1853, in *JD* 1:172-85. See also the editorial by Thomas Ward in *Millennial Star* 3 (February 1843): 169-70.

80. *Proclamation of the Twelve Apostles of the Church of Jesus Christ of Latter-day Saints. To All the Kings of the World; to the President of the United States; to the Governors of the Several States and to the Rulers and Peoples of All Nations* (New York: Prophet Office, 1845). That Parley Pratt was the author of this item is made clear in the letter of Brigham Young to Parley P. Pratt, 26 May 1845, MS at Archives, Harold B. Lee Library, Brigham Young University.

81. See the account of his discourse of 11 April 1841, in the Journal of Wilford Woodruff, MS in HDC.

82. See esp. his *Kingdom of God* series (Liverpool: James, 1848-49); *Divine Authenticity of the Book of Mormon* (Liverpool: James, 1850); and *Latter-day Kingdom, or the Preparations for the Second Advent* (Liverpool: LDS Book and Star Depot, 1857). For references in his early journals, see n. 30.

83. See *The Seer* 1 (October 1853): 148; 2 (August 1854): 307-11;

and the following sermons in *JD* 7:210-27 (14 August 1859); 13:125-26 (10 April 1870); 15:67-76 (4 February 1872); 16:86-87 (15 June 1873); 17:181-88 (11 October 1874); 17:308-9 (28 February 1875); 18:181-82 (26 March 1876); 18:335-48 (25 February 1877).

84. "Nebuchadnezzar's Dream," *Gospel Reflector* [Philadelphia] 1 (1 and 15 April 1841): 192-200, 201-13. This essay was reprinted in the *Times and Seasons* 3 (1 December 1841): 607-14. See also Benjamin Winchester, *An Examination of a Lecture Delivered by the Rev. H. Perkins* (N.p., 1840), 9-10. A copy of this rare tract is in the Harvard University Library. It should be noted that in his writings Winchester stresses a spiritual rather than a temporal kingdom, which would only be established at the time of the Second Coming of Christ. His own disaffection from the Church was thus related to the same anticentralist tendencies discussed above. For more information on him see David J. Whittaker, "Early Mormon Pamphleteering," Ph.D. diss., Brigham Young University, 1982, 139-235.

85. *A Dissertation on Nebuchadnezzar's Dream: Showing That the Kingdom Spoken of by Daniel the Prophet Was Not Set Up in the Days of the Apostles; and the Order of the Kingdom Set Up Then Explained* (Philadelphia: Brown, Bicking and Guilbert, 1844). See also the manuscript of Appleby's unpublished "History of the Signs of the Times for the Benefit of the Church of the Latter Day Saints," dated June 1848, Recklesstown, NJ. MS in HDC. Daniel references occur on 55-56, 77, 97, 113, 159-60.

86. Dated before 8 August 1839. See Ehat and Cook, *The Words of Joseph Smith*, 8-11. Peter Cartright recalled hearing Joseph Smith preach in 1839, "I will show you, sir, that I will raise up a government in these United States which will overturn the present government and I will raise up a new religion that will overturn every other form of religion in the country." See W. P. Strickland, ed., *Autobiography of Peter Cartright* (New York: Carlton and Porter, 1857), 345. Peter Crawley has examined the role of Joseph Smith's trip to the East Coast in 1839-40 in the context of being freed from the restraints of the Whitmer faction in "The Passage of Mormon Primitivism," *Dialogue* 13 (Winter 1980): 26-37.

87. Ehat and Cook, *The Words of Joseph Smith*, 67 (discourse of 21 March 1841). Cf. Daniel 7:9, 14, 21-22, 27.

88. Ehat and Cook, *The Words of Joseph Smith*, 123-26, citing *The Wasp*, 9 July 1842. See also Journal of Wilford Woodruff, 3 July 1842. Cf. Daniel 2:44; 7:9-14, 22-27.

89. Ehat and Cook, *The Words of Joseph Smith*, 183-90 (discourse of 8 April 1843). Cf. Daniel 7:3-8, 12, 16-28; 8:3-27; and Revelation 4:6; 7:1-14.

90. See Ehat and Cook, *The Words of Joseph Smith*, 367 (discourse of 12 May 1844).

91. Dan Jones, in the *Prophet of Jubilee* (1847), 18. I am grateful to Ronald Dennis who translated this material from the Welsh and shared it with me. See also Dan Jones, "The Martyrdom of Joseph and Hyrum Smith," MS in HDC, written in 1855; and the "History of Joseph Smith," *Millennial Star* 24 (7 June 1862): 359, which refers to William Law's charges relating to Daniel's kingdom.

92. For details see the Oliver Olney papers, Yale University Library. Cf. *HC* 5:269-70.

93. James J. Strang, *Book of the Law of the Lord*, 1856 edition, 171. See further the early letter of George J. Adams to James J. Strang, 20 June 1846. MS in Strang Papers, Yale University.

94. See Klaus J. Hansen, *Quest for Empire: The Political Kingdom of God and the Council of Fifty in Mormon History* (East Lansing: Michigan State University Press, 1967); and D. Michael Quinn, "The Council of Fifty and Its Members, 1844 to 1945," *BYU Studies* 20 (Winter 1980): 163-97. Quinn suggests (p. 164) that the 7 April 1842 organizational meeting fulfilled the prophecy of Daniel 2:44-45. See also Andrew F. Ehat, " 'It Seems Like Heaven Began on Earth': Joseph Smith and the Constitution of the Kingdom of God," *BYU Studies* 20 (Spring 1980): 253-79.

95. See D. Michael Quinn, "Echoes and Foreshadowings: The Distinctiveness of the Mormon Communities," *Sunstone* 3 (March-April 1978): 12-17.

96. Ehat and Cook, *The Words of Joseph Smith*, 367 (discourse of 12 May 1844). It is interesting to compare Joseph Smith with William Miller, a contemporary who also stressed the book of Daniel. Mormons probably never could forget that Miller's great publicist, Joshua V. Himes, had written the preface to the first anti-Mormon tract, a work by Alexander Campbell: *Delusions, An Analysis of the Book of Mormon* (1832); or Himes's own *Delusions and Monstrosities* (1842), which had been responded to by John Hardy, *Hypocrisy Exposed* (Boston: Albert Morgan, 1842). In 1841 Joshua Himes reprinted the 1796 work of Joshua Spalding which used Daniel's volume: *Sentiments Concerning the Coming and Kingdom of Christ, Collected from the Bible, and from the Writings of Many Ancient, and Some Modern Believers.* So far the only serious study comparing the two groups is Grant Underwood, "Apocalyptic Adversaries: Mormonism Meets Millerism," *John Whitmer Historical Association Journal* 7 (1987): 53-61, but this essay does not treat the issues from the perspectives suggested here. Other important studies of Mormon apocalypticism

are Keith Norman, "How Long, O Lord? The Delay of the Parousia in Mormonism," *Sunstone* 8 (January-April 1983): 48-58; Stephen J. Stein, "Signs of the Times: The Theological Functions of Early Mormon Apocalyptic," ibid., 59-65; and W. H. Oliver, *Prophets and Millennialists* (Auckland: Auckland University Press, 1978), 236-38.

97. Relevant studies that apply the recent insights relating to social and cultural conflict to early Mormon history include Warren Jennings, "The City in the Garden: Social Conflict in Jackson County, Missouri," in F. Mark McKiernan et al., eds., *The Restoration Movement: Essays in Mormon History* (Lawrence, KS: Coronado, 1973), 99-119; Leonard J. Arrington and Davis Bitton, *The Mormon Experience: A History of the Latter-day Saints* (New York: Knopf, 1979), 44-64; James B. Allen, "Why Did People Act That Way?" *Ensign* 8 (December 1978): 21-24; and the material in *Sunstone* 4 (July-August 1979): 43-46.

98. For example, Parley Pratt argued that the Book of Mormon "set the time for the overthrow of our government and all other Gentile governments on the American continent." Parley P. Pratt, *Mormonism Unveiled: Zion's Watchman Unmasked, and its editor, Mr. L. R. Sunderland, exposed: truth vindicated: the devil mad, and priestcraft in danger!* (New York: printed for the author, 1838), 15.

11

Aspects of an Early Christian Initiation Ritual

William J. Hamblin
Brigham Young University, Provo, Utah

Joseph Smith and other leaders of the early Church were convinced that the temple endowment was an authentic restoration of ancient Christian and Jewish initiation ceremonies, a concept which is still generally held among most Latter-day Saints.[1] In recent decades Latter-day Saint scholars, foremost among whom has been Hugh Nibley, have pointed to numerous interesting parallels between some aspects of the Latter-day Saint temple endowment and different forms of ancient Near Eastern initiation rituals.[2]

But the fact that similarities may exist between ancient and Latter-day Saint ideas and ritual motifs[3] does not answer the more significant question concerning the precise nature of interdependence between the texts or ritual systems manifesting the parallels. Generally speaking, there are five possible explanations for these parallels. The first three could be called naturalistic:

1. The parallels are either coincidental or on closer examination prove to be based on false comparisons and strained interpretations.

2. Whatever valid parallels may exist are due to the fact that human beings frequently express their religious and social solidarity by ritual acts. Latter-day Saint and ancient rituals may be broadly similar but are fundamentally distinct in all significant details. Existing parallels are general and universal rather than specific and historical.

3. Joseph Smith invented the Latter-day Saint endowment based on readily available early nineteenth-century sources such as the Bible as well as Masonic or magical practices and rituals. Some of these nineteenth-century sources may be tenuously linked back to more ancient ritual traditions, which could account for some of the apparent resemblances.

These three naturalistic explanations are by no means mutually exclusive. Some combination or variation of them is generally accepted by most non-Mormons as well as a small portion of Latter-day Saints.

The other two possible explanations are supernaturalistic:

1. The Latter-day Saint endowment represents an inspired restoration of authentic ancient revealed initiation rituals. The parallels between ancient and modern rituals exist because the ancient rituals are either themselves revealed or are counterfeit copies and corruptions of revealed rituals. Some variation of this explanation is accepted by most practicing Latter-day Saints who have considered the matter. This is the position which I personally believe best accounts for all of the available evidence.

2. Joseph Smith received the endowment from a supernatural source other than God, such as the devil. Some evangelical Christians and other groups might accept some variation of this proposition.[4]

Given that some level of parallels exists between ancient and Latter-day Saint ritual motifs, the question now becomes, which of these five explanations, or combination and variation thereof, best accounts for the parallels? It is impossible to deal adequately with all the ramifications of this question in the short space available here. I will therefore limit myself to a discussion of only one aspect of the broader historical problem: a possible method of transmission and transformation of some late first- and early second-century Christian secret rituals into Gnostic writings and rituals.[5] Specifically I will examine some of the evidence for the following seven propositions:

1. Jesus himself established a secret, graded initiation ritual.

2. This ritual system was transmitted through Peter to Mark the Evangelist, who brought the ritual system to Alexandria in Egypt sometime shortly after ca. A.D. 65.

3. These rituals were secretly practiced by at least some branches of "orthodox" Alexandrian Christianity until at least the late second century A.D.

4. During the early second century A.D., Carpocrates, an early Gnostic Christian, gained access to at least part of this ritual system through an apostate elder at Alexandria.

5. Carpocrates and other Gnostics transformed and transmitted various modified forms of these ideas and rituals to some of the branches of Gnostic Christianity.

6. Possible manifestations of this transformed ritual system can be found in various early Christian writings by or about the Gnostics.

7. The parallels between the Latter-day Saint temple endowment and some Gnostic rituals and writings can be seen as reflections of parallels with the original rituals established by Jesus.

Let me now briefly examine the evidence for each of these seven propositions.

1. Jesus himself established a secret, graded initiation ritual. Did some early Christians believe that Jesus during his lifetime established secret, graded rituals of salvation? The answer to this question is most certainly yes.[6] The early Christian eucharist (or sacrament) is the clearest example of this. Although today the eucharistic rituals of most branches of Christianity are public rites, the opposite was true in the first through the third centuries A.D. As the Catholic scholar Jean Daniélou writes, "It might seem astonishing that there is nothing like [the early descriptions of baptism] to be found in relation to the Eucharist, but the reason is that the discipline of the *arcana*, or secrecy, forbade the revelation of the Mysteries. The only teaching given on this subject, therefore, could not be preserved for use in writing."[7] The idea that the eucharist and other sacraments should be secret rituals is expressed in numerous early Christian writings. For example, the *Apostolic Constitutions* advises that "the doors be watched [during the eucharist], lest any unbelieving or uninitiated person enter."[8] Thus, according to nearly all branches of earliest Christianity, Jesus instituted a ritual of salvation, known as the eucharist (or sacrament), which was to be performed in secret.

Was the eucharist the only secret ritual established by Jesus? Here the evidence is much more controversial, but a wide range of documents discovered and studied in the last few decades clearly shows that many branches of earliest Christianity maintained that Jesus did indeed institute other secret rituals, known variously as the "Mystery of Redemption," the "Great Mysteries," or the "Mystery of the Kingdom of God."

One of the most interesting of these new documents was discovered several decades ago by Professor Morton Smith.[9] The document is a fragment of a letter of Clement of Alexandria who lived from about A.D. 150-213 and who is generally considered an "orthodox" Christian. In this letter Clement quotes a fascinating passage from a previously unknown work he calls the *Secret Gospel of Mark*. Although nothing is known for certain about the date, authorship, or provenance of this *Secret Gospel of Mark*, the following is a summary of the current evidence and scholarly hypotheses:

Author: Clement claims the document was written by Mark the Evangelist. Most modern scholars feel that the document is an early second-century pseudepigraphic gospel.[10]

Date: For the *Secret Gospel of Mark* to have been quoted by Clement, it must have been in existence by at least A.D. 150. Morton Smith provides convincing evidence that it probably dates to the late first or early second century, an hypothesis that is generally accepted today.[11] If it was actually written by Mark, it could not have been written much later than about A.D. 80. It is important to note that many scholars believe that they can establish that the canonical Gospel of Mark was literarily dependent on, and therefore written after, the *Secret Gospel of Mark*.[12] Hans-Martin Schenke believes that "this apocryphal version of Mark from Alexandria would by no means have been an enlargement of our Second Gospel; rather, our Gospel [of Mark] would have been a purified abridgement of the Alexandrian apocryphon," and may represent an old tradition which "reflect[s] a historical event."[13] John Crossan agrees that the *Secret Gospel of Mark* "is independent of [the Gospels of] John . . . [and] of Mark. . . . Dependence, in fact, is in the opposite direction, from Secret Mark to John and Mark."[14] In other words, there is good evidence that the material in the *Secret Gospel of Mark* represents Christian ideas from the first century A.D.

Provenance: Clement says that the document was written in Egypt, which location is generally accepted today as accurate.

In summary, the *Secret Gospel of Mark* is an Egyptian Christian document of uncertain authorship, written sometime in the late first or early second centuries A.D.

The following passage is part of the only extant fragment from the *Secret Gospel of Mark*, which tells the story of what happened to Lazarus after he was raised from the dead by Jesus:

> And they [Jesus and the Apostles] come into Bethany, and a certain woman, whose brother had died, was there. And, coming, she prostrated herself before Jesus and says to him, "Son of David, have mercy on

me." But the disciples rebuked her. And Jesus, being angered, went off with her into the garden where the tomb was, and straightway a great cry was heard from the tomb. And going near, Jesus rolled away the stone from the door of the tomb. And straightway, going in where the youth was, he stretched forth his hand and raised him, seizing his hand. But the youth, looking upon him, loved him and began to beseech him that he might be with him. And going out of the tomb they came into the house of the youth, for he was rich. And after six days Jesus told him what to do and in the evening the youth comes to him, wearing a linen cloth over [his] naked [body]. And he [the young man] remained with him [Jesus] that night, for Jesus taught him the mystery of the kingdom of God.[15]

This passage provides us a very clear description of Jesus performing a secret initiation ritual called the "Mystery of the Kingdom of God." From the passage we can isolate four ritual motifs which were part of this "Mystery of the Kingdom of God" according to the *Secret Gospel of Mark*:

A. There was a period of six days of preparation, with the initiation taking place on the seventh day. This waiting period may be coincidental, but in its ancient setting probably represents a period of some type of ritual purification.[16]

B. The "Mystery of the Kingdom of God" begins with the young man (who is called Lazarus in John's version of the story) wearing a "linen cloth over his naked body," which again in its ancient context clearly implies an initiatory ritual.[17]

C. Instruction in the "Mystery of the Kingdom of God" lasts all night. In other words, participation in the full ritual requires many hours.

D. The "Mystery of the Kingdom of God" is something which was taught and established by Jesus himself.

2. This ritual system was transmitted through Peter to Mark the Evangelist, who brought the ritual system to Alexandria in Egypt sometime shortly after ca. A.D. 65, and, 3. These rituals were secretly practiced by at least some branches of "orthodox" Alexandrian Christianity until at least the late second century A.D. The newly discovered letter of Clement also provides us a literary history of the *Secret Gospel of Mark* as understood by Clement's branch of Christianity in Alexandria.

> As for Mark, during Peter's stay in Rome he wrote [an account of] the Lord's doings, not, however, declaring all [of them], nor yet hinting at the secret [ones], but selecting those he thought most useful for increasing the faith of those who were being instructed. But when Peter died as a martyr, Mark came over to Alexandria, bringing both his own notes and those of Peter, from which he transferred to his former book the things suitable to whatever makes for progress toward knowledge [*gnosis*]. [Thus] he composed a more spiritual Gospel for the use of those who were being perfected. Nevertheless, he yet did not divulge the things not to be uttered, nor did he write down the "Hierophantic Teaching of the Lord," but to the stories already written [in canonical Mark] he added yet others and, moreover, brought in certain sayings of which he knew the interpretation would, as a mystagogue, lead the hearers into the innermost sanctuary of that truth hidden by seven [veils]. . . . (When he died) he left his composition to the church in Alexandria, where it even yet is most carefully guarded, being read only to those who are being initiated into the "Great Mysteries."[18]

This fascinating passage implies the following:

A. Clement believed that Jesus taught secret teachings which were not recorded in the New Testament.[19]

B. There existed a document in Alexandria which was not made available to ordinary Christians, but only to a select group whom Clement describes as those seeking the true knowledge and those who were being perfected. This book is known today as the *Secret Gospel of Mark*.

C. In addition to the written teachings in Mark's *Secret Gospel*, there were other secret oral teachings known to Clement as the "Hierophantic Teaching of the Lord."

D. These most secret oral teachings were only for "those who are being initiated into the Great Mysteries," which were somehow related to an "innermost sanctuary . . . hidden by seven [veils]."

Thus, if Clement's report is accurate, by at least A.D. 180 in Egypt there existed among the Alexandrian branch of Christianity a set of highly sacred and secret teachings known as "the Hierophantic Teaching of the Lord" and secret initiation rituals known as "the Great Mysteries." The Hierophantic Teaching and the Great Mysteries are *not* based on the *Secret Gospel of Mark*, nor are they contained in any other document in Clement's possession. Clement specifically states that these are "things not to be uttered," and Mark did not write them down. The Hierophantic Teaching and Great Mysteries must therefore have been transmitted by a secret oral tradition. In fact, the importance of maintaining the secrecy of these teachings was so great that Clement insists in his letter that "one must (never) concede that the *Secret Gospel* is by Mark, but should even deny it on oath."[20] Even before the discovery of the *Secret Gospel of Mark*, there was good evidence that Clement of Alexandria viewed initiation into the mysteries of God as a fundamental part of Christianity. As described by G. Bornkamm, Clement saw

> the truths of the Christian religion as mysteries. Led by Christ the Mystagogue (*Stromata* IV, 162, 3ff.) the Gnostic [in this sense, simply "knower"] receives initiation and perfection (*Protrepticon* XII, 120, 1) by going through the stages from the little mysteries (e.g., the doctrine of creation) to the great mysteries, in which the mystical ini-

tiation takes place (*Stromata* IV, 3, 1; *Protrepticon* XII). The supreme mysteries, to be protected against profanation, must be passed on only in veiled form (*Stromata* V, 57, 2).[21]

The discovery of this new letter by Clement has now clearly shown that Clement did not see these mysteries in an allegorical sense as has often been previously assumed, but had in mind actual secret initiation *rituals* which he believed to have been instituted by Christ himself.

Schenke also sees the importance of this new evidence of early secret Christian initiation rituals:

> How may it be explained that in Alexandria the Secret Gospel gained such great importance and functioned as a ritual text used in the initiation of the Perfect? Indeed, the rite connected with the Secret Gospel of Mark is so strange that many scholars refuse to acknowledge it as real. . . . The rite must have been something that was never introduced to [Alexandria] but rather something that was simply there. Applied to the Secret Gospel of Mark, this would mean that it never came to Alexandria, but was there all along. It is the very own gospel of orthodox Christianity in Alexandria and is linked in a fundamental way to the origin of that [branch of] Christianity.[22]

4. *During the early second century* A.D., *Carpocrates, an early Gnostic Christian, gained access to at least part of this ritual system through an apostate elder at Alexandria, and,* 5. *Carpocrates and other Gnostics transmitted modified forms of these ideas and rituals to some branches of Gnostic Christianity.* Again from the newly discovered letter of Clement we learn that the Carpocratian Gnostic branch of early Christianity[23] acquired knowledge of some of the Hierophantic Teaching and Great Mysteries. Clement claims that:

> Carpocrates [one of the original Gnostic teachers who flourished ca. A.D. 117-138] . . . using deceitful arts,

so enslaved a certain elder of the church in Alexandria that he [Carpocrates] got from him [the elder] a copy of the secret Gospel which he both interpreted according to his blasphemous and carnal doctrine and, moreover, polluted, mixing with the spotless and holy words utterly shameless lies. From this mixture is drawn off the teaching of the Carpocratians.[24]

If Clement's statement is accurate, it implies that:

A. The *Secret Gospel of Mark* must have been extant for some years before about A.D. 125, when Carpocrates got a copy of it.

B. An unnamed Alexandrian elder defected to Carpocrates, giving him a copy of the *Secret Gospel of Mark* and perhaps orally transmitting parts of the Hierophantic Teaching and the Great Mysteries.

C. Before the recent discovery of Clement's letter it had usually been maintained by modern scholars that the theologians of Alexandrian Christianity were influenced by Gnostic and Hellenistic concepts.[25] The new letter of Clement shows that the Great Mysteries and Hierophantic Teaching were not copied by the Alexandrians from the Gnostics or Greek Pagans, but, as maintained by Schenke, were part of the earliest ideas and practices of Alexandrian Christianity.[26]

D. The ideas and rituals of at least some branches of Gnostic Christianity can thus in part be seen as variations and modifications of the secret teachings and rituals of the early Alexandrian Christians.

6. *Possible manifestations of this transformed ritual system can be found in various early Christian writings by or about the Gnostics.* Is it possible to determine any details of the Hierophantic Teaching or the Great Mysteries? Clement refused to discuss the subject openly, although there are many interesting allusions to such matters in his surviving writings, as we have seen.[27] However, explicit discussions of purported secret doctrines and rituals have survived in the

teachings of the Gnostics, which, according to Clement, were derived at least in part from Carpocrates' access to the secret teachings of the Alexandrian Christians.

Modern scholars are now beginning to recognize that, in addition to the esoteric doctrines of the Gnostics, there also existed a body of esoteric ritual, which receives frequent allusions in Gnostic writings.[28] Indeed, J. J. Buckley maintains that the Nag Hammadi *Gospel of Philip* is essentially a preparatory manual for a secret initiation ritual.[29]

The ritual background to the *Gospel of Philip* is quite explicit. For example, we learn that "The Lord [did] all things by means of a mystery ⟨*or ritual*⟩: baptism, chrism ⟨*or anointing*⟩, eucharist, ransom ⟨*or redemption*⟩, and bridal chamber."[30] According to the *Gospel of Philip*, these rituals thus form the essence of Christ's teachings. The Great Mysteries are also allegorically equated with the temple in Jerusalem. "The holy building ⟨*or the temple of Jerusalem*⟩ is baptism, the holy of the holy is ransom ⟨*or redemption*⟩, the holy of holies is the bridal chamber."[31]

7. *The parallels between the Latter-day Saint temple endowment and some Gnostic rituals and writings can be seen as possible reflections of parallels with the original rituals established by Jesus.* It is precisely in the Gnostic writings that we find some of the most fascinating parallels to some ritual motifs in the Latter-day Saint temple endowment. Among the many doctrines and ritual motifs mentioned in Gnostic writings which parallel Latter-day Saint temple endowment ritual motifs, we note only the following twelve general aspects here:[32]

A. *The secret tradition originates with Jesus.* Irenaeus reports: "Jesus, [the Gnostics] say, spoke in a mystery to his disciples and apostles privately, and charged them to hand these things on to the worthy and those who assented."[33]

B. *The secret initiatory rituals are the center of Christ's gospel.* The *Gospel of Philip* says: "The Lord [did] all things by means of a mystery ⟨*ritual*⟩: baptism, chrism ⟨*anointing*⟩, eucharist, ransom ⟨*redemption*⟩, and bridal chamber."[34]

C. *Rituals of baptism and anointing with oil.* "The chrism ⟨*or anointing*⟩ is superior to baptism, for it is from the word 'chrism' that we have been called 'Christians,' certainly not because of the word 'baptism.' And it is because of the chrism that 'the Christ' has his name. For the father anointed the son, and the son anointed the apostles, and the apostles anointed us. He who has been anointed possesses everything. He possesses the resurrection, the light, the cross, the holy spirit. The father gave him this in the bridal chamber; he merely accepted (the gift). The father was in the son and the son in the father. This is [the] kingdom of heaven."[35]

D. *Ritual prayer circles* (described at length by Hugh Nibley).[36]

E. *Use of ritual clothing.* "The (demonic) powers do not see those who are clothed in the perfect light, and consequently are not able to detain them. One will clothe himself in this light sacramentally in the union."[37]

F. *Handclasps as tokens of recognition.* Epiphanius explains: "The hand is held out, in greeting, of course, and a tickling stroke is made in the palm of the hand, so as to indicate secretly that the visitor is of the same religion as they."[38]

G. *Knowledge of the sacred name of God is necessary for exaltation.* "One single name is not uttered in the world, the name which the Father gave to the Son, the name above all things: the name of the Father. For the Son would not become Father unless he wears the name of the Father. Those who have this name know it, but they do not speak it. But those who do not have it do not know it."[39]

H. *Preexistence of mankind.* "[The Gnostics claim that] I derive my being from him who was pre-existent, and I go again to that which is my own, whence I came forth."[40]

I. *Sacred marriage is necessary to complete the ordinance.*

"If anyone becomes a son of the bridal chamber, he will receive the light. If anyone does not receive it while he is here, he will not be able to receive it in the other place."[41] "Those who have united in the bridal chamber will no longer be separated."[42] "Some of [the Gnostics] prepare a bridal chamber and perform a mystic rite, with certain invocations, for those who are being consecrated, and they claim that what they are effecting is a spiritual marriage, after the image of the conjunctions above."[43]

J. *The initiation rituals symbolize a heavenly ascent.* Origen provides a detailed description of such an ascent, which is too long for full quotation here.[44]

K. *A veil separates the initiate from God.* "Therefore the perfect things have opened to us [through the veil], together with the hidden things of truth. The holies of the holies were revealed, and the bridal chamber invited us in."[45]

L. *Mankind can become like God.* "You saw the spirit, you became spirit. You saw Christ, you became Christ. You saw [the father, you] shall become father."[46]

I believe we can make the following conclusions based on the evidence of Clement's letter and the fragment of the *Secret Gospel of Mark*. Clement's early branch of Christianity in Alexandria believed that there existed three levels of Christian knowledge: First, the canonical gospels, which were intended to bring new converts to Christianity. Second, a secret written tradition, exemplified by the *Secret Gospel of Mark*, which was only to be read by advanced Christians seeking higher, more esoteric, knowledge. Third, an even more secret oral tradition known as the "Hierophantic Teaching," and rituals, known as the "Great Mysteries," or "Mystery of the Kingdom of God." The "Mystery of the Kingdom of God" included secret teachings and some type of ritual initiation ceremony which lasted all night. The known elements of this initiation ceremony were being clothed in a ritual linen cloth or robe, and the use of seven veils (or perhaps doctrines, doors, angels, etc.) hiding an innermost sanctuary. At some time around A.D. 125, Carpocrates acquired knowledge of some or all of these secret teachings and rituals from an apostate elder in Alexandria. A part of Carpocratian Gnostic teachings was thus derived from a modified form of the secret Alexandrian Christian teachings and rituals. Gnostic writings and rituals, which manifest many parallels to Latter-day Saint temple ritual motifs, may in part represent a Gnosticized version of the Hierophantic Teaching and the Great Mystery mentioned by Clement.

Thus by means of the newly discovered letter of Clement of Alexandria, it is possible to reconstruct a detailed outline of the origin, nature, transmission, and transformation of an early Christian secret initiation ritual system, purportedly established by Jesus himself.

Notes

1. For a selection of statements see Jeff Keller, "Mormonism and Masonry," *Seventh East Press*, 28 September 1982, 9-14; and Reed C. Durham, "Is There No Help for the Widow's Son," a presentation given at the 1974 Mormon History Association Annual Meeting at Nauvoo, Illinois, 20 April 1974, typescript.

2. This is a major theme running through much of Nibley's work. See especially Hugh Nibley, *The Message of the Joseph Smith Papyri* (Salt Lake City: Deseret Book, 1975). Although I do not agree with all of his interpretations, Eugene Seaich, *Ancient Texts and Mormonism* (Murray, UT: Sounds of Zion, 1983), presents further interesting parallels. Additional sources could be further multiplied.

3. In order to better analyze the possible relationships between ancient and restored rituals I will be using the term *ritual motif*, by which I mean a discrete symbolic action, image, or phrase used in the context of a larger ritual system. For example, the Latter-day Saint sacrament can be described as a ritual system composed of the following ritual motifs: All participants must be in a state of spiritual purity; ritual preparation of the bread and water by priesthood bearers; formulaic prayer over the bread and water; ritual distribution of the sacrament; and communal partaking of the food. In a similar sense, the Latter-day Saint temple ceremony can be

described as a complex ritual system composed of dozens, if not hundreds, of discrete ritual motifs. As a general rule, the greater the number of parallel ritual motifs, the greater the likelihood of some type of historical interdependence between two ritual systems.

4. Ed Decker and Dave Hunt, *The Godmakers* (Eugene, OR: Harvest House, 1984) give an interpretation of the Latter-day Saint endowment based on this theory.

5. For a collection of the writings of the Gnostics, with excellent discussions, notes, and bibliographies, see Bentley Layton, *The Gnostic Scriptures* (New York: Doubleday, 1987).

6. For a general background to secret doctrines and rituals in Judaism and early Christianity, see Morton Smith, *Clement of Alexandria and a Secret Gospel of Mark* (Cambridge: Harvard University Press, 1973), 197-202.

7. Jean Daniélou, *The Bible and the Liturgy* (Notre Dame, IN: University of Notre Dame Press, 1956), 9.

8. *Apostolic Constitutions* II, 57. See also Justin Martyr, *Apologia* 66; Tertullian, *Apologia* 7; Cyril of Jerusalem, *Catechetical Lectures*, passim; John Chrysostom, *Homilia in Matthaeum* 23; Ambrose, *De his Qui Mysteriis Initiantur*, ch. 1; and Theodoret, *Quaestio in Numeros*. Related sources could be further multiplied, see A. Haddan, "Disciplina Arcani," in W. Smith and S. Cheetham, eds., *A Dictionary of Christian Antiquities*, 2 vols. (Millwood, NY: Kraus Reprints, 1968), 1:564-66, for numerous additional references.

9. Smith, *Clement of Alexandria and a Secret Gospel of Mark*, 1-85, discusses the discovery of the manuscript and evidence for its authenticity.

10. It should be noted that most of these same scholars maintain that the four canonical gospels are also pseudepigraphic. For summary discussions of the current state of analysis see Morton Smith, "Clement of Alexandria and Secret Mark: The Score at the End of the First Decade," *Harvard Theological Review* 75/4 (1982): 449-61, who gives a complete bibliography up to 1982. Also V. P. Furnish, "Mark, Secret Gospel of," in *The Interpreter's Dictionary of the Bible: Supplementary Volume* (Nashville: Abingdon, 1976), 573. See especially F. F. Bruce's brief lecture, *The Secret Gospel of Mark* (London: Athlone Press, 1974); and R. Brown, "The Relation of 'The Secret Gospel of Mark' to the Fourth Gospel," *Catholic Biblical Quarterly* 36 (1974): 466-85.

11. Smith, *Clement of Alexandria and a Secret Gospel of Mark*, 88-97; Furnish, "Mark, Secret Gospel of."

12. This was, of course, Morton Smith's original hypothesis. The

best discussion of the arguments and evidence is in Helmut Koester, "History and Development of Mark's Gospel (From Mark to Secret Mark and 'Canonical' Mark)," in Bruce Corley, ed., *Colloquy on New Testament Studies: A Time for Reappraisal and Fresh Approaches* (Macon, GA: Mercer University Press, 1983), 35-57.

13. Hans-Martin Schenke, "The Mystery of the Gospel of Mark," *The Second Century* 4/2 (1984): 73, 69.

14. John D. Crossan, *Four Other Gospels: Shadows on the Contours of Canon* (Minneapolis, MN: Winston, 1985), 110.

15. Smith, *Clement of Alexandria and a Secret Gospel of Mark*, 447 (2:23-3:10).

16. On similar periods of six days of spiritual preparation before initiation in early Christianity, see ibid., 175.

17. Ibid., 175-78, discusses the overwhelming evidence for this.

18. Ibid., 446-47 (1:15-2:3).

19. Ibid., 81-82, presents additional evidence that this was Clement's opinion.

20. Ibid., 447 (2:12).

21. G. Bornkamm, " Mysterion," in G. Kittel, *Theological Dictionary of the New Testament*, 10 vols. (Grand Rapids, MI: Eerdmans, 1967), 4:825.

22. Schenke, "The Mystery of the Gospel of Mark," 75. Here I must insert the aside that although many modern biblical scholars may find the rituals described in Clement's letter as being "so strange [that they] refuse to acknowledge [them] as real," they not only make sense but indeed are to be expected in light of the Latter-day Saint concept of the importance of the temple endowment.

23. For a discussion of the extant sources on Carpocrates and the Carpocratians see Smith, *Clement of Alexandria and a Secret Gospel of Mark*, 269-78.

24. Ibid., 446-47 (2:5-11).

25. Bornkamm, "Mysterion," 4:825.

26. Schenke, "The Mystery of the Gospel of Mark," 75; see n. 22 above.

27. Clement makes frequent references to teachings which he cannot put in writing: *Stromata* VI, 15; VII, 9; he specifically states that he had an oral esoteric doctrine transmitted from several of the Apostles (see also *Stromata* I, 1; VI, 17), which is also stated by Clement's disciple Origen, *Contra Celsum* I, 7.

28. For several dozen references to rituals in the Gnostic writings, see the index of Layton, *Gnostic Scriptures*, 475 ("Baptism"), 478 ("Chrism"), 477 ("Bridal Chamber"), 505-6 ("Sacraments"), 507 ("Seals").

29. J. J. Buckley, "A Cult-Mystery in the Gospel of Philip," *Journal of Biblical Literature* 99/4 (1980): 569-81.

30. *Gospel of Philip* (Nag Hammadi Codex 2, document 3, folio 67, lines 27-30; hereafter designated as 67:27-30); all references and quotations are from the translation of Layton, *Gnostic Scriptures*, unless otherwise noted (my comments in *italics* and brackets like these ⟨⟩). Another useful translation is Wesley W. Isenberg, in James M. Robinson, ed., *The Nag Hammadi Library*, 3rd rev. ed. (New York: Harper and Row, 1988), 139-60.

31. *Gospel of Philip* 69:22-25.

32. I am currently preparing a paper which fully discusses the many ritual motifs in Gnostic writings. Many Latter-day Saints will find some variation of such concepts and rituals not only understandable and acceptable, but even an essential part of early Christianity. However, I should emphasize that I am not here implying that Gnosticism is an early form of Mormonism. Many fundamental ideas of the Gnostics are quite different from those of Latter-day Saints.

33. Irenaeus, *Against Heresies* I, 25, 5. Hippolytus, *Refutatio Haeresium* VII, 20, 1: "Matthew communicated to them [the Basileides Gnostics] secret discourses, which, being specially instructed, he heard from the Saviour." See also *Gospel of Thomas* 32:10 [380]; *Apocryphon of John* 1:1 [28]; *Thomas the Contender* 138:1 [403]; *1 Jeu* 1:1; Irenaeus, *Against Heresies* III, 3, 1.

34. *Gospel of Philip* 67:28-30. Clement of Alexandria, *Exhortation to the Greeks* XII, 118-23: "Then thou shalt have the vision of my God and shalt be initiated in those holy mysteries, and shalt taste the joys that are hidden away in heaven, preserved for me, 'which neither ear hath heard nor have they entered into the heart' of any man. . . . I will show thee the Word, and the Word's mysteries. . . . O truly sacred mysteries! O pure light! In the blaze of the torches I have a vision of heaven and of God. I become holy by initiation. The Lord reveals the mysteries; He marks the worshiper with His seal, gives light to guide his way, and commends him, when he has believed, to the Father's care, where he is guarded for ages to come. These are the levels of my mysteries. If thou wilt, be thyself also initiated, and thou shalt dance with angels around the unbegotten and imperishable and only true God. . . . I desire to conform you to the archetype, that you may become even as I am. I will anoint you with the ointment of faith, whereby you cast away corruption; and I will display unveiled the figure of righteousness, whereby you ascend to God. . . . And to say and believe that when

he has been made by Christ Jesus 'just and holy with understanding,' he also becomes in the same degree already like to God. So the prophet openly reveals this gracious favor when he says, 'I said, ye are gods, and ye are all sons of the Most High.' Now we, I say, we are they whom God has adopted"; *Gospel of Philip* 69:25-29: The relation of the five mysteries: "[Baptism] possesses resurrection [and] ransom; ransom is in the bridal chamber. [The] bridal chamber is within what is superior to [. . .]"; Irenaeus, *Against Heresies* I, 13, 1: "They practice magic arts and incantations, love potions and love feasts, familiar spirits and dream inducers"; *Pistis Sophia*, chaps. 97, 103, 133, 135.

35. *Gospel of Philip* 74:12-24 (Isenberg tr.). Baptism or washing: *Gospel of Philip* 64:22-32; 72:29-73:1; 75:21-24; 77:7-15; Irenaeus, *Against Heresies* I, 21, 3. Anointing with oil: *Gospel of Philip* 67:19-27 (Isenberg tr.): "Not only must those who produce the name of the father and the son and the holy spirit do so, but ⟨those who⟩ have produced them for you. If one does not acquire them, the name ('Christian') will also be taken from him. But one receives the unction of the [. . .] of the power of the cross. This power the apostles called 'the right and the left.' For this person is no longer a Christian but a Christ"; *Gospel of Philip* 73:15-19: "The tree of life is in the middle of the garden. However, it is from the olive tree that we get the chrism, and from the chrism, the resurrection"; *Gospel of Philip* 85:27: "All those who are in it ⟨the holy of holies⟩ will [receive the chrism]"; *Gospel of Philip* 57:27-28; 67:19-26; 69:4-14; Irenaeus, *Against Heresies* I, 21, 3-5.

36. Hugh Nibley, "The Early Christian Prayer Circle," in *Mormonism and Early Christianity*, vol. 4, *The Collected Works of Hugh Nibley* (Salt Lake City: Deseret Book and F.A.R.M.S., 1987), 45-99. See also *2 Jeu* 42; *Sophia Christia*, P. Berolinensis 8502, 77-78; and *Pistis Sophia* 136.

37. Nibley, "Sacred Vestments," F.A.R.M.S. paper, 1985; *Gospel of Philip* 70:5-9; 76:22-32 ("putting on the perfect light"); 75:23-24; *2 Jeu* 47; Layton, *Gnostic Scriptures*, 486 ("Garment").

38. Epiphanius of Salamis, *Against Heresies* XXVI, 4, 2. For an excellent discussion of this topic, see Todd Compton, "The Whole Token: Mystery Symbolism in Classical Recognition Drama," *Epoché* 13 (1985): 1–81; cf. also Compton, "The Handclasp and Embrace as Tokens of Recognition," in this volume. See also *1 Jeu* 33; *2 Jeu* 47; Galatians 2:9; *Gospel of Nicodemus* 2:7.

39. *1 Jeu* 33. Irenaeus, *Against Heresies* I, 21, 3: "Others employ Hebrew words in order to baffle even more those who are being

consecrated"; and Irenaeus, *Against Heresies* I, 21, 3: "Others refer to the redemption as follows: 'The name which is hidden from every deity'." See also *Gospel of Philip* 53:24-54:13; 56:4-15; 62:7-17; 67:19-26; 76:6-17.

40. Irenaeus, *Against Heresies* I, 21, 5. *Gospel of Philip* 64:10-12 (Isenberg tr.): "The Lord said, 'Blessed is he who is before he came into being. For he who is, has been and shall be.' "

41. *Gospel of Philip* 85:32-86:18 (Isenberg tr.).

42. *Gospel of Philip* 70:19-20 (Isenberg tr.).

43. *Irenaeus, Against Heresies* I, 21, 3; see also *Gospel of Philip* 64:31-33 (Isenberg tr.): "Great is the mystery of marriage! For [without] it the world would [not exist]"; *Gospel of Philip* 65:7-12 (Isenberg tr.): "And none shall be able to escape ⟨the demonic powers⟩, since they detain him if he does not receive a male power or a female power, the bridegroom and the bride. — One receives them from the mirrored bridal chamber"; *Gospel of Philip* 69:35-70:1 (Isenberg tr.): "⟨Before⟩ [. . . the] veil was rent [. . .] ⟨we had no other⟩ bridal chamber except the image . . . ⟨of the bridal chamber which is⟩ above"; *Gospel of Philip* 70:9-20 (Isenberg tr.): "If the woman had not separated from the man, she should not die with the man. His separation became the beginning of death. Because of this Christ came to repair the separation which was from the beginning and again unite the two, and to give life to those who died as a result of the separation and unite them. But the woman is united to her husband in the bridal chamber. Indeed those who have united in the bridal chamber will no longer be separated"; *Gospel of Philip* 74:18-23: The anointing is given in the bridal chamber.

Gospel of Philip 82:5 (Isenberg tr.): "How much more is the undefiled marriage a true mystery!"; *Gospel of Philip* 85:10-20 (Isenberg tr.): Bridal chamber is beyond a veil. "But it ⟨the veil⟩ was rent from top to bottom. Those above opened to us the things below, in order that we may go in to the secret of the truth. . . . We shall go in there by means of lowly types and forms of weakness. . . . Therefore the perfect things have opened to us, together with the hidden things of truth. The holies of the holies were revealed, and the bridal chamber invited us in"; *Gospel of Philip* 85:32-86:18 (Isenberg tr.): "Every one who will [enter] the bridal chamber will kindle the [light], for [. . .] ⟨it burns⟩ just as in the marriages which are [. . .] ⟨observed, though they⟩ happen at night. That fire [. . .] ⟨burns⟩ only at night and is put out. But the mysteries of that marriage are perfected rather in the day and the light. Neither that day nor its light ever sets. If anyone becomes a son of the bridal chamber, he will receive the light. If anyone does not receive it while he is here, he will not be able to receive it in the other place. He who will receive that light will not be seen, nor can he be detained. And none shall be able to torment a person like this even while he dwells in the world. And again when he leaves the world he has already received the truth in the images. The world has become the eternal realm (aeon), for the eternal realm is fullness for him. This is the way it is: it is revealed to him alone, not hidden in the darkness and the night, but hidden in a perfect day and a holy light"; Irenaeus, *Against Heresies* I, 21, 3: "Some of them prepare a bridal chamber and perform a mystic rite, with certain invocations, for those who are being consecrated, and they claim that what they are effecting is a spiritual marriage, after the image of the conjunctions above"; Irenaeus, *Against Heresies* I, 13, 6: "And immediately she carries them upwards, conducts them into the bride-chamber"; Irenaeus, *Against Heresies* I, 13, 3: "Adorn thyself as a bride who expects her bridegroom, that thou mayest be what I am, and I what thou art." See also *Gospel of Philip* 67:3-5; 68:23-26; 69:1-4; 82:23-26; 84:20-23.

44. Origen, *Contra Celsum* VI, 30-33; cf. Henry Chadwick, ed., *Origen: Contra Celsum* (Cambridge: Cambridge University Press, 1965), 345-49, who has some excellent notes on this subject, referencing many other parallels. See also Irenaeus, *Against Heresies* I, 21, 5; I, 13, 6.

45. *2 Jeu* 47. See also *Gospel of Philip* 84:23-85:20.

46. *Gospel of Philip* 61:29-31 (Isenberg tr.); cf. Keith E. Norman, "Deification, the Content of Athanasian Soterology," Ph.D. diss., Duke University, 1980. *Gospel of Philip* 61:29-35: "You saw the Spirit, you became spirit. You saw Christ, you became Christ. You saw [the Father, you] shall become Father. So [in this place] you see everything and [do] not [see] yourself, but [in that place] you do see yourself—and what you see you shall [become]"; *Gospel of Philip* 75:25-76:5 (Isenberg tr.): "A horse sires a horse, a man begets man, a god brings forth a god. . . . Christians, [. . .] these [. . .] ⟨people⟩ are referred to as 'the chosen people of [. . .] ⟨the living God⟩' and 'the true man' and 'the son of man' and 'the seed of the son of man.' This true race is renowned in the world . . . that the sons of the bridal chamber dwell"; *Gospel of Philip* 81:14-24 (Isenberg tr.): "There is the son of man and there is the son of the son of man. The lord is the son of man and the son of the son of man is he who creates through the son of man. The son of man received from God the capacity to create. He also has the ability to beget. He who has received the ability to create is a creature. He who has received the ability to beget is an offspring." See also *Gospel of Philip* 57:28-58:10; 67:30-32.

12

Early Christian Millenarianist Interpretation of the Two Witnesses in John's Apocalypse 11:3-13

Thomas W. Mackay
Brigham Young University, Provo, Utah

One of the curious aspects of early Christian interpretation of the Apocalypse (or the book of Revelation) of John is that a literal view of the Millennium, together with the precise identification of the two witnesses or prophets at Jerusalem who herald the Second Coming of the Lord, later came to be rejected by the "spiritualized" — the "demythologized" and, to use Hugh Nibley's expression,[1] "de-eschatologized" — forms of Christian exegesis of the scriptures that predominated after the late fourth century. Thereafter, the two witnesses were taken to be the Old and New Testaments, or the Church preaching the gospel to the world, or some other such allegorical interpretation. Thus, in the explanation of Apocalypse 11 and related scriptures, we find a direct and specific manifestation of the shift from literal to allegorical exegesis that characterized Christianity in the patristic era, an era corresponding roughly to the end of the ancient world (from the accession of Diocletian to the death of Justinian). This period of cultural and political transition heralds the emergence of the Byzantine Empire in the East, and simultaneously in the West it displays the fragmented remnants of the Roman world, the "Dark Ages" of European civilization that ended with the Carolingian Renaissance in the late eighth and early ninth centuries. The dramatic results of the change from literal to allegorical interpretation of the scriptures are manifest in the medieval Christian exegetical and homiletic traditions in Europe. I shall sketch some of these developments by analyzing references to the two witnesses from the second century to the beginning of the Carolingian Renaissance.

In order to appreciate more fully the nature of differing approaches to the scriptures, I will treat some background material. I will first consider the textual tradition of the Apocalypse. Next, a brief historical overview of the exegesis of the Apocalypse will familiarize us both with the names and with the literary and intellectual relationships of many of the authors I will later quote. With a sketch of the exegetical tradition, its sources, tensions and development, we can better grasp why the interpretation changes over the centuries. Although the passages I have selected and translated are extensive, the sheer weight of the evidence leads irresistibly to the conclusions that are also corroborated by artistic evidence in manuscripts.

History of the Text of the Apocalypse

The Apocalypse was not warmly received in many Christian circles. While the second-century apologist Justin Martyr, and he alone, relates "tradition reposing on historical memory"—namely that John wrote it and that he believed in a literal Millennium—later objections to literalist exegesis "were based either on dogmatic or on literary grounds."[2] In the third century, the Roman presbyter Gaius was "still attacking the book in violent terms, and attributing its authorship to St. John's traditional enemy, the heretic Cerinthus."[3] To comprehend the distrust Christians held for the Apocalypse in the third to fifth centuries, we need only to note how reluctantly, and how late, the book gained approval of the councils to become part of the

New Testament. Eusebius records that while many of the books gained ready acceptance (the *anantirrēta*, or "undisputed books" and *homologoumena*, or "agreed-upon books"), James, 2 Peter, Jude, and some others were in the "disputed" class or *antilegomena*, but they were not rejected as outright spurious—*en tois nothois*.[4] The Apocalypse was esteemed to be undisputed by some leaders, spurious by others: at *Historia Ecclesiastica* III, 25, 2, Eusebius classes it among the *homologoumena*,[5] but later in that same chapter he notes that others claim it is not genuine:

ἐν τοῖς νόθοις κατατετάχθω καὶ τῶν Παύλου Πράξεων ἡ γραφὴ ὅ τε λεγόμενος Ποιμὴν καὶ ἡ Ἀποκάλυψις Πέτρου καὶ πρὸς τούτοις ἡ φερομένη Βαρναβᾶ ἐπιστολὴ καὶ τῶν ἀποστόλων αἱ λεγόμεναι Διδαχαὶ ἔτι τε, ὡς ἔφην, ἡ Ἰωάννου Ἀποκάλυψις, εἰ φανείη· ἥν τινες, ὡς ἔφην, ἀθετοῦσιν, ἕτεροι δὲ ἐγκρίνουσιν τοῖς ὁμολογουμένοις.[6]

Among the books that are not genuine, let there be included ⟨in this class⟩ the scripture of the Acts of Paul, the work called the Shepherd ⟨sc., of Hermas⟩, the Apocalypse of Peter, and in addition to these the epistle attributed to Barnabas and the so-called *Didachai* or Teachings of the Apostles and besides, as I stated, the Apocalypse of John, if it should seem ⟨to be best included among the spurious books⟩. As I said, some people reject it, while others judge it to be one of the undisputed [*lit.*, agreed-upon] books.

Because of this hesitation to receive the Apocalypse, the text is not as strongly attested in Greek manuscripts as other books.[7] While there are more than five thousand manuscripts containing at least a portion of the Greek New Testament—and granted most have some of the gospels—only about 250 have the Apocalypse. Vaticanus is missing the last leaves, including the Apocalypse; the text is found in Sinaiticus, Alexandrinus, and Codex Ephraemi Rescriptus as well as Leningrad *P*, the Chester Beatty papyrus P^{4}7 (late third century), P^{1}8 (end of third/beginning of fourth century), and P^{2}4 (fourth century). It is also in uncials 046, 051, 052, 0207, and 0229 and in some notable minuscules: 1, 88, 94, 104, 1006, 1611, 1828, 1854, 1859, 2020, 2042, 2053, 2065, 2073, 2081, 2138, 2344, 2432, and 2495.

> On ne connait jusqu'ici que 250 manuscrits eviron du texte original de l'Apocalypse; très peu sont antérieurs au xe siècle (sept [ou 8] onciaux et un ou deux miniscules) et les derniers sont du xviie siècle. La modicité relative de ce chiffre s'explique naturellement par toutes les discussions qui se prolongèrent dans l'Eglise grecque au sujet de la canonicité du livre. Il existe aussi quelques fragments sur papyrus, et des citations des anciens Pères, Origène, Hippolyte et Méthodius.[8]

> Up to the present we only know of about 250 manuscripts of the original text of the Apocalypse. Very few are earlier than the tenth century (seven [or eight] uncials and one or two minuscules) and the latest [*i.e.,* most recent] are from the seventeenth century. The relative paucity of this number can be naturally explained by all the discussions that took place over time in the Greek church on the subject of the canonicity of the book. Also extant are some papyrus fragments and citations of the early fathers, Origen, Hippolytus, and Methodius.

The suspicion of the Apocalypse in the Christian east was such that it never came to be used in the liturgy, and it was never admitted into the Peshitta or Syriac New Testament.[9] So, while only a restricted number of fathers referred to one passage or another of the Apocalypse, far fewer composed extensive commentaries on it than they did on the Gospels.

COMMENTATORS ON THE APOCALYPSE

The earliest references to the Apocalypse are not in systematic exegetical commentaries but are, rather, passing or incidental comments in **apocrypha** or in early patristic treatises. According to Eusebius, **Papias**, bishop of Hieropolis in Asia Minor in the early second century,[10] was heir to such unwritten traditions as a belief in a literal thousand-year reign after the resurrection of the dead, and he personally listened to John teach.

ἐν οἷς καὶ χιλιάδα τινά φησιν ἐτῶν ἔσεσθαι μετὰ τὴν ἐκ νεκρῶν ἀνάστασιν, σωματικῶς τῆς Χριστοῦ βασιλείας ἐπὶ ταυτησὶ τῆς γῆς ὑποστησομένης· ἃ καὶ ἡγοῦμαι τὰς ἀποστολικὰς παρεκδεξάμενον διηγήσεις ὑπολαβεῖν, τὰ ἐν ὑποδείγμασι πρὸς αὐτῶν μυστικῶς εἰρημένα μὴ συνεορακότα.[11]

Among these ⟨rather mythical beliefs⟩ he asserts that there will also be some sort of millennium after the resurrection from the dead, when the kingdom of Christ will be physically set up on this earth. I suppose that he got these notions by accepting ⟨literally⟩ the apostolic accounts, simply because he failed to understand that the utterances in their memoirs had been spoken mystically [*or*, allegorically] by them.

Jerome reports that:

Hic dicitur annorum mille iudaicam edidisse *deuterōsin*. Quem secuti sunt Irenaeus et Apollinaris et ceteri, qui post resurrectionem aiunt in carne cum sanctis Dominum regnaturum. Tertullianus quoque in libro de Spe fidelium et Victorinus Pitabionensis et Lactantius hac opinione ducuntur.[12]

[Papias] is said to have promulgated the Jewish tradition of a millennium, and he is followed by Irenaeus, Apollinaris, and others, who say that after the resurrection the Lord will reign in the flesh with the saints. Tertullian too in his book on the "Hope of the Faithful" and Victorinus Pitabionensis [*sic* = Petovionensis, *i.e.*, of Pettau] and Lactantius are led by this belief.

We do not have information about the Apocalypse from other orthodox writers contemporary with Papias — writers such as Ignatius, Clement of Rome, and Polycarp, and even the archheretic **Cerinthus** (early second century) was reputed to have believed in a literal millennium.[13] In the middle of the second century, scarcely sixty years after the composition of the Apocalypse, **Justin Martyr** attributes the millennial belief to John — a doctrinal position in harmony with Isaiah and others:

καὶ ἔπειτα [*v.l.*, ἐπειδὴ] καὶ παρ' ἡμῖν ἀνήρ τις, ᾧ ὄνομα Ἰωάννης, εἷς τῶν ἀποστόλων τοῦ Χριστοῦ, ἐν ἀποκαλύψει γενομένῃ αὐτῷ **χίλια ἔτη** [Apocalypse 20:4] ποιήσειν ἐν Ἰερουσαλὴμ τοὺς τῷ ἡμετέρῳ Χριστῷ πιστεύσαντας προεφήτευσε, καὶ μετὰ ταῦτα τὴν καθολικὴν καί, συνελόντι φάναι, **αἰωνίαν** ὁμοθυμαδὸν ἅμα πάντων ἀνάστασιν γενήσεσθαι καὶ **κρίσιν**.[14]

And next, also [*v.l.*, and this is true since] a certain man among us named John, one of Christ's apostles, when he had received a revelation, prophesied that those who had faith in our Christ would dwell in Jerusalem for a thousand years, and that afterwards the universal and, to state it briefly, everlasting resurrection and judgment of all would take place with one accord.

[This is probably the source of Jerome's statement at *De Viris Illustribus* 9 and in his *Chronicle* that Justin had written a commentary on the Apocalypse, an assertion for which there is no other evidence.] A few decades later, **Irenaeus** interprets a number of passages and words from the Apocalypse,[15] stating that John received it near the end of the reign of Domitian.

εἰ δὲ ἔδει ἀναφανδὸν ἐν τῷ νῦν καιρῷ κηρύττεσθαι τοὔνομα αὐτοῦ, δι' ἐκείνου ἂν ἐρρέθη τοῦ καὶ τὴν ἀποκάλυψιν ἑωρακότος. οὐδὲ γὰρ πρὸ πολλοῦ χρόνου ἑωράθη, ἀλλὰ

σχεδὸν ἐπὶ τῆς ἡμετέρας γενεᾶς, πρὸς τῷ τέλει
τῆς Δομετιανοῦ ἀρχῆς.[16]

> But if it had been necessary to proclaim his [i.e.,
> John's] name openly at the present time, it would have
> been spoken by him who in fact beheld the apocalypse.
> For it was seen not long ago but almost in our own
> generation, near the end of the reign of Domitian.

As Jerome stated in the passage quoted above about
Papias, Irenaeus, too, follows the early Christian tradition
of a literal millennium and attendant doctrines, although
in other matters his exegesis was allegorical:

> Millenarianism is one of the most robust elements
> in his [i.e., Irenaeus'] thought and piety. . . . The sheet-
> anchor of all is the assertion, so utterly contrary to his
> general expository usage when other parts of the Bible
> are in review, that apocalyptical Scripture must not be
> interpreted in an allegorical or symbolical manner. It is
> fundamental that a literal interpretation is alone legiti-
> mate. . . . In final token that the religious experience of
> Irenaeus was robust and prophetic rather than quiet and
> speculative is his Millenarianism. This too is a Biblical
> and primitive element.[17]

Bishop **Melito of Sardis,** a contemporary of Irenaeus,
is reported to have written on the Apocalypse,[18] but the
text is not extant.

At the close of the second and the beginning of the
third century, **Tertullian,** the famous Latin lawyer-convert
from North Africa who died some time after 220, often
cited the Apocalypse, giving a literal interpretation to the
Millennium. The idea of *recapitulatio* or *anakephalaiōsis* is
usually traced to Tertullian and Irenaeus, although it is
later developed by others, including Victorinus and Lactantius, but particularly Tyconius (see below). John of Damascus has preserved a tantalizing quotation from Irenaeus about the beast that is to come forth: *anakephalaiōsis*

ginetai pasēs adikias. . . . ["it is the recapitulation of all evil"].[19] In contrast to his predecessors, Tertullian's contemporary, **Hippolytus** (who died after 235), produced a commentary on the Apocalypse that has not survived intact.[20] But his ideas are retained in a number of fragments and in his other works (especially *De Christo et Antichristo*),[21] including citations by Bar Salibi (see below). Hippolytus comments on the two witnesses and Antichrist in his fragmentary commentary on Daniel.[22] His, too, is a chiliastic approach: the earth awaits its "sabbath" rest after six thousand years of existence. For Hippolytus, following the early Christian tradition, the two witnesses are to be Enoch and Elijah; and, as in Irenaeus, the Antichrist will come from the tribe of Dan.[23] This interpretation persisted: Quoduultdeus in the fifth century states,

> Hic ostenditur quod ex Iudaeis, de tribu Dan quae hodieque in Perside est, ueniat Antichristus iuxta propheticam benedictionem Iacob patriarchae dicentis: **Dan iudicabit populum sicut aliae tribus. Fiat Dan coluber in uia, cerastes in semita, mordens ungulas equi ut cadat ascensor eius retro.**[24]

> It is shown here that Antichrist will come from the Jews, from the tribe of Dan which even today is in the land of Persia, according to the prophetic blessing of the patriarch Jacob when he said, "Dan shall judge his people, just as the other tribes. Dan shall be a serpent along the road, an adder in the path, biting the horse's hooves so that [*or,* with the result that] the rider fall backwards" (Genesis 49:16-17).

And Primasius succinctly writes "De tribu enim Dan antichristus traditur nasciturus" ("For it is the tradition that from the tribe of Dan will the Antichrist be born").[25] Quoting Ambrosius Autpertus, his major source, Alcuin puts it thus:

> Dan ergo de spiritali catalogo eiectus, ipsa nominis

sui interpretatione docet, quia in sexta mundi aetate occulto quidem, sed iusto iudicio, iudaica plebs perfida
prorsus sedibus expulsa sacerdotii dignitatem perdidit.[26]

Therefore Dan, who has been excluded from this
spiritual catalogue, instructs us by the very meaning of
his name, because in the sixth age of the world by a
hidden but just judgment, the Jewish people lose the
honor of the priesthood, for they have been rejected from
their abode because they are faithless.

And Bede on Apocalypse 7:5 states:

Conuenienter et a Iuda inchoat ex qua tribu ortus
est dominus noster: et Dan praetermisit ex quo dicitur
antichristus esse nascendus sicut scriptum est: **Fiat Dan
coluber in uia cerastes in semita mordens ungulas equi
ut cadat ascensor eius.**[27]

Appropriately he begins from Judah, from which
tribe our Lord came forth; and he omits Dan from whom
it is said that the Antichrist must be born, just as it is
written: (Bede then quotes Genesis 49:17).

In his work *De Antichristo*, Hippolytus apparently used
an extracanonical source, an unnamed "prophet," and expressed a similar doctrinal stance.[28] About the middle of
the third century, **Commodian** wrote his *Carmen de duobus
populis*, using the Sibylline books and various apocryphal
texts, but it is virtually useless for exegetical purposes.[29]
Similarly, in his *Diuinae Institutiones*, **Lactantius** (early
fourth century) uses the Sibylline books, apocrypha, and
the Apocalypse to produce a fanciful eschatology that is
neither fully in harmony with the primitive church nor
with post-fourth-century Christianity, though he does retain some ties to Irenaeus and Hippolytus, for Lactantius,
too, is chiliastic:

Haec eos ratio fefellit, quod resurgent defuncti non
post mille annos mortis suae, sed ut restituti rursus in
uitam mille annis cum Deo regnent. Deus enim ueniet,

ut orbe hoc ab omne labe purgato rediuiuas iustorum animas corporibus innouatis ad sempiternam beatitu-dinem suscitet.[30]

This explanation completely escapes them [*i.e.*, the pagan poets], because the dead will rise not one thou-sand years after their own death (each individual, re-spectively), but so that, when restored again to life, they will reign with God during one thousand years. For God will come, so that when this world has been cleansed of every spot, he may raise up the souls of the just, alive once more with their renewed bodies to eternal blessed-ness.

Clement of Alexandria, whose life ended by 215, ap-pears to have taken a "spiritual" or allegorical approach in his *Hypotyposes*.[31] He was followed by **Origen** (ca. 185-253), who proposed writing a commentary on the Apoc-alypse (according to a Latin fragment of his Commentary on Matthew 24), and a text of the scholia was published from a manuscript at the Meteora monastery in 1911.[32] But Origen, like Clement, eschewed limiting himself to the literal approach, favoring an allegorical mode built upon but transcending the literal.[33] When Origen departed from Alexandria for Caesarea, his successor as head of the Ca-techetical School was **Dionysius of Alexandria,** who was later bishop of the city. In response to Nepos' treatise against allegorical interpretation of the scriptures (*Refuta-tion of the Allegorists*), Dionysius composed various treatises on the scriptures, including the Apocalypse, but little re-mains of his writings; the few extant fragments of the Apocalypse commentary are doubtfully ascribed to him.[34] **Methodius of Olympus,** who died about 311, wrote a Pla-tonic dialogue explaining some passages of the Apocalypse (but particularly Apocalypse 12:1-6) in a purely spiritual or allegorical mode, although he did retain a chiliastic belief in the literal millennium.[35] He also rejected Origen's doc-trine of the antemortal existence of the soul and also his nonmaterialistic or "spiritualistic concept of the resurrection of the body."[36] He uses *recapitulatio* as in Irenaeus: the sense is a summing up of past revelations in the incarnation of Christ and of restoring fallen humanity by obedience to Christ. So the text of the Apocalypse stands still in time, as it were, to summarize God's past dealings with mankind.

In contrast to most of the earlier writers, **Victorinus,** Bishop of Pettau (Poetovio) in Pannonia and martyr under Diocletian (*i.e.,* probably about the beginning of the fourth century), composed a running commentary on the Apocalypse.[37] Like Tertullian, Commodian, and later Lactantius, Victorinus used recapitulation as a means of explaining the scriptural text and its relation to history. Furthermore, he still maintained a literal view of the Millennium, as did Lactantius in the ensuing decades. However, they are among the last writers of note who were chiliastic. The growing animosity towards the literal millennium propounded by the early Christians is manifest in Eusebius' and Jerome's scorn of Papias and in the writings of many fathers of the fourth century.[38] A notable exception is **Apollinarius** (or **Apollinaris**) **of Laodicea** (ca. 310-390), who also wrote on the Apocalypse among his many commentaries on the books of the Old and New Testaments. But most of his works are lost; fragments of the commentaries may be found in the *Catenae* or chains of quotations by the fathers on scriptures,[39] and there are also some fragments of his work *Recapitulatio*.[40] According to Jerome, in his description of Papias quoted above, Apollinarius held the earlier, literalist position in contrast to the later allegorical approach. However his contemporary, **Didymos the Blind of Alexandria** (ca. 313-397), followed Origen's multifaceted mode of exegesis, and, as head of the Christian Catechetical School at Alexandria, he propagated the allegorical approach and taught it to Jerome, among others.[41] Didymos dictated numerous works, particularly explanations of the scriptures, and among his many compositions was a commentary on the Apocalypse that, unfortunately, has not survived. But he attests to the work in his commentary on Zechariah, for there Didymos says:

σαφήνεια δὲ ἀναντίρρητος περὶ τούτων γέγονεν ἐν τοῖς ὑπομνήμασιν τῆς Ἀποκαλύψεως τοῦ Ἰωάννου καὶ τῆς πρὸς Ῥωμαίους Παύλου ἐπιστολῆς.[42]

> Undeniable clearness [or, irrefutable interpretation] of these ⟨numbers⟩ has been made in my commentaries on the Apocalypse of John and on the Epistle of Paul to the Romans.

For the history of the text and commentary of the Apocalypse in the West, the pivotal figure is **Tyconius**, a Donatist Christian living in North Africa in the second half of the fourth century.[43] Although his commentary, written about 380, is not extant in its entirety, it was the basis for the commentaries by Primasius, Caesarius, Bede, Beatus, and perhaps even Ambrosius Autpertus, as well as the **Turin Fragments**[44] of Tyconius where the commentary appears greatly abbreviated and retouched by a Roman Catholic writer.[45] For **Tyconius**, the two witnesses are the two Testaments, the Old and New. Tyconius made a complete rupture with the old tradition of literal interpretation, giving preference to the Alexandrian allegorical and "spiritualizing" approach. He even established seven basic rules for interpreting the scriptures, his *Liber Regularum*, which Augustine summarized in *De Doctrina Christiana*.[46]

> Tout en recommandant de ne lire Tyconius qu'avec précaution, saint Augustin incorpora les sept règles exégétiques son *de Doctrina christiana*, perpétuant ainsi l'influence de cet esprit vigoureux, original, et, en plus d'un cas, déconcertant.[47]

> While recommending that Tyconius should only be

read with due care, St Augustine embodied his seven
rules of exegesis in his *De Doctrina Christiana*, thus per-
petuating the influence of this vigorous, original, and in
more than one case, disconcerting mind.[48]

Bede adopted the approach from Augustine; his verbal
echoes demonstrate that only Tyconius' commentary, and
not the *Liber Regularum*, was known in Bede's Anglo-Saxon
England. But because of the dramatic and complete shift
in exegesis which Tyconius' commentary on the Apocalypse represents, and because of Jerome's and Augustine's
influence on later writers, the de-eschatologizing or "spiritualizing" mode of interpretation held sway.

Thus, **Jerome** (331-420), the justly famous exegete and
scholar who prepared the monumental Vulgate version of
the Bible (the form known and used in the West for more
than a millennium), revised Victorinus' commentary and
in so doing rejected the earlier chiliastic interpretation.[49]
He had learned his allegorical approach from Didymos the
Blind at Alexandria both in person and from his writings;
he even translated Didymos' *De Sancto Spiritu*.[50] Jerome
may have known Tyconius' commentary, but there are few
verbal echoes of Tyconius in Jerome, and those which do
exist were apparently passages already in Victorinus. Tyconius in fact seems to have borrowed a few quotes from
Victorinus, but most of what can be recovered was Tyconius' own expression. We are also hindered from a complete analysis of the Victorinus-Jerome commentary because the text is incomplete and because the manuscript
tradition is complex. Perhaps an uncollated manuscript I
have noted will be of some assistance, but it is not likely.
Yet Jerome's views of the Apocalypse pepper his works,
and his approach is allegorical.

> Apocalypsis Iohannis tot habet sacramenta, quot
> uerba. Parum dixi et pro merito uoluminis laus omnis
> inferior est. In uerbis singulis multiplices latent intelle-
> gentiae.[51]

The Apocalypse of John has as many mysteries as words. Yet I have said almost nothing, and any praise is less than the book deserves. In each individual word multiple levels of meaning lie hidden.

In his introduction to book XVIII of his Commentary on Isaiah, Jerome states

> nec ignoro quanta inter homines sententiarum diuersitas sit. Non dico de mysterio trinitatis . . . sed de aliis ecclesiasticis dogmatibus . . . et qua ratione intelligenda sit Apocalypsis Iohannis, quam, si iuxta litteram accipimus, iudaizandum est; si spiritualiter, ut scripta est, disserimus, multorum ueterum uidebimur opinionibus contraire; Latinorum, Tertulliani, Victorini, Lactantii; Graecorum . . . Irenaei, etc.[52]

I well understand how great a difference of opinion men have. I am not speaking of the mystery of the trinity but concerning other church doctrines and also how the Apocalypse of John is to be understood: if we take it literally, it has to be viewed as Jews would take it [*i.e.,* literal millennium, etc.]; if we discuss it allegorically, as it is written, then we will seem to contradict the opinions of many earlier writers: Tertullian, Victorinus, and Lactantius, among the Latin writers, and among the Greeks, Irenaeus, etc.

Both in the same prologue and elsewhere, Jerome labels the Millennium a *fabula.*[53] For the two witnesses, he vacillates between Enoch-Elijah or Elijah-Moses and the two testaments or some other allegorical meaning.[54]

Of all the figures in late antiquity, however, **Augustine** is the one who exercised the greatest lasting influence on Western civilization. In his *City of God* book 20, he discusses at length matters pertaining to the Apocalypse—the Antichrist, the beast, the two cities, the Millennium, and the judgment. Yet, in treating 2 Thessalonians 2:3, he cites the scripture using the Old Latin word *refuga* (*i.e.*, *apostates*, an individual Antichrist) instead of *apostasia*. (Let it be noted that when Paul, who came from a Greek city, Tarsus, wrote to Greeks, they understood the word *apostasia* in its fundamental meaning: a military and political revolt against leaders, in the deliberate attempt to subvert and overthrow the ruling powers and the cultural *mores* they espoused.) Although Augustine refers to Malachi's prophecy of Elijah, he states, *Ipse quippe ante aduentum iudicis saluatoris non immerito speratur esse uenturus, qui [v.l., quia] etiam nunc uiuere non immerito creditur* "Indeed it may very properly be hoped that he will come before the coming of the Savior as judge, because he is believed on good cause to be living even at the present moment."[55] Also, while he had earlier spoken of a sabbath-like millennium,[56] in *de Ciuitate Dei* 20.7 he scorns chiliasm as ridiculous fables: *in quasdam ridiculas fabulas*.[57] The "thousand years" are equated with the spiritual reign of the Church, inauguated by the First Coming of the Lord; the "abyss" where Satan is chained is the heart of the infidels.[58] Augustine does assent to the notion of recapitulation to explain the events that John prophesies:

> Et in hoc quidem libro, cuius nomen est apocalypsis, obscure multa dicuntur, ut mentem legentis exerceant, et pauca in eo sunt, ex quorum manifestatione indagentur cetera cum labore; maxime quia sic eadem multis modis repetit, ut alia atque alia dicere uideatur, cum aliter atque aliter haec ipsa dicere uestigetur.[59]

> And in this book, the name of which is the Apocalypse, many things are obscurely stated, with the result that they exercise the mind [*i.e.*, test the understanding] of the reader; and there are few things in it which, when understood, clarify the rest with some effort; and this is especially true since he so repeats the same things in so many different ways that he seems to be dealing with various different subjects, although the very same subject is being dealt with in various ways.

But viewed in the larger perspective, Augustine has

borrowed heavily from Tyconius' approach. In the hands of the great Latin church father, the interpretation of the Apocalypse has become "spiritualized" and allegorized (or de-eschatologized), for the literalism of chiliastic interpretation has been rejected. All other points, including the identity of the two witnesses, have been readjusted accordingly. Though Augustine speaks of Elijah's return, he does not equate him directly with the two witnesses who oppose Antichrist.[60] A successor as bishop at Carthage, **Quoduultdeus**, also explained some passages from the Apocalypse in his writings, especially *Dimidium Temporis in Signis Antichristi*.[61]

In the Greek church, the Apocalypse was not warmly received and only later was it admitted into the canon. Hence, **Theodoret of Cyr** included in his writings some discussion about the Apocalypse,[62] as did **Procopius of Gaza** in the sixth century.[63] Of Theodoret Quasten writes:

> Theodoret is one of the most successful writers of the Eastern Church and his literary bequest has greater variety than that of the other theologians of Antioch. . . . Though Theodoret does not pretend to originality, his exegetical writings are among the finest specimens of the Antiochene School and remarkable for their combination of terseness and lucidity. In his interpretation of Holy Scripture he adopts a middle course, avoiding the radicalism of Theodore of Mopsuestia and his excessive literalness and allowing an allegorical and typological explanation, whenever this appears preferable.[64]

But the earliest systematic Greek commentator was **Oecumenius**, bishop of Tricca (Thessaly), who produced his commentary in the late sixth century, and the editio princeps was finally published in 1928.[65] According to Hoskier, the editor of Oecumenius, his work antedated that of Andreas.[66] The author of another full Greek commentary is **Andreas of Caesarea**, a contemporary, or perhaps pred-

ecessor, of Oecumenius writing in Cappadocia about 550-
600.[67] (The dating traditionally depends on two matters:
he cites Pseudo-Dionysius the Areopagite, hence he writes
later than 476; but he makes no allusion to the Islamic
invasion of 637.) Andreas is important in that he eclectically
records differing interpretations of the same passage, and
he apparently uses Oecumenius (scholarly debate used to
favor Andreas preceding Oecumenius; now he is viewed
as following and quoting from Oecumenius, as Hoskier
noted). While he is attached to the spiritualizing approach,
he records many of the ideas of Irenaeus and Hippolytus
(e.g., he states that the Antichrist will issue from the tribe
of Dan, and so that tribe is omitted in the list of the 144,000
in Apocalypse 7), though he rejects their millenarianism.
But he does assent to recapitulation. Furthermore, Andreas' text of the Apocalypse greatly influenced later manuscripts of that book.[68] Other incidental comments about
the Apocalypse are found in the **Chronicon Paschale**[69] and
in **John of Damascus,** who preserves excerpts from previous writers.[70] In the ninth century, **Photius** compiled his
magnificent *Bibliotheca* at Constantinople where he summarizes, among other books, patristic comments on scriptures.[71] Finally, **Arethas of Caesarea** made use of Andreas
in Cappadocia about 900.[72] So great is the antipathy toward
the Apocalypse in Greek Christianity that in the eleventh
century the exegete Theophylact composed "a series of
commentaries on several OT Books and on the whole of
the NT except Rev. [the Apocalypse]."[73]

Elsewhere in the East we do not have much written
about the Apocalypse. **Ephraem the Syrian** (306-373), a
fourth-century contemporary of Didymos the Blind who
wrote at Nisibis and especially at Edessa, composed a wide
array of works in Syriac, including comments on the Apocalypse. Many of his writings were translated into Greek
and Armenian, and some from Greek into Latin and Slavonic. But his style, "characterized by repetitions and the

accumulation of metaphors, is alien to modern taste."[74] As Angelo de Berardino observes: "The works of Ephrem in Latin present a complete mystery. It is certain that after the deaths of Augustine and Cassian, the Western world showed a greater interest for this type of work than for the speculations of Greek theology."[75] In the ninth century, the Byzantine writer Photius, mentioned above, devoted a section of his famous *Bibliotheca* to a summary of Ephraem's works translated into Greek. **Dionysius bar Salibi** (who died in 1171) is notable for providing us with fragments from Hippolytus' *Capita contra Gaium*.[76] Also, Stan Larson has discovered and edited a twelfth-century Syriac commentary. But the Nestorians and Monophysites did not comment much on the Apocalypse, and the other commentaries which may have been composed were lost or ignored. Recently Leslie MacCoull called attention to a Coptic commentary in an unpublished manuscript at the J. P. Morgan Library. Though written after the Arab Conquest, the text is purportedly from Cyril of Alexandria, and it apparently does incorporate earlier patristic sources as well as an utterly fantastic numerology.[77]

It is in the Latin West, especially in the Roman church, that the exegetical tradition of the Apocalypse became well developed. **Primasius,** bishop of Hadrumetum in North Africa (modern Sousse, Tunisia), prepared a massive commentary about 540.[78] He was greatly dependent on Tyconius and Augustine, and though it appears that he knew Victorinus, it may have been through Tyconius. He has an elaborate development of recapitulation. The two witnesses are Enoch and Elijah; the Antichrist is personal— a king of the Jews. But on the whole, his interpretation is allegorical, not literal. A contemporary, the famous scholar **Cassiodorus,** also composed some notes on Acts and the Apocalypse, but he probably did not use Tyconius though he did know Primasius and the Victorinus-Jerome commentary. His work lies outside the mainstream of the exegetical tradition and, in fact, only survives in a single manuscript at Verona.[79] Another writer of the sixth century, **Caesarius of Arles**, produced nineteen discourses on the Apocalypse. Although they were long known as Pseudo-Augustine or incorrectly attributed to Gennadius, they were finally identified as belonging to Caesarius, and Germain Morin has edited them.[80] Caesarius has used Tyconius but not Primasius, and so he becomes an important witness in establishing the text of Tyconius. Yet another commentator contemporary with these three was **Apringius Bishop of Beja** (now Portugal). The incomplete text was edited by Férotin[81] and depends on the Victorinus-Jerome tradition but has no affinities to the Tyconius tradition. At the end of the sixth century, **Gregory the Great**, who widely used the allegorical method of exegesis, referred to the Apocalypse in several compositions, though he devoted none to that book alone. His quotations on the Apocalypse were later gathered by **Alulfus** and circulated separately.[82]

In the late seventh or eighth century an extremely compressed **anonymous Irish** commentary on the Apocalypse was composed,[83] and this may have been preceded by a commentary, not now extant, composed in the late sixth or early seventh century by a disciple of Saint Columba (ca. 521-97), namely, by a certain Cominus Scotus, although the evidence is highly questionable.[84] The anonymous Irish commentary cites Jerome and names as interpreters of the Apocalypse:

> (1) librum antiquitum nobis exploratum super hoc qui in priscis temporibus tractatum est, tamen auctor non inuenitur, (2) XII omaeliae Originis, (3) tractatus Anticonii Donatiste, (4) expositio . . . Primasii.[85]

> (1) a very old book examined by us on this topic; it was composed in the pristine Christian times, but its author is nevertheless not known; (2) twelve homilies of Origen; (3) the commentary by Tyconius [for ms. An-

ticonius] the Donatist; and (4) the exposition of the Apocalypse by Primasius.

This commentary most likely antedates what may be called the **Irish Reference Bible**, a work that draws on Bede and other patristic sources for its brief, basically allegorical comments.[86] Recently Joseph Kelly has asserted that the early insular oral sources of Irish Reference Bible work were known to **Bede of Jarrow** (673-735), the most imposing exegete of the early eighth century.[87] However, the evidence is extremely thin and tenuous and does not conform to Bede's normal method of citation, as may also be stated of Bede's possible use of the anonymous Irish commentary on the General Epistles.[88] Still, Bede *did* know the Apocalypse commentaries by Tyconius and Primasius as well as Augustine's extensive discussion of the text in the *City of God*, and Bede and the anonymous Irish work probably drew upon similar written material as well as perhaps also being influenced by an oral exegetical tradition of insular origin. Since Bede did not have access to Caesarius of Arles, these two writers may be treated as independent witnesses of the text of Tyconius. Furthermore, Bede's position in the exegetical tradition and the extent of his library make him very important for any examination of patristic and early medieval scriptural interpretation. In his fine assessment of Bede's method and contribution, Roger Ray summarizes thus:

> Bede's biblical commentaries are the largest single group of his extant writings, the embodiment of his avowed lifework, and the cornerstone of his immense medieval fame. Critical study of them has just begun, but it has already become clear that they shed important light on his better known works, like the *Historia ecclesiastica*. It is also certain that they can no longer be dismissed as merely derivative and allegorical. This essay argues that their patristic contents serve a well-conceived program of pastoral instruction for a new Christian

people and that their allegorical aspects spring from a lively method of rhetorical analysis.[89]

In northern Italy in the second half of the eighth century, **Ambrosius Autpertus** wrote a lengthy treatise on the Apocalypse. He compiled the ten books, composed in two major segments, during the years 758-67. Until a few years ago, the most recent printed edition was 1677; it has now been critically edited for *Corpus Christianorum*.[90] The monumental commentary by **Beatus of Liebana** in Spain (ca. 776) is based on Tyconius as well as Victorinus and Apringius.[91] Finally, **Alcuin of York**, the famous minister of education under Charlemagne, undertook to compose his own commentary at the end of the eighth century. Cardinal Angelo Mai discovered and published it in 1838; it exists only in a single manuscript, Vat. lat. 651 of the ninth century, and the commentary covers only through Apocalypse 12:12.[92] Alcuin's primary source was not his fellow Anglo-Saxon Bede (whom he greatly admired and read)[93] but rather Ambrosius Autpertus, from whom he drew many of the words and phrases for his own commentary.[94] Yet Alcuin names many of his predecessors in the preface, and the prominence of Bede patently indicates his respect:

> Beatus Beda in septem periochis dicit Apocalypsin consistere. In prima post salutationem commemorat Domini passiones et glorias ad confirmandos infirmos: deinde commemoratis quae in septem ecclesiis gesta uel gerenda sunt, describit pugnas et uictorias uniuersalis ecclesiae. In secunda uidet quattuor animalia, et uiginti quattuor seniores, et agnum stantem, et librum septem sigillis signatum: narrat etiam pugnas et triumphos ecclesiae. In tertia sub specie septem angelorum tuba canentium uarios euentus ecclesiae describit. In quarta sub figura mulieris et draconis, pugnas et uictorias ecclesiae narrat, ubi ⟨per⟩[95] septem angelos dicta et facta commemorat, etsi non ut prius. In quinta per septem angelos septem plagis terram percutit. In sexta damnationem

meretricis narrat. In septima uxorem agni dicit ornatam de caelo descendere.

De septem regulis Tychonii; quarum prima est de Domino, eiusque corpore; secunda de Domini corpore uero et simulato; tertia de promissis et lege; quarta de specie et genere; quinta de temporibus; sexta recapitulatio. Septima de diabolo, eiusque corpore. Hae septem regulae, non solum in Apocalypsi, sed et in aliis libris inueniuntur, maxime autem in propheticis.

In Apocalypsin primus commentatus martyr Victorinus; quem sequens beatus Hieronymus quaedam quae ille iuxta litteram intellexerat auferens, quaedam ex proprio adiciens, unum in eam condidit librum, promittens, se in ea potissime laboraturum, si uitae spatium adesset: sed opus illud utrum impletum fuerit, incertum est. Donatista etiam Tichonius multiplicem in eam edidit expositionem; sed perfidiae ueneno commiscuit. Post quem Primasius africanae ecclesiae antistes, uir per omnia catholicus, et in diuinis scripturis eruditus, quinque eam libris enodauit, in quibus, ut ipse asserit, non tam propria, quam aliena contexuit, eiusdem scilicet Tichonii bene intellecta deflorans; nihilominus et beati Augustini quaedam exposita capitula adnectens. Et quamuis eam plenius quam alii exposuerit, altissimo tamen sermone composuit. Denique etsi numero pauca, luculentissime tamen a sancto Gregorio exposita sunt capitula per eius diuersa opuscula. Postremo beatus Ambrosius Autpertus presbyter quaedam ex his, multa uero ex suo ponens, pulcherrime pertractauit.[96]

Saint [lit., blessed] Bede states that the Apocalypse is comprised of seven units. In the first, after his greetings, he recalls the sufferings and glories of the Lord to strengthen the weak. Next, after mentioning the deeds that have happened in the seven churches and what must ⟨shortly⟩ happen, he describes the battles and victories of the universal [i.e., Catholic] church. In the second section, he sees four animals and twenty-four elders and the lamb standing and a book sealed with seven seals. He also narrates the battles and triumphs of the church. In the third, he describes various events of the church under the appearance of seven angels sounding trumpets. In the fourth, under the figure of a woman and a dragon [*i.e.*, a great snake], he narrates battles and victories of the church when he recalls the sayings and deeds through the seven angels although differently than before [*lit.*, although not as before = but differently than previously]. In the fifth, through the seven angels he strikes the earth with seven plagues. In the sixth, he recounts the damnation of the whore. In the seventh, he says that the woman, adorned with the lamb, descends from heaven.

Concerning Tyconius' seven rules [*sc.*, of exegesis], the first of which is about the Lord and his body; the second ⟨is⟩ about the true and apparent body of the Lord; the third ⟨is⟩ about covenants and the law; the fourth ⟨is⟩ about species and type [group]; the fifth ⟨is⟩ about times; the sixth ⟨treats⟩ recapitulation. The seventh ⟨is⟩ about the devil and his body. These seven rules are found ⟨*sc.*, to be valid⟩ not only in the Apocalypse but also in other books, and especially in the prophetic ones.

The first commentator on the Apocalypse was the martyr Victorinus. While he [*sc.*, generally] followed Victorinus, Saint Jerome removed some matters that Victorinus had understood literally, added some things on his own, and constructed one book on the Apocalypse; furthermore, he promised that he was going to exert himself very much, if he lived long enough. But it is unknown whether that work was ever completed. Also, the Donatist Tyconius brought forth an extensive exposition on the Apocalypse, but he mixed into it some of his heretical poison. After him, Primasius, a leader [*i.e.*, priest, bishop, or spokesman] for the African church, and a man who was absolutely orthodox Catholic and extremely learned in the holy scriptures, elucidated the Apocalypse in five books. In these he stitched together, as he himself plainly says, not so much his own thoughts and observations but those of others, namely by culling matters that this same Tyconius had correctly understood. Nevertheless, he also added Augustine's exposition in some chapters. And although he made a fuller exposition on the book than others, still he composed in a very elevated style. Next, Saint Gregory the Great explained some portions, though numerically few, in his various works. Finally, blessed Ambrosius Autpertus, a priest, very beautifully made exegetical interpretation by putting into his work some quotations and paraphrases from his predecessors but also adding much on his own.

Relations among the Commentators

Alcuin's preface gives the general perspective of early Christian allusions to as well as commentaries and discussions of the Apocalypse.[97] The early writers follow Papias, Tertullian, and Hippolytus in a literal approach to the Millennium, resurrection, and judgment. At the beginning of the fourth century, Victorinus and Apollinarius were the last major exegetes in this tradition. Following the lead of Clement, the Alexandrian school developed an allegorical method of interpretation and applied it systematically to all scriptures, including the Apocalypse. This became the underlying approach of virtually all patristic authors after the midfourth century. Jerome's commentary reworked Victorinus' to produce a more allegorical and less literal explanation, but neither Victorinus' commentary, nor even Jerome's, had wide circulation. Even Cassiodorus did not draw heavily on Jerome.

But Jerome's contemporary, Tyconius, had a major influence on subsequent writers. Augustine used the commentary of Tyconius, his fellow North African, and also his *Liber Regularum* in commenting on the scriptures, especially on the Apocalypse in *de Ciuitate Dei* XX, and in describing the allegorical approach in *de Doctrina Christiana* III. Furthermore, Primasius, Caesarius of Arles, Bede of Jarrow, and Beatus of Liebana all made direct quotations and paraphrases from Tyconius, and Primasius also became the primary immediate source of Ambrosius Autpertus. In turn, Ambrosius Autpertus and Bede underlie Alcuin and Carolingian commentators. This line of interpretation from Tyconius and Primasius through Bede and, to a much lesser degree, Ambrosius Autpertus is the major exegetical tradition in the West. Consequently, a deepened appreciation for and awareness of Tyconius' interpretation can be very helpful to any serious study both of the exegetical tradition itself and of the changing meaning ascribed to individual passages from ante-Nicean times to late antiquity and continuing to the early Middle Ages.

A METHOD OF FINDING TYCONIAN QUOTATIONS

Tyconius' *Commentary on the Apocalypse*

The last recorded possession of a manuscript of Tyconius' commentary on the Apocalypse is in the first catalogue of Saint Gall in the ninth century, where the notation is added that the manuscript was "old" — *uetus*.[98] Because of the close interrelations of the continental monasteries with insular origins and because of the doctrinally and textually "maverick" nature of Northern Italy and nearby Switzerland, it is not surprising to discover a copy of Tyconius at Saint Gall. It was probably akin to the one known to Bede and to the one that was the source for the anonymous Turin fragments in a manuscript from Bobbio.

Since there is no extant manuscript of Tyconius' commentary on the Apocalypse, we must design a method for recovery. Tyconius was known to Caesarius, Bede, Beatus, and to the redactor of the Turin fragments. He was also used by Primasius, who in turn was known to and used by Bede and Ambrosius Autpertus. The question of Ambrosius Autpertus' first-hand knowledge of Tyconius has not been answered, although the modern editor of Ambrosius for *Corpus Christianorum* was inclined to believe that Ambrosius did not have a copy of Tyconius. Since Bede, Caesarius, Beatus, and the Turin fragments are fully independent of each other, if we can find passages in two or more commentaries where the wording is precisely the same or so close as to leave no doubt as to quotation from a common source, we may conclude that these comments derive directly from Tyconius. Also, Bede, Caesarius, and Beatus all attribute statements to Tyconius, and these, too, we may accept, even though there is no collaborating witness. Where Primasius has statements that are reflected in Beatus and Caesarius, though they did not have his commentary, we may safely take them to have been drawn from Tyconius. We suspect the same for many quotations of Primasius in Bede, but without confirming evidence of Caesarius or Beatus, we cannot be certain whether Bede has incorporated the words from Tyconius or Primasius, since he knew both. In my edition of Bede's *Explanatio Apocalypseos* for *Corpus Christianorum*, I will cite the identifiable Tyconian verbal parallels of Primasius, Caesarius, Bede, Beatus, and other early commentaries.

Tyconius' *Liber Regularum*

Finally, there are a number of passages in those commentaries where the interpretation accords entirely with the principles (and occasionally even with the wording) of Tyconius' *Liber Regularum*.[99] There are only three manuscripts of the *Liber Regularum*. It was not a popular medieval treatise. However, Augustine summarized the seven rules at the conclusion of the third book of *De Doctrina Christiana*, and this was widely known and followed both directly and in Eugippius' extracts. Hence, the method was adopted and propounded by Augustine through whose influence and text Bede, too, summarized the rules in the preface to his Apocalypse commentary. Because Tyconius' methodical description of his allegorical approach accorded with that used by Ambrose, Jerome, Augustine, and Gregory, it became part of the exegetical tradition in the West. Hence, even in a late thirteenth-century manuscript at Laon, the seven rules are listed and attributed to Tyconius, though without any mention of his Donatist affiliation:

Regulae Ticonii

Regula prima caput nostrum cum corpore iungit.
Corpore de uero loquitur mistoque secunda.
Tertia describit quid lex, quid gratia possit.
Quarta genus, speciem, totum partemque rependit.
Tempora disiungit maiora minoraque quinta.
Sexta refert iterum qu(a)e primo facta fuerunt.
Septima serpentis sibi membra caputque resoluit.[100]

The first rule joins our head with the body.

The second speaks concerning the true body and the mixed one.

The third describes what the Law and what Grace can do.

The fourth depends on genus and species and the part and the whole.

The fifth separates [or, distinguishes] greater and lesser times.

The sixth speaks again of what happened in the beginning.

The seventh undoes the strength of the serpent's head and limbs.

The *Liber Regularum* contained ideas appropriate to a pivotal shift of scriptural interpretation at a crucial time of development in the western church. This shift includes the notion of *recapitulatio* mentioned by Tertullian but developed by Tyconius. The likelihood is that when commentators use Tyconius' catch-words and categories, much of the passage has originally come from Tyconius' commentary on the Apocalypse, not the *Liber Regularum*. Such an approach to identifying Tyconian quotations is strengthened by the fact that Bede and Beatus often quote their sources at length with little or no verbal change, an editorial practice which Bede progressively but only moderately deserted in his later commentaries.

Tyconian Quotations in Modern Editions of the Commentaries

One of the fundamental problems in such a search for Tyconian quotations has been the deplorable condition of the texts of these commentaries. Yet, we now have good critical editions for Caesarius, the Turin fragments, Ambrosius Autpertus, Primasius, and a new edition of Beatus, supplementing that by Sanders, has recently been published.[101] My editions of the commentaries by Bede and Alcuin will include source references and exegetical parallels. For with critical editions and with the aid of computer-generated concordances and word-searches, we can more completely and accurately ascertain the verbal remnants of Tyconius imbedded in later commentaries. Fortunately, modern editors have been cognizant of the Tyconian origin of many statements in late antique and early medieval commentaries, and often they have identified such passages. However, since Apringius, Cassiodorus, Jerome, and the anonymous Irish commentary lie outside of the circle of Tyconius' influence, they have nothing to offer the effort to recover Tyconius. But for our broader interest in early Christian interpretation of Apocalypse 11, they too are important, even if they only touch on the issue briefly.

LITERAL AND SPIRITUAL INTERPRETATION OF THE SCRIPTURES

Anciently there were various approaches to understanding the scriptures. One very respected mode of interpretation, associated with the School of Antioch, emphasized the traditional early Christian practice of interpreting the text literally.[102] A leading exponent was a late contemporary of Didymos and Jerome, Theodore of Mopsuestia (350-428), but unfortunately he apparently did not comment on the Apocalypse.[103] He was followed by Theodoret of Cyr, a notable fifth-century proponent of Antiochene literalist exegesis, although, as was noted above, Theodoret cautiously admitted some allegorical meanings. He thus sought to unify the competing traditions by fusing the best parts of the two approaches into a new amalgam.

However, since it is primarily from fourth-century Alexandria—location both of the Museion, the justly famous center for scholarship on classical literature, and of the Christian Catechetical School—that later mainstream Christianity, both Greek Orthodox and Roman Catholic, derives its exegetical tradition, and since most of the patristic commentators date to the fourth century or later, they use an extremely refined mode of allegorical interpretation of the scriptures. This tradition had been developed at the famous Christian Catechetical School at Alexandria in the late second and early third centuries by Clement of Alexandria, following the example of the Jewish scholar, Philo, and it was furthered by Origen in the third century. Origen left Alexandria and went to Caesarea, taking manuscripts of texts and commentaries with him, and there he propagated his method. Ironically, in later centuries Origen was anathematized for teaching incorrect doctrines; however, many of these doctrines were early Christian teachings later rejected by the church.[104] But the tradition of the Catechetical School also persisted and flourished at Alexandria. During the last half of the fourth century, Didymos the Blind was the teacher of Jerome, Rufinus, and some of the Greek fathers, including Gregory of Nazianzus; he was, in essence, the disseminating force by which the allegorical method developed by Clement and Origen was widely transmitted to influential Christian writers and teachers. But he came under the same condemnation as Origen, and for the same early doctrines;

his commentaries were repressed and unknown until the discovery of five papyrus codices in 1941.[105] Thus the survival of texts became linked to doctrinal stance and exegetical method, for "orthodox" and "heretical" were labels subject to changing and conflicting values in the complex world of Christian polemics of the first centuries of our era.[106]

Moreover, Christians were not alone in approaching texts allegorically. This had been a time-honored practice in the ancient Near East, especially in Egypt, and the great scholars associated with the Museum (or *Mouseion*) also employed it. But it was particularly with the Neoplatonists of the second and third centuries that allegorical interpretation flourished, and it was widely applied to classical authors.[107] It was in this intellectual environment and with the tradition of the Jewish scholar Philo of Alexandria[108] that the Catechetical School systematized their allegorical and spiritual interpretation of the scriptures.

Among Christian exegetical authors of the Alexandrian School and their intellectual heirs in the Middle Ages, there was, as Henri de Lubac and others have noted, a systematic approach that allowed for four different levels of interpretation. The first is the literal (*iuxta litteram* or *ad litteram* — "to the letter") mode of understanding, that is, reading the text grammatically and making appropriate references to linguistic (including morphological, syntactical, and lexical or philological), historical, and cultural matters. The other three we tend to group broadly into the term allegorical, but anciently the three levels were called allegorical, tropological and anagogical; their generic term was "spiritual."[109] We recognize in Didymos' commentaries all four levels, just as they are used by Origen, but Didymos and church fathers of the late fourth and fifth centuries paid greater attention to the allegorical than to the literal meaning. And even Jerome, who used the allegorical method himself, lamented that Didymos distanced himself too much from the literal approach.[110] Occasionally a medieval commentator began to develop and to apply the literal mode of interpretation, but it was only in the twelfth century at Paris that it again became strongly linked to the allegorical levels.[111]

One example of the shift from literal to allegorical interpretation is the rejection of a literal millennium, mentioned above.[112] This could not be reconciled with the de-eschatologized exegesis of the scriptures:

> Throughout its long history, the church has been the steady enemy of the old Christian eschatology which, as Harnack says, emerges only at critical moments. When, as has happened in every century, groups and individuals within the church have sought the old literalism in normal times, they have been held to display exceedingly bad taste, and vigorously suppressed.[113]
>
> The same churchmen who gloried in the irrestible forward march of their invincible church suddenly remembered, when that church suffered collapse and dissolution before their eyes, that the real church of Christ was not to be a triumphant world church at all; they remember what they had forgotten: that Christ's church is only to be victorious at the end of the world. "The Apocalyptic element of Chiliasm," Harnack wrote, "it is true, lay dormant for long periods, but at critical moments constantly emerged."[114]

Similarly, the Christian fathers viewed the temple with apprehension and misgiving, and they could only interpret the temple in the Apocalypse allegorically:[115]

> It is commonly admitted that John's reference to the Temple is to be taken symbolically and not literally. Nearly all Catholic interpreters explain the Temple allegorically, although all do not explain the allegory in the same way, some referring it to the Church militant and others to the Church triumphant. This symbolical interpretation can be traced from Victorinus through the

Middle Ages, for instance through Albert the Great,[116] to the present time. This also is the meaning given to the Temple by most orthodox Protestants and by some independent critics. Unless it is taken symbolically it has no meaning in the passage, for when John wrote, the Temple of Jerusalem was already in ruins for many years.[117]

Another significant example of the allegorical approach coming into conflict with pristine Christian literalism is in the identification of the two witnesses in Apocalypse 11:3-13, also identified as the two lampstands and the two olive trees (Zechariah 4:3). The earliest Christian tradition holds firmly that the witnesses are to be identified with Enoch and Elijah. Such was the meaning given by Tertullian, Hippolytus, Irenaeus, and others whom Eusebius castigated for the millenarianist or chiliastic views, for the fourth century was inimical to pristine Christian literalism and eschatology. Yet, the tradition of Enoch and Elijah was strong enough to gain mention in Primasius, Cassiodorus, and even in one of Jerome's letters.[118] Similarly, some late apocalypses inspired by this scripture include such an identification. Although Origen's brief scholia do not discuss Apocalypse 11:3-13, Andreas later asserts that many Doctors of the eastern or Greek church even in his day held the position that the witnesses are Enoch and Elijah, and Arethas notes that it is the traditional view. Even the Coptic commentary of Pseudo-Cyril of Alexandria gives Enoch and Elijah as the witnesses. In the Latin west, Victorinus asserts that the witnesses are Elijah and Jeremiah or Elijah and Moses, the latter probably influenced by the type of plagues that the prophets invoke against their enemies as well as by the Transfiguration account in Matthew 17. Yet, even this shift points to the progressive loss that the church endured in those first centuries, for the interest shown early in Enoch and Melchizedek subsides and then is lost. So when Augustine speaks of the eschatological return of

Elijah, it is with reference only to Malachi, not to the Apocalypse.[119]

In Tyconius, the typological and allegorical interpretation is systematically expanded and applied. Hence, to follow Caesarius, Beatus, Bede, and the Turin fragments, we must conclude that Tyconius, motivated by a strong ecclesiological interest, used the witnesses as types of the unified power and tradition of the church, in particular calling them the two testaments, New and Old. Variations of this idea can be found throughout the Middle Ages, and the notion persists today. But it was not what the Primitive Church believed. Since the fifth century, interpreters have variously identified the two witnesses with individuals such as Peter and Paul; "for Nicholas of Lyra, the Two Witnesses are Pope Sylvester and Mennas, the Patriarch of Constantinople at the time of the Monothelite heresy"; yet others suggest two prophets similar to Elijah and Moses. Alcazar asserts "that the Two Witnesses are types of persecuted and resuscitated Christianity. . . . For Bousset, the Two Witnesses are not Elias and Henoch but the might and power of the Church, although he hesitates to deny the tradition relating to Elias and Henoch."[120] In the twelfth century, Peter Cantor, one of the great "masters of the sacred page,"[121] wrote in his commentary on the Apocalypse:

> **Et dabo** ad consolationem et auxilium electorum; **dabo** supple officium predicationis **testibus** Helye et Enoch per quos alii praedicatores intelliguntur. **hii sunt** commendat Helyam et Enoch ostendens quanti sint meriti quantaeue potestatis et in ill(is) commendat omnes praedicatores.[122]

> "And I shall give" to the comfort and help of the elect; "I shall give" supply the responsibility of preaching; "to the witnesses" Elijah and Enoch, through whom other preachers are understood. "These are" he commends Elijah and Enoch by demonstrating how much

merit and power is in them, and in them he commends all the preachers.

Jewish pre-Christian traditions, including the Pseudo-Philo *Liber Antiquitatum Biblicarum*,[123] often associated Elijah and Enoch as two precursors who would return and be slain; and the Apocalypse of Elijah recognizes sixty such precursors.[124] Because of this confusing welter of explanations, and because the allegorical and typological interpretations permeate the tradition, at the expense of the literal approach, we present the actual quotations from the early Christian writers through Alcuin of York in the West and through Photius and Arethas in the East.

PASSAGES FROM THE COMMENTATORS AND OTHER CHRISTIAN WRITINGS RELATING TO APOCALYPSE 11

Descensus Christi ad inferos

9. Dominus autem tenens manum Adae tradidit Michaeli archangelo: et omnes sancti sequebantur Michaelem archangelum, et introduxit omnes in paradisi gratiam gloriosam. Et occurrerunt eis obuiam duo uiri uetusti dierum. Interrogati autem a sanctis: Qui estis uos qui nobiscum in inferis mortui nondum fuistis et in paradiso corpore collocati estis? respondens unus ex eis dixit: Ego sum Enoch, qui uerbo domini translatus sum huc; iste autem qui mecum est Elias Thesbites est, qui curru igneo assumptus est hic, et usque nunc non gustauimus mortem, sed in aduentum Antichristi reseruati sumus, diuinis signis et prodigiis proeliaturi cum eo, et ab eo occisi in Ierusalem, post triduum et dimidium diei iterum uiui in nubibus assumendi.[125]

Christ's Descent into Hell: The Gospel of Nicodemus

Thus the Lord went into paradise holding the hand of Adam and entrusted him to Michael the archangel;

and all the saints were following Michael the archangel,
and he led them all through the glorious door into paradise. Two very old men met them there. When they
were asked by the saints, "Who are you who, though
dead, have not yet been with us in hades but have been
placed in paradise with your bodies?" one of them replied and said, "I am Enoch who was translated hither
by the word of the lord. And this man who is with me
is Elijah the Tishbite, who was caught up here in a chariot
of fire. And we have not tasted death until the present
moment, but rather we have been preserved to counter
the coming of Antichrist. Using divine signs and pro-
digies [miracles], we shall battle against him, and when
we have been killed at Jerusalem, after three and a half
days we shall assuredly be raised up in clouds, alive
once again."[126]

Historia Iosephi Fabri Lignarii

32. Et diximus: O domine noster, deus et seruator
noster, quinam sunt illi quattuor, quos dixisti e medio
sublaturum esse Antichristum ob exprobationem
eorum? Respondit seruator: Illi sunt Henoch, Elias,
Schila, et Tabitha.[127]

And we said, "Our Lord, our God and Savior,
whoever are these four whom you have said the Antichrist will bear off from the midst [sc., of the people]
because of them being proved? The Savior replied, these
are Enoch, Elijah, Schila, and Tabitha.

Tertullian

Translatus est Enoch et Helias nec mors eorum re-
perta est, dilata scilicet; ceterum morituri reseruantur,
ut antichristum sanguine suo exstinguant. Obiit et Iohannes, quem in aduentum domini remansurum frustra
fuerat spes.[128]

Enoch and Elijah were translated nor did they experience death; it was postponed. However that may

be, although they are going to die, they are preserved so that by their blood they may destroy the Antichrist. Even John died who had vainly hoped that he would remain alive until the second coming of the Lord.

Irenaeus, *Adversus Haereses*

Τί δὲ καὶ περὶ ἐκείνων λέγομεν, ὅπουγε Ἐνὼχ εὐαρεστήσας τῷ θεῷ, ἐν σώματι μετετέθη, τὴν μετάθεσιν τῶν δικαίων προμηνύων, καὶ Ἠλίας ὡς ἦν ἐν τῇ τοῦ πλάσματος ὑποστάσει, ἀνελήφθη, τὴν ἀνάληψιν τῶν πνευματικῶν προφητεύων; καὶ οὐδὲν ἐνεπόδισεν αὐτοῖς τὸ σῶμα πρὸς τὴν μετάθεσιν καὶ ἀνάληψιν. δι' ὧν γὰρ χειρῶν ἐπλάσθησαν τὴν ἀρχήν, διὰ τούτων τὴν ἀνάληψιν καὶ μετάθεσιν ἐλάμβανον.[129]

Quid autem de illis dicimus, quando quidem Enoch placens Deo in quo placuit corpore translatus est, translationem iustorum praemonstrans, et Helias sicut erat in plasmatis substantia assumptus est, assumptionem patrum prophetans? Et nihil impediit eos corpus in translationem et assumtionem eorum: per illas enim manus per quas in initio plasmati sunt, per ipsas assumptionem et translationem acceperunt.

And what do we say of them? Wherever Enoch is, the one who well pleased God, he was translated in his body, thus proclaiming in advance the change of the righteous. And Elijah, when he was in the hypostasis [*i.e.*, the substance, essence, *or* foundation] of the creation [*lit.*, plasma, image, *or* the shaped creation], was caught up, prophesying the event of the spiritual [*i.e.*, the righteous] people being caught up to heaven. And their bodies did not impede them at all in the change and being caught up. For they received their change and ascension through the hands of those by whom they were fashioned in the beginning.

Irenaeus, *Adversus Haereses*

Manifestius adhuc etiam de nouissimo tempore et de his qui sunt in eo decem regibus in quos diuidetur quod nunc regnat imperium significauit Iohannes, domini discipulus, in Apocalypsi, edisserens quae fuerint decem cornua quae a Daniele uisa sunt dicens sic dictum esse sibi [quotes Apocalypse 17:12-14; then Daniel 2:33-45].

Illo enim ueniente, et sua sententia apostasiam recapitulante in semetipsum et sua uoluntate et arbitrio operante quaecumque operabitur et in templo dei sedente, ut sicut Christum adorent illum qui seducentur ab illo, quapropter et iuste **in stagnum proicietur ignis** [Apocalypse 19:20], deo autem secundum suam prouidentiam praesciente omnia et apto tempore eum qui talis futurus erat, immittente, **ut credant falso, ut iudicentur omnes, qui non crediderunt ueritati, sed consenserunt iniquitati** [2 Thessalonians 2:11-12].

Cuius aduentum Iohannes in Apocalypsi significauit ita [quotes Apocalypse 13:2-10].

Nouissimus enim agon hic iustorum, in quo uincentes coronantur incorruptelam. Et propter hoc in bestia ueniente recapitulatio fit uniuersae iniquitatis et omnis doli ut in ea confluens et conclusa omnis uirtus apostatica in caminum mittatur ignis.[130]

Rather plainly to this point has John, the Lord's disciple, indicated in the Apocalypse concerning the very last time and concerning those who are at that time the ten kings among whom the current ruling power is to be divided. John explains what the ten horns, seen by Daniel, were to be, stating that it had been told to him as follows [Irenaeus then quotes Apocalypse 17:12-14 and Daniel 2:33-45]. . . . For he [*sc.*, the Antichrist] will come, and his intention will summarize [*lit.*, recapitulate] the apostasy in and for himself, and his will and desire will accomplish whatever is to be done [*i.e.*, whatever he wants he will do], and he will sit in the temple of God so that those who are seduced by him may worship him as though he were Christ. Hence, justly "he will be cast into the lake of fire" [Apocalypse 19:20]. But God, who because of his providence, knows all things, and at the apt time he will send forth him who was to be such "that they believe in a falsehood and that there be judged all who did not have faith in the truth but consented to iniquity" [2 Thessalonians 2:11-12]. In the Apocalypse John thus indicated the coming of that person [*sc.*, the Antichrist; Irenaeus then quotes Apocalypse 13:2-10]. . . .

For this is the very last conflict of the righteous, and if they are victorious in it, they will be crowned with an incorruptible crown [*sc.*, of glory]. And consequently with the arrival of the beast there is produced a recapitulation of all evil and of every deceitfulness so that the entire power of apostasy, flowing together and being enclosed in the beast may be sent with it into the fiery furnace.

Irenaeus, *Adversus Haereses*

His autem sic se habentibus, et in omnibus antiquis et probatissimis et ueteribus scripturis numero hoc posito, et testimonium perhibentibus his qui facie ad faciem Iohannem uiderunt . . . (numerus enim qui dicitur sex similiter custoditus recapitulationem ostendit uniuersae apostasiae eius quae initio et quae in mediis temporibus et quae in fine erit). . . .

Cum autem deuastauerit Antichristus hic omnia in hoc mundo, regnauerit annis tribus et mensibus sex et sederit in templo Hierosolymis, tunc ueniet dominus de caelis in nubibus in gloria patris, illum quidem et obaudientes ei in stagnum ignis mittens, adducens autem iustis regni tempora, hoc est requietionem, septimam diem sanctificatam, et restituens Abrahae promissionem hereditatis.[131]

Since that is the way matters stand, and since this number is found in all of the most ancient and proven [*or*, approved] ⟨manuscript⟩ copies of the scriptures, and

since those who saw John face to face bear testimony of
it . . . (for the number that constitutes the digit six, consistently preserved ⟨in the Apocalypse text⟩ points out the
recapitulations of its universal [worldwide] apostasy that
occurred in the beginning, in the meridian of time [*lit.*,
the middle times], and that will occur at the end). . . .

But when this Antichrist shall have destroyed everything in this world, he will reign for three years and six
months, and he will even sit down in the temple at
Jerusalem. Then shall the Lord come from heaven in
clouds, in the glory of the Father, sending this man [the
Antichrist] and those who obey him into the lake of fire.
But he shall bring forth for the righteous the times of
his kingdom, that is, the rest, the hallowed seventh day,
and restore to Abraham the covenanted inheritance.

Irenaeus, *Adversus Haereses*

Si autem quidam tentauerint allegorizare haec quae
eiusmodi sunt, neque in omnibus poterunt consonantes
sibimetipsis inueniri, et conuincentur ab ipsis dictionibus
disserentibus [*v.l.*, differentibus]. . . . Haec enim alia
uniuersa in resurrectionem iustorum sine controuersia
dicta sunt, quae fit post aduentum Antichristi et per-
ditionem omnium gentium sub eo exsistentium, in qua
regnabunt iusti in terra, crescentes ex uisione domini,
et per ipsum assuescent capere gloriam dei patris, et
cum sanctis angelis conuersationem et communionem
et unitatem spiritalium in regno capient. et illi quos dominus in carne inueniet exspectantes eum de caelis et per-
pessos tribulationem, qui et effugerint iniqui manus.[132]

But if certain individuals shall attempt to allegorize
these matters, which are of that sort, they shall not be
found agreeing among themselves on all issues, and they
will be found guilty by the very people who argue with
their public statements [*v.l.*, by themselves because of
their conflicting statements]. . . . For all these other
points and issues have been stated without controversy
about the resurrection of the just, that it happens after

the coming of Antichrist, and also about the destruction of all nations that exist under him [*i.e.*, under his domination and control]. At the time of that destruction the righteous shall reign upon the earth, growing because of the overseeing and revelations of the Lord, and through him they will become accustomed to receive the glory of God the father, and, with the holy angels, they shall receive in the kingdom the behavior, communion, and unity of spiritual beings. And those whom the Lord will find [*sc.*, still living] in the flesh, waiting for him [*sc.*, to come] from the heavens, and suffering tribulation, these will also flee from the hands of the evil one.

Hippolytus, *De Christo et Antichristo*

μίαν μὲν οὖν ἑβδομάδα εἰπών [*v.l.*, ἐτῶν], τὴν ἐσχάτην τὴν ἐπὶ τῷ τέρματι τοῦ σύμπαντος κόσμου ἐσομένην ἐπ' ἐσχάτων ἐσήμανεν ἧς ἑβδομάδος τὸ μὲν ἥμισυ λήμψονται οἱ δύο προφῆται, Ἐνὼχ καὶ Ἠλίας. οὗτοι γὰρ κηρύξουσιν **ἡμέρας χιλίας διακοσίας ἑξήκοντα, περιβεβλημένοι σάκκους** [Apocalypse 11:3], μετάνοιαν τῷ λαῷ καὶ πασὶ τοῖς ἔθνεσι καταγγέλλοντες.[133]

When he said one week [*v.l.*, By one week of years], therefore, he signified the last week that is to be at the end of the whole world. The two prophets, Enoch and Elijah, will take up half of the week. For they will preach 1,260 days clothed in sackcloth, proclaiming repentance to the [*sc.*, chosen] people and to all the nations.

Hippolytus, *De Christo et Antichristo*

ἀναγκαίως δεῖ τοὺς προδρόμους αὐτοῦ πρώτους φανερωθῆναι, καθὼς διὰ Μαλαχίου τοῦ ἀγγέλου [*v.l.*, καὶ Ἀγγαίου] φησίν· **Πέμψω ὑμῖν Ἠλίαν τὸν Θεσβίτην πρὶν ἢ ἐλθεῖν τὴν ἡμέραν Κυρίου τὴν μεγάλην καὶ ἐπιφανῆ, ὃς ἀποκαταστήσει καρδίας**

πατέρων πρὸς [v.l., ἐπὶ] τέκνα, καὶ
ἀπειθεῖς ἐν φρονήσει δικαίων, μήποτε
ἐλθὼν πατάξω [v.l., πατάξῃ] τὴν γῆν
ἄρδην. Οὗτοι συμπαραγενόμενοι [v.l., οὖν
παραγενόμενοι] κηρύξουσι τὴν μέλλουσαν
ἔσεσθαι ἀπ' οὐρανῶν Χριστοῦ ἐπιφάνειαν, οἳ
καὶ ποιήσουσι σημεῖα καὶ τέρατα εἰς τὸ κἂν
οὕτω δυσωπῆσαι καὶ ἐπιστρέψαι τοὺς ἀνθρώπους εἰς μετάνοιαν, διὰ τὴν ὑπερβάλ-
λουσαν αὐτῶν ἀνομίαν τε καὶ ἀσέβειαν.

Λέγει γὰρ Ἰωάννης· **Καὶ δώσω τοῖς δυσὶ
μάρτυσί μου, καὶ προφητεύσουσιν ἡμέρας χιλίας διακοσίας ἐξήκοντα, περιβεβλημένοι σάκκους,** τουτέστι τὸ ἥμισυ τῆς
ἑβδομάδος, ὃ [v.l., ἧς] εἴρηκε Δανιήλ.[134]

He must assuredly cause his forerunners to appear
first, just as he says through Malachi, his messenger: "I
shall send to you Elijah the Tishbite before the arrival
of the great and glorious day of the Lord. And he shall
restore [establish] the hearts of the fathers upon the
children, and the disobedient in [= to or by] the thought
[= wisdom] of the righteous, so that I might not ever come
and utterly strike down the earth" [Malachi 4:5-6]. These
will [v.l., therefore] come and proclaim the impending
appearance of Christ from heaven. And they shall also
perform signs and wonders that they might shame men
and turn them to repentance, because of their haughty
lawlessness [wickedness] and disobedience [impiety].

For John says, "And I shall grant to my two witnesses, and they shall prophesy for 1,260 days, dressed
in sackcloth" [Apocalypse 11:3]. That is, the half of a
week, that which [v.l., of which] Daniel spoke.

Hippolytus, *Capita contra Gaium*

Et dabo duos testes meos et prophetabunt, et cetera.
H(oc) e(st) uenient duo testes, prophetae Henoch et
Elias. Et uocat eos duas oliuas, sicut eos uocauit Za-

charias [Zechariah 4:3, 11, 14]. Et de Elia dixit Dominus
noster: "Eliam oportet uenire ut stabiliat omnia" [Mat-
thew 17:11]. Illos dicit facturos esse miracula et signa et
adducturos plagas super infideles ut sit requies fidelibus.

Illi duo prophetae surgent aduersus Antichristum. . . . Dicit Iohannes: **accipient potestatem** Henoch
et Elias et **praedicabunt dies mille et ducentos et sexaginta, amicti saccis,** et docentes poenitentiam populum
et gentes. Illi dies sunt **dimidium hebdomadis,** et illae
duae oliuae et duo candelabra sunt, sicut dixit Zacharias,
Henoch et Elias.[135]

"And I shall give my two witnesses and they shall
prophesy, etc." That is, two witnesses shall come, the
prophets Enoch and Elijah. And he calls them two olive
trees, just as Zechariah called them. And our Lord said
of Elijah, "it is necessary for Elijah to come to restore all
things." He says that they are going to perform miracles
and signs and that they will bring plagues on the faithless
[disobedient] so that there may be peace for the faithful.

These two prophets shall rise up against the Antichrist. . . . John says, Enoch and Elijah "shall receive
power and shall prophesy during 1,260 days, dressed
in sackcloth," and teaching repentance to the [God's]
people and to the gentile nations. These days are "half
a week," and "the two olive trees and the two candlesticks," just as Zechariah said, are Enoch and Elijah.

Hippolytus, *In Danielem*

τῶν γὰρ ἑξήκοντα δύο ἑβδομάδων πληρω-
θεισῶν καὶ Χριστοῦ παραγενομένου καὶ τοῦ
εὐαγγελίου ἐν παντὶ τόπῳ κηρυχθέντος ἐκ-
κενωθέντων τῶν καιρῶν, μία ἑβδομὰς περιλειφ-
θήσεται ἡ ἐσχάτη, ἐν ᾗ παρέσται Ἠλίας καὶ
Ἐνὼχ καὶ ἐν τῷ ἡμίσει αὐτῆς ἀναφανήσεται **τὸ
βδέλυγμα τῆς ἐρημώσεως,** ὁ ἀντίχριστος,
ἐρήμωσιν τῷ κόσμῳ καταγγέλλων · [136]

For when the sixty-two weeks shall be completed,

and Christ shall have come, and the gospel shall be preached in every place—when these critical times shall be fulfilled, one week—the last—shall remain. During this time there shall appear Elijah and Enoch, and at the middle of the week shall appear the "abomination of desolation," that is the Antichrist, proclaiming desolation to the world.

Hippolytus, *In Danielem*

ταῦτα μὲν οὖν οὕτως ὁ προφήτης διηγεῖται περὶ τοῦ ἀντιχρίστου, ὡς [*v.l.*, ὃς] ἔσται ἀναιδής, πολεμοτρόφος καὶ τύραννος . . . ὃς ὑπὲρ πάντας βασιλεῖς καὶ πάντα θεὸν ἐπαρθείς οἰκοδομήσει τὴν Ἰερουσαλὴμ πόλιν καὶ τὸν ναὸν ἀναστήσει· . . . καὶ τούτῳ προσκυνήσουσιν ὡς θεῷ οἱ ἀπειθεῖς καὶ τούτῳ γόνυ κλινοῦσιν, ὑπονοοῦντες αὐτὸν εἶναι τὸν Χριστόν· . . .

οὗτος ἀνελεῖ τοὺς δύο μάρτυρας, καὶ προδρόμους Χριστοῦ κηρύσσοντας τὴν ἔνδοξον αὐτοῦ ἀπ' οὐρανῶν παρουσίαν [*v.l.*, βασιλείαν]: ὡς λέγει διὰ τοῦ προφήτου·[137] **καὶ δώσω τοῖς δυσὶ μάρτυσί μου . . . σάκκους** [Apocalypse 11:3]· καθ' ἃ [*v.l.*, καθὼς] καὶ τῷ Δανιὴλ εἴρηκε· **καὶ διαθησει διαθήκην . . . καὶ σπονδή** [Daniel 9:27], ἵνα δειχθῇ ἡ μία ἐβδομὰς εἰς δύο μεριζομένη, τῶν μὲν δύο μαρτύρων τρία ἥμισυ ἔτη κηρυσσόντων, τοῦ δὲ ἀντιχρίστου τὸ ἐπίλοιπον τῆς ἐβδομάδος τοὺς ἁγίους πολεμοῦντος καὶ πάντα τὸν κόσμον ἐρημοῦντος· ἵνα πληρωθῇ τὸ εἰρημένον· **καὶ δώσουσι βδέλυγμα ἐρημώσεως ἡμέρας χιλίας διακοσίας ἐνενήκοντα** [Daniel 12:11–12].[138]

Therefore the prophet thoroughly explains about the Antichrist: he will be shameless; he will nurture himself on war [*i.e.*, be a war-monger]; he will be a tyrant . . . who will audaciously exalt himself above all kings and every god; he will build up the city of Jerusalem and will restore the sanctuary of the temple; . . . and the disobedient will worship him as though he were God and will bow their knee to him, deeming him to be the Christ.

He shall destroy the two witnesses and precursors of Christ as they proclaim his glorious coming [*v.l.*, kingdom] from heaven, as ⟨John in the Apocalypse⟩ says: [quotes Apocalypse 11:3] and according to what [*v.l.*, just as] was also stated by Daniel: [quotes Daniel 9:27] — that the one week might be shown to be divided into two parts. So, the two witnesses preach during three and a half years, and during the rest of the week the Antichrist makes war upon the saints and devastates the world, that the scripture [*lit.*, utterance, what has been spoken ⟨by the prophet⟩] may be fulfilled: [quotes Daniel 12:11-12].

(Pseudo-)Methodios, *Apocalypsis*

> ἐξαποστελεῖ οὖν ἐν συντόμῳ τοὺς ἰδίους αὐτοῦ καὶ γνησίους θεράποντας τὸν Ἐνὼχ καὶ τὸν Ἐλίαν εἰς ἔλεγχον τοῦ ἀντικειμένου.[139]

Therefore he shall soon send forth his very own and legitimate servants, Enoch and Elijah, to expose [refute] the adversary.

> ἐξαποστελεῖ οὖν ἐν συντόμῳ τοὺς ἰδίους αὐτοῦ καὶ γνησίους θεράποντας τόν τε Ἐνὼχ καὶ τὸν Ἐλίαν, οἵτινες ἐπὶ πάντων τῶν ἐθνῶν ἐλέγχουσιν αὐτοῦ τὴν πλάνην.[140]

Therefore he shall soon send forth his very own and legitimate servants, Enoch and Elijah, who shall expose his error to all nations.

> ἀλλ᾽ἐξαποστελεῖ τοὺς ἰδίους δούλους αὐτοῦ τόν τε Ἐνὼχ καὶ Ἐλίαν καὶ Ἰωάννην τὸν θεολόγον εἰς ἔλεγχον τοῦ ἀντιχρίστου.[141]

But he shall send his own servants, Enoch, Elijah, and John the theologian, to the confrontation with the Antichrist.

Commodian

> Sed priusquam ille ueniat, prophetabit Helias
> Tempore partito, medio ebdomadis axe[m].
> Conpleto spatio succedit ille nefandus,
> Quem et Iudaei simul tunc cum Romanis adorant.
> Quamquam erit alius, quem expectent ab oriente,
> In nostra caede tamen saeuient cum rege Nerone.
> Ergo cum Helias in Iudea terra prophetat,
> Et ⟨signo⟩ signat populum in nomine Christi;
> De quibus quam multi quoniam illi credere nolunt,
> Supplicat iratus Altissimum, ne pluat inde:
> Clausum erit caelum ex eo nec rore madescet,
> Flumina quoque iratus in sanguine uertit.[142]

But before he comes, Elijah shall prophesy at the division of time, the midaxis of the week. After the space of time is filled, that accursed man will come forth whom the Jews together with the Romans worship. Although there will be another whom they anticipate from the east, nevertheless, they will rage with the King [=Emperor] Nero in our slaughter. Therefore while Elijah prophesies in the land of Judah and with a mark seals the people in the name of Christ, since many of them refuse to believe in him, in anger he will pray to the most high [God] that it not rain henceforth. From that time heaven will be closed nor will it become wet from dew. Furthermore, because of his anger he will turn rivers to blood.

Victorinus

> Aquila uolans medio caelo: spiritus sanctus significatur in duobus prophetis contestans magnam plagarum iram imminere, si quo modo, quamuis sit nouissimum tempus, aliquis adhuc saluus esse possit.[143]

An eagle flying through the midst of heaven; by the

two prophets is the Holy Spirit signified, opposing the great anger of the plagues that is ready at hand, [to see] whether perchance, although it is the very last time, someone can yet be saved.

Jerome

[*Et uidi unam aquilam uolantem per medium caelum.*] Aquila magna medio caelo uolans: spiritus sanctus significatur in duobus prophetis contestans magnam plagarum iram imminere, si quo modo, quisque uolens sit nouissimo tempore conuersus, ut aliquis adhuc saluus esse possit.[144]

A great eagle flying in the midst of heaven; by the two prophets is the Holy Spirit signified, opposing the great anger of the plagues that is ready at hand, [to see] whether perchance, anyone willingly might be converted at the last time, so that anyone could be saved up to the present moment.

Victorinus

Multi putant cum Helia esse Heliseum aut Moysen, sed utrique mortui sunt. Hieremiae autem mors non inuenitur. Per omnia ueteres nostri tradiderunt illum esse Hieremiam.[145]

Many people think that Elisha or Moses is [going to be coming] with Elijah, but both of them died. However, the death of Jeremiah is not found [recorded in the scriptures]. Through all matters, our predecessors have passed down the tradition that this [other] person is Jeremiah.

Jerome

Multi putant cum Helia esse Heliseum aut Moysen, sed utrique mortui sunt. Hieremiae autem mors non inuenitur. Perque omnia ueteres nostri tradiderunt illum esse Hieremiam.[146]

Many people think that Elisha or Moses is [going to

be coming] with Elijah, but both of them died. However,
the death of Jeremiah is not found [recorded in the scrip-
tures]. And through all matters, our predecessors have
passed down the tradition that this [other] person is
Jeremiah.

Victorinus

Deinde ait: **factum est in caelo bellum: Michael et
nuntii eius pugnauerunt cum dracone, et draco pugnauit et nuntii eius, et non est inuentus ei locus in caelo.
et iactatus est draco magnus, anguis antiquus, recidit
in terram.** hoc est initium aduentus Antichristi. ante
tamen oportet praedicare Heliam et pacifica tempora
esse, et sic postea consummato triennio et mensibus sex
praedicationis Heliae iactari Antichristum de caelo, ubi
habuit potestatem ascendendi usque ad illud tempus, et
angelos refugas uniuersos. sic Antichristum de inferno
suscitari, hoc et Paulus apostolus ait: **nisi prius uenerit
homo peccati, filius perditionis, aduersarius, qui se
eleuabit super omne quod nominatur deus aut colitur.**[147]

Then he says: "There was war in heaven. Michael
and his angels fought with the dragon, and the dragon
and his angels fought; and there was not found any place
in heaven for the dragon. And that great dragon, the
old viper, was hurled out and fell to the earth." This is
the beginning of the coming of the Antichrist. For before
that time it is necessary for Elijah to preach and for the
times to be peaceful; and thus after the completion of
three years and six months of the preaching of Elijah,
the Antichrist is thrown from heaven, where he had the
power of ascending until that time, he and all his apostate angels. That Antichrist is thus raised up from hell,
even the apostle Paul says: "except there should first
come the man of sin, the son of perdition, the adversary,
who will lift up himself above all that is called God or
that is worshipped."

Jerome

Deinde ait: [**factum est proelium in caelo: Michael
et angeli eius pugnabant cum dracone, et draco proe-**

liatus est et angeli eius, et non ualuerunt neque inuentus est eorum locus etiamnunc in caelo. et proiectus est draco ille magnus, serpens antiquus, proiectus est in terram.] factum est bellum in caelo: Michael et nuntii eius pugnauerunt cum dracone, et draco pugnauit et nuntii eius, et non est inuentus ei locus in caelo. et iactatus est draco magnus, anguis antiquus, iactatus in terram. hoc est initium Antichristi. ante tamen oportet praedicare Heliam et pacis tempora esse, et postea consummato triennio et sex mensibus praedicationis Heliae iactari eum de caelo, ubi habuit potestatem ascendendi usque ad illud tempus, et angelos refugas uniuersos. sic et Antichristum de inferno suscitari Paulus apostolus ait: nisi prius uenerit homo peccati, filius perditionis, aduersarius, qui se eleuabit super omne quod nominatur deus aut colitur.[148]

Then he says [twice quoting Apocalypse 12:7-9]: This is the beginning of Antichrist. However, before that time, it is necessary that Elijah preach and that there be times of peace; later, after the completion of the three years and six months of Elijah's preaching, he [the Antichrist], together with all his apostate angels, is cast from heaven where he had power of ascending up until that time. Thus Paul the apostle says that the Antichrist is raised up from Hades: "except there first come the time of the apostasy and that there appear the man of sin, the son of perdition, the adversary who will raise himself up above all that is called God or above all that is worshipped" [2 Thessalonians 2:3-4].

(Tyconius) Turin Fragments

332 Et dabo duobus testibus meis, et prophetabunt dies mille ducenti sexaginta. 333 Id est, ante dixerat: Oportet te iterum prophetare, hoc nunc de duobus testibus suis uoluit demonstrare. 334 Duos enim testes quos dicit, duo testamenta intellegi uoluit, in quibus ecclesia ipsius gubernatur ac regitur. 335 Non enim dixit: facio mihi testes, tanquam qui non fuerint, sed Dabo testibus,

qui ab initio mecum sunt et a me penitus non disces-
serunt. **336 Dies** autem **mille ducenti sexaginta,** non
tempus est pacis sed nouissimae persecutionis, in quibus
in christianos diabolus exardescet, quando ad proban-
dum ecclesiam potestatem acceperit. **337** Et sicut ante
diluuium, quando **peccata** hominum **usque ad caelum**
extulerant caput, non defuit qui iram Domini pereun-
tibus praedicaret, ita tunc non deerunt qui regnum Dei
et nouissimum diem adnuncient, exemplo suo pecca-
toribus paenitentiae uiam demonstrent. **338 Saccis,** inquit, **induti.** Id est, in exomologesim constituti, **339** sicut
propheta dicit: **cum mihi molesti essent, induebam me**
cilicium. 340 Et Iob: **Adsuerunt,** inquit, **cutibus meis**
cilicium. 341 Deinde qui sunt isti duo testes in conse-
quentibus dicit.[149]

332 "And I shall grant . . . " **333** That is what he had
previously said: "you must prophesy again," this is what
is now wanted to demonstrate about his two witnesses.
334 For the two witnesses whom he mentions he wanted
to be understood as the two testaments, whereby his
own church is governed and ruled. **335** For he did not
say: I shall make witnesses for myself, as if they didn't
exist, but "I shall grant unto my witnesses" who have
been with me from the beginning and have not at all
defected from me. **336** Moreover, the 1,260 days are not
a time of peace but of the very last persecution. On those
days the devil will burn with rage against the Christians,
since he will have power to try the church. **337** And just
as before the flood, when the sins of men had raised
their head [*i.e.,* the summary titles in a list] to heaven,
there was no lack of a person who was to prophesy the
wrath of God to those who were about to perish, so then
there will not be a lack for people who will proclaim the
kingdom of God and the very last day [*i.e.,* the judgment
day] and who, by their own example, will point out the
way of repentance unto the sinners. **338** "Dressed," he
said, "in sackcloth." That is ⟨to say⟩, established to bear
witness [*or,* to confess], **339** just as the prophet said:

"although they were a nuisance to me, I dressed myself in sackcloth" [Vulgate Psalm 34:13]. **340** And Job: "they have placed," he says, "sackcloth on my skin [Old Latin Job 16:16]. **341** Then he states who these two witnesses are in what follows.

(Tyconius) Turin Fragments

342 Hi sunt duo olivae et duo candelabra, qui in conspectu Domini terra⟨e⟩ stant. 343 Hi sunt qui stant, ait. Non autem dixit **stabunt,** sicut stare non possint. **344** In **duo candelabra** ecclesia signata est, quae duorum testamentorum munitione uallata est. **345** Nam et in septem angelis et septem candelabris unam ecclesiam designauit, ita ut cum unum nominauerit etiam caetera nominauit. **346** Nam cum Zacharias propheta in figura nostra e somno excitaretur ut ecclesiae lumen aspiceret, unum candelabrum septiformem uidit, in quo mysterium septiformis ecclesiae declarauit. **347** Nam duae oliuae duo sunt testamenta, oleum scientiae candelabro infundentia.[150]

342 "These are the two olive trees and the two candlesticks. . . . " **343** "These are those who stand," he says. However, he did not say "they will stand" as if they could not stand. **344** In "two candlesticks" the church is signified, which is protected by the fortification of the two testaments. **345** For both in the seven angels and in the seven candlesticks he has designated one church, so that when he named the one he also named the others. **346** For when the prophet Zechariah was aroused from sleep in our image, so that he might look upon the light of the church, he beheld a sevenfold candlestick whereby he stated that the mystery of the sevenfold church was made plain. **347** For the two olive trees are the two testaments, pouring forth the oil of knowledge upon [or, into] the candlestick.

Ambrosius, *Commentarii in Epistolam I ad Corinthios*

Sicut passuri sunt Enoch et Elias, qui ultimo tempore futuri sunt apostoli. Mitti enim habent ante Christum ad praeparandum populum Dei, et muniendas omnes Ecclesias, ad resistendum Antichristo, quos et persecutiones pati et occidi lectio Apocalypsis testatur (Apocalypse 11:8-9).[151]

Just as Enoch and Elijah, who will be sent forth [*lit.*, apostles] at the last time, are going to suffer. For people hold that they are sent before Christ to prepare the people of God and to fortify all the churches to combat against the Antichrist. Reading the Apocalypse bears witness that these two will suffer persecutions and be killed.

Didymos the Blind, *In Genesim*

[quoting Genesis 5:21–24, concluding with 5:24] ... καὶ εὐηρέστησεν Ἐνὼχ [τ]ῷ θεῷ, καὶ οὐχ ηὑρίσκετο, | ὅτι μετέθηκεν αὐτὸν ὁ θεός. ... περὶ δὲ τούτου λέγε|[ται ὅτι μ]ετετέθη, περὶ οὗ νοοῦμεν ὅτι ἢ ὡς Ἠλίας ἀναλήμφθη | ἢ καθ' ἕ[τ]ερον τρόπον εἰς θεῖον ἡρπάγη χῶρον. ...

θε|ωρίαν ἄρα πρέπουσαν ἔχει τὸ προκείμενον, εἰ καὶ μὴ τῷ εἰθισ|μένῳ τὸ νῦν τοῖς ἄλλοις ἀνθρώποις θανάτῳ κεκοινωνήκασιν, ἀλλὰ | τῷ τὴν ἔνυλον ζωὴν ἀποτεθεῖσθαι κατὰ τὸν ἀπόρρητον ἡμῖν | τοῦ θεοῦ λόγον τὸ θνητὸν αὐτῶν δεῖ νοῆσαι.

εἰ δέ τῳ φίλον κα[ὶ] τὴν βίβλον τῆς δια-θήκης ἀναγιγνώ|σκειν, γνώσεται ὡς [εἰς] τὸν παράδεισον ἡρπᾶσθαι λέγεται· | καὶ τοῦτο γὰρ εἰδέναι, [εἰ κα]ὶ μὴ ἐξ ἀναντιρρήτου βιβλίου ἐστίν, | οὐκ ἄτοπον.[152]

"And Enoch pleased God, and he was not found any more, because God transported him" [Genesis 5:24]. ... Concerning him [*sc.*, Enoch] it is said that "he was transported" [Genesis 5:24], about whom we understand that either, like Elijah, "he was taken up" [*sc.*, to heaven; 2 Kings 2:11] or "he was caught up" [2 Corinthians 12:4] in some other manner to a divine place. . . .

Therefore, this matter [or, what has earlier been put forth, *namely the verb in Genesis 5:24 translated* "and he was transported"] has an explanation appropriate ⟨to Enoch and Elijah⟩ [or, an appropriate consideration], although they [sc., Enoch and Elijah] have not partaken of [lit., shared in] the ⟨sort of⟩ death usual to men nowadays; but rather it is requisite for us to understand, according to the ineffable word of God [or, using God's explanation that is secret to us], their mortal condition by their having laid aside their material life [or, by the fact that their material life has now thoroughly been laid aside].

And if someone enjoys reading [or, is willing to read] *The Book of the Testament* [sc., of Enoch], he will realize that Enoch is said to have been caught up to paradise. And in fact it is not bizarre to know this [i.e., to learn or ascertain this fact from this source], even though it is not from an irrefutable book.

Didymos the Blind, *In Zachariam*

διὰ τοῦ εἰπεῖν τὴν λυχνί[αν χρυ]σῆν ὅλην εἶναι, δηλοῖ ὅτι ὅλη δι' ὅλων ἡ φωτῶν πε-πληρωμέν[η λυ]χνί[α] νοερὰ καὶ ἀσώματός ἐστιν.[153]

Because he says that the entire lampstand is gold, it is obvious that the lampstand, entirely filled with lights, is spiritual and immaterial.

Didymos the Blind, *In Zachariam*

[lemma: Zechariah 4:11–14] 335. ἐπηρωτή-σαντος τοῦ ἀγγέλου τοῦ λαλοῦτος ἐν τῷ προφήτῳ· "Τί βλέπεις σύ;" ἀπεκρίθη καὶ εἶπεν πευστικῶς· "Τίνες αἱ δύο ἐλαῖαι αἱ ἐκ δεξιῶν καὶ ἐξ εὐωνύμων τῆς λυχνίας;" ἀπεκρίσεως

αὐτῷ μὴ δοθείσης, ἐκ δευτέρου ἐπερωτᾷ περὶ
δύο κλάδων τῶν ἐλαιῶν οἱ ἐν ταῖς χερσὶν τῶν
δύο μυξωτήρων τῶν ἐπιχεόντων καὶ ἐπανα-
γόντων τὰς ἐπαρυστρίδας τὰς χρυσᾶς. πρὸς ὃν
ὁ ἄγγελος· "οὐ γινώσκεις τί ἐστιν ταῦτα;" "Οὐχί,
κύριε," εἰπόντος τοῦ προφήτου, ὁ ἄγγελος ἔφη·
"Οὗτοι οἱ δύο υἱοὶ τῆς πιότητος παρεστήκασιν
τῷ κυρίῳ πάσης τῆς γῆς."

336. τῷ ἀρχὴν ἔχοντι μυσταγωγίας οὐ
δυνατόν πω γνῶναι τίνες ἐκ δεξιῶν καὶ ἐξ
εὐωνύμων τῆς λυχνίας ἐλαῖαι· διὸ ἐκ δευτέρου
ἐπερωτᾷ περὶ κλάδων δύο τῶν ἐλαιῶν. σεσα-
φήνισται ἐν τοῖς πρότερον λόγους εἶναι μελέτης
θείας, ἐλαίας ὀνομαζομένους διὰ τὸ τὸν καρ-
πὸν αὐτῶν αὔξειν καὶ τρέφειν τὸ φῶς. 337. ἐπεὶ
οὖν [οὐ] δυνατὸν τὸν **ἐκ μέρους γινώσκον-
τα καὶ προφητεύοντα** θεωρῆσαι ἐξ ὅλων τὰ
στελέχη καὶ τὰ ἔρνη τῶν [ἐ]κκειμένων φυτῶν,
ἐκ δευτέρου ἐπηρώτησιν προσάγει [περ]ὶ δύο
κλάδων ἐλαιῶν, τούτων γὰρ μόγις γνῶσιν
[ἔχε]ιν δυνατὸν τὸν **δι' ἐσόπτρου καὶ αἰ-
νίγματος** ἐπιβάλλον[τα] τῇ ἀληθείᾳ, ἵν' ἐκ
τῶν μερικῶν ὠφεληθεὶς δύνηθῇ ποτὲ γνῶναι
τίνες αἱ ἐλαῖαι τυγχάνουσιν.

338. καὶ ἐπεὶ μία ἀποδόσεων κατά τινα τῶν
ἐξηγησαμένων τὸ ῥητὸν ὃς τὰς δύο ἐλαίας εἰς
τὸν περὶ υἱοῦ καὶ ἁγίου πνεύματος λόγον
ἐξέλαβεν, ὅρα εἰ οἱ κλάδοι τῶν ἐλαιῶν τούτων
ἐκλαμβάνοιντο τὰ ἐφικτὰ τῷ ἐκ μέρους γινώ-
σκοντι. καὶ Χριστοῦ μὲν ἐλαίας ὄντος, κλάδος
εἴη τὸ σάρκα γεγονέναι τὸν λόγον· τοῦ δ' ἁγίου
πνεύματος, ἡ εἰσαγωγικὴ θεωρία αὐτοῦ, ὀνο-
μαζομένη "ἀρραβὼν" αὐτοῦ. . . .

342. ἐπίστησον εἰ δύνασαι πιότητος υἱοὺς
δύο ἐκλαβεῖν παρεστηκότας τῷ κυρίῳ πάσης
τῆς γῆς, τοὺς ὀφθέντας ἐν δόξῃ μετὰ Ἰησοῦ ἐν

τῷ ὄρει Μωϋσέα καὶ Ἡλίαν, τὸν νομικὸν καὶ προφητικὸν δηλονότι λόγον. ὥσπερ γὰρ ὁ πνευματικὸς νόμος υἱὸς τυγχάν[ει] τῆς ἀπο-δοθείσης πιότητος, οὕτω καὶ ὁ ἀνηγμένος προ-φήτ[ου] λόγος. ἀνέγνων ἐν ἀποκρύφῳ βιβλίῳ τὸν Ἐνὼχ καὶ τὸν Ἡ[λίαν] τοὺς δύο υἱοὺς τῆς πιότητος εἶναι, ὡς εἰκὸς διὰ τὸ προσόνα[σθαι] παρὰ τοὺς ἄλλους ἀνθρώπους. [Didymos quotes Hebrews 11:5 and 2 Kings 2:11 as proof.][154]

335. When the angel who spoke with the prophet asked the question, "what do you see?" he replied by inquiring, "who are the two olive trees at the right and at the left of the lampstand?" Since no response was given to him, he asked a second time concerning the two branches of the olive trees who have in their hands the golden lamp-oil containers of the two spouts that pour out and bring up the oil ⟨for burning in the lamp wicks⟩. The angel replied, "don't you know what these things are?" So when the prophet said, "not at all, my Lord," the angel said, "these two sons of the anointing [lit., children of fatness] stand before the lord of all the earth."

336. To him who has ⟨only⟩ the beginning of initiation into the mysteries it is not at all possible for him to know the identity of the olive trees on the right and left of the lampstand. Hence, a second time he inquires about the branches of the two olive trees. It has been made ade-quately clear in the preceding comments that there are topics of divine practice [study] that are called olive trees because their fruit increases and nurtures the light. 337. Therefore, since it is not possible for the person who "knows and prophesies in part" [1 Corinthians 13:9] to contemplate completely the trunks and branches of the aforementioned plants, he (the prophet) asks a second time about the two branches of the olive trees. For to acquire knowledge is scarcely possible [= only with great

difficulty] for a person who devotes himself to the truth "through [or, in] a mirror and with uncertainty" [1 Corinthians 13:12 "see through a glass darkly"]. And this is that by not being concerned about details, he might sometime be about to come to know who the olive trees happen to be.

338. And since this is one ⟨possible⟩ explanation according to one of the exegetes [probably Athanasius] of this passage, a person who took the two olive trees to mean the study of the Son and of the Holy Spirit, consider whether the branches of these olive trees might receive [= admit, understand] matters accessible to one who knows only in part. And so if the olive tree should be [= signify] Christ, then the branch would be the word made [lit., become] flesh [or, the incarnation of the word], but if it should be [= signify] the Holy Spirit, then it would be the introductory (spiritual) contemplation, something called "the earnest" [or, down payment, first installment of the Spirit] [2 Corinthians 5:5]. . . .

342. Come to understand whether you are able to accept that the two sons of the anointing who stand in the presence of the lord of all the earth are ⟨to be identified with [or, the same as]⟩ Moses and Elijah — obviously the word of the Law and the prophetic word — who were seen in glory on the mount with Jesus. For just as the spiritual law happens to be the son of the anointing as has been explained, even so it is with the word of the prophet that has been brought up [or, that we have been discussing; alternatively, even so it is with the anagogical or allegorical word of the prophet]. I have read in an apocryphal book that Enoch and Elijah are the two sons of the anointing, as is likely because of their having an advantage in comparison with the rest of mankind.

Jerome, *Commentarii in Zachariam*

Dicamus igitur singula percurrentes, primum quid uideatur Hebraeis, a quibus in ueteri testamento eruditi sumus; deinde per hos quasi gradus ad Ecclesiae culmina conscendamus. Candelabrum aureum solidum, legem,

id est, *nomon* interpretantur. Lampadem autem, id est
flammam in uertice candelabri lucentem atque fulgen-
tem, Christum, qui caput legis sit, et omnem mundum
illuminet. Septem lucernas super candelabrum, septem
gratias Spiritus sancti, de quibus supra diximus, quod
in lapide uno septem oculi sint. Nulli enim dubium quin
lex, Spiritu sancto dictante, conscripta sit. Septem autem
infusoria in quibus oleum sit, quod mittatur in lucernas,
quae super candelabro luceant, hoc intellegi uolunt, septem istas gratias de caelo ad homines per legem descendere. Duas autem oliuas super candelabrum a dextera
parte et sinistra, inter quas media lampas luceat, legem
et prophetiam interpretantur.[155]

Therefore, as we examine each particular issue, let
us state first what seemed best to the Jews, from whom
we have been educated in the Old Testament. Next, let
us ascend through these people the steps, as it were, to
the heights of the church. The solid gold candlestick they
interpret to be the Law, that is, the *nomos*. But the lampstand on the candlestick, which is the flame shining and
burning, illumines Christ, who is the head of the Law,
and the entire world. The seven lamps upon the candlestick are the seven graces of the Holy Spirit, concerning
which we spoke above, that there are seven eyes in one
rock. For no one has any doubts but that the Law was
written as the Holy Spirit dictated it. Moreover, the seven
pipes through which there is oil that can be put into the
lamps, they want this to be understood as the seven
graces that descend from heaven upon men through the
Law. Moreover, ⟨the commentators⟩ interpret the two olives above the candlestick on the right and left, such
that a balanced brilliance shines between them, to be the
law and prophecy.

Jerome, *Commentarii in Zachariam*

Haec ab Hebreis dicta reperimus. Nunc quid ab ec-
clesiasticis uiris in commentariis scriptum sit disseramus. . . . Duas oliuas super candelabrum, et ipsi Moy-

sen et Heliam intellegunt, qui cum Domino loquebatur
in monte, et significabant quid in Hierusalem passurus
esset. Omnis enim lex et prophetae de Christi praedicant
passione. Alii duas oliuas a dextris, et a sinistris, legem
et euangelium interpretantur, ut in dextra euangelium
sit, in sinistra lex . . . . Mons ibi aperte diabolus accip-
itur. Alii autem temeritate non parua, hoc quod mani-
feste de diabolo dicitur, ad Christum referunt, qui in
scripturis sanctis mons saepius dicitur. Nec necesse est
dare exempla, quorum magna copia est. . . . Et ab Hebraeis et a nostris multa dicuntur, quorum pleraque sec-
tantes, et alia repudiantes, quid nobis placeat, infera-
mus, seruantes historiae ueritatem, ut ex hac possimus
eum, qui per historiam prophetatur, agnoscere.[156]

This is what we find stated by the Jewish ⟨scholars⟩.
Now let us discuss what has been written in commentaries by men of the Church. . . . They themselves understand the two olive trees above the candlestick as
Moses and Elijah, who spoke with the Lord on the Mount
[sc., of Transfiguration], and they indicated what he
would have to suffer at Jerusalem. For all of the law and
the prophets foretell of the passion of Christ. Other exegetes interpret the two olives—on the right and on the
left—to be the law and the gospel, such that the gospel
is on the right and the law on the left. . . . There obviously the mount is to be taken as the devil. But others,
with extreme audacity, apply this [sc., notion], that
clearly is spoken about the devil, to Christ, as he is very
often called a mountain in the scriptures. And there is
no need to provide examples, for there is a great abundance of them. . . . Many things are stated both by the
Jews and by ours [i.e., by the Christian scholars]; though
we follow much of what they say, and though we re-
pudiate other parts, let us accept and admit what might
please us, while preserving the historical truth, so that
we may be able to recognize him, for he was prophesied
throughout history.

Jerome, *Commentarii in Zachariam*

Cumque et de duobus ramis propheta quaereret, et rursum interrogaretur ab angelo, utrumnam sciret quid duo rami significarent, et ille dixisset: **Non, domine** [Zechariah 4:13], respondit angelus Domini: **Isti sunt duo filii olei,** ut Symmachus uoluit, siue *zilpnotētos,* ut interpretatus est Aquila, id est splendoris; uel *piotētos,* hoc est pinguedinis, ut uerterunt Septuaginta; aut *lamprotētos,* id est claritatis, ut Theodotio transtulit, **qui assistunt Dominatori uniuersae terrae** [Zechariah 4:14]. De duabus oliuis quae erant ad dextram lampadis et sinistram, supra legimus. Et idcirco nunc interrogans super his propheta, non meretur audire, quia priora non retinet, siue quod ibi obscurius dictum est, hic manifestius audire desiderat, aut certe silentio angeli confutatur eius pertinacia, quod maiora se scire contendat : quamquam Hebraei ideo eum de oliuis interrogantem, nihil audisse confirment, quia non bene interrogauit, nec totum quaesierit quod scire debuerat. Denique postea plenius sciscitatur addens, spicas uel ramos oliuarum, de quibus supra tacuerat. Ibi enim dixit: **Quid sunt duae oliuae istae?** Hic interrogat: **Quid sunt duae spicae oliuarum?** *Metaphorikōs* quod in morem spicarum rectae sint arbores, et quasi spicae aristis, sic istae uallo quodam ramorum atque foliorum tectae sint et in sublime surgentes. Duas oliuas quidam e nostris Filium interpretantur, et Spiritum sanctum, et mediam lampadem Deum Patrem. Sed nescio quomodo absque blasphemia, alterum a dextris, et alterum accipiant a sinistris. Ramos quoque siue spicas oliuarum, incarnationem Saluatoris et similitudinemque columbae Spiritus sancti edisserunt, quia totas oliuas uidere nequeamus, sed partem quandam et, ut ita dicam ramusculos incarnationis Christi, et ostensionis Spiritus sancti nobis esse monstratos. Alii duo intellegunt testamenta, a dextris euangelium, a sinistris legem, eo quod in altero spiritalis sensus sit, in altero corporalis; et quod nec totum euangelium, nec totam legem explanare possimus: **Et nunc**

ex parte cognoscamus, et ex parte prophetemus, et necdum possimus intellegere quod perfectum est. Sunt qui
duos ramos oliuarum uel duas spicas, et filios pinguedinis uel splendoris, sacerdotium interpretentur et legem, quae praebeant gaudium uniuersae terrae. Alii
Henoch et Heliam, quorum alter in praeputio, alter in
circumcisione placuit Deo, et cum corpore raptus in caelum est. Pro splendore et oleo, et pinguedine et claritate,
in Hebraico legimus Isaar, iuxta illud quod de gaudio et
felicitate sanctorum in psalmis scriptum est: **Inebria-
buntur ab ubertate,** siue **pinguedine domus tuae**: *piotēs*
enim magis pinguedinem quam ubertatem sonat. Haec
ut quiuimus, et ut uires ingenioli nostri ferre potuerunt,
locuti sumus, et Hebraeorum et nostrorum uarias opin-
iones breuiter perstringentes, si quis melius immo uerius
dixerit, et nos libenter melioribus acquiescimus.[157]

And when the prophet inquired about the two
branches, and again while he was being questioned by
the angel as to whether he knew what the two branches
signified, when he said "No, Lord [Zechariah 4:13]," the
angel of the Lord replied, "These are the two sons of
the olive oil," as Symmachus wanted ⟨to say⟩ it, or *zilpnotētos*, as Aquila translated it—that is "of brilliance"—
or else *piotētos*, that is "of fatness or richness," as the
Septuagint translated it; or *lamprotētos*, that is "of shining
or gleaming light," as Theodotion translated it [*sc.*, in
his version of the Septuagint Old Testament], "who
stand beside the Lord of the whole earth" [Zechariah
4:14]. Concerning the two olive trees that were at the
right and left of the lampstand, we read above. And
therefore when the prophet now asks about them, he
does not deserve to hear because he does not retain the
previous answers whether here he wants to hear it stated
more openly, because it was stated there too obtusely
[*or*, in a rather obscure fashion], or his impertinence is
castigated [refuted] by the angel's silence, because the
prophet seeks to know greater matters [*sc.*, than he ought
to know]. However, the Jewish writers thus assert that

the prophet heard nothing when he inquired about the olive trees, on the grounds that he was not asking well his question nor did he ask everything that he ought to know.

Next, he later seeks to know more fully, adding a question about the spikes or branches of the olives, about which he had been silent earlier. For there he said, "what are these two olive trees?" [Zechariah 4:12] He inquires, "what are the two twigs of the olives?" [Zechariah 4:13] ⟨They are to be understood⟩ metaphorically, because the trees are standing straight up, in the same way as spikes of grain, and as though they were shoots with ears of grain, so these have been covered by a sort of wall of branches and leaves, and they ascend upwards. Some of our people interpret the two olives as the Son and the Holy Spirit, and the lampstand in the midst as God the Father. But I do not comprehend how they can take one on the right and the other on the left without blaspheming. They explain that the branches or twigs of the olives are the incarnation of the Savior and the likeness of the Holy Spirit to a dove, because we are unable to see the entire olive trees, but just a certain part, and, if I say it this way, the branches of the incarnation of Christ and also of the manifestation of the Holy Spirit have been shown to us. Others understand [sc., the two olive branches or trees to be] the two testaments, the gospel on the right, on the left the law [sc., of Moses], because in the one is a spiritual [or allegorical] sense, in the other a corporal [or material sense], and because we can neither explain the totality of the gospel nor all of the law: "And now we know in part, and we prophesy in part" [1 Corinthians 13:9], and we are not yet capable of understanding that which is perfect. Some people interpret the two branches of the olives or the two twigs, as well as the sons of richness or brilliance, as the priest and the law, that furnish joy to all the earth. Others ⟨interpret them to be⟩ Enoch and Elijah — the one pleased God because of the foreskin [i.e., although he lived prior to the covenant with Abraham] and the other because of circumcision [*i.e.*, he complied with circumcision as a mark of the covenant with Abraham]—and each was taken to heaven with [in] his body. Pertaining to brilliance and olive oil, and also richness and glory, in the Hebrew we read "Isaar" following which concerning the joy and felicity of the saints it is written in the Psalms: "They will become drunk from the plenty" or "from the richness of thy house." For *piotēs* corresponds more closely to richness than to plenty and copiousness. We have said what we could and as the strength of our feeble mind has allowed, briefly grazing [*or*, touching] diverse opinions held by Jewish and Christian scholars, whoever said anything a little better and more accurately, and we now freely yield to others better than us.

Jerome, *Commentarii in Amos*

Et si ascenderint, inquit, usque ad caelum, inde detraham eos, quia et Henoch et Helias rapti cum corporibus in caelum, Dei reguntur arbitrio.[158]

And so, he says, if they shall ascend into heaven, from whence I shall draw them down, because both Enoch and Elijah were caught up to heaven with their bodies [*i.e.*, corporeally; and there] they are ruled [*or*, governed] by the will of God.

Jerome, *Epistula LIX*

Cum et dominus noster mortuus sit et Enoch atque Helias secundum Apocalypsin Iohannis morituri esse dicantur. . . . De Enoch autem et Helia, quos uenturos Apocalypsis refert et esse morituros, non est istius temporis disputatio, cum omnis ille liber aut spiritaliter intellegendus sit, ut nos aestimamus, aut, si carnalem interpretationem sequimur, Iudaicis fabulis adquiescendum sit, ut rursum aedificetur Hierusalem et hostiae offerantur in templo et spiritali cultu inminuto carnales obtineant caeremoniae.[159]

Since even our Lord died, and Enoch and Elijah are

said to be going to die, according to the Apocalypse of John. But now is not the time to discuss Enoch and Elijah, who, as the Apocalypse states, will come [back to earth] and die, since that entire book either must be allegorically understood, as we believe and assert, or, if we follow a literal [mundane] interpretation, we must acquiesce to Jewish myths that Jerusalem will again be built up and that [blood] sacrifices will be made in the ⟨restored, rebuilt⟩ temple and that the carnal rituals will prevail because spiritual worship will abate.

Augustine, *Epistula CXCIII*

Illud uero, quod in litteris tuis commemorasti obicere nobis Enoch et Heliam, quod mortui non fuerint, sed cum suis corporibus ex ista hominum conuersatione translati, quid eos ad hoc, unde agitur, adiuuet, non intellego, ut enim omittam, quod ipsi quoque morituri postea perhibentur, sicut plerique exponunt Apocalypsin Iohannis de duobus illis prophetis, de quibus tacitis eorum nominibus loquitur, quod isti duo sancti cum suis tunc corporibus apparebunt, in quibus nunc uiuunt, ut etiam ipsi quem ad modum ceteri martyres pro Christi ueritate moriantur, ut ergo hoc omittam, ista questione dilata.[160]

As to the matter you have called to our attention in your letters, that Enoch and Elijah are not dead but have been translated with their bodies from this life among men, I don't understand what that can do to help them in the present issue. For let me postpone the question because they, too, are said to be going to die later, just as many commentators explain the Apocalypse of John about these two prophets, concerning whom John spoke although he did not mention their names, that these two saints shall appear with their bodies as they now have them and in which they now live, so that they, too, may die for Christ's truth the same as the other martyrs. As I say, let me pass over the matter and postpone the question for later.

Augustine, *De Genesi ad litteram*

Nam si Enoch et Elias, in Adam mortui mortisque propaginem in carne gestantes, quo debitum ut soluant creduntur etiam redituri ad hanc uitam et, quod tamdiu dilatum est, morituri, nunc tamen in alia uita sunt ubi, ante resurrectionem carnis, antequam animale corpus in spiritale mutetur, nec morbo nec senectute deficiunt.[161]

For if Enoch and Elijah, who died in [=because of] Adam and who bear the seed of death in their flesh, whereby it is required that they should die, are believed to be going to return to this life and to die—though it is temporarily postponed—but that they are now in another condition of life where, before the resurrection of the flesh, before the animate [living, mortal] body be changed into a spiritual one, they are not overwhelmed by disease or old age.

Theodoret of Cyr (Pseudo-Justin Martyr)

Δι' ἣν αἰτίαν οὐδὲ ἐτελεύτησαν πάλιν, ἀλλὰ μένουσιν ἐν ἀθανασίᾳ, καθάπερ ὁ 'Ενὼχ καὶ 'Ηλίας, καί εἰσι σὺν αὐτοῖς ἐν τῷ παραδείσῳ ἀναμένοντες τὴν ἤδη αἰωνίαν τῆς τοῦ Χριστοῦ ἀναστάσεως γινομένην κατὰ ἐναλλαγὴν, καθ' ἣν, ὥς φησιν ὁ θεῖος ἀπόστολος, **Πάντες ἀλλαγησόμεθα**.[162]

For that reason they did not die again but remain in an immortal condition, just like Enoch and Elijah, and they are with them in paradise awaiting the eternal life of the resurrection of Christ, the condition produced by an interchange, according to which, as the divine apostle says, "we shall all be changed" [1 Corinthians 15:51].

Quoduultdeus, *Liber Promissionum*

Pro Abel quem Cain occidit natus est Seth, ex quo per ordinem successionis uenit Enoch; qui deo dum placeret, translatus est ne gustaret mortem, Heliae socian-

dus ut duo testes idonei secundo Christi aduentui prae-
pararentur, in confutatione Antichristi et in gloria
iudicantis filii dei: de quibus suo loco testimonia pro-
feremus.[163]

In the place of Abel, whom Cain killed, was born
Seth; from him in the order of succession came Enoch.
While he pleased God, he was translated so that he
should never tasted death, and he is to be associated
with Elijah so that the two may be prepared as ideal
witnesses for the second coming of Christ, readied for
the confrontation with Antichrist and ⟨to come⟩ in the
glory of the son of God who will judge. Concerning these
two we will bring forth testimony in the appropriate
place.

Quoduultdeus, *Dimidium Temporis in Signis Antichristi*

22. [Apocalypse 11:3-4, 6, Old Latin version]. Ecce
et hic tripertita etiam testium diuisio. Contra Pharaonem
duo testes Dei missi sunt, Moyses et Aaron, et duo magi
Pharaonis Iamnes et Mambres resistentes Moysi qui si-
mul cum suo rege perierunt. Et contra Neronem duo
Petrus et Paulus apostoli; a contrario Simon magus qui
et se perdidit et Neronem decepit. Et contra Antichristum duo Enoch et Helias prophetae aduersus quos tres
pseudoprophetae Antichristi exsurgent.[164]

22. [Quotes for lemma Apocalypse 11:3-4, 6, Old
Latin version]. Here, too, we find a tripartite division of
witnesses. Against Pharaoh two witnesses were sent,
Moses and Aaron, and there were two magicians of Pharaoh, Iamnes and Mambres, who opposed Moses; they
perished with the king. And against Nero there were
the apostles Peter and Paul; opposing was Simon Magus
(the magician) who both deceived Nero and destroyed
himself. Also, against Antichrist there will be two prophets, Enoch and Elijah, against whom three false prophets
of Antichrist will rise up.

Quoduultdeus, *Dimidium Temporis in Signis Antichristi*

24. In Apocalypsi Iohanni dicitur: [Apocalypse 11:7-8, Old Latin version]. Haec platea conscientia est omnium impiorum in mundo plaudentium in morte sanctorum quod acerrimos quasi caruerint inimicos. . . .

25. Apocalypsis Iohannis dicit: **Post tres et dimidium diem spiritus uitae a Deo intrauit in illos et steterunt super pedes suos.** De his arbitror apostolum dixisse Paulum: **Et mortui in Christo resurgent primi.** Tres igitur et dimidius dies tribus annis et sex mensibus respondent quibus potestas erit Antichristo; eisque suppletis coram oculis inimicorum Helias et Enoch ascendentes in caelum occursum ire Christo uero regi et iudici uenienti; qui Antichristum omnesque eius **interficiet spiritu oris sui,** ut regnet in domo Iacob ipse de quo dictum est: **Regni eius non erit finis.**[165]

24. In the Apocalypse it is stated by John: [quotes for lemma Apocalypse 11:3-4, 6, Old Latin version]. This plaza [open city square] is the conscience of all the wicked in this world who give praise at the death of the saints because, ⟨as they suppose⟩, they are freed, as it were, from their most terrible enemies. . . .

25. The Apocalypse of John says: "After three and a half days, the spirit of life from God entered them and they stood up on their feet" (Apocalypse 11:11). Concerning them I think the apostle Paul said: "And those who died in Christ will resurrect the first" (1 Thessalonians 4:16). Therefore, three and a half days correspond to the three years and six months in which power is granted to Antichrist. And when they are filled ⟨with the spirit of life⟩ before the eyes of their enemies, Elijah and Enoch ⟨will show themselves⟩ ascending into heaven to meet Christ, the true king and judge, as he comes. And he will "slay with the breath of his mouth" (2 Thessalonians 2:8) Antichrist and all his ⟨servants⟩ so that he may rule and reign in the house of Jacob, ⟨for⟩ of him it

is said: "And of his kingdom there will be no end" (Luke 1:33).

Procopius of Gaza

ἡρπάγη καὶ ὁ δίκαιος Ἐνὼχ, ὡς ἂν μὴ ἀναιρεθῇ διὰ Λάμεχ· ἐπίστευσε τοῦ μὴ ἰδεῖν **θάνατον** [Hebrews 11:5], καὶ παρέσχεν ἡ πίστις τῇ φύσει τὴν χάριν· ὃς καὶ ἤλεγξε τὸν Ἀδὰμ, θνητὸς ὤν, καὶ μὴ ἀποθανὼν, τὸν ἀποθανόντα μὴ ὄντα θνητὸν, ἐπειδὴ τὴν ἐντολὴν οὐκ ἐφύλαξεν· ὁ μὲν γὰρ εἰσῆλθεν εἰς τὸν παράδεισον, ὁ δὲ ἐκβέβληται· ἀλλ' οὔτε Ἐνὼχ, οὔτε Ἡλίας τὸν θανατὸν κατήργησαν· ὥσπερ ὁ Χριστὸς τὴν φύσιν αὐτὴν ἐν ἑαυτῷ διορθούμενος, κἀκείνοις φύσει θνητοῖς οὖσι τὴν ἀθανασίαν μετὰ πάντων δωρούμενος· εἰ καὶ δι' αὐτῶν τύπον τῆς μελλούσης ἀθανασίας παρέσχετο· ὡς ἂν μὴ εἰς τὴν ἀθυμίαν ἐμβάλῃ τῶν δικαίων χορόν· ἔδειξε γὰρ διὰ μὲν τοῦ Ἐνὼχ πῶς ἐπὶ τοῦ μέλλοντος οἱ δίκαιοι τῶν ἁμαρτωλῶν χωρίζονται· ἐν δὲ τῷ Ἡλίᾳ, πῶς τὰ σώματα ἐν ἀέρι κουφίζονται.[166]

Also, the righteous Enoch was taken up so that he might not be slain because of Lamech. He had faith "so that he not see death" [Hebrews 11:5], and his faith furnished grace to his natural condition. And since he did not die, though mortal, he also reproached Adam, who had died and ⟨originally⟩ was not mortal, because he had not kept the commandment. For whereas the one entered into paradise, the other was cast out. But neither Enoch nor Elijah were ⟨completely⟩ snatched away from death. Just as Christ set on the proper path nature itself in himself, so, too, upon them, who were mortal by nature, he bestowed immortality with all ⟨the rest⟩, although through them he provided a type of future immortality, so that he might not hurl the choir of the righteous into despair. For he demonstrated through

Enoch how the just are going to be separated from the wicked in the future; and in the case of Enoch, how the bodies are lifted up into the air.

Caesarius of Arles

Et dabo duobus testibus meis, id est, duobus testamentis. . . . **Duo candelabra** ecclesia est, sed pro numero testamentorum dixit duo; sicut quattuor angelos dixit ecclesiam, cum sint septem pro numero angelorum terrae, ita ex septem candelabris, si unum uel amplius pro locis nominet, tota ecclesia est. Nam Zacharias unum candelabrum uidit septiforme; et has duas oliuas, id est testamenta, infundere oleum candelabro, id est ecclesiae.[167]

"And I shall give to my two witnesses," that is, to the two testaments. . . . The two candlesticks are the church, but he said two because of the number of the testaments. Just as he says four angels for the church, since there are seven for the number of the angels, so the whole church is from the seven candlesticks, if he names one or two for the places. For Zechariah saw one sevenfold candlestick; and these two olive trees, that is, the testaments, pour the olive oil into the candlestick, that is, upon the church.

Primasius

Et dabo inquit **duobus martyribus meis, ut prophetent diebus mille ducentis sexaginta, saccis amicti.** Quod dixerat **oportet te iterum prophetare, hoc est dabo duobus testibus meis et prophetabunt**; quod est enim Ioannes, hoc duo testes, id est ecclesia duobus Testamentis praedicans et prophetans. Aliter duo genera esse martyrii ueritas protestatur, unum in habitu, alterum in actu.[168]

"And I shall grant," he says, "to my two witnesses, that they prophesy 1,260 days, dressed in sackcloth." What he had said, "it is necessary for you to prophesy again," that is, "I shall grant to my two witnesses and they shall prophesy," that is what John says—they are the two witnesses, that is ⟨by interpretation⟩ the church preaching and prophesying with its two testaments. Another way to interpret is that the truth puts forth two types of witness, the one in manner of dress, the other in action and deed.

Magnus Aurelius Cassiodorus

Hi sunt qui in finem saeculi per tres et semis annos, Antichriste regnante, in martyrum sanguinem bacchabuntur. Fit quoque Enoch et Eliae commemoratio, quod palam iacebunt, et insepulti triduo, donec uocati subito ascendere uideantur in caelum.[169]

These are those who at the end of the world during three and a half years, while the Antichrist reigns, will revel in the blood of the witnesses. He also recalls Enoch and Elijah who will openly lie and be unburied for three days, until when they are called [summoned], they will seem immediately to ascend into heaven.

Gregory the Great, *Homiliae in Hiezechihelem prophetam*

8. Reprobis ergo tunc praedicatorum scientia tacere compellitur. Unde et hic subditur: **Et linguam tuam adhaerescere faciam palato tuo et eris mutus, nec quasi uir obiurgans, quia domus exasperans est** [Ezekiel 3:26]. Sed quia, Enoch et Helia praedicante, multi ex his qui tunc ex Iudaeis in infidelitate remanserint ad cognitionem ueritatis redeunt, sicut de eodem Helia dicitur: **Helias ueniet, et ipse restituet omnia** [Matthew 17:11], qui utrique per Zachariam duae oliuae, et per Iohannem duo candelabra nominantur, recte hic quoque subiungitur:

9. **Cum autem locutus fuero tibi, aperies os tuum, et dices ad eos: Haec dicit Dominus Deus** [Ezekiel 3:27]. Tunc enim uelut in extremo os prophetae aperitur, cum in praedicatione Enoch et Heliae a Iudaeis ad fidem re-

deuntibus prophetia sacri eloquii de Christo fuisse cog-
noscitur. Sed quia haec typice diximus, nunc uerba
eadem caritati uestrae moraliter disseramus.[170]

Therefore the knowledge of the preachers is then
obliged to silence the wicked. Consequently it is also
added for them: "And I shall cause that your tongue
shall cleave to your palate and you will be mute, nor
will you be like a man who rebukes and finds fault,
because his house is blazing" [Ezekiel 3:26]. But while
Enoch and Elijah preach many of those who ⟨until⟩ then
shall have remained in the infidelity from the Jews shall
return to the knowledge of the truth, just as it is said of
the same Elijah: "Elijah shall come and he himself shall
restore all things" [Matthew 17:11]. The two of them are
the two olive trees, according to Zechariah, and they are
called the two candlestickes by John; and so he also
correctly adds:

9. "But when I shall have spoken to you, open your
mouth and you shall say to them: 'Thus saith the Lord
God' " [Ezekiel 3:27]. For then the mouth of the prophet
is opened, as it were at the last moment, when in [= by
or through] the preaching of Enoch and Elijah the prophecy of the holy word is recognized by the Jews, who
come back to the faith, to have been concerning Christ.
But because we have said these things allegorically [or,
by types and shadows], now we shall explain morally
the same things for [sc., the benefit of] your love.

Gregory the Great, *Moralia in Iob*

Hi qui in fine mundi electi reperientur in morte carnis
prosternendi sunt, et illi etiam qui a prioribus mundi
partibus processerunt; Enoch scilicet et Elias, ad medium
reuocabuntur et crudelitatis eius saeuitiam in sua adhuc
mortali carne passuri sunt.[171]

Those who at the end of the world will be found to
be chosen must be cast down to the earth in the death
of the flesh, even those who had departed from the
earlier parts [times and places] of the world; namely,

Enoch and Elijah will be summoned back to the midst
and will suffer the fierceness of his [the Antichrist's]
cruelty in their own flesh that is still mortal.

Isidore of Seville

Enoch filius Iared, septimus ab Adam, placens Deo,
malorum nescius, mortis ignarus, qui sceleratorum hominum non ferens angustias, a perniciosis contractibus
mundi subtractus . . . trecentorum sexaginta quinque.
Manet autem hactenus in corpore; in consummatione
mundi restituet cum Elia mortalem uitae conditionem.[172]

Enoch was the son of Jared, the seventh from Adam;
because he pleased God and knew not evil, he did not
experience death, although he was subjected to the tight
straights of wicked men, he was snatched away from
the difficulties of the world at age 365. Moreover, he is
still in his body, even to today. And at the end of the
world, he and Elijah will recover a mortal condition of
life.

Cosmas Indicopleustes

< Ἠλίας > ὁ μακροχρόνιος καὶ ἀγήρως
ἄνθρωπος, ὁ τῷ Ἀντιχρίστῳ διατηρούμενος
στρατηγός, ὁ ἀντικαθιστάμενος καὶ διελέγχων
τὴν ἀπάτην καὶ τὴν ὑπερηφανίαν αὐτοῦ.[173]

The long-lived and unaging man, the general preserved for [i.e., against] the Antichrist, he who is posi-
tioned as his adversary and reproaches his deceit and
his arrogance.

Pseudo-Hilarius (Pseudo-Isidore,
An Anonymous Irish Commentator)

⟨17⟩ **Helias homo erat,** licet diuina opera perfecerit.
Similis nobis passibilis. Inferiorem se prophetis imponit
apostolus. Sed sciendum est, passio ista de ieiunio et
edulio specialiter intellegi. **Et orationem orauit.** Philo-
sophicae et mysticae loquitur, ut est illud: **Locutus est**

ore mysticae. Haec est oratio exortatio quae sanctis hominibus in angelos transfertur; et oratio⟨ne⟩ exortationeque, quod orat, implorat. **ut non plueret super terram**. et ipse Dominus noster dicit: Serui mei **potestatem habent** claudere **caelum**. Sicut in peccatum primi hominis factum est, ita in peccato scelestissimi actum est, ut cooperatores sint creaturae peccato, sicut dictum est: **Maledicta terra in operibus tuis. Annos tres et menses sex**, id est ante legem et in lege et post legem. Moraliter autem intellegi debet annos tres paenitentiae delinquentibus imponi. Sciendum est temptationem istam omni terrae insidisse, sicut in euangelio Lucae legitur, quae **facta est in omni terra**.[174]

"Elijah was a man," although he fulfilled divine works. "Like us he was subject to passions." The apostle places himself lower than the prophets. But we must learn that this passion must be especially understood about fasting and feasting. "And he prayed" a prayer. He speaks philosophically and allegorically, as in this: "he spoke with his mouth allegorically." This prayer is the imprecation that is passed by holy men to the angels, and he implores what he prays for by prayer and imprecation. "That it should not rain upon the earth." And our Lord himself said: My servants "have power to close the heaven." Just as the deed of the first man was [sc., counted or esteemed] for sin, so it happened in the sin of the most wicked one that we became coworkers in the sin, just as it says: "Cursed be the earth because of your deeds." "During three years and six months," that is, before the law and in [= during or under] the law and after the law. It ought to be understood morally [i.e., allegorically] that the "three years" are placed upon those who need repentance. We must understand that this temptation has afflicted all the earth, just as we read in the Gospel of Luke that "it happened upon the entire earth."

Anonymous Irish Commentator (Pseudo-Isidore)

Heliam et Enoch, spiritualiter uidelicet[175]

Elijah and Enoch, spiritually [allegorically] understood, of course

duos testes Heliam et Enoch.[176]

"the two witnesses" ⟨are⟩ Elijah and Enoch.

Andreas of Caesarea

Τούτους [τοὺς δύο μάρτυρας] Ἐνὼχ καὶ Ἠλίαν, πολλοὶ τῶν διδασκάλων ἐνόησαν, καιρὸν θεόθεν τοῦ προφητεύειν [τὰ] ἐν τῇ συντελείᾳ ληψομένους, ἐπὶ ἔτη τρία ἀπὸ τριακοσίων ἑξήκοντα ἡμερῶν ἀριθμούμενα· καὶ διὰ τῆς περιβολῆς **τῶν σάκκων**, τὸ σκυθρωπὸν καὶ πένθους ἄξιον ἐπὶ τοῖς ἀπατω- μένοις ἐμφαίνοντας, καί τοὺς τότε εὑρισκο- μένους τῆς πλάνης τοῦ Ἀντιχρίστου ἀπάγον- τας· οὓς Ζαχαρίας [ὁ προφήτης] ἐν εἴδει **τῶν δύο ἐλαιῶν** καί [τῶν δύο] **λυχνιῶν** ἠνίξατο, διὰ τὸ τὴν τροφὴν τοῦ φωτὸς τῆς γνώσεως τῷ ἐλαίῳ τῶν θεαρέστων πράξεων ἐπιφέρεσθαι.[177]

These [two witnesses], Enoch and Elijah, many of the teachers have thought, will receive from God ⟨the charge⟩ to prophesy at the end of the world for three years, counting from the 360 days. And because of their being encircled with sackcloth, ⟨he means that⟩ they show to those who are being deceived a countenance that is sad and worthy of mourning, and those who are found at that time they lead from the deception of the Antichrist. Zechariah spoke of these allegorically in his vision of the two olive trees and the two lampstands, because of providing the nourishment of knowing the light by the olive oil of deeds pleasing to God.

Chronicon Paschale (ca. s. vii[1] A.D.)

Οὗτός ἐστιν Ἐνὼχ ὁ μετατεθεὶς εἰς ζωὴν εἰς δεῖγμα τῆς τοῦ θεοῦ δυνάμεως ταῖς μετὰ ταῦτα γενεαῖς τῆς δυναμένης διατηρῆσαι τοὺς θνητοὺς μὴ ἀποθανεῖν ἀλλὰ ζῶντας τὴν ἐπὶ τὸ κρεῖτον ἀλλαγὴν ὑπομένειν.

Οὗτός ἐστιν ὁ ἅμα τῷ Ἠλίᾳ ἐν ἐσχάταις ἡμέραις ἀντικαθιστάμενος τῷ Ἀντιχρίστῳ καὶ ἐλέγχων τὴν πλάνην αὐτοῦ κατὰ τὴν τῆς Ἐκκλησίας παράδοσιν.[178]

This is Enoch who was translated to life as a demonstration of God-s power to later generations, for it has the power so that mortals die not but rather, while still alive, that they may wait for a change to a better condition.

This is the one who, together with Elijah, will be set up to oppose the Antichrist in the last days, and he shall reproach his erroneous way against the entrusted tradition of the church.

John of Damascus (ca. 675-749)

Ἀποσταλήσεται δὲ Ἐνὼχ καὶ Ἠλίας ὁ Θεσβίτης, καὶ ἐπιστρέψουσι τὰς καρδίας πατέρων ἐπὶ τέκνα [cf. Malachi 4:6], τουτέστι τὴν Συναγωγὴν ἐπὶ τὸν Κύριον ἡμῶν Ἰησοῦν Χριστὸν, καὶ τὸ τῶν ἀποστόλων κήρυγμα, καὶ ὑπ' αὐτοῦ ἀναιρεθήσονται.[179]

Enoch and Elijah the Tishbite will be sent forth, and they shall turn the hearts of the fathers to their children [cf. Malachi 4:6], that is to say, they shall turn the synagogue to our Lord Jesus Christ, and the preaching of the apostles, and they shall be destroyed by him [Antichrist].

Enoch et Elias cum Antichristo pugnaturi. Mittentur autem Enoch et Elias Thesbites, qui Patrum corda in filios, hoc est, Synagogam ad Dominum nostrum Iesum Christum, atque apostolorum doctrinam conuertent: ab eoque trucidabuntur.[180]

Enoch and Elijah will battle with the Antichrist. But Enoch and Elijah the Tishbite will be sent forth to turn the hearts of the fathers to the children, that is, they shall convert the synagogue to our Lord Jesus Christ and to the teaching of the apostles; and by him [the Antichrist] they will be cut down.

Oecumenius

ὥσπερ ἐξ ὑποστροφῆς νῦν τὰ περὶ αὐτῶν διδάσκεται, ὅτι μὲν οὖν ἥξειν Ἠλίαν τὸν Θεσβίτην προηγόρευσεν ἡμῖν ἡ θεία γραφὴ παντίπου δῆλον ... [Oecumenius then quotes Malachi 4:5–6; Matthew 11:14] ... περὶ ἑτέρου δὲ προδρόμου οὐδαμοῦ σαφές ἀκηκόαμεν, πλὴν ὅτι περὶ τοῦ Ἐνὼχ εἶπεν ἡ Γένεσις ὅτι **εὐαρεστήσας τῷ Θεῷ μετετέθη** [Genesis 5:24] καὶ ὁ σοφὸς ἀπόστολος περὶ αὐτοῦ **πίστει Ἐνὼχ μετετέθη τοῦ μὴ ἰδεῖν θάνατον, καὶ οὐχ ηὑρέ-σκετο διότι μετέθηκεν αὐτὸν ὁ Θεός** [Hebrews 11:5]. λόγος δὲ παλαιὸς ἐκ παραδόσεως ἐν τῇ ἐκκλησίᾳ κρατεῖ· μετὰ Ἠλίου τοῦ Θεσβίτου ἥξειν καὶ τὸν Ἐνὼχ προτρέχοντα τῆς δευτέρας Χριστοῦ παρουσίας μέλλοντος ἐφίστασθαι τοῦ ἀντιχρίστου· φασὶ γὰρ αὐτοὺς προελθεῖν καὶ προδιαμαρτύρασθαι ἀπάτην εἶναι τὰ παρ' αὐτοῦ γενησόμενα σημεῖα καὶ ὡς οὐ δεῖ πιστεῦσαι τῷ ἀλητηρίῳ. περὶ τούτων νῦν ἡ ὀπτασία διαλέγεται· ὅτι προφητεύσουσιν ἡμέρας τοσάσδε ἢ μυστικόν τινα λέγουσα ἀριθνὸν ἢ τὸν πάντως ἐσόμενον. τοῦτο δὲ ποιήσουσι **περιβεβλημένοι** φησὶ **σάκκους.** πενθήσουσι γὰρ ἐπὶ τῇ ἀπειθείᾳ τῶν τότε

ἀνθρώπων. οὗτοί φησίν εἰσιν αἱ δύο ἐλαῖαι
καὶ αἱ δύο λυχνίαι αἱ ἐνώπιον τοῦ
κυρίου ἐπὶ τῆς γῆς ἐστῶσαι. Ζαχαρίας ὁ
θεσπέσιος προφήτης εἶδε λυχνίαν, ἑπτὰ
λύχνους ὑπερδίδουσαν, καὶ δύο κλάδους
ἐλαιῶν, ἀλλὰ τοὺς κλάδους ἐστῶτας ἐν δύο
λύχνων μυξωτῆρσιν.[181]

Just as if because of returning [i.e., because of the body returning to the earth upon death], these matters are now taught ⟨in the church⟩ about them—that the holy scripture has proclaimed to us how Elijah the Tishbite will indeed come, it is everywhere obvious [quoting Malachi 4:5-6; Matthew 11:14]. Concerning the other precursor, we have nowhere heard anything clear, except that Genesis says of Enoch that "because he pleased God he was taken to another place [i.e., translated]" and the wise apostle ⟨says⟩ about him, "on account of his faith Enoch was translated so that he not see death, and he was not ⟨ever⟩ found because God had translated him" [Hebrews 11:5]. The time-honored [lit., old] word from tradition is still valid in the church: with Elijah the Tishbite Enoch, too, will come as a precursor of the second coming of Christ who will oppose the Antichrist. For they say that they [sc., Enoch and Elijah] will precede and will affirm by their testimony that the signs that shall be produced by him are a deception and also that people should not have faith in the vagrant deceiver. Now of these two ⟨prophets⟩, the divine vision relates that they shall prophesy so many days either uttering a mystical [or, allegorical] number or else one that is actually going to occur. And they shall do this "clothed," he says, "in sackcloth." For they shall mourn at the lack of faith of people at that time. "These," he says, "are the two olive trees and the two lampstands standing before the face of the Lord upon the earth" [Apocalypse 11:4]. Zechariah the divine prophet saw the lampstand, providing seven lamps, and also the two branches of the olive trees, but the branches ⟨he saw⟩ standing in the two nostrils [*i.e.*, wick feeder pipes] of the lamps.

Andreas of Caesarea

καὶ ὅτι μὲν Ἠλίας ἥξει ὁ προφήτης δῆλον. . .
[quoting Malachi 4:5–6; Matthew 11:14] . . .
περὶ μὲν οὖν Ἠλία ταῦτα. περὶ δὲ τοῦ Ἐνὼχ
μαρτυρίαν μὲν ὅσον πρὸς τὴν παρουσίαν ἀπὸ
τῆς γραφῆς οὐκ ἔχομεν, πλὴν τοῦ διὰ μεταθέσεως ἀπαθανατισθῆναι. λόγος δὲ φέρεται ἐκ
παραδόσεως φοιτῶν τῇ ἐκκλησίᾳ ἀπαρατρέπτως καὶ αὐτὸν ἥξειν μετὰ Ἠλίου τοῦ Θεσβίτου
(φασὶ γὰρ αὐτοὺς κατὰ τὸν καιρὸν τοῦ Ἀντιχρίστου ἥξειν καὶ προδιαμαρτύρασθαι τοῖς
οὖσι τότε, μὴ τοῖς ἀπατηλοῖς τοῦ Ἀντιχρίστου
παράγεσθαι σημείοις), καὶ τῇ διαμαρτυρίᾳ
ταύτῃ τριβῆναι χρόνον τριετίας καὶ ἡμίσεως.
τοῦτο γὰρ αἱ χίλιαι διακόσιαι ἑξήκοντα ἡμέραι
χρονικὸν ἀποτελοῦσι διάστημα.[182]

And it is clear that Elijah the prophet will come . . . [quoting Malachi 4:5-6 and Matthew 11:14]. So much about Elijah. Concerning Enoch, we do not have witness [evidence] from the scriptures so much concerning his coming except that he became immortal because of a change of state [*i.e.*, he was transported to a different condition or sphere], but the report is that he too will come with Elijah the Tishbite (for they [*i.e.*, earlier ecclesiastical writers] state that they will come at the time of the Antichrist and first suffer martyrdom with those who live at that time, so that they not be overcome [*or*, led astray] by the false miracles of the Antichrist) and they will suffer this martyrdom over a time of three and a half years. For the 1,260 days fill this time interval.

Arethas of Caesarea (Cappadocia) [= shorter version of Andreas]

Καὶ δώσω τοῖς μάρτυρσί μου . . . [quotes Apocalypse 11:3–6 for the lemma]. Καὶ ὅτι μὲν Ἡλίας ἥξει ὁ προφήτης δῆλον. . . . [quotes Malachi 4:5–6] Περὶ δὲ τοῦ Ἐνὼχ μαρτυρίαν μὲν ὅσον πρὸς τὴν παρουσίαν ἀπὸ τῆς φραφῆς οὐκ ἔχομεν, πλὴν τοῦ διὰ μεταθέσεως ἀπαθανατισθῆναι. λόγος δὲ φέρεται ἐκ παραδόσεως φοιτῶν τῇ ἐκκλησίᾳ ἀπαρατρέπτως καὶ αὐτὸν ἥξειν μετὰ Ἠλίου τοῦ Θεσβίτου (ἥξουσι γὰρ ἄμφω προδιαμαρτύρασθαι τοῖς οὖσι τότε, μὴ τοῖς ἀπατηλοῖς τοῦ Ἀντιχρίστου παράγεσθαι σημείοις), καὶ τῇ διαμαρτυρίᾳ ταύτῃ τριβῆναι χρόνον τριετίας καὶ ἡμίσεως. τοῦτο γὰρ αἱ χίλιαι διακόσιαι ἐξήκοντα ἡμέραι χρονικὸν ἀποτελοῦσι διάστημα.[183]

[Arethas quotes Apocalypse 11:3-6 for his lemma.] And it is clear that Elijah the prophet will come . . . [quoting Malachi 4:5-6]. So much about Elijah. Concerning Enoch, we do not have witness [evidence] from the scriptures so much concerning his coming except that he became immortal because of a change of state [*i.e.*, he was transported to a different condition or sphere], but the report is that he too will come with Elijah the Tishbite (for they both will come suffer martyrdom with those who live at that time, so that they not be overcome [*or*, led astray] by the false miracles of the Antichrist) and they will suffer this martyrdom over a time of three and a half years. For the 1,260 days fill this time interval.

Beda, *Expositio in Apocalypsin*

11:3A **Et dabo duobus testibus meis et prophetabunt diebus mille ducentis sexaginta.** Ne saeuitia prauorum terreret audientem ecclesiam quoque duobus ex populis unitam gratia commemorat inlustrandam esse uirtutum. Quae et ipsa caput suum Christum uidelicet in carne docentem semper intuens tribus semis annis prophetatura narratur. Menses enim trium semis annorum id est tricies quadrageni et bini mille ducentos sexaginta dies efficiunt. Danihel autem scribit dies mille ducentos nonaginta temporis eiusdem quo ponenda sit abominatio in desolatione.[184]

"And I shall grant unto my two witnesses and they shall prophesy 1,260 days." So that the fierceness of depraved people not frighten the church, united from the two peoples, as it listens, he recalls that it [the church] must be made illustrious by the grace of virtues. The church, he relates, while ever beholding Christ, its head, as he taught in the flesh, will prophesy during three and a half years. For the months of three and half years, that is thirty ⟨days⟩ times forty and two ⟨months⟩, make 1,260 days. Moreover, Daniel writes 1,290 of the same period of time when the abomination must be placed in [or, sent to] desolation.

Beda, *Expositio in Apocalypsin*

11:4 **Hi sunt duae oliuae et duo candelabra in conspectu domini terrae stantes.** Ecclesia duorum testamentorum lumine radiata domini semper iussis adsistit. Nam et propheta Zacharias unum candelabrum uidit septiforme et has duas oliuas id est testamenta infundere oleum candelabro. Haec est ecclesia cum oleo suo indeficiente quod eam facit in lumine orbis ardere.[185]

"These are the two olive trees and the two candlesticks standing in the view of the Lord of the earth." The church, radiant with the light of the two testaments, carefully abides by [hearkens to] the Lord's commands. For the prophet Zechariah, too, saw a single sevenfold candlestick and the two olive trees, that is the testaments, pouring the oil into the candlestick. This is the church with its never-failing supply of oil which makes the church burn in the light of the world.

Beda, *Expositio in Apocalypsin*

11:6 **Hi habent potestatem claudendi caelum ne pluat diebus prophetiae ipsorum**. Data est ecclesiae in Christo omnis potestas in caelo et in terra clauibus ei ligandi atque soluendi dimissis. Sed et spiritaliter caelum clauditur ne imbrem pluat ne super terram sterilem de ecclesia benedictio descendat.[186]

"These have the power of sealing the heavens so that it not rain in the days of their prophecy." All power in heaven and on earth has been given to the church in Christ with the keys of binding and of loosing sent forth. But heaven is also spiritually closed lest it rain, lest any blessing from the church fall upon sterile ground.

Beda, *Expositio in Apocalypsin*

11:13e **Et dederunt gloriam deo caeli**. Isti sunt super petram aedificati qui aliis terrae motu ruentibus de stabilitate sua recta deum confessione clarificant. Laetabitur enim iustus cum uiderit uindictam impiorum. Quidam duos prophetas Enoch et Heliam interpretantur qui tribus semis annis praedicantes contra mox secuturam antichristi perfidiam fidelium corda confirment illisque occisis tantundem temporis saeuitiam eiusdem grassaturam . . . dicente Danihele, **confirmabit** [*v.l.*, confirmauit] **pactum multis ebdomadas una et in dimidio ebdomadis deficiet hostia et sacrificium et in templo erit abominatio desolationis** [Daniel 9:27]. Et in subsequentibus, **Et posita fuerit abominatio in desolatione dies mille ducentos nonaginta** [Daniel 12:11]. Qui numerus circa trium annorum et sex mensium curricula diuersatur. Denique Helias igne quondam perdidit aduersarios et tres semis annos latitans imbres continuit, tandemque pseudoprophetis interfectis per sacrificium quod ablatum fuerat conuertit Israel ad dominum. Hucusque recapitulatio.[187]

"And they gave glory to the God of heaven." These are those built upon the rock who glorify God with correct confession because of their own stability while oth-

ers are falling into ruins because of the earthquake. For
the just will rejoice when he sees the vindictive judgment
of [upon] the wicked. Some people interpret the two
prophets as Enoch and Elijah who will strengthen the
hearts of the faithful, while preaching for three and half
years against Antichrist's heresy that is soon to follow.
When at last they are killed, the fierceness of that time
will proceed violently.

According to the statement of Daniel, "he will confirm the covenant of one week ⟨made⟩ to many, and in
the half of the week [*i.e.*, under the rule of Antichrist]
the eucharist and sacrifice will fail, and in the temple
there will be the abomination of desolation" [Daniel 9:27;
KJV: "And he shall confirm the covenant with many for
one week, and in the midst of the week he shall cause
the sacrifice and the oblation to cease, and for the ov-
erspreading of abominations he shall make it desolate"].
And in the following ⟨verses, Daniel says⟩, "And the
abomination in desolation shall be placed for 1,290 days"
[Daniel 12:11]. This number is about equivalent to three
years and six months. Next, Elijah once destroyed his
enemies by fire and while in hiding for three and a half
years, he withheld the rains; at long last Israel killed the
false prophets and returned [*or*, converted] to the Lord
with the sacrifice that had been omitted. A recapitulation
to this point ⟨is inserted by John⟩.

Beda, *De Temporum Ratione*

Duo sane certissima necdum instantis diei iudicii
habemus indicia, fidem uidelicet Israheliticae gentis et
regnum persecutionemque Antichristi, quam uidelicet
persecutionem trium semis annorum futurum [*v.l.*, fu-
turam] fides ecclesiae tenet. Sed ne haec improuisa uen-
iens omnes passim quos inparatos inuenerit, inuoluat,
Enoch et Heliam maximos prophetas et doctores ante
huius exortum uenturos in mundum, qui Israheliticam
plebem ad fidei conuertant gratiam atque ad pressuram
tanti turbinis in parte electorum insuperabilem reddant.
Qui cum ipsi primo tres semis annos praedicauerint, et

sicut de uno eorum Helia propheta Malachias praedixit, **conuerterint corda patrum in filios,** id est, antiquorum fidem dilectionemque sanctorum in eorum qui tunc uicturi sunt mente plantauerint, tunc excandescens illa horrenda persecutio ipsos inprimis martirii uirtute coronet, dein ceteros fideles corripiens uel martyres Christi gloriosissimos uel damnatos apostatas faciat. Quod significare uidetur apostolus Iohannes ita scribens in Apocalypsi: **Atrium autem quod est foris templum eice foras et ne metieris eum, quoniam datum est gentibus, et ciuitatem sanctam calcabunt mensibus XLII,** id est eos qui nomine tenus fideles sola exteriora diligunt, ab electorum sorte separatos ostende. Quia et ipsi ad persequendam ecclesiam conuertentur nouissima illa persecutione trium semis annorum. **Et dabo,** inquit, **duobus testibus meis, et prophetabunt diebus mille CCLX amicti saccis,** id est, artissimis continentiae et praessurarum laboribus accincti praedicabunt.[188]

Indeed, we have two absolutely positive indications that the day of judgment is not at hand, namely the faith of the house of Israel and the kingdom and persecution of Antichrist. The ⟨traditional⟩ faith of the church holds that this persecution will last for three and a half years. But lest this come unforeseen and swirl upon all, here and there, whom it discovers unprepared, ⟨he reassures that⟩ Enoch and Elijah, the greatest prophets and teachers, shall come into the world before he [Antichrist] arises. They shall ⟨be able to⟩ convert the people of Israel to the grace of faith and render it invincible to the tribulation of such a great storm [sc., of persecution] in the midst of the elect. After they have first preached for three and a half years, and when—as Malachi prophesied about one of them, namely the prophet Elijah—they "have turned the hearts of the fathers to the children," that is, when they have grafted the faith of the ancestors and the love of the saints in the minds of those who will then be victorious, then at that time that horrifying persecution will flare up and ⟨be able to⟩ crown these two [sc., Enoch and Elijah] with the virtue [or, power] of martyrdom. Next , as it violently attacks others of the faithful, it will ⟨be such as to⟩ make them either the most glorious martyrs of Christ or utterly damned apostates. The apostle John seems to indicate this when he wrote in the Apocalypse thus: "But the court . . . and they shall trample under foot the holy city for forty-two months" [quoting Apocalypse 11:2], that is, show as separated from the lot of the elect those who, while nominally faithful, love only the exterior matters. Because they, too, shall be turned [*or,* converted] at the last persecution of three and a half years to persecute the church. "And I shall grant," he says, "unto my two witnesses, and, being clothed in sackcloth, they shall prophesy for 1,260 days" [Apocalypse 11:3], that is, they shall preach girded about by the most strict labors of continence and tribulations.

Beda, *In Genesim*

[The relevant passage was directly quoted from Augustine; see above, Augustine, *De Genesi ad litteram*].[189]

Beatus

Et dabo duobus testibus meis, et prophetabunt dies mille ducentos nonaginta. Hi dies mille ducenti nonaginta anni sunt tres et menses sex. hoc erit praedicatio Eliae, et regnum antichristi alterum tantum, quod fiunt sub uno septem anni. ceterum uero spiritualiter in ecclesia **duo testes** duo sunt testamenta, id est, lex et euangelium. . . . haec omne tempus est a passione domini usque ad antichristum. et nunc spiritualiter in tipo Eliae, et qui cum eo uenerit, duo testes, id est, lex et euangelium, ab eis occiditur, a quibus non obseruabatur; hoc sunt duo testes, id est, ecclesia duobus testamentis prophetans. qui sunt enim testes domini nisi Christiani?[190]

"And I shall grant to my two witnesses, and they shall prophesy for 1,290 days." The 1,290 days are three years and six months. This will be the prediction of Elijah, and the kingdom of the Antichrist is something entirely different because the seven years will occur under one [*i.e.*, under just the kingdom]. Moreover allegorically [*lit.*, spiritually] in the church the "two witnesses" are the two Testaments, that is, the Law and the Gospel. . . . All these ⟨measures of time⟩ are the entire period of time from the passion of our Lord until the Antichrist. And now spiritually in the type [*i.e.*, likeness, manner, or imitation] of Elijah and him who shall come with him, the two witnesses, that is, the Law and the Gospel, are killed by those who do not preserve it [*i.e.*, keep the commandments]. These are the two witnesses, that is, the church, prophesying, with the two testaments. For who are the witnesses of the Lord if not the Christians?

Beatus

Hi sunt duae oliuae et duo candelabra etc. hi sunt, inquit, qui stant, quod nunc est in praedicatione. duo candelabra ecclesia est . . . nam Zacharias propheta **unum candelabrum uidit septiformem et duas oliuas,** id est, duo testamenta infundere oleum candelabro, haec est ecclesia cum olio suo indeficiente . . . et de oliuis, quod sunt duo testamenta, interroganti sic ait.[191]

"These are the two olive trees and the two candlesticks," etc. These are, he says, those who stand ⟨in God's presence⟩ because now it [*i.e.*, the church] is ⟨involved⟩ in preaching. The two candlesticks are the church, for Zechariah the prophet saw "one sevenfold candlestick and two olive trees," that is, the two testaments pouring the oil into the candlestick, that is the church with its unfailing oil, and concerning the olive trees, because they are the two testaments, it is so said to the one who inquires.

Alcuin (summarizing Ambrosius Autpertus)

Et dabo duobus testibus meis, et prophetabunt diebus mille ducentis sexaginta, amicti saccos. Victorinus martyr duos testes Eliam, et Hieremiam intellegit; dicit

enim quia nusquam Hieremiae legatur interitus. Sed
melius alii Eliam et Enoch. Nos autem etiam in specie
genus intellegamus; id est per duos testes ecclesiam, et
per dies mille ·CC··⟨LX⟩·[192] non solum Antichristi tempus sed etiam retroacta tempora uoluuntur. Et bene per
duos testes ecclesia, propter duo testamenta, duos po-
pulos, duo mandata dilectionis, et duo martyrii genera.
Per saccum uero intellegimus humilitatis confessionem,
uel despectam malis claritatem sanctorum.

**Hi sunt duo oliuae, et duo candelabra in conspectu
Domini terrae stantes.** Ecclesia siue in illis duobus, siue
generaliter in omnibus praedicatoribus propter uncti-
onem sancti Spiritus, per oliuam; propter lumen fidei et
operationis, per candelabra exprimitur. Cum autem una
sit ex duobus populis, oliua et unum candelabrum propter duo testamenta duae oliuae et duo candelabra dicuntur. In conspectu Domini stant, quia intima contem-
platione conditori suo inhaerent. Hinc Elias cui
specialiter ista adscribuntur dicit; **uiuit Dominus in cuius
conspectu sto** [4 Reg. 3:14]. Potest hoc sub alio intellectu
specialiter ad Eliam et Enoch referri, qui humanis as-
pectibus subtracti Deo secretius inhaerent.[193]

"And I shall grant unto my two witnesses and they
shall prophesy 1,260 days, dressed in sackcloth." Victorinus the martyr understands that the two witnesses
are Elijah and Jeremiah; for he says that nowhere do we
read of the burial of Jeremiah. But better, others maintain
that the two are Elijah and Enoch. Moreover, let us understand the genus in the species, that is, through the
two witnesses the church and through the 1,260 days
not only the time of the Antichrist but also past times
roll back again. And well does he identify the church
with the two witnesses, because of the two testaments,
the two peoples, the two mandates of choosing, and the
two types of witness. Through the sackcloth we understand the confession of humility or the brightness of the
saints looking down upon the evil.

"These are the two olive trees and the two candlesticks standing in the presence of the Lord." Through

the olive the church ⟨is to be understood⟩, whether in these two ⟨witnesses⟩, or whether more generally in all preachers because of the anointing of the Spirit. It is expressed by the candlestick because of the light of faith and works. However, since it comes from the two peoples, the olive tree and a single candlestick are called the two olive trees and the two candlesticks because of the two testaments. "They stand in the presence of the Lord" because they cling to their creator with intimate contemplation. At this place he mentions Elijah, to whom these responsibilities are ascribed; "the Lord lives in whose presence I stand" [2 Kings 3:14]. Taken in another way, this can especially be making reference to Elijah and Enoch who, when they were taken from human view, came to cling closely to God.

Photius, *Bibliotheca* (summarizing Ephraem the Syrian)

Καὶ οὐκ ἄν τις εἴποι τὸ σῶμα τότε εἰς τὴν οὐσίαν μεταβαλεῖν τῆς ψυχῆς· εἰ γὰρ καὶ λεπτότερον καὶ διαυγέστερον γίνεται, ἀλλ' οὖν τὰ ἰνδάλματα σῴζει τοῦ σώματος, καὶ ἄνθρωπός ἐστι, τὰ ἀνθρώπου φέρων γνωρίσματα. Μαρτυρεῖ δὲ τοῖς εἰρημένοις Ἐνὼχ καὶ Ἡλίας καὶ ὁ τῆς βροντῆς υἱὸς Ἰωάννης, ἔτι περιόντες ἐν τῷ σώματι· καὶ γὰρ τούτους ὡς ἀπαρχὴν τοῦ ὅλου φυράματος ἡμῶν ὁ δημιουργὸς λαβὼν ἔδειξε πᾶσιν ὡς εἰ μὴ ἥμαρτεν ὁ Ἀδάμ, ἔτι ἂν περιῆν μετὰ τοῦ σώματος. Πλὴν καὶ οὗτοι πολυχρόνιον βίον ἀνύοντες γεύσονταί ποτε θανάτου, κἂν ἐν ριτῇ ὀφθαλμοῦ.

Ὅρα δὲ τὴν δι' αὐτῶν πίστιν, ὡς ἐκ τῶν τριῶν προάγεται γενεῶν, ἐκ μὲν τῶν πρὸ νόμου ληφθέντος τοῦ Ἐνώχ, ἐκ δὲ τῶν μετὰ τὸν νόμον τοῦ Ἡλία, ἐκ δὲ τῶν μετὰ τὴν χάριν τοὺς ἐπιστηθίου τῶν μαθητῶν. Οὐκοῦν καὶ ὁ Ἀδάμ,

εἰ τὴν ἐντολὴν ἐφύλαττε, τούτοις ἂν
ἀδιστάκτως συμπεριῆν.

"Ὅτι δὲ περίεστιν ὁ παρθένος Ἰωάννης, ὅπερ
ἐζήτησας, ὥσπερ τὸν Ἐνὼχ καὶ τὸν Ἠλίαν
παράδοσις μαρτυρεῖ, οὕτω καὶ τοῦτον. . . . Οὐ
γάρ τις αὐτὸν ἀθάνατον εἶναί φησιν, ἀλλὰ
διαμένειν μετὰ Ἐνὼχ καὶ Ἠλία μέχρι τῆς
δευτέρας τοῦ δεσπότου παρουσίας.[194]

And a person could not say that the body has
changed into the essence of the spirit at a specific moment. For although it becomes lighter and more lumi-
nous, it still preserves the characteristic appearance of
the body; and it is human [i.e., mortal], since it bears
the identifying marks of a human being. Since they still
remain [or, survive] in their bodies, Enoch and Elijah
and John, the son of thunder, bear witness to these
statements. For in fact the creator took these as [or, so
as to become] the firstfruits of our entire human compound [or, existence; i.e., with reference to our mortal
bodies as being temporarily mixed and joined together].
Thus he showed to all that if Adam had not sinned, he
would have continued to exist with his mortal body. But
these, too, [i.e., Enoch, Elijah, and John] while effecting
a lengthy life will at some time taste of death, even if it
should be in the blink [or, twinkling] of an eye (1 Corinthians 15:52).

But consider the ⟨reaffirmation of our⟩ faith ⟨that comes⟩
because of them—how it is brought forth from the three
different generations: Enoch was taken up before the
law ⟨of Moses⟩, Elijah after the law ⟨had been given⟩, and
the preferred disciple after grace [i.e., "the gospel"] was
given. And so it is obvious that if Adam had been keeping the commandment, he would have assuredly continued to survive with them ⟨to the present time⟩.

Furthermore, as to the precise point you attempted
to search out—that the virgin John still survives alive—
our ⟨Christian⟩ tradition attests that he, too, is alive, just
as it also attests to Enoch and Elijah. . . . For no one

asserts that he [John] is immortal but rather that he continues to live [*lit.*, to continue to remain *or* to abide] with
Enoch and Elijah until the second coming of our Lord.

EVIDENCE FROM ILLUSTRATED MANU-
SCRIPTS OF BEATUS

This much we see in the texts themselves. But an especially curious circumstance is found in some of the manuscripts of Beatus of Liebana. Beatus' commentary on Apocalypse 11 is clearly allegorical, as we have just quoted.
Several manuscripts of Beatus also exhibit some beautiful
illustrations of the text.[195] One is called the Gerona Apocalypse. I will refer to it inasmuch as it is available in facsimile form.[196] On three different folios the two witnesses
are portrayed, and twice [on fol. 164r and on 167v] the
artist has included their names: *Henoch et Elias*! Obviously,
since this interpretation does not correspond to Beatus'
contextual identification, the tenth-century artist did not
derive the names from the text of his commentary. Moreover, the Gerona Apocalypse is only one of thirty-four
illuminated manuscripts of Beatus, so the complex artistic
heritage is to be sought in their common source, the original manuscript of Beatus. But that still would not explain
the discrepancy between picture and text, for Beatus himself would not have designed miniatures in direct conflict
with his own composition. What, then, is the origin of the
iconographic tradition? It is probable that the pictures were
copied directly from Beatus' manuscript of Tyconius where
the pictures *again* did not illustrate the text but rather reproduced some earlier series of paintings developed from
a traditional Christian interpretation of the Apocalypse,
antedating the fourth century, that may underlie some of
Tyconius' text just as Victorinus' underlies Jerome's. Thus,
the early Christian identification of the two witnesses with
Enoch and Elijah was so deeply imbedded that even when
Tyconius shifted to an allegorical and typological approach
in the late fourth century, the earlier view persisted in art.

Such a transmission of the artistic tradition from antiquity to the early Middle Ages is not limited to Tyconius and Beatus. There are a number of manuscripts from late antiquity which have full- or half-page color illustrations. Among classical authors, such manuscripts exist for Vergil, Homer, and Terence,[197] and it is curious to see a ninth-century copy of Terence exhibiting actors with authentic antique Roman masks.[198] For the artist must have copied these from his source manuscript since the live comic tradition had long before ceased.

In the same manner, the Gerona Apocalypse of Beatus and its kindred manuscripts reproduce pictures from the fourth or fifth centuries whose artistic tradition seems to hark back to the second or third centuries. The implication is that at least one late antique manuscript of Tyconius displayed such pictures and that they too were derivative. Were they perchance developed for an early fourth-century manuscript of Victorinus? The answer to that question is probably not, since Victorinus identified the witnesses with Elijah and Jeremiah or alternatively with Elijah and Moses, and also since Beatus' exegetical discussion is highly dependent textually on Tyconius and apparently not on Victorinus. But the mere fact that there is such an extensive set of illustrations of the Apocalypse in Beatus and that at least the representation of the two witnesses antedates the late fourth century demonstrates that the artistic tradition developed rather early before Alexandrian allegorical interpretation gained sway among commentators. So even the art becomes an independent attestation of the early Christian identification of the two witnesses as Enoch and Elijah.[199]

CONCLUSIONS

Thus we can see that Tyconius, by precept and by example, helped to infuse into the Christian exegetical tradition in the West Alexandrian allegorical, typological, and "spiritual" interpretation of the scriptures. Through his *Liber Regularum* and its summary by Augustine in *De Doctrina Christiana*, these principles were widely taught. Through his commentary on the Apocalypse, which became the basis for the major exegetical tradition of that book, he provided an allegorical paradigm, applying the theory in practice. Although we do not possess that commentary, its influence can be traced in quotations and in the approach found in later writers. Tyconius' allegorical method — his systematic exposition of the Alexandrian exegesis — underlies Augustine's synthesis and mode of interpretation and, through him, the western exegetical tradition.

But while the "spiritualizing" approach of Origen, Didymos, Jerome, Tyconius, and Augustine changed the future of Christian exegesis, our earliest sources — and some remnants even in later sources, such as the commentary Pseudo-Cyril of Alexandria and the artistic tradition accompanying the text of Beatus — concur in naming Enoch and Elijah as two literal prophets ushering in a literal millennium upon the earth. This identification goes back to the second century, to an era not far removed from John's composition and promulgation of the Apocalypse, and Papias, who knew and listened to John, is squarely in the literal tradition of scriptural exegesis. Given the evidence, the preallegorical interpretation and identification of Enoch and Elijah, of Dan as the source of Antichrist, of the restoration of a literal temple, and of a literal millennium on earth may well reflect John's own oral explanations of his text.

Notes

Note: Some common abbreviations used in the footnotes are: *AB = Anchor Bible* (Garden City, NY: Doubleday); *BT = Bibliotheca Teubneriana* (Leipzig: Teubner); *CCCM = Corpus Christianorum, Continuatio Medievalis* (Turnhout, Belgium: Brepols); *CCSL = Corpus Christianorum, Series Latina* (Turnhout, Belgium: Brepols); *CPG = Clavis Patrum*

Graecorum (Turnhout, Belgium: Brepols); *CPL = Clavis Patrum Latinorum* (Turnhout, Belgium: Brepols) [SE = *Sacris Eruditi* 3, 2nd ed. (1961)]; *CSEL = Corpus Scriptorum Ecclesiasticorum Latinorum* (Vienna); *DS = Dictionnaire de Spiritualité* (Paris: Beauchesne, 1937–); *GCS = Die Griechischen Christlichen Schriftsteller der ersten drei Jahrhunderte* (Leipzig: J. C. Hinrichs, and Berlin: Akademie, 1897–); *ICC = International Critical Commentary* (Edinburgh: T. & T. Clark); *ODCC* = F. L. Cross and E. A. Livingstone, eds., *Oxford Dictionary of the Christian Church*, 2nd ed., rev. (Oxford: Oxford University Press, 1983); *PG = Patrologiae Cursus Completus, Series Graeca* (Paris; repr. Turnhout, Belgium: Brepols); *PL = Patrologiae Cursus Completus, Series Latina* (Paris; repr. Turnhout, Belgium: Brepols); *PLS = Patrologiae Cursus Completus, Supplementa* (Paris; repr. Turnhout, Belgium: Brepols); *PTS = Patristische Texte und Studien* (Berlin and New York: Walter de Gruyter); *RBMA* = F. Stegmüller, *Repertorium Biblicum Medii Aevi*, 11 vols. (Madrid: Consejo Superior de Investigationes Cientficas, 1940–); *SC = Sources Chrétiennes* (Paris: Société d'Édition, "Les Belles Lettres"); *TU* = Texte und Untersuchungen (Leipzig and Berlin).

1. Hugh Nibley, "The Way of the Church," in *Mormonism and Early Christianity*, vol. 4, *The Collected Works of Hugh Nibley* (Salt Lake City: Deseret Book and F.A.R.M.S., 1987), 300–13; see also Hugh Nibley, "The Passing of the Primitive Church: Forty Variations on an Unpopular Theme," in *Mormonism and Early Christianity*, 183–90, and Hugh Nibley, "Prophets and Crisis," in *The World and the Prophets*, vol. 3, *The Collected Works of Hugh Nibley* (Salt Lake City: Deseret Book and F.A.R.M.S., 1987), 191–99.

2. Austin Farrer, *The Revelation of St. John the Divine* (Oxford: Clarendon, 1964), 2–3.

3. Farrer, *The Revelation of St. John*, 2; cf. Eusebius, *Historia Ecclesiastica* III, 25, 2, in *SC* 41:204–5, quoting Dionysius of Alexandria.

4. Eusebius, *Historia Ecclesiastica* III, 25, 4, in *SC* 31:134; for the development of the canon, see Henry C. Thiessen, *Introduction to the New Testament* (Grand Rapids, MI: Eerdmans, 1943), 3–30, and especially Bruce M. Metzger, *The Canon of the New Testament: Its Origin, Development, and Significance* (Oxford: Oxford University Press, 1987). English translations accompanying the quotations in the text and footnotes were prepared by the author. Significant variant readings [*v.l.*] of manuscripts (and editions) are in square brackets within the Greek or Latin text, and alternate English renderings are also enclosed in square brackets in the translation. Scriptural quotations within the Greek and Latin passages are in boldface type.

5. Eusebius, *Historia Ecclesiastica* III, 25, 2, in *SC* 31:133.

6. Eusebius, *Historia Ecclesiastica* III, 25, 4, in *SC* 31:134.

7. Thiessen, *Introduction to the New Testament*, 8.

8. E.-B. Allo, *Saint Jean l'Apocalypse*, 2nd ed. (Paris: J. Gabalda, 1921), ccli; for a fuller discussion of the manuscripts, see Bernhard Weiss, *Die Johannes-Apokalypse*, *TU* 7.1 (1891); Wilhelm Bousset, *Textkritische Studien zum neuen Testament*, *TU* 11.4 (1894): 1–44; R. H. Charles, *A Critical and Exegetical Commentary on the Revelation of St. John*, ICC 1 (1920; repr. 1985): clx-clxxxiii; Allo, *Saint Jean l'Apocalypse*, ccli-cclxiv; and especially H. C. Hoskier, *Concerning the Text of the Apocalypse*, 2 vols. (London: Bernard Quaritch, 1929).

9. Thiessen, *Introduction to the New Testament*, 15–16, 318. See also Henry B. Swete, *Commentary on Revelation* (Grand Rapids, MI: Kregel, 1977; repr. of *The Apocalypse of St. John*, 3rd ed. [London: Macmillan, 1911]), clxxxvi-cxcvi for matters of text and versions.

10. For the Greek Christian writers discussed below, an older but still valuable survey is Aimé Puech, *Histoire de la Littérature Grecque Chrétienne*, 3 vols. (Paris: Société d'Édition "Les Belles Lettres," 1928–30); similarly for the Latin, see Pierre de Labriolle, *Histoire de la Littérature latine chrétienne*, rev. by Gustav Bardy, 3rd ed., 2 vols. (Paris: Société d'ÁEdition "Les Belles Lettres," 1947) and the English translation, *The History and Literature of Christianity from Tertullian to Boethius*, tr. Herbert Wilson (New York: Barnes and Noble, 1968); see also Pierre Monceaux, *Histoire littéraire de l'Afrique chrétienne*, 7 vols. (Paris, 1901–1923; repr. Brussels: Culture et Civilization, 1963); and Frances M. Young, *From Nicaea to Chalcedon: A Guide to the Literature and Its Background* (London: SCM, 1983). The best starting point is Johannes Quasten, *Patrology*, 3 vols. (Utrecht: Spectrum, 1950, 1953, 1960) and Angelo de Berardino and Johannes Quasten, *Patrology* 4 (tr. Placid Solari; Westminster, MD: Christian Classics, 1986).

11. Eusebius, *Historia Ecclesiastica* III, 39, 12, in *SC* 31:156; for the fragments of Papias see *CPG* 1:10.1047; cf. *ODCC* 1028.

12. Jerome, *De Viris Illustribus* 18, ed. E. C. Richardson, *TU* 14.1A (1896): 19; and ed. Wilhelm Herding, *BT* (1879), 22.

13. Gustave Bardy, "Cérinthe," *Revue Biblique* 30 (1921): 344–73; Hippolytus, *Refutatio Omnium Haeresium* VII, 33 in *PG* 16:3342A; see the recently published critical edition, Miroslav Marcovich, ed., *Hippolytus. Refutatio Omnium Haeresium*, *PTS* 25 (1986): 317; cf. Irenaeus, *Adversus Haereses* I, 26, in *PG* 7:686A-B; *SC* 264:344–46.

14. Justin Martyr, *Dialogus cum Tryphone Iudaeo* 81, in *PG* 6:609A; Edgar J. Goodspeed, ed., *Die ältesten Apologeten* (Göttingen: Van-

denhoeck & Ruprecht, 1914), 193–94, the text I have quoted; *CPG* 1:31–32.1076.

15. Irenaeus, *Adversus Haereses* especially in V, in *SC* 152–53; cf. *CPG* 1:110–111.1306.

16. Irenaeus, *Adversus Haereses* V, 30, 3, in *PG* 7:1207A-B; *SC* 153:384, with the Greek text quoted in Eusebius, *Historia Ecclesiastica* III, 18, 3, in *SC* 31:122, and repeated at Eusebius, *Historia Ecclesiastica* V, 8, 6, in *SC* 41:36, where Eusebius' text reads almost exactly as at III, 18, 3, noted above. Only after the end of Domitian's reign did John return: Eusebius, *Historia Ecclesiastica* III, 23, 1, in *SC* 31:126.

17. John Lawson, *The Biblical Theology of Saint Irenaeus* (London: Epworth, 1948), 279 and 293, with specific reference to Irenaeus, *Adversus Haereses* V, 35, 1–2, in *PG* 7:1218B-1219A; *SC* 153:436–52, from which the key excerpt is quoted below.

18. Eusebius, *Historia Ecclesiastica* IV, 24, in *SC* 31:206; for Melito see *ODCC* 900; *DS* 10:979–90.

19. John of Damascus, *Sacra Parallela*, in *PG* 96:525B.

20. Jerome, *De Viris Illustribus* 61, in Richardson, 35; Herding, 41–42; cf. *CPG* 1:268–69.1890; see P. Prigent and R. Stehly, "Les Fragments du De Apocalypsi d'Hippolyte," *Theologische Zeitschrift* 29 (1973): 313–33; cf. John A. Green, "Hippolytus of Rome and the Apostolic Tradition," *Improvement Era* 67 (August 1964): 648–51, 672–74; *ODCC* 652–53; *DS* 7:531–71.

21. Text in *PG* 10:725–88 and *GCS* 1.2:3–47; cf. *CPG* 1:259.1872.

22. Hippolytus, *In Danielem*, in *PG* 10:637–69, 669–700; *GCS* 1.1:2–340; *SC* 14; cf. *CPG* 1:259–60.1873. See Marcel Richard, "Les Difficultés d'une édition des oeuvres de S. Hippolyte," *Studia Patristica* (1971 Oxford Conference on Patristic Studies), 12.1, *TU* 115 (1975): 51–70; Marcel Richard, "Les difficultés d'une édition du commentaire de S. Hippolyte sur Daniel," *Revue d'Histoire des Textes* 2 (1972): 5–7; and also Marcel Richard, "Pour une nouvelle ÁEdition du Commentaire de S. Hippolyte sur Daniel," in Patrick Granfield and Josef A. Jungmann, ed., *Kyriakon: Festschrift Johannes Quasten,* 2 vols. (Münster: Aschendorff, 1970), 1:69–78.

23. Irenaeus, *Adversus Haereses* V, 30, 2, in *PG* 7:1205B; *SC* 153:376–78; cf. Hans Achelis, *Hippolytstudien,* *TU* 16.1.4 (1897): 3–16, 169–84 and also Charles, *ICC* 1:208–9. The reference to Enoch in 1 Clement 9 comes from Genesis 5:24 and does not associate him with Elijah. At Irenaeus, *Adversus Haereses* V, 5, 1, in *PG* 7:1123B-C; *SC* 153:62, quoted below, Enoch and Elijah are mentioned, though they are not specifically identified as the two prophets or witnesses at Jerusalem.

24. Quoduultdeus, *Dimidium Temporis in Signis Antichristi* IX, 17: "Praedictio implenda in moribus Antichristi," in *CCSL* 60:202.13–18; *SC* 102:620.

25. Primasius, *Commentarii in Apocalypsin* III, 11:7, in *CCSL* 92:169.91; *PL* 68:867D.

26. Alcuin, *Commentarii in Apocalypsin* IV, 7:5, in Angelo Mai, ed., *Alcuini Commentariorum in Apocalypsin Libri Quinque*, Scriptorum Veterum Nova Collectio e Vaticanis Codicibus edita 9 (Rome: Vatican, 1837): 308–11; *PL* 100:1132C; for Alcuin's principal source cf. Robert Weber, ed., *Ambrosii Autperti Opera, pars I: Expositionis in Apocalypsin Libri I-V; pars II: Expositionis in Apocalypsin Libri VI-X*, in *CCCM* 27–27A. For the parallel and source of the passage cited from Alcuin, see Ambrosius Autpertus, *Expositio in Apocalypsin* IV, 7:5–8, in *CCCM* 27:306.238–42. Alcuin omits *mediatore nostro adueniente* between *aetate* and *occulto*, and he also makes a minor inversion and omission for his source's *iudaica perfida plebs propriis sedibus expulsa*.

27. Beda, *Expositio in Apocalypsin* I, 7:5, in *PL* 93:150B-C.

28. Hippolytus, *De Antichristo* 15 and 54, in *PG* 10:737C-740A; *GCS* 1.2:11.20; and *PG* 10:773AB; *GCS* 1.2:28.10.

29. Commodian, *Carmen de duobus populis*, ed. Joseph Martin; *CCSL* 128:73–113.

30. Lactantius, *Diuinae Institutiones* VII, 22, 8, ed. S. Brandt and G. Laubmann; *CSEL* 19:654; cf. *CPL* 18.85; *ODCC* 791–92; *DS* 9:48–59 (54 for a discussion of "les fins dernières").

31. Eusebius, *Historia Ecclesiastica* VI, 14, in *SC* 41:106–7; *ODCC* 303; *DS* 2:950–61; see *CPG* 1:138.1380 for the extant fragments.

32. C. Diobouniotis and A. von Harnack, eds., *Der Scholien-Kommentar des Origenes zur Apokalypse Johannis*, *TU* 38.3 (1911): 21–44, and C. H. Turner, "Document: Origen, Scholia in Apocalypsin," *Journal of Theological Studies* 25 (1923):1–15; *CPG* 1:167.1468. But see also A. de Boysson "Avons-nous un commentaire d'Origène sur l'Apocalypse?" *Revue Biblique* 22 [n.s. 5] (1913): 555–67.

33. See Karen Jo Torjesen, *Hermeneutical Procedure and Theological Method in Origen's Exegesis*, *PTS* 28 (1986); also P. Nautin, *Origène: Sa Vie et son Oeuvre*, Christianisme Antique 1 (Paris: Beauchesne, 1977); Jean Daniélou, *Origen*, tr. Walter Mitchell (New York: Sheed and Ward, 1955); and Charles Kannengiesser and William L. Petersen, eds., *Origen of Alexandria: His World and His Legacy*, Christianity and Judaism in Antiquity 1 (Notre Dame, IN: University of Notre Dame Press, 1988). For other studies on Origen, see Henri Crouzel, *Bibliographie Critique d'Origène*, 2 vols., Instrumenta Patristica 8–8A (Le Hague: Martinus Nijhoff and Steenbrugge, Belgium: Abbatia Sancti Petri, 1971 and 1982).

34. Eusebius, VII, 24–25, in *SC* 41:201–10, for his two books *On the Promises*, the first against Nepos, the second treating the Apocalypse. Eusebius gives a lengthy summary and quotation from Dionysius on the Apocalypse. See Wolfgang A. Bienert, *Dionysius von Alexandrien zur Frage des Origenismus im dritten Jahrhundert*, PTS 21 (1978), especially 197–200.

35. Anastasios Lolos, ed., *Die Apokalypse des Ps.-Methodios*, Beiträge zur klassischen Philologie 83 (1976) and also *Die dritte und vierte Redaktion des Ps.-Methodios*, Beiträge zur klassischen Philologie 94 (1978). See Paul J. Alexander, *The Byzantine Apocalyptic Tradition* (Berkeley: University of California, 1985); Quasten, *Patrology*, 2:129–37; *CPG* 1:252–53.1830. See also Methodius *Symposium* 8.4–11, in *PG* 18:143B-158B) and 9.1–5, in *PG* 18:175C-192B; for Methodius see *ODCC* 910–11; *DS* 10:1109–1117.

36. Quasten, *Patrology*, 2:129.

37. Victorinus Petovionensis, *Commentarii in Apocalypsim*, ed. Iohannes Haussleiter, *CSEL* 49; *PLS* 1:103–72; *CPL* 80. An early edition is *PL* 5:317–44, but it is not textually reliable.

38. Cf. Manlio Simonetti, "Il Millenarismo in Oriente da Origene a Metodio," in Eligius Dekker, ed., *Corona Gratiarum*, 2 vols., Instrumenta Patristica 10–11 (Brugge: Sint Pietersabdij, 1975), 1:37–58.

39. *ODCC* 72–73; see J. A. Cramer, *Catena in Epistolas Catholicas accesserunt Oecumenii* [sic] *et Arethae Commentarii in Apocalypsin ad fidem Codd. Mss.*, vol. 8 of Catenae Graecorum Patrum in Novum Testamentum, 8 vols. (Hildesheim: Georg Olms, 1967; repr. of Oxford, 1840).

40. *CPG* 2:308.3658.

41. *ODCC* 402; *DS* 3:868–71; see also Thomas W. Mackay, "Didymos the Blind on Psalm 28 (LXX): Text from Unpublished Leaves of the Tura Commentary," *Studia Patristica* 20 (1987 Oxford Conference on Patristic Studies; Louvain, Belgium: Peeters, 1989): 40–41. In addition to five papyrus codices of the writings of Didymos, the cache at Tura also included a previously unkown work by Origen on Easter: Octave Guéraud and Pierre Nautin, *Origène sur la Pâque*, Christianisme Antique 2 (Paris: Beauchesne, 1979).

42. Didymus Caecus Alexandrinus, *In Zachariam* III, 73 = ZaT 200.14–16, in Louis Doutreleau, ed., *Didyme l'Aveugle sur Zacharie* [*SC* 83–85], *SC* 84:654. ZaT is the technical abbreviation for the Didymos commentary on Zechariah in the papyrus from Tura. Doutreleau has also given book and paragraph notations to the commentary, hence the double reference. Doutreleau, in *SC* 83:123,

credits Devresse, in an article on the *Catena* or "chain" of patristic quotations, with the tentative discovery that Didymos had written on the Apocalypse: "peut-être aussi un fragment de Didyme (Schol. 1)," R. Devresse, "Chaînes exégétiques grecques," in F. G. Vigouroux, ed., *Dictionnaire de la Bible*, 5 vols. (Paris: Letouzey et Ané, 1895–1912), with Supplément, ed. Louis Pirot, A. Robert, Henri Cazelles, and André Feuillet, 10 vols. to date (Paris: Letouzey et Ané, 1928–), Suppl. 1:1228.

43. *ODCC* 1400; Monceaux, *Histoire littéraire de l'Afrique chrétienne*, 5:165–219.

44. Francesco Lo Bue, *The Turin Fragments of Tyconius' Commentary on Revelation* (Cambridge: Cambridge University Press, 1963); repr. *PLS* 1:621–52, 1749–50. The text is found in Turin Biblioteca Nazionale F.iv.18, from Bobbio.

45. See Gerald Bonner, *Saint Bede in the Tradition of Western Apocalyptic Commentary*, Jarrow Lecture, 1966 (Jarrow: The Rector, 1966), 6; cf. Lo Bue, 23: the Turin manuscript "does not preserve the Tyconian text which other commentators had before them, but a text which at a certain period of its history underwent some degree of modification." See also Alexander Souter, "Tyconius's Text of the Apocalypse: A Partial Restoration," *Journal of Theological Studies* 14 (1913): 338–58; Gerald Bonner, "Towards a Text of Tyconius," *Studia Patristica* 10.1 (1967 Oxford Patristic Studies Conference), *TU* 107 (1970): 9–13; and, in a recent study, K. Steinhauser, *The Apocalypse Commentary of Tyconius: A History of Its Reception and Influence* (Frankfurt: Peter Lang, 1987).

46. Thomas W. Mackay, "Bede's Biblical Criticism: The Venerable Bede's Summary of Tyconius' *Liber* Regularum," in Margot H. King and Wesley M. Stevens, eds., *Saints, Scholars and Heroes: Studies of Medieval Culture in Honour of Charles W. Jones*, 2 vols. (Collegeville, MN: Saint John's Abbey and University, 1979), 1:209–231; see George Brown, *Bede the Venerable*, Twayne's English Authors Series 443 (Boston: G. K. Hall, 1987), 50 and 119, n. 17. For Tyconius' influence on Augustine, see Alberto Pincherle, "Da Ticonio a Sant'Agostino," *Ricerche Religiose* 1 (1925): 443–46, but particularly now Charles Kannengiesser and Pamela Bright, *A Conflict of Christian Hermeneutics in Roman Africa: Tyconius and Augustine* (Berkeley: Center for Hermeneutical Studies and University of California, 1989).

47. De Labriolle, *Histoire de la Littérature latine chrétienne*, 1:427.

48. De Labriolle, *The History and Literature of Christianity from Tertullian to Boethius*, 293-94.

49. J. Hausleitter, "Die Commentare des Victorinus, Tichonius

und Hieronymus zur Apokalypse," *Zeitschrift für kirchliche Wissenschaft und kirchliches Leben* 7 (1886): 241.

50. Jerome, *De Viris Illustribus* 135, in Richardson, 55-56, and Herding, 66: "*De Spiritu Sancto Didymi*, quem in Latinum transtuli, librum unum" "*On the Holy Spirit* by Didymos, one book that I translated into Latin"; cf. Jerome, *De Viris Illustribus* 109, in Richardson, 50, and Herding, 59: "et *De Spiritu Sancto* librum unum quem ego in Latinum uerti." See J. N. D. Kelly, *Jerome: His Life, Writings, and Controversies* (New York: Harper and Row, 1975), 85, 121-26, 142-43. The text is preserved in several manuscripts, probably because of the association with Jerome. Bede quoted three passages from a copy of the text for his *Expositio in Actuus Apostolorum*, and his text is quite close to (but usually better than) British Library Royal 5 B VII, fol. 22v-56r (quotations are parallel to text found on fol. 23r-v, 39v, and 54r-v). But curiously no extant manuscript of *De Sancto Spiritu*, including Oxford Jesus College 3, Durham Cathedral Library B.III.2 (fol. 1r-18v) and B.IV.16, and the British Library manuscript Royal 5 B VII — all from the early or mid-twelfth century, comes from Anglo-Saxon England; Helmut Gneuss, "A Preliminary List of Manuscripts Written or Owned in England up to 1100," *Anglo-Saxon England* 9 (1981): 1-60.

51. Jerome, *Epistula* LIII, 9 [*ad Paulinum*], in *CSEL* 54:463.

52. Jerome, *Commentarii in Isaiam* XVIII, prologue, in *CCSL* 73A:740.9-741.19.

53. Jerome, *Commentarii in Danielem* II, on Daniel 7:17-18A, in *CCSL* 75A:848.713-14: "Cessat ergo mille annorum fabula" "so let the fable of a millennium cease!" Elsewhere he says: [Dionysius Alexandrinus] "irridens mille annorum fabulam et . . . instaurationem templi." "[Dionysius of Alexandria] ridiculing the fable of the millennium and the restoration of the temple." Jerome, *Commentarii in Isaiam* XVIII, prologue, in *CCSL* 73A:741.22-24.

54. Jerome, *Commentarii in Zachariam* I, on Zechariah 4:11-14, M. Adriaen, ed., in *CCSL* 76A:784.267-85.286; cf. *Commentarii in Amos* III, on Amos 9:2-5, M. Adriaen, ed., in *CCSL* 76:337.79-82.

55. Augustine, *De Ciuitate Dei* XX, 29, in *CCSL* 48:752.11-13.

56. Augustine, *Sermo* CCLIX, in *PL* 38:1196-1201, esp. 1197-98.

57. Augustine, *De Ciuitate Dei* XX, 7, in *CCSL* 48:708.4.

58. Augustine, *De Ciuitate Dei* XX, 9, in *CCSL* 48:715.1-719.139.

59. Augustine, *De Ciuitate Dei* XX, 17, in *CCSL* 48:728.48-729.53; cf. *De Ciuitate Dei* XX, 9, in *CCSL* 48:717.56-59.

60. Augustine, *De Ciuitate Dei* XX, 29, in *CCSL* 48:752.1-753.43.

61. His writings are edited in *CCSL* 60 and *SC* 101-2. For Quod-uultdeus, see de Berardino and Quasten, *Patrology*, 4:501-3; *DS* 12:2882-89.

62. The texts *Expositio Rectae Fidei* and *Quaestiones et responsiones ad orthodoxos* were formerly attributed to Justin Martyr; see *CPG* 3:218.6284-85 and Quasten, *Patrology*, 3:536-54. For Theodoret, see *ODCC* 1360-61.

63. *ODCC* 1130; *CPG* 7430 (for his commentary on Genesis).

64. Quasten, *Patrology*, 3:538-39.

65. H. C. Hoskier, *The Complete Commentary of Oecumenius on the Apocalypse*, University of Michigan Humanistic Series 23 (Ann Arbor: University of Michigan Press, 1928): 29-260. *CPG* 3:394.7470; *ODCC* 993; *DS* 11:681-82.

66. Hoskier, *Commentary of Oecumenius*, 4.

67. In *PG* 106:207-458; *CPG* 3:395-96.7478.

68. See Allo, *Saint Jean l'Apocalypse*, ccxxv. Some sixty manu-scripts of the Apocalypse text—about one-fourth of the total—also contain Andreas' commentary (Swete, *Commentary on Revelation*, cxcix). An anonymous abridgment of Andreas is in Cramer, *Catena*, 8:497-582. This was formerly, but quite incorrectly, attributed to Oecumenius.

69. *ODCC* 284.

70. *ODCC* 748-49; *DS* 8:452-66.

71. *ODCC* 1087-88; *DS* 12:1397-1408.

72. In *PG* 106:487-786.

73. *ODCC* 1364.

74. *ODCC* 463. For Ephraem, see *DS* 4:788-822; *ODCC* 462-63. Older but still of value is Guiseppe Ricciotti, *Sant' Ephrem Siro. Biografia, Scritti, Teologia* (Turin and Rome: Marietti, 1925).

75. De Berardino and Quasten, *Patrology*, 4:207.

76. Latin translation from Syriac by I. Sedlacek, in *CSCO* 60:1-22; *CPG* 1:269.1891.

77. Stan Larson, "The Earliest Syriac Commentary on the Apoc-alypse," *Studia Patristica* 18.4 (1983 Oxford Conference on Patristic Studies; Louvain, Belgium: Peeters, forthcoming). Leslie S. B. MacCoull, "MS. Morgan 591: The Apocalypse Commentary of Pseudo-Cyril of Alexandria," *Studia Patristica* 20 (1987 Oxford Con-ference on Patristic Studies; Louvain, Belgium: Peeters, 1989): 33-39.

78. A. W. Adams, ed., *Primasius Episcopus Hadrumetinus, Com-mentarius in Apocalypsin*, in *CCSL* 92; the previous edition, with de-fective text is *PL* 68:793-936. For additions and corrections to the *PL*

text of Primasius, see *PLS* 4:1207-21; but Adam's text in *CCSL* now supersedes all other editions. For Primasius, see *RBMA* 4:480-82.6988; *ODCC* 1124; *DS* 12:2351-53; *CPL* 873; Johannes Haussleiter, *Die lateinische Apokalypse der alten afrikanischen Kanon*, in T. Zahn, ed., Forschungen zur Geschichte des neutestamentlichen Kanons, 4 (Erlangen and Leipzig: Andr. Deichert'ches Verlagsbuchhandlung Nachf. [G. Böhme], 1891). A fine study of the manuscript Oxford Bodl. Douce 140, an important early copy of Primasius very close to that known to the Venerable Bede in Anglo-Saxon England in the late seventh century, is A. C. Clark, *The Descent of Manuscripts* (Oxford: Clarendon, 1918; repr. 1969), 104-23.

79. E. A. Lowe, *Codices Latini Antiquiores* 4 (Oxford: Clarendon 1947): 27.496; *RBMA* 2:238.1918; *PL* 70:1405-1918; *ODCC* 246-47; *DS* 2:276-77; James O'Donnell, *Cassiodorus* (Berkeley: University of California Press, 1979), 225-29.

80. Caesarius of Arles, *Expositio in Apocalypsim*, in Germain Morin, ed. *Opera Omnia*, 2 vols. (Maredsous, Belgium: Abbaye de Maredsous, 1942): 2:209-77; see also Germain Morin, "Le Commentaire Homilétique de S. Césaire sur l'Apocalypse," *Revue Bénédictine* 45 (1933): 43-61; *CPL* 1016; *RBMA* 2:146-47.1495, and also 2:335.2445, where it was attributed to Gennadius. For Caesarius see *ODCC* 218; *DS* 2:420-29. The earlier edition is reprinted in *PL* 35:2417-52.

81. M. Férotin, *Apringius de Béja: Son Commentaire de l'Apocalypse* (Paris: Alphonse Picard, 1900); text is reprinted in *PLS* Roman 4:1221-48. *RBMA* 2:127-28.1422.

82. Alulfus, *De Expositione Noui Testamenti*, in *PL* 79:1137-1424, with 1397C-1424C for the Apocalypse citations, but there is nothing on the two witnesses. Alulfus (d. 1143/44) was a monk at Saint Martin's in Tournai (*DS* 1:403).

83. Joseph F. Kelly, "Bede and the Irish Exegetical Tradition on the Apocalypse," *Revue Bénédictine* 92 (1982): 393-406. This text was edited by Hartung from Bamberg MS Patr. 102 (B.V. 18), with frequent reference to Munich clm 14469: K. Hartung, *Ein Traktat zur Apokalypse des Apostels Johannes in einer Pergamenthandschrift der K. Bibliothek in Bamberg* (Bamberg: Gustav Duckstein, 1904). Later G. Lo Menzo Rapisarda made a full analysis of the manuscript tradition, Miscellanea di Studi di Letterature Cristiana Antica, 15 (Catania: Centro di Studi sull'Antico Cristianesimo, 1965): 119-40, and edited the text: G. Lo Menzo Rapisarda, *Incerti Auctoris Commentarius in Apocalypsin*, Miscellanea di Studi di Letteratura Cristiana Antica, 16 (Catania: Centro di Studi sull'Antico Cristianesimo, 1967), and the text was reprinted in *PLS* 4:1850-63, with a note on the manuscripts

and editions at *PLS* 4:1844; *RBMA* 3:491.5271 (= 3:86.3461); *CPL* 276.1221. The seminal study for early Irish exegesis is Berhard Bischoff, "Turning-Points in the History of Latin Exegesis in the Early Irish Church: A.D. 650-800," in Martin MacNamara, ed., *Biblical Studies: The Medieval Irish Contribution* (Dublin: Dominican Publications, 1976), 74-160, a translation of "Wendepunkte in der Geschichte der lateinischen Exegese im Frühmittelalter," published in Bischoff's *Mittelalterliche Studien* 1 (Stuttgart: Hiersemann, 1966): 205-73, and revised from original article in *Sacris Erudiri* 6 (1954): 189-279. For this text see Bischoff, "Turning-Points in the History of Latin Exegesis," 143 (= Bischoff, *Mittelalterliche Studien* 1:268).

84. J. F. Kelly, "Bede and the Irish Exegetical Tradition on the Apocalypse," 394 and n. 2, names and characterizes the source: "according to the notorious Thomas Dempster, Scottish patriot and liar." *RBMA* 2:250.1990.

85. Bischoff, "Turning-Points in the History of Latin Exegesis in the Early Irish Church: A.D. 650-800," 143 (= Bischoff, *Mittelalterliche Studien* 1:268).

86. J. F. Kelly, "Bede and the Irish Exegetical Tradition on the Apocalypse," 395, citing Paris BN lat. 11561, fol. 1v-217v, a manuscript from the second half of the ninth century. Primasius is the only patristic authority named in the Reference Bible commentary on the Apocalypse (Paris BN lat. 11561, fol. 203r). Consult also Joseph F. Kelly, "Hiberno-Latin Exegesis and Exegetes," *Annuale Mediaevale* 21 (1981): 46-60, and Charles D. Wright's entry on Hiberno-Latin exegesis in the forthcoming volume, Fred Biggs, Tom Hill, and Paul E. Szarmach, eds., *Sources of Anglo-Saxon Literary Culture: A Trial Version* (Binghamton, NY: Center for Medieval and Early Renaissance Studies, 1990).

87. J. F. Kelly, "Bede and the Irish Exegetical Tradition on the Apocalypse," 405-6; see Bonner, *Saint Bede*; Brown, *Bede the Venerable*, 42-61; Henry Mayr-Harting, *The Coming of Christianity to England* (New York: Schocken, 1971), 140, 209-19; and Claudio Leonardi, "Il Venerabile Beda e la Cultura del Secolo VIII," *I Problemi dell'Occidente nel Secolo VIII*, Settimane di Studio del Centro Italiano di Studi sull'Alto Medioevo, 20 (Spoleto: Centro Italiano di Studi sull'Alto Medioevo, 1973): 603-58. A fine assessment of Bede's method and of the importance of his contribution is Roger Ray, "What Do We Know about Bede's Commentaries?" *Recherches de Théologie ancienne et médiévale* 49 (1982): 5-20. Roger Ray has also prepared an excellent article on Bede for a future volume in the series Aufstieg und Niedergang der Römischen Welt (Berlin and

New York: De Gruyter, forthcoming). Bede's Apocalypse commentary is *CPL* 1393, *RBMA* 2:185.1640.

88. Robert McNally, *Scriptores Hiberniae Minores*, Pars I, *CCSL* 108B: xii-xiii; but for a different assessment, see Rand H. Johnson, *Bedae Venerabilis Explanatio Epistolae Iudae Apostoli*, master's thesis, Brigham Young University, 1979, 4-6.

89. Ray, "What Do We Know about Bede's Commentaries?" 20.

90. Weber, *Ambrosii Autperti Opera* (*CCCM* 27-27A). *RBMA* 2:95.1275; *DS* 1:429. The date of composition is established by the author's words preserved at the end of book X (*CCCM* 27A:872) only by Vat. Reg. lat. 96 and Oxford Bodl. Laud. misc. 464 (767).

91. H. A. Sanders, ed., *Beati in Apocalypsim Libri XII*, Papers and Monographs of the American Academy at Rome 7 (Rome: American Academy at Rome, 1930); also E. Romero-Pose, ed., *Sancti Beati A Liebana Commentarius in Apocalypsin*, 2 vols.; Scriptores Graeci et Latina Consilio Academiae Lynceorum Editi (Rome: Accademia dei Lyncei, 1985). *RBMA* 2:172-74.1597.

92. Mai, *Alcuini Commentariorum in Apocalypsin Libri Quinque*, 257-338; reprinted in *PL* 100:1055C-1156C; cf. *RBMA* 2:62.1102. See Marcus Vatasso and Pius Franchi de' Cavalieri, *Codies Vaticani Latini* 1 (codd. 1-678; Rome: Vatican, 1902): 505.

93. For Alcuin letters requesting Bede's commentaries, see E. Dümmler, ed., *Epistolae Alcuini*, MGH, Epistolae 4 (Karolingi Aevi 2), 2, no. 216. A few decades earlier Saint Boniface, Anglo-Saxon missionary to Germany, called Bede a "candle of the Church" [*candela ecclesiae*]: M. Tangl, ed., *Die Briefe des heiligen Bonifatius und Lullus*, in *Monumenta Germaniae Historica*, Epistolae selectae, 1, nos. 75, 76, 125, and 131.

94. The details of this will appear in my forthcoming article on Alcuin's commentary. For an example of his close quotation and paraphrasing, see above, n. 26.

95. Mai inserts ⟨per⟩; alternatively, read "septem angelor(um) dicta et facta commemorat" or else punctuate the passage "septem angelos—dicta et facta [*sc.* eorum]—commemorat."

96. Alcuin, *Commentarii in Apocalypsin* praefatio, in Mai, *Alcuini Commentariorum in Apocalypsin Libri Quinque*, 257-58; *PL* 100:1057A-58A. The first two paragraphs summarize Bede's *praefatio*, including his brief account of Tyconius' rules; see Mackay, "Bede's Biblical Criticism," 1:209-31. The final paragraph comes from Ambrosius Autpertus' own preface (*CCCM* 27:5.8-31).

97. For the exegetical tradition, see Swete, *Commentary on Rev-*

elation, cxcvii-ccxix; Allo, *Saint Jean l'Apocalypse*, ccxvii-ccl; and Devresse, "Chaînes exégétiques grecques," Suppl. 1:1228-31.

98. Gustav Becker, *Catalogi Bibliothecarum Antiqui* (Bonn: M.
Cohen, 1885; repr. Hildesheim: Georg Olms, 1973), 48. Becker has
reprinted the catalog from Saint Gall MS 728 (also recopied in the
early tenth century in MS 267). Becker's entry reads: 242. Expositio
tichonii donatistae in apocalipsim vol. I vetus. 243. Expos(itio) pri-
masii in apocalipsim libri. V. et glosule gregorii in apocalipsi(m)
sp(ir)italis intelligentie in volumine I.

99. F. C. Burkitt, ed., *The Book of Rules of Tyconius Newly Edited
from the Manuscripts*, Texts and Studies: Contributions to Biblical and
Patristic Literature 3 (Cambridge: Cambridge University Press,
1894); D. L. Anderson, "The Book of Rules of Tyconius: An Introduction and Translation with Commentary," Ph.D. diss., Southern
Baptist Theological Seminary, Louisville, 1974. For fine recent analysis see Pamela Bright, *The Book of Rules of Tyconius: Its Purpose and
Inner Logic* (Notre Dame: University of Notre Dame, 1987).

100. Laon Bibliothèque Municipale 89 (from Laon) on verso of
last leaf; *Catalogue Général des Manuscrits des Bibliothèques publiques
des Départements*, 1 (Paris: Imprimérie Nationale, 1849): 88; see also
Bright, 15-16.

101. See n. 91 above.

102. Beryl Smalley, *The Study of the Bible in the Middle Ages*, 2nd
ed. (Oxford: Oxford University Press, 1952; repr. Notre Dame, 1964),
14-19.

103. Louis Pirot, *L'Oeuvre Exégétique de Théodore de Mopsueste*
(Rome: Sumptibus Pontificii Instituti Biblici, 1913) and Robert Devresse, *Essai sur Théodore de Mopsueste*, Studi e Testi 141 (Rome:
Vatican, 1948): 53-92 (=ch. 2 "La Méthode d'Exégèse"); cf. *ODCC*
1358-59.

104. The teachings include antemortal existence of spirits and
apokatastasis, the doctrine that punishment is not ever-enduring but
that after punishment the souls may still be granted some sort of
reward in the kingdom of God. This doctrine was propounded by
Clement of Alexandria, Origen, Didymos, and Gregory of Nyssa
but rejected by Augustine; it was formally condemned at the Council
of Constantinople in A.D. 553 (*ODCC* 69-70). For the rejection of the
early Christian doctrine of the antemortal existence of spirits, see
Edictum Iustiniani imperatoris contra Origenem (*CPG* 3:303.6880). For
the text of the *Edict* of the Third Council of Constantinople, see
Joannes Dominicus Mansi, *Sacrorum Conciliorum noua et amplissima
collectio*, 54 vols. (Graz: Akademische, 1960-61; repr. of Paris and

Leipzig: Hubert Welter, 1901-27), 9:488D-533D; Eduardus Schwartz, *Acta Conciliorum Oecumenicorum* 4 tomes, 15 vols., in 29 parts (Berlin and Leipzig: Walter de Gruyter, 1914–), 3:189-214; also *PG* 86:945-94 and *PL* 69:177-226. The *Edict* states:

εἰ δὲ προϋπῆρχεν ἡ ψυχή, καθὼς Ὠριγένης ληρεῖ

in *PG* 86:953A; Mansi, 9:496A; "si autem anima praeexistebat, ut delirat Origenes," in *PL* 69:186A; Mansi, 9:495A: "But if the soul existed before this life [preexisted], as Origen deliriously babbles."

105. Thomas W. Mackay, "Didymos the Blind on Psalm 28," 2:40-41; J. N. D. Kelly, *Jerome*, 142; *ODCC* 402; *DS* 3:868-71; for Didymos' method see also W. A. Beinert, *"Allegoria" und "Anagoge" bei Didymos dem Blindem von Alexandrie, PTS* 13 (1972).

106. The seminal work on this subject is Walter Bauer, *Orthodoxy and Heresy in Earliest Christianity*, tr. Robert A. Kraft, Gerhard Krodel, et al. (Philadelphia: Fortress, 1971).

107. R. Pfeiffer, *History of Classical Scholarship from the Beginnings to the End of the Hellenistic Age* (Oxford: Clarendon, 1968); D. A. Russell, *Criticism in Antiquity* (Berkeley: University of California Press, 1981); cf. D. A. Russell and M. Winterbottom, *Ancient Literary Criticism: The Principal Texts in New Translations* (Oxford: Clarendon, 1972), and G. M. A. Grube, *The Greek and Roman Critics* (Toronto: University of Toronto Press, 1965), esp. 122-49, 325-56.

108. *ODCC* 1083-84; a fine overview is Samuel Sandmel, *Philo of Alexandria: An Introduction* (Oxford and New York: Oxford University Press, 1979); see also Ronald Williamson, *Jews in the Hellenistic World: Philo,* Cambridge Commentaries on Writings of the Jewish and Christian World 200 B.C. to A.D. 200, vol. 1, part 2 (Cambridge: Cambridge University Press, 1989).

109. *ODCC* 37; see D. E. Nineham, *The Church's Use of the Bible, Past and Present* (London: SPCK, 1963) and K. Froelich, *Biblical Interpretation in the Early Church*, in Sources of Early Christian Thought (Philadelphia: Fortress, 1984). For the setting of the Alexandrian school and Christianity in Egypt in the first four centuries, see C. Wilfred Griggs, *Early Egyptian Christianity* (Leiden: E. J. Brill, 1989) and Birger A. Pearson and James E. Goehring, eds., *The Roots of Egyptian Christianity*, Studies in Antiquity and Christianity (Philadelphia: Fortress Press, 1986); note also Colin H. Roberts, *Manuscript, Society and Belief in Early Christian Egypt*, Schweich Lecture of the British Academy 1977 (London: Oxford University Press for the British Academy, 1979).

110. J. N. D. Kelly, *Jerome*, 125.

111. Smalley, *The Study of the Bible in the Middle Ages*, 87-88, 97,

106-95 (on Andrew of St. Victor). For medieval exegesis, see also C. Spicq, *Esquisse d'une Histoire de l'Exégèse latine au Moyen Age* (Paris: J. Vrin, 1944), and Henri de Lubac, *L'Exégèse médiévale: Les Quatre Sens de l'Écriture*, 2 vols. in 4 parts (Paris: Aubier, 1959-60); Robert Kaske et al., *Medieval Christian Literary Imagery: A Guide to Interpretation*, Toronto Medieval Bibliographies 11 (Toronto: University of Toronto Press, 1988).

112. For a discussion of the issue, see Simonetti, "Il Millenarismo in Oriente da Origene a Metodio," 37-58; also Robert E. Lerner, "Refreshment of the Saints: The Time after Antichrist as a Station for Earthly Progress in Medieval Thought," *Traditio* 32 (1976): 97-144.

113. Nibley, *The World and the Prophets*; 178; also n. 1 above and Thomas W. Mackay, "Early Christian Exegesis of the Apocalypse," *Studia Biblica 1978, Journal for the Study of the New Testament*, Supplement Series 3 (1980): 257-63.

114. Nibley, *The World and the Prophets*; 176, citing A. von Harnack, *Monasticism and the Confessions of St. Augustine* (London, 1901), 69; see Norman Cohn, *The Pursuit of the Millennium: Revolutionary Millenarians and Mystical Anarchists of the Middle Ages*, 2nd ed., rev. (Oxford: Oxford University Press, 1970), and Werner Verbeke, Daniel Verhelst, and Andries Welkenhuysen, ed., *The Use and Abuse of Eschatology in the Middle Ages*, Mediaevalia Lovaniensia, Series 1, Studia 15 (Louvain, Belgium: Leuven University Press, 1988).

115. Hugh Nibley, "Christian Envy of the Temple," in *Mormonism and Early Christianity*, 391-434.

116. Albertus Magnus, *Enarrationes in Apocalypsim*, Opera Omnia, 38 vols. (Paris: Ludovicum Vives, 1895-99), 38:465-792; listed in *RBMA* 2:47.1041 under Pseudo-Albertus Magnus.

117. Joseph S. Considine, "The Two Witnesses: Apoc. 11:3-13," *Catholic Biblical Quarterly* 8 (1946): 390.

118. Jerome, *Epistula* LIX, 3, in *CSEL* 54:543-44.

119. Augustine, *De Ciuitate Dei* XX, 29, in *CCSL* 48:752.1-753.43.

120. Considine, "The Two Witnesses: Apoc. 11:3-13," 390-91; see Matthew Black, "The 'Two Witnesses' of Rev. 11:3f. in Jewish and Christian Apocalyptic Tradition," in E. Bammel, C. K. Barrett, and W. D. Davies, eds., *Donum Gentilicium. New Testament Studies in Honour of David Daube* (Oxford: Clarendon, 1978), 227-37; Charles, *ICC* 1:281; Kenneth A. Strand, "The Two Witnesses of Rev 11:3-12," *Andrews University Seminary Studies* 19 (1981): 127; J. M. Ford, *Revelation*, AB (1975), 177-78; André Feuillet, "Essai d'Interpretation du Chapître XI de l'Apocalypse," *New Testament Studies* 4 (1957-58):

183-200; and G. B. Caird, *A Commentary on the Revelation of St. John the Divine* (New York: Harper and Row, 1966), 134-35.

121. The expression is the title of Smalley's chapter 5 (196-263), entitled "Masters of the Sacred Page: The Comestor, The Chanter, Stephen Langton." On pages 196-97 of *The Study of the Bible in the Middle Ages*, Smalley writes, "The masters who made themselves responsible for continuing the Victorine tradition are the trio we met in the last chapter: Peter Comestor, Peter the Chanter, Stephen Langton. Mgr. Grabmann has grouped them together as the 'biblical moral school'; they have a common interest in biblical studies and in practical moral questions, which distinguishes them from those who were primarily theologians and dialecticians: Peter Lombard, Peter of Poitiers, Adam of the Petit Pont."

122. Peter Cantor, *In Apocalypsim* on Apocalyse 11:3; unpublished text in a manuscript at Brigham Young University, fol. 117^v. I will publish a critical edition of this important text in *CCCM* and *SC*.

123. Black, "The 'Two Witnesses' of Rev. 11:3f.," 231; Guido Kisch, *Pseudo-Philo's "Liber Antiquitatum Biblicarum"*, Publications in Mediaeval Studies, 10 (Paris and Notre Dame: University of Notre Dame, 1949).

124. Allo, *Saint Jean l'Apocalypse*, 131; Considine, "The Two Witnesses: Apoc. 11:3-13," 390.

125. *Descensus Christi ad inferos* 9 (= *Evangelium Nicodemi* or *Acta Pilati*, 25; *Evangelia Apocrypha*, C. von Tischendorff, ed., 2nd ed. [Leipzig, 1876; repr. Hildesheim: Olms, 1966], 404-6).

126. Because of the preponderance of the Latin tradition, I have taken my translation from Tischendorff's Latin text given above, and it represents well the meaning of the Greek, though it adds a few words (as correctly construing the genitive absolute at the beginning of chapter 10: *tauta toutōn legontōn* by "Et cum haec loquerentur sanctis Enoch et Elias" "and while Enoch and Elijah were saying these things to the saints"). Edgar Hennecke and Wilhelm Schneemelcher, *New Testament Apocrypha*, tr. R. McL. Wilson, 2 vols (Philadelphia: Fortress, 1963), have used the Greek: "While they were saying this . . . " (1:475).

127. *Historia Iosephi* 32 (Tischendorff, *Evangelia Apocrypha*, 139).

128. Tertullian, *De Anima* L, 5; see J. H. Waszink, ed., *Septimi Florentis Tertulliani De Anima* (Amsterdam: J. M. Meulenhoff, 1947), 68 and commentary on 525, with reference to W. Bousset, *Der Antichrist*, 134-39. Bousset's valuable book has been translated into English by A. H. Keane as *The Antichrist Legend: A Chapter in Christian and Jewish Folklore* (London: Hutchinson, 1896; repr. New York: AMS, 1985).

129. Irenaeus, *Adversus Haereses* V, 5, 1, in *PG* 7:1134B-C; *SC* 153:62 (with Greek quoted from John of Damascus' *Sacra Parallela*; cf. *CPG* 3:517-18.8056).

130. Irenaeus, *Adversus Haereses* V, 26, in *PG* 7:1192B; *SC* 153:324; V, 28, 2, in *PG* 7:1198BC; *SC* 153:350-52; V, 29, 1-2, in *PG* 7:1201C-1202A; *SC* 153:364-66.

131. Irenaeus, *Adversus Haereses* V, 30, 1, in *PG* 7:1203AB; *SC* 153:370 (with Greek quoted at Eusebius, *Historia Ecclesiastica* V, 8, in *SC* 41:36) and *PG* 7:1203B; *SC* 153:372; V, 30, 4, in *PG* 7:1207B-1208A; *SC* 153:386.

132. Irenaeus, *Adversus Haereses* V, 35, in *PG* 7:1218B-1219A; *SC* 153:436-38.

133. Hippolytus, *De Christo et Antichristo* 43, in *PG* 10:761A; *GCS* 1.2:27-28.

134. Hippolytus, *De Christo et Antichristo* 46-47, in *PG* 10:764C-765A; *GCS* 1.2:29-30, with some manuscripts quoting an old form of the Septuagint or Greek Old Testament.

135. Hippolytus, *Capita contra Gaium* (Latin translation of Syriac I. Sedlacek, in *CSCO* 60:13-14).

136. Hippolytus, *In Danielem*, on Daniel 4:35, in *PG* 10:656D; *GCS* 1.1:278-80; *SC* 14:201.

137. In a sixteenth-century manuscript, Munich Staatsbibliothek gr. 53, fol. 271r, but in no other manuscript copy of this text, there is a passage — perhaps inserted from a gloss — that reads:

'Ενὼχ δὲ καὶ 'Ηλίας οἱ προφῆται κηρύξουσιν [κηρύξωσιν *ed.*] τὴν δευτέφαν παρουσίαν τοῦ κυρίου περιβεβλημένοι σάκκους ὡς γέγραπται διὰ τοῦ προφήτου

"Enoch and Elijah, the two prophets, will proclaim [*or*, let them proclaim] the second coming of the Lord while wearing sackcloth, as it has been written through the prophet" (*GCS* 1.1:314.14, critical apparatus).

138. Hippolytus, *In Danielem*, on Daniel 4:49-50, in *PG* 10:665A-B; *GCS* 1.1:314-16; *SC* 14:215-17; the text is somewhat more extensive for this passage than I have quoted.

139. Pseudo-Methodios 14.11, ed. 1 (Lolos 1976, 138.49-50).

140. Pseudo-Methodios 14.11, ed. 2 (Lolos 1976, 139.37-39).

141. Pseudo-Methodios 14.11, ed. 3 (Lolos 1978, 73.46-47).

142. Commodian, *De Duobus Populis* 833-44, in *CCSL* 128:103-4.

143. Editio Victorini 8.3, on Apocalypse 8:13, in *CSEL* 49:86; *PLS* 1:140.

144. Recensio Hieronymi 8.3, on Apocalypse 8:13, in *CSEL* 49:87; *PLS*1:140.

145. Editio Victorini 11.3, on Apocalyse 11:3, in *CSEL* 49:98; *PLS* 1:146.

146. Recensio Hieronymi 11.3, on Apocalyse 11:3, in *CSEL* 49:99; *PLS* 1:146.

147. Editio Victorini 12.6, on Apocalyse 12:7-9, in *CSEL* 49:114; *PLS* 1:153-54.

148. Recensio Hieronymi 12.6, on Apocalyse 12:7-9, in *CSEL* 49:115; *PLS* 1:153-54. The quotation in square brackets is the Vulgate; the repetition with its variants (n.b. *nuntii* for *angeli, anguis* for *serpens,* etc.) is the Old Latin biblical text known to Victorinus and other early Latin writers.

149. (Tyconius) Turin Fragments 332-41, in Lo Bue, 142-44; *PLS* 1:643.

150. (Tyconius) Turin Fragments 342-47 in Lo Bue, 145-46; *PLS* 1:643-44.

151. Ambrose, *Commentarii in Epistolam I ad Corinthios* 4:8, in *PL* 17:216A.

152. Didymus Caecus Alexandrinus (Didymos the Blind), *In Genesim* GnT 148.1-149.18 (actual quotes come from 148.6-7, 15-17, 23-27 and 149.5-8) on Genesis 5:21-24, in Pierre Nautin and Louis Doutreleau, eds., *Didyme l'Aveugle sur la Genèse* [*SC* 233, 244], *SC* 244:14-18.

153. Didymus Caecus Alexandrinus, *In Zachariam* 1.277 = ZaT 63.12-14, in *SC* 83:336-38.

154. Didymus Caecus Alexandrinus, *In Zachariam* 1.334-42 = ZaT 75.16-77.24, in *SC* 83:370-76.

155. Jerome, *Commentarii in Zachariam* I, on Zechariah 4:2-7, in *CCSL* 76A:778.54-779.70.

156. Jerome, *Commentarii in Zachariam* I, on Zechariah 4:2-7, in *CCSL* 76A:780.93-94, 780.106-782.170.

157. Jerome, *Commentarii in Zachariam* I, on Zechariah 4:11-14, in *CCSL* 76A:784.246-785.294.

158. Jerome, *Commentarii in Amos* III, on Amos 9:2-5, in *CCSL* 76:337.79-82.

159. Jerome, *Epistula* LIX, 3, in *CSEL* 54:543-44.

160. Augustine, *Epistula* CXCIII, 3, 5, in *CSEL* 57:170.

161. Augustine, *De Genesi ad litteram,* in *CSEL* 28:271-72, later quoted by Bede in his *In Genesim* I, 2, 18, in *CCSL* 118A:53-54; see below. To judge from the variants in the critical apparatus, Bede's textual source must have been a manuscript closely akin to Rome Biblioteca Vittorio Emmanuele 2094 (*olim* Sessorianus XIII) and Saint Gall 161 since, for example, they both give *in terra,* as does Bede at

118A:53.1681 while other manuscripts of Augustine omit *in*; but for Bede 118A:54.1702 *corporalium* vs. *corporalibus* in Augustine, in *CSEL* 28:272.11, the closest manuscript is that underlying the 1689 St. Maur edition of Augustine.

162. Theodoret of Cyr (Pseudo-Justin Martyr), *Quaestiones et Responsiones ad Orthodoxos* 85, in *PG* 6:1328A.

163. Quoduultdeus, *Liber Promissionum* I, VI, 9 "Praedictio Figurata Duorum Scilicet Populorum," in *CCSL* 60:18.35-40; *SC* 101:170-72.

164. Quoduultdeus, *Dimidium Temporis in Signis Antichristi* XIII, 22 "Promissio Implenda in Missione Heliae et Enoch," in *CCSL* 60:206.11-207.24; *SC* 102:632.

165. Quoduultdeus, *Dimidium Temporis in Signis Antichristi* XV, 24 "Praedictio Implenda in passione Heliae et Enoch" and XVI, 25 "Promissio ⟨implenda⟩ in eorum resurrectione Heliae et Enoch," in *CCSL* 60:208-9; *SC* 102:636-38.

166. Procopius of Gaza, *Commentarii in Genesin* IV, 91, in *PG* 87:260C-D.

167. Caesarius, *Expositio in Apocalypsim* 8, in Morin, *Opera Omnia*, 2:239.

168. Primasius, *Commentarius in Apocalypsin* III, 11:3, in *CCSL* 92:166.28-34; *PL* 68:866C.

169. Magnus Aurelius Cassiodorus, *Complexiones in Apocalypsin* 15, in *PL* 70:1411.

170. Gregory the Great, *Homiliae in Hiezechihelem prophetam* I, Homilia XII, 8-9, in *CCSL* 142:187-88; *SC* 327:500.

171. Gregory the Great, *Moralia in Iob* 14.(xxiii) 27 on Job 18:20, in *CCSL* 143A:714; *PL* 75:1053D.

172. Isidore of Seville, *De Ortu et Obitu Patrum* 3, in *PL* 83:131-32.

173. Cosmas Indicopleustes, *Topographia Christiana* V, 140, in *PG* 88:260AB; *SC* 159:205.

174. *Tractatus Hilarii in Septem Epistolas Canonicas*, Robert E. McNally, ed., in *CCSL* 108B:75 on James 5:17; *RBMA* 3:93-94.3525-31; cf. Bischoff, "Turning-Points in the History of Latin Exegesis in the Early Irish Church: A.D. 650-800," 141-43.

175. Anonymous Irish, Rapisarda, ed., 94, in *PLS* 4:1858.

176. Anonymous Irish, Rapisarda, ed., 94, in *PLS* 4:1859.

177. Andreas of Caesarea, *Commentarii in Apocalypsin* 30, "De Enocho et Elia," in *PG* 106:312B-C.

178. *Chronicon Paschale*, "De Prophetia Enoch," in *PG* 92:105A; cf. G. Mercati, "A Study of the *Paschal Chronicle*," *Journal of Theological Studies* 7 (1906): 397-412; *CPG* 3:496.7960.

179. John of Damascus, *De Fide Orthodoxa* 4, in *PG* 94:1217B-C; *CPG* 3:512.8043.

180. John of Damascus, *De Fide Orthodoxa* 4, in *PG* 94:1218B-C.

181. Oecumenius, *Commentarius in Apocalypsin*, in Hoskier, *The Complete Commentary of Oecumenius on the Apocalypse*, 128-29, on Apocalypse 11:1-7.

182. Andreas of Caesarea, *Commentarius in Apocalypsin* 30: [Concerning Enoch and Elijah who are going to refute and expose the Antichrist] in Cramer, *Catena*, 8:339-40, commentary on Apocalyse 11:3-6, based on Oecumenius.

183. Arethas, *Commentarius in Apocalypsin* 30, in *PG* 106:648C-689B, abbreviating Andreas of Caesarea on Apocalyse 11:3-6.

184. Beda, *Expositio in Apocalypsin* II, 11:3, in *PL* 93:162C.

185. Beda, *Expositio in Apocalypsin* II, 11:4, in *PL* 93:162D.

186. Beda, *Expositio in Apocalypsin* II, 11:6, in *PL* 93:163A.

187. Beda, *Expositio in Apocalypsin* II, 11:13e, in *PL* 93:164C-D, with the expression *hucusque recapitulatio* taken from the early manuscripts of Bede.

188. Beda, *De Temporum Ratione* LXIX, 600-601 'De Temporibus Antichristi,' in *CCSL* 123B:538.1-539.27.

189. Beda, *In Genesim* I, 1703-9, on Genesis 2:18, in *CCSL* 118A:54.

190. Beatus of Liebana V, Explanatio 11, 1-5, in Sanders, *Beati in Apocalypsim Libri XII*, 445; Romero-Pose, *Sancti Beati A Liebana Commentarius in Apocalypsin*, 2:67-68.

191. Beatus of Liebana V, Explanatio 11, 8, 10, 13, in Sanders, *Beati in Apocalypsim Libri XII*, 446-47; Romero-Pose, *Sancti Beati A Liebana Commentarius in Apocalypsin*, 2:69-70.

192. The manuscript reads mille ·CC· ·XL· perhaps by misreading Ambrosius Autpertus or Victorinus with reference to *MCCLX dies, id est XLII menses*, thus causing a confusion in the number.

193. Alcuin, *Commentarii in Apocalypsin* V, 11:3-4; Mai, *Alcuini Commentariorum in Apocalypsin Libri Quinque*, 328-29; *PL* 100:1147C-1148A); cf. Ambrosius Autpertus, *Expositio in Apocalypsin* V, 11:3-4, in *CCCM* 27:413.1-416.33. Alcuin draws upon Ambrosius but plainly shows the radical compression of his exegetical source in his paraphrasing. For example, whereas Ambrosius has eighty-six lines of printed commentary on Apocalyse 11:3, Alcuin has scarcely the equivalent of ten or eleven printed lines. Nevertheless, Alcuin still tends to use significant words and phrases that can be directly traced to Ambrosius. Also, Alcuin proceeds in the same order as Ambrosius, and so the summary must be deliberate, intentionally based upon his immediate literary and exegetical source.

194. Photius, *Bibliotheca* 229, in *PG* 103:985AB, D; ed. R. Henry, 4 (Paris: Société d'Édition "Les Belles Lettres," 1965): 139-40 in the series 'Collection Byzantine' of the Association Guillaume Budé. This section comprises some of his notes from reading works by Ephraem the Syrian, a prominent fourth-century church writer mentioned above. The quotation is from his summary of a treatise in reply to the attorney Anatolius, and Ephraem apparently quoted from various authorities, but especially from the Cappadocian Fathers. So this quotation is a ninth-century statement of fourth-century theological views.

195. Luis Revenga, ed., *Los Beatos: Europalia 85 España*, 26 September-30 November 1985, Chapelle de Nassau, Bibliothèque royale Albert Ier, Brussels (Madrid: Graficen, 1985), 102-35 for a brief description of each manuscript and a collation of illustrations.

196. Gerona Cathedral MS 7, written in A.D. 975 at the monastery of San Salvador, Zamora, by the priest Senior at the request of Abbot Dominicus, and decorated with 114 full-page miniatures by the monk Emeterius and the lady En; manuscript published in facsimile and with analyses in J. M. Casanovas, C. E. Dubler, W. Neuss, J. Marqués, eds., *Sancti Beati a Liebana in Apocalypsin Codex Gerundensis* (Olten and Lausanne: Urs Graf, 1962), and also G. Sanders, ed., with J. Camón, T. Marn, and J. Marqués, *Beati in Apocalipsin libri duodecim, Codex Gerundensis* (Madrid: Ediln, 1975).

197. Kurt Weitzmann, *Ancient Book Illumination*, Martin Classical Lectures 16 (Cambridge, MA: Harvard University Press, 1959). The Homer manuscript is the *Ilias Ambrosiana*, Milan, Biblioteca Ambrosiana, F 205 inf. Only some of the miniatures and a bit of text remain: see the reproductions and descriptive analyses in Ranuccio Bianchi-Bandinelli, *Hellenistic-Byzantine Miniatures of the Iliad (Ilias Ambrosiana)* (Bern and Olten: Urs Graf, 1955). For Vergil, see L. D. Reynolds, ed., *Texts and Transmission: A Survey of the Latin Classics* (Oxford: Clarendon, 1983), 433-36; the great manuscript, frequently studied, is Vat. lat. 3867, the *Vergilius Romanus*. See Erwin Rosenthal, *The Illuminations of the Vergilius Romanus (Cod. Vat. Lat. 3867): A Stylistic and Iconographical Analysis* (Dietikon and Zürich: Urs Graf, 1972). For Terence, see Reynolds, *Texts and Transmission*, 412-20, and also L. W. Jones and C. R. Morey, *The Miniatures of the Manuscripts of Terence prior to the Thirteenth Century*, 2 vols. (Princeton: Princeton University Press, 1930-31). "Someone soon after A.D. 400, to judge from the style of the illustrations, illustrated the text in accordance with the scene-headings of his manuscript, and these illustrations survive in descendants of ⟨manuscript family⟩ Γ." Reynolds, *Texts*

and Transmission, 413, citing A. W. Byvanck, "Antike Malerei, II:
Das Vorbild der Terenzillustrationen," *Mnemosyne* 3rd series, 7
(1939): 115-35. The manuscripts include Bibliotheca Apostolica Va-
ticana, Vaticanus lat. 3868 (ca. 820-30, Corvey; written by Hrod-
garius, illustrated by Adelricus; facsimile ed. Gunther Jachmann,
Terentius: Codex Vaticanus Latinus 3868 picturis insignis [Leipzig: Otto
Harrassowitz, 1929]); Paris, Bibliothèque Nationale lat. 7899 (s. ix²
from near Reims]); Paris, Bibliothèque Nationale lat. 7900 (s. ix³/⁴
from Corbie); and Lyon, Bibliothèque de la ville, MS 788 (s. ix³/⁴
from near Paris).

198. Specifically in manuscript family Γ and its antecedent, Σ;
see John N. Grant, "The Miniatures and the Date of Σ," *Studies in
the Textual Tradition of Terence* (Toronto: University of Toronto Press,
1986), 18-59.

199. For other examples of the persistence of Enoch and Elijah
in the artistic tradition even in the Greek world, see Harold R.
Willoughby, *The Elizabeth Day McCormick Apocalypse,* vol. 1: A Greek
Corpus of Revelation Iconography (Chicago: University of Chicago
Press, 1940).

13

The Case of Leviticus Rabbah

Jacob Neusner
The Institute for Advanced Study, Princeton, New Jersey

While the world at large treats Judaism as "the religion of the Old Testament," the fact is otherwise. Judaism inherits and makes the Hebrew Scriptures its own, just as does Christianity. But just as Christianity rereads the entire heritage of ancient Israel in the light of "the resurrection of Jesus Christ," so Judaism understands the Hebrew Scriptures as only one part, the written one, of "the one whole Torah of Moses, our rabbi." Ancient Israel no more testified to the oral Torah, now written down in the Mishnah and later rabbinic writings, than it did to Jesus as the Christ. In both cases, religious circles within Israel of later antiquity reread the entire past in the light of their own conscience and convictions. Accordingly, while the framers of Judaism as we know it received as divinely revealed ancient Israel's literary heritage, they picked and chose as they wished what would serve the purposes of the larger system they undertook to build. Since the Judaism at hand first reached literary expression in the Mishnah, a document in which Scripture plays a subordinate role, the founders of that Judaism clearly made no pretense at tying up to scriptural proof texts or at expressing in the form of scriptural commentary the main ideas they wished to set out. Accordingly, Judaism only asymmetrically rests upon

---

This was published earlier in a somewhat different form in Jacob Neusner, Judaism and Scripture: The Evidence of Leviticus Rabbah *(Chicago: University of Chicago Press, 1986).*

the foundations of the Hebrew Scriptures, and Judaism is not alone or mainly "the religion of the Old Testament."

Since Judaism is not "the religion of the Old Testament," we cannot take for granted or treat as predictable or predetermined the entry of the Hebrew Scriptures into the system of Judaism at hand. That is why we must ask exactly how the Scriptures did enter the framework of Judaism. In what way, when, and where, in the unfolding of the canon of Judaism, were they absorbed and recast, and how did they find the distinctive role they were to play from late antiquity onward?

The Importance of Leviticus Rabbah

If we wish to know in detail how the framers of Judaism confronted the challenge of Scripture, we logically turn to the books they wrote in which they expressed their ideas by making use of verses of Scripture. Some of these are organized around the structure of the Mishnah, others around that of Scripture. Clearly, the latter bring us closer to the answer, since in them the confrontation with Scripture proves immediate and ever-present. The issue of the Tosefta and the Talmud is the Mishnah, however, to which Scripture forms a merely critical component, but not the definitive issue. The issue of Sifra, the two Sifres, Genesis Rabbah, and Leviticus Rabbah is Scripture, specifically, the rereading of Scripture in the light of the rabbis' established system. All the texts, both those formed around the Mishnah and those ordered in accord with a book of Scripture, find a place within and point toward a larger matrix of values and convictions — the rabbinic system as a whole. Each one testifies in its own way. Sifra and the two Sifres address the Mishnah through Scripture. They explain how the Mishnah relates to Scripture. In Genesis Rabbah and Leviticus Rabbah the issue is not the Mishnah but Scripture itself.

But how do rabbis propose to speak within, about, and

through Scripture, when the Mishnah is *not* a principal issue? And what modes of discourse do they find useful when the exegesis of the Mishnah or the accommodation of the Mishnah to Scripture does not dictate the appropriate redactional and rhetorical forms? Only Genesis Rabbah and Leviticus Rabbah provide evidence of the answers to these questions.

The former, however, stands altogether too close to its predecessors—the Tosefta, Sifra, the two Sifres. How so? Just as they take shape essentially around the phrase-by-phrase exegesis of an established text, so too does Genesis Rabbah. The group that focuses upon the Mishnah adopts a rhetoric of word-for-word or phrase-by-phrase exegesis. The largest arena of discourse then is defined by a complete sentence or two, not a topic or a problem. In this regard, Genesis Rabbah takes only one step away from established conventions. It organizes ideas around a book other than a Mishnah tractate, the book of Genesis. That is stunning and original. But then the framers express their ideas in exactly the same rhetorical pattern—exegesis of words and phrases—that had long predominated in the study and amplification of the Mishnah. There are no large-scale discursive constructions on themes or problems, no evidences of a philosophical reading of Scripture such as Philo or Origen accomplished. It is only when we reach Leviticus Rabbah that we come to an essentially new situation.

A Sample of Leviticus Rabbah

Leviticus Rabbah deals with a biblical book, not a Mishnah tractate. But it approaches that book with a fresh plan, one in which exegesis does not dictate rhetoric, and in which amplification of an established text (whether Scripture or Mishnah) does not supply the underlying logic by which sentences are made to compose paragraphs—completed thoughts. To state matters affirmatively, the framers of Leviticus Rabbah treat topics, not particular verses. They make generalizations which are free-standing. They express cogent propositions through extended compositions, not episodic ideas. Earlier, things people wished to say were attached to predefined statements based on an existing text, constructed in accord with an organizing logic independent of the systematic expression of a single, well-framed idea. Now the authors so collect and arrange their materials that an abstract proposition emerges. That proposition is not expressed only or mainly through episodic restatements, assigned, as I said, to an order established by a base-text, rather it emerges through a logic of its own. In this paper, I claim to uncover that logic which transforms exegesis of a biblical text into a syllogistic, propositional discourse about the vivid issues of Israel's life, that is, that moves from Scripture to Judaism.

Before proceeding, let us consider a complete *parashah* of Leviticus Rabbah, taking account of the traits of its individual units and noting how it develops its large ideas. The translation is my own, based on the critical text and commentary of M. Margulies.[1] My individual comments on each unit of thought of the *parashah* should not obscure our main interest, which is to see how the plan of the framer of the document pursues a theme, rather than verse-by-verse exegesis of individual verses. The theme, moreover, does not impose an order based on the sequence of specific verses of Scripture. So the mode of organizing and laying out comments on Mishnah tractates, familiar in the Talmud of the Land of Israel and of Babylonia, and biblical books, well known in such exercises as Sifra on Leviticus, Sifre on Numbers, Sifre on Deuteronomy, and Genesis Rabbah, is abandoned. A quite different mode is at hand.

Parashah One

I:I

1.   A. The Lord called Moses [and spoke to him from the tent of meeting, saying, Speak to the children of

Israel and say to them, When any man of you brings
an offering to the Lord, you shall bring your offering
of cattle from the herd or from the flock].

B. R. Tanhum bar Hinilai opened [discourse by citing
the following verse:] "Bless the Lord, you his messengers, you mighty in strength, carrying out his word,
obeying his word" (Psalm 103:20).

C. Concerning whom does Scripture speak?

D. If [you maintain that] Scripture speaks about the
upper world's creatures, [that position is unlikely, for]
has not [Scripture in the very same passage already
referred to them, in stating], "Bless the Lord, all his
hosts [his ministers, who do his word]" (Psalm 103:21)?

E. If [you maintain that] Scripture speaks about the
lower world's creatures, [that position too is unlikely,]
for has not [Scripture in the very same passage already
referred to them, in stating], "Bless the Lord, you his
messengers"? (Psalm 103:20). [Accordingly, concerning whom does Scripture speak?]

F. [We shall now see that the passage indeed speaks
of the lower ones.] But, since the upper world's creatures are perfectly able to fulfill the tasks assigned to
them by the Holy One, blessed be he, therefore it is
said, "Bless the Lord, all his hosts." But as to the
creatures of the lower world [here on earth], who cannot fulfill the tasks assigned to them by the Holy One,
blessed be he, [the word all is omitted, when the verse
of Scripture states,] "Bless the Lord, you his messengers" — but not all of his messengers.

2.   A. Another matter: Prophets are called messengers
[creatures of the lower world], in line with the following passage, "And he sent a messenger and he took
us forth from Egypt" (Numbers 20:16).

B. Now was this a [heavenly] messenger [an angel]?
Was it not [merely] Moses [a creature of the lower
world]?

C. Why then does [the verse of Scripture, referring to what Moses did] call him a "messenger"?

D. But: It is on the basis of that usage that [we may conclude] prophets are called "messengers" [in the sense of creatures of the lower world].

E. Along these same lines, "And the messenger of the Lord came up from Gilgal to Bochim" (Judges 2:1). Now was this a [heavenly] messenger [an angel]? Was it not [merely] Phineas?

F. Why then does [the verse of Scripture, referring to Phineas] call him a "messenger"?

G. Said R. Simon, When the holy spirit rested upon Phineas, his face burned like a torch.

H. [There is better proof of the allegation concerning Phineas, deriving from an explicit reference, namely:] rabbis said, What did Manoah's wife say to him [concerning Phineas]? "Lo, a man of God came to me, and his face was like the face of a messenger of God" (Judges 13:6).

I. [Rabbis continue,] She was thinking that he was a prophet, but he was in fact a [heavenly] messenger [so the two looked alike to her].

3.   A. Said R. Yohanan, From the passage that defines their very character, we derive evidence that the prophets are called "messengers," in line with the following passage: "Then said Haggai, the messenger of the Lord, in the Lord's agency, to the people, I am with you, says the Lord" (Haggai 1:13).

B. Accordingly, you must reach the conclusion that on the basis of the passage that defines their very character, we prove that the prophets are called "messengers."

4.   A. [Reverting to the passage cited at the very outset,] "You mighty in strength, carrying out his word [obeying his word]" (Psalm 103:20).

B. Concerning what [sort of mighty man or hero] does Scripture speak?

C. Said R. Isaac, Concerning those who observe the restrictions of the Seventh Year [not planting and sowing their crops in the Sabbatical Year] does Scripture speak.

D. Under ordinary conditions a person does a religious duty for a day, a week, a month. But does one really do so for all of the days of an entire year?

E. Now [in Aramaic:] this man sees his field lying fallow, his vineyard lying fallow, yet he pays his *anona*-tax [a share of the crop] and does not complain.

F. [In Hebrew:] Do you know of a greater hero than that!

G. Now if you maintain that Scripture does not speak about those who observe the Seventh Year, [I shall bring evidence that it does].

H. Here it is stated, "Carrying out his word" (Psalm 103:20) and with reference to the Seventh Year, it is stated, "This is the word concerning the year of release" (Deuteronomy 15:2).

I. Just as the reference to "word" stated at that passage applies to those who observe the Seventh Year, so reference to "word" in the present passage applies to those who observe the Seventh Year.

5.   A. [Continuing discussion of the passage cited at the outset:] "Carrying out his word" (Psalm 103:20):

B. R. Huna in the name of R. Aha: It is concerning the Israelites who stood before Mount Sinai that Scripture speaks, for they first referred to doing [what God would tell them to do], and only afterward referred to hearing [what it might be], accordingly stating "Whatever the Lord has said we shall carry out and we shall hear" (Exodus 24:7).

6.   A. [Continuing the same exercise:] "Obeying his word" (Psalm 103:20):

B. Said R. Tanhum bar Hinilai, Under ordinary circumstances a burden which is too heavy for one person is light for two, or too heavy for two is light for four.

C. But is it possible to suppose that a burden that is too weighty for six hundred thousand can be light for a single individual?

D. Now the entire people of Israel were standing before Mount Sinai and saying, "If we hear the voice of the Lord our God any more, then we shall die" (Deuteronomy 5:22; verse 25 in KJV). But [for his part], Moses heard the voice of God himself and lived.

E. You may find evidence that that is the case, for, among all [the Israelites], the [Act of] Speech [of the Lord] called only to Moses, on which account it is stated, "The Lord called Moses" (Leviticus 1:1).

Leviticus 1:1 intersects with Psalm 103:20 to make the point that Moses was God's messenger *par excellence*, the one who blesses the Lord, is mighty in strength, carries out God's word, obeys God's word. This point is made first implicitly at No. 1 by proving that the verse speaks of earthly, not heavenly, creatures. Then it is made explicit at No. 6. No. 1 and No. 2 present two sets of proofs. The second may stand by itself. It is only the larger context that suggests otherwise. No. 3 is continuous with No. 2. No. 4 and No. 5 refer back to the cited verse, Psalm 103:20, but not to the context of Leviticus 1:1. So we have these units:.

1.A. Psalm 103:20 refers to earthly creatures.

2–3. Prophets are called messengers.

4. Psalm 103:20 refers to a mighty man who observes the Sabbatical Year.

5. Psalm 103:20 refers to the Israelites before Mount Sinai.

6. Psalm 103:20 refers to Moses.

If then we ask what is primary to the redaction resting on Leviticus 1:1, it can only be Nos. 1 and 6. But since No.

1 does not refer to Moses at all, but only sets up the point made at No. 6, No. 6 does not require No. 1. It makes its point without No. 1's contribution. Furthermore, No. 1, for its part, is comprehensible by itself as a comment on Psalm 103:20, and hardly requires linkage to Leviticus 1:1. If, therefore, I may offer a thesis on the history of the passage, it would begin with Leviticus 1:1 + No. 6. Reference to Psalm 103:20 then carried in its wake Nos. 1, 2, 3, 4, and 5—all of them to begin with autonomous sayings formed into a kind of handbook on Psalm 103:20. So first came the intersection of Leviticus 1:1 and Psalm 103:20 presented by No. 6, and everything else followed in the process of accretion and aggregation, mostly of passages in Psalm 103:20.

I:II

1.   A. R. Abbahu opened [discourse by citing the following verse]: "They shall return and dwell beneath his shadow, they shall grow grain, they shall blossom as a vine, their fragrance shall be like the wine of Lebanon" (Hosea 14:7).

B. "They shall return and dwell beneath his shadow"—these are proselytes who come and take refuge in the shadow of the Holy One, blessed be he.

C. "They shall grow grain"—they are turned into [part of] the root, just as [any other] Israelite.

D. That is in line with the following verse: "Grain will make the young men flourish, and wine the women" (Zechariah 9:17).

E. "They shall blossom as a vine"—like [any other] Israelite.

F. That is in line with the following verse: "A vine did you pluck up out of Egypt, you did drive out the nations and plant it" (Psalm 80:9; verse 8 in KJV).

2.   A. Another item [= Genesis Rabbah 66:3]: "They shall grow grain"—in Talmud.

B. "They shall blossom as a vine" — in lore.

3.   A. "Their fragrance shall be like the wine of Lebanon [and Lebanon signifies the altar]" —

B. Said the Holy One, blessed be he, The names of proselytes are as dear to me as the wine-offering that is poured out on the altar before me.

4.   A. And why [is that mountain called "Lebanon"]?

B. In line with [the following verse]: "That goodly mountain and the Lebanon" (Deuteronomy 3:25).

C. R. Simeon b. Yohai taught [= Sifre Deuteronomy 6:28], Why is it called Lebanon (LBNN)? Because it whitens (MLBYN) the sins of Israel like snow.

D. That is in line with the following verse: "If your sins are red as scarlet, they shall be made white (LBN) as snow" (Isaiah 1:18).

E. R. Tabyomi said, It is [called Lebanon (LBNN)] because all hearts (LBB) rejoice in it.

F. That is in line with the following verse of Scripture: "Fair in situation, the joy of the whole world, even Mount Zion, at the far north" (Psalm 48:3; verse 2 in KJV).

G. And rabbis say, It is [called Lebanon] because of the following verse: "And my eyes and heart (LB) shall be there all the days" (1 Kings 9:3).

So far as we have a sustained discourse, we find it at Nos. 1 and 3. No. 2 is inserted whole because of its interest in the key verse, Hosea 14:7. Reference at that verse to "Lebanon" explains the set-piece treatment of the word at No. 4. These units may travel together, but the present location seems an unlikely destination. But someone clearly drew together this anthology of materials on, first, Hosea 14:7, and, by the way, second, the word Lebanon. Why the two sets were assembled is much clearer than how they seemed to the compositor of the collection as a whole to belong to the exposition of Leviticus 1:1. Margulies' thesis that the theme of the righteous proselyte

intersects with the personal biography of Moses through
Pharaoh's daughter (a proselyte) on the surface seems far-
fetched. So, in all, the construction of the passage surely
is prior to any consideration of its relevance to Leviticus
1:1, and the point of the construction certainly is the exegesis of Hosea 14:7 — that alone. Whether the materials
shared with other collections — Nos. 2, 5 — fit more com-
fortably in those compositions than they do here is not a
pressing issue, since, as is self-evident, there is no link to
Leviticus 1:1 in any event.

I:III

1.   A. R. Simon in the name of R. Joshua b. Levi, and
R. Hama, father of R. Hoshaiah, in the name of Rab:
The Book of Chronicles was revealed only for the
purposes of exegetical exposition.

2.   A. "And his wife Hajehudijah bore Jered, the father
of Gedor, and Heber, the father of Soco, and Jekuthiel
the father of Zanoah — and these are the sons of Bithiah, the daughter of Pharaoh, whom Mered took" (1
Chronicles 4:17).

B. "And his wife, Hajehudijah [= the Judah-ite]" —
that is Jochebed.

C. Now was she from the tribe of Judah, and not
from the tribe of Levi? Why then was she called Hajehudijah [the Judah-ite]?

D. Because she kept Jews (Jehudim) alive in the
world [as one of the midwives who kept the Jews
alive when Pharaoh said to drown them].

3.   A. "She bore Jered" — that is Moses.

B. R. Hanana bar Pappa and R. Simon:

C. R. Hanana said, He was called Jered (YRD) because he brought the Torah down (HWRYD) from on
high to earth.

D. Another possibility: "Jered" — for he brought
down the Presence of God from above to earth.

E. Said R. Simon, The name Jered connotes only royalty, in line with the following verse: "May he have dominion (YRD) from sea to sea, and from the river to the end of the earth" (Psalm 72:8).

F. And it is written, "For he rules (RWDH) over the entire region on this side of the river" (1 Kings 5:4; 1 Kings 4:24 in KJV).

4.   A. "Father of Gedor" —

B. R. Huna in the name of R. Aha said, Many fence-makers (GWDRYM) stood up for Israel, but this one [Moses] was the father of all of them.

5.   A. "And Heber" —

B. For he joined (HBR) Israel to their father in heaven.

C. Another possibility: "Heber" — for he turned away (HBYR) punishment from coming upon the world.

6.   A. "The father of Soco" —

B. This one was the father of all the prophets, who perceive (SWKYN) by means of the Holy Spirit.

C. R. Levi said, It is an Arabic word. In Arabic they call a prophet "sakya."

7.   A. "Jekuthiel" (YQWTY'L) —

B. R. Levi and R. Simon:

C. R. Levi said, For he made the children hope (MQWYN) in their Father in heaven.

D. Said R. Simon, When the children sinned against God in the incident of the Golden Calf . . .

E. "The father of Zanoah" —

F. Moses came along and forced them to give up (HZNYHN) that transgression.

G. That is in line with the following verse of Scripture: "[And he took the calf which they had made and burned it with fire and ground it to powder] and strewed it upon the water" (Exodus 32:20).

8.   A. "And these are the sons of Bithiah (BTYH), the daughter of Pharaoh" —

B. R. Joshua of Sikhnin in the name of R. Levi: The Holy One, blessed be he, said to Bithiah, the daughter of Pharaoh, Moses was not your child, but you called him your child. So you are not my daughter, but I shall call you my daughter [thus BTYH, daughter of the Lord].

9.   A. "These are the sons of Bithiah . . . whom Mered took" —

B. [Mered] is Caleb.

C. R. Abba bar Kahana and R. Judah bar Simon:

D. R. Abba bar Kahana said, This one [Caleb] rebelled [MRD] against the counsel of the spies, and that one rebelled [MRDH] against the counsel of her father [Pharaoh, as to murdering the babies]. Let a rebel come and take as wife another rebellious spirit.

E. [Explaining the link of Caleb to Pharaoh's daughter in a different way], R. Judah b. R. Simon said, This one [Caleb] saved the flock, while that one [Pharaoh's daughter] saved the shepherd [Moses]. Let the one who saved the flock come and take as wife the one who saved the shepherd.

10.   A. Moses [thus] had ten names [at 1 Chronicles 4:17]: Jered, Father of Gedor, Heber, Father of Soco, Jekuthiel, and Father of Zanoah [with the other four enumerated in what follows].

B. R. Judah bar Ilai said, He also was called [7] Tobiah, in line with the following verse: "And she saw him, that he was good (TWB)" (Exodus 2:2). He is Tobiah.

C. R. Ishmael bar Ami said, "He also was called [8] Shemaiah."

11.   A. R. Joshua bar Nehemiah came and explained the following verse: "And Shemaiah, the son of Nethanel the scribe, who was of the Levites, wrote them

in the presence of the king and the princes and Zadok the priest and Ahimelech the son of Abiathar" (1 Chronicles 24:6).

B. [Moses was called] Shemaiah because God heard (ŠMᶜ YH) his prayer.

C. [Moses was called] the son of Nethanel because he was the son to whom the Torah was given from hand to hand (NTN 'L).

D. "The scribe," because he was the scribe of Israel.

E. "Who was of the Levites," because he was of the tribe of Levi.

F. "Before the king and the princes" — this refers to the King of kings the Holy One, blessed be he, and his court.

G. "And Zadok the priest" — this refers to Aaron the priest.

H. "Ahimeleh" — because [Aaron] was brother (Ḥ) of the king.

I. "The son of Abiathar" ('BYTR) — the son through whom the Holy One, blessed be he, forgave (WYTR) the deed of the Golden Calf.

12. A. R. Tanhuma in the name of R. Joshua b. Qorhah, and R. Menehemiah in the name of R. Joshua b. Levi: He also was called [9] Levi after his eponymous ancestor: "And is not Aaron, your brother, the Levite" (Exodus 4:14).

B. And [he of course was called] [10] Moses — hence [you have] ten names.

C. Said the Holy One, blessed be he, to Moses, By your life: Among all the names by which you are called, the only one by which I shall ever refer to you is the one which Bithiah, the daughter of Pharaoh, gave to you: "And she called his name Moses" (Exodus 2:10), so God called Moses.

D. So: "He called Moses" (Leviticus 1:1).

Now we see some slight basis for Margulies' view of

the relevance of I:II, that the daughter of Pharaoh was named Moses, and she was a proselyte. But the passage at hand stands fully by itself, leading to the climax at the very end, at which the opening words of the opening verse of the book of Leviticus are cited. The point of the entire, vast construction is the inquiry into the various names of Moses. From that standpoint we have a strikingly tight composition. But still, the unit *is* a composite, since it draws together autonomous and diverse materials. The first passage, No. 1, is surely independent, yet it makes for a fine superscription to the whole. Then the pertinent verse, at No. 2.A, 1 Chronicles 4:17, is cited and systematically spelled out in Nos. 2, 3, 4, 5, 6, 7, 8, 9. Not only so, but at No. 10, we review the matter and amplify it with an additional, but completely appropriate, set of further names of Moses, Nos. 10 + 12, to be viewed, in line with No. 12, as a unified construction. No. 11 is inserted and breaks the thought. Then 12.C tells us the point of it all, and that brings us back to Leviticus 1:1, on the one side, and to No. 8. But, as we have seen, we cannot refer to No. 8 without drawing along the whole set, Nos. 2-9. So the entire passage forms a single, sustained discussion, in which diverse materials are determinedly drawn together into a cogent statement. We notice that No. 7 presents a text problem, since Levi's statement is not matched by Simon's. Levi speaks of Jekuthiel and Simon of "the father of Zanoah." But the only problem is at 7.B. If we omit that misleading superscription—which served perfectly well at 3.B + C-F—and have 7.D and E change places, we get a perfectly fine autonomous statement.

I:IV

1.   A. R. Abin in the name of R. Berekhiah the Elder opened [discourse by citing the following verse]: "Of old you spoke in a vision to your faithful one, saying, I have set the crown upon one who is mighty, I have

exalted one chosen from the people" (Psalm 89:20; verse 19 in KJV).

B. [The Psalmist] speaks of Abraham, with whom [God] spoke both in word and in vision.

C. That is in line with the following verse of Scripture: "After these words the word of God came to Abram in a vision, saying . . . " (Genesis 15:1).

D. "To your faithful one" — "You will show truth to Jacob, faithfulness to Abraham" (Micah 7:20).

E. "Saying, I have set the crown upon one who is mighty" — for [Abraham] slew four kings in a single night.

F. That is in line with the following verse of Scripture: "And he divided himself against them by night . . . and smote them" (Genesis 14:15).

2. A. Said R. Phineas, And is there a case of someone who pursues people already slain?

B. For it is written, "He smote them and he [then] pursued them" (Genesis 14:15):

C. But [the usage at hand] teaches that the Holy One, blessed be he, did the pursuing, and Abraham did the slaying.

3. A. [Abin continues,] "I have exalted one chosen from the people" (Psalm 89:20).

B. "It is you, Lord, God, who chose Abram and took him out of Ur in Chaldea" (Nehemiah 9:7).

4. A. ["I have exalted one chosen from the people" (Psalm 89:20)] speaks of David, with whom God spoke both in speech and in vision.

B. That is in line with the following verse of Scripture: "In accord with all these words and in accord with this entire vision, so did Nathan speak to David" (2 Samuel 7:17).

C. "To your faithful one" (Psalm 89:20) [refers] to David, [in line with the following verse:] "Keep my soul, for I am faithful" (Psalm 86:2).

D. "Saying, I have set the crown upon one who is mighty" (Psalm 89:20) —

E. R. Abba bar Kahana and rabbis:

F. R. Abba bar Kahana said, David made thirteen wars.

G. And rabbis say, Eighteen.

H. But they do not really differ. The party who said thirteen wars [refers only to those that were fought] in behalf of the need of Israel [overall], while the one who held that [he fought] eighteen includes five [more, that David fought] for his own need, along with the thirteen [that he fought] for the need of Israel [at large].

I. "I have exalted one chosen from the people" (Psalm 89:20) — "And he chose David, his servant, and he took him . . . " (Psalm 78:70).

5.   A. ["Of old you spoke in a vision to your faithful one"] speaks of Moses, with whom [God] spoke in both speech and vision, in line with the following verse of Scripture: "With him do I speak mouth to mouth [in a vision and not in dark speeches]" (Numbers 12:8).

B. "To your faithful one" — for [Moses] came from the tribe of Levi, the one concerning which it is written, "Let your Thummim and Urim be with your faithful one" (Deuteronomy 33:8).

C. "Saying, I have set the crown upon one who is mighty" —

D. The cited passage is to be read in accord with that which R. Tanhum b. Hanilai said, Under ordinary circumstances a burden which is too heavy for one person is light for two, or too heavy for two is light for four. But is it possible to suppose that a burden that is too weighty for six hundred thousand can be light for a single individual? Now the entire people of Israel were standing before Mount Sinai and saying, "If we hear the voice of the Lord our God any more, then we shall die" (Deuteronomy 5:22; verse 25 in KJV).

But, for his part, Moses heard the voice of God himself and lived [= I:I.6.B-D].

E. You may know that that is indeed the case, for among them all, the act of speech [of the Lord] called only to Moses, in line with that verse which states, "And [God] called to Moses" (Leviticus 1:1).

F. "I have exalted one chosen from the people" (Psalm 89:20) — "Had not Moses, whom he chose, stood in the breach before him to turn his wrath from destroying them [he would have destroyed Israel]" (Psalm 106:23).

The whole constitutes a single, beautifully worked out composition, applying Psalm 89:20 to Abraham, David, then Moses, at Nos. 1, 3 (Abraham), 4 (David), and 5 (Moses). No. 2 is a minor interpolation, hardly spoiling the total effect. No. 5.D is jarring and obviously inserted needlessly. That the purpose of the entire construction was to lead to the climactic citation of Leviticus 1:1 hardly can be doubted, since the natural chronological (and eschatological) order would have dictated Abraham, Moses, David. That the basic construction, moreover, forms a unity is shown by the careful matching of the stichs of the cited verse in the expositions of how the verse applies to the three heroes. If we had to postulate an "ideal form," it would be simply the juxtaposition of verses, A illustrated by X, B by Y, etc., with little or no extraneous language. But where, in the basic constituents of the construction, we do find explanatory language or secondary development, in the main it is necessary for sense. Accordingly, we see as perfect a construction as we are likely to find: whole, nearly entirely essential, with a minimum of intruded material. To be sure, what really looks to be essential is the notion of God's communicating by two media to the three great heroes. That is the clear point of the most closely corresponding passages of the whole. In that case, the reorganization and vast amplification come as an afterthought, provoked by the construction of a passage serving Leviticus 1:1. Since 5.E contradicts the message of the rest, that must be regarded as a certainty. Then the whole, except 5.E (hence, 5.D, too), served Psalm 89:20, and 5.F is the original conclusion, with 5.D-E inserted by the redactor.

I:V

1.   A. R. Joshua of Sikhnin in the name of R. Levi opened [discourse by citing the following] verse: "For it is better to be told, Come up here, than to be put lower in the presence of the prince" (Proverb 25:7).

B. R. Aqiba repeated [the following tradition] in the name of R. Simeon b. Azzai, Take a place two or three lower and sit down, so that people may tell you, Come up, but do not go up [beyond your station] lest people say to you, Go down. It is better for people to say to you, Come up, come up, than that they say to you, Go down, go down.

C. And so did Hillel say, When I am degraded, I am exalted, but when I am exalted, I am degraded.

D. What is the pertinent biblical verse? "He who raises himself is to be made to sit down, he who lowers himself is to be [raised so that he is] seen" (Psalm 113:5-6).

E. So too you find that, when the Holy One, blessed be he, revealed himself to Moses from the midst of the bush, Moses hid his face from him.

F. That is in line with the following verse of Scripture: "Moses hid his face" (Exodus 3:6).

2.   A. Said to him the Holy One, blessed be he, "And now, go (LKH), I am sending you to Pharaoh" (Exodus 3:10).

B. Said R. Eleazar, [Taking the word "Go," (LK), not as the imperative, but to mean, "to you," and spelled LKH, with an H at the end, I may observe that]

it would have been sufficient to write, "You (LK),"
[without adding] an H at the end of the word. [Why
then did Scripture add the H?] To indicate to you, "If
you are not the one who will redeem them, no one
else is going to redeem them."

C. At the Red Sea, Moses stood aside. Said to him
the Holy One, blessed be he, "Now you, raise your
rod and stretch out your hand [over the sea and divide
it]" (Exodus 14:16).

D. This is to say, If you do not split the sea, no one
else is going to split it.

E. At Sinai Moses stood aside. Said to him the Holy
One, blessed be he, "Come up to the Lord, you and
Aaron" (Exodus 24:1).

F. This is to say, If you do not come up, no one else
is going to come up.

G. At the [revelation of the instructions governing
sacrifices at] the tent of meeting, [Moses] stood to the
side. Said to him the Holy One, blessed be he, How
long are you going to humble yourself? For the times
demand only you.

H. You must recognize that that is the case, for
among them all, the speech of God called only to
Moses, as it is written, "And [God] called to Moses"
(Leviticus 1:1).

We have once more to work backward from the end
to find out what, at the outset, is necessary to make the
point of the unit as a whole. It obviously is the emphasis
upon how the humble man is called to take exalted position
and leadership, that is, No. 2. Then what components of
No. 1 are thematically irrelevant? None, so far as I can see.
We may regard 1.A as standing by itself, a suitable introduction to a statement on the theme at hand, namely, it
is better to be called upon, as at Leviticus 1:1. Then Nos.
1.B, C-D, E-F illustrate the same theme, leading to the
introduction of the figure of Moses. E-F are so formulated

("so too you find") as to continue the foregoing, but, of course, they form a bridge to what follows, No. 2. Accordingly, a rather deft editorial hand has drawn together thematically pertinent materials. I find it difficult to imagine that the composition was not worked out essentially within a unitary framework, with the exegetical program of the whole, expressed at No. 2, fully in hand before the anthology of No. 1 was gathered. But the fact is that Nos. 1.B, C-D, do come from already framed materials.

I:VI

1.   A. R. Tanhuma opened [discourse by citing the following verse:] "There are gold and a multitude of rubies, but lips [that speak] knowledge are the [most] valuable ornament" (Proverb 20:15).

B. Under ordinary circumstances [if] a person has gold, silver, precious stones, pearls, and all sorts of luxuries, but has no knowledge—what profit does he have?

C. In a proverb it says, If you have gotten knowledge, what do you lack? But if you lack knowledge, what have you gotten?

2.   A. "There is gold"—all brought their free-will offering of gold to the tabernacle.

B. That is in line with the following verse of Scripture: "And this is the offering [which you shall take from them, gold] . . . " (Exodus 25:3).

C. "And a multitude of rubies"—this refers to the free-will offering of the princes.

D. That is in line with the following verse of Scripture: "And the rulers brought [onyx stones and the stones to be set]" (Exodus 35:27).

E. "But lips [that speak] knowledge are the [most] valuable ornament" (Proverb 20:15).

F. Now Moses was sad, for he said, Everyone has

brought his free-will offering for the tabernacle, but I have not brought a thing:

G. Said to him the Holy One, blessed be he, By your life: Your words [of address to the workers in teaching them how to build the tabernacle] are more precious to me than all of these other things.

H. You may find proof for that proposition, for among all of them, the Word [of God] called only to Moses, as it is written, "And [God] called to Moses" (Leviticus 1:1).

Once more we see a complete construction, with a seemingly irrelevant introduction, No. 1, serving to cite a verse in no way evoked by the passage at hand. The exposition of the verse, further, does not appear to bring us closer to the present matter. But at No. 2, both the cited verse and the exposition of the verse are joined to the verse before us. If we may venture a guess at the aesthetic *jeu d'esprit* involved, it is this: how do we move from what appears to be utterly irrelevant to what is in fact the very heart of the matter? The aesthetic accomplishment is then to keep the hearer or reader in suspense until the climax, at which the issue is worked out, the tension resolved. It must follow, of course, that we deal with unitary composition.

I:VII

1.   A. What subject matter is discussed just prior to the passage at hand? It is the passage that deals with the building of the tabernacle [in which each pericope concludes with the words], "As the Lord commanded Moses" (cf. Exodus 38:22; 39:1, 5, 7, 21, 26, 29, 31, 32, 42, 43; 40:16, 19, 21, 23, 25, 27, 29, 32).

B. To what may this matter be compared? To a king who commanded his servant, saying to him, Build a palace for me.

C. On everything that [the employee] built, he wrote

the name of the king. When he built the walls, he inscribed the name of the king, when he set up the buttresses, he wrote the name of the king on them, when he roofed it over, he wrote the name of the king on [the roof]. After some days, the king came into the palace, and everywhere he looked, he saw his name inscribed. He said, Now my employee has paid me so much respect, and yet I am inside [the building he built], while he is outside: He called him to enter.

D. So when the Holy One, blessed be he, called to Moses, Make a tabernacle for me, on [every] thing that Moses made, he inscribed, ". . . as the Lord commanded Moses."

E. Said the Holy One, blessed be he, Now Moses has paid me so much respect, and yet I am inside, while he is outside.

F. He called him to come in, on which account it is said, "And [God] called Moses" (Leviticus 1:1).

The passage begins with the imputation to the verb QR' of the sense of invitation. The focus of exegesis shifts from Moses to God's calling him. The exegetical resource is the repeated reference, as indicated, to Moses' doing as God had commanded him. But this is now read as Moses' inscribing God's name everywhere on the tabernacle as he built it, and the rest follows.

I:VIII

1.   A. R. Samuel bar Nahman said in the name of R. Nathan, Eighteen times are statements of [God's] commanding written in the passage on the building of the tabernacle, corresponding to the eighteen vertebrae in the backbone.

B. Correspondingly, sages instituted eighteen statements of blessing in the Blessings of the Prayer, eighteen mentions of the divine name in the recitation of the Shemaᶜ, eighteen mentions of the divine name in the Psalm, "Ascribe to the Lord, you sons of might" (Psalm 29:1).

C. Said R. Hiyya bar Ada, [The counting of the eighteen statements of God's commandment to Moses] excludes [from the count the entry prior to the one in the verse], "And with him was Oholiab, son of Ahisamach of the tribe of Dan" (Exodus 38:23), [thus omitting reference to Exodus 38:23; verse 22 in KJV: "And Bezalel, son or Uri son of Hur of the tribe of Judah, made all that the Lord commanded Moses"]. But the counting then includes all further such references to the end of the book [of Exodus].

2.   A. To what is the matter comparable? To a king who made a tour of a province, bringing with him generals, governors, and lesser officers, and [in watching the procession], we do not know which one among them is most favored. But [when we see] to whom the king turns and speaks, we know that he is the favorite.

B. So everyone surrounded the tabernacle, Moses, Aaron, Nadab, and Abihu, and the seventy elders, so we do not know which one of them is the favorite. But now, since the Holy One, blessed be he, called to Moses and spoke to him, we know that he was the favorite of them all.

C. On that account it is said, "And [God] called Moses" (Leviticus 1:1).

3.   A. To what may the matter be compared? To a king who made a tour of a province. With whom will he speak first? Is it not with the market-inspector, who oversees the province? Why? Because he bears responsibility for the very life of the province.

B. So Moses bears responsibility for Israel's every burden,

C. Saying to them, "This you may eat" (Leviticus 11:2), "and this you may not eat" (Leviticus 11:4), "This you may eat of whatever is in the water" (Leviticus

11:9), and this you may not eat, "This you shall treat as an abomination among fowl" (Leviticus 11:13), and so these you shall treat as an abomination, and others you need *not* abominate, "And these are the things that are unclean for you" (Leviticus 11:29), so these are unclean, and those are *not* unclean.

D. Therefore it is said, "And [God] called Moses" (Leviticus 1:1).

No. 1 bears no relationship to what follows. It continues I:VII, with its interest in the repetitions of the statement about Moses' having done as God had commanded him. However, 1.A-B stands completely outside the present frame of reference, Leviticus 1:1. 1.C harmonizes the number of times the cited phrase actually occurs with the number of vertebrae in the backbone. No. 1 further occurs at TB *Berakhot* 28b, TY *Berakhot* 4:3, so we may be certain the passage was tacked on because of the interest in the verse at the center of the preceding item.

No. 2 and No. 3 match one another, making essentially the same point and leading up to the citation of the verse by establishing the same connotation, "called" in the sense of "recognized, gave preference to." 3.C is wildly out of place, since, as it is now composed, the emphasis is on the fact that, if Scripture says you may *not* eat a certain thing, whatever is not covered in the negative statement then *may* be eaten. That is why the language of the verse is repeated, ". . . not this . . . but then that is permitted." In fact, we should move from 3.A-B to D. The passage as a whole then is a composite of three distinct items.

I:IX

1.   A. "And [the Lord] called to Moses" (Leviticus 1:1) [bearing the implication, to Moses in particular].

B. Now did he not call Adam? [But surely he did:] "And the Lord God called Adam" (Genesis 3:9).

C. [He may have called him, but he did not speak

with him, while at Leviticus 1:1, the Lord "called Moses and spoke to him"], for is it not undignified for a king to speak with his tenant-farmer [which Adam, in the Garden of Eden, was]?

D. ". . . and the Lord spoke to him" (Leviticus 1:1) [to him in particular].

E. Did he not speak also with Noah? [But surely he did:] "And God spoke to Noah" (Genesis 8:15).

F. [He may have spoken to him, but he did not call him,] for is it not undignified for a king to speak with [better: *call*] his ship's captain [herding the beasts into the ark]?

G. "And [the Lord] called to Moses" (Leviticus 1:1) [in particular].

H. Now did he not call Abraham? [But surely he did:] "And the angel of the Lord called Abraham a second time from heaven" (Genesis 22:15).

I. [He may have called him, but he did not speak with him,] for is it not undignified for a king to speak with his host (Genesis 18:1)?

J. "And the Lord spoke with him" (Leviticus 1:1) [in particular].

K. And did he not speak with Abraham? [Surely he did:] "And Abram fell on his face, and [God] spoke with him" (Genesis 17:3).

L. But is it not undignified for a king to speak with his host?

2.   A. "And the Lord called Moses" (Leviticus 1:1), but not as in the case of Abraham.

B. [How so?] In the case of Abraham, it is written, "And an angel of the Lord called Abraham a second time from heaven" (Genesis 22:15). The angel did the calling, the Word [of God] then did the speaking.

C. Here [by contrast], said R. Abin, the Holy One, blessed be he, said I am the one who does the calling, and I am the one who does the speaking.

D. "I, even I, have spoken, yes, I have called him,
I have brought him and he shall prosper in his way"
(Isaiah 48:15).

The point of No. 1 is clear, but the text is not. What is
demanded is three instances in which God called someone
but did not speak with him, or spoke with him but did
not call him, in contrast with the use of both verbs, "call"
and "speak," in regard to Moses at Leviticus 1:1. If that is
what is intended, then the pattern does not work perfectly
for all three: Adam, Noah, and Abraham. 1.A-D and E-G
are smooth. With Abraham, however, the exposition
breaks down, since the point should be that he called Abraham but did not actually speak with him, and it is only
No. 2 that makes *that* point. The repetition of I at L therefore
is only part of the problem of the version. We can readily
reconstruct what is needed, of course, in the model of the
passages for Adam and Noah.

No. 2 of course is independent of No. 1, and hand-
somely worked out. But No. 2 cannot have served the form
selected by the framer of the triplet at No. 1.

My guess is that No. 1 fails as it does because of yet
another problem. F does have God *speaking* with Noah,
while G says that that is undignified, and the same problem
recurs with Abraham. In all, No. 2 is a success, and No.
1 is not. Here it is difficult to claim that someone delib-
erately worked up the entire unit, leading to the climax at
the very end. Two existing sets have been combined, and
the first of the two turns out to be flawed.

I:X

1.   A. "[And the Lord called Moses and spoke to him]
from the tent of meeting" (Leviticus 1:1).

      B. Said R. Eleazar, Even though the Torah [earlier]
had been given to Israel at Sinai as a fence [restricting
their actions], they were liable to punishment on ac-

count of [violating] it only after it has been repeated for [taught to] them in the tent of meeting.

C. This may be compared to a royal decree, which had been written and sealed and brought to the province. The inhabitants of the province became liable to be punished on account of violating the decree only after it had been spelled out for them in a public meeting in the province.

D. Along these same lines, even though the Torah had been given to Israel at Sinai, they bore liability for punishment on account of violating it[s commandments] only after it had been repeated for them in the tent of meeting.

E. That is in line with the following verse of Scripture: "Until I had brought him into my mother's house and into the chamber of my teaching [lit.: parent]" (Song of Songs 3:4).

F. ". . . into my mother's house" refers to Sinai.

G. ". . . and into the chamber of my teaching" refers to the tent of meeting, from which the Israelites were commanded through instruction [in the Torah].

The passage is formally perfect, running from the beginning, a general proposition, 1.B, through a parable, C, explicitly linked to the original proposition, D, and then joined to the exposition of a seemingly unrelated verse of Scripture, which turns out to say exactly what the general proposition has said. So the original statement, B, is worked out in two separate and complementary ways, first, parabolic, second, exegetical.

I cannot see any problem but one: what has the stated proposition to do with the present context? In fact, the theme is the tent of meeting, that alone. We may expect an anthology of materials on the tent of meeting, none of which bears any distinctive relationship to what happens there, so far as the verses following Leviticus 1:1 will tell us. In other words, the redaction of materials following the order of verses of Scripture in the present instance imposes no thesis upon what will be said *about* those materials, what is important *in* them. Rather we have nothing more than a list of topics, each to be treated through the formation of an anthology of materials relevant to a topic, not through the unpacking of a problem indicated by the substance and the context at hand.

I:XI

1. A. Said R. Joshua b. Levi, If the nations of the world had known how valuable the tent of meeting was to them, they would have sheltered it with tents and balustrades.

    B. [How so?] You note that before the tabernacle was erected, the nations of the world could hear the noise of [God's] speech and [fearing an earthquake(?)] they would rush out of their dwellings.

    C. That is in line with the following verse of Scripture: "For who is there of all flesh, who has heard the voice of the living God [speaking out of the midst of the first as we have, and lived]?" (Deuteronomy 5:23).

2. A. Said R. Simon, The word [of God] went forth in two modes, for Israel as life, for the nations of the world as poison.

    B. That is in line with the following verse of Scripture: "as you have, and lived" (Deuteronomy 4:33).

    C. You hear [the voice of God] and live, while the nations of the world hear and die.

    D. That is in line with what R. Hiyya taught [= Sifra Dibura dinedabah 2:10], "from the tent of meeting" (Leviticus 1:1) teaches that the sound was cut off and did not go beyond the tent of meeting.

Nos. 1 and 2 go over the same ground but are unrelated. For the sense of 1.B, I follow Margulies. But then the relevance of the verse cited at 1.C is not clear. I should have thought that the nations of the world would benefit from the possibility of hearing God's speech, which would then have warned them about an impending earthquake, for example, getting them out of their houses in time. But 1.C and No. 2 make the point that the tent of meeting *prevented* the gentiles from hearing God's voice, and this was good for them, since the Torah was life for Israel and death for the gentiles. Accordingly, the sense of 1.B as Margulies reads it seems incongruous to the meaning required by its context. Israelstam[2] gives: "rushed in fright out of their camps." I cannot suggest anything better. As noted above, the larger context of Leviticus 1:1 makes no impact upon the exegesis of the passage, which is focused upon the theme, the tent of meeting, and not on the meaning of the place or tent in this setting.

I:XII

1.   A. Said R. Isaac, Before the tent of meeting was set up, prophecy was common among the nations of the world. Once the tent of meeting was set up, prophecy disappeared from among them. That is in line with the following verse of Scripture: "I held it [the Holy Spirit, producing], and would not let it go [until I had brought it . . . into the chamber of her that conceived me]" (Song of Songs 3:4).

B. They said to him, Lo, Balaam [later on] practiced prophecy:

C. He said to them, He did so for the good of Israel: "Who has counted the dust of Jacob" (Numbers 23:10). "No one has seen iniquity in Jacob" (Numbers 23:21). "For there is no enchantment with Jacob" (Numbers 23:23). "How goodly are your tents, O Jacob" (Numbers 24:5). "There shall go forth a star out of Jacob" (Numbers 24:17). "And out of Jacob shall one have dominion" (Numbers 24:19).

"The chamber" of 1.A is the tent of meeting, as before. In fact the passage at hand is continuous with the fore-

going. As we shall see, the established theme then moves
forward in what follows. The construction is of course
unitary. "They said to him" of B simply sets up discourse;
it is not meant to signify an actual conversation, rather
serves as a convention of rhetoric. B then allows C to string
out the relevant verses. We now continue the same matter
of Balaam, prophet of the gentiles, and Israel.

I:XIII
1.   A. What is the difference between the prophets of
Israel and those of the nations [= Genesis Rabbah 52:5]?

B. R. Hama b. R. Hanina and R. Issachar of Kepar
Mandi:

C. R. Hama b. R. Hanina said, The Holy One,
blessed be he, is revealed to the prophets of the nations
of the world only in partial speech, in line with the
following verse of Scripture: "And God called [WYQR,
rather than WYQR', as at Leviticus 1:1] Balaam" (Numbers 23:16). On the other hand, [he reveals himself] to
the prophets of Israel in full and complete speech, as
it is said, "And [the Lord] called (WYQR') to Moses"
(Leviticus 1:1).

D. Said R. Issachar of Kepar Mandi, Should that
[prophecy, even in partial form] be [paid to them as
their] wage? [Surely not, in fact there is no form of
speech to gentile prophets, who are frauds]. [The connotation of] the language, "And [God] called (WYQR)
to Balaam" (Numbers 23:16) is solely uncleanness. That
is in line with the usage in the following verse of Scripture: "That is not clean, by that which happens
(MQRH) by night" (Deuteronomy 23:11). [So the root
is the same, with the result that YQR at Numbers 23:16
does not bear the meaning of God's calling to Balaam.
God rather declares Balaam unclean.]

E. But the prophets of Israel [are addressed] in language of holiness, purity, clarity, in language used by

the ministering angels to praise God. That is in line with the following verse of Scripture: "And they called (QR') one to another and said" (Isaiah 6:3).

2.   A. Said R. Eleazar b. Menahem, It is written, "The Lord is far from the wicked, but the prayer of the righteous does he hear" (Proverb 15:29).

B. "The Lord is far from the wicked" refers to the prophets of the nations of the world.

C. "But the prayer of the righteous does he hear" refers to the prophets of Israel.

D. You [furthermore] find that the Holy One, blessed be he, appears to the prophets of the nations of the world only like a man who comes from some distant place.

E. That is in line with the following verse of Scripture: "From a distant land they have come to me, from Babylonia" (Isaiah 39:3).

F. But in the case of the prophets of Israel [he is always] near at hand: "And he [forthwith] appeared [not having come from a great distance]" (Genesis 18:1), "and [the Lord] called" (Leviticus 1:1).

3.   A. Said R. Yose b. Biba, The Holy One, blessed be he, is revealed to the prophets of the nations of the world only by night, when people leave one another: "When men branch off, from the visions of the night, when deep sleep falls on men" (Job 4:13), "Then a word came secretly to me" (Job 4:12). [Job is counted among the prophets of the gentiles.]

4.   A. R. Hanana b. R. Pappa and rabbis [= Genesis Rabbah 74:7]:

B. R. Hanana b. R. Pappa said, The matter may be compared to a king who, with his friend, was in a hall, with a curtain hanging down between them. When [the king] speaks to his friend, he turns back the curtain and speaks with his friend.

C. And rabbis say, [The matter may be compared]

to a king who had a wife and a concubine. When he walks about with his wife, he does so in full public view. When he walks about with his concubine, he does so discreetly. So, too, the Holy One, blessed be he, is revealed to the prophets of the nations of the world only at night, in line with that which is written: "And God came to Abimelech in a dream by night" (Genesis 20:3). "And God came to Laban, the Aramean, in a dream by night" (Genesis 31:24). "And God came to Balaam at night" (Numbers 22:20).

D. To the prophets of Israel, however, [he comes] by day: "[And the Lord appeared to Abraham . . .] as he sat at the door of his tent in the heat of the day" (Genesis 18:1). "And it came to pass by day that the Lord spoke to Moses in the land of Egypt" (Exodus 6:28). "On the day on which he commanded the children of Israel" (Leviticus 7:38). "These are the generations of Aaron and Moses. God spoke to Moses by day on Mount Sinai" (Numbers 3:1).

Once the topic of comparing Israel's receiving of revelation to that of the nations of the world has arisen, at I:XII, we pursue it further, and, as we shall see, I:XIV adds still more pertinent material. We have a fine superscription, 1.A, with three independent items strung together, 1.B-D, 2-3, and 4. Nos. 1.B-D and 4 follow an obvious, simple pattern, and Nos. 2-3 simply assign a protracted saying to a given name. We have no reason to suppose the entire set has come from a single hand. Since the same points are made by two or more authorities, it is likely that a redactor has chosen pertinent materials out of what he had available.

I:XIV

1.   A. What is the difference between Moses and all the other [Israelite] prophets?

B. R. Judah b. R. Ilai and rabbis:

C. R. Judah said, All the other prophets saw [their visions] through nine mirrors [darkly], in line with the following verse of Scripture: "And the appearance of the vision which I saw was like the vision that I saw when I came to destroy the city; and the visions were like the vision that I saw by the River Chebar, and I fell on my face" (Ezekiel 43:3) [with the root RᶜH occurring once in the plural, hence two, and seven other times in the singular, nine in all].

D. But Moses saw [his vision] through a single mirror: "in [one vision] and not in dark speeches" (Numbers 12:8).

E. Rabbis said, All other [Israelite] prophets saw [their visions] through a dirty mirror. That is in line with the following verse of Scripture: "And I have multiplied visions, and by the ministry of the angels I have used similitudes" (Hosea 12:11; verse 10 in KJV).

F. But Moses saw [his vision] through a polished mirror: "And the image of God does he behold" (Numbers 12:8).

2.   A. R. Phineas in the name of R. Hoshaia: [The matter may be compared] to a king who makes his appearance to his courtier in his informal garb [as an intimate].

B. For in this world the Indwelling Presence makes its appearance only to individuals [one by one], while concerning the age to come, what does Scripture say? "The glory of the Lord shall be revealed, and all flesh shall see [it together, for the mouth of the Lord has spoken]" (Isaiah 40:5).

The continuous discourse continues its merry way, ignoring not only the passage at hand—Leviticus 1:1—but the several topics provoked by exposition of the theme under discussion in connection with the tent of meeting. Having compared Balaam to Israelite prophets, we proceed to compare Israelite prophets to Moses, with the predictable result. No. 1 preserves the matter. But No. 2 on the surface is wildly out of place, since Moses now is forgotten, and the contrast is between prophecy in this age and in the time to come—a subject no one has hitherto brought up. But the messianic finis is a redactional convention.

Note that Margulies rejects as spurious I:XV, in the standard printed text. This passage is absent in all manuscript evidence of Leviticus R. except for one and was added in the earliest printed texts.[3]

Judaism and Scripture

To state the outcome at the very beginning, when Judaism had defined its matrix of myth and rite—a system of worldview and way of life focused on a particular social group—then Judaism attained its independent voice, its inner structure and logic. At that moment Scripture would reenter and assume its proper position as source of truth and proof for all (autonomously framed, independently reached) propositions. Scripture became paramount when it no longer provided a source of proof texts for the Mishnah but began to dominate discourse and define rhetoric. But Scripture succeeded the Mishnah as the focus of discourse only when discourse itself had expressed determinants autonomous of both the Mishnah and also Scripture—determinants, or propositions—prior to all else. To revert to the operative myth, it is only when the Torah had reached full expression as an autonomous entity of logic that the (mere) *components* of Torah—Scripture, the Mishnah and associated writings alike—found their proper place and proportion.

Accordingly, when we listen to the framers of Leviticus Rabbah, we see how statements in the document at hand thus become intelligible not contingently, that is, on the strength of an established text, but *a priori*, that is, on the basis of a deeper logic of meaning and an independent principle of rhetorical intelligibility. How so? Leviticus Rabbah is topical, not exegetical. Each of its thirty-seven *par-*

ashiyyot pursues its given topic and develops points relevant to that topic. It is logical, in that (to repeat) discourse appeals to an underlying principle of composition and intelligibility, and that logic inheres in what is said. Logic is what joins one sentence to the next and forms the whole into paragraphs of meaning, intelligible propositions, each with its place and sense in a still larger, accessible system. Because of logic one mind connects to another, public discourse becomes possible, debate on issues of general intelligibility takes place, and an anthology of statements about a single subject becomes a composition of theorems about that subject. In this sense, after the Mishnah, Leviticus Rabbah constitutes the next major logical composition in the rabbinic canon. Accordingly, with Leviticus Rabbah, rabbis take up the problem of saying what they wish to say not in an exegetical, but in a syllogistic and freely discursive logic and rhetoric. It follows that just as much as the Mishnah marks a radical break from all prior literature produced by Jews, so Leviticus Rabbah marks a stunning departure from all prior literature produced by a particular kind of Jew, namely, rabbis. Since these same rabbis defined Judaism as we have known it from their time to ours, we rightly turn to the book at hand for evidence about how the Scripture entered into, was absorbed by, and reached full status as the foundation document of the Judaism taking shape at just this time.

What Is New in Leviticus Rabbah?

To seek, through biblical exegesis, to link the Mishnah to Scripture, detail by detail, represented a well-trodden and firmly packed path. One document opened a new road to Scripture, and that is Leviticus Rabbah. How so? Leviticus Rabbah is the first major rabbinic composition to propose to make topical and discursive statements, not merely a phrase-by-phrase or verse-by-verse exegesis of a document, whether the Mishnah or Scripture itself. Rather,

the framers of that composition undertook to offer propositions, declarative sentences (so to speak), in which, not
through the exegesis of verses of Scripture in the order of
Scripture but through an order dictated by their own sense
of the logic of syllogistic composition, they would say what
they had in mind. To begin with, they laid down their
own topical program, related to, but essentially autonomous from, that of the book of Leviticus. Second, in expressing their ideas on these topics, they never undertook
simply to cite a verse of Scripture and then to claim that
that verse states precisely what they had in mind to begin
with. Accordingly, through rather distinctive modes of
expression, the framers said what they wished to say in
their own way—just as had the authors of the Mishnah
itself. True, in so doing, the composers of Leviticus Rabbah
treated Scripture as had their predecessors. That is to say,
to them as to those who had gone before, Scripture provided a rich treasury of facts.

The Mode of Thought of Leviticus Rabbah

The paramount and dominant exegetical construction
in Leviticus Rabbah is the base-verse/intersecting verse exegesis. Parashah I:I provides an ample instance. In this
construction, a verse of Leviticus is cited (hence: base-
verse), and another verse, from such books as Job, Proverbs, Qohelet, or Psalms, is then cited. The latter, not the
former, is subjected to detailed and systematic exegesis.
But the exegetical exercise ends up by leading the intersecting verse back to the base-verse and reading the latter
in terms of the former. In such an exercise, what in fact
do we do? *We read one thing in terms of something else.* To
begin with, it is the base-verse in terms of the intersecting
verse. But it also is the intersecting verse in other terms
as well—a multiple-layered construction of analogy and
parable. The intersecting verse's elements always turn out
to stand for, to signify, to speak of, something other than

that to which they openly refer. If water stands for Torah, the skin disease for evil speech, the reference to something for some other thing entirely, then the mode of thought at hand is simple. One thing symbolizes another, speaks not of itself but of some other thing entirely.

How shall we describe this mode of thought? It seems to me we may call it an *as-if* way of seeing things. That is to say, it is *as if* a common object or symbol really represented an uncommon one. Nothing says what it means. Everything important speaks metonymically, elliptically, parabolically, symbolically. All statements carry deeper meaning, which inheres in other statements altogether. The profound sense, then, of the base-verse emerges only through restatement within and through the intersecting verse—*as if* the base-verse spoke of things that, on the surface, we do not see at all.

Accordingly, if we ask the single prevalent literary construction to testify to the prevailing frame of mind, its message is that things are never what they seem. All things demand interpretation. Interpretation begins in the search for analogy, for that to which the thing is likened, hence the deep sense in which all exegesis at hand is parabolic. It is a quest for that for which the thing in its deepest structure stands.

Exegesis as we know it, in Leviticus Rabbah (and not only there), consists of an exercise in analogical thinking—something is like something else, stands for, evokes, or symbolizes that which is quite outside itself. It may be the opposite of something else, in which case it conforms to the exact opposite of the rules that govern that something else. The reasoning is analogical or it is contrastive, and the fundamental logic is taxonomic. The taxonomy rests on those comparisons and contrasts we should call, as I said, metonymic and parabolic. In that case, what lies on the surface misleads. What lies beneath or beyond the surface—there is the true reality, the world of truth and meaning. To revert to the issue of taxonomy, the tracts that allow classification serve only for that purpose. They signify nothing more than that something more.

How shall we characterize people who see things this way? They constitute the opposite of those who call a thing as it is. Self-evidently, they have become accustomed to perceiving more—or less—than is at hand. Perhaps that is a natural mode of thought for the Jews of this period (and not then alone), so long used to calling themselves God's first love, yet now seeing others with greater worldly reason claiming that same advantaged relationship. Not in mind only, but still more, in the politics of the world, the people that remembered its origins along with the very creation of the world and founding of humanity, that re-called how it alone served, and serves, the one and only God, for more than three hundred years had confronted quite a different existence. The radical disjuncture between the way things were and the way Scripture said things were supposed to be—and in actuality would some day become—surely imposed an unbearable tension. It was one thing for the slave born to slavery to endure. It was another for the free man sold into slavery to accept that same con-dition. The vanquished people, the nation that had lost its city and its temple, that had, moreover, produced another nation from its midst to take over its Scripture and much else, could not bear too much reality. That defeated people will then have found refuge in a mode of thought that trained vision to see things other than as the eyes perceived them. Among the diverse ways by which the weak and subordinated accommodate to their circumstance, the one of iron-willed pretense in life is most likely to yield the mode of thought at hand: things never are, because they cannot be, what they seem.

The Role of Scripture in Leviticus Rabbah:
Renewal and Reconstruction

Everyone has always known that Jews read Scripture.
Every system of Judaism has done so. But why did they
do so? What place did Scripture take in the larger systems
of reality presented by various Judaisms? Why one part of
Scripture rather than some other, and why read it in one
way rather than another? These questions do not find ready
answers in the mere observation that Jews read Scripture
and construct Judaisms out of it. Nor is that observation
one of a predictable and necessary pattern, since some of
the documents of the rabbinic canon did not focus upon
Scripture or even find it necessary to quote Scripture a
great deal. The Mishnah, Tosefta, and important units of
discourse of both Talmuds, for example, did not express
their ideas in the way in which people who "read Scripture" ought to. They make use of Scripture sparingly, only
with restraint adducing proofs for propositions even when
these are based upon scriptural statements. So the paramount and dominant place accorded to Scripture in Leviticus Rabbah and documents like it cannot pass without
comment and explanation.

Exactly what can we say for the position of Scripture
in this composition in particular, and what did Scripture
contribute? We ask first about the use of Scripture in the
mode of thought at hand: where, why, and how did Scripture find its central place in the minds of people who
thought in the way in which the framers of our document
did? The answer is that Scripture contributed that other
world that underlay this one. From Scripture came that
other set of realities to be discovered in the ordinary affairs
of the day. Scripture defined the inner being, the mythic
life, that sustained Israel. The world is to be confronted *as
if* things are not as they seem, because it is Scripture that
tells us how things always are—not one-time, in the past

only, not one-time, in the future only, but now and always. So the key to the system is what happens to, and through, Scripture. The lock that is opened is the deciphering of the code by which people were guided in their denial of one thing and recognition and affirmation of the presence of some other. It was not general, therefore mere lunacy, but specific, therefore cultural.

To spell this out: the mode of thought pertained to a particular set of ideas. People did not engage ubiquitously and individually in an ongoing pretense that things always had to be other than they seemed. Had they done so, the Jewish nation would have disintegrated into a collectivity of pure insanity. The insistence on the *as-if* character of reality collectively focused upon one, and only one, alternative existence. All parties (so far as we know) entered into and shared that same and single interior universe. It was the one framed by Scripture.

What happens in Leviticus Rabbah (and, self-evidently, in other documents of the same sort)? Reading one thing in terms of something else, the builders of the document systematically adopted for themselves the reality of the Scripture, its history and doctrines. They transformed that history from a sequence of one-time events, leading from one place to some other, into an ever-present mythic world. No longer was there one Moses, one David, one set of happenings of a distinctive and never-to-be-repeated character. Now whatever events the thinkers propose to take account of must enter and be absorbed into that established and ubiquitous pattern and structure founded in Scripture. It is not that biblical history repeats itself. Rather, biblical history no longer constitutes history as a story of things that happened once, long ago, and pointed to some one moment in the future. Rather it becomes an account of things that happen every day—hence, an ever-present mythic world, as I said.

A rapid glance at Leviticus Rabbah (and its fellows)

tells us that Scripture supplies the document with its structure, its content, its facts, its everything. But a deeper analysis also demonstrates that Scripture never provides the document with that structure, contents, and facts, that it now exhibits. Everything is reshaped and reframed. Whence the paradox?

Scripture as a whole does not dictate the order of discourse, let alone its character. Just as the talmudic authors destroyed the wholeness of the Mishnah and chose to take up its bits and pieces, so the exegetical writers did the same to Scripture. In our document they chose in Leviticus itself a verse here, a phrase there. These then presented the pretext for propositional discourse commonly quite out of phase with the cited passage. Verses that are quoted ordinarily shift from the meanings they convey to the implications they contain, speaking—as I have made clear— about something, anything, other than what they seem to be saying. So the *as-if* frame of mind brought to Scripture brings renewal to Scripture, seeing everything with fresh eyes.

And the result of the new vision was a reimagining of the social world envisioned by the document at hand, I mean, the everyday world of Israel in its Land in that difficult time. For what the sages now proposed was a reconstruction of existence along the lines of the ancient design of Scripture as they read it. What that meant was, from a sequence of one-time and linear events, everything that happened was turned into a repetition of known and already experienced paradigms, hence, once more, a mythic being. The source and core of the myth, of course, derive from Scripture—Scripture reread, renewed, reconstructed along with the society that revered Scripture.

So, to summarize, the mode of thought that dictated the issues and the logic of the document, telling the thinkers to see one thing in terms of something else, addressed Scripture in particular and collectively. And thinking as they did, the framers of the document saw Scripture in a new way, just as they saw their own circumstance afresh, rejecting their world in favor of Scripture's, reliving Scripture's world in their own terms.

That, incidentally, is why they did not write history, an account of what was happening and what it meant. It was not that they did not recognize or appreciate important changes and trends reshaping their nation's life. They could not deny that reality. In their apocalyptic reading of the dietary and leprosy laws, they made explicit their close encounter with the history of the world as they knew it. But they had another mode of responding to history. It was to treat history *as if* it were already known and readily understood. Whatever happened had already happened. How so? Scripture dictated the contents of history, laying forth the structures of time, the rules that prevailed and were made known in events. Self-evidently, these same thinkers projected into Scripture's day the realities of their own, turning Moses and David into rabbis, for example. But that is how people think in that mythic, enchanted world in which, to begin with, reality blends with dream, and hope projects onto future and past alike how people want things to be.

The upshot is that the mode of thought revealed by the literary construction under discussion constitutes a rather specific expression of a far more general and prevailing way of seeing things. The literary form in concrete ways says that the entirety of the biblical narrative speaks to each circumstance, that the system of Scripture as a whole not only governs, but comes prior to, any concrete circumstance of that same Scripture. Everything in Scripture is relevant everywhere else in Scripture. It must follow that the Torah (to use the mythic language of the system at hand) defines reality under all specific circumstances. Obviously we did not have to come to the specific literary traits of the document at hand to discover those prevailing characteristics of contemporary and later documents of the rabbinic canon. True, every exercise in referring one biblical passage to another expands the range of discourse to encompass much beyond the original referent. But that is commonplace in the exegesis of Scripture, familiar wherever *midrash* exegesis was undertaken, in no way particular to rabbinic writings.

The System of Leviticus Rabbah

The message of Leviticus Rabbah comes to us from the ultimate framers. It is delivered through their selection of materials already available as well as through their composition of new ones. What we now require is a clear statement of the major propositions expressed in Leviticus Rabbah. That will emerge through classification of the statements, with the notion that the principal themes, and the messages on those themes, should coalesce into a few clear statements.

The recurrent message may be stated in a single paragraph. God loves Israel, so he gave them the Torah, which defines their life and governs their welfare. Israel is alone in its category (*sui generis*), as in Parashah One, so what is a virtue to Israel is a vice to the nation, life-giving to Israel, poison to the gentiles. True, Israel sins, but God forgives that sin, having punished the nation on account of it. Such a process has yet to come to an end, but it will culminate in Israel's complete regeneration. Meanwhile, Israel's assurance of God's love lies in the many expressions of special concern, for even the humblest and most ordinary aspects of the national life: the food the nation eats, the sexual practices by which it procreates. These life-sustaining, life-transmitting activities draw God's special interest, as a mark of his general love for Israel. Israel then is supposed to achieve its life in conformity with the marks of God's love. These indications moreover signify also the character of Israel's difficulty, namely, subordination to the nations in general, but to the fourth kingdom, Rome, in particular. Both food laws and skin diseases stand for the nations. There is yet another category of sin, also collective and generative of collective punishment, and that is social. The moral character of Israel's life, the treatment of people by one another, the practice of gossip and small-scale thuggery—these too draw down divine penalty. The nation's fate therefore corresponds to its moral condition. The moral condition, however, emerges not only from the current generation. Israel's richest hope lies in the merit of the ancestors, thus in the Scriptural record of the merits attained by the founders of the nation, those who originally brought it into being and gave it life.

The world to come upon the nation is so portrayed as to restate these same propositions. Merit overcomes sin, and doing religious duties or supererogatory acts of kindness will win merit for the nation that does them. Israel will be saved at the end of time, and the age, or world, to follow will be exactly the opposite of this one. Much that we find in the account of Israel's national life, worked out through the definition of the liminal relationships, recurs in slightly altered form in the picture of the world to come.

If we now ask about further recurring themes or topics, there is one so commonplace that we should have to list the majority of paragraphs of discourse in order to provide a complete list. It is the list of events in Israel's history, meaning, in this context, Israel's history solely in scriptural times, down through the return to Zion. The one-time events of the generation of the flood, Sodom and Gomorrah, the patriarchs and the sojourn in Egypt, the exodus, the revelation of the Torah at Sinai, the golden calf, the Davidic monarchy and the building of the Temple, Sennacherib, Hezekiah, and the destruction of northern Israel, Nebuchadnezzar and the destruction of the Temple in 586, the life of Israel in Babylonian captivity, Daniel and his associates, Mordecai and Haman—these events occur over and over again. They turn out to serve as paradigms of sin and atonement, steadfastness and divine intervention, and equivalent lessons. We find, in fact, a fairly standard repertoire of scriptural heroes or villains, on the one side, and conventional lists of Israel's enemies and their actions and downfall, on the other. The boastful, for instance, include (VII:VI) the generation of the flood, Sodom and Gomorrah, Pharaoh, Sisera, Sennacherib, Nebuchadnezzar, the wicked empire (Rome) — contrasted to Israel, "despised and humble in this world." The four kingdoms recur again and again, always ending, of course, with Rome, with the repeated message that after Rome will come Israel. But Israel has to make this happen through its faith and submission to God's will. Lists of enemies ring the changes on Cain, the Sodomites, Pharaoh, Sennacherib, Nebuchadnezzar, Haman.

Accordingly, the mode of thought brought to bear upon the theme of history remains exactly the same as before: list making, with data exhibiting similar taxonomic traits drawn together into lists based on common monothetic traits or definitions. These lists then, through the power of repetition, make a single enormous point or prove a social law of history. The catalogues of exemplary heroes and historical events serve a further purpose. They provide a model of how contemporary events are to be absorbed into the biblical paradigm. Since biblical events exemplify recurrent happenings, sin and redemption, forgiveness and atonement, they lose their one-time character. At the same time and in the same way, current events find a place within the ancient, but eternally present, paradigmatic scheme. So no new historical events, other than exemplary episodes in lives of heroes, demand narration because, through what is said about the past, what was happening in the times of the framers of Leviticus Rabbah would also come under consideration. This mode of dealing with biblical history and contemporary events produces two reciprocal effects. The first is the mythicization of biblical stories, their removal from the framework of ongoing, unique patterns of history and sequences of events and their transformation into accounts of things that happen all the time. The second is that contemporary events too lose all of their specificity and enter the paradigmatic framework of established mythic existence. So (1) the Scripture's myth happens every day, and (2) every day produces reenactment of the Scripture's myth.

In seeking the substance of the mythic being invoked by the exegetes at hand, who read the text as if it spoke about something else and the world as if it lived out the text, we uncover a simple fact. At the center of the pretense, that is, the *as-if* mentality of Leviticus Rabbah and its framers, we find a simple proposition. Israel is God's special love. That love is shown in a simple way. Israel's present condition of subordination derives from its own deeds. It follows that God cares, so Israel may look forward to redemption on God's part in response to Israel's own regeneration through repentance.

Salvation and Sanctification

The message of Leviticus Rabbah attaches itself to the book of Leviticus, as if that book had come from prophecy and addressed the issue of salvation. But it came from the priesthood and spoke of sanctification. The paradoxical syllogism—the *as-if* reading, the opposite of how things seem—of the composers of Leviticus Rabbah therefore reaches simple formulation. In the very setting of sanctification we find the promise of salvation. In the topics of the cult and the priesthood we uncover the national and social issues of the moral life and redemptive hope of Israel. The repeated comparison and contrast of priesthood and prophecy, sanctification and salvation, turn out to produce a complement, which comes to most perfect union in the text at hand.

The basic mode of thought — denial of what is at hand in favor of a deeper reality — proves remarkably apt. The substance of thought in Leviticus Rabbah confronts the crisis too.

Are we lost for good to the fourth empire, the now-Christian Rome? No, we may yet be saved.

Has God rejected us forever? No, aided by the merit of the patriarchs and matriarchs and of the Torah and religious duties, we gain God's love.

What must we do to be saved? We must do nothing, we must be something: sanctified.

That status we gain through keeping the rules that make Israel holy. So salvation is through sanctification, which is all embodied in Leviticus and read as rules for the holy people.

The Messiah will come not because of what a pagan emperor does, nor, indeed, because of Jewish action, but because of Israel's own moral condition. When Israel enters the right relationship with God, then God will respond to Israel's condition by restoring things to their proper balance. Israel cannot, and need not, so act as to force the coming of the Messiah. Israel can attain the condition of sanctification, by forming a moral and holy community, that God's response will follow the established prophecy of Moses and the prophets. *So the basic doctrine of Leviticus Rabbah is the metamorphosis of Leviticus.* Instead of holy caste, we deal with holy people. Instead of holy place, we deal with holy community, in its holy land. The deepest exchange between reality and inner vision, therefore, comes at the very surface: the rereading of Leviticus in terms of a different set of realities from those to which the book, on the surface, relates. No other biblical book would have served so well; it had to be Leviticus. Only through what the framers did on that particular book could they deliver their astonishing message and vision.

The complementary points of stress in Leviticus Rabbah—the age to come will come, but Israel must reform itself beforehand—address that context defined by Julian, on the one side, and by the new anti-Judaic Christian policy of the later fourth and fifth centuries, on the other. The repeated reference to Esau and Edom and how they mark the last monarchy before God's through Israel underlines the same point. These truly form the worst of the four kingdoms. But they also come at the end. If only we shape up, so will history. As I said, that same message would hardly have surprised earlier generations and it would be repeated afresh later on. But it is the message of our document, and it does address this context in particular. We therefore grasp an astonishing correspondence between how people are thinking, what they wish to say, and the literary context—rereading a particular book of Scripture in terms of a set of values different from those expressed in that book—in which they deliver their message. Given the mode of thought, the crisis that demanded reflection, the message found congruent to the crisis, we must find entirely logical the choice of Leviticus and the treatment accorded to it. So the logic and the doctrine—the *logos* and *topos* of our opening discussion—prove remarkably to accord with the society and politics that produced and received Leviticus Rabbah.

Scripture in Judaism

Scripture proves paramount on the surface, but subordinated in the deep structure of the logic of Leviticus Rabbah. Why so? Because Scripture enjoys no autonomous standing, e.g., as the sole source of facts. It does not dictate the order of discussion. It does not (by itself) determine the topics to be taken up, since its verses, cited one by one in sequence, do not tell us how matters will proceed. Scripture, moreover, does not allow us to predict what proposition a given set of verses will yield. On the contrary, because of the insistence that one verse be read in light of another, one theme in light of another, augmentative one, Leviticus Rabbah prohibits us from predicting at the outset, merely by reading a given verse of Scripture, the way in which a given theme will be worked out or the way in which a given proposition will impart a message through said theme.

So, in all, the order of Scripture does not govern the sequence of discourse, the themes of Scripture do not tell us what themes will be taken up, the propositions of Scripture about its stated themes, what Scripture says, in its context, about a given topic, do not define the propositions of Leviticus Rabbah about that topic. The upshot is simple. Scripture contributes everything and nothing. It provides the decoration, the facts, much language. But whence the heart and soul and spirit? Where the matrix, where source? The editors, doing the work of selection, making their points through juxtaposition of things not otherwise brought into contact with one another, they are the ones who speak throughout. True, the voice is the voice of Scripture. But the hand is the hand of the collectivity of the sages, who are authors speaking through Scripture.

If, moreover, Scripture contributes facts, so too do the ones who state those ineluctable truths that are expressed in parables, and so too do the ones who tell stories, also exemplifying truths, about great heroes and villains. No less, but also no more, than these, Scripture makes its contribution along with other sources of social truth.

Greek science focused upon physics. Then the laws of Israel's salvation serve as the physics of the sages. But Greek science derived facts and built theorems on the basis of other sources besides physics; the philosophers also, after all, studied ethnography, ethics, politics, and history. For the sages at hand, along these same lines, parables, exemplary tales, and completed paragraphs of thought deriving from other sources (not to exclude the Mishnah, Tosefta, Sifra, Genesis Rabbah and such literary compo-

sitions that had been made ready for the Talmud of the
land of Israel) these too make their contribution of data
subject to analysis. These sources of truth, all together,
were directed toward the discovery of philosophical laws
for the understanding of Israel's life, now and in the age
to come.

So, to state the main conclusion, standing paramount
and dominant, Scripture contributed everything but the
main point. That point comes to us from the framers of
Leviticus Rabbah—from them alone. So far as Leviticus
Rabbah transcends the book of Leviticus—and that means,
in the whole of its being—the document speaks for the
framers, conveys their message, pursues their discourse,
makes the points they wished to make. For they are the
ones who made of Leviticus, the book, Leviticus Rabbah,
that greater Leviticus, the document that spoke of sanctification but, in its augmented version at hand, meant
salvation. As closely related to the book of Leviticus as the
New Testament is to the Old, Leviticus Rabbah delivers
the message of the philosophers of Israel's history.

I have emphasized that Leviticus Rabbah carries a message of its own, which finds a place within, and refers to,
a larger system. The method of thought and mode of argument act out a denial of one reality in favor of the affirmation of another. That dual process of pretense at the
exegetical level evokes the deeper pretense of the mode of
thought of the larger system, and, at the deepest layer,
the pretense that fed Israel's soul and sustained it. Just as
one thing evokes some other, so does the rabbinic system,
overall, turn into aspects of myth and actions of deep symbolic consequence what to the untutored eye were commonplace deeds and neutral transactions. So too, the
wretched nation really enjoyed God's special love. As I
stated at the outset, what is important in the place and
function accorded to Scripture derives significance from

the host and recipient of Scripture, that is to say, the rabbinic system itself.

But so far as Leviticus Rabbah stands for and points toward that larger system, what are the commonplace traits of Scripture in this other, altogether new context?

1. Scripture, for one thing, forms a timeless present, with the affairs of the present day read back into the past and the past into the present, with singular events absorbed into Scripture's paradigms.

2. Scripture is read whole and atomistically. Everything speaks to everything else, but only one thing speaks at a time.

3. Scripture is read as an account of a seamless world, encompassing present and past alike, and Scripture is read atemporally and ahistorically.

All of these things surprise no one; they have been recognized for a very long time. What is new here is the claim to explain why these things are so, meaning the logic of the composition that prevails *also*, when Scripture comes to hand.

1. Scripture is read whole, because the framers pursue issues of thought that demand all data pertain to all times and all contexts. The authors are philosophers, looking for rules and their verification. Scripture tells stories, to be sure. But these exemplify facts of social life and national destiny: the laws of Israel's life.

2. Scripture is read atomistically, because each of its components constitutes a social fact, ever relevant to the society of which it forms a part, with that society everywhere uniform.

3. Scripture is read as a source of facts pertinent to historical and contemporary issues alike, because the issues at hand, when worked out, will indicate the prevailing laws, the rules that apply everywhere, all the time, to everyone of Israel.

Accordingly, there is no way for Scripture to be read

except as a source of facts about that ongoing reality that forms the focus and the center of discourse, the life of the unique social entity, Israel. But, as we have seen, the simple logic conveyed by the parable also contributes its offering of facts. The simple truth conveyed by the tale of the great man, the exemplary event of the rabbinic sage, the memorable miracle — these too serve as well as facts of Scripture. The several truths, therefore, stand alongside and at the same level as the truths of Scripture, which is not the sole source of rules or cases. The facts of Scripture stand no higher than those of the parable, on the one side, or of the tale of the sage, on the other. Why not? Because to philosophers and scientists, facts are facts, whatever their origin or point of application.

What we have in Leviticus Rabbah, therefore, is the result of the mode of thought not of prophets or historians, but of philosophers and scientists. The framers propose not to lay down, but to discover, rules governing Israel's life. I state with necessary emphasis: *as we find the rules of nature by identifying and classifying facts of natural life, so we find rules of society by identifying and classifying the facts of Israel's social life.* In both modes of inquiry we make sense of things by bringing together like specimens and finding out whether they form a species, then bringing together like species and finding out whether they form a genus — in all, classifying data and identifying the rules that make possible the classification. That sort of thinking lies at the deepest level of list-making, which is, as I said, work of offering a proposition and facts (for social rules) as much as a genus and its species (for rules of nature). Once discovered, the social rules of Israel's national life yield explicit statements, such as, that God hates the arrogant and loves the humble. The readily assembled syllogism follows: if one is arrogant, God will hate him, and if he is humble, God will love him. The logical status of these statements, in context, is as secure and unassailable as the logical status of statements about physics, ethics, or politics, as these emerge in philosophical thought. What differentiates the statements is not their logical status — as sound, scientific philosophy — but only their subject matter, on the one side, and distinctive rhetoric, on the other.

So Leviticus Rabbah is anything but an exegetical exercise. We err if we are taken in by the powerful rhetoric of our document, which resorts so ubiquitously to the citation of biblical verses and, more importantly, to the construction, out of diverse verses, of a point transcendent of the cited verses. At hand is not an exegetical composition at all, nor even verses of Scripture read as a corpus of proof texts. We have, rather, a statement that stands by itself, separate from Scripture, and that makes its points only secondarily, along the way, by evoking verses of Scripture to express and exemplify those same points. We miss the main point if we posit that Scripture plays a definitive or even central role in providing the program and agenda for the framers of Leviticus Rabbah. Their program is wholly their own. But, of course, Scripture then serves their purposes very well indeed.

So too, their style is their own. Scripture merely contributes to an aesthetic that is at once pleasing and powerful for people who know Scripture pretty much by heart. But in context, the aesthetic too is original. The constant invocation of Scriptural verses compares with the place of the classics in the speech and writing of gentlefolk of an earlier age, in which the mark of elegance was perpetual allusion to classical writers. No Christian author of the age would have found alien the aesthetic at hand. So while the constant introduction of verses of Scripture provides the wherewithal of speech, these verses serve only as do the colors of the painter. The painter cannot paint without the oils. But the colors do not make the painting. The painter does. As original and astonishing as is the aesthetic

of the Mishnah, the theory of persuasive rhetoric governing Leviticus Rabbah produces a still more amazing result.

Conclusion

We may say that Leviticus Rabbah provides an exegesis
of the book of Leviticus just as much as the school of
Matthew provides an exegesis of passages cited in the book
of Isaiah. Yet, I must reiterate at the end, Leviticus serves
as something other than a source of proof texts. It is not
that at all. And that is the important fact I mean to prove.
What is new in Leviticus Rabbah's encounter with Scripture emerges when we realize that, for former Israelite
writers, Scriptures do serve principally as a source of proof
texts. That certainly is the case for the school of Matthew
and also for the Essene writers whose library survived at
Qumran. The task of Scripture for the authors of the Tosefta, Sifra, Genesis Rabbah, and the Talmud of the Land
of Israel emerged out of a single need. That need was to
found the creations of the new age upon the authority of
the old. Thus the exegetical work consequent upon the
Mishnah demanded a turning to Scripture. From that necessary and predictable meeting, exegetical work on Scripture itself got under way, with the results so self-evident
in most of the exegetical compositions on most of the Pentateuch, including Leviticus, accomplished in the third and
fourth centuries. None of this, in fact, defined how Scripture would reach its right and proper place in the Judaism
of the Talmuds and exegetical compositions. It was Leviticus Rabbah that set the pattern, and its pattern would
predominate for a very long time. How so? The operative
rules would be these:

1. From Leviticus Rabbah onward, Scripture would
conform to paradigms framed essentially independent of
Scripture.

2. From then onward, Scripture was made to yield
paradigms applicable beyond the limits of Scripture.

In these two complementary statements we summarize the entire argument. The heart of the matter lies in laying forth the rules of life — of Israel's life and salvation. These rules derive from the facts of history, as much as the rules of the Mishnah derive from the facts of society (and, in context, the rules of philosophy derive from the facts of nature). Scripture, then, never stands all by itself. Its exalted position at the center of all discourse proves contingent, never absolute. That negative result, of course, bears an entirely affirmative complement.

Judaism is *not* the religion of the Old Testament because Judaism *is* Judaism. Scripture enters Judaism because Judaism is the religion of "the one whole Torah of Moses, our rabbi," and part of that Torah is the written part, Scripture. But that whole Torah, viewed whole, is this: *God's revelation of the rules of life: creation, society, history alike.*

Obviously, every form of Judaism would be in some way a scriptural religion. But the *sort* of scriptural religion a given kind of Judaism would reveal is not to be predicted on the foundations of traits of Scripture in particular. One kind of Judaism laid its distinctive emphasis upon a linear history of Israel, in a sequence of unique, one-time events, all together yielding a pattern of revealed truth, from creation, through revelation, to redemption. That kind of Judaism then would read Scripture for signs of the times and turn Scripture into a resource for apocalyptic speculation. A kind of Judaism interested not in one-time events of history but in all-time rules of society, governing for all time, such as the kind at hand, would read Scripture philosophically and not historically. That is, Scripture would yield a corpus of facts conforming to rules. Scripture would provide a source of paradigms, the opposite of one-time events.

True enough, many kinds of Judaism would found their definitive propositions in Scripture and build upon them. But while all of Scripture was revealed and authoritative, for each construction of a system of Judaism, only some passages of Scripture would prove to be relevant. Just as the framers of the Mishnah came to Scripture with a program of questions and inquiries framed essentially among themselves, one which turned out to be highly selective, so did their successors who made up Leviticus Rabbah. What they brought was a mode of thought, a deeply philosophical and scientific quest, and an acute problem of history and society. In their search for the rules of Israel's life and salvation, they found answer not in the one-time events of history but in paradigmatic facts, social laws of salvation. It was in the mind and imagination of the already philosophical authors of Leviticus Rabbah that Scripture came to serve, as did nature, as did everyday life and its parables, all together, to reveal laws everywhere and always valid—if people would only keep them.

Notes

1. Mordecai Margulies, *Midrash Wayyikra Rabbah: A Critical Edition Based on Manuscripts and Genizah Fragment with Variants and Notes*, 5 vols. (Jerusalem: Louis M. and Minnie Epstein Fund of the American Academy for Jewish Research, 1953-60).

2. J. Israelstam and Judah J. Slotki, *Midrash Rabbah Leviticus: Translated into English with Notes, Glossary, and Indices*, H. Freedman and Maurice Simon, eds. (London: Sorcino, 1939), 14.

3. Margulies, *Midrash Wayyikra Rabbah*, p. 32, n. to line 5.

14

Ancient Jewish Seafaring and River-faring Laws

Raphael Patai[1]
Forest Hills, New York

Ancient Jewish literature contains many references to seafaring, river-faring, and related subjects. From them it is possible to conclude that these activities played a definite role in the life of the Hebrews in biblical times and a more important one in that of the Jews of Palestine and Babylonia in the days of the Second Jewish Commonwealth and in talmudic times. The following paper presents data, culled primarily from talmudic and midrashic sources, pertaining to the commercial and religious laws that governed Jewish seafaring up to ca. A.D. 500.

COMMERCIAL LAWS

Talmudic law devotes considerable attention to the legal side of commercial transactions concerning ships. The purchase of a ship was concluded either by duly signing a contract, or, presumably in the case of smaller craft, by the traditional act of taking movable property into possession, namely by pulling: the buyer pulled the ship toward himself and thus his ownership of it became legally established.[2]

This paper is based on a chapter in my Hebrew book Ha-Sappanut ha-ʿIvrit: Pereq be-Toldot ha-Tarbut ha-Artziyisr'elit b-Ime Qedem (Jewish Seafaring: A Chapter in Ancient Palestinian Culture), *published in Jerusalem in 1938 by the Hebrew Society for the Study of Palestine and Its Antiquities.*

Of the parts of the ship and the gear that went with the hull in case of a purchase, some are expressly mentioned. If a person sold a ship owned by him, it was understood that he sold with it the mast, the yard, the anchor, the oars, the rudder, the ladder, the water tank, and, according to the opinion of some sages, also the small boat (*dugit* or *bitzit*) that was part of its equipment.[3] However, the following items of equipment remained the property of the seller: the ballast-stones (*yǝshiwin*), the poles (*ᶜuvin*), the mattresses (*yǝtzuᶜin*), the dunnage bags (*martzufin*), the light boat called *isqofa*. Also the cargo and the slaves who manned the ship remained the property of the seller.[4] If the intention of the shipowner was to sell the ship together with all these items and the personnel, he had to state explicitly at the time of the sale: "I am selling you the ship and all that is in it."[5]

The right of ownership of ships was often the subject of litigation. The Babylonian Talmud records that once it happened that two men argued over an *arva*, a boat. Each of them claimed that the craft belonged to him alone. One of the two went to the court and requested it to foreclose on the boat in order to prevent the other from selling it until he was able to produce witnesses to establish his claim. The decision of the court in this case was not to interfere, that is, not to foreclose on the boat. In another similar case the court declared itself willing to foreclose on the boat, whereupon the litigant who requested the foreclosure set out to find his witnesses, but was unable to locate any. He then returned to the court and requested the judges to cancel the foreclosure in order to enable the two contesting parties to try their luck in seizing the boat by force. However, the decision of the court concerning this second request was not to annul the foreclosure. The only case in which the court allowed the two parties to use force against each other in trying to seize the boat was when each of them argued that he had inherited the boat in question from his father.[6]

Information on the price of ships is scanty. One statement, quoted in the Babylonian Talmud in the name of Rabbi Romanos, that the price of a ship was no less than 4,000 golden dinars,[7] is not very helpful since we are left in the dark about the size of the ship in question. Further, from a statement in the Mishnah it appears that some owners or operators of ships accepted fruits or vegetables from the passengers in place of the fare.[8]

In Babylonia, where the rivers and canals served as the main thoroughfares for the transportation of all kinds of cargo, owners of cargo boats would charter their vessels to merchants for the shipping of their goods. However, some shipowners served as their own skippers.[9] If somebody chartered a ship, he had to pay the charter money either in advance or upon completion of the voyage, when he handed the ship back to its owner.[10] If a person seized another man's ship and made use of it for his own purposes, the owner of the ship could claim payment for either the hire or a compensation for wear and tear.[11] Talmudic rabbis were so familiar with the chartering of ships that they used it as the basis for a simile: "There are men who own ships but the merchandise in them is not theirs, or, if the merchandise is theirs, the ships are not theirs. Not so the Holy One, blessed be He, who owns both the earth and everything that is in it."[12]

Legislation was necessary to regulate the relationship between the lessor and the lessee of a ship. The general rules as to their rights and obligations were laid down by the Tannaim (the talmudic sages who lived in Palestine prior to A.D. 200), and they were later amplified and refined by the Amoraim (the talmudic sages of the third to fifth centuries) of Babylonia. Several of these rulings deal with the problems of damages arising from the loss of ship or cargo. According to tannaitic legislation, for instance, if a person hired a ship and it was wrecked and sank in the course of the voyage, the following rules applied: if he had paid the charter money, he was not entitled to demand its refund; but if he had not yet paid it, he was not required to do so. The Amoraim approached this ruling from several legal angles and came to the conclusion that it was valid only in case the lessor and the lessee had contracted concerning a *definite* ship for the transportation of a *definite* cargo, for in that case, if the ship sank together with the cargo, neither the lessor nor the lessee was able to fulfill his agreed-upon obligation. On the other hand, if they had contracted concerning a ship without specifying one particular vessel, as well as concerning an unspecified cargo, the ruling was that the lessee had to pay the lessor half of the fee due to the lessor for the voyage actually made by the ship.[13]

Again, according to the Tannaim, if somebody hired a ship to transport cargo to a certain destination, but then unloaded the ship when it had covered half the distance, he had to pay the lessor only the fee due for half the way.[14] The amoraic elaborations of this ruling are too lengthy and complex to be quoted here in full, but let us point out briefly that while trying to define the exact cases to which this ruling applied, they discussed such technicalities as the wear and tear on the ship, any change in its route, and the relationship between any increase of the cargo and the amount of the ropes worn out. From the context it becomes clear that the owner of the ship sailed with his ship, probably in the capacity of skipper, or as supercargo. The sailors, in general, had the status of hired laborers.[15] When ships entered or left ports, they had to pay customs dues.[16] From a Midrash, it appears that occasionally these customs dues were so severe that they caused ruin to the merchants. It runs as follows:

Our sages said: It happened that merchants were

sailing on a ship, and there was also a scholar with them. The merchants said to the scholar: "What is your merchandise?" He replied: "It is hidden away." The merchants thereupon began to search the ship, and when they found nothing, they mocked him. When they arrived in port, the customs collectors arose and took away all that the merchants had with them, so that they had nothing to eat and nothing to wear. That scholar, however, went to the synagogue, sat down, and began to teach the congregation, which honored him and provided for his needs. The merchants who had been with him on the ship now came to him, entreated him, and said: "Pray, plead in our favor, since you know us!" What caused the scholar to be saved? The Tora (Law), which he had in his heart.[17]

Considering the great risks connected with sea trade, it is not surprising that merchants engaged in it were often in need of loans. In such cases, the merchants would apply for a loan first of all to the shipowners as the persons most likely to be interested in the success of their enterprises. Since, however, biblical law prohibited the taking of interest on a loan (Leviticus 25:35-37), without the incentive of an increased return the shipowners could not be expected to run the risk of losing their money in addition to their ships. This obstacle was overcome, not only in case of sea trade, but also in other similar cases, by offering the owner a higher rent, or freight rate, than originally stipulated, in consideration of a loan to be used to improve the property. A tenant, for instance, may offer higher rent for a field on condition that the owner of the field give him a loan which the tenant was bound to use for improvements. The loan was, in this case, regarded as a loan without interest, for the higher rent paid by the tenant to the owner was considered due him owing to the improvement in the field, and consequently in its yield, made possible by the loan.[18] The same sort of agreement might be entered into also by the owner of a ship and the merchant who hired it from him. Talmudic law, however, expressly stipulates that no higher rent might be charged by the owner of a ship if the merchant used the loan for buying merchandise or for any other investment into his business. If, however, he made use of the loan to embellish the ship, he was allowed to offer, and the owner to accept, higher rent, because in this case the ship would bring greater gain to the merchant.[19]

One form of loan made use of by maritime merchants was called *qalito shel yam* (literally, "suction" or "gorge of the sea"), which largely corresponded to the Greek *tókos nautikós*, or the Roman *fenus nauticum*.[20] The Palestinian Talmud explains: "What is *qalito shel yam*? If somebody advances a certain amount of dinars to his neighbor in the same manner as those who give goods to those who sail to the isles,[21] at a share of two or three *sextarii*, this is no usury, but *tarsha*."[22] To understand this ruling, one must add explanations to the terse language of the Talmud. "A share of two or three *sextarii*" means payment of this amount per each *modius* of profit earned by the merchant. A *sextarius* was one sixteenth of a *modius*, so that the two or three *sextarii* taken by the lender per each *modius* earned by the merchants represented an interest of one-eighth or three-sixteenths on the money lent. This type of interest was termed by the talmudic sages *tarsha*, that is, silent interest, which they considered permissible. The principle underlying the *tarsha* was the higher price charged in case of deferred payment. Rabbi Yehuda ha-Nasi, who owned several merchant-ships plying the Mediterranean, was therefore interested in legalizing the *qalito shel yam*-type of hidden interest, but was overruled by the sages.[23]

In Babylonia, where cargo transport on the rivers and canals was a highly developed business, shippers used to undertake the responsibility for the transport of a given cargo to a certain port, and for discharging it there. Such responsibility covered even cases of *force majeure*. Rav Papa and Rav Huna, two Babylonian Amoras of the midfourth century A.D., once bought a load of sesamum seed on the banks of the Old King's Canal and hired sailors to track it to its place of destination. The sailors undertook to be responsible in case of any accident that might occur. It so happened that the canal became blocked, whereupon the two merchant-rabbis demanded from the sailors that, having undertaken the responsibility in case of any accident, they hire donkey drivers to carry the cargo to its destination. The sailors, however, objected, and when the case was brought before Rava, the head of the Jewish academy of Mehoza, he absolved them, finding that it was a most unusual occurrence for that big canal to become blocked.[24]

Talmudic law regulates the responsibility of the owner of a boat, of the sailors who charter it from him, and of the passengers, in case the boat suffers damage. If a man charters a ship, he has to pay its hire when he takes over the ship and has to pay damages if the vessel suffers shipwreck.[25] This ruling can be compared to paragraph 236 in the Code of Hammurabi, preceding talmudic legislation by at least two millennia: "If a seignior let his boat for hire to a boatman, and the boatman was so careless that he has sunk or wrecked the boat, the boatman shall make good the boat to the owner of the boat."[26] According to talmudic law, if the boatman who has hired a boat overloads it by at least one-thirtieth of its usual load, he becomes responsible for any damage suffered by the ship.[27]

In cargo shipping there were usually three parties involved: the owner of the boat, the boatman or boatmen who hired the boat from him, and the owner of the merchandise who hired the boatmen. We may thus take it for granted that the boatmen were responsible to the owner of the cargo not only for the transport of the cargo to its agreed-upon destination (cf. above), but also for the safety of the cargo itself. The Code of Hammurabi ruled (paragraph 237): "When a seignior hired a boatman and a boat and loaded it with grain, wool, oil, dates, or any kind of freight, if that boatman was so careless that he has sunk the boat and lost what was in it as well, the boatman shall make good the boat which he sank and whatever he lost that was in it."[28]

The carelessness or care of the boatmen was considered a decisive factor in talmudic legislation in connection with the significant institution of mutual insurance that played an important role in the commercial shipping practices of Babylonian Jews some fifteen hundred years before Lloyd's Underwriting Association. The idea of mutual insurance seems to have originated among the Jewish sailors of Palestine, who in sailing the Mediterranean must have suffered many more accidents than their Babylonian colleagues on the quiet canals or rivers of their country. Tannaitic legislation gave its approval: "The sailors are permitted to say, 'Whosoever loses his ship, we shall supply him with another in its stead.' If, however, he lost his ship through negligence (busya or bisya), they are not bound to supply him with another ship. Only if his ship was lost not due to his own negligence are they bound to supply him with another ship. If he sailed to a place where people do not usually sail, they are not bound to supply him with another ship."[29]

The Babylonian Jewish sages adapted this ruling to the Babylonian conditions and interpreted accordingly the phrase, "if he sailed to a place where people do not usually sail," as follows: It was the usage on the Babylonian waterways to sail in the spring, when the water level was high, at a distance of one cable length from the shore, whereas in the autumn, when the rivers ran low, they sailed at a distance of two cables from the shore. If a boatman did not follow these rules, he was regarded as having been negligent, and if as a consequence his boat was wrecked, it did not have to be replaced by another boat.[30]

In the canals of Babylonia, collision between two boats was an ever-present danger. Two millennia before the talmudic age, the Code of Hammurabi considered such contingencies and ruled (paragraph 240): "If a rowboat rammed a sailboat and has sunk (it), the owner of the boat whose boat was sunk shall in the presence of the god set forth the particulars regarding whatever was lost in his boat and the one in charge of the rowboat which sank the sailboat shall make good to him his boat and his lost property."[31] The talmudic sages went into still greater detail in their legal provisions concerning such damages, and even passed preventive measures in the form of traffic regulations: Two ships sailing in opposite directions on a river meet; if both of them continue to sail, they will collide, and both will sink. If one of them draws near the shore and lets the other pass, no harm will befall either of them. The question thus arises, which of the two ships has to give way to the other? The talmudic ruling is that if one of the ships is empty and the other loaded, the empty one must draw aside and let the full one pass. Or, if one of them is nearer the shore and the other farther away, the one nearer the shore must let the other pass. If both of them are at equal distance from the shore, they have to come to an agreement, and the one that wishes to pass has to pay the other for the right of passage.[32] The same ruling is contained in a Palestinian tannaitic source: "Two ships that sail towards each other, one empty and one loaded, the empty one must give way to the loaded one; if both are empty or both are loaded, they must come to an understanding."[33]

To appreciate the importance of these regulations, one must remember that in Babylonia boats were in many cases towed along narrow irrigation canals (*nigrē*, sing. *nigra*), so that for a boat to pull aside and let another boat pass involved considerable additional work as well as much loss of time. Although these canals or channels were the private property of the landowner through whose fields they passed, he was obliged to leave their banks free of cultivation to a width of four cubits at least so that the vegetation should not obstruct the waterway itself. The larger canals and their banks were considered public property, and they, too, had to be kept free of all growth to a width of four cubits. Rabbi Ammi bar Nathan, the outstanding Palestinian Amora of the third century, who lived for some years in Babylonia, decreed: "Cut down [the vegetation] on both banks of the river to the width of the shoulders of the *naggadē* [the draggers of boats]."[34] Once it happened that one of the sages gave orders to cut down the trees bordering a river to a width of sixteen cubits, whereupon the enraged owners of the trees thus destroyed fell upon him and beat him.[35] From the talmudic stories it becomes evident that the availability of free passageways along riverbanks was considered such a basic public right that when they were found obstructed by trees or other vegetation, the sages, in their capacity as community leaders, felt justified in ordering their removal even without the consent of the landowners.[36]

Since the Babylonian canals tended to become obstructed with sediment, it was necessary from time to time to dredge them. Talmudic legislation provided that this should be carried out by the owner of the land which adjoined the silted-up stretch of the canal. He was to be helped by the owners of the lands that lay lower down along the banks of the canal, for they too would suffer from any diminution of the water needed for irrigation. However, the owners of the adjoining lands higher up along the canal were not expected to help, since they only benefitted from the accumulation of water caused by the obstruction of the canal lower down.[37] On occasion, major repairs had to be undertaken: canals had to be cleaned up by digging a course through a sandbank, or in some other manner. This repair was considered so essential for the general public that its performance was permitted even on a half-holiday.[38]

In Palestine, where navigation was mainly maritime, the sailors suffered much from storms. One of the most common methods of saving a ship caught in a storm was to jettison its cargo or part of it. Rabbinic legislation dealt with the legal aspects of such rescue maneuvers. It decreed that if several merchants sail on a ship, each with a certain amount of merchandise with him, and the need arises to jettison part of the cargo, then each of the merchants has to take his share in the sacrifice in relation to the weight and value of his merchandise. If, on the other hand, several merchants charter a ship for the transportation of their wares, each of them has to pay his share according to the weight of his merchandise, without regard to its value.[39] These talmudic rulings, however, are accompanied by the caution, "One does not, however, deviate from the usage of the sailors."[40] That is, the local usage must be regarded as taking precedence over the rabbis' rules.

RELIGIOUS LAWS

A major part of talmudic legislation concerning ships and shipping deals with religious issues.

Prayers

The fulfillment of Jewish religious duties could not be interrupted even when setting out on a sea voyage. On the contrary, as soon as a person came in sight of the sea (i.e., the Mediterranean), he had to recite the benediction: "Blessed be He who created the Great Sea."[41] When sailing on any vessel a man must direct his heart toward the temple of Jerusalem and say the obligatory prayers.[42] This rule, evidently, dates from before A.D. 70, when the temple of Jerusalem was destroyed.

At times passengers had to embark very early in the morning, even before dawn, in which case they had to recite the morning prayer prior to embarkation, even though it was still dark, and later, on board the ship, after it dawned, they had to recite the *Shema^c* prayer, the part of the morning prayer that can be recited only after dawn.[43] Again, when the traveller had happily reached his port of destination he had, according to R. Yehuda, to say a special grace for having been saved from the perils of the sea.[44]

An inscription from the second century A.D. shows that the Jews of that period occasionally expressed their gratitude for having been saved from a storm on the sea in a more permanent form than mere oral blessings. The inscription, found in the temple of Pan at Apollonopolis Magna (Edfu) in Upper Egypt, reads in Greek: "Thanks to God, the Jew Theodotos son of Dorion was saved from the sea."[45] That the Jew Theodotos placed an inscription in the temple of Pan indicates the extent of Hellenization among the Egyptian Jews of the period.

In Jewish law the presence of a corpse causes defilement. Jews who died abroad often expressed the wish to be buried in Palestine, and their bodies were transported in ships to a Palestinian port. The large Bet She^carim necropolis near Haifa contains hundreds of inscriptions testifying to the burial of Jews from all parts of the Diaspora in tannaitic and talmudic times.[46] The depiction of sailing ships on the walls of the catacombs may be an oblique reference to the way in which the dead were transported from the places in which they died to the shores of Palestine. If a corpse was transported on a ship, they put it in one corner of the ship, and when the time for prayers arrived they retired to another corner to recite the prayers at a distance from the source of impurity.[47]

In addition to reciting the obligatory daily prayers, Jewish sailors and passengers used to pray frequently and spontaneously. It seems to have been customary to say a prayer before setting out on a sea voyage. R. Nathan Kohen, the third-to-fourth-century Palestinian Amora, once wished to sail after the Feast of Tabernacles, that is, in the relatively stormy fall season, and before embarking asked his brother R. Hiyya bar Abba to pray for him. R. Hiyya, however, replied: "What use is my praying for you? Has it not been said, 'When you bind your *lulav*, bind your feet' (according to a variant version: 'bind your ship'). If you enter the synagogue and hear that they are praying for rain, do not rely on my prayer (for your safety)."[48] From the apocryphal Wisdom of Solomon (date uncertain) it appears that also among the pagans of antiquity it was customary to pray before setting out on a voyage on the sea.[49]

If a ship was caught in a storm, both Jews and Gentiles aboard prayed, each to his own god. The earliest evidence of this is found in the book of Jonah. The prophet sailed from Jaffa to Tarshish, and, when a mighty tempest blew up so that the ship was in danger of foundering, "the mariners were afraid and cried every man unto his god" (Jonah 1:5). A tannaitic source records that once a small Jewish child was travelling on a ship of Gentiles, and a gale arose which threatened to wreck the ship. Thereupon all the sailors cried out, each to his own god, but the child said to them: "How long will you continue in your foolishness? Cry to Him who created the sea."[50] In Numbers 10:9, the talmudic sages saw an allusion to the effect that god will help those of his people who are in danger on the high sea.[51] It was well known to the sages of the Mishnah that the day on which a Gentile reached his destination after a sea voyage was celebrated by him as a feast-day with prayers and thanksgiving offerings.[52]

The Sabbath

Sea voyages in ancient days usually lasted several days or even weeks, and thus Jewish sailors and passengers were compelled to spend the day of rest, the Sabbath, on board. In this connection a number of regulations were promulgated by the sages in order to define precisely what was allowed and what forbidden to a Jew sailing on the Sabbath. Since riding or sitting on any vehicle on the Sabbath was forbidden, precautions had to be taken to avoid even the suspicion that one boarded a ship with the intention of spending the Sabbath on it. Hence it was ruled that one had to board the ship at least three days before the Sabbath, that is, not later in the week than on Wednesday. Only if the purpose of the voyage was to perform a religious or pious act was it allowed to embark later in the week, even on a Friday.[53] Moreover, according to one talmudic opinion, it was necessary to come to an agreement with the skipper to the effect that he would break the voyage for the duration of the Sabbath, even though one knew that this agreement was not likely to be kept.[54]

In order to give an outward indication of observing the Sabbath rest on board the ship, the more strict among the sages remained put during that whole day within a space of four by four cubits, which they occupied before the beginning of the Sabbath. It once happened that four sages sailed from Brundisium (Brindisi) in southern Italy to Palestine. On the Sabbath, two of them, Rabban Gamliel and R. Eleazar ben Azarya, walked about freely on the ship, while the two others, R. Joshua and R. Akiba, who wanted to observe the Sabbath rest as strictly as possible, did not move outside of their four cubits.[55] The sages in question lived in the second half of the second century A.D. The halakhah (religious tradition) was fixed according to the more liberal spirit of Rabban Gamliel and R. Eleazar ben Azarya.[56]

Another problem that had to be solved by religious legislation was whether it was permissible to disembark, that is, to leave the ship and go ashore, on the Sabbath. Again, the halakhah was fixed following an actual event. A ship on which Rabban Gamliel sailed reached port shortly after sunset on Friday. His companions asked Rabban Gamliel; "Are we permitted to go ashore?" His answer was: "You are permitted to disembark, for I observed that we had already reached the Sabbath limits before it became dark,"[57] that is to say, the ship was within two thousand cubits from the port before the Sabbath began. Accordingly, this is how the *halakhah* was fixed: "When a ship enters port,[58] the passengers may disembark only if it was within the Sabbath limits before it became dark."[59] If the landing gangway was put out especially for a Jew on the Sabbath, he was not allowed to go ashore by it; if, however, it was run out for the convenience of non-Jews, he was permitted to cross by it to the shore.[60]

With regard to the Sabbath laws, the cabins of a ship were equated to the private homes on dry land: the carrying of objects within them was permitted. The deck of the ship, on the other hand, was equated to a courtyard common to several houses: hence carrying objects on it was prohibited.[61] In addition, it is expressly stated that it was forbidden to carry about on the Sabbath any wooden parts of the ship.[62] On the other hand, it was permissible to move the anchor,[63] probably because it was deemed essential for the safety of the ship and its passengers.

If a ship stood in the water higher than ten handbreadths (ca. thirty inches), it was prohibited to remove anything from it or to bring anything aboard on the Sabbath.[64] However, one was permitted to throw anything from the sea to the shore or vice versa, or from the sea to a ship, or from one ship to another.[65] These rules were *ad hoc* applications of the general Sabbath laws that prohibited on that day the carrying of anything from one house to the next, or from a private property to a public domain, e.g., from a house to the street or to a courtyard, and vice versa. To avoid the considerable inconvenience caused by these rules, a legal fiction was resorted to: a symbolic act was performed by which a continuity or communality was created among the dwellings that surrounded a common courtyard. It consisted of preparing a dish of food to which all families who lived in the homes in question contributed a share. The dish then was deposited in one of the dwellings. By this act, termed *eruv*, all the houses around the courtyard became a common dwelling, and the thus the carrying of objects among them was permitted. A similar *eruv* was used to make it permissible for people to carry objects on the Sabbath from one ship to another, if the ships were lashed to one another with cables. If, however, the ships were not lashed together, but anchored alongside and touched each other, the resort to such an *eruv* remained ineffective, and the carrying of objects from one ship to the other remained prohibited.[66]

Since it was considered forbidden to fetch anything from the sea to the ship on the Sabbath, the question arose whether it was allowed to draw water from the sea on that holy day of rest. To make that permissible, it was ruled that a plank should be run out from the deck over the water, and then the water that lay under the plank was considered as forming part of the ship and could be drawn aboard.[67] Also, it was permitted to pour waste water over the side of the ship whence it flowed down into the sea.[68]

It was forbidden on the Sabbath to make a permanent "sailor's knot"; a temporary knot, however, which was frequently slipped and knotted again, might be made on the Sabbath.[69] This made it impermissible on a Sabbath to bind the rigging loops to the head of the mast, since that was done by a permanent lashing. On the other hand, it was allowable to pass ropes through these loops, for that had to be done each time anew.[70] As to the mats used as awnings to protect the cargo, the opinions of Rav and Shemuel, the two religious leaders of third-century Babylonian Jewry, were divided: According to Shemuel it was permitted to move them on the Sabbath, while according to Rav it was forbidden.[71]

There was, however, no difference of opinion as to the liberty to violate the Sabbath in order to save the ship from being wrecked in a storm,[72] in accordance with the general principle that "the duty of saving life supersedes the Sabbath laws."[73] How strictly these laws were obeyed at least by some Jewish sailors even generations later we learn from a letter written by Sinesius, Bishop of Corynna, dated in the year 404. We know from the Codex of Theodosius that about that time there was a Jewish shipmasters' guild ("*corpus naviculariorum*") in Alexandria, Egypt,[74] and it was on board the ship of one of these Jewish shipmasters, Amarantus Navicularius by name, that Bishop Sinesius sailed from Alexandria to Corynna. Subsequently, he recorded his experiences on board the Jewish ship in a lengthy letter from which the following passages have interest for us:

> All the sailors of the ship, their number being twelve, and together with the captain thirteen, were Jews, the children of that accursed nation which thinks that it is doing a good deed by causing death to the Greeks. . . . They were all deformed in one or another part of their bodies. As long as we were not in danger they amused themselves by calling one another not by their proper names but by their bodily defects: Lame, Ruptured, Left-handed, Squint, and so forth. . . . [75] We too amused ourselves with them a great deal. We were about fifty passengers on board; among us a third part were women, mostly beautiful and charming. But, nevertheless, you should not envy me. Even Priapus himself would have behaved piously in a ship steered by Amarantus, who did not allow us even one short hour of pleasure in which to be free of mortal fear. . . . On the day which the Jews call the sixth day, a great storm arose. The Jews believe that on that day the evening already belongs to the following day on which it is forbidden to them to do any work. When Amarantus perceived that the sun had gone done, he dropped the steering rudder from his hands. The passengers believed that he had done thus because of despair. When it became known

to them what the real reason was, namely the keeping of the Sabbath, and all their requests that he should return to the rudder were in vain—because as we entreated him to save the ship from the danger he only continued to read his book [probably the Bible]—they tried to threaten him. One brave soldier—there sailed with us a few Arab horsemen—drew his sword and threatened to cut off the man's head unless he instantly took the rudder again into his hands. But the captain, like a true Maccabean, could not be moved to transgress the commandments of his religion. Later, however, at midnight, he returned to the rudder voluntarily, saying, "Now our law permits it to me, because there is a danger of life."

In later passages of his letter Sinesius relates the further events of the voyage until they reached Asarius. Amarantus was happy and confident, for he hoped that after completing this voyage successfully, he would be able to save himself from the hands of his creditors by repaying them his debts from the fares received from his passengers. The ship of Amarantus seemed to have been in a somewhat neglected state of repair. Despite the strong wind it sailed with all the sails set, for the loops and rings did not work, and, although the sailors with the help of the passengers tried all they could to haul on the ropes, they were unable to furl the sails. Neither could the sails be changed, for the ship carried no spare sails. Finally, they came to anchor with the only anchor the ship still possessed, since the other anchor had been sold, and the ship never had a third one. Later, when the ship sailed again, a second storm broke out, the ship drew near the shore, whence one of the "peasants" (a pilot?) came aboard and took the rudder in his hands, while the "Syrian," that is, Amarantus, willingly let him have this honor. Finally, all of them went ashore at Asarius.[76]

Holidays

Passover. If a person set out on a sea voyage within thirty days before the Feast of the Unleavened Bread, he had to remove from his house anything containing leavened substance—an observance ordinarily carried out on the eve of the Pesach (Passover)—for he could not count on being able to return from his voyage before the feast.[77] R. Yehuda (a Palestinian Tanna of the early second century A.D.) tried to forbid sailing on the six days of half-holiday intervening between the first and the last (eighth) days of the holiday of Passover, but this was not accepted by the *halakhah*. Only the inhabitants of Mesha, a locality northeast of Tyre, undertook voluntarily to observe this stricture. Some time later their descendants found that it was too difficult for them to follow the usage of their fathers, and they approached R. Yehuda ha-Nasi, the head of the Palestinian Jewish community in the second half of the second century A.D., who, incidentally, was a pupil of the aforementioned R. Yehuda, and asked him: "Our fathers refrained from sailing on the Great Sea [the Mediterranean, on the Passover half-holiday]; now as for us, what are we to do?" R. Yehuda ha-Nasi's response was: "Seeing that your fathers took upon themselves this prohibition, do not deviate from the usage of your fathers."[78]

The religious duty to sell before the Passover all the *ḥametz*, that is, everything containing leavened substance, had to be observed also by Jews sailing on a boat. A tannaitic source discusses the situation in which a Jew and a Gentile travel in a ship on the day before Passover. The ruling is that the Jew must sell the Gentile all his *ḥametz*, or else give it to him as a present, and then can buy it back or take it back after the Passover.[79] A Jewish passenger also had to behave on board exactly as it was incumbent on him in his own home: he had to search his quarters on the ship and collect any *ḥametz* he might find. In his home the next step was to burn the *ḥametz*; aboard the ship he had instead to grind it into dust and cast it overboard.[80]

The Jewish calendar was regulated by the phases of the moon. The day on which the new moon was first sighted was taken to be the first day of the new month. The fixing of this day was the prerogative of the central religious authority of Palestine, which then sent signals or messengers to all parts of the country to inform the people of the date and to enable them to celebrate the ensuing feasts on the proper days. Such messages could, of course, not reach Jews sailing on the high sea, who therefore remained in uncertainty as to the correct date on which the Passover began (on the eve of the fifteenth day of the month of Nissan). To solve the problem, R. Nahman[81] advised the Jewish seafarers: "Since you don't know which day has been fixed as that of the new moon, burn the *ḥametz* as soon as you see that the moon shines until dawn."[82] In the sequel to this passage the Talmud states that although on land the moon is visible until dawn only on the fifteenth day of the month, at sea, where the sailors have an unobstructed view of the whole horizon, they can see the moon until dawn already on the fourteenth day of the month, and thus they are able to observe the burning of the *ḥametz* on that day as demanded by the law.

Feast of Tabernacles (or *Sukkot*, "Booths"). The ritual of this feast, celebrated in the autumn, consisted of reciting, on each of the seven days of the feast, the prescribed benediction over the festal wreath, the *lulav*. Moreover, for the duration of the feast, one had to dwell and take one's meals in a booth, covered with green branches and boughs, and built especially for the feast. Jews sailing on ships during the Sukkot festival used to provide themselves in advance with the *lulav*[83] and also used to build themselves booths on the foredeck. On one occasion R. Akiba built himself a *sukkah* (booth) on the foredeck of a

ship, but the next day a strong wind blew away his structure.[84]

Purim. Even though this feast fell at the end of the
winter season (fourteenth of Adar, February-March), when
the sea was considered "closed" to maritime traffic, it
nevertheless happened that urgent business overseas
forced Jews to sail and to brave the inclement weather of
this season. In that case it was their religious duty to celebrate the feast of Purim on board ship by reading the book
of Esther in the same manner they did on land in the
synagogue of their home town.[85]

Ritual Purity

The question of ritual purity and impurity played an
important role in Jewish religious life in talmudic days.
There were objects that might become ritually impure,
while others were not subject to ritual defilement even if
brought into contact with a ritually impure object. Ships,
in general, were regarded as immune to ritual impurity.[86]
Certain types of boats, however, were susceptible of ritual
impurity. Among the latter were the small Jordan boats,
called *ᶜarevat ha-Yarden,* as well as small vessels made of
clay.[87] When a ship was launched the first time, in order
to make its hull watertight, the same water that caused it
to be wet could also make it susceptible to ritual impurity.[88]

The principal source of ritual impurity was the human
corpse. In order to become ritually impure one need not
even touch the corpse directly; it was sufficient to enter a
room in which there was a corpse, and immediately the
ritual impurity of the corpse communicated itself across
the empty space of the room. If there was a corpse in a
ship, however, as long as the ship sailed on the sea, it did
not render the passengers ritually impure. But as soon as
the ship was made fast to the shore or its anchor was
dropped, it did communicate its ritual impurity to all the

passengers aboard.[89] The same held good, not only for ships in general, but also for a cabin on board a ship.[90]

Moreover, while houses in general were liable to become ritually impure through what was called in biblical legislation a "plague of leprosy in a house" (Leviticus 14:34-57),[91] cabins built on board ships or rafts remained ritually pure even though they were attacked by such plagues of leprosy.[92] The water tank of an "Alexandrian ship" which contained at least forty *seahs*[93] of water and had a flat bottom, transmitted ritual impurity to a person or object if the latter remained underneath it together with a corpse.[94] This legal provision indicates that such a big water tank stood on legs. The water tank itself, however, was not liable to becoming ritually impure.[95] On the other hand, the water tank of a small ship was liable to become ritually impure either from a corpse or from a plague of leprosy,[96] since such a tank contained less than forty *seahs* of water. Also the sails of a ship were liable to ritual impurity.[97] The packing bags aboard a ship, if they became loosened and opened, were liable to become ritually impure if an impure person trod on them.[98] Similarly, implements or vessels made out of the *ʿeqel*[99] were liable to become ritually impure.[100] On the other hand, the water that entered the ship through the oar ports, or collected in the bilge well, could not render any object wetted by it ritually impure.[101] The baked-clay "swimmer's barrel," probably used by swimmers as a float, was itself liable to become ritually impure.[102]

On board ship many people met who knew nothing of each other, and therefore the danger was always present that a man could become polluted by the touch or proximity of a ritually impure person. Talmudic legislation lays down the rules covering such ritual contagion on board a ship. If a ritually pure person finds himself on board a big ship together with a *zav*, a man suffering from a discharge (gonorrhea?), and hence ritually impure, he does not become impure.[103] Other rules deal with the possible defilement caused by menstruating women on board to ritually pure persons or vessels;[104] with pollution by the touch of Gentiles of wine owned by Jews and transported on ships;[105] with the effect of a wave that sweeps overboard and wets objects found there and thereby renders them liable to ritual impurity;[106] and with other such questions.

In order to be able to partake of meat on board a ship during a long sea voyage, Jewish passengers used to take with them live animals to be ritually slaughtered and consumed. Since ritual slaughter required the covering of the blood of the animal with earth, they were obliged to take earth with them for this purpose. If however, they had no earth at hand, they were permitted to slaughter the animal in such a manner as to allow the blood to flow directly into the sea, or else to cover the blood with earth as soon as they reached land. According to one talmudic opinion, however, the covering of the blood with earth was so indispensable that the slaughterer was enjoined to burn his prayer shawl and cover the blood with its ashes if he had no earth with him.[107]

Missing Persons and Tithing

Talmudic legislation relating to seafaring also deals with the legal position of a woman whose husband was missing at sea and with the application of the law of tithes to property on board ships. As long as there was no definite proof that the husband was actually dead, his wife was regarded as a married woman with all the obligations and rights that this status entailed.[108] To spare his wife the complications attendant on his situation, a man would give instructions, before embarking on a sea voyage, that his wife be given a *get*, a letter of divorce, in the event that he failed to return home.[109] As soon as a ship coming from foreign lands reached the shores of Palestine, the Talmud provided that the law of tithes became applicable at that point to fruit grown or carried on board and belonging to Jews.[110]

Conclusion

The frequency with which maritime laws are found in the talmudic and other ancient Jewish sources, and the detail into which the rabbis go in making the rulings, are indications of the importance seafaring had for the Jews of Palestine and river shipping had for those of Babylonia in talmudic times.

Notes

Abbreviations in these notes include M = Mishnah; R = Rabbi; T = Tosefta; and TB = Babylonian Talmud; TY = Yerushalmi, the Palestinian Talmud.

1. In 1946 or 1947, at the suggestion of James Hornell (1865-1949), the well-known British expert on maritime history and seafaring in Eastern lands, I rendered my Hebrew book into English and sent him the manuscript for comments and criticism. In the course of the ensuing correspondence (most of it lost) we agreed that we would produce and publish, under joint authorship, a revised and expanded book on the subject. Regrettably, in 1949, before we were able to complete the planned manuscript, Mr. Hornell died at the age of 84.

In the chapter here published, Mr. Hornell's contribution happened to be very limited: it was confined to a few notes he added. They are printed below in brackets and are marked "J. H."

2. T *Qiddushin* 1:7; cf. TY *Ketubot* 34b mid.; TB *Baba Bathra* 76a.

3. M *Baba Bathra* 5:1; T *Baba Bathra* 4:1; TB *Baba Bathra* 73a; TY *Baba Bathra* 15a top.

4. M *Baba Bathra* 5:1; T *Baba Bathra* 4:1; TY *Baba Bathra* 15a top; TB *Baba Bathra* 73a.

5. M *Baba Bathra* 5:1.

6. TB *Baba Bathra* 34b and Rashi's comment, ibid. [This was in accordance with the talmudic legal principle, "He who is stronger wins the right of possession in cases in which the judge is unable to decide because the two parties have an equal claim," for instance, TB *Gittin* 60b. J. H.]

7. TB *Nedarim* 38a.

8. M *Shevi'it* 8:5.

9. Cf. TB *Baba Qama* 97a.

10. TB ʿArakhin 18a; TB Baba Metziʿa 69b-70a, 79a.

11. TB Baba Qama 97a.

12. Midrash Tehillim, Psalm 24:2.

13. TB Baba Metziʿa 79a-b.

14. TB Baba Metziʿa 79b. Cf. T Baba Metziʿa 7:2.

15. T Baba Metziʿa 9:14.

16. TB ʿAvoda Zara 10b; Numbers Rabba 2. Cf. also Matthew 9:9-10.

17. Midrash Tanhuma, Teruma, ed. Buber, 88.

18. M Baba Metziʿa 5:5; TB Baba Metziʿa 69b.

19. TB Baba Metziʿa 69b, and Rashiʿs comment, ibid. Cf. T Baba Metziʿa 5:13; TY Baba Metziʿa 10c top.

20. Georg F. Schoemann, Griechische Altertümer, 4th ed., 2 vols. (Berlin: Weidmann: 1897-1902), 1:474; William Smith, Dictionary of Greek and Roman Antiquities, 3rd ed. (London: Murray, 1872), s.v. Fenus, esp. p. 833.

21. The printed text of the Yerushalmi Talmud has risim, which has been emended by Joseph Perles in "Beiträge zur rabbinischen Sprach- und Altertumskunde," Monatschrift für Geschichte und Wissenschaft der Judentums 37/6 (1893): 6-14, 64-68, 111-16, 174-79, 356-78, to nesim, i.e., Greek nesos, islands, and by Immanuel Loew to Qafrisim, i.e., Cyprus, cf. Saul Lieberman, Talmudah shel Qisrin (Jerusalem, 1931), 14-15.

22. TY Baba Metziʿa 10c bot.

23. Cf. TB Baba Metziʿa 65a, 68a; TY Baba Metziʿa 10c bot; TY ʿAvoda Zara 42a mid. On interest rates on ship loans in ancient Greece and Rome, cf. sources listed in n. 20 above.

24. TB Gittin 73a; cf. TB Baba Metziʿa 106a.

25. TB Baba Metziʿa 69b-70a.

26. Cf. Theophile Meek, "The Code of Hammurabi," in James B. Pritchard, ed., Ancient Near Eastern Texts (Princeton, NJ: Princeton University Press, 1955), 176.

27. TB Baba Metziʿa 80b.

28. Meek, "The Code of Hammurabi," 176.

29. T Baba Metziʿa 11:26. These rulings should be compared with Codex Theodosius XIII:5:32, which provides that in the case of shipwreck "if any measure of grain is said to have been lost in a storm at sea . . . the expense of such loss shall be allotted to the entire guild of shipmasters." Cf. Clyde Pharr, The Theodosian Code: A Translation with Commentary (Princeton, NJ: Princeton University Press, 1952), 396a. Codex Theodosius XIII:9:2-3 also provides that the sailors should be tortured in order to bring out "the full measure of the truth" concerning a shipwreck.

30. TB *Baba Qama* 116b.

31. Meek, "The Code of Hammurabi," 176.

32. TB *Sanhedrin* 32b.

33. T *Baba Qama* 2:10. Cf. TY *Baba Qama* 3d mid.

34. TB *Baba Metzi°a* 107b.

35. TB *Baba Metzi°a* 107b-108a.

36. TB *Baba Metzi°a* 108a.

37. TB *Baba Metzi°a* 108b.

38. TB *Mo°ed Qatan* 4b. [*Hol ha-Mo°ed* or half-festival days are those intervening between the first and last days of Passover and the Feast of Tabernacles. J. H.]

39. TY *Baba Metzi°a* 11a mid. Cf. also T *Baba Metzi°a* 7:14; TB *Baba Qama* 116b, where the text has to be emended according to the version of the Yerushalmi Talmud.

40. T *Baba Metzi°a* 7:14. Also the Codex Theodosius XIII:9:4 contains provisions about tossing cargo overboard in order to lighten the ship and thus save it from sinking in a storm.

41. M *Berakhot* 9:2.

42. M *Berakhot* 4:6.

43. T *Berakhot* 3:19.

44. TB *Berakhot* 54b.

45. Emil Schürer, *Geschichte des jüdischen Volkes*, 4th ed., 4 vols. (Leipzig: Hinrichs, 1901-11), 3:50.

46. Cf. "Bet She°arim," in *Encyclopaedia Judaica* (Jerusalem: Keter, 1972), and literature there in the bibliography.

47. TB *Berakhot* 18a.

48. *Genesis Rabba* 6:5, and parallel sources listed there in the notes of the Theodor-Albeck edition, 44-45.

49. *Sapientia Salomonis* 14:1-2.

50. T *Nidda* 5:17. Cf. also TY *Berakhot* 13b mid.

51. *Sifre Numeri* 76, ed. Friedman, 19b.

52. M. *°Avoda Zara* 1:3. Cf. also Philo Judaeus, *Vita Mosis* II, 224.

53. T *Shabbat* 13:10; TB *Shabbat* 19a.

54. TB *Shabbat* 19a.

55. M *°Eruvin* 4:1. Cf. TB *°Eruvin* 43a.

56. TB *°Eruvin* 42b.

57. M *°Eruvin* 4:2.

58. Reading *lalimen* for *layam*.

59. T *Shabbat* 13:11.

60. M *Shabbat* 16:8; T *Shabbat* 13:11.

61. T *Shabbat* 10:16.

62. T *Shabbat* 16:8. Cf. also TY *Shabbat* 13c top.

63. TY *Shabbat* 16a mid.
64. T *Shabbat* 10:14; T *ᶜEruvin* 10:2, TB *Shabbat* 100b-101a.
65. M *Shabbat* 11:5; T *Shabbat* 10:13.
66. M *Shabbat* 11:5; T *Shabbat* 10:15.
67. TB *Shabbat* 100b; TY *Shabbat* 13b top.
68. TB *Shabbat* 100b-101a.
69. M *Shabbat* 15:1; TB *Shabbat* 111b.
70. TB *Shabbat* 111b.
71. TB *Shabbat* 156b.
72. T *ᶜEruvin* 4:8.
73. M *Yoma* 3:6; TB *Yoma* 85a, and so forth.
74. Codex Theodosius XIII:5:18 (*De naviculariis*), from the year 390. Cf. Pharr's ed., p. 394a. Cf. also Semen Markovich Dubnov, *Weltgeschichte des jüdischen Volkes*, 10 vols. (Berlin: Jüdischer Verlag, 1925-29), 3:254, 325; Salo W. Baron, *A Social and Religious History of the Jews* (New York: Columbia University Press, 1952), 2:249-50.
75. [Concerning the use of nicknames it is noteworthy that the sailors and fishermen of Malta, an old Phoenician colony, are greatly addicted to this custom of addressing one another by some nickname rather than by their proper names. J. H.]
76. Cf. Jean Juster, *Les Juifs dans l'Empire Romain*, 2 vols. (Paris, Geuthner, 1914), 2:324.
77. T *Pesaḥim* 1:4.
78. TY *Pesaḥim* 30d mid.
79. T *Pesaḥim* 1:24.
80. TB *Pesaḥim* 28a.
81. There were several Babylonian Amoras by the name of Nahman.
82. TB *Rosh ha-Shanah* 21a.
83. T *Berakhot* 3:19.
84. M *Sukkah* 2:3; TB *Sukkah* 23a; cf. TY *Sukkah* 52d bot; TY *ᶜEruvin* 19b mid.
85. M *Megilla* 1:2; T *Berakhot* 3:91. Concerning the "closure of the sea" during the stormy season, cf. Codex Theodosius XIII: 9:3, which decrees that "the month of November shall be exempt from navigation, but the month of April, since it is nearest the summer, shall be employed for the acceptance of cargo. . . . Navigation shall be extended to the day of the ides of the aforementioned months." That is, navigation was suspended from November 15 to April 15.
86. M *Shabbat* 9:2; TB *Shabbat* 83b; TY *Shabbat* 11d bot. Cf. also T *Kelim Baba Qama* 2:3; M *Kelim* 2:3.
87. TY *Shabbat* 7a mid.; TB *Shabbat* 83b, 84a.

88. M *Makhshirin* 5:7.

89. M *Oholot* 8:5.

90. TY *Sukkah* 52d bot.

91. [Leviticus 14:34-57 contains detailed ritual rules regarding the "plague of leprosy" in a house. If the walls of a house should show greenish or reddish stains (probably caused by some species of fungus) the house was regarded as unclean and ritual means had to be taken in order to clean it and thereby render it habitable again. J. H.]

92. M *Negaᶜim* 12:1.

93. [A "seah" is a measure of volume for dry substances (such as grain) and also for liquids. It is equivalent of ca. 12 liters. J. H.]

94. M *Oholot* 8:1.

95. M *Kelim* 15:1.

96. M *Kelim* 15:1.

97. M *Negaᶜim* 11:11; T *Kelim Baba Metziᶜa* 11:9.

98. M *Kelim* 20:1.

99. [ᶜ*Eqel* was the ballast of the ship and usually consisted of iron bars. Here the reference is to pots and the like made from the iron bars of the ᶜ*eqel*. J. H.]

100. T *Kelim Baba Metziᶜa* 1:1.

101. M *Makhshirin* 5:7.

102. M *Kelim* 2:3.

103. M *Zavin* 3:3.

104. M *Taharot* 5:8; T *Zavin* 4:4.

105. M ᶜ*Avoda Zara* 5:4; T ᶜ*Avoda Zara* 7:13.

106. M *Miqvaot* 5:4, 6.

107. M *Hullin* 2:9; T *Hullin* 1:4; 2:29; 6:6; TB *Hullin* 13b, 88b.

108. M *Gittin* 3:4; TB *Baba Bathra* 153b.

109. M *Gittin* 6:5.

110. M *Halla* 1:2; T ᶜ*Orla* 1:2, 3.

15

Which Came First, the Music or the Words? (A Greek Text and Coptic Melody: Musical Transcription and Analysis of the Setting)

Marian Robertson
Coptic Encyclopedia, University of Utah, Salt Lake City, Utah

Prelude

I am happy and honored to write this article as a tribute to Dr. Hugh W. Nibley, my longtime friend and teacher. As the only courageous soul enrolled in Advanced Greek at Brigham Young University (1946-1948), I was privileged to sit at his feet for a lesson thrice-weekly — time which he readily granted to me alone even though he usually carried a teaching load of much more than thirty hours per quarter. For these very special classes, we often went outdoors, and as I chanted aloud mighty lines, carefully prepared, from Homer, Hesiod, Aeschylus, Sophocles, and many, many others, we both would gaze northward to imperial Mount Timpanogos, or southwestward to hazy, distant Mount Nebo. These memories, the challenge of his genius, and his constant support have been, and will always be, important in my life. God bless you, Hugh and Phyllis.

Introduction

This article is an expansion of a paper presented at the Third International Congress of Coptic Studies (Warsaw, Poland, 1984), which dealt with a Coptic melody that is performed at Easter time to two completely different texts.[1] It is hoped that the following discussion will provide a clue as to the antiquity of the music in question.

The dating of Coptic melodies is a difficult problem for musicologists, for no Coptic manuscripts have as yet been identified as definitely containing musical notation, and those texts that may perhaps show some rudimentary form of ekphonetic notation have not as yet been deciphered.[2] Consequently, deprived of manuscript documentation, scholars must at present rely on internal evidences gleaned from studies of the oral tradition and analyses of the texts and music at hand.[3] The transcription and analysis herewith presented are an example of the latter.

The melody is a short but subtle little tune that has remained essentially the same through the years, no matter what the language.[4] It is metrical and consists of eight measures broken into two phrases by a distinct caesura in the fourth measure.[5] On Maundy Thursday it is sung as a response during the Morning Office of Incense with a text in Greek and Arabic; during the Sixth Hour on Good Friday, it is heard again as a response, but with quite another text in Coptic and Greek. In both the Maundy Thursday and Good Friday settings, this brief melody is repeated many times over as the hymn text unfolds, line after line, verse after verse. It is the Maundy Thursday setting of the Greek text which will now be discussed.

Description of the Greek Text

The Greek text is comprised of seventeen verses, each having two lines of varying length.[6] It treats the betrayal of Christ by Judas Iscariot, and is identified by its opening lament, "Judas, Judas. . . ." Anton Baumstark has reconstructed the Greek from a liturgical text printed in Coptic letters, which he dates from the seventh or eighth century.[7] It may be translated as follows (each verse is indicated by a Roman numeral):[8]

I. Judas, Judas, Judas, Judas, Judas, Judas, the cruel traitor,[9]

II. Sold Christ to the unjust[10] Jews for a piece of silver.

III. Lo, those violent ones[11] seized Christ, and, with a cross,

IV. They drove [Him] towards Golgotha.[12]

V. *Refrain*: Judas, Judas, etc.

VI. They released Barabbas, the condemned [murderer],

VII. And crucified Him, [our] Judge and Lord.

IX.[13] Like a thief, they drove [Him] forward with a cross,[14]

VIII. And thrust a sword into His side, then placed [Him]

X. In a sepulcher,[15] Him, who called Lazarus forth[16] from the tomb.

XI. *Refrain*: Judas, Judas, etc.

XII. [And indeed], just as Jonah remained three days in the belly of the whale,

XIII. So did our Savior stay three days

XIV. Among the dead. They sealed the tomb.[17]

XV. Verily, He is risen, and the mob[18] did not know that

XVI. Thus the Savior of the world was raised [from the dead], He who suffered,

XVII. And was resurrected for mankind.[19] [O] Lord, glory unto Thee. Amen.

Transcription of the Music and Text[20]

Analysis of How the Text Is Set to the Music

The foregoing translation and transcription both show discrepancies in the setting of the text with the music, some of which are more disturbing than others. Throughout the hymn, the syllables do not always correspond to the notes of the melody, either as to quantity (long or short) or stress. Long syllables may fall on a short note,[21] or a short syllable may be lengthened, and even extended over many beats.[22] Likewise, a stressed syllable (i.e., one bearing an accent) may or may not fall on a strong beat.[23]

But the most surprising discrepancies are found in the various phrasings of the text and melody, which often do not correspond at all. There seems to be little feeling for the mutual needs of either the words or the melody, with the persistent demands of the music prevailing throughout. The above-mentioned caesura of the melody in measure four often separates words that belong together in a single phrase,[24] and on two occasions, words themselves are cut in two.[25] However, the most prominent breaks in the text occur at the end of the melody, i.e., at the final cadence of measure eight, where the words are separated not only in midsentence, but sometimes in midphrase.[26] Thus musically one verse ends and another begins, but if scanned apart from the music, the text continues unbroken. Especially with verses eight through ten, which comprise but one sentence, it is very difficult to reconcile the words with the definite breaks in the music.

A brief note should be made about the influence of Arabic upon the pronunciation of the text. Whereas in Greek many syllables begin with two or more consonants, in Classical Arabic a syllable may begin with only one consonant. Therefore, it is natural for the present-day Copts — whose language is Arabic — to insert an extra vowel between consonants,[27] either (1) within a word,[28] (2) between words,[29] or (3) at the beginning of a phrase.[30] Sometimes this inserted vowel is even prolonged as a sort of vocalise over several notes.[31]

Comments and Conclusions

In view of the foregoing data, the following statements may be made: The distortions of the language caused by the music show that the melody was certainly not composed for this particular text. Indeed, the situation was somewhat reversed in that the melody must have already been in existence and was simply "borrowed" by whoever set the text to it. One may even speculate that this haunting tune was probably already well known and familiar to the people when these words were put with it.[32] When one also considers the Good Friday setting, which is simpler both as to the music (less ornamentation) and text (fewer verses, shorter phrases), it is tempting to propose that this melody had already become an established part of the Good Friday services, and that the more extended "Judas, Judas . . . " was a later addition to the Maundy Thursday rites.

In conclusion, it does seem logical to postulate that the music is at least as old as the text, which would date it from the seventh or eighth century if one accepts Baumstark's dating (see above). Likely it is much older.[33] Admittedly, the ultimate origin of this melody yet remains a mystery, but there can be no doubt that it is sung and heard today as a living remnant from the distant past.

Notes

1. Marian Robertson, "A Coptic Melody Sung Interchangeably in Different Languages: Comparisons Thereof and Proposed Dating Therefor," to be published in the *Proceedings of the Third International Congress of Coptic Studies*, Warsaw, Poland. Henceforth referred to as "Coptic Melody."

2. See the Coptic manuscripts in the John Rylands Library and the Copto-Greek liturgical and biblical manuscripts in the Insinger Collection at the Museum of Antiquities in Leiden.

3. See Robertson, "Coptic Melody," 6-7. For comparative stud-

ies indicating the antiquity of certain Coptic melodies, see Marian Robertson, "The Reliability of the Oral Tradition in Preserving Coptic Music . . . , Parts I and II," *Bulletin de la Société d'Archéologie Copte* 26 (1984): 83-93, and 27 (1985): 73-85. For a general historical discussion, see Ilona Borsai, "Die musikhistorische Bedeutung der orientalischen christlichen Riten," *Studia Musicologica Academiae Scientarum Hungaricae* 16 (1974): 3-14.

4. Robertson, "Coptic Melody," 3-5.

5. See transcription below.

6. These verses are followed by an Arabic translation of the Greek which is condensed into fourteen verses, thus making a total of some thirty-one verses for the entire piece.

7. Anton Baumstark, "Drei griechische Passionsgesänge ägyptischer Liturgie," *Oriens Christianus* 3 (1929): 69-77. Baumstark took this text from *Kitāb Dalāl wa-Tartīb Jumᶜat al-Ālām wa-ᶜĪd al-Fasḥ al-Majīd . . . (Book of the Order [of Services] for Good Friday and Holy Week . . .)* (Cairo: n.p., 1920), 111ff. It contains some Greek grammatical and spelling errors which, however, reflect the Coptic pronunciation. This text is also found in *Epgōm ente pipaskha ethouab (The Book of Holy Easter)* (Cairo: The Patriarchate, 1981), 303.

8. Because of inherent differences in Greek and English, the author has adapted the text, rather than translate it verbatim, in order to have a smooth, comprehensible English reading. Thus some words (mentioned in footnotes) have been paraphrased; some words (enclosed in brackets) have been added; certain Greek participles have been rendered as verbs; and the order of verses eight and nine has been reversed. Every effort has been made to keep the original meaning intact.

9. ὁ παράνομος (*ho paranomos*, "contrary to law and custom, unjust, violent, cruel").

10. παρανόμοις (*paranomois*; see n. 9).

11. παράνομοι (*paranomoi*; see n. 9).

12. ἐν τῷ κρανίῳ τόπῳ (*en tō kraniō topō*, "the place of a skull," which is the Greek rendering of the Hebrew *Golgotha*). In this phrase, the genitive κρανίου (*kraniou*, "skull") is usually used instead of the dative κρανίῳ (*kraniō*). Cf. B. F. Westcott and F. J. A. Hort, eds., *The New Testament in Greek* (New York: Macmillan, 1943), 68, 111, 234.

13. Cf. n. 8.

14. ξύλῳ (*xulō*, "cudgel" or "cross").

15. μνημείῳ (*mnēmeiō*, "monument").

16. ἐγείρας (*egeiras*, "awakened" or "raised from the dead").

17. Baumstark includes an additional refrain at this point in the text. However, it is not sung in the recordings from which the transcriptions were made (see n. 20).

18. στρατιά (stratia, "army" or "band").

19. διὰ τὸ γένος ἡμῶν (dia to genos hēmōn, "for our [human] race").

20. This hymn was transcribed from cassette recordings of the Holy Week Services, edited by Ragheb Moftah (Cairo: Institute of Coptic Studies, 1972). The author is indebted to Mr. Moftah, who generously presented her with copies thereof, and to the late Dr. Aziz S. Atiya and Mme. Lola Atiya, who also lent her their recordings for comparison purposes.

The criteria of transcription are as follows: (1) "A" above "middle C" equals 440. (2) All notes actually sound one octave lower than notated (the singing is done by men only—the treble clef was used for convention's sake). (3) A minus sign (−) above a note indicates that the note is sounded one quarter-tone lower; conversely, a plus sign (+) above a note indicates that the note is sounded one quarter-tone higher. (4) Measures are indicated by bar lines, but close scrutiny reveals that the number of beats in a measure may vary (see verses one and two, measure four; verses eight and nine, measure seven, etc.); also, the number of eighth notes in a beat may vary (see verse ten, measure seven; verse seventeen, measure two, etc.). (5) Letters written in parentheses above the text indicate extra vowels that are inserted into the text by the singers.

21. For example, verse two, measure one, beat three; measure two, beat two, etc.

22. For example, verse one, measure seven; verse two, measures six to seven, etc.

23. For example, verse one in its entirety; verse two, measure one, beat two; or measure two, beat one; or measure three, beat three, etc.

24. See verse two, τοῖς / Ἰουδαίοις (tois / Ioudaiois, "to the / Jews"); verse four, ἐν τῷ / κρανίῳ τόπῳ (en tō / kraniō topō, "in the / place of a skull," see n. 12); verse fourteen, τὸν / τάφον (ton / taphon, "the / tomb"); verse sixteen, ὁ σωτὴρ / τοῦ κόσμου (ho sōtēr / tou kosmou, "the Savior / of the world").

25. Verse three ἐπιλαβού / μενοι (epilabou / menoi, "seiz/ing"); verse six, τὸν κατά / κριτον (ton kata / kriton, "the con/demned").

26. Verse nine ends with the word ἔθηκαν (ethēkan, "they placed [Him]"), and verse ten begins with the phrase ἐν μνημείῳ (en mnēmeiō, "in a sepulcher"). In Baumstark's text the order of these

two phrases is reversed, which intensifies the problem. Verse fifteen ends with the words οὐκ ἔγνωσαν στρατιά, ὅτι(*ouk egnōsan stratia hoti,* ". . . the mob did not know that"), and verse sixteen continues the clause οὕντωσ ἐγέρθη ὁ σωτήρ. . . (*ountōs egerthē ho sōtēr . . . ,* "Thus the Savior . . . was raised . . .").

27. This vowel is usually pronounced as the "e" in "let"; however, in verse sixteen, measure two, it becomes a prolonged "a," pronounced as the "a" in "father."

28. For example, in verse fifteen, measures four through six, *stratia* becomes *s(e)t(e)ratia.* Other examples are found in verse nine, measure three; verse ten, measure one; verse twelve, measure one; verse fourteen, measure five; verse sixteen, measure three (cf. also n. 29).

29. In verse three, measures five to eight, *ton Christon staurō* becomes *ton(e) Christon (e) stavrō.* Other examples are found in verse eight, measure three; verse nine, measure three; verse ten, measure one; verse twelve, measures two and three; verse fifteen, measures two and three. In this last example, measure two becomes a syllabic chant, cf. transcription.

30. At the beginning of verse four, *prosēlōsan* becomes *(e)p(e)rosēlōsan.* Other examples are found in verse four, measure four; verse six, measures four to five; verse nine, measure three.

31. See verse three, measures six to seven; verse seven, measure three, etc.

These brief indications in nn. 27-31 as to the pronunciation are meant only as cursory remarks. A more exhaustive analysis could well be the subject of another article.

32. It is interesting to note that even today when a Copt is asked to sing something from the Holy Week Services (particularly those of Good Friday), this song is usually the first one to come to mind. In contemporary liturgical books, the Arabic rubrics specifying the use of this melody refer to it as *al-Laḥn al-Maʿrūf* ("The Familiar Melody"), e.g., *Khidmat al-Shammās (Services of the Deacon)* (Cairo: The Patriarchate, 1965), 296.

33. René Ménard has suggested that those melodies with Greek or Coptic texts predate the Arab conquest of Egypt (A.D. 642-43). Ménard, "Note sur la mémorisation et l'improvisation dans le chant copte," *Etudes grégoriennes* 3 (1959): 143.

16

What Is Reality?[1]

John M. Lundquist
New York Public Library, New York, New York

The Real, or Reality, I take to describe the place where
God dwells, the state of mind which he possesses, and
the way he acts. I take the world, in the state of mortality
it has known since the beginning of human history to be —
in large part — the contravention of this reality, to be a place
where God does not and cannot dwell, where his perceptions do not prevail, and where humankind acts in a way
contrary to his desires. The primary question is and always
has been: How to discover the mind of God.

Throughout history God has mediated his knowledge
about the Real to humankind through various means:
through dreams, visitations, and various degrees and
forms of revelation to private individuals and to prophets.
The scriptures contain an account of God's dealings with
humankind and are a historical record of his revelations
to prophets, or, in other words, of his transmission to them
of knowledge of the Real.

It is my contention that the temple has been the means
which, throughout history, God has used as the primary
vehicle through which to pass on to humankind knowledge
concerning Reality; that the temple is the paradigm *par
excellence,* the pattern by and through which humankind
has learned (1) where God lives (represented in the temple
by the innermost sanctuary, the most holy place); (2) how
one arrives there (the ritual process — rites of passage — the
ordinances); and (3) what life there is like (a paradisiacal
existence without evil and death, represented in the temple

428

by actual or artistically produced springs, lush gardens, trees of life, etc.).[2] It is in and through the temple that people have gained the greatest and most significant knowledge about Reality.[3]

In the biblical tradition, as well as in many — if not all — cultures of humankind which have known or still know the institution of the temple, a far-reaching commonality of architectural symbolism, ritual practices, and religious symbolism has been noted.[4] Two features of this common tradition that are particularly relevant to my thesis here are that temple practices are revealed to prophets by God (the absence of prophecy within a religious community is commonly taken to be a sufficient explanation for the absence of full temple practices in that community)[5] and that the central feature of the revelation is an architectural plan which is itself an imitation or a model of a temple which exists in heaven.[6]

I have stated above that Reality consists in part of the place where God lives. The innermost sanctuary of the temple, the most holy place, is a model on earth of the place where God lives. He does not live in the earthly temple's most holy place — this is clear from the Hebrew text of Exodus 19:18, 20, where the Lord descends out of heaven onto the mountaintop. He lives in heaven, the Real, but offers a glimpse into heaven through the earthly most holy place, where his presence is experienced by the prophet or the king on special occasions.

In or near the most holy place are arranged architectural and natural features which symbolize what I have elsewhere called "the Primordial Landscape": (1) the cosmic mountain (the most holy place of the ancient Near Eastern temple was thought to be located directly over the primordial hillock, the "Rock of Foundation" in the biblical tradition, the first ground to appear after the waters of chaos had receded, where earthly creation first took place; this hillock became the mountain, the archetype of the built temple), (2) the waters of life, and (3) the tree of life.[7] These features symbolize the beauty and pristine purity of creation and of God's dwelling, as well as the saving gifts of the temple. Ultimately, the temple and its symbolism represent the eternal life that is the main characteristic of Reality.

Heaven is, as it were, one vast "temple without walls," because God's presence fills that space, and the temple is, by definition, a *model* of the place where God dwells. But he does not dwell permanently in the earthly shrine. He reveals the knowledge of how it should be built (Exodus 25:8-9), according to the pattern of heaven itself. The highly organized contact with this earthly temple throughout history thus gives God's people knowledge of heaven, of the Real, and instills within them the desire to live ultimately in that place. They realize that this world is for the most part far removed from the Real, from the place where God dwells, from his perceptions and actions.

But how is the Real, or heaven, to be reached? The answer to this is to be found in the mountain, the archetype and prototype of the built temple. Exodus 19 points us conveniently and profoundly in the right direction. The way up the mountain involves ritual, or rites of passage, through which the prophet mediates knowledge of the Real to the people who have been prepared by this ritual to approach the holy place.

Initiation ritual is to the initiate a journey to the center. In many of the great religious traditions of humankind, the gods are thought to live on a mountain, or to descend from heaven to a mountain, there to meet those who have made the arduous journey to the center to be instructed. The mountain is the center because it was the first place of creation, the central place in the universe from the perspective of the adherents of that religious tradition. It is the vertical pole connecting the heavens with the earth, the navel of the earth. To become one with God, one must join him at the mountain. The journey to the mountain and the ascent of the mountain once one has reached its base are arduous, difficult, and fraught with danger and obstacles. Here we are introduced to the labyrinthine nature of initiation.

The journey to the center involves three kinds of movement: *around* (the practice of ritual circumambulation possibly originates in the necessity to circle around a mountain, as a process of reconnoitering, as one attempts to climb it), *up* (obvious), and *into* (moving ever closer to the center as one moves toward the summit). Herein we have the rationale for such temple complexes as Barabudur in Java—the initiate moves around, into, and up. These movements all find their origins in the very practical requirements of mountain climbing, which has always carried mystical overtones, even when viewed solely as a sport. If the mountain one is being asked to climb, as in Exodus 19, is perceived as the place to which Deity actually descends in order to meet with people, then the kinds of movement required to climb the mountain will themselves be enshrined and canonized.

One sees this clearly in connection with Mount Kailash in Tibet, the holy mountain *par excellence*, thought to be the site of the sacred mountain of the Hindu and Buddhist traditions, anciently known as Mount Meru.[8] The impetus to build sacred mountains, to erect structures that resemble holy mountains (the Old Testament Mount Zion in Jerusalem becomes likened to the mountain of God in the wilderness), will result in similar architectonic arrangements, imitating the topography of the mountain—this is so clear in the Hindu tradition of temple building—as well as the types of physical movement necessary to negotiate it: circumambulation, walking upward (the threshold of each successive section of an Egyptian temple rises in absolute level as one approaches the rear of the building), and walking into the building toward the rear to the most holy place.

The difficulty of mortality, with its pitfalls and plateaus, is compared to the difficulty of climbing mountains, where the gods are to be found. Certain high points along life's path are commemorated and memorialized, formally and ritually, at the mountain and in the temple. Life for the religious person is an arduous journey to the center, with certain high points along this journey commemorated ritually through rites of passage: the passage to adulthood, marriage, introduction into the mysteries. The ultimate stage of one's journey, the ultimate rite of passage, is death. In the great formal canonical traditions — Hinduism, Buddhism, the ancient religions, many contemporary forms of culture (such as the American Indian), and to a lesser extent contemporary Christianity — this journey is commemorated in a physical way, in buildings with formal ritual. In the mystical variants of these traditions, the whole process is carried out in the mind of the traveler. The canonical traditions combine the physical with the metaphysical, the mystical traditions eliminate the physical.[9]

The temple is a visual representation of *all* the symbolism of the mountain, and thus the architecture reflects this symbolism in a thoroughgoing and repetitive way (e.g., the Pagoda structures of Indian, Chinese, Southeast Asian, and Japanese temple architecture, with the multi-level hipped roofs present on every building and gateway in the complex) and is a constant visual reminder that the visitor/initiate is engaged in a journey up a mountain, to heaven. It is this symbolism that we meet in Exodus 19-24: the difficult, arduous, highly charged, and dangerous (because of the sacredness of the place) preparations which must be gone through before reaching the point of readiness to receive knowledge about heaven, its ways and requirements.

Thus the purpose of life is to return to heaven, to the

Real. Knowledge of this place and its requirements is revealed periodically through prophets in temples. The laws,
for example, are often revealed through a prophet or king
in a temple setting.[10] This process reveals the pattern of
life: a difficult, arduous journey to the Real, assisted at
various times by rites of passage that strengthen the person, leading, ideally, to even higher plateaus until the
ultimate initiation, death, which will eventually bring the
person into heaven itself. And here the *instructional* nature
of the temple should be emphasized. The journey to the
mountain, the ritual process, is accompanied by instruction
about Reality which may take many forms: dramatic plays
in which actors reenact the story of creation;[11] visual representations of the exemplary life and of life's course, as
is the case of the sculptures representing the Buddha's life
in the galleries at Barabudur;[12] verbal instruction, as was
the case between Moses and the Israelites at Sinai (Exodus
19-24); or some combination of these.

During the historical existence of the human race the
temple has offered a respite from the harshness and *unreality* of life, beckoning the devotee to partake of the waters
of life which bubble up into the most holy place from the
deep springs on which it is built (Ezekiel 47:1; Joel 3:18;
Zechariah 14:8; Psalm 46:5). Within a dark, misty, misleading world, the temple offers to the initiate a taste of
paradise, so well exemplified by the formative dream, set
in Liverpool, experienced by the great psychologist Carl
Gustav Jung in 1927: After a difficult ascent to the top of
a hill in a dirty, sooty city (Liverpool), he encountered "a
broad square dimly illuminated by street lights, into which
many streets converged." The city's quarters were arranged radially around the square. A round pool stood in
the center of the square, thus creating the squared circle,
the mandala configuration, indicating the location of the
temple in the topography of the dream. A small island
stood in the center of the pool. On the brightly illuminated

island, which stood out amidst the darkness that surrounded it, a magnolia tree stood. The tree seemed to be the source of light on the island. This combination of symbols, the "primordial landscape," provided for Jung the central message of his life, the central revelation: "Through this dream I understood that the self is the principle and archetype of orientation and meaning."[13] He had reached the Center, the Real, the Ultimate, which provided him with the insight and strength to continue his life's arduous journey once he was no longer under the influence of the temple setting of his dream. As a matter of fact, as I have pointed out elsewhere, the main formative insights of Jung's life were all mediated to him either as a result of profoundly moving visits to temple ruins, such as the stupas of Sanchi in India, or in dreams that were saturated with temple symbolism.[14]

And why do people seek out this path amidst the difficulties and complexities of life? Mircea Eliade answers: "The profound reason for all these symbols is clear: the temple is the image of the sanctified world. The holiness of the temple sanctifies both the cosmos and cosmic time. . . . Religious man wants to live in a cosmos that is similar in holiness to that of the temple."[15] The religious person wants to recover and return to heaven, the Real.

The paradigmatic nature and purpose of the temple is made clear in Paul's discourses on Christ's atonement and the temple in Hebrews 7-10. Each part of the Mosaic tabernacle is seen as a precursor to, and teacher about, the Savior. The ultimate holy place is clearly defined here in Hebrews 9:12, 24, and 10:19—it is the place where God dwells: "by his own blood he entered once into the holy place" (Hebrews 9:12), "but into heaven itself, now to appear in the presence of God for us" (Hebrews 9:24). Through his death the Savior passed into the presence of his Father, the real holy place of which the earthly is an imitation and a model. That there is a temple in heaven is made clear in Revelation 11:19: "And the temple of God was opened in heaven, and there was seen in his temple the ark of his covenant." The temple on earth will continue to function during the Millennium, as is so dramatically demonstrated in Ezekiel 40-48, and in the chapters of Revelation which deal with the Millennium. The basic principle will still hold during the thousand-year reign of the Savior on the earth—the temple, with its most holy place, will serve as a reminder of the ultimate holy place, of the Real, of heaven where God dwells. But Revelation gives additional remarkable insight about heaven, the earth, and the temple. Following the resurrection and the judgment, "a new heaven and a new earth" are created, in which the heavenly Jerusalem descends from heaven to the earth, at which time God the Father himself will dwell on the earth with those worthy to be there with him (Revelation 21:1-3, 10). But now, in contradistinction to the historical plus millennial periods of the earth, when the temple existed as a copy on earth of the heavenly temple, a "piece of heaven on earth," there will no longer be any temple. The need for it will have disappeared with the presence on the renewed earth of the Father himself (Revelation 21:22). Heaven, the Real, will have been brought down to earth in the form of the New Jerusalem, and the entire city is now suffused with the saving, paradisiacal symbols that in the period of earthly history were limited to the rather smallish temple itself.

> And I saw no temple in the city, for its temple is the Lord God the Almighty and the Lamb. And the city has no need of sun or moon to shine upon it, for the glory of God is its light, and its lamp is the Lamb (Revelation 21:22).
>
> Then he showed me the river of the water of life, bright as crystal, flowing from the throne of God and of the Lamb through the middle of the street of the city; also, on either side of the river, the tree of life with its

twelve kinds of fruit, yielding fruit each month; and the leaves of the tree were for the healing of nations (Revelation 22:1-2).

Thus, from the perspective of the scriptures, the world is a poor substitute for Reality, which is to be found in heaven, where God lives. Life's purpose is to return to this heaven. The difficult journey is made lighter by access to the temple, which mirrors Reality. Access to the temple is gained by rites of passage and by observing the laws of God, which themselves were revealed in the temple and are sanctified by it. The ultimate initiation, death, will, following the resurrection and judgment, bring the worthy into the presence of God, on an earth made heavenly by being turned into one vast temple. The symbol and its referent will merge into one. Reality will reign supreme.

Notes

1. Anyone in the scholarly LDS tradition who writes about the temple stands on the shoulders of Hugh Nibley, whose brilliance and personal example on this subject represent a beacon light to those who would follow. This article is a struggling attempt to show my indebtedness to the man who introduced me to this subject, and to the lifelong joy that its study has given me.

2. John M. Lundquist, "The Common Temple Ideology of the Ancient Near East," in Truman G. Madsen, ed., *The Temple in Antiquity* (Provo: Religious Studies Center, 1983), 53-76.

3. I am taking an approach here which is remarkably close to, yet independent from, that of A. J. Bernet Kempers, "Barabudur: A Buddhist Mystery in Stone," in Luis O. Gomez and Hiram W. Woodward, Jr., eds., *Barabudur: History and Significance of a Buddhist Monument*, Berkeley Buddhist Studies Series (Berkeley: Asian Humanities Press, 1981), 109-19. Kempers writes, for example, that "I frequently use in connection with Barabudur other words such as Reality (as opposed to the phenomenal world, the 'real' world of nonreligious people), Ultimate Reality, Absolute Reality, Totality" (p. 109). "The meeting of Reality and Man is a central element in many religions, in which, consequently, the most essential sanctuaries provide a meeting place for the Holy and the worshipper" (p. 111). "The sanctuary establishes as a fact that there is — always —

a relation between the world we live in and an Ultimate Reality which introduces meaning and certainty into our existence" (ibid.). "The major mystery expressed in Barabudur—both in its general layout, construction, and symbolism, and in its additional decoration and reliefs—is the meeting of the Holy and Mankind, enacted by the descent of the Holy—of Ultimate Reality, Totality—and the ascent of Man" (p. 112).

4. Hugh W. Nibley, "What Is a Temple?" and "Looking Backward," in Madsen, *The Temple in Antiquity*, 19-51; reprinted in *CWHN* 4:355-90. Lundquist, "The Common Temple Ideology"; John M. Lundquist, "What Is a Temple? A Preliminary Typology," in H. B. Huffmon, F. A. Spina, and A. R. W. Green, eds., *The Quest for the Kingdom of God: Studies in Honor of George E. Mendenhall* (Winona Lake, IN: Eisenbrauns, 1983), 205-19.

5. Dennis J. McCarthy, "Covenant in Narratives from Late OT Times," in Huffmon, Spina, and Green, *The Quest for the Kingdom of God*, 90-94. See the comments by Yigael Yadin that were appended to David Noel Freedman, "Temple without Hands," in *Temples and High Places in Biblical Times* (Jerusalem: Nelson Glueck School of Biblical Archaeology of Hebrew Union College-Jewish Institute of Religion, 1981), 29.

6. Freedman, "Temple without Hands," 21-29; Lundquist, "What Is a Temple?" 211-12.

7. Lundquist, "The Common Temple Ideology"; John M. Lundquist, "Temple Symbolism in Isaiah," in Monte S. Nyman, ed., *Isaiah and the Prophets* (Provo: Religious Studies Center, 1984), 33-55.

8. John Snelling, *The Sacred Mountain* (London: East West Publications, 1983).

9. For a good example of this latter point, see R. C. Zaehner, "Standing on the Peak," in *Studies in Mysticism and Religion Presented to Gershom G. Scholem* (Jerusalem: Magnes Press, 1967), 381-85.

10. John M. Lundquist, "Temple, Covenant, and Law in the Ancient Near East and in the Hebrew Bible," in Avraham Gileadi, ed., *Israel's Apostasy and Restoration in Prophetic Thought: Essays in Honor of R. K. Harrison* (Grand Rapids, MI: Baker Book, 1988), 293-305.

11. Lundquist, "What Is a Temple?" 212-15.

12. J. G. de Casparis, "The Dual Nature of Barabudur"; Kempers, "Barabudur: A Buddhist Mystery in Stone"; Hiram W. Woodward, Jr., "Barabudur as a Stupa"; Alex Wayman, "Reflections on the Theory of Barabudur as a Mandala," in Gomez and Woodward,

Barabudur: History and Significance of a Buddhist Monument, 47-172.
"The monument is only a framework for the sculpture": Jacques
Dumarçay, *Borobudur*, ed. and tr. Michael Smithies (Singapore: Ox-
ford University Press, 1978), 31.

13. C. G. Jung, *Memories, Dreams, Reflections*, recorded and edited
by Aniela Jaffe, tr. Richard and Clara Winston (New York: Vantage
Books, 1965), 198-99.

14. John M. Lundquist, "C. G. Jung and the Temple: Symbols
of Wholeness," in Karin Barnaby and Pellegrino D'Acierno, eds.,
C. G. Jung and the Humanities: Toward a Hermeneutic of Culture (Princeton: Princeton University Press, 1989), 113-23.

15. Mircea Eliade, "The Prestige of the Cosmogonic Myth," *Di-
ogenes* 23 (1958): 12.

17

Native American Rites of Passage: Implications for Latter-day Saints

Suzanne E. Lundquist
Brigham Young University, Provo, Utah

In traditional Native American cultures, the way to achieve maximum human potential is directed by the gods. Growth from childhood to adulthood, from ignorance to wisdom, from irresponsibility to responsibility, from arrogance to humility, from fragmentation to wholeness requires the aid of supernaturals. For most tribes, the creator established, in the beginning, certain rituals or rites of passage that would aid man in comprehending the underlying harmony of the universe and in finally assuming his place in it. By means of these ceremonies, frequently representative of the struggles and discoveries of members of the divine family, holy men who understand the divine will instruct the initiate, often by having him assume the identity of one of the characters in the stories of creation. As the initiate reenacts the sacred drama, he is endowed with the knowledge and power possessed by the gods. The initiate becomes one who knows.

Initiation, according to Mircea Eliade, is "equivalent to a spiritual maturing."[1] For religious man, the rites of passage that mark the stages of this maturing "play a consid-

This paper was originally given at the third annual Spheres of Influence conference at Brigham Young University in 1985 and was published in Spheres of Influence: Perspectives on Change 1 *(1986): 79-92.*

erable part in . . . life."[2] For such a person, rites of passage are performed at birth, when an infant takes upon him a name and an identity as a living person; at puberty, when a child moves from adolescence to adulthood; at marriage, when a male and female create a new family unit; and, finally, at death. Each state of growth implies a crisis because it requires the death of a former mode of being and the birth of a new behavior and identity. Because the initiate is continually overcoming ignorance by gaining new, more advanced, sacred knowledge, he often takes upon himself a new name. These are true names, sacred names, names which imply that the initiate has become transformed and is therefore more fully human.[3]

Members of The Church of Jesus Christ of Latter-day Saints are not unfamiliar with sacred rituals. Priesthood blessings at the birth of a child, baptism and confirmation, the endowment, celestial marriage, and grave dedications are our rites of passage. The symbolism is rich in these rites; and if the initiate is purified and made ready to receive the knowledge endowed upon him during such an experience, not only does his life become more meaningful, but also his ability to overcome crises becomes greater, so that his journey towards godhood is facilitated by his correct mental map of how to travel. The initiate recognizes the influence of the divine and desires to become like God — to become a member of the community of those who have gained an identity as Christ's children. But the importance of this process is as poorly understood by Latter-day Saints as it is by most other members of Western cultures, and the possibilities for aid and instruction inherent in the rituals we do have are inadequately explored. Even Latter-day Saints, then, could learn something important from the rites of traditional American Indian cultures.

Modern Western man is in crisis — a crisis of spirit — a crisis of identity. Sociologists, ethnographers, artists, and religious leaders are making very disquieting observations. The prevalence in society of violence, sexual promiscuity and perversions, suicide, and of the dissolution of family life alarms us all. And these problems are not confined to "others out there" in the world. That these same problems exist in the Church is increasingly obvious. New questions asked during temple recommend interviews reflect ecclesiastical concern for such offenses as child and spouse abuse, incest, and failure of one parent to discharge financial and emotional obligations to children left with the other parent through or following divorce.

Many causes for this crisis have been assigned by critics of modern society. Industrialization, technology, television, and the decline in moral values are only some of the causes cited. I would like to suggest another cause. It is my assertion that we have become an asymbolic society, and, as a result, we do not understand the power of our own rites of passage. I also contend that we might have lost one of the most powerful rites of passage from our own canon of rituals. According to cultural psychologist Rollo May, the preoccupation with self that is so characteristic of our time comes because human beings have cut themselves adrift from the basic, underlying sacred myths that give definition to what it means to be human. May claims that the reason for the popularity of psychology today is that it is all that remains for coping with the problems facing modern man. From "the myth of an afterlife to the more modern beliefs in the virtues of family and state, the myths and symbols that once drained off anxiety, assuaged guilt feelings, comforted people, and gave them strength to face the problems of life have lost their vitality."[4]

The students I have taught over the past eighteen years at four major universities have seldom been familiar with the symbolic process or with the sacred texts and metaphors that have formulated their own worldview. Few have read the Old or New Testaments—documents closely connected with Western values and thought. Most are unaware of why and how values are transmitted from one generation to the next.

The use of the word " myth," as May uses it, should not unsettle Latter-day Saints as it often does. In this context, "myth" refers to sacred stories that explain the interventions of the divine into human affairs—the interventions that reveal covenant laws, temple rites, and the purpose of human existence. May suggests that it is time for a rebirth of such "cultural myths and symbols."[5] Theodore Hesburgh, president of the University of Notre Dame, makes a similar assertion. When Hesburgh became chairman of the board of the Rockefeller Foundation, he persuaded his fellow trustees to set up a commission on the humanities. It cost the foundation one million dollars to come to the conclusion that the future of man "is dictated by the most profound need of our age": the need to "rediscover man and the meaning of human life," the need to bring man to a consciousness of "his ultimate destiny, his vision beyond time, his idealism that transcends power, money, or pleasure." Hesburgh concludes that the burden of the humanities lies in bringing men to the "awareness of what men and women can be" with the "determination to re-create the world in that vision."[6]

For Latter-day Saints, the vision of what it means to be human ought to be obvious. Most of us get tears in our eyes when we sing, "I Am a Child of God." Seldom, however, do we pose the question, "Which child of God am I?" Nor do we struggle to understand the meaning of our own rituals or what ritual behavior implies.

In rituals such as those performed in ancient Near Eastern temples, the initiate identifies himself with the first man or first woman. The participant is washed, anointed, and made ready to understand the mysteries of godliness. He is endowed with information to aid him in his quest to understand what it means to be human, what man's relationship to his fellowman ought to be, what the bounds of his own sexuality are, what the purpose of this life is, why the earth was created, and, more particularly, what true moral behavior requires. As sacred history is recited, the initiate learns how to journey to the tree of life, how to arrive at the center of the universe. This central place has generally been holy ground—the mountain of the Lord's house—the temple. It is there that man can meet God, the true Father, and, as a result, learn to transform himself into the image of God.

Implied, then, is the possibility of change—of movement away from the tragedies, calamities, crises, and confusions of profane human existence toward true identity.[7] One of Rollo May's patients once made this statement during a struggle to discover self: "The grace of God is the capacity to change."[8] This, I believe, is a simple yet profound definition of repentance.

But even when all of these ritual realities are accessible, many people fail to lay fast hold of the tree of life because they are not able to comprehend or internalize the messages contained in ritual symbols. These rituals, it must be noted, are intended for mature, righteous adults. What rituals precede the temple ritual? What, if any, rituals aid the adolescent in his journey to the adult world? Modern Western cultures do not have them. Mormons do not have them. I believe there is a need for a rite of passage between the ages of eleven and fifteen and again between the ages of sixteen and twenty. Traditional Native American cultures, those that have overcome the pressures to assimilate, have such rites. These rites allow the members of the tribe to attain peace and harmony in a world of chaos and greed. Such rites are worthy of examination.

Adolescence, in modern Western cultures, is an ambiguous period. According to Neil Postman, what we have experienced in modern society is the collapse of successive levels of existence—the loss of childhood as well as adulthood. Through early exposure to "adult entertainment," children lose their innocence and the opportunity for natural growth and development. Adult life, for the most part, is characterized by being old enough to break normal taboos—old enough to drink, to have multiple sex partners, to choose an individual brand of moral behavior independent of what traditional religion or education recommends, and old enough to cause violent and perverse misery in the name of liberty. What we have, claims Postman, is the "rise of the 'childified' adult."[9] What we have become, especially in the United States, is a nation of adolescents. As the emphasis of most advertising shows, fashions and tastes are largely youth-oriented. We have become a nation that worships youth. And, tragically, youth today is characterized by turmoil, confusion, anxiety, and moral experimentation. Adolescence in modern Western societies has become synonymous with irrationality.

According to Ira Progoff, "Depth psychology was brought into being in nineteenth-century Europe essentially because the quality of behavior and the quality of consciousness of modern man had become disturbed and needed to be healed—or as was later discovered, the consciousness of modern man needed to be transformed." The metaphor most used to describe the condition of modern man has been a medical one. Modern man has a malady, a disease, a cancer, needing not only a diagnosis but a cure. However, says Progoff, "during the past generation experience has shown that man does not require healing; what he requires is a new metaphor for human development—a metaphor that would transform the quality of modern man's consciousness."[10]

What Progoff and other depth psychologists discovered through their research concerning human growth, creativity, and spiritual development was that certain patterns began to emerge. In particular, they discovered that "the development of personality through [adolescent stages] of life moves in the direction of an experience of initiation, both a primary experience of initiation to life and successive initiations to larger dimensions of awareness." These experiences "are the key to the emergence of form and meaning in individual existence."[11] Identity, at this time, opens in two directions: inward and outward. Of necessity, there is a strong need for individual identity, a clear sense of independence and distinctness in relationship to others. However, with this strong sense of personal existence also comes "the realization of the individuality of others, and of an existence in others that is both separate from us and intimately connected to us." This awareness is essential during adolescence "when the transition into adult life is made."[12]

Traditional American Indian cultures assume that while biological transitions are being made during adolescence, so are cultural and existential transitions. Because this is a time of crises, of confusion and lack of identity, traditional cultures accomplish or aid this transition by means of a rite of passage. These cultures take youth through life activities, ritual dramas, to bring about emotional changes that correspond to outward biological growth. Our culture provides nothing comparable. Boy Scouting for boys (incorrectly modeled after Native American beliefs) and "personal progress" for girls are not rites of passage. Priesthood ordinations could serve this function, but they are not inclusive enough. These ordinations bless young boys with spiritual power and ecclesiastical duties but not with knowledge of sexuality or interpersonal development and individual identity. Patriarchal blessings provide some important knowledge typical to traditional rites of passage, but the ritual framework is absent. Missionary experiences come very close to acting as a rite of passage for many young men and some young women in the Church. This experience, however, comes too late in life to serve the purposes I am describing. S. N. Eisenstadt, in "Archetypal Patterns of Youth," identifies tasks that must be accomplished during adolescence: a youth must discover the seed of his own independent identity apart from the collective; he must come to terms with his relationship to family and community and assume his relationship to the creator; and, finally, he must come to terms with his own sexuality.[13] None of these discoveries should come as the result of exploitive or damaging forms of experimental behavior so typical of the current Western adolescent culture. "Sowing wild oats" can damage rather than enhance personal discovery. Properly channeled, however, the energies of the young at this point in their lives can even successfully challenge existing societal norms and thus rejuvenate societies.[14]

The Winnebago Indians expose exploitive adolescent behavior through a body of sacred literature that incorporates the adventures of a character, the Trickster, who existed at the time of the sacred beginnings — the premortal existence. The Trickster, throughout most of the Trickster myth cycle, is a sacred fool whose exploits draw attention to the consequences of being a human primarily concerned with satisfying his appetites for food, sex, and pleasure. He has no notion, for most of the myth cycle, of any responsibility toward himself, his family, his community, or nature. As a result, he brings pain and suffering not only on himself but on others. The purpose of such tales is to bring about psychotherapeutic change in the individuals who hear the tales. As the Trickster transforms from being an amoral, instinctual, amorphous, desocialized, subhuman being to a character who has the right to govern an earth of his own, the students of the tale are expected to see their own behavior in the Trickster and desire such a transformation in themselves. All this is accomplished with great humor; laughter, among the Winnebago, brings about healing. The Trickster's activities explain the origins of human anatomy and also show why man must respect the laws of culture and of nature. The Trickster's sexual exploits demystify romantic passion while illustrating what silliness and pain accompany personal preoccupation with sex.

According to Paul Radin, the symbol of the Trickster "contains within itself the promise of differentiation, the promise of god in man."[15] The Trickster moves through the ambiguities of existence: good/evil, denial/affirmation, destruction/creation, fool/hero. As a contrary figure, the Trickster exposes the chaos of life without an ideal to work from. The Winnebago teach the highest type of conduct: "the right of every man to happiness and to freedom of expression in consonance with individual capacities; the recognition of limits imposed upon individual freedom by human relationships; and the responsibility of an individual for his own actions."[16] Trickster tales are told against this ideal, allowing for a kind of moral sorting out.

Progoff suggests, as does the talmudic creation text, that "when God was creating man, he did not complete his task. He refrained from making man perfect, but left that as a task remaining to be done. He left it for man himself to do, specifically for man to achieve in his existence as an individual. The human being is therefore neither perfect nor complete according to his nature, as other more limited species are. His life is open-ended in its possibilities, and this is precisely why man is the species that holds the possibility of carrying the evolution of life to further levels."[17] Man's destiny is to become something greater than the Tricksterlike qualities inherent in the early phases of human development. This evolutionary process, claims Progoff, requires initiatory events. In modern Western culture, however, the crucial passage from adolescence to adulthood has become no longer significant.

Progoff explains that "the requirements of life in a technological culture have so extended the necessary period of preparation for life, both in terms of formal education and in terms of daily interpersonal experiences, that the age of early adolescence is no longer an appropriate time for initiating the young . . . into the adult world."[18] While in earlier cultures adolescence "was a time for launching out in life, in modern culture it can be no more than a time of waiting."[19] The resultant "damming-up of life energies . . . creates a restlessness of personality. It is a time of treading water in life, a time when there are large amounts of energy available to be expended, but the doors are closed on them." During the ages of eleven to nineteen, modern youth exist in a "psychological vacuum."[20] Most youth fill this vacuum with irrational behavior, foolish fads, sexual experimentation, and profound restlessness. Their behavior, in other words, is very Tricksterlike. Being set apart in "community" with other adolescents further intensifies the vacuum. William Golding's *Lord of the Flies* is an extreme metaphor for what can happen to youth when left without a true community of all age groups.

If initiation does not take place during these years, it generally does not take place until much later. Often heads of families find themselves in midlife still selfish and in search of self-identity. Many leave families in search of their more authentic selves; the costs of such a search are great. The family unit fragments, crippling male/female relationships as well as parent/child relationships. Children require the security of loving parents to mature. Without such stability, children feel orphaned. The entire complexion of human existence in modern Western society is being altered because of these realities.

Dramatic, prototypical initiation, then, becomes impossible for an entire culture. The rites of passage that should take place at this time establish the pattern for all other initiatory events and are, therefore, crucial. If the initiation to life "does not take place at this time, the individual continues to live in an in-between world. . . .

Many people in modern society . . . live into the later years of their lives without undergoing the initiatory experience that makes the transition for them into adult awareness." The result of this is an "era of inadequate men" and "confusion among women. An essential ingredient for life, a certain quality of awareness, a perspective, a stability, and an inward power, are lacking until this initiation takes place."[21]

The Sioux Indians have two significant rites of passage for their youth, rites they say were revealed through their prophets. Initiates essentially reenact the process of growth established by sacred characters who learned how to become whole. The holy man Black Elk explained these rites to Joseph Epes Brown, who later recorded them in a book, *The Sacred Pipe*. Slow Buffalo had a vision given to him through which he came to understand that "he had been given rites which should be used for the benefit of the young women of his nation."[22] Shortly after Slow Buffalo received his vision, Feather-on-Head brought his fourteen-year-old daughter to Slow Buffalo. The daughter, White Buffalo Cow Woman Appears, had experienced her first menstrual period. Slow Buffalo wanted her purified for womanhood.

This is when the first rite of passage into womanhood took place among the Sioux. From this a complex ritual filled with profound symbolism was developed. To explain it only briefly, the entire community, especially the older men and women, are involved in a sacred ritual acknowledging a young girl's womanhood. The young woman is placed at the center of the nation's hoop while the powers of the universe are called upon; the North, South, West, and East, with their attendant meanings, are ritually recreated with the young woman at the center. Only the young woman's closest relatives are permitted to enter the lodge (*tipi*). These rites are too sacred to be witnessed by all. During this rite, a young woman's relationship to her

own body, to all living creatures, and to her nation is
established.

When the initiate, representing White Buffalo Cow
Woman Appears, is given her sacramental meal, she is
told that she, having prayed to Wankan Tanka, will now
go forth among her people in a sacred manner. She is
instructed to "cherish those things which are most sacred
in the universe" and that she "will be as Mother Earth —
humble and fruitful." Her task as a woman is outlined.
She should be like Wankan Tanka, "merciful to others,
especially to those children who are without parents."
Generosity is the key to womanhood. The young woman
is required to give her last mouthful of food to a needy
child. In essence, she must provide for the wants of others,
for her children. As the prayer of instruction continues,
the young girl is told to "follow the sacred path with Light,
not with the darkness of ignorance."[23]

As the young woman emerges from the *tipi*, the entire
community rejoices because a "great thing has been accomplished." Because of this rite, there is much holiness
in her, therefore the entire community rushes up to the
woman so that they can put their hands on her. Following
the ritual and celebration, a feast and give-away are held.
The poor in the community are taken care of, and the entire
community is renewed. The young woman is a symbol for
the continuation of all life, of the nation's hoop, and of
man's continued favor with deity. This ceremony makes
pale the teas that are held for our daughters during fifth
grade. Cookies are served; a short film about reproduction
is shown; and a brief talk about love, how bodies change,
and about the use of deodorant is given. Mothers are often
not even informed when their daughters begin their periods. This has become an event associated with secrecy,
shame, and, often, uncleanliness. For the Sioux, red (the
color of blood) is a symbol of goodness, life, and abundance
and is the color of the East — the goal of life's journey. In

the West, the color red (or scarlet) has confused connotations.

The Sioux also have vision quests for their young men.
Vision quests are not limited to this phase of life, but the
primary, prototypical vision quest is established during
this time. The young initiate goes to a holy man when he
is ready to go on his vision quest. He is instructed in how
to prepare a sweat lodge in which to purify himself before
going on his quest. Here the symbolism is similar to that
of the rite for the young woman. The cosmic circle is re-
created, and the initiate must journey to the center of that
circle. The initiate, when this ordeal is completed, will
receive his man name. A sacred relationship with the
waters of life, the trees, the grasses, the birds, and all
animal life is asked for by the young man so that the coming
generations might "live in a holy manner." Once the youth
is purified, he is taken to a sacred spot—a mountain, the
center of the universe—and left for up to four days. During
this period of time the youth does not eat. He cries to the
Six Grandfathers for a revelation of his purpose as an individual. When the holy man returns to receive the initiate,
he interprets the experiences, dreams, and signs given to
the youth. It is the desire of Wankan Tanka that his people
not live in ignorance, either personal or communal.

When Lame Deer embarked on his initial vision quest,
it was the first time in his life he had ever gone anywhere
without his parents. He was sixteen at the time. His grandmother made a beautiful quilt for him to take with him, a
quilt which he treasured until the end of his life. More
than anything, he wanted to become a holy man like his
father and grandfather. He was afraid he would be asked
to become a sacred clown, a Heyoka. The Medicine man
gave him the sacred pipe to take with him—a wonderful
gift. During the four days that Lame Deer was seeking his
vision, he had numerous spiritual experiences. The most
important one, however, was when he was raised in the

spirit above the world, and a voice came to him, saying: "You are sacrificing yourself here to be a medicine man. In time you will be one. You will teach other medicine men. . . . You will learn about herbs and roots and you will heal people. You will ask for nothing in return. A man's life is short. Make yours a worthy one."[24] While Lame Deer was sleeping, "yet fully awake," he explains, his great-grandfather Lame Deer, an old chief of the Minneconjou, came to him wishing Lame Deer to take upon him his name. Through this experience, Lame Deer gained his own personal identity, a man's name, and came to understand what his relationship to his people was to be. He learned through this experience what his life's work was to be. This rite was one of the most dramatic experiences in Lame Deer's life—a truly prototypical event. He would no longer be the same boy who came up on the mountain to sit in the Vision Pit where his father, grandfather, and great-grandfather had sat before him.[25]

One other example, this from the Taos Pueblo tribe, will establish the wide variety of experiences available for Indian youth. When a young Taos boy arrives at the age of twelve, he is taken away from his family (his "mother") into the Kiva, the womb of mother earth. The Kiva (an underground temple) is a structure which also re-creates the cosmic circle. On the walls the scenes from creation stories and emergence myths, as well as scenes from the history of the tribe, are painted. The young initiate will be schooled there for eighteen months, twice as long as he was in his mother's womb.

Frank Waters, in his fine novel *The Man Who Killed the Deer*, takes a young boy, Napaita, through this event. Napaita is not, however, the major character in the novel. Martiniano, a young man who has been away at a white man's school, is the main character. It is Waters's contention in the novel that because Martiniano did not receive his rite of passage, he was unable to find his true identity.

Because of this, he causes his wife, tribe, and local government to suffer. He continually acts out of selfishness and pride, failing to see what life requires of a mature tribe member. Napaita does receive his rite. In the Kiva, Napaita learns the proper relationship between the body, mind, and spirit. Napaita's father, Palemon, explains to him, "Now you belong to your greater mother. And you return to her womb to emerge once again, as a man with no mother's hold upon him, as a man who knows himself not as an individual but as a unit of his tribe and part of all life which ever surrounds him."[26] In the Kiva, Napaita learns about the primal life of his tribe, their history, how the world was created, a new dimension of time, and his place in the cosmos. Says Palemon to his son, "We will meet again. But as brothers. As men together. As equal parts of one great life. No longer separated. But in that consciousness of our oneness which gives us our only freedom."[27] In the end of the novel, Martiniano also discovers this unity. He and Napaita save one another through an act of quiet heroism. When Napaita becomes lost and hurt during his final test of manhood, it is Martiniano who is led by the powers of the spirit to find Napaita unconscious and bleeding. Martiniano, without pride and with real compassion, simply picks Napaita up from the snow during a winter night and delivers him, without anyone knowing, to the door of the Kiva. Martiniano returns home, determined that his baby son will have a similar rite of passage.

The goal of life for most Native Americans is to reach old age with wisdom and understanding, understanding of the connections possible between male and female, man and his fellowman, man and nature, and, finally, man and the cosmos — a cosmos with a divine center. Change toward these ends can only be made when there is a constant — traditional values and paradigms of being. In Christian theology, the constant is Jesus Christ — the Self-existent

One, the Great I Am. Ideally, the end of all our changing is to come to a stage in development where we can say, "I have created something divine out of the experiences of my life. I Am."

These rites, these values and goals, have aided many traditional Native Americans in their struggle to re-create the world in an image of wholeness, of relatedness. Despite constant legislation by the United States government against tribal religions and governments, traditional ways of believing have persisted among most North American tribes. While the number of traditional believers remains small, they are a source of constancy, resisting assimilation into a dominant culture that offers individualism, competition, luxury, and economic mobility at the expense of family and tribal life. Stress, violence against self and others, irresponsibility, and chaotic lives seem to be the result of mainstreaming. However, in an effort to offer "individual liberty" to all, the United States government has continually legislated against Native American religions and governments. Termination, relocation, the Dawes Severalty Act, the Indian Removal Act, the Mexican American War, and simply the failure to keep any of the 389 treaties made with Native American governments, demonstrate reasons that Native American rites have remained largely unknown in the dominant culture.[28]

C. G. Jung claimed that as long as the Pueblos continued their sacred rituals, they would have "pride and the power to resist the dominant whites." These rituals, said Jung, gave the people "cohesion and unity." Jung felt certain that "the Pueblos as an individual community will continue to exist as long as their mysteries are not desecrated."[29] Religious beliefs and rites are sacred. Most cultures, including the Latter-day Saints, will not reveal their sacred rites to uninitiated observers. Moreover, even though their implications are universal, the forms of sacred rituals are culturally specific. Western drive and individualism have created a people able physically to subdue the Native American cultures. But our culture, as I have shown, has paid a great price for its successes. It seems clear to many observers that the future of our culture depends upon our ability to rediscover our own rites of passage and to come to understand the rich ritual implications of our own sacred symbols.

For Latter-day Saints, wards are ideal social units for the movements necessary toward mature, joyous life. In its parameters, a ward is tribal. Called a "family," a ward is based on a clan metaphor, suggesting mutual responsibility for deep human relationships. In this context, the old, who have experienced life, could aid the adolescents in their journey toward adult life. In the Native American tribe, the elders impart their wisdom to the young to ensure the continuance of the culture. Whether related to the initiate by blood, the elders feel a loving responsibility to enlarge the vision of the young.

Instead of following such a rich model, however, our wards too often imitate the models of our surrounding culture, a culture of separation. We continue to segregate men from women, teenagers from adults and from the opposite sex, children from those not their age, and the aged and single adults from the rest of the community.

The gospel itself is built upon the metaphor of reunion—godly parents with their children. The desire of these parents is that we move through successive stages of development to become like them. For this purpose the gospel structure was revealed. Are we willing to refine our understanding of this structure, perhaps looking for models in places we have previously overlooked? I suggest that we have a great deal to learn about this from the cultures of the Native Americans.

Notes

1. Mircea Eliade, *The Sacred and the Profane: The Nature of Religion* (New York: Harcourt Brace, 1959), 185.

2. Ibid., 184.

3. Ibid., 184-85.

4. Rollo May, "Psychology Has Moved into Matters That Used to Be Left to Poetry," *Psychology Today* (May 1982): 57.

5. Ibid.

6. Theodore M. Hesburgh, "The Future of Liberal Education," *Change* (April 1981): 40.

7. See Truman G. Madsen, ed., *The Temple in Antiquity* (Provo: Bookcraft, 1984), especially Hugh W. Nibley, "What Is a Temple," 19-37, and "Looking Backward, 39-51; and John M. Lundquist, "The Common Temple Ideology of the Ancient Near East,"53-76.

8. Rollo May, *Man's Search for Himself* (New York: Dell, 1953), 214.

9. Neil Postman, *The Disappearance of Childhood* (New York: Delacorte, 1982), 126.

10. Ira Progoff, "Form, Time, and Opus: The Dialectic of the Creative Psyche," in Adolf Portmann, ed., *Forms als Aufgabe des Geistes Eranos-Jahrbuch 1965* (Zürich: Rhein, 1966), 270.

11. Ibid., 274.

12. Ibid., 277.

13. S. N. Eisenstadt, "Archetypal Patterns of Youth," in Dorothy Rogers, ed., *Issues in Adolescent Psychology* (New York: Appleton-Century-Crofts, 1969), 565-75.

14. Ibid., 574.

15. Paul Radin, *The Trickster* (New York: Schocken, 1972), 168.

16. Paul Radin, *Primitive Man as Philosopher* (New York: Dover, 1957), 96.

17. Progoff, "Form, Time and Opus," 265.

18. Ibid., 278.

19. Ibid.

20. Ibid., 279.

21. Ibid., 281.

22. Joseph E. Brown, *The Sacred Pipe: Black Elk's Account of the Seven Rites of the Oglala Sioux* (New York: Penguin Books, 1983), 117.

23. Ibid., 126.

24. Lame Deer (John Fire) and Richard Erdoes, *Lame Deer: Seeker of Visions* (New York: Simon and Schuster, 1972), 15-16.

25. Ibid.

26. Frank Waters, *The Man Who Killed the Deer* (New York: Pocket, 1974), 80.

27. Ibid., 82.

28. Harold E. Fey and D'Arcy McNickle, *Indians and Other Amer-*

icans (New York: Harper and Row, 1970); Harold E. Driver, *Indians of North America* (Chicago: University of Chicago Press, 1972), 479-505.

29. Carl G. Jung, *Memories, Dreams, Reflections,* ed. Aniela Jaffe (New York: Vintage, 1965), 342.

18

"Putting on the Names": A Jewish-Christian Legacy

Truman G. Madsen
Brigham Young University, Provo, Utah

Aristotle observed that "nothing is by nature a name or a noun." That is, words or word-names have no inherent or necessary meaning. Instead they are arbitrarily assigned to objects or persons. For different reasons, it is a standard view today that names, as well as concrete or abstract terms, are no more than a *flatus vocis*, a mere sound.

This tendency to reduce language to whimsical convention without concern for more profound origins may be symptomatic of the secularization of men and even the trivialization of life itself. At any rate, it reflects a diminishing of the religious consciousness that some names were thought anciently to be of divine origin.

In antiquity, several ideas about names recur, among which are the following:

1. In names, especially divine names, is concentrated divine power.

2. Through ritual processes one may gain access to these names and take them upon oneself.[1]

3. These ritual processes are often explicitly temple-related.

The tradition that certain temple-centered names have a divine status is present in the inscriptions of Tel Mardikh, which reach back into the third millennium B.C. There are place names in the tablets of Ebla (Upper Syria), which translate "Temple of the Word." These Canaanites apparently divinized the word *ni'm* (Heb. *ne'um*) meaning oracle. And they ascribed a divine status to the voice, the name, the oracle, and *the word* of their god or gods associated with the temple.[2]

The proscription against pronouncing the personal name of deity is also ancient.[3] It relates to the third commandment, "Ye shall not swear falsely by the name of Yahweh or God" (Exodus 20:7 and Deuteronomy 5:11). This seems to suggest that one use of God's name is in making a covenant. Related is the idea that one may make a serious and solemn vow by using, taking upon oneself, or acting in the name of God. The proper use of the name YHWH constitutes a covenant between Israel and her God.[4]

In Egyptian initiation rites one puts off his former nature by discarding his name, after which he receives a new name. Prior to coronation, the candidate is presented to the gods without his own personal name. In order to pass the obstacles, he recites the name of his god and thus is allowed to pass. If the candidate cannot produce the name, the gatekeepers are aggressive and unyielding.[5]

In the temple ritual setting, names are not seen as mere labels. They mark degrees or attributes or roles in one's transformation process. They are symbolic of new births or beginnings. Thus, an individual, while retaining his identity, may take on several names as he moves through stages toward the divine. "To possess knowledge of another's name is to hold some power over him, even if it be the high god himself."[6] The Egyptians went further: "the name is a person's essence." If his name perishes, he himself does not exist.[7] The person was told "Thy name lives on earth. . . . Thou dost not perish, thou art not destroyed forever and ever!"[8] Hence, it was important that one's name live in memory because if the "name lives on earth" the person could "live hereafter."[9] The name enabled his body to survive.[10]

The Hebrew Word for "Name"

The Hebrew word for "name" is *shem*. *Ha-Shem* is still used sometimes as a "meta-word,"[11] part of a prayer pattern, used to avoid saying the most sacred name. In Judaism the "sh" (which in English looks like a "W") has often had ritual importance because it pictures a position of prayer—arms raised above the head.[12] Thus one symbolizes the name in prayer whether or not he uses it.

Speculation continues on the derivation of the name of the oldest son of Noah, Shem, from whose name the designation of "Semite" for the peoples of the Near East has been derived.[13] ("Sh" and "s," depending upon the "pointing" of the letter,[14] are different sounds but reflect both the Hebrew and the Arabic values). Abraham and his descendants are, in turn, descendants of Shem. It is at least possible that some scriptural references to the person Shem and the word "name" reflect the idea that whoever bears that name is like the angel of the Lord's presence. Abraham received, glorified, and sanctified this name. He is a blessing, and his seed bless themselves, precisely because the imprint of that name is upon all of them.

It is hard to exaggerate the richness of a single order of consonants in Hebrew and how many meanings may derive from a given root. By examining variations of vowel "pointing" on divine names, analysis of the ancient sources continues to this day. Among the Jews, other techniques expand it even more: Gematria assigns numbers to consonants and then draws conclusions about matching sets.[15] By acronyms words are derived from first letters. In *notarikon* letters of words are interpreted as abbreviations of whole sentences, and letters are varied or interchanged according to certain systematic rules.[16]

The twenty-two letters of the Hebrew alphabet were early assigned masculine and feminine values. And much is made of the contrast between such couplets as dark and light, right and left, male and female.[17] Today there is renewed discussion of ways in which words not only name, but also function, as in the performative roles they play in ritual expression. Such "linguistic acts," for example, "I baptize you," especially in ceremonial form, undergird and override very important life changes.[18]

Names as Titles

In the Psalms, eleven of which were sung on festive days in honor of royalty, there are many composite names—sentence names or titles—such as the "God of Gods," "the Most High God," "Yahweh the Exalted," and "the Most High Yahweh." Some Psalms are "a litany of sacred names"[19] as is Psalm 145, which introduces new titles in verses 1, 3, 5, 6, and 7. Praise here becomes synonymous with prayer and vice versa. In the Psalms, the most frequent order of praising is first of Yahweh, then of his works, and finally his name. Frank Cross, Jr., sees Psalm 132 as a "royal hymn" with connections to the tabernacle and Psalm 89 as "from an early temple liturgy."[20]

In the context there is a close association between the name and the glory of God (cf. Psalm 26:8 and 79:7). "The dwelling place of God" means the place where his glory—his name—dwells.

The Name and Solomon's Temple

After the construction of the First Temple of Jerusalem, Solomon either stood or knelt down[21] upon a platform in the sight of the whole congregation, spread out his hands toward the heavens, and offered a dedicatory prayer. Repeatedly, Solomon called the Temple "the house I have built for your name"[22] (cf. 2 Chronicles 6:34, 38). Even the foreigner who implored Yahweh was to know "as your people Israel do" that this house "bears your name." The exact Hebrew reads "that your name has been *called over*"[23] (2 Chronicles 6:33). The temple is "the place where you promised to put your name, so that you may hear [KJV reads "hearken unto"] the prayer your servant offers toward this place" (2 Chronicles 6:20; 1 Kings 8:29).

From then on, prayers were directed to the temple in the belief that God's presence was there as it was in heaven. Covenanters spoke of "seeing God" as an extension of worshipping in the temple (Isaiah 6:1; Psalm 24:3-6; Matthew 5:8).

The Jews, during the period of the Second Temple, faced the dilemma of avoiding the pagan idolatrous practices of "placing" statues or idols in their sacred structures. For the Jews, the belief that a temple was dedicated to Yahweh, and that his presence was somehow localized therein, confronted the commandment to avoid images or statues. In Deuteronomy, and especially Jeremiah, the name became a substitute, a legitimate replacement for forbidden images or replications of the deity. Somehow, it was believed, the name brought the presence of the *kavod* or glory—a tangible and visible presence—within the most sacred place. A cluster of interrelated expectations revolved around this presence: the priestly literature speaks of the light, the aura, the perpetual flame of tabernacle and temple. Thus, the use of the name of deity in the temple setting helped to reconcile the ideas of divine transcendence and immanence in the setting of the temple, for the name could be present within the temple while the power of God extended everywhere.

Names and Sacrifice

For Israelites, the highest moment of feast or sacrifice in the sanctuary was to behold the presence of Yahweh, that is, to be presented at the sanctuary (Exodus 34:23; cf. Deuteronomy 31:11 and Isaiah 1:12).[24] When an altar was built to Yahweh and sacrifice and invocation of his name were appropriately made, it was believed he would come and bless the worshipper. As Kaufmann puts it, "the effect of the offering on the divine realm is depicted not in terms of union, but in terms of God's pleasure at man's submission and obedience." An offering is "a token of honor and reverence. . . . The sacrifice is 'acceptable,' 'delightful,' and 'pleasant' to God."[25] This is the substratum assumption behind most temple laws and narratives. Kaufmann concludes, "the custom of calling altars and sanctuaries by theophoric names is attested to in early times."[26]

In the temple setting it is clear that by proper use of the name or names, one does not speak *of* or *about* God. He speaks *to* or *for* or *with* God.[27] Divine names are uniquely hallowed because they are more than descriptions, however lofty. They are invocations. The question is not "What do you call this 'object'?" but "How may I summon or commune with the Divine?"

The Name *Yahweh*

The supreme or transcendent name of God is in the four Hebrew letters *YHWH*, later known as the tetragrammaton. The letters have obscure origins, pronunciations, and meanings that continue to confound scholars.[28] But they are usually thought to express the eternity of God— that he was, he is, he shall be, or that his presence shall never depart from Israel. Whatever its meanings, this sacred name, both in early and late Jewish thought, was surrounded with safeguards: It could be spoken only on one day a year—Yom Kippur—and in the most sacred place—the Holy of Holies. The High Priest spoke it in behalf of the people-community of all Israel. It was in the performance of his most sacred function, the cleansing of the sanctuary. This meant purifying Israel of her sins.

When the *Kohen Gadol* (High Priest) went into the temple on the Day of Atonement, he had already undergone elaborate preparations for purification. The experience was considered awesome, even perilous. Imminent

danger as well as redemption was at stake. The pronunciation of the name was thought to bring him into direct
contact with the Divine. Through the power of the name,
he was able to experience God as "a consuming fire."[29] If
spoken in unpreparedness or without concentration, the
name could bring dire, even disastrous, results.[30]

One of the oldest passages of the Mishnah says that
the high priest at the appointed place and time on the Day
of Atonement offered thrice a certain formula containing
the name. The congregation answered after him: "Blessed
be the name of the glory of his kingdom for ever and
ever."[31] Thus the name of the King of Righteousness became, symbolically, the name of His Righteous Kingdom
and of its members. After the third recitation, "the priests
and the people who stood in the Court at the time when
they heard the Name, coming forth from the mouth of the
High Priest, bent the knee, prostrated themselves and fell
on their faces and said: 'Blessed be the Name of His Glorious Kingdom forever and ever.' "[32] "The climax of the
ceremony was the mighty official proclamation of the sacred cultic name of Yahweh."[33]

The Qumran community, a century and a half before
the birth of Jesus, considered themselves a righteous remnant plucked from the midst of a corrupt temple culture.
They, too, celebrated the Name.[34] Regarding the Second
Temple as defiled and looking forward to a future messianic temple, they performed an annual ritual for renewing their covenant with Yahweh. The process involved
ritual ablutions, purifying baths, clothing themselves in
white, and praising Yahweh.[35]

Bearing the Name

During the First and Second Temple periods, receiving
the name was a privilege of obedience. It was to be inscribed on and in the person—in the hands (Isaiah 56),
and on the "inward parts" (Jeremiah 31:31-34). It was to

permeate the new heart and new spirit of those who had heretofore profaned the name (Ezekiel 36:21-28). It was also associated with priestly robes. The headdress both of the ordinary priest and of the high priest[36] (cf. Exodus 28:6) was a cap "made in the same fashion as that of all the priests." Over this was stitched blue or violet embroidery extending from the nape of the neck to the two temples. The forehead had a plate of gold in which was graven in sacred characters the name of God.[37] The name was expected to be inscribed and present in the new temple (Ezekiel 43:7) and the new city (Ezekiel 48:35) where it would signify "The Lord is there." In deed and in prayer it was to be retained and honored just as the ark contained the covenant and as the temple contained the ark. Ultimately, it was to be as everlasting as the covenants accompanying it. Finally, desecration of names brought the penalty of death (Leviticus 24:16; 1 Kings 21:10). To sanctify the name, one must be willing to submit to martyrdom.

In Jewish practice to this day, a person who recovers from a severe illness is given a new name which, in effect, celebrates his return from near death. Such new names assigned in prayer are chosen from worthy patriarchs (e.g., Abraham, Isaac, and Jacob) and from worthy matriarchs (e.g., Sarah, Rachel, and Leah). The names are new to the person because it is assumed the person is himself new, having overcome or been healed from death. Sometimes the names are compounds of the names of God (cf. Revelation 2:17).

Names and Creation

The notion that divine names have creative power and that the world itself was made by the use of the holy language is present in a Talmudic statement: "Bezalel knew how to combine the letters [of Hebrew] by which the heavens and earth were created" (cf. Exodus 31:3; 35:31). It is said that this man was filled with the Spirit of God in *wisdom*, and *understanding*, and in *knowledge*. It goes on to say that by knowledge "the depths were broken up," by wisdom the earth was founded, and by understanding the heavens were established.[38]

In fact, Jewish tradition has sometimes elevated the words of the Torah into divine entities. The words of the Pentateuch were first seen as a total tapestry and unity, not one syllable of which was dispensable. Later the words or names were thought to be organic, in some sense vitalized, so that the names were understood as living supermundane beings. [The Zohar says "Scripture is like a man and has flesh, soul, and spirit."] The next step was not only to regard the Torah as a composite of the names of God but, as a whole, the one great Name of God.[39]

By the speaking of words (names), God himself acted in creation. His *saying* made light, or the heavens, or the world. The Talmud says all creation was completed by ten utterances.[40] Thus, in Jewish tradition, as one praises the name of God, he reaches the very ultimate nature of God. As he verbalizes the name, he is calling upon that nature "at which moment all the creation is at our feet, prepared to do our bidding, because all of creation emanates from that nature."

A prescribed order was required in the use of the names. Rabbi Eleazar said in a well-known midrash on Job 28, "The various sections of the Torah were not given in their correct order. For if they had been given in their correct order, anyone who read them would be able to wake the dead and perform miracles."[41] Exodus 34:5 says "The Lord came down in a cloud and placed himself beside him [Moses] and proclaimed the name of the Lord." One legend says Moses used that name as his instrument in dividing the Red Sea. Traditions dealing with the creation of the world are matched by traditions concerning the recreation of man.

There is evidence that the Qumran community and

other groups, as well as John the Baptist, set great store upon initiation hymns leading to rebirth or the gift of life. They saw this process as the restoration of God's image. To take the name upon oneself was to take the image of God. Later, the *Odes of Solomon,* a Gnostic group of hymns that date to the first or second century, describe baptism as a sign and as a seal of names.[42] It may be that Paul had this in mind in Ephesians 1:13.

The Name of Jesus

In nothing is Jesus more Jewish than in his use and reverence of the "name of the Father." Jesus says, "I am come in my Father's name" (John 10:25). He speaks of "the works that I do in my Father's name"(John 5:43). He prays, "Father glorify thy name" (John 12:28). He instructs that prayer addressed to the Father begin "hallowed be thy name" (Luke 11:2). His high priestly prayer asks, "keep through thine own name those whom thou hast given me" (John 17:11), and "I have declared unto them thy name" (John 17:26). And John 20:31 promises "life through his name." But what of Jesus' own name?[43]

At one point Jesus tells his disciples: "Hitherto have ye asked nothing in my name" (John 16:24). Later he says that some will claim in vain to prophesy in his name and thus to cast out devils and in his name to do many wonderful works (Matthew 6:9; 7:22). He asks his disciples to gather "in my name" (Matthew 18:20). Luke describes the disciples' return, saying that even the demons are "subject unto us through thy name" (Luke 10:17). John speaks of those who "believe on his name" (John 1:12; cf. John 2:23). All this bespeaks a kinship of Messiah and Father in the tradition of the sacral name and name-entitlement.

Jesus, in the book of John, as well as in the epistles of John, bears God's name to the point that he can say "the Father and I are one" (John 10:30). Does this mean their names are one? The specific divine name which is assumed

in these passages is a matter of controversy. Perhaps it is
the divine name in Exodus 3:14: "I am." But the Masoretic
text can be read to mean "I will become what I will become."[44] This is compatible with the view that Yahweh
became the messianic figure of the New Testament. But it
is incompatible with the philosophical thesis that God is
exclusively "being" without the dimension of becoming.

In the New Testament, the tradition is carried forward
that one can be named by God, or be named after God,
or "called" by a name which gives a person a specific
mission or commission. Associated with the latter idea is
the conviction that by wearing or bearing the name, one
is placed under God's special protection, as also his judgment. (Adam named animals and by so doing attained
dominion over them;[45] cf. Genesis 2:19; Psalm 1:26; 8:6.) It
would appear that to take or to give a name without divine
authority is, in effect, to illegitimately assume or presume
a divine honor.

Baptism into the Name

Albright observes: "There are two kinds of formal statements about baptismal status in the New Testament." One
mentions "baptism 'in the name of' and the other 'into the
name of' the Messiah. . . . The first formula ('in the name
of') may include both faith in Jesus as Messiah, and also
the ceremonial action which accepted this profession of
faith—i.e., the baptismal rite. 'Into the name of' . . . calls
attention to the results" of baptism. "The neophyte baptized *into the name of* the Messiah thus not only pledges
allegiance to Jesus as Messiah," but is also established or
born "into fellowship with him"[46] and with the Father in
whose name he acts.

Writing one's own name on a temple wall was thought,
in Second Temple times, to unite one with the temple deity.
"To bear the name" was a sign of citizenship in the sacred
city. Revelation 3:12 makes the new name of Jesus as Lord

the insignia of victory. For by bearing the name, one shares in the name and character of Jesus (cf. Philippians 2:9-10). This is comparable to the promise of being "registered" in the Book of Life (Revelation 13:8; 17:8; 20:12; cf. Luke 10:20; Hebrews 12:23).

Baptism, as described in Acts 2:38, 8:16, and 1 Corinthians 1:13, 15, requires one to acknowledge (1) knowing the name, (2) accepting the name, and (3) testifying of the name. This is a blessing, a burden, a commission. The name may have been "Messiah" or the title "Son of Man" or both.

The Disciples' Transmittal of the Name

Peter heals in the name of Jesus Christ and explains that there is no other name under heaven given among men by which we can be saved (Acts 4:12; cf. 2 Nephi 31:21). It is also clear that forgiveness of God comes in the name of Christ, which is also somehow the name of God. (Compare the "forgiveness" of God described in Ezekiel 20:8-9.) To refuse to punish would bring contempt from the gentiles for the name of God and his power.

By the end of the first century, the *Psalms of Solomon,* a pseudepigraphal work, says "While your name dwells in our midst, we shall find mercy." This is often interpreted as both a lament and a consolation for the destroyed temple.[47] Thereafter, divine names were associated, among the Jews, with the Ark of the Covenant in the synagogue and among Christians with emerging sacraments and preachments. The Didache at about A.D. 100 has this sentence: "We thank you, Father most holy, for the sake of your holy name which you made to dwell in our hearts."[48]

The close connection between desecrating the name and desecrating the temple is reflected in the Jewish tradition that the correct pronunciation of the name of God was lost as the Temple was demolished by the Romans in A.D. 70. Concern for the recovery of this knowledge, viewed as crucial, is reflected in the mystical tradition that it was rediscovered about A.D. 300.[49] Then the Kabbalists gave the name the title "tetragrammaton," "the word of four letters," or the square name, or more simply, the square.[50] The tradition was carried on that the name must remain ineffable, that is unspeakable, except in ritual contexts. A Gnostic echo of this with allusions to the temple is in the second- or third-century *Gospel of Philip*.

> One single name they do not utter in the world, the name which the Father gave to the Son, which is above all things, which is the name of the Father. For the Son would not become Father except he clothe himself with the name of the Father. This name those who have it know indeed, but they do not speak of it. But those who have it not do not know it.[51]

This passage is close to another in the *Gospel of Philip* which says Christ did all things in a mystery or sacrament. It names five of these. One involved the receiving of a new name with an anointing that rendered the person Christlike.[52]

The *Gospel of Bartholomew*, also from the third century, embodies a Jewish legend that "Adam and Eve had characters and signs written on their brows, and the names of the Father, Son, and Holy Ghost were written" in certain parts of their bodies.[53] In Egypt as well, similar holy insignia were placed on or in ritual garments.[54]

Name and Destiny

The Hebrew *Apocalypse of Enoch* (fifth century A.D.) became a basic document in Jewish Merkabah throne mysticism, which depends heavily on passages in Ezekiel. There are three main notions of names: (1) that sacred names are engraved "with a pen of flame on the throne of glory," (2) that sacred names "fly off (from the throne of glory) like eagles,"[55] and (3) that there is a heavenly curtain "on which are printed all the generations of the world and all their deeds, whether done or to be done, till the last generation."[56] The curtain was seen as a heavenly counterpart of the temple veil, which in the earthly tabernacle and temple divided the holy place from the Holy of Holies. It was a veil that somehow contained "in blueprint" the whole course of human history.[57] In Jewish thinking, this was a condensation of names, a forecast of destiny which is neither a violation of freedom nor a compromise of individual prophecy.[58] Rabbi Akiba epitomized the prevailing view: "All (is) foreseen (and) choice (is) granted."[59] A corresponding notion is that heavenly records are kept and guarded by a heavenly scribe. (The idea that names of the faithful may be written in the Book of Life appears at least as early as in Daniel 12:1-4.)[60]

Name Transmission

Medieval Jewish mysticism continued and embellished — in the absence of the temple — ritual processes for receiving and giving divine names.[61] Thus Eleazar of Worms (about A.D. 1200) describes an initiation which Scholem concludes is "very old," for the transmitting of the name of God from master to pupil.

> The name is transmitted only to the reserved — this word can also be translated as "the initiate" — who are not prone to anger, who are humble and God-fearing, and carry out the commandments of their Creator. And it is transmitted only over water. Before the master teaches it to his pupil, they must both immerse themselves and bathe in forty measures of flowing water, then put on white garments and fast on the day of instruction. Then both must stand up to their ankles in the water, and the master must say a prayer ending with the words: "The voice of God is over the waters! Praised be Thou, O Lord, who revealest Thy secret to those who fear Thee, He who knoweth the mysteries." Then both

must turn their eyes toward the water and recite verses
from the Psalms, praising God over the waters.[62]

There may be a link between such patterns and Jewish
ritual baths practiced in the time of Jesus. These ceremonies
required sizable cisterns or pools and abundant water re-
serves. Remnants of many such cisterns have been uncovered in and near Jerusalem. Numerous baths have been
found in the southeast corner of the Old City dating back
to the Second Temple period.[63] Such ritual baths were preparatory to entry into the Temple Mount. One precept of
ritual purity required a "bath . . . [with] no less than forty
'seahs' [about 750 liters] of spring water or rainwater."[64]
The insistence not only on water but on running water
reflects an earlier Qumran preoccupation. It was also embraced by the Hassidic movement for whom, as Buber
writes, "Immersion in a river or a stream is higher in value
than the ordinary ritual bath."[65] In this context it should
be recalled that the Jerusalem Temple was built over flowing water. "A river rises from below the temple," writes
Richard Clifford, "and flows out to make the earth fertile."[66] Ezekiel prophesies that out from under the future
Messianic Temple water will flow (cf. Ezekiel 47:1-12; Genesis 2:10-14).

Another Jewish name-ritual in medieval times was titled "Putting On and Fashioning the Mantle of Righteousness." "A piece of pure deerskin parchment" was cut into
a sleeveless garment similar to the high priest's ephod. It
covered shoulders, chest, and navel, and included a "hat
connected with the garment." On this garment the names
of God were inscribed. After a period of fasting and ritual
purification, and at the end of seven days, one went to
the water. On receiving certain signs which confirmed his
inward purity, he was considered fit to put on the venerable name. He proceeded into the water and emerged
from it with the name which it was believed assured him

"irresistible strength" and authorized him to invoke angels associated with the name thus acquired.[67]

A thoroughgoing attempt to ascribe a number or a name to every human muscle or nerve, as if the name "governs" the organism, permeates many Jewish movements as, for example, the writings of Isaac of Luria (sixteenth century). Similar ritual procedures are thought, under certain combinations, to bring the Holy Spirit. Breathing or blowing the utterance with the face in the proper position is thought to bring about "communion with His great Name."[68]

Names and Magic

In warning and protest against abuses and magical expectations arising from the use of names,[69] Maimonides (1135-1204) and other influential Jewish interpreters tried to draw the line between authentic and spurious practices. Nevertheless, Jewish and Christian lore contains many references to occult incantations, to amulets, charms, spells, exorcisms, all related to speculative angelologies and demonologies.[70] Maimonides tended to interpret passages, both biblical and talmudic, in a figurative way and thus denied the existence of either demons or of angels. But wonder-working aspirations continued (and continue) to flourish. Martin Buber's *For the Sake of Heaven* is a striking and lamentable account of the efforts of nineteenth-century Jews to effect and even reverse the outcomes of Napoleonic Wars with occult incantations.[71] In contrast to the magician, the sorcerer, and the conjurer, Jewish rabbis sought to understand name rituals for altruistic and not for manipulative purposes. Merely knowing and repeating the names were not sufficient.

The observant Jew, as the dedicated Christian, claimed to employ these names and invoke these powers either in his quest for divine aid or in his attempt to establish a meaningful relationship between "the above and the below," or in his striving to organize and vitalize his own life.

Physical Correlates

In religious as well as in legal practice, most contemporary cultures have abandoned severe punishments of mutilation for blasphemy of sacred names. Anciently, it was not so. Among Israelites, blasphemy could bring death by stoning.[72] In other cultures, for abuse of the sacred name one could lose his eyes, his nose, his ears, or his tongue. More radical still were those punishments which left a man a eunuch, impotent, and left a woman barren and hardly recognizable as a woman.

Why such extreme, even fatal, consequences? This brief outline points the way to one answer: Both in Jewish and Christian parlance, divine names were and are a matter of life and death — in every physical and spiritual sense. Life is violated in taking or speaking names "in vain." One who thus profanes is acting in self-destruction, striking at the fountain of his own soul, his nature, the vital places of selfhood. In Hebrew lore, the loci of these soul powers were the *neshamah* (breath), *ruach* (also breath or vital spirit), and *nefesh* (soul).[73]

Such abuse of the divine instrument, which is the self, is all the more serious because the *selem* and the *demut* (the image and the likeness)[74] of God reside in every human self — "Be ye holy for I am holy" (*qadosh*; Leviticus 11:44-45). Once one has partaken of the name, he wears it, he manifests it. An identification tag is attached, as it were, to every element of his being (those who truly know him know him by name). The highest spiritual aspiration is that there will one day be full harmony of nature in the One who names, the name, and the named. This is the vision of the Temple in Isaiah 56:

> For thus says the Lord:
> As for the eunuchs who keep my Sabbaths

and choose to do what I will—
holding fast to my covenant—
to them I will give a handclasp and a name
within the walls of my house
that is better than sons and daughters;
I will endow them with an everlasting name
that shall not be cut off.
And the foreigners who adhere to the Lord
to serve him,
who love the name of the Lord,
that they may be his servants—
all who keep the Sabbath without profaning it,
holding fast to my covenant—
these I will bring to my holy mountain
and gladden in my house of prayer.
Their offerings and sacrifices
shall be accepted on my altar,
for my house shall be known
as a house of prayer for all nations.
Thus says my Lord the Lord,
who gathers up the outcasts of Israel:
I will gather others to those already gathered.[75]

Notes

1. Cf. Dallin Oaks, "Taking upon Us the Name," *Ensign* 15 (May 1985): 80-83; Numbers 6:27, and Mosiah 5:6-12.

2. Mitchell Dahood, "The Temple and Other Sacred Places in the Ebla Tablets," in Truman G. Madsen, ed., *The Temple in Antiquity* (Salt Lake City: Bookcraft, 1984), 86.

3. E. A. Speiser, *Genesis*, Anchor Bible (Garden City, NY: Doubleday, 1964), 16.

4. Yehezekel Kaufmann, *The Religion of Israel*, tr. Moshe Greenberg (Chicago: University of Chicago, 1960), 298.

5. Hugh Nibley, *The Message of the Joseph Smith Papyri* (Salt Lake City: Deseret Book, 1975), 219.

6. Ibid., 140.

7. Ibid., 139.

8. Ibid., 139-40.

9. Ibid.

10. Ibid., 140.

11. F. Brown, S. R. Driver, and C. A. Briggs, *A Hebrew and English Lexicon of the Old Testament* (Oxford: Clarendon, 1974), 1028.

12. The prayer posture symbolized by the Hebrew letter for "sh," "shin," may be traced to an Old Testament verse; Abraham replies to the king of Sodom, "I have lift[ed] up mine hand unto the Lord, the most high" (Genesis 14:22). In Hebrew it means literally, "I raised up my hand." It is an oath formula, cf. Speiser, *Genesis*, 104-5, n. 22.

13. Samuel N. Kramer, *The Sumerians: Their History, Culture and Character* (Chicago: University of Chicago Press, 1963), 298-99, an expert on Sumerian, believes that the word *shem* derives from the name Sumer.

14. In Hebrew, vowels are designated by dots or points below the consonants, hence the term "pointing." The arrangement and number of dots determine the vowel sound.

15. Gershom Scholem, "Gematria," in *Encyclopaedia Judaica*, 16 vols. (Jerusalem: Macmillan/Keter, 1971-72), 7:370-74.

16. Cf. "Notarikon," in *Encyclopedia Judaica*, 12:1231; Gershom Scholem, *Major Trends in Jewish Mysticism* (New York: Schocken Books, 1946), 99.

17. Cf. Charles Poncé, *Kabbalah* (London: Quest Books, 1973), 249.

18. Cf. John L. Austin's account of "performative utterance"; e.g., "I christen you," "I pronounce you man and wife," "I baptize you." In each case saying is a form of doing. *Philosophical Papers* (Oxford: Oxford University Press, 1979), ch. 10.

19. Cf. Mitchell Dahood, *Psalms*, Anchor Bible, 3 vols. (Garden City, NY: Doubleday, 1970), 3:xxxviii; cf. 259 and 336.

20. Cf. Frank M. Cross, Jr., "The Priestly Tabernacle in the Light of Recent Research," in Madsen, *The Temple in Antiquity*, 98-99. Cf. Psalm 132:12-13.

21. Both standing and kneeling are represented on ancient monuments. See Jacob Myers, *II Chronicles*, Anchor Bible, 2 vols. (Garden City, NY: Doubleday, 1965, 1974), 2:36.

22. On building a house to the name of the Lord, see 2 Samuel 7:13; 1 Kings 3:2; 5:3, 5; 6:1-38; 7:13-51; 8:16-18, 20, 29, 43-44; 9:3, 7; 18:32 ("an altar in the name of the Lord"); 2 Kings 21:4; 1 Chronicles 22:7-8, 10, 19; 28:3; 29:16; 2 Chronicles 2:1, 4; 6:5, 7-10, 20, 33-34, 38; 7:16; 20:8-9; Ezra 6:12; Nehemiah 1:9. The people of Israel and the Holy City itself also bear the name.

23. See Jacob Myers, *II Chronicles*, 2:35, n. 33.

24. Richard D. Barnett, "Bringing the God into the Temple," in

Avraham Biran, ed., *Temples and High Places in Biblical Times* (Jerusalem: Hebrew Union College, 1981), 10-20.

25. Kaufmann, *The Religion of Israel*, 112.

26. Ibid., 138, n. 3.

27. Louis Jacobs, explaining Buber, in *A Jewish Theology* (New York: Behrman House, 1973), 54. See also his "Excursus: The Names of God," ch. 10.

28. A Palestinian targum identifies the divine name YHWH as expressing God's eternal presence with Israel. Robert Hayward, *Divine Name and Presence* (Totowa, NJ: Allanheld, Osmun, 1981), 17-20, 82, has written that this name is at the core of covenant terminology of covenant oaths and was associated with the Jerusalem temple.

29. See *3 Enoch* 42 in James H. Charlesworth, ed., *Old Testament Pseudepigrapha*, 2 vols. (Garden City, NY: Doubleday, 1983), 1:293.

30. Talmudic traditions say that the unpronounceable or secretly pronounced tetragrammaton was trusted only to priests who were pious, chaste, and discreet. When singing from the Torah, the rabbi would "gulp the pronunciation amid the singing of his brethren." Rabbis continue to do so today in "a chant reminiscent of the singing of the Temple priests." See C. G. Montefiore and H. Loewe, *A Rabbinic Anthology* (New York: Schocken Books, 1965), 14.

31. M *Yoma* 3:8; 6:2, citing Leviticus 16:30 in Herbert Danby, tr. and ed., *The Mishnah* (Oxford: Oxford University, 1933), 165, 169; cf. Hayyim Schauss, *The Jewish Festivals* (New York: Schocken, 1962), 136-38, who gives greater emphasis to the name with his translation. "Blessed be the Name, the glory of His kingdom forever and ever."

32. I. Abrahams, *Studies in Pharisaism and the Gospels*, 2 series in 1 vol. (New York: KTAV, 1967), 2:25.

33. Hans Joachim-Kraus, *Worship in Israel*, tr. Geoffrey Buswell (Richmond, VA: John Knox, 1966), 213.

34. Yigael Yadin, ed., *The Temple Scroll*, 3 vols. plus supplement (Jerusalem: Israel Exploration Society, 1977-83), 1:279, "The city which I will hallow by settling my name and [my] temp[le within it] shall be holy and clean." In many Qumran texts the name of God is written in a distinctive script to remind the reader that it is too holy to pronounce. In the Temple Scroll, however, the author, who perhaps thought of his writing as the very law of God, wrote the letters for YHWH in the exact style of the rest of the text; see ibid., 3:36 (plate 36) for two examples of YHWH in the standard script of the text.

35. J. Massyngberde Ford, *Revelation*, Anchor Bible (Garden City, NY: Doubleday, 1975), 123.

36. Josephus, *Jewish Antiquities* III, 157-58.

37. Josephus, *The Jewish War* V, 235-36. A "crown [with] sacred letters . . . in four vowels," i.e., YHWH. The golden diadem (Exodus 28:36 and 39:70) contained "seal engravings." Hebrew sources claim that the diadem had in it the words "Holiness to Yahweh." The exact rabbinical phrase is *kodesh le-Yahweh*. Cf. TB *Shabbat* 63b. Other sources, including Philo, *De Vita Mosis* II, 114, 132, claim it was simply the tetragrammaton. Gregory of Nyssa, II, 201, describes the gold letters as "ineffable," in Gregory of Nyssa, *The Life of Moses*, tr. Abraham J. Malherbe and Everett Ferguson (New York: Paulist Press, 1978), 106. See Menahem Haran, *Temples and Temple Service in Ancient Israel* (Oxford: Clarendon, 1978), 169. The Holy Name may have been abbreviated (ibid., 34, n. 38) on the headplate (TB *Shabbat* 63b).

38. TB *Berakhot* 55a.

39. Abraham J. Heschel, "The Mystical Element in Judaism," in Louis Finkelstein, ed., *The Jews, Their History, Culture, and Religion*, 3rd ed., 2 vols. (New York: Harper, 1960), 2:943, writes of this approach to the Torah: "The Torah is the 'Holy of Holies'; it consists entirely of the name of the Holy One, blessed be He. Every letter in it is bound up with that Name."

40. Cf. TB *Abot* 5:1.

41. Gershom Scholem, *On the Kabbalah and Its Symbolism* (New York: Schocken, 1946), 37.

42. See discussions on baptism in the *Odes of Solomon* in Charlesworth, *The Old Testament Pseudepigrapha*, 2:728 and n. 31, and 732: cf. J. H. Bernard, *The Odes of Solomon*, in *Texts and Studies*, 10 vols. (Cambridge: Cambridge University, 1912), 8(3):42.

43. A Jewish midrash claims that the name of the Messiah "existed . . . in an incomplete form" before the creation. See Samuel Rapaport, *Genesis Rabba I*, in *A Treasury of the Midrash* (New York: KTAV, 1968), 42.

44. W. F. Albright, "Further Observations on the Name Yahweh and Its Modifications," *Journal of Biblical Literature* 44 (1925): 158-62.

45. Markus Barth, *Ephesians 1-3*, Anchor Bible (Garden City, NY: Doubleday, 1974), 383.

46. William F. Albright and C. S. Mann, *Matthew*, Anchor Bible (Garden City, NY: Doubleday, 1971), 362.

47. Not only destruction but desecration and defilement of the temple led to a loss of names. Ezekiel 8 describes how the temple was entered by idolaters. Images were engraved all around the walls, and the seventy men of the elders of the house of Israel were stand-

ing before them. In the inner court of the temple between the porch and the altar, twenty-five men were prostrating themselves eastward toward the sun. This was, in Greenberg's phrase, the "climactic abomination" — turning one's back to the sanctuary and bowing toward the sun; cf. Moshe Greenberg, *Ezekiel 1-20,* Anchor Bible (Garden City, NY: Doubleday, 1983), 171; cf. 164-74.

48. Raymond Brown, *The Epistles of John,* Anchor Bible (Garden City, NY: Doubleday, 1982), 711.

49. David Noel Freedman concludes that the pronunciation was lost "some time during the Middle Ages" and efforts were made "in the modern period . . . to recover the pronunciation." See *Theological Dictionary of the Old Testament,* 5:500.

50. Greenberg, *Ezekiel 1-20,* 174-75.

51. The *Gospel of Philip* 102:5-13, section 12. The translation and numbering system are in R. M. Wilson, *The Gospel of Philip* (New York: Harper & Row, 1962), 30; cf. *The Nag Hammadi Library,* tr. James M. Robinson (San Francisco: Harper and Row, 1977), 133, *Gospel of Philip* 54:5-13, with a translation by Wesley W. Isenberg and an alternate numbering system.

52. *Gospel of Philip* 115:27-30, cited as section 68 in Wilson, *The Gospel of Philip,* 43; cited as 67.27-30 in Robinson, *The Nag Hammadi Library,* 140.

53. Nibley, *The Message of the Joseph Smith Papyri,* 190.

54. Ibid.

55. *3 Enoch* 39:1, in Charlesworth, *Old Testament Pseudepigrapha,* 1:290-91, cf. 246, 249-52.

56. *3 Enoch* 45:1, in Charlesworth, *Old Testament Pseudepigrapha,* 1:296.

57. *3 Enoch* 45:1-2, Exodus 26:31, and 2 Chronicles 3:14.

58. The length of the "garment" in later Kabbalah included two hundred and thirty-one "gates" which were, in fact, "possible combinations of the 22 letters of the Hebrew alphabet." Its width was a numerical "elaboration of the Tetragrammaton"; see Gershom Scholem, "Kabbalah, in *Encyclopaedia Judaica,* 10:591.

59. Louis Finkelstein, *Akiba: Scholar, Saint and Martyr* (New York: Covici Friede, 1936), 204.

60. *3 Enoch* 44, in Charlesworth, *Old Testament Pseudepigrapha,* 1:295-96, note 44t. Apocryphal literature, especially Enoch material, eventually links Enoch and Metatron, both of whom write and record the merits or demerits of Israel. In *3 Enoch,* Enoch, now called Metatron, is even called "the lesser Yahweh," *Yahweh ha-Qatan,* thus *3 Enoch* 12:5: "And he called me 'the lesser Yahweh' in the presence

of all his heavenly household; as it is written *For my name is in him* (Exodus 23:21)." Cf. John Bowker, *The Targums and Rabbinic Literature* (Cambridge: Cambridge University Press, 1969), 150 and note a; cf. 144-49.

61. Scholem describes the notion of a "cosmic veil or curtain before the throne which conceals the glory of God from the host of angels." Allowing that the idea is very old, at least as old as the Aggadah of the second century and citing *Pistis Sophia* of the Gnostics, he says, describing a passage in the book of *Enoch*, it "contains the images of all things which since the day of creation have their pre-existing reality, as it were, in the heavenly sphere. All generations and all their lives and actions are woven into this curtain; he who sees it penetrates at the same time into the secret of Messianic redemption, for like the course of history, the final struggle and the deeds of the Messiah are already pre-existently real and visible." This summarizes his account of Merkabah mysticism. Cf. Scholem, *Major Trends in Jewish Mysticism*, 72; source for the *Pistis Sophia* is from Karl Schmidt's German translation of 1925, 35; the reference for the book of *Enoch* is 3 *Enoch* 45, in Charlesworth, *Old Testament Pseudepigrapha*, 1:296-99. In Scholem's discussion of the theory of magic, n. 130 refers to *Midrash Tehillim*, edited by Buber.

Letters and combinations have cosmic power. Scholem says that one of the "related processes to ascending to the throne is 'the putting on, or clothing, of the name', a highly ceremonious rite in which the magician impregnates himself, as it were, with the great name of God." The Hebrew phrase is *lavosh et-hashem*. There is a Syriac phrase in the *Odes of Solomon* 39:7. He also compares it to Paul's statement in Romans 13:14 about "put ye on the Lord Jesus Christ." Cf. Scholem, *On the Kabbalah*, 136, and n. 3. The magician "performs a symbolic act by clothing himself in a garment into whose texture the name has been woven." He claims the rite is described in a manuscript in the British Museum. Cf. Scholem, *Major Trends in Jewish Mysticism*, n. 132; also n. 112 to lecture IV, p. 77.

62. Scholem, *On the Kabbalah*, 136.

63. Nahman Avigad, *Discovering Jerusalem* (Jerusalem: Shikmona, 1980), 139-43.

64. Ibid., 139.

65. Martin Buber, *Tales of the Hasidim, Early Masters* (New York: Schocken, 1947),J328.

66. Richard Clifford, "The Temple and the Holy Mountain," in Madsen, *The Temple in Antiquity*, 122.

67. Scholem, *On the Kabbalah*, 136-37.

68. Ibid., 188.

69. Louis I. Rabinowitz et al., "Maimonides," in *Encyclopaedia Judaica*, 11:754-81.

70. An introduction to the subject of demons both in the Bible and in extracanonical literature is in T. H. Gaster, "Demon, Demonology," in *Interpreter's Dictionary of the Bible*, 4 vols. (New York: Abingdon, 1962), 1:817-24.

71. Martin Buber, *For the Sake of Heaven*, tr. Ludwig Lewisohn (New York: Harper, 1953).

72. Leviticus 24:11-16; cf. "Blasphemy," in *Encyclopaedia Judaica* 4:1073-74.

73. Brown, Driver, and Briggs, *A Hebrew and English Lexicon of the Old Testament*, 675, 924-26, 659-61, respectively; cf. Scholem, *On the Kabbalah*, 195-96.

74. Brown, Driver, and Briggs, *A Hebrew and English Lexicon of the Old Testament*, 853-54, 198, respectively.

75. Avraham Gileadi, tr., *The Apocalyptic Book of Isaiah* (Provo, UT: Hebraeus Press, 1982), 142. Compare King James Version. Cf. also Avraham Gileadi, *The Book of Isaiah: A New Translation with Interpretive Keys from the Book of Mormon* (Salt Lake City: Deseret Book, 1988), 206.

19

Sinai as Sanctuary and Mountain of God

Donald W. Parry
Provo, Utah

Central to Israelite religion was its temple worship. Large sections of the Old Testament describe temple service, detailing the various sacrifices, the laws relating to purity, the rites and ceremonies of the priests, and their vestments. Many passages specify the precise dimensions of both the tabernacle and temple of Jerusalem. John Lundquist, in his paper "What Is a Temple? A Preliminary Typology," listed several types and motifs that are common among many ancient Near Eastern temples.[1] This paper demonstrates that Mount Sinai also served as a sanctuary — the first Israelite sanctuary — and that many of the motifs listed by Lundquist in his article are also found at Sinai. Such motifs as the cosmic mountain, the waters of life, the sacred repast, sacrificial ordinances, religious laws, divine revelation, and other features associated with Sinai will be examined. Indeed, in many ways, events at Mount Sinai were related to the temple worship later found at the tabernacle and the temple of Jerusalem.

Of course, Mount Sinai was not a temple built of marble or cedar, for it is not necessary for a sanctuary to be an edifice or structure.[2] Rather, Sinai was a sacred place built by Yahweh himself (Exodus 15:17) and, as such, was the precursor and prototype of later Israelite sanctuaries, the model from which later temples were copied. As Freedman has stated, Sinai was "the sanctuary which served as a model for all the replicas, especially the tabernacle and the temple in Jerusalem."³ To this Lundquist added, "the temple of Solomon would seem ultimately to be little more than the architectural realization and the ritual enlargement of the Sinai experience."⁴

None will deny that many vagaries and problems exist in the text of Exodus 19-33, which describes the experience of the Israelites at Sinai. Scholars cannot agree upon how many authors are involved,⁵ nor can they come to a consensus concerning the date of the composition of the material.⁶ But the current text gives convincing evidence that Mount Sinai was indeed the first sanctuary of Israel. With this in mind, we will proceed with Lundquist's first motif.

*"The temple is the architectural embodiment of the cosmic mountain."*⁷ The mountain/temple imagery is found throughout the Old Testament. In the well-known "Song of the Sea," Moses and the Israelites rejoiced by singing: "Thou [Yahweh] will bring them [thy people] and plant them on the mountain that is thine own, in the place, O Lord, which thou hast made for thee to dwell in, in the Sanctuary [*miqdāš*], O Lord, which thy hands have established" (Exodus 15:17). The Hebrew word for "sanctuary" is *miqdāš*, the root of which denotes "apartness" or "sacredness."⁸ In this passage Mount Sinai is called the *miqdāš*; elsewhere both the tabernacle (Exodus 25:8; Leviticus 16:33) and the Jerusalem temple (1 Chronicles 22:19; Isaiah 63:18) are referred to as the *miqdāš*. However, unlike the man-made sanctuaries, Sinai was created by Yahweh—it was the temple established "not by human but by divine hands." It was "the sanctuary which served as a model for all replicas, especially the tabernacle and the temple in Jerusalem."⁹

Other biblical passages treat "holy mountain" and "sanctuary" as analogous structures. In a chapter of Ezekiel, God requires "all the house of Israel" to serve him, to bring "offerings," "firstfruits," "oblations," and other "holy [temple] things," to his "holy mountain, the mountain of the height of Israel" (Ezekiel 20:40). Similarly, the Psalmist says: " Exalt the Lord our God, and worship at his holy mountain; for the Lord our God is holy" (Psalm 99:9). Isaiah refers to "the house of the God of Jacob" as "the mountain of the Lord" (Isaiah 2:3), and Psalm 68:16 mentions "the mountain which God desireth to dwell in; yea, the Lord will dwell in it forever."

Also, in a parallelism attributed to King David, "tabernacle" and "holy mountain" are used synonymously.[10] "Lord, who shall abide in thy Tabernacle? Who shall dwell in thy holy mountain?" (Psalm 15:1; cf. also Psalm 43:3-4). These passages demonstrate that during the Old Testament period, the word "mountain" (Heb. *har*) was often employed to describe the tabernacle *or* the temple of Jerusalem.

As noted above, the tabernacle of Moses and the temple of Solomon were but copies of the genuine mountain temple. Each structure became, in its time, the "architectural embodiment" of the cosmic mountain. They became small, man-made mountains designed to replace Sinai as the dwelling place of Yahweh. In the case of the tabernacle, it was a mobile mountain, so to speak, a moving dwelling place; and in the instance of the temple of Jerusalem, it also became a residence for Yahweh. Consequently, Sinai became known as the "mountain of God"; the tabernacle was called "the tent of God"; and the Jerusalem temple was referred to as "the house of God."

It is possible that the temple of Jerusalem (and to some extent the tabernacle) had the very appearance of a mountain—lofty and towering above the ground, sturdy and unyielding to the elements of the earth, and immutable in its composition. Built upon a high mountain of Jerusalem, the size of this magnificent structure was sixty cubits long, twenty cubits wide, and thirty cubits high (1 Kings 6:2). Its stone walls were six cubits thick.

The temple was built of raw material transported from the mountains. The foundation and outer walls consisted of white limestone, hewn by "fourscore thousand hewers in the mountains" surrounding Jerusalem (1 Kings 5:15). The interior of the building was made of the finest of mountain materials. The walls and ceiling were covered with cedar wainscoting, the floors with cyprus, and leading to the inner sanctum was a door made of olive wood. Much of the interior was overlaid with gold (1 Kings 6:15-22). Carved upon the walls were figures of flowers and palm trees (1 Kings 6:29).

There is some evidence that the walls of the sacred precinct contained a garden with living trees. Referring to Psalms 52:8 and 92:13, Widengren states that there are "many allusions to . . . trees growing within the area of the sanctuary."[11] This would give the appearance of a small grove or forest, which is often found on or near a mountain.[12]

Like the temple itself, Israelite sacrificial altars had the appearance of miniature mountains. The altar built by Moses was constructed either of unhewn stones or of the earth itself (Exodus 20:24-25), and Joshua built an "altar of unhewn stones upon which no man had lift up any iron" (Joshua 8:31), thus giving the impression of a natural mountainlike altar, both in form and substance. Concerning this altar, Robertson wrote that "the *mizbakh adama* was the natural beginning of a sanctuary. Where God had appeared in person was manifestly the place to continue to worship him. And what would seem more appropriate to the Hebrews than an altar of the material as it left the hands of the Creator?"[13] Finally, the two tablets of the covenant, which were later kept in the ark of the covenant (1 Kings 8:9), were made from the mountain of God, showing that in a very real sense the law originated at the sanctuary.

"The temple is often associated with the waters of life which

flow forth from a spring within the building itself—or rather the temple is viewed as incorporating within itself or as having been built upon such a spring."[14] In the Sinai pericope, the waters of life are found at a rock at Horeb-Sinai where thirsty Israel was miraculously filled. This event, which occurred in a place where there was "no water for the people to drink" (Exodus 17:1), enabled the Lord to demonstrate his power to the chosen people. The account states:

> And the people thirsted there for water: and the people murmured against Moses. . . . And Moses cried unto the Lord, saying, What shall I do unto this people? . . . And the Lord said unto Moses. . . . Behold, I will stand before thee there upon the rock in Horeb; and thou shalt smite the rock, and there shall come water out of it, that the people may drink. And Moses did so in the sight of the elders of Israel (Exodus 17: 3-6).

The image of God, the rock, and the water in this passage is a reminder that both the rock and the water are symbols of Yahweh. He is like a rock, permanent, lofty, immovable, and steadfast. Yahweh is "the rock" (Deuteronomy 32:4), "the rock of his [Jeshurun's] salvation" (Deuteronomy 32:15), "the rock of Israel" (2 Samuel 23:3), "my rock and my salvation" (Psalm 62:2, 6), and "the rock of my refuge" (Psalm 94:22). And Yahweh is the "fountain of living waters" (Jeremiah 2:13; cf. also Isaiah 12:2-3; 33:21; 55:1). He provides both the actual water for Israel to invigorate and renew their souls in the dry desert of Horeb, and he is the representation of spiritual waters, or spiritual life. Later traditions recall this great occurrence at the rock (Psalm 78:15-16, 20; 105:41; 114:8; Isaiah 48:21).

"The temple is built on separate, sacral, set-apart space."[15] According to the biblical text, Sinai is first mentioned in the biblical text when the shepherd Moses received his prophetic call in the episode of the fiery bush (Exodus 3:1-14).[16] It was at this moment that the inquisitive prophet,

when approaching the bush that would not be consumed with fire, learned that the immediate area was "separate, sacral, set-apart space." "Come no nearer," commanded Yahweh. "Take off your shoes, for the place on which you stand is holy ground" (Exodus 3:5). At first glance, to remove one's shoes may seem to be an unusual order, but there are two possible hypotheses as to why Moses (and later Joshua; cf. Joshua 5:15) was told to remove his shoes. First, common ground or dirt must not fall from the shoe onto sacred ground, because common ground represents the flesh, mortality, and humanness. Second, by wearing shoes on holy ground, the person might carry away "the sacredness of the holy place."[17]

All of Mount Sinai was holy, but according to Milgrom there were "gradations of holiness"[18] in the mountain area. That is to say, around the mountain were a series of concentric circles, with the most sacred area being found within the center circle, and the other circles declining in holiness as they extended outward from the focal point. These "gradations of holiness" found at Sinai are not unlike the distinguishable areas of sacred space known to exist at the tabernacle and temple of Jerusalem. Nachmanides and Milgrom have likened the tabernacle's "gradations of holiness" to those of Sinai, and Haran has demonstrated that within the temple of Solomon were certain hallowed areas.

First Nachmanides:

> Hereafter the Tabernacle in the wilderness is zoned as Mount Sinai was zoned, since the Divine Glory was also thereon. And He commands: "the outsider shall be put to death" (Numbers 1:51) as He said there: "for he shall surely be stoned" (Exodus 19:13); and he commands "let not (the Kohathites) go inside and witness the dismantling of the sanctuary" (Numbers 4:20) as He warned there: "lest they break through to the Lord to gaze" (Exodus 19:21); and He commands: "you shall

guard over the sanctuary and the altar" (Numbers 18:5)
as He said there: "The priests also, who come near the
Lord, must purify themselves . . . let not the priests or
the people break through to come up to the Lord" (Exodus 19:22, 24).[19]

Milgrom, while agreeing with the comments above,
asserts that Nachmanides did "not exhaust the comparison" between the tabernacle and Sinai. Therefore, he adds:

> Mount Sinai is the archetype of the Tabernacle, and
> is similarly divided into three gradations of holiness. Its
> summit is the Holy of Holies; God's voice issues forth
> from there (Exodus 19:20) as from the inner shrine (Ex-
> odus 25:22; Numbers 7:89); the mountaintop is off limits
> to priest and layman alike (Exodus 19:24) and its very
> sight is punishable by death (Exodus 19:21), and so with
> its Tabernacle counterpart (cf. Leviticus 16:2 and Num-
> bers 4:20); finally, Moses alone is privileged to ascend
> to the top (Exodus 19:20; see 34:2) just as later, the high
> priest is permitted to enter the inner shrine under special
> safeguards (Leviticus 16:2-4). The second division of
> Sinai is the equivalent of the outer shrine, marked off
> from the rest of the mountain by being enveloped in a
> cloud (Exodus 20:21; 24:15-18) just as the cloud over-
> spreads the entirety of the Tabernacle (Numbers 9:15-
> 22). . . . Below the cloud is the third division. . . . Here
> is where the altar and stelae are erected (Exodus 24:4).
> It is equivalent to the courtyard, the sacred enclosure of
> the Tabernacle.[20]

Both Nachmanides and Milgrom fail to mention the
idea of "gradations of holiness" connected with the temple
of Jerusalem. However, Haran wrote in his *Temples and
Temple Service in Ancient Israel:* "the plans of both Solomon's
temple and the tabernacle demonstrate [the pattern] of
concentric circles of declining order the further they move
away from the focal point of the cherubim in the inner
sanctum."[21]

"The tablets of destiny are consulted in the cosmic sense by the gods. . . . It is by this means that the will of the deity is communicated to the people through the king or the prophet for a given year."[22] The Israelite "tablets of destiny," variously called the "two tablets of stone" (Exodus 34:1, 4), "the two tablets of the pact" (Exodus 31:18; 32:15; 34:29), and "the tablets of the covenant" (Deuteronomy 9:9, 11, 15), are perhaps the focal point of the entire Sinai pericope. One scholar has claimed that the basic law of Israel (which was found on these tablets) is "the climax of the entire Book, the central and most exalted theme, all that came before being, as it were, a preparation for it, and all that follows, a result of, and supplement to it."[23]

According to Widengren, "the tablets of the Law, as well as the Urim and Thummin, play the same role as the tablets of destiny in being the instrument by which the will of the deity is communicated to the leader of the people, be it Moses or the king."[24] That is, the destiny of the children of Israel was in some way tied up with subsequent obedience or disobedience to the laws of Yahweh as revealed to king Moses (Deuteronomy 33:4-5). Deuteronomy 28 and 29, which contain a lengthy list of blessings and curses, illustrate this concept beautifully.

The tablets became a symbol of the Sinai pact and an emblem of the Yahweh-Israel convention. As a constant reminder of the connection between the law of Yahweh and his holy house, the tablets were later stored in the Holy of Holies of Solomon's temple. "There was nothing in the ark save the two tablets of stone, which Moses put there at Horeb, when the Lord made a covenant with the children of Israel" (1 Kings 8:9). Furthermore, to demonstrate the importance of the Ten Commandments, the words of the law were written upon the stones of the sacrificial altar (Deuteronomy 27:8).

"Sacral, communal meals are carried out in connection with temple ritual, often at the conclusion of or during a covenant

ceremony."[25] Exodus 24:9-11 describes a divine theophany unequaled in magnificence in Old Testament records. On this occasion more than sixty Israelite men were allowed to see God. Then followed a sacred meal *par excellence.* The covenantal ceremony of Exodus 19:1-24:10 was immediately followed by the eating and drinking of a sacrificial meal before God himself:

> Then went up Moses, and Aaron, Nadab, and Abihu, and seventy of the elders of Israel: and they saw the God of Israel: and there was under his feet as it were a paved work of a sapphire stone, and as it were the body of heaven in his clearness. And upon the nobles of the children of Israel he laid not his hand: also they saw God, and did eat and drink (Exodus 24:9-11).

Most contemporary scholars believe that this covenantal meal actually included "eating" and "drinking" real food. Nicholson, however, differs from the mainstream thought in that he argues that verse 11 should not read "they saw God, and did eat and drink," but, "they saw God, and lived (i.e., survived)."[26] Booij also doubts that there was an "actual sacrificial meal" upon the mountain, but argues that a later redactor added verses 9-11 to the text.[27] Nonetheless, the covenantal meal ties in remarkably well with the sacral meal at the time of the dedication of the temple of Solomon. At the mountain scene there are "burnt offerings" and "sacrificial peace offerings of oxen" upon the altar of Yahweh, followed by a meal of "that portion of the flesh of the offering which had not ascended to heaven in smoke."[28] Centuries later Solomon offered a dedicatory prayer of his newly built temple with his "hands spread up to heaven" (1 Kings 8:54). Immediately following his prayer, "he offered burnt offerings, and meat offerings . . . and at that time Solomon held a feast, and all Israel with him . . . before the Lord" (1 Kings 8: 64-65).

"There is a close interrelationship between the temple and

law in the ancient Near East.''[29] Clearly, the laws of ancient Israel were revealed to Moses during his many visits to the mountain height. The Lord had charged him: "Come up to me into the mount, and be there: and I will give thee tables of stone, and a law, and commandments" (Exodus 24:12). Many times Moses ascended to the dwelling place of Yahweh to receive both temporal and spiritual laws. On one such occasion, following a rather extended period of preparation (forty days and forty nights), Yahweh revealed to the prophet numerous policies and regulations (Exodus 25-31). Later, as recorded in Exodus 34:1-2, Yahweh instructed Moses to "hew thee two tablets of stone like unto the first: and I will write upon these tables the words that were in the first tables, which thou brakest." Following yet another divine theophany experience, Moses received further laws and instructions to assist him in regulating and governing the people.

The mountain sanctuary of Sinai and the law are related in three principal ways. First, as mentioned, it is obvious from the account that the laws were revealed to the prophet during his many engagements in the clouds of the mountain. The lawgiver was Yahweh, the mountain deity, and the recipient was Moses, who in turn became the lawgiver to his people.

Second, the tradition of the mutual relationship between law and temple continued when Moses and subsequent prophets and kings stored the two tablets of law in the ark of the covenant, which was kept in the most sacred precinct of all, the Holy of Holies. The tablets became the symbol of the law of Israel and were stored under the throne of the lawgiver—Yahweh.

Third, although Moses received a broad range of laws, many of them were rules and polices which governed the precincts of the temple. The laws received by Moses upon the mountain may be summarized as follows: The Ten Commandments (Exodus 20:1-21); ritual ordinances (Exodus 20:22-26); the social code, including civil and criminal laws pertaining to slavery, capital offenses, compensation for injuries, property loss, duties concerning foreigners, widows, orphans, sabbaths, and festivals (Exodus 21:1-23:33); laws concerning the ordinances; details concerning the ark, the table, the lampstand, the altar, the tabernacle, the tent, priestly garments and vestments, and the veil (Exodus 25:1-28:43); rules governing the consecration of the priests, the daily offerings and sacrifices, the poll tax, the holy oil, incense, and the tabernacle furniture (Exodus 29:1-31:18). Exodus 35:1-40:38 is largely a repetition of chapters 25-31 with some abridgments and elaborations.

"God's word is revealed in the temple, usually in the holy of holies, to priests or prophets attached to the temple or to the religious system that it represents."[30] Connected with the Sinai pericope were manifold divine communications between Deity and man. First of all, God "called" Moses up to the mountain (Exodus 19:3, 20; 24:15). According to Cassuto, the verb "called" [*wayyiqrā'*] here, "does not mean 'summoned,' but 'spoke in a loud voice.' " After Moses ascended to the top of the mountain, God then "spoke" [*wadabbēr*] with him (Exodus 20:1; 25:1); also the Lord "said" [*wayyōmer*] things to Moses (Exodus 19:9, 10, 21, 24; 20:22; 24:1). This divine disclosure was not a one-way experience only, as is shown by Exodus 33:11, "And the Lord spoke unto Moses face to face, as a man speaketh unto his friend," and Exodus 19:19, "Moses spoke, and God answered him by a voice." Revelation culminated upon the mountain sanctuary when a group of Israelite males "saw the God of Israel" (Exodus 24:10).

Closely associated with the manifestations and communications between God and man was the incubation of Moses. Gnuse, who has made an extensive study of dream incubation in the ancient Near East, writes that "the basic components of the incubation process can be seen. The incubant spends the night in a sanctuary, perhaps a special room for such activity. Sacrifices are offered to the deity. . . . Special preparatory rites, perhaps purification, are undertaken. The recipient does something to his clothing."[31] All this was for the purpose of receiving revelation or some divine disclosure from the deity. Gnuse lists five "possible incubation texts" which are found in the Old Testament: Genesis 15; 28:10-19; 46:1-4; 1 Samuel 3; and 1 Kings 3.[32] He fails to mention Psalm 3:4-5, which is a reference to the process of incubation, and Exodus 24:18; 34:28; and Deuteronomy 9:9, 18, which refer to the incubation of Moses.

Moses, as an incubant, spent the night in the sanctuary (Exodus 24:18), offered sacrifices to his deity (Exodus 24:4-8), purified himself (Exodus 19:10-15), and washed his clothing (Exodus 19:10-15), thus fulfilling the four "constitutive parts of the procedure"[33] of incubation. In return, Yahweh revealed his law to the prophet.

"The temple is a place of sacrifice."[34] The text is clear on this point; the Lord instructed Moses: "Make for me an altar of earth and sacrifice on it your burnt offerings and your peace offerings of sheep and oxen" (Exodus 20:24). In accordance with this command, Moses set up an altar at the foot of the mountain, and "sent young men of the children of Israel, which offered burnt offerings, and sacrificed bulls as offerings to the Lord" (Exodus 24:5).

It may seem almost superfluous to mention here the sacrifices connected with the tabernacle and the temple of Jerusalem. Several chapters of the Old Testament are devoted to the sacrificial ordinances, with all its associated regulations. Suffice it to say here that the sacrificial ordinances connected with Sinai were probably an archetype to those of the later temples. As Clements has commented, "It is probable . . . that the daily sacrifices came to be thought of as a renewal of the sacrifice on Mount Sinai, so that all the daily worship was linked to the idea of Yahweh's covenant with Israel."[35]

"The plan and measurements of the temple are revealed by God to the king, and the plan must be carefully carried out."[36] While upon the mount, the Lord told Moses, "In making the tabernacle and its furnishings you must follow exactly the pattern I shall show you" (Exodus 25:9), and for emphasis this dictum was repeated three more times (Exodus 25:40; 26:30; 27:8). The blueprint given to the prophet was very specific in its details. He was given the precise dimensions and measurements of the tabernacle, the tent, the ark, the table, the altar, the veil, the courtyard, and more. He was shown precise details concerning the priestly robe, ephod, diadem, and other vestments of the priesthood. All this and more concerning the tabernacle was revealed to Moses while upon the mount.[37]

Yahweh "tents" among his people. An important connection between the mountain of Sinai, the tabernacle, and the temple of Jerusalem can be seen when examining the Hebrew triliteral root *škn. This word plays a threefold role in the portrayal of the dwellings of Yahweh. First, the noun *miškān*, which is derived from this root, is defined as "dwelling place" or "tabernacle,"[38] and has special reference to the tabernacle built by Moses. Cross wrote, "In the Priestly strata, the term *mishkan* applies to the one Tent, the Mosaic sanctuary. The word has become a proper name."[39]

Second, the word *šəkînāh* is "very closely related with the Priestly use of *mishkan* and *shakan*."[40] *Šəkînāh* was perceived as being the divine manifestation of Yahweh, whether at the burning bush, Mount Sinai, or any other theophanic appearance of the Israelite God. In the case of Mount Sinai, the tabernacle, and the temple of Solomon, the *Šekînāh* was always accompanied with a cloud, which was a visible sign of the glory of God.[41]

And third, from the triliteral root *škn comes the verb *šākan*, which signifies, according to Davies, to "tabernacle, dwell among,"[42] and according to Cross, "to tent," or "to encamp."[43] In the Sinai pericope, *šākan* is used in connection with Yahweh "tenting" or "tabernacling" among his people, even before the idea of the tabernacle was revealed to Moses. Consequently, it is possible to translate Exodus 24:16, "and the glory of Yahweh tented on the mountain of Sinai," and Cross and Freedman translate Deuteronomy 33:16, "from the abundance of the earth and its fullness, and the favour of the one who tented on Sinai."[44] Later biblical writers employed the verb *šākan* when referring to the Mosaic tabernacle and the temple of Jerusalem. Therefore the God of Israel is found "tenting" in both the tabernacle (Numbers 5:3) and the temple (Joel 3:17, 21; Isaiah 8:18; Psalm 68:16-18; 135:21).

Such theological usage of this verb implies that Yahweh "tabernacles" or "tents" in his sanctuary, wherever it may be. Whether he temporarily camps on the mountain at Sinai, dwells in the mobile tabernacle, or chooses to *pro tempore* abide on the mount at Jerusalem, the notion was the same — God "tented" among his people. Even the seemingly permanent structure built at Jerusalem under the direction of Solomon "served only as a sort of temporary resting-place"[45] for the Ark of the Covenant, which was a symbol of the Divine Presence. According to Phythian-Aeams, "Solomon did not dare infringe the primary significance of the Ark. It might 'rest' in a house of cedar . . . but it must never cease to be the mobile vehicle of His presence, ready at any moment to resume its activity."[46]

Thus Yahweh first tented on Sinai, then the Divine Presence (*Šəkînāh*) tabernacled in the mobile sanctuary for a period, and later, the Lord was known to have camped at the temple found on Moriah. Finally, in a day yet future, the God of Israel will tent in the eschatological temple (Ezekiel 43:9).

Notes

1. Lundquist was not unaware of the problems which exist when writing and composing such a list of types; therefore, he wrote

in his introduction, "the following list of motifs . . . does not purport to be a complete motif list (hence the word 'preliminary' in the title), nor to have identified all examples to which a given motif may apply. Nor is it my intention to claim that a common 'pattern' can be applied indiscriminately to all ancient Near Eastern temples without regard to time, space, and cultural uniqueness." John M. Lundquist, "What Is a Temple? A Preliminary Typology," in H. B. Huffmon, F. A. Spina, and A. R. W. Green, eds., *The Quest for the Kingdom of God: Studies in Honor of George E. Mendenhall* (Winona Lake, IN: Eisenbrauns, 1983), 206. For a larger work on this subject, see John Lundquist, "Studies on the Temple in the Ancient Near East," Ph.D. diss., University of Michigan, 1983.

2. Lundquist explained: "It should be noted that the Greek root *temno*, from which *temenos* derives, [is] 'a piece of land marked off from common uses and dedicated to a god, precinct,' " "What Is a Temple? A Preliminary Typology," 205. Furthermore, the Hebrew root **qdš*, from which the word *miqdaš*, "sanctuary," is derived, denotes "apartness" or "sacredness," with no connotations of edifice or building whatsoever. Also, W. B. Kristensen deals with the term "temple" in his *Meaning of Religion* (The Hague: Martinus Nijhoff, 1960), 369-71.

3. Freedman, David N., "Temple without Hands," in *Temples and High Places in Biblical Times* (Jerusalem: Nelson Glueck School of Biblical Archaeology of Hebrew Union College-Jewish Institute of Religion, 1981), 28-29.

4. Lundquist, "What Is a Temple? A Preliminary Typology," 207.

5. Concerning the authorship of the Sinai pericope, Cassuto, for one, argues that "there is no reason to regard it as a collection of fragments derived from various sources, as many commentators have supposed." Umberto Cassuto, *A Commentary on the Book of Exodus* (Jerusalem: Magnes Press, 1967), 235. Others, such as Childs, Beegle, Haran, Davies, and Noth see two or more authors represented in these chapters. For example, see Brevard S. Childs, *The Book of Exodus* (Philadelphia: Westminster Press, 1974), 344-48; Dewey M. Beegle, *Moses, the Servant of Yahweh* (Grand Rapids, MI: Eerdmans, 1972), 237-78; Menahem Haran, *Temples and Temple-Service in Ancient Israel* (Oxford: Clarendon Press, 1978), 74-71; G. Henton Davies, *Exodus* (London: SCM Press, 1967), 153-97; Martin Noth, *The Laws in the Pentateuch and Other Studies* (Edinburgh: Oliver and Boyd, 1966), 36-41. In spite of this disagreement among scholars, I agree with Sklba's outlook. He wrote, "A critical reading of the

account of Israel's primal experience of Yahweh has often suggested the presence of pericopes apparently inserted into the narrative by later redactors. These must be momentarily set aside if one is to attain a fuller appreciation of the theological affirmations inherent in the original experience of Sinai." Richard J. Sklba, "The Redeemer of Israel," *Catholic Biblical Quarterly* 34 (January 1972): 1-18. In other words, one should not miss the theological significance of the Sinai pericope while dealing with the problems of authorship, dating, and so on.

6. Concerning the dating of this material, see Freedman, "Temple without Hands," 22; E. W. Nicholson, "The Antiquity of the Tradition in Exodus 24:9-11," *Vetus Testamentum* 25 (1975): 69-79; E. W. Nicholson, "The Origin of the Tradition in Exodus 24:9-11," *Vetus Testamentum* 26 (1976): 148-60; and Anthony Phillips, "A Fresh Look at the Sinai Pericope," *Vetus Testamentum* 34 (1984): 282-94.

7. Lundquist, "What Is a Temple? A Preliminary Typology," 207; others have written about the mountain/temple motif. See Richard J. Clifford, *The Cosmic Mountain in Canaan and the Old Testament* (Cambridge: Harvard University Press, 1972), esp. 98-181; Richard J. Clifford, "The Temple and the Holy Mountain," in Truman G. Madsen, ed., *The Temple in Antiquity* (Provo: Religious Studies Center, 1984), 47-71; Othmar Keel, *The Symbolism of the Biblical World*, tr. Timothy J. Hallett (New York: Seabury Press, 1978), 111-19.

8. Francis Brown, S. R. Driver, and Charles A. Briggs, *A Hebrew and English Lexicon of the Old Testament*, tr. Edward Robinson (Oxford: Clarendon Press, 1951).

9. Freedman, "Temple without Hands," 28-29.

10. For a very interesting discussion on Psalm 15:1 as referring to the temple, see Moshe Weinfeld, "Instructions for Temple Visitors in the Bible and in Ancient Egypt," *Scripta Hierosolymitana* 28 (1984): 224-50. Weinfeld translates this passage: "Lord, who may dwell in your tent, who may reside on your holy mountain?" (224). Another Psalm discussed by Weinfeld pertains to temple/mountains. He translates Psalm 24:3: "Who may ascend the mountain of the Lord, who may stand in his holy place?" (225).

11. Geo Widengren, *The King and the Tree of Life in Ancient Near Eastern Religion* (Uppsala: Otto Harrassowitz, 1951), 31.

12. Perhaps connected with this was the so-called "house of the Forest of Lebanon" (1 Kings 7:1-4), which housed several rows of cedar wood pillars. The actual purpose of this structure is unknown to the scholars of today.

13. Edward Robertson, "The Altar of Earth," *The Journal of Jewish Studies* 1 (1948): 21.

14. Lundquist, "What Is a Temple? A Preliminary Typology," 208.

15. Ibid., 209. For a rather general section on sacred space in ancient Israel, see Roland de Vaux, *Ancient Israel*, tr. John McHugh (New York: McGraw-Hill, 1961), 274-88.

16. Concerning Moses' commission (received at the burning bush) to lead the Israelites out of Egypt, see George W. Coats, "Moses in Midian," *Journal of Biblical Literature* 92 (March 1973): 3-10.

17. J. A. MacCulloch, "Shoes and Sandals," in James Hastings, ed., *Encyclopedia of Religion and Ethics*, 13 vols. (New York: Scribners, 1951), 11:474.

18. This phrase is used frequently by Jacob Milgrom. For instance, see Jacob Milgrom, *Studies in Cultic Theology and Terminology* (Leiden: E. J. Brill, 1983), 44.

19. Nachmanides, quoted in Jacob Milgrom, *Studies in Levitical Terminology* (Berkeley: University of California Press, 1970), 44.

20. Milgrom, *Studies in Levitical Terminology*, 44-45.

21. Haran, *Temples and Temple-Service in Ancient Israel*, 190. In the sanctuary of Yahweh, there were "gradations of holiness" of three types. First, there was graded sanctity of sacred space, as was noted above. Second, the actual materials employed in the building of the tabernacle and temple were "similarly graded. Its most precious components were made of gold, the least sacred, of copper. There were three degrees of workmanship, according to their sacredness"; W. Gunther Plaut, *The Torah* (New York: Union of American Hebrew Congregations, 1981), 601. And third, three types of sins were represented in each of the three parts of the tripartite sanctuary, "individual inadvertent misdemeanors" were purged upon the outer altar. "Communal inadvertent" transgressions were expiated for in the holy place, and "wanton, unrepented" sins were atoned for in the Holy of Holies by the High Priest. Milgrom, *Studies in Cultic Theology and Terminology*, 78-79. See also Jacob Milgrom, *Cult and Conscience* (Leiden: E. J. Brill, 1976), 17-18, 36-37. For a different approach to the same concept, see David P. Wright, "The Disposal of Impurity in the Priestly Writings of the Bible with Reference to Similar Phenomena in Hittite and Mesopotamian Cultures," Ph.D. diss., University of California, Berkeley, 1984, 217-29.

22. Lundquist, "What Is a Temple? A Preliminary Typology," 216.

23. Cassuto, *A Commentary on the Book of Exodus*, 235.

24. Geo Widengren, *The Ascension of the Apostle and the Heavenly Book* (Uppsala: Lundequistska Bokhandeln, 1950), 27. In this case Moses was the king (Deuteronomy 33:4-5). For an exhaustive work concerning Moses as king, see Wayne A. Meeks, *The Prophet-King* (Leiden: Brill, 1967).

25. Lundquist, "What Is a Temple? A Preliminary Typology," 215.

26. In 1974, Nicholson argued that the phrase " 'they ate and drank' is best understood, as in other cultic contexts in the Old Testament, as meaning that those who experienced this remarkable manifestation of God 'rejoiced' or 'worshipped' in the presence of God," E. W. Nicholson, "The Interpretation of Exodus 24:9-11," *Vetus Testamentum* 24 (1974): 94. However, two years later he altered his opinion: "I wish to revise my opinion on the meaning of the phrase 'they ate and drank' which I discussed in the first article mentioned above. . . . My proposal for the interpretation of that phrase [now is] that the representatives of Israel on the mountain in spite of having seen God 'lived' (i.e., survived)," Nicholson, "The Origin of the Tradition in Exodus 24:9-11," 148-49.

27. Th. Booij, "Mountain and Theophany in the Sinai Narrative," *Biblica* 65 (1984): 8.

28. Martin Buber, *Moses* (London: Phaidon Press, 1946), 115.

29. Lundquist, "What Is a Temple? A Preliminary Typology," 216.

30. Ibid., 217. Concerning the idea of revelation in ancient Israel, one scholar has written, "Revelation, Covenant, and Law are the three pillars upon which the structure of the people's history is reared. Without them, Israel would have been a nation like other nations; with them, it became a focal point of human destiny," Plaut, *The Torah*, 516.

31. Robert K. Gnuse, *The Dream Theophany of Samuel* (Nashville: n.p., 1980), 62. For an excellent work on dream incubation in ancient Ugarit, see Julian Obermann, "How Daniel Was Blessed with a Son: An Incubation Scene in Ugarit," *Journal of the American Oriental Society*, Supplement VI (April-June 1946): 1-30. See also Robert K. Gnuse, *The Dream Motif in the Theology of the Elohist* (Chicago: n.p., 1975), 35-37.

32. Gnuse, *The Dream Theophany of Samuel*, 63.

33. Ibid., 62.

34. Lundquist, "What Is a Temple? A Preliminary Typology," 217.

35. R. E. Clements, *God and Temple* (Philadelphia: Fortress, 1965), 72.

36. Lundquist, "What Is a Temple? A Preliminary Typology," 211.

37. Not only were the dimensions of the tabernacle given to Moses, but as the king he was authorized to build it. For the king as temple builder, see A. S. Kapelrud, "Temple Building, a Task for Gods and Kings," *Orientalia* 32 (1963): 56-62; and Keel, *The Symbolism of the Biblical World*, 269-79.

38. Brown, Driver, and Briggs, *A Hebrew and English Lexicon of the Old Testament*, 1015-16.

39. Frank M. Cross, "The Tabernacle," *Biblical Archaeologist* 10 (Sept. 1947): 66.

40. Ibid., 68. Although this Hebrew word was first attested in the intertestamental writings, Cross believes that the word "*šǝkînāh*" predates this period.

41. For the cloud at Sinai, see Exodus 19:16; 24:15-18; for the cloud accompanying the tabernacle during the desert wanderings, cf. Exodus 33:9; 40:34-35; Numbers 12:4-10; and for the cloud found at Jerusalem's temple, see 1 Kings 8:10.

42. Davies, *Exodus*, 197.

43. Cross, "The Tabernacle," 66.

44. Frank M. Cross and David N. Freedman, "The Blessing of Moses," *Journal of Biblical Literature* 67 (1948): 194, 206. Cf. also Clements, *God and Temple*, 19.

45. Hugh Nibley, "Tenting, Toll, and Taxing," *Western Political Quarterly* 19 (1966): 605. See also H. G. May, "The Ark—A Miniature Temple," *American Journal of Semitic Language and Literature* 3 (1936): 215-34, where May argues that the temple of Solomon was no more permanent than was the tabernacle.

46. W. J. Phythian-Adams, *The People and the Presence* (New York: Oxford University Press, 1942), 16.

20

Names in Antiquity: Old, New, and Hidden

Bruce H. Porter and Stephen D. Ricks
LDS Institute of Religion, San Marcos, California, and
Brigham Young University, Provo, Utah

In the cultures of the ancient Near East, existence was thought to be dependent upon an identifying word, that word being a "name." The name of someone (or something) was perceived not as a mere abstraction, but as a real entity, "the audible and spoken image of the person, which was taken to be his spiritual essence."[1] According to Philo of Alexandria, the name "is like a shadow which accompanies the body."[2] Similarly, Origen viewed the name as the designation of the individual's essence.[3] The phenomenon and religious significance of naming, as well as the practices of renaming and of giving secret or hidden names, are richly attested in the extant sources among the peoples of the ancient Near East, particularly in Israel and Egypt; but they are also found in chronologically and geographically contiguous societies in the ancient world.

Naming and Existence

The intimate connection between naming and existence can be inferred from its role in many ancient Near Eastern creation texts, where the creation of each element of the cosmos was dependent upon the gods naming those things which were to be created. The *Enuma Elish*, the Babylonian epic of creation, describes the precreation period as a time when "the heaven had not been named, Firm ground below had not been called by name, . . . when no gods what-

501

ever had been brought into being, Uncalled by name, their destinies undetermined."[4] According to Alexandre Piankoff, "The god Re creates the heavens and its host merely by pronouncing some words whose sound alone evokes the names of things—and these things then appear at his bidding. . . . As its name is pronounced, so the thing comes into being. For the name is a reality, the thing itself."[5] The primeval condition is described in the Amon Ritual of Berlin Papyrus 3055 as the time when "the name of anything was not yet named."[6] In the text of the Shabako Stone, an early Egyptian religious document, the notion of creation is expressed by the phrase *r mt rn n iḫt nbt*, "it is the mouth which pronounced the name of everything."[7] If naming creates something, it also distinguishes that thing, since the name is that feature which reflects individuality.[8]

When a man received his name, he was considered complete, since he was deemed to be "constituted of body and soul and name."[9] The name of a child or adult (or of an animal or thing) could be given to him either by man or by God. The Hebrew scriptures provide numerous examples of naming by God and man. Naming by man is first recorded in Genesis 2:19: "And out of the ground the Lord God formed every beast of the field, and every fowl of the air; and brought them unto Adam to see what he would call them: and whatsoever Adam called every living creature, that was the name thereof." This act, according to Alan Jenkins, "demonstrates [man's] preeminence in the created order by virtue of the power entrusted to him by his creator."[10] It is interesting to note that in the Old Testament the responsibility for naming a child frequently seems to have devolved upon women as well as men. Thus, Leah and Rachel gave names to Jacob's sons (Genesis 29:32-35; 30:6, 8, 11, 13, 18, 20, 24; 35:18).[11] Similarly, the judges Samson and Samuel were named by their mothers (Judges

13:24; 1 Samuel 1:20), and Ruth and Boaz's son was named by Naomi's neighbor women (Ruth 4:17).

Names given by God or angels from God are often mentioned in the Bible and in noncanonical Jewish writings. In *1 Enoch*, it is reported of Noah that he received his name in a blessing from God given through Enoch.[12] Abraham's concubine Hagar was told by an angel that the name of her son would be Ishmael (Genesis 16:11). Perhaps the most memorable angelic namings are those of John the Baptist and Jesus, where the angel Gabriel announced both their forthcoming births as well as their names (Luke 1:11-13, 19, 26-31).

In Egypt, too, there are reports of naming by divine beings. The Coffin Texts report that Shu, the son of the Egyptian creator god, is given authority and intellectual capacity to "go around the circle of total being, giving everything its name."[13] Further, when King Amenhotep III was being conceived, the god Amon appeared to the queen, who said: "How gracious (*hotep*) is thy heart towards me." To this Amon replied, "Amon is gracious (*Amon-hotep*) is the name of the child, for these are the words which came forth from thy mouth." A similar event occurred at the birth of Queen Hatshepsut. Her mother addressed Amon: "How magnificent (*shepses*) it is to see thy front (*hat*): Thou hast embraced my majesty with thy light." The god then named the child in the following fashion: "Hatshepsut-whom-Amon-embraced (*Henemet-Amon*) is the name of this daughter of thine, which I put into thy womb, [according to thy words] which came out of thy mouth." The Berlin Westcar Papyrus tells of Re sending three goddesses to the birth of the first three kings of the fifth dynasty in order to assist in the birth and naming of the children.[14]

That the existence and essence of an individual is dependent upon his name[15] is a theme particularly evident in the Egyptian Pyramid Texts, reflected in the Egyptians'

almost obsessive concern with the perpetual existence of
the name. For example, Osiris the king is referred to as
one who "will not die, nor will his name perish."[16] It is
further recorded in the Pyramid Texts, "O King, succeed
to your throne at the head of living, for it is the dread of
you which is on their hearts. May your name live upon
earth, may your name endure upon earth, for you shall
not perish, nor shall you be destroyed for ever and ever."[17]
On the other hand, to blot out a man's name was in effect
to destroy the man himself (cf. Mosiah 5:11-12). Historical
evidence for this belief can be seen in the acts of Thutmosis
III against the name and memory of his mother and co-
regent, Hatshepsut. Following her death, Thutmosis defaced her monuments, removed her name from royal inscriptions, effaced her portraits, and otherwise did all in
his power to destroy her name and to remove her memory
from the historical recollection of the Egyptians.[18] The
grave religious implications of Thutmosis' actions can be
fully appreciated only when it is borne in mind that "a
nameless being could not be introduced to the gods, and
as no created thing exists without a name, the man who
had no name was in a worse position before the divine
powers than the feeblest inanimate object."[19]

Renaming

In many parts of the ancient world there are accounts
of men receiving new names in place of their former des-
ignations. This act of renaming often occurred at a time of
transition in the life of the one renamed and frequently
carried with it special privileges and honors for the one
receiving the new name. The person who gave the new
name was usually in a position of authority and could
exercise power and dominion over the individual named.[20]
Dependence was sometimes, but not invariably, implied
in renaming, since, as Otto Eissfeldt has noted, "Renaming
can also indicate a kind of adoption into the household

which is equivalent to conferring on them a high honor."[21] This "adoption" would carry with it the idea of responsibility as well as inheritance.

Abram and his name change is usually the first to come to mind in the Old Testament. The act of changing Abram's name to Abraham begins with the introduction of God: "I am the Almighty God. . . . Neither shall thy name any more be called Abram, but thy name shall be Abraham; for a father of many nations have I made thee" (Genesis 17:1, 5). The new name given to Abraham was intimately connected with the covenant he received from God.[22] On the other hand, the name change of Sarai differs from that of Abraham. It is recorded that "God said unto Abraham, As for Sarai thy wife, thou shalt not call her name Sarai, but Sarah shall her name be" (Genesis 17:15). God changed the name of Sarah, but Abraham was given the responsibility to initiate that change. The new Sarah was thus ready to receive God's blessing: "I will bless her, and she shall be a mother of nations; kings of people shall be of her" (Genesis 17:16).

Joseph of Egypt was renamed Zaphnath-paaneah by the Pharaoh (Genesis 41:45), who placed him in a position of authority and gave him special privileges as well as freedoms. Eliakim and Mattaniah were respectively renamed Jehoiakim by Pharaoh Neco and Zedekiah by the king of Babylon (2 Kings 23:34, 24:17). Daniel was renamed Belteshazzar, and the three heroes of the fiery furnace — Shadrach, Meshach, and Abednego — were first known by their Hebrew names Hananiah, Mishael, and Azariah (Daniel 1:6-7). There are numerous instances in Greek mythology of youths being renamed, often by their tutors: Achilles' son Pyrrhos was renamed Neoptolemus by his tutor Phoenix; Jason received his name from his tutor Cheiron; Achilles himself was named Ligyron before he was renamed Achilles by Cheiron; Paris's name was Alexan-

dros when he was a *neaniskos* ("young man"); and Heracles
was originally called Alcaeus, Alcides, or Neilos.[23]

The renaming of Jacob is unique because of the series
of questions and answers that accompanied it:

> And he [the angel] said, Let me go, for the day
> breaketh. And he [Jacob] said, I will not let thee go,
> except thou bless me. And he said unto him, What is
> thy name? And he said, Jacob. And he said, Thy name
> shall be called no more Jacob, but Israel: for as a prince
> hast thou power with God and with men, and hast pre-
> vailed (Genesis 32:26-28).

Jacob then asked the name of the man with whom he had
wrestled (or embraced, as this may also be understood),
to which the man replied, "Wherefore is it that thou dost
ask after my name? And he blessed him there" (Genesis
32:29). Jacob then named the place where these things
occurred "Peniel" (face of God) for he had entered into
the presence of God and lived (Genesis 32:30). A similar
account in the Hebrew *3 Enoch* involves the question/an-
swer motif, as well as the names given to Enoch "by
God."[24] In this work, Rabbi Ishmael begins by questioning
Enoch about his name: "What is your name?" Enoch responds by listing the seventy names he had received from
God. Enoch is then asked why he had these names, to
which he responds that he has received these names because "he [the Holy One] assigned me to be a prince and
ruler among the angels."[25]

In Genesis 35:9-15, God appears to Jacob in order to
reaffirm what had already taken place: "And God appeared
unto Jacob again, . . . and blessed him. And God said unto
him, Thy name is Jacob: thy name shall not be called any
more Jacob, but Israel shall be thy name: and he called his
name Israel. And God said unto him, I am God Almighty"
(Genesis 35:9-11). As was also the case with Abraham, God
is introduced as the one who has the authority to change

the name and to bestow the blessing: "Be fruitful and multiply; a nation and a company of nations shall be of thee, and kings shall come out of thy loins; And the land which I gave Abraham and Isaac, to thee I will give it, and to thy seed after thee will I give the land" (Genesis 35:11-12). Jacob then sets up a stone, anoints it, and names the place of this sacred event Bethel (the House of God).[26]

The name change or the receipt of a new name marks a turning point in the life of the initiate: he is "re-created," so to speak, and becomes a new man. S. G. F. Brandon, in describing the rite of baptism, notes that "emergence from the waters of death, the re-clothing, and the reception of a new name . . . represented the resurrection of Christ . . . so that the baptised person should also be raised to a new and glorious life."[27] This name change was the "determination to cut one's self off from one's worldly identification and one's former way of life."[28]

New names were frequently conferred upon individuals at the time of their enthronement. The king of Egypt assumed at the time of his accession a titulary that consisted of five "great names" (*rn wr*).[29] Similarly, Sumerian, Hittite, and Iranian kings were all given new names at the time of their coronation or accession.[30] In the Book of Mormon, all kings were to be called "Nephi," giving honor both to the original Nephi as well as to the new king (Jacob 1:11). One of the best known public examples of a name change in the modern Western world is that which occurs at the time the Roman Catholic pontiff takes office. The pope not only receives a new name but also, as part of the enthronement ceremony, dons the new robes of his office and calling.[31] The receipt of a throne name is, of course, a regular feature of modern as well as ancient and medieval, royal accession rites.[32]

New and Hidden Names

The giving or possessing of a second name, to be kept hidden from others, is widely attested in antiquity among both mortals and divinities (and, occasionally, among objects, too). One Egyptian designation for a god was *Amn-rn-f*, "He whose name is hidden."[33]

The myth of Re and Isis, attested from a twentieth-dynasty papyrus, shows the importance of the "hidden name of the god" as well as the ignorance, even among the other gods, of the "true" name of Re. According to this myth, Isis desired to learn the hidden name of Re so that she might gain some of the power which he possessed. Since Re had become old, he frequently drooled. Isis took some of Re's saliva which had fallen to the ground, kneaded it with earth, and formed a serpent in the shape of a pear. Subsequently, the serpent bit him, causing him to cry out in pain as the "flame of life" began to depart from him. Isis offered to alleviate Re's suffering through magic (an art at which she was particularly adept) if he would agree to reveal to her his secret name. At first he attempted to satisfy her by a repetition of names which were already well known to her. Isis refused to provide him any relief until Re, tormented and in the depths of despair, revealed his secret name to her.[34]

In Vedic India, besides the name for general use (*vyavaharikam nama*) that was given on the tenth day, a secret name (*guhyam nama*) known only to the parents and, occasionally, to a trusted tutor, was given the child immediately after his birth.[35] In Greek magical texts, spirits and demons are often described as having "hidden names" (*krupta onomata, onomata aphthengkta*).[36]

Intertestamental literature and other writings of ancient Judaism and early Christianity refer to the hidden name. In *1 Enoch*, the fallen angel Kasb'el (Beqa) requests that Michael "disclose to him his secret name so that he would memorize this secret name of his so that he would call it up in an oath in order that they shall tremble before it and the oath. He (then) revealed these to the children of the people (and) all the hidden things and this power of this oath, for it is power and strength itself."[37] In rabbinic literature, the four-letter, twelve-letter, forty-two-letter, and seventy-two-letter "Hidden Name[s] of God" (*šēm hamməp̄ōrāš*) is frequently mentioned, although the tetragrammaton (YHWH) was not spoken, not because it was unknown, but for pious reasons.[38] The motif of the hidden name of God is also evident in Christian scripture, particularly in the book of Revelation. In Revelation 2:17, those who overcome are promised that they will be given "the hidden manna" as well as a "white stone, and in the stone a new name written, which no man knoweth saving he that receiveth it" (cf. Revelation 19:12; Isaiah 62:2; 65:15).[39] This is of particular interest since, as Hugh Nibley has pointed out, according to the Book of Breathings, the "Osirian dead" receive the name "stone of Righteousness," and since "the use of such a tangible seal as a means of identification and certification in the course of the mysteries is infrequently met with."[40] The faithful are further promised: "Him that overcometh will I make a pillar in the temple of my God, and he shall go no more out: and I will write upon him the name of my God, and the name of the city of my God, which is new Jerusalem, which cometh down out of heaven from my God: and I will write upon him my new name" (Revelation 3:12).[41] Christ himself has a new name, as can be seen from this description: "His eyes were as a flame of fire, and on his head were many crowns; and he had a name written, that no man knew, but he himself" (Revelation 19:12). The notion of the secret name was also found among the Gnostics. The Marcosians, a Gnostic sect attacked by Irenaeus, taught that Christ was clothed in a "hidden name" (*to onoma to apokekrummenon*).[42]

The hidden name of the gods was often known only to the gods and was frequently given by them. In the view of the ancient Egyptian, when the deceased was allowed to enter into the presence of the gods, he then became like them. Once he was there, he was given his "True Name," which "no man knoweth." This is made clear in the Pyramid Texts: "The king is a master of wisdom, Whose mother knows not his name."[43] In the first book of the *Iliad*, reference is made to Aegaeon, "whom the gods call Briareus, but whom men call Aegaeon."[44] According to the prayer of Joseph, Jacob is the earthly name of the patriarch, while his heavenly name is Israel.[45] The Gnostic *Pistis Sophia* contains both the heavenly names and the earthly names of the five archons: Orimuth is Kronos, Munichunaphor is Ares, Tarpetanuph is Hermes, Chosi is Aphrodite, and Chonbal is Zeus.[46] Similarly, in the Mandaean texts, Bhaq-Ziwa, who wishes a world to be created, sends down Ptahil-Uthra to nonexistence, and at the same time "he put names on him, which are hidden and preserved on their place. He called him 'Gabriel the Apostle.' "[47]

The idea that the name was used as a key to permit the initiate to enter into the true fold of God is also attested in the Egyptian sources. Entrance in the "Hall of the Two Truths" in order to see the face of "every God" was dependent on a knowledge of names and formulas. This is clearly evident from the 125th chapter of the *Book of the Dead* in which, after the deceased approaches the Hall of the Two Truths, he is told, "Let him come." Thereafter he is asked, "Who art thou?" The deceased replies with his name and then answers other questions the gatekeepers ask. Upon answering the questions correctly, the guards say, "Come, enter this gate of the Broad Hall of the Two Truths—thou knowest us." The initiate is then stopped by the jambs of the gate, and afterwards the beams, the rails, and the floor. All make the same demand, "We will not let thee enter past us . . . unless thou tellest our name."

The doorkeeper of the Broad Hall of the Two Truths refuses to announce the name of the deceased unless he tells his name. After correctly giving the doorkeeper his name, the initiate petitions him to announce the initiate to the "Interpreter of the Two Lands." Again, questions are posed: "And who is the Interpreter of the Two Lands?" "It is Thoth." "Why didst thou come?" inquires the doorkeeper. "I have come to report." "What is thy condition?" To this query the deceased replies, "I am pure from sin, from quarrels in their day. I am not involved in them." "To whom shall I announce thee?" asks the doorkeeper. "To him whose Hall is of fire." "Who is he?" asks the guard. "It is Osiris," replies the initiate. "Proceed then, thou art announced."[48]

The proper announcement of names in order to enter the halls of the gods is a motif much older than the *Book of the Dead*. A similar situation is mentioned in the *Pyramid Texts*: "The kings speaks: Hail to you, doorkeeper of Horus at the gate of Osiris! Tell my name here to Horus, for I have come."[49] The dead king must prove his divine origin and authority. The gatekeepers are to act as mediators between the deceased and the gods. Further, one finds in the *Pyramid Texts*: "They summon me. And they bring to me these four who pass by, wearers of the side-lock, Who stand by their staffs on the eastern side of the sky, That they may tell my name, that of the good one, to Re, And that they may announce my name, that of the good one to *Nhbw-kw*, I am vindicated."[50]

The Ethiopian *Bandlet of Justification* has been described as an "Ethiopian *Book of the Dead*."[51] This "tractacte," purportedly the "prayer of our Lady Mary,"[52] contains information that will enable the deceased to enter the kingdom of heaven. Chief among the topics discussed in this work is an account of Mary who, believing that Christ "possessed a secret name, by the use of which He created the world and governed it"[53]—like Isis in the story of Re and

Isis — asks Christ to reveal to her his hidden name. At first he demurs but, after Mary's continued importuning, he finally reveals his numerous hidden names, as well as other information necessary for the deceased's successful ascent to heaven.

In the so-called "Liturgy of Mithras," the ascent from one degree to the next is effected only through a proper knowledge of the name of the objects and beings which are encountered:

> After saying this, you will see the doors thrown
> open, and seven virgins coming from deep within
> dressed in Linen garments, and with the faces of
> asps. They are called the Fates of heaven, and
> wield golden wands. When you see them, greet them
> in this manner:
> "Hail, O seven Fates of heaven, O noble and good
> virgins, O sacred ones and companions of MINIMIK-
> RROPHOR, O most holy guardians of the four pillars:
> Hail to you, the first, CHREPSENTHAES!
> Hail to you, the second, MENESCHEES!
> Hail to you, the third, MECHRAN!
> Hail to you, the fourth, ARARMACHES!
> Hail to you, the fifth, ECHOMMIE!
> Hail to you, the sixth, TICHNONDAES!
> Hail to you, the seventh, EROYROMBRIES![54]

The danger inherent in revealing the hidden name lay in the potential power over the individual which knowledge of the name might give. "The deceased king," writes Erich Hornung, "shares with no one the knowledge of his name," thereby eluding the terrifying supernatural powers of evil that can only operate if the name and nature of the object is known.[55] As we have noted above, Isis is at pains to learn the secret name of Re, since she believes thereby to be able to "usurp the power of Ra."[56] The first-century Rabbi Hillel said, "He . . . who spreads his name loses his name . . . and who makes use of the . . . secret name of

God vanishes, and who knows [something new] will be asked for [it] in the world to come."[57]

In Greek magical papyri, the invocation and supplication of divinities and demons are frequently coupled with threats of exposing their true name: "O mightiest Typhon, hear me, N[ame]; and do x for me: for I tell your true names."[58] Rome (i.e., the city's patron deity) was possessed of two names, one of which (given by Joannes Lydus as Flora) was preserved by the priests but was never spoken aloud, not even during the most solemn rites.[59] For instance, when Valerius Soranus, a plebian tribune and distinguished grammarian of the first century B.C., betrayed the secret name, he was immediately put to death.[60] According to Pliny, before the Romans besieged a town, their priests would address the tutelary deity of the town, promising it that it would be shown greater honor there than it had been in its own town. Fearful that priests of hostile cities would attempt to do the same thing at Rome, it was given a secret name.[61]

Conclusion

When contrasted with their general devaluation in the modern West, the significance of naming and the wide attestation of renaming and the giving of hidden names in the ancient world is astonishing. Not merely identification, but existence itself, was widely thought to be contingent upon the name. If naming constituted the giving of an identity, the giving of a new name gave a new identity to the recipient, and was frequently associated with an important transition in the recipient's life. As has been shown, in many of the cultures of antiquity the knowledge of certain secrets, including secret names, was requisite to entering into everlasting bliss and to learning his own "True Name," a notion succinctly reflected in the *Wisdom of Sirach*: "He will find gladness and a crown of rejoicing and will acquire an everlasting name" (*Wisdom of Sirach* 15:6).

Notes

1. W. Brede Kristensen, *The Meaning of Religion*, tr. John B. Carman (Hague: Nijhoff, 1971), 416.

2. Philo, *De Decalogo* 82.

3. Origen, *Contra Celsum* I, 24, in *PG* 11:701-3; cf. also *Contra Celsum* V, 45 in *PG* 11:1249-53.

4. "The Creation Epic (Enuma Elish)," Tablet 1:1-2, 7-8, Ephraim A. Speiser, tr., in James B. Pritchard, ed., *Ancient Near Eastern Texts* (Princeton: Princeton University Press, 1974), 60-61.

5. Alexandre Piankoff, *The Litany of Re* (New York: Pantheon Books, 1964), 4. In other myths it is Thoth who gives names to things that were previously nameless, cf. E. A. Wallis Budge, *Osiris and the Egyptian Resurrection*, 2 vols. (New York: Putnam, 1911), 1:10.

6. Berlin Papyrus 3055, col. 16:3-4, in Hermann Grapow, "Die Welt vor der Schöpfung," *Zeitschrift für ägyptische Sprache und Altertumskunde* 67 (1931): 36.

7. Siegfried Morenz, *Egyptian Religion*, tr. Ann E. Keep (Ithaca: Cornell University Press, 1978), 164; Grapow, "Die Welt," 36, notes that the creation language used in the Shabako Stone and in Berlin Papyrus 3055, col. 16:3-4 (cited above) is nearly identical.

In the *Book of the Overthrowing of Apep*, cited in Budge, *Osiris and the Egyptian Resurrection*, 2:174, in which Atum says he developed his desire to create the world "by making his mouth utter his own name as a word of power and straightway the world and all therein came into being."

8. Robert T. R. Clark, *Myth and Symbol in Ancient Egypt* (London: Thames and Hudson, 1977), 63.

9. Hans Bietenhard, "*Onoma*," in Gerhard F. Kittel, ed., *Theological Dictionary of the New Testament*, tr. Geoffrey W. Bromiley, 10 vols. (Grand Rapids, MI: Eerdmans, 1967), 5:243.

10. Alan K. Jenkins, "A Great Name," *Journal for the Study of the Old Testament* 10 (1978): 43. In the *Clementine Homilies* III, 21, in *PG* 2:124-25, the naming of the animals by Adam is itself interpreted as a creative act.

11. In Genesis 35:18, the child, first named Benoni ("son of my sorrow") by his mother, was renamed Benjamin ("son of the right hand") by his father.

12. *1 Enoch* 106-7, in James H. Charlesworth, ed., *The Old Tes-*

tament Pseudepigrapha, 2 vols. (Garden City, NY: Doubleday, 1983), 1:86-88.

13. Clark, *Myth and Symbol in Ancient Egypt*, 75.

14. Piankoff, *The Litany of Re*, 4-5.

15. Jan Zandee, *Death as an Enemy* (Leiden: Brill, 1960), 14; Albrecht Alt, "Menschen ohne Namen," *Archiv Orientální* 18/1 (1950): 9.

16. Raymond O. Faulkner, *The Ancient Egyptian Pyramid Texts* (Oxford: Oxford University Press, 1969), par. 1812.

17. Faulkner, *Pyramid Texts*, par. 764; cf. ibid., par. 1660. These sections of the *Pyramid Texts* may be compared with the plaintive cry of Penelope to Medon about her son Telemachus, whom she imagines to have perished: "Was it that not even his name should be left among men?" *Odyssey* 4.710.

18. B. G. Trigger et al., *Ancient Egypt: A Social History* (New York: Cambridge University Press, 1983), 218-19.

19. E. A. Wallis Budge, *Egyptian Magic* (London: Routledge and Kegan Paul, 1977), 166.

20. Otto Eissfeldt, "Renaming in the Old Testament," *Words and Their Meanings* (Cambridge: Cambridge University Press, 1968), 70; Alan H. Gardiner, "A Lawsuit Arising from the Purchase of Two Slaves," *Journal of Egyptian Archaeology* 21 (1935): 140-46.

21. Eissfeldt, "Renaming," 73.

22. According to Philo, cited in Erwin R. Goodenough, *Jewish Symbols in the Greco-Roman Period*, 13 vols. (New York: Pantheon Books, 1953), 1:25, Abraham reached his final state of mystical achievement by the receipt of his new name.

23. Jan Bremmer, "Heroes, Ritual, and the Trojan War," *Studi Storico-Religiosi* 2 (1978): 7-8, where the references to the classical sources are also given.

24. Hugo Odeberg, *The Hebrew Book of Enoch* (New York: KTAV, 1973), 169.

25. Ibid., 5-7.

26. The blessings that are recorded as having been bestowed on the patriarchs were also claimed by the Egyptian ruler in a slightly different form. Alan Gardiner, *Egyptian Grammar* (London: Oxford University Press, 1973), 50, notes that the attributes *ꜥnḫ wḏ' snb* ("may he live, be prosperous, [and] be healthy") were believed to be bestowed on the king and on persons honored by the gods. This tripartite petition was not to be used for this life only, but was a desired benediction for all eternity.

27. Samuel G. F. Brandon, "The Significance of Time on Some

Ancient Initiatory Rituals," in C. J. Bleeker, ed., *Initiation*, Studies in the History of Religions 10 (Leiden: Brill, 1965), 47. An example of a baptismal rite in which the element mentioned by Brandon figures prominently may be found in "Homily XXII B (On Baptism)" of Narsai (fl. A.D. 450), in R. H. Connolly, ed. and tr., *The Liturgical Homilies of Narsai in Texts and Studies*, 10 vols. (Cambridge: Cambridge University Press, 1909), 8:40, who wrote:

> He [i.e., the initiate] waits for the priest to bring in his words before the judge; and he [the priest] restores to him the chart of Liberty with the oil and the water.
>
> A sponsor also he brings with him into the court that he may come in and bear witness to his preparation and his sincerity. With sincerity he protests that he will abide in love of the truth; and his companion becomes a surety [saying]: "Yea, truth is the protestation of his soul." He becomes as a guide to his words and his actions; and he shews him the conduct of spiritual life. He calls [or reads] his name and presents him before the guards [i.e., the priests] that they may name him heir and son and citizen.
>
> In the books the priest enters the name of the lost one and he brings it in and places it in the archives [*archeîa*] of the king's books. He makes him to stand as a sheep in the door of the sheep-fold; and he signs his body and lets him mix with the flock, the sign [*rushmā*] of oil he holds in his hand before the beholders, and with manifest things he proclaimed the power of things hidden [cf. Mosiah 5:8-13].

28. F. X. Murphy, "Names, Christian," in *New Catholic Encyclopedia* (New York: McGraw-Hill, 1967), 10:203.

29. Gardiner, *Egyptian Grammar*, 71; cf. Alan H. Gardiner, *Egypt of the Pharaohs* (Oxford: Clarendon Press, 1961), 51; Henri Frankfort, *Kingship and the Gods* (Chicago: University of Chicago Press, 1978), 46-47; John A. Wilson, *The Culture of Ancient Egypt* (Chicago: University of Chicago Press, 1962), 102; E. A. Wallis Budge, *The Book of the Kings of Egypt* (London: Kegan Paul, Trench, Trubner, 1908), xii-xxiv.

30. Frankfort, *Kingship and the Gods*, 246; Ivan Engnell, *Studies in Divine Kingship in the Ancient Near East*, 2nd ed. (Oxford: Blackwell,

1967), 59; Geo Widengren, "The Sacral Kingship of Iran," *La regalità sacra/The Sacral Kingship*, Studies in the History of Religions 4 (Leiden: Brill, 1959), 253.

31. Edwin O. James, *Christian Myth and Ritual* (London: Murray, 1937), 90; Lord Raglan, *Death and Rebirth* (London: Watts, 1945), 62.

32. Arthur M. Hocart, "Initiation," *Folk-Lore* 35 (1924): 312. The receipt of a new name by the monarch at the time of enthronement is a nearly universal phenomenon. Tor Irstram found in his study of African kingship, *The King of Ganda* (Lund: Ohlsson, 1944), 58, numerous instances of new names given at the time of coronation; similarly, Robert Ellwood, *The Feast of Kingship* (Tokyo: Sophia University, 1973), 152, notes that the receipt of a new name was a characteristic feature of the Japanese enthronement ceremonies. The Japanese never refer to their emperor by his regnal name (e.g., Hirohito or Akihito) during his lifetime, though after his death his reign is known by this name.

33. Piankoff, *The Litany of Re*, 5; hidden names in Egypt from the Pharaonic to the Coptic eras are given in François Lexa, *La magie dans l'Égypte antique*, 2 vols. (Paris: Geuthner, 1925), 1:145; 2:155, 163-66, 168, 172, 183.

34. Willem Pleyte and Francesco Rossi, *Papyrus de Turin*, 2 vols. (Leiden: Brill, 1876), 2: pl. 131-38; E. Lefébure, "Un chapitre de la chronique solaire," *Zeitschrift für ägyptische Sprache und Altertumskunde* 21 (1883): 27-33; Gunther Roeder, *Urkunden zur Religion der alten Ägypten* (Jena: Dederichs, 1915), 138-41; Lexa, *La magie dans l'Égypte antique*, 1:113-14; E. A. Wallis Budge, *Egyptian Tales and Romances* (London: Thornton and Butterworth, 1935), 111-17: Hendrik Willem Obbink, *De magische Beteekenis van den Naam inzonderheid in het Oude Egypte* (Amsterdam: Paris, 1925), 4-8.

35. Alfons Hilka, *Beiträge zur Kenntnis der indischen Namengebung: Die altindischen Personennamen* (Breslau: Marcus, 1910), 12; Wilhelm Kroll, "Aberglaube," *Rheinisches Museum für Philologie* 52 (1897): 346; Wilhelm Schmidt, *Die Bedeutung des Namens in Kult und Aberglauben: Ein Beitrag zur vergleichenden Volkskunde* (Darmstadt: Otto, 1912), 45. Hilka also notes, *Beiträge zur Kenntnis*, 40, that the practice of bestowing secret names persists among the modern Hindus. According to Jan Gonda, *Vedic Ritual: The Non-Solemn Rites* (Leiden: Brill, 1980), 375, the name given a child immediately after birth was not revealed so as to protect the child from the attack of evil spirits. See also Moritz Zeller, *Die Knabenweihen: Eine psychologisch-ethnologische Studie* (Bern: Haupt, 1923), 3.

36. Carl Wessely, ed., *Griechische Zauberpapyrus von Paris und Lon-*

don, in *Königliche Akademie der Wissenschaften,* Wien. Philosophisch-historische Klasse. *Denkschriften* 36/2 (1888): v. 1609; Carl Wessely, ed., *Neue griechische Zauberpapyri,* in *Königliche Akademie der Wissenschaften,* Wien. Philosophisch-historische Klasse. *Denkschriften* 42/2 (1893): v. 569; cf. Albrecht Dieterich, *Abraxas: Studien zur Religionsgeschichte des späten Altertums* (Leipzig: Teubner, 1891), 195; Schmidt, *Bedeutung des Namens,* 43.

37. *1 Enoch* 69:14-15, in Charlesworth, ed., *Old Testament Pseudepigrapha,* 1:48.

38. Chaim Kaplan, "The Hidden Name," *Journal of the Society of Oriental Research* 13 (1929): 181-84. The pious suppression of a divine name is frequently attested in antiquity, cf. Rudolf Hirzel, "Der Name: Ein Beitrag zu seiner Geschichte im Altertum und besonders bei den Griechen," in *Abhandlungen der Philologisch-historischen Klasse der Sächsischen Gesellschaft der Wissenschaften* 36/2 (1918), 252-57, and the explanation given in Doctrine and Covenants 107:2-4 why the first priesthood, called before Melchizedek's time "the Holy Priesthood, after the order of the Son of God" was later called after the name of Melchizedek "out of respect or reverence to the name of the Supreme Being, to avoid the too frequent repetition of his name."

39. Cf. Attilio Gangemi, "La manna nascosta e il nome nuovo," *Rivista Biblica Italiana* 25 (1977): 348, where he reviews various suggestions concerning the meaning of the white stone in ancient and modern commentators, including those of Aretas, Andreas of Caesarea, Pseudo-Augustine, Strabo, Primasius, the Venerable Bede, Alcuin, Grotius, Zahn, and Swete, concluding that its most probable meaning is that of "una attestatazione di vittoria" ("a sign of victory").

40. Hugh Nibley, *The Message of the Joseph Smith Papyri* (Salt Lake City: Deseret Book, 1975), 120.

Henry C. Trumbull, *The Blood Covenant* (New York: Scribner, 1885), 336, mentions a striking aspect in the manhood initiation rites practiced among the natives of New South Wales: "There, the initiate is given a white stone or quartz crystal, called a *mundie,* at the time that he receives his new name. This stone is thought to be a gift from deity and is viewed as being particularly sacred. In order to test the moral stamina of the initiate, the old men of the community try by all sorts of means to induce him to give it to them after he has received it."

41. That the children of Christ are known and called by name is implied by John 10:3: "The sheep heareth his voice: and he calleth his own sheep by name, and leadeth them out."

42. Irenaeus, *Contra Haereses* I, 21, 3, in *PG* 7:661-64.

43. Faulkner, *Pyramid Texts*, par. 394.

44. *Iliad* I, 403-4; cf. XX, 74: "whom the gods call Xanthus, but men call Scamander."

45. Jonathan Z. Smith, "The Prayer of Joseph," in Jonathan Z. Smith, ed., *Map Is Not Territory* (Leiden: Brill, 1978), 31.

46. *Pistis Sophia* 137, in Carl Schmidt and Walter Till, eds. and trs., *Koptisch-Gnostische Schriften*, 2 vols. (Berlin: Akademie Verlag, 1962), 1:237

47. Mark Lidzbarski, *Ginza* (Göttingen: Hinrich, 1925), 98, cited in Geo Widengren, *The Ascension of the Apostle and the Heavenly Book* (King and Savior III) (Uppsala: Lundequist, 1950), 59; cf. also Lidzbarski, *Ginza*, 284, where Ptahil is identified as Gabriel, and see Kurt Rudolf, *Theogonie, Kosmogonie und Anthropogonie in den mandäischen Schriften* (Göttingen: Vandenhoeck and Ruprecht, 1965), 198, for further examples in Mandaean literature. This same dichotomy between heavenly names and earthly names is also implied in John Milton, *Paradise Lost* 1:79-83, where "the Infernal Serpent" begins to recognize the companions of his revolt by him, including,

weltring by his side,
One next himself in power, and next in crime,
Long after known in Palestine, and named
Beelzebub. To whom the Arch-Enemy,
And thence in Heaven called Satan, with bold words
Breaking the horrid silence, thus began.

48. Thomas G. Allen, ed. and tr., *The Egyptian Book of the Dead* (Chicago: University of Chicago Press, 1960), 200-202.

49. Faulkner, *Pyramid Texts*, par. 520-21.

50. Ibid.

51. Sebastian Euringer, "Die Binde der Rechtfertigung (*Lefâfa sedek*)," *Orientalia* 9 (1940): 76-99, 244-59.

According to E. A. Wallis Budge, *The Bandlet of Righteousness: An Ethiopian Book of the Dead* (London: Luzac, 1929), 1-2, the bandlet of justification (or, righteousness) was "a strip of linen or parchment which was exactly as long as the body of the person for whose benefit it was prepared was high, and on this were inscribed a series of eight magical compositions, and, presumably, drawings of crosses. The width of the strip is unknown; it may have been wide enough to cover the body, but it is more likely that it was only from 3 inches to 6 inches wide, like the linen strips inscribed in hieratic with texts from the Book of the Dead, which the Egyptians buried with their dead in the Saïte and Ptolemaïc periods. This Bandlet was wound round the body of the deceased on the day of burial and was believed to protect it from the attacks of devils, and enable him to pass through the earth without being stopped at any of the gates or doors, and ultimately to pass into heaven."

Both Euringer and Budge consistently refer to this work as "magical," without providing a shred of evidence for their use of this terminology. While the contents of the *Bandlet of Justification* may, in certain regards, reflect the post-Reformation European view of "magic," discussed by David Aune in "Magic; Magician," in Geoffrey W. Bromiley, ed., *The International Standard Bible Encyclopedia*, rev. ed., 4 vols. (Grand Rapids, MI: Eerdmans, 1987), 3:213-14, it has little to do with activities and writings that were anciently described as "magical." According to Jonathan Z. Smith, "Good News Is No News: Aretalogy and Gospel," in Smith, *Map Is Not Territory*, 163, and Jules Maurice, "La terreur de la magie au IV. siècle," *Comptes rendus de l'Academie des Inscriptions et Belles-Lettres* (1926): 188, in antiquity certain ritual activities were described as "magical" if they were illegal or societally marginal.

Morton Smith, *Clement of Alexandria and a Secret Gospel of Mark* (Cambridge, MA: Harvard University Press, 1973), 163, avers that "magic" was primarily a term of abuse, a most interesting statement in light of the title of his book, *Jesus the Magician*, which came out in 1978, only a few years after the other statement was made. As Hans Penner has pointed out in a recent brilliant article, "Rationality, Ritual, and Science," in Jacob Neusner, Ernest S. Frerichs, and Paul V. M. Flesher, *Religion, Science, and Magic* (New York: Oxford University Press, 1989), 11-24, no objective criteria can be established for distinguishing "magic" and ritual.

52. Euringer, "Binde," 244.

53. Budge, *Bandlet of Righteousness*, 50.

54. Marvin W. Meyer, *The "Mithras Liturgy"* (Missoula, MT: Scholars Press, 1976), 14, 16. According to Meyer, ibid., vii-viii, although the tractate may contain Mithraic elements, it was "apparently collected for use in the working library of an Egyptian magician."

55. Erich Hornung, *Conceptions of God in Ancient Egypt*, tr. John Baines (Ithaca: Cornell University Press, 1982), 88-89; cf. also Otto Böcher, *Dämonenfurcht und Dämonenabwehr: Ein Beitrag zur Vorgeschichte der christlichen Taufe* (Stuttgart: Kohlhammer, 1970), 104-6; idem, *Christus Exorcista: Dämonismus und Taufe im Neuen Testament* (Stuttgart: Kohlhammer, 1972), 88-89, for a similar view of the power inherent in the knowledge of names in New Testament exorcisms.

56. Budge, *Egyptian Tales and Romances*, 111.

57. Cited in Gershom G. Scholem, *Jewish Gnosticism, Merkabah Mysticism and Talmudic Tradition* (New York: Jewish Theological Seminary of America, 1965), 80.

58. Arthur D. Nock, "Greek Magical Papyri," *Journal of Egyptian Archaeology* 15 (1929): 227.

59. Joannes Lydus, *De Mensibus* (*Peri Mēnōn*) IV, 30; cf. IV, 73, 75, in Richard Wünsch, *Ioannis Lydi Liber de Mensibus* (Stuttgart: Teubner, 1967), 89.19, 125.7-8, 126.16. Joannes Lydus posits a relationship between Flora, Rome's secret name, and Anthousa, the secret name of the New Rome, Constantinople. According to Jacob Bernays, "Quellennachweise zu Politianus und Georgius Valla," *Hermes* 11 (1876): 129-34, and A. Riese, "Anthusa," *Hermes* 12 (1877): 143-44, several other Greek and Byzantine authors also mention Anthousa as the name of Constantinople, among them Julius Honorius, Eustathius, and Stephanus Byzantinus. Georg Wissowa, "Flora," in Georg Wissowa, ed., *Paulys Realencyclopädie der klassischen Altertumswissenschaft* (Stuttgart: Metler, 1909), 6:2749, coolly avers that there "ist nichts Rechtes anzufangen" with the name Flora. Macrobius, *Saturnalia* III, 9, 8, includes several suggestions about the secret name (tutelary deity) of Rome, including Jupiter, Luna (Lua), Angerona, and (his personal preference) Ops Consivia. But see Friedrich Pfister, "Zur Grabschrift des Aberkios," *Berliner Philologische Wochenschrift* 33 (1913): 29, who distinguishes in the writings of the classical authors between the *onoma telestikon*, which might under no circumstances be divulged, the *onoma hieratikon*, which might, without penalty, be revealed to another person, and the *onoma politikon*, the name commonly used. Rome's three names, corresponding to these three categories were, respectively, Eros, Flora, and Roma.

60. Plutarch, *Quaestiones Romanae* 61; Pliny the Elder, *Historia Naturalis* III, 5, 65; Servius, *Commentarius in Aeneidem* I, 277, in Georg Thilo and Hermann Hagen, eds., *Servii Grammatici Commentarii*, 3 vols. (Hildesheim: Olms, 1961), 1:103.

61. Pliny the Elder, *Historia Naturalis* XXVIII, 4, 18; cf. Macrobius, *Saturnalia* III, 9, 4.

The power of the knowledge of a name over a being can also be seen in the widely attested folk tales of the Rumpelstiltskin variety (Tom Tit Tot, Purzingele, Kruzimugeli, Gilitrutt, Ropiquet, and Wind and Weather), wherein elves, trolls, dwarves, and sprites are rendered impotent to work their (generally malevolent) will on their would-be victims because their names have been discovered; cf.

Edward Clodd, *Tom Tit Tot: An Essay on Savage Philosophy* (London: Duckworth, 1898), 53-56; idem, "The Philosophy of Rumpelstiltskin," *Folk-Lore Journal* (1889): 135-62; Jacob Grimm, *Deutsche Mythologie*, 3 vols. (Basel: Schwabe, 1953), 1:418, n. 1, and 454; Schmidt, *Bedeutung des Namens*, 43-44; Stith Thompson, *Motif-Index of Folk Literature*, 6 vols. (Bloomington: Indiana University Press, 1966), C 432.1 (vol. 1:518), G 303.16.19.9 (vol. 3:339); Jan de Vries, *Altgermanische Religionsgeschichte*, 2 vols. (Berlin: de Gruyter, 1957), 2:49-50, notes that the names Freyer and Freya were not the true names of these deities, but were used so that no harm might come to them.

21

Togetherness Is
Sharing an Umbrella:
Divine Kingship, the Gnosis, and
Religious Syncretism

Gordon C. Thomasson[1]
Marlboro College, Marlboro, Vermont, and
School for International Training, Brattleboro, Vermont

עשה לך רב וקנה לך חבר

Secure a teacher for yourself, and acquire a companion for yourself.

To inhabitants of the ancient world, perhaps nothing would have seemed more appropriate than the fact that a man named Chamberlain, prime minister to a king, carried an umbrella—were it not for the fact that Neville (1869-1940) usually carried it closed and pointed downward. Living at what many recent observers have considered the end of an age, or a particular (secular) consciousness, Western society in general and scholars in particular are, more often than not, insensitive, if not oblivious, to reality as it was understood in antiquity. And this lack of understanding is especially troublesome since our social and political theories, institutions, and laws are all ultimately rooted deeply in the past—to say nothing of a collective nature

---

This essay originally appeared in a slightly different form in the unpublished "Tinkling Cymbals: Essays in Honor of Hugh Nibley," John W. Welch, ed., 1978.

of our consciousness (or either a theoretical unconscious or some supposed deep structures of our languages).

Our difficulties in comprehending the past are themselves a product of the past. Unquestioned assumptions deriving from Platonic idealism and Aristotelian either/or logic, for example, have trapped scholarship in its own categories for countless generations—and not just regarding ethics and aesthetics. In studies of divine kingship one can find seemingly endless confusion as to what a king is, what a god is, and how a king could be divine.[2] Puzzlement is often expressed at how a king could be so naive as to claim world-rulership while being fully aware of another sovereign who ruled (and threatened) just beyond the border. Many students of Southeast Asia despair of understanding how a seeming plethora of religions could coexist and thrive. Some questions seem to be insoluble, for instance, how an avowedly Theravāda ruler such as Kyanzittha of Burma could simultaneously claim to be Avatār of Viṣṇu and also allow Abèyadana to build a Mahāyānist temple at his capital of Pagán, or how the Buddhist Borobudur and the Hindu Prambanan complexes could be built in such relative space/time proximity in ancient Java. This should not really be surprising, though, for even contemporary Asian scholars are handicapped by their Western-style education which conditions them to perceive data within Greek philosophical constructs that are inadequate to deal with the world (and especially religion and kingship) as it was understood by those who did not imbibe that *lethe* which characterized the Greek style of rationalism.

Many conflicting ideas exist as to the nature of the institution of divine kingship. This is not surprising, however, because our blindness to ancient forms also has its roots deep in the past. I see misunderstandings dating at least as far back as the early Greek *polis*—or at least the first performances of *Oedipus*. Post-Renaissance scholarship has seen this drama as the working out of almost every theme except as a political satire (and the radical implications of this position for psychoanalytic theory, mythology, and comparative literature are intended!). Yet if one examines the type of royal/ritual marriage common in the ancient world and the relationship of the *hieros gamos* to succession (and this, whether by sister-marriage of a Pharaoh in Egypt, marriage of a hero to the queen of a deceased king as in the case of Jocasta, the union of a conqueror or hero to a crown princess, or whatever variation of the theme one finds), it is apparent that an early Greek audience would not have seen the play uniquely as a tragedy, Aristotle's rather late evaluation notwithstanding. *Oedipus* was clearly a commentary on the political systems of some of the Greeks' neighboring states, though it may not have been recognized as being relevant to their own past. At that period there was already visible movement toward "modern" consciousness.

An ancient case in point reaches back to the earliest Hellenistic contact with the Eastern world. In few things did Alexander offend his fellow Macedonians as much as in his accepting and encouraging conquered peoples to treat him as divine (or more accurately, as a divine king). In Egypt he was given the title (among others) of Horus — as conqueror he was the *de facto* Pharaoh and was accepted as such — and legitimized with the spread of the story that he was the natural son of Nectanebo, the last legitimate Pharaoh, who had in typical Osiris style visited Olympias as a snake and begotten Alexander. Philip was left out of the picture.[3] In Asia there was contention as Alexander's countrymen refused to prostrate themselves before him according to oriental custom. Alexander probably recognized the practical political value of conforming to local custom, but the irritation it caused highlights the growing difference between Eastern and Greek-influenced consciousness.

What Is a Divine King?

In antiquity kings were usually men. Rarely, however, were they merely men. Ken Angrok, the thirteenth-century Javanese hero/trickster/criminal/goldsmith/usurper/king, for instance, is described in the *Pararaton* (Book of Kings)[4] as a literal son of the god Brahma and a peasant woman, the adopted son of Śiva, and an incarnation of Viṣṇu. Lesser-born figures such as Burma's Kyanzittha were nevertheless likely to be given "the anointing of the head with Indra's anointment,"[5] and in spite of Theravāda concepts of atheism, to be addressed with the same title — *purhā* — which was used to refer to the Buddha. Few ancient scribes took the care to distinguish between the most exalted *purhā* and a living *purhā*, either.[6] The "Theravādin" Burmese went so far as to describe their king Kyanzittha as

> the exalted mighty universal monarch, who rides upon a white elephant, the omniscient [one], the Bodhisattva, who shall verily become a Buddha that saves [and] redeems all beings, who is great in love [and] compassion for all beings at all times, who upholds the religion of the Lord Buddha, who is exalted above all other kings that [dwell in?] all the four quarters . . . without exception . . . who was foretold by the Lord Buddha . . . who is to become a true Buddha.[7]

Kings were, first of all, exceptional men. They were supposed to be physically perfect, without blemishes or impairments.[8] The well-being of the cosmos was to be seen reflected in their physical well-being. This requirement of physical completeness was one way of diminishing competition for the throne by near relatives (especially half-brothers). Coedès records from Cambodia, for instance: "On the day that a new king is proclaimed, all his brothers are mutilated. From one a finger is removed, from another the nose is cut off. Then their maintenance is provided for, each in a separate place, and they are never appointed to office."[9] John Cady emphasized how it was customary to purge contenders, especially the sons of ranking queens, when a change of rulers occurred.[10]

Beyond bearing all of the physical traits and signs of kingship, the king must be a man of prowess. Notwithstanding Georges Dumézil's analysis of the Indo-European tradition into threefold categories of warrior, king, and priest, the functions of these three often merge or are indistinguishable. The king usually takes the role of priest on behalf of his people, and the warrior/hero is a candidate for king extraordinaire. When Professor Luce discusses the controversial Makuṭa inscription in his *magnum opus, Old Burma — Early Pagán*, he betrays a predictable Western puzzlement at the lack of boundaries between what are, for moderns, disrete categories. He asserts that Makuṭa "does not sound quite like a hereditary sovereign. Was he not just a war-lord, popularly elected to meet a sudden threat of war?"[11] His question sounds strange from a comparative perspective if one goes back — to the "beginning," as it were — to when Marduk was elected as a "war lord" *and* king of the gods. Whether one is born to rule and "proved" in the ritual combats of the year rite, or is recognized by having conquered or defended the kingdom and by marrying the just-widowed queen or being rewarded by marriage to the crown-princess and named heir, it is the hero — the man of prowess — who is destined to become king.[12]

Anciently, being elevated to kingship was like ascending to heaven. In early India, ascribing the identity of a king with the Hindu gods was nearly universal. This idea of incarnation carried over into Buddhism, in fact it was implicit in Gautama's being a Kṣatriya by birth. Professor Luce, in his discussion of the Jambupati or crowned Buddha image, points out that very early the idea of Buddha as a divine king spread throughout Southeast Asia, but that

> Crowned Buddhas, in ancient India as in Burma, are never wholly royal. The correlation and contrast between Monk and King are there, and are intended. Seen in the ultimate perspective, the Wheel of Dharma, turned by the Buddha, merges in the Wheel of Authority, turned by the Cakravartin [world-ruler]. Pryzyluski has shown that before the first century A.D., many traditions identified the Buddha with the Universal Monarch. "For the primitive image of the *śramaṇa* Gautama, humbly clad in coarse *pāṁśukūla* (rags from the dust-heap), was substituted that of Buddha-Cakravartin, dressed in royal robes."[13]

The divine king, as representative if not the person of a people's god or gods, has many responsibilities. He insures the welfare of the kingdom—political, economic, social—and this is a manifestation of his broader legitimacy and potency. His worthiness is questioned as problems arise, and his illness or weakness bodes ill (if not requiring the king's death or replacement).[14] Scholars are handicapped in understanding such systems not only by the concepts of immutability and perfection/completeness which Greek philosophy ascribed to God, but by the obviously tenuous political status of divine kings as well. Many are chary of believing that any people would have been so credulous as to accept an individual as divine *and* to consider him answerable with his life for the well-being of the cosmos as reflected both in the heavens and in the stability and fecundity of the kingdom. This contrast becomes stark through comparison to the politically expedient and particularly "Greek" "divine right of kings" espoused by the Stuart kings—the model that most reflects the Western perspective. While in the West it came to be said that a king was only bound to answer to God, a divine king, while not subject to a plebiscite *per se,* operated in a completely different milieu.[15]

The Ideology of Expansion

Western writers read the claims of ancient kings to world-rulership with amusement at people's gullibility or with disgust at pretentious oriental rhetoric and flattery. One is often asked how a Burmese or a Javanese ruler, for example, could pretend to the title of world-ruler, knowing that among other kingdoms, China (to whom they usually paid tributes) lay to the north and India to the west. While the religious and ritual significance of these claims will be discussed below, the spatial perspective must first be outlined.

The roles of the king have their cosmic analogues. As many peoples viewed their god as having organized matter out of chaos and as having created the world, so too their king by his personal presence and power must organize the world both religiously and politically and insure its order. The canopies of the umbrellas carried over the heads of the kings, whether in Africa, Southeast Asia, or elsewhere, signified—as did, to a lesser degree, the umbrellas of ministers with delegated authority and those of vassal-kings—the expanse of the heavens. This symbol can be found in earliest times in the umbrella-like roof of the tent of a nomad chief and later in the tentlike canopy over a king's throne.[16] The staff of the umbrella was the link or connection between earth and heaven and an indication that the world was ordered. If the king were not seen as personifying that link, he was principally responsible for maintaining it—the guardian and priest of the cosmic tree.[17] However his responsibility was formally pictured, the king maintained contact between earth and heaven and thereby ordered the earth. From the very person of the king extended the lands to the cardinal points, and accordingly many kings were known as lord "of the four points of the compass."[18] No matter that other kingdoms existed, the *mandāla* of creation and the center of the cosmos were recognized in the king. Those areas outside the king's control, though ruled and inhabited by others, were chaotic by definition. They became ordered when his reign was extended to them. The kingdom, capital, palace, temple, and ultimately the king's tomb all reflected the organization of space and life around the divine center and point of connection with the heavens. In his role as organizer and definer of the world, the king was also able to perform such tasks as recognizing holy sites and founding cities.[19] It should not be surprising that the religious responsibility to sacralize territory was held by the same person—the king—who was under an imperative to maintain and expand the realm through military action. The divine king's political roles were a mere reflection of macrocosmic reality.

The forces of evil and disorder never rest, and the king must therefore periodically renew the order of the cosmos. This ritual renewal (acted out in year rites in which the king victoriously combats chaos/death, participates in a sacred marriage with its promise of fertility, etc.) preserves and extends order in the world. Often in the earliest records, and as late as the nineteenth century in the kingdoms of Central Africa which claimed an Egyptian origin for themselves, the king would be sacrificed when signs were discerned that his strength or potency was diminishing. It is not surprising, however, that substitute sacrifices were developed, or that kings encouraged such changes. Games, races, and ritual combats all symbolized the struggle by the forces of order for victory over chaos.[20] When the king's death was simulated (a substitute being killed in his stead), he would emerge victorious from the tomb, and stability would be insured. But the king's victory was not immediate and did not go unchallenged.

A usurper, often having "murdered" the king, asserted control momentarily. This lord of misrule would subsequently be killed or driven away, and the king would reassume the throne. But before the king's triumphant revival, the usurper baldly asserted that he was the god of this world and took control. Ceremonially, the world was often represented in the form of the throne itself (frequently a lion throne), which often served as altar and royal bed as well. Recently, N. Falk recognized the king's conquest of the wilderness as a royal ordeal.[21] The conquest is a struggle for possession of the throne. It is acted out frequently, in the king's pleasure park/garden/paradise/hunting preserve or symbolic wilderness.

Ms. Falk points out that Buddhist sculpture which depicts the conflict between the Buddha and Māra under the Bodhi tree shows the Buddha picked as the perfect spot to attain enlightenment a *yaksha-caitya*, or tree with the usual stone throne beneath it—in this case the throne from which Māra claims to rule. The Buddha's choice was an explicit challenge to Māra's claim. Ms. Falk explains:

> Māra, lord of death and desire—that is, of the realm of *saṃśara*—becomes aware of what is going on. He therefore attacks the *bodhisattva* in an attempt to remove him from the seat. . . . Māra challenges the *bodhisattva* saying in effect: "The seat is mine, for I have given the most gifts." The *bodhisattva* claims the seat, on the same basis, and calls the earth to witness his generosity. He retains the seat and that same night attains to enlightenment.[22]

Ms. Falk concludes that this clearly depicts a struggle for kingship—generosity being the basis for claiming a royal throne in India, as elsewhere.[23] For some time I have been interested in a Burmese variant of this same text in which Māra (rather than the Buddha) strikes the earth with his hand and makes a terrible noise and, having failed to drive away the Buddha and the hosts that attended him, withdraws his armies in a great temper of anger.[24] When the

Buddha refuses to worship Māra, the latter's claim to be the god of this world stands refuted.

While in many texts the animal kingdom accedes to the sovereignty of a divine king, men are not always so submissive, and political dominion is most often achieved through warfare or the threat (implied or explicit) of force. The Buddha differs from Māra in that he wins converts by precept and example rather than by force. Every divine king makes the pretense of being a Cosmocrator and center of the universe—it is *de rigueur*, part of his role by definition. Usually such a world-ruler demonstrates the legitimacy of his kingship not just by ritual combats, however, but by military protection and expansion of his territories, rolling forth, as it were, to fill the entire earth. The purpose of such expansion is not to acquire *Lebensraum*, but to drive back the forces of chaos. The divine king must always demonstrate his merit, and is thereby driven to a constant bellicose attitude, if not an actual state of war. Overlordship (even while in a vassal or tribute relation with another more powerful suzerain), either by military conquest or through accepting voluntary submission and granting protection to a weaker lord, is a sign of heaven's favor.

Finding Unity in a Man

An unavoidable consequence of the expansionism incumbent on divine kings was the difficulty of maintaining unity. Once the frontiers of the king's own ethnic/religious group's territory were crossed and other peoples were conquered or voluntarily rendered fealty, the problem of winning hearts and minds — gaining their loyalty — became important. Oaths of loyalty, like chastity belts, are a *contradictio in adjecto*, and do not solve the problem.[25] "Nationalism" as a means for uniting diverse peoples, if it succeeds at all, is always based on perceived self-interest — and few foundations could better be termed a will-of-the-wisp. Conquered or vassal states that submitted to an overlord were, as often as not, of different language and culture backgrounds. They might have had little or nothing in common with a king's people except the taxes they paid and the person of the king. Ultimately, the only common denominator which divine kings had to offer to unite their various subjects was their royal and divine person. It was in the king that fusion could occur, and through him that syncretism took place.

The divine king, serving as an interface between cultures, was inevitably a multivalent symbol. One could recall the multiple political titles of the Queen of England (a political though not a divine kingdom). Each title reflects a people conquered or assimilated (though hardly unified, as events in Ulster and calls for Scots separatism that flowed from the economic promise of North Channel oil eloquently testify). The titles themselves reflect that the ruler of anything larger than the smallest kin-based group must stand for very different things to different people. On the other hand, the titles of divine kings represent the symbolic ritual functions which the divine king performs as the vicar if not the incarnation of each subject people's deity. The multiple crowns and ritual functions of Egypt's pharaohs are an obvious case in point.

Every people required connection with the divine, and that connection was embodied in the king.[26] The king's year was the sacred ritual year, from New Year to New Year, and he was the primary religious and political actor. The royal progress, which will be discussed below, reflected not only political necessity but ritual responsibility as well. While virtually every religious group had its priesthood and presiding figures, the high priest was most often merely a facilitator. The king was the nexus of the cosmic and the mundane, and the priests performed the highest initiation and conferred the highest keys on the person of the king. It was in his presence or on his person that the most sacred rituals and the highest mysteries had to be performed, and the divine king became the gnostic *par excellence*, holding the knowledge, power, and authority upon which the welfare and salvation of his subjects depended. With each royal progress through his domains, and at the beginning of each new age (year) in his capital, the king was reordained as the head of each cult and therefore of each people under his suzerainty.

While divine kings initially may have been partial toward their own concept of divinity, being a "defender of the faith" as it were, these same rulers almost inevitably brought about the dilution of their belief as their power spread and they extended their rule and "religion" over greater areas. By becoming head of the cults of conquered peoples, the king began the process of assimilation and confusion whether he wanted to or not. A very necessary *Realpolitik* was in direct conflict with any "missionary" zeal the king might have had, and divine kingship patterns, I am suggesting, were a primary cause of religious syncretism in antiquity. Professor Luce recognizes one aspect of the problem when he discusses how Kyanzittha tried, with his priest Shin Arahan, "to lead Burma fast into the Theravāda fold": "[he] found by experience (like the Indo-Greeks of Gandhāra) that the most effective way to teach them Buddhism was to give them a large number of images to worship."[27]

Their Theravādin commitment, however, rapidly seems to have given way to larger national priorities:

> Under the aegis of Buddhism — chiefly, but not only the Theravāda — [of] Buddhism of a wide syncretistic kind, embracing not only Mahāyānism and the earlier Tāntric schools of East Bengal, but also the old Vedic and Brahmanic cults (excluding sacrifice), especially Vaisnavism, whose influence was deep in lower Burma, both among the Mon and Pyu, heedful also of the old Nāga-worship of the north, of native Burmese animism . . . of the clan-spirits (*kindok*) and spirit-mediums

(ḍoṇ) of the ancient Mons, perhaps even of aboriginal totemism—he seems to have striven, with the help of his mahathera Arahan, to lay a broad and strong foundation for a united Burma.[28]

This unification through syncretism cannot be accounted for in terms of the character of any one of these religions, however. Professor Coedès exhibits a basic misunderstanding of popular Southeast Asian religion, what I have called the Theravādin trap,[29] when he writes: "Hinduism and Mahayana Buddhism, in the special form of royal and personal cults, were religions that were hardly suited to the masses; this explains the ease and speed with which the masses adopted Singhalese Buddhism."[30] In fact, only by being mixed with indigenous cults through royal patronage did Theravāda Buddhism become widespread in Southeast Asia. Theravāda Buddhism itself, as it was exported from Sri Lanka, was above all a royal cult, and a continuation of a very old *yaksha* cult.[31]

Just because divine kingship practices filled very pragmatic political needs, or at least attempted to, it does not necessarily follow that those who were involved were cynical or opportunistic in their religious practices. Even in deposing a ruler, many probably felt they were following heaven's mandate, rather than self-interest. Regardless of the sincerity of a pretender or usurper, however, the system entailed several imperatives. In attempting coups, as well as in disputes of succession, beyond the strategic considerations and necessities (e.g., military alliances, some loyal following) and tactical opportunities, certain more specifically religious actions were necessary. The first involved filling the "power vacuum" that resulted with the removal of a king, which entailed being ordained or initiated into as many cults as possible, both to secure the loyalty of those peoples and to insure the uninterrupted ritual stability of the cosmos. If there were several claimants (as in the case of several sons each claiming the right of succession at the death of his father) with different power-bases and regional alliances within the kingdom, this could result in very quick tours around the country to various religious establishments in order to be ordained and have conferred the keys of as many cults as possible, thus enhancing the image of the claimant's legitimacy, as well as resulting in battles with other pretenders and their allies. Royal progresses by a new king from cult center to cult center insured a kind of restoration of the keys to preside over the kingdom as a whole. The second imperative was intimately related to the first and could be summarized by saying that "marrying Jocasta was the rule." Acquiring wives from various local leaders would tend to build alliances, of course, but the ritual role of the sacred-marriage cannot be ignored. On this point Professor Coedès also seems confused. Writing of Pushkara (or Pushkaraksha), who became king at Sambhupura on the Mekong in the eighth century, he remarks: "It has been suggested that he obtained this royal status 'by marriage' but this is a gratuitous hypothesis; we can just as easily hypothesize that he seized power because the throne was vacant."[32] Rather than one action precluding the other, of course, both are compatible means to the same end. With scarcely more evidence than in the former case, Coedès recognizes the obvious regarding Suryavarman's eleventh-century claim to legitimacy in ruling Cambodia both by descent from Indravarman, and through his wife back to the son of Yasovarman: "We may have here an example of the legitimization of power by means of marriage to the wife or daughter of a predecessor."[33]

The legitimization of rule, the potential for practical alliance-making, and the normal structure of year rites and royal ritual combine to make not only marriage but some sort of polygyny almost inevitable. Elaborate protocols were usually maintained, however, to distinguish between "hostage" queens and "tribute" queens of inferior status on the one hand, and "alliance" marriages between equals and so forth on the other. Concubines generally occupied another status altogether. Such multiple marriages seemed to promote political stability in the short run, but as often as not led to disputes over succession between potential heirs. It should surprise no one that the great kingdoms of antiquity so frequently broke up at the end of the reign of particularly successful kings. The crucial factor at this point, however, is that a queen, given in marriage by a vassal to his overlord, would be the partner *par excellence* with whom to participate in the cult of that particular people.

A divine king, after he was initiated into the highest gnosis of each of his subjects' cults, became the patron of those cults as well. When he periodically renewed, through ritual, the fertility and well-being of that land, he would often set aside lands for the support of that priesthood, and so forth. Thus, the cults became beholden to him. More importantly, in most cases the rituals of such cults were daily or at least periodic in their rehearsal of the vital aspects of the year rite. For that purpose the king would bring priests of each group to his capital and maintain cult centers there. As priests traveled back and forth, they were exposed to other systems. Religions coexisted and mixed (coincidentally or not), precisely because it was necessary for the king to participate in and patronize the cults of the gods of every people under his dominion. The price of unity, as has been pointed out, was syncretism. Nevertheless, the royal propensity to keep records and the cost of such activities (which was usually borne by the king) often means that more can be known about a particular cult through royal sources than from anywhere else. While many of these sources have been relatively neglected in the study of Gnosticism, their pro-royal bias is easier to deal with than when a writer's bent is unknown, and such documents would seem to provide not only evidence on the process of religious syncretism, but also possibly the clearest picture of the nature of gnosis as it was understood in a particular cult — and how it was communicated to the highest initiate of that cult, the divine king.[34]

The Royal Progress

I do not pretend to offer any radically new insights into the structure of the royal progress in general. Dr. Nibley and others have far surpassed what I can hope to contribute there. Particular Indian and Burmese cases will be mentioned as a prelude to treatment in the next section of one Javanese text in particular, and a general corollary to a working diffusionist hypothesis will be suggested: "often, the more things change, the more they stay the same!"[35] Nothing paradoxical is intended in that statement. It simply implies that adaptation of a given cultural pattern to its larger ecosystem is a prerequisite to its survival. Thus, if in one culture the center of a cult-complex is a war-horse surrogate for a king, in another place and time an elephant may be substituted for the horse because it is the preferred animal for warfare, or somehow fits the new ecosystem or culture-setting better. It should be easy to see how use of an elephant might dictate other changes in ritual, as well, and yet the essential form could be maintained.

There is historical evidence that the institution of kingship persisted in India for at least three millennia. Over such a time span it should not be surprising that the kingship rituals of India as we know them are many and varied. Yet these rituals — the Cakravartin year cycle or wheel ritual, the Dasapeya which bestowed the power of the New Year on the king, the Nirajana with its yearly expiation, the Rajasuya in which the king's power is renewed, the Abishekaniya with its rebirth, the Vajapeya where the king takes the ritual place of Prajapati (who was sacrificed to create the cosmos), which entails among other things chariot races the king is supposed to win, the Mangala, and for our purposes most important, the Aśvamedha or horse sacrifice — contain little to surprise the comparativist. Each can and should be studied in isolation as a *Ding in sich*, as well as in the Indian context, but to neglect the insights a comparative perspective and diffusionist approach can provide may lose for us a vital dimension in our understanding of them. W. F. Albright and P. E. Dumont's fertile collaboration on "A Parallel between Indic and Babylonian Sacrificial Ritual" should make this evident to every student, though little work of this caliber has been produced by more recent generations of scholars.[36]

Let us begin with the Aśvamedha, an Indian version of a royal progress. In it, a stallion, perfect of body, was "allowed" to run "free" for a year through all the king's realms. The horse's activities during the year were nowhere so random as that might imply, however. The horse was accompanied by a sizeable contingent of warriors, if not the king and his entire Court. The horse was allowed to mate, it was to traverse all the lands ruled by the king, and it was to end the year precisely where it began. Its course had to have been carefully guided. Any lord who rejected the authority of the suzerain and wished to assert his independence or superiority had only to resist the passage of the stallion and its escorts across his lands. In fact, as each lord allowed the court's passage, tribute was paid and gifts were requited by the overlord. As was the case with other progresses, the Aśvamedha dramatized and ritually reenacted

> the original seizure and subduing of the land; it is always the triumphant procession of a victor, pacifying the land, receiving formal submission, suppressing rebellion, rewarding loyalty, imposing justice and order on the world. . . . "The journeys and entertainment of the ruler . . . appear as the result of the superimposing of the authority of nomadic warriors over sedentary agrarians."[37]

While from one perspective the Aśvamedha seems to entail tremendous expense, it is precisely in making the circuit that revenues are collected, and it is not a once-and-for-all enterprise. Just as elsewhere, it is to be repeated. As Jan Gonda points out:

> On every anniversary of the first "coronation" the king should repeat the rites; this leads to welfare, to increase of the country, to the destruction of enemies and so on. Then the "inauguration" has become cyclic, annually carrying the ruler and his realm beyond a difficult stage, and re-creating the beneficial power inherent in kingship.[38]

Royal progresses are documented from millennia before and after Christ. Whether or not one can demonstrate a continuity from one in particular to another, sufficient similarities can be noted to demonstrate their relatedness. For example, Professor Luce, in his study "Old Kyauksè and the Coming of the Burmans," argues that the name of one town among those originally conquered by the Burmans: "*Mrankhuntuin*, 'Horse-leaping Post' . . . recalls the great Aśvamedha rite of horse-sacrifice . . . so the practice of horse-[sacrifice], and doubtless other sacrifice was still widespread among the early Burmans."[39] At least one contemporary Burmese scholar (a fervent nationalist) contests this interpretation and goes so far as to state that the "*Arvamdha* [sic] was a ritual known to vedic India but not to Southeast Asia."[40] This position is absurd if by "known" the writer means to imply awareness. The Mahabharata epic was known throughout the Indianized states of Southeast Asia, and its description of the Aśvamedha is more than sufficient to diffuse essential details of the ritual. More substantial questions would involve whether the ritual was actually practiced, whether the Burmese horse-sacrifice was similar in anything more than that it entailed killing a horse, or whether some distinct variant of the ritual evolved. To suggest a continuity from Albright's Babylonia through India in its epic period to Burma in the second millennium A.D. might seem overly courageous. The question reduces, however, to whether the apparent survival of certain elements and the seeming adaptation of others justifies asserting that a continuity exists, rather than the perpetuation of an anachronism or a revival of misunderstood and out-of-context fragments culled from ancient lore.

A record that suggests the persistence and adaptation of such practices comes from the reign of Kyanzittha, the ruler, who first unified what constitutes most of modern Burma in the late eleventh and early twelfth centuries A.D. Among other things, besides building many national shrines and temples and endowing priestly colleges and cult centers, he imported much of Singhalese Buddhist practice. In the intercourse that followed, a replica of the Buddha tooth-relic from the Temple of the Tooth at Kandy was miraculously produced and sent to Burma. According to the *Glass Palace Chronicle*, Kyanzittha, at the behest of his high priest Arahan, placed the tooth-relic on the back of a sacred white elephant (one of the vital signs of Southeast Asian kingship) and determined and covenanted to build a *zedi* to house it wherever the animal might kneel (in the first instance at the national shrine, the Shwezigon). We should not find it surprising that at that point the tooth miraculously reduplicated itself and one relic was left at the shrine, while the elephant proceeded to Mt. Tangyi where the process repeated itself as it did again and again throughout Burma.[41] What is being suggested, of course, is that the peregrinations of the white elephant are substituted for those of the horse, while the basic religio-political significance of the act persists. Escorting the royal elephant over the countryside and building shrines where it knelt was an outright assertion of sovereignty. There were other ways to do this, of course. But this one was chosen. More than the symbolic presence of the king/cult was involved. In the end there was the physical presence of the person of the king traveling the land.

The *Nagara-Kertagama*

From Java comes a text with remarkable comparative potential. The *Nagara-Kertagama* (The Kingdom Which Is Ordered according to Holy Tradition, as it is called in a colophon) is the product of a court poet and priest, the *rakawi* Prapanca, for the benefit of Rajasanagara (or Hayam Wuruk, as he is also known), king of the fourteenth-century Majapahit empire of Java. The other title given in the only manuscript known—*Deca Warnana* (Description of Country)—while preferred by most scholars, does not, from my perspective, adequately reflect the ritual content and nature of the text. While the *Nagara-Kertagama* is unique in its length and richness as a resource for fourteenth-century and earlier Majapahit historical and cultural studies, from another perspective it is predictable and stereotyped—almost a cliché. I do not mean to diminish its value in any way by that statement. The text is invaluable because it contains a detailed record of one of many royal progresses made by Rajasanagara, a description of an annual court festival (year rite), and other details of life and politics in general. It illustrates the survival of ancient rituals of kingship into the fourteenth century A.D.—not as bits and pieces but as meaningful wholes—and exposes how they were perhaps adapted to changing environments, while maintaining an essential integrity. Moreover, if one were to prepare a composite or ideal-type model of ancient kingship patterns, this very recent case would seem to be more complete than many, though not all,[42] that are older. That is meant as a commentary on the condition of many ancient records, however, rather than a denial of the persistence of ritual and the ancient *Weltanschauung*.

The *Nagara-Kertagama* text has gone through several

editions, the latest and most complete being that of Professor Pigeaud, to whose work I shall refer here.[43] While the text is in Javanese, Professor Pigeaud points out that it is "a product of high poetical schooling conforming as far as possible to Sanskrit prosody and *kawya* rules."[44] The earliest records from Java are engraved copper plates and stone slabs that date to the ninth century. The *Nagara-Kertagama* text was preserved on a palm-leaf manuscript of the type familiar throughout South and Southeast Asia. The text employs chronograms and other mnemonic devices (many of which may remain undeciphered today because as students of Southeast Asia have recognized, many ritual texts were mere prompters that accompanied a much more secret oral tradition, as exemplified in the Naxi script used in the southwestern Yunnan), which suggest that it may have been intended for recitation. While *Saka* dates are given, the Javanese calendar cannot be correlated exactly to India's. One might expect that either the royal progresses or the annual court rite at the capital would take place in the first month of the year (Kasa), for example. But the progress for which we have the best record (that of *Saka* A.D. 1281 or 1359) took place in the month Bhadra (August-September), which, as Pigeaud points out, is at the end of the "cold" season and "in the middle of the East Java monsoon, the dry season. This season of course was the only time suited for travelling. During the West monsoon the roads were made impassable by the rains, and the rivers were difficult to cross."[45] Such adaptations, as will be seen below, are to be expected. While the *Saka* calendar is a solar/lunar calendar of 365 days, other complications arise because another calendar year of 210 days (30 weeks of 7 days each) was concurrently followed to observe the sacred *wuku* year.[46] The two new years were rarely, if ever, exactly in phase with each other. Thus, this text presents many unsolved (and perhaps insoluble) problems for scholars. The value of the information it provides far outweighs the difficulties, though.

Majapahit was at the point of its greatest development during the reign of Rajasanagara.[47] Many diverse cultures and peoples were united under his rule. While scholars may debate the degree of overstatement and objectivity on the part of the court poet in his description and adulation, the common discussion of whether the king actively ruled over an equivalent of modern Indonesia and part of Malaysia, or was at the center of a "sphere of influence" and received tribute or some form of "token submission" from the more distant domains, and whether those domains were in large part "internally self-governing," betrays a significant lack of understanding of the institution of ancient kingship generally and is irrelevant to our discussion. The main thing, for our purposes, is that what those kingdoms are reported to have done fits a pattern and reflects certain understandings as to the "ideal" nature of relations between kingdoms and kings that is revealing in itself. One thing is certain. An attempt was made to describe the order of the kingdom according to holy tradition.

Majapahit court religion, as commonly described, was a syncretism of Siva-Bhairava worship and Tantric Buddhism of the Kalachakra school.This picture is manifestly oversimplified, and the Majapahit royal compound itself was described as containing various Buddhist, Sivite, Visnuite, and chthonic shrines. Residences were provided for numerous groups of priests nearby. The text also makes reference to numerous Hindu and Buddhist centers of Tantric and non-Tantric orientation throughout the country: cult centers, monasteries, shrines, estates, and vestiges of earlier systems as well. The king is described as participating in some form of worship at virtually every cult-establishment mentioned in the record. In fact, the whole text could be viewed as a *history of the ritual of the realm*.

The text begins with a dedication to the Siva-Buddha

(1.1.1), but by the end of the first stanza it says "there is an apparition of Him in the world" (1.1.4).[48] The entire first canto stresses the divine identities of Rajasanagara and how he was a Prabhu at birth (1.4.1), born to the purple. Throughout the text the king's superiority is emphasized, as might be expected. It is said "verily he is a divine incarnation in the material (world)" (73.1.1-4). Besides his divinity he is described as a "world-conquering *Prabhu*" (7.1.1) and "supreme Ruler of the world" (12.4.4). Cantos 13 through 16 list tributaries. Whatever the real extent of his rule, Rajasanagara maintained trade relations with all of Asia (83.4). The world was ordered because of his presence and virtue, the protocols of caste were observed and sinners repented (1.5.3, 4).

Cantos 8 through 12 discuss the capital and the royal compound. The palace, a long hall where court was held, the residences of other royal officers, and the large field where the annual festivals were held seem to have been located in four quadrangles of uncertain scale, intersected near the palace by "the cross-roads, sacred, imposing" (8.2.4). Here, at the center of the town and kingdom, "every month *Caitra* [March-April] it is the meeting-place of the Royal servants' assembly" (8.2.4). This annual coronation/renewal is elsewhere said to occur "every month *Phalguna* [February-March]" when "the Illustrious Prince is offered *paripuja* (procession worship), celebrated in his own Royal residence" (83.5.1). The festival actually extended through parts of both months (85.1).[49] Traders and royal emissaries from other seagoing powers were in the port of Majapahit at this time, waiting for the change of the monsoon winds to return to their ports or their next stop. It would have been impossible for monsoon-blown traders, travelers, and tributaries to attend New Year rites at Majapahit (or Singasari) at another time of year. For many reasons such as this one, year rites were repeated and rehearsed in several parts of a given kingdom a number of times in a particular year. First-fruits offerings from a given crop will be harvested when they will, for example, and a calendar might be modified in accord with such circumstances. Often, though, the original New Year and other rites persist, and other observances are added, keeping the king constantly on the move and coincidentally in continual review of his many stewards and dominions.[50]

Thus, the entire year comes to be occupied with rituals which perpetuate and renew the cosmos and the kingship — to say nothing of practical political ends. The king's year and the ritual year were one. If one restricts the definition of a new year rite to the period of time commencing with the parties on the evening of December 31 until the bowl games are over on January 1, or, for that matter, to the eleven days of the *akitu* festival, the multiple purposes of the year rites and the adaptability of diffused culture-patterns to local environmental constraints will be missed. This is not to say that *everything* the king did was necessarily part of a year rite (though in Egypt, for instance, certain acts were repeated daily). There would be little explanatory value in the concept were that the case. But records of particular events should not be ignored in regard to their relationship to the ancient pattern simply because they do not jibe with a strict calendar definition of the New Year. When a kingdom is known to have followed several calendars this becomes more obvious, of course.

The royal progress of *Saka* 1281 is described beginning with Canto 17. I take definite exception to Pigeaud's and Zoetmulder's view that Cantos 38.3 through 54.3 are "intermezzos" inserted because of antiquarian or literary considerations by the poet.[51] To the contrary I see the narrative extending continuously from Canto 17 through Canto 60. The royal progress was clearly an annual affair: "Every time at the end of the cold season He makes a tour, diverting himself" (17.4.1). The obvious goal of the progress of *Saka* 1281 is Singasari, the old capital as well as the cult center of Rajasanagara's ancestors, and it is from Singasari that the king is said to be "making ready to go home, longing for the charms of his own town" (55.2.1). While I shall discuss other features of the progress momentarily, the so-called "intermezzos" must first be explained.

While with other commentators we can wish Prapanca had said more about the details of ancestor worship and other cultic observances in Singasari, there is no question that when the king arrived "in Singasari he entered His sojourning-place finally" (38.3.2) and that while there he stayed in the royal *dharma* or religious domain (35.1.4). The supposed literary devices begin with the king's arrival. The first poetic "insertion" (38.3 through 49) is dismissed by other scholars as nothing more than the poet's inclusion of a recitation by an old Buddhist official of the genealogy of the dynasty of Singasari, their royal fortunes, their religious domains, and the cultic work for the dead that was established for each ancestor's benefit. The living king, of course, worshipped these ancestors, and to neglect the possibility of a relationship between the rituals of ancestor worship and the inclusion of a long genealogical/historical passage is astounding. The purpose of the visit to Singasari was ritual. Generally in Java, once a capital was conquered and then retaken, it was abandoned as the capital and another erected. The oldest seat of the dynasty was the ideal place for rehearsing the drama of creation itself. The second supposed poetic insertion directly follows the first. It is assumed to be a "fancied" description of a royal hunt in the countryside around Singasari. In fact it is clearly a ritual hunt, and quite appropriately part of a royal progress. It begins with a *battue* (50.2). Once encircled, the animals hold a conference, presided over by the lion, the "game-animals' Monarch" (50.6.3), at whose side "the jackal, entering into the Presence, [was] not frightened" (50.6.4). The question of the day was the policy to follow — what conduct was proper. It was crucial to uphold the law (*dharma*). Some advocated flight, others resistance. The lion, having heard the two plans proposed, answered that if the threat came from "bad people, *wahya* (worldly) should be the conduct: run or struggle" (41.4.3).

> Concerning the case, though, that you should be found in the activity of the Prince, hunting, simply await death, offer your life, do not be reluctant [51.5.3, 4]. For a Prince is proper to be an instrument to take away life of creation. Lord Giripati (Shiwa) is incarnated in Him, being the paramount *Prabhu*. It is clear that shall disappear the evil (the sins) of anybody who will die by His killing [51.6.1-3].

As is typical of royal (ritual) hunts, what we have here is a classic assertion of the divine king's "right" to rule, being the god of this world and holding, Nimrod-like, that great secret, the power over life and death in his hands.[52] There follows an almost comic scene in which servants, mandarins, and priests alike are scattered or wounded by the animals. Into the chaos rides the king."He made for the centre of that innermost wilderness, following the game, whichsoever caused fear" (54.1.3). "Exterminated were the animals, thrusted, lanced, cut, crissed, dying without a gasp" (54.2.4). Rather than poetic intermezzos, these two passages represent the most explicit kinds of ritual assertions of Rajasanagara's status as lord of creation and Cosmocrator, taking place at the cult center where the kingdom and the world-order originated. Instead of being accidental insertions, these sections are essential to the purpose of the narrative as a whole, and to the maintenance of the order of creation in the kingdom.

The progress itself consisted of a large caravan of carts — its number increasing at each stop. Queens, mandarins, headmen, priests of many cults, the poet-scribe — in other words the entire court — all make the journey. The king rode in a palanquin — the focus of the entourage. At each religious center on the route rituals were performed.

At each stop local leaders and commoners alike pressed forward to give gifts. The rulers of Bali and Madura came as well. "All of them submissively offered *hatur* (homage) presents, all of them trying to outvie each other: pigs, sheep, buffaloes, cattle, fowls, dogs . . . were accepted in succession (28.2.1-3)." At each place the king requited the gifts with cloth, money, lands, titles, or whatever was needed locally, perhaps. There were sporting contests, and at several points the king took new wives (27.1.4, 31-34). All the subjects were pleased, and "the common people then praised (His bounty)" (28.3.4). The text contains much more regarding this and the progresses of other years, along with more specifically political records, the final funeral rites for the dead Queen Mother—work necessary for the welfare of her soul—and a description of the year rite in the capital of Majapahit.

Cantos 83.4 through 91.9 give a general description of the year rite at the sacred crossroads in the center of the kingdom. The mandarins of the entire land came (83.5.2). There were first-fruits offerings (83.5.3). An order of worship involving portable pavilions (83.6.1), sacrifices (83.6.3), and such was followed. The king was carried about in the "jewel-*singhasana* (lion throne palanquin)" (84.3.1). All the people, commoners and those of rank, gathered at the great field (84.6). The poet omits a direct description of the consecration (84.7.2), though we do not know whether this was because of the sacred or secret character of the rite, or its commonplaceness. A great assembly is held with the purpose of preventing the people from falling into error, and they are told "they have to follow the 'Teachings of the Raja Kapa-kapa (Kings of yore),' [which are] always every *Caitra* [March-April] read (to them)" (85.2.1, 2). On the empty plain or great field at Bubat a temporary camp is erected on the same plan as the royal compound itself (86.3.3). There are games and gambling (87.2-3), feasting (89.5, 90.1-2), and drinking of spirits (90.3). There is always enough of everything, even for the drunkard. "If there are people addicted (to drinking) just as well they are visited, their liquor is all-surpassing. Nor does it occur that (the Princes) censure them for their faults, completely they are covered up (90.5.2-3)."[53] All praise the king's bounty and finally return home. As was said at the outset, this text is, if anything, a cliché. But while it is quite predictable, its detail, placed in the context of comparative data, is quite illuminating.

Inconclusive Unscientific Postscript

In summary, as one reviews the cultures of antiquity, it is apparent that systems of divine kingship were the rule, and that the Greek *polis* was an exception. The divine king came to power through religious ritual, especially the ritual of marriage. The divine king was the highest initiate into the secret, saving knowledge (gnosis) of his religion and the religions of the peoples he conquered. Usually he was regarded as an incarnation of the god of that people as well. One of the primary roles of the gods was to create — that is to organize or order the cosmos. That duty to organize matter and defeat chaos translated itself in the "real" world into an imperative for political stability and territorial expansionism, usually by military means — driving back the forces of disorder. Success in maintaining and extending his reign, however, created another problem for the divine king — achieving unity. Having achieved a military/political sovereignty, the divine king was in a position to be a unifying force, since as ruler he automatically fell heir to the ritual role of god-on-earth to each conquered people, as well as his own. As the divine king filled the religious responsibilities incumbent on him, however, he also brought about the confusing of the various religions in his person, as well as the intermingling of the priesthoods and cults of each people within the context of the royal establishment — in the court at his capital, and in the circuit of the court about his realm in the royal progress (whatever form it took). As the various priesthoods and religions not only coexisted but had to adapt their rites so as not to conflict with those of other groups, all of whom had their part in court ritual, in time beliefs were changed as well. Also, the king's involvement with the various groups went beyond ritual participation and fiscal patron-age—often as far as settling disputes over belief and ap-pointing or legitimizing the leaders of the priesthoods of these religions. While the process of religious syncretism resulting from a divine king's effort to achieve national unity can be seen most clearly in cases such as that of Kyanzittha of Burma, a close examination of the structure of divine kingship shows this to be a predictable rather than an exceptional result. In simple words, then, political unity is achieved through compromising the integrity of the religions.

For us as students of broader social and personal re-ligious questions (a task we cannot avoid, but usually do badly), other lessons follow. As A. M. Hocart perceptively observed about Adolf Hitler in the early 1930s while writing his important work *Kings and Councillors*,[54] seeking a savior/ king to solve our problems and unify us in this secular age is fraught with danger—a painfully accurate if secular "pro-phetic" warning which is still timely.

Finally, while a call to return to "old" or "conservative" political values—with a promise of unity which will lead to stability, security, law, and order—sounds attractive, we must not forget that the basis of such a condition among men has been compromise and the dilution of religious principles in order to promote political unity. Any *man* who would present a program or movement to unite us against the forces of chaos that seek to overcome us, any society that unites many people of very different religions, must accommodate.[55] Today there are no divine kings that can order the earth; there is only politics. And as to politics, the First Presidency's letter of 20 July 1849 still rings true:

> Never, no never, no never drag Priesthood into a political Gentile warfare. Let no religious test be required, or the holy influence and power of the Priesthood be brought to bear in any political question. If the intrinsic merits of all such matters will not furnish argument sufficient—for all necessary purposes, then let them go, for it is better that the whole political fabric, corrupt as we know it to be, should totter and go to destruction, than for one Saint to be offended.[56]

Notes

1. I must acknowledge that Hugh Nibley opened my academic eyes and ears—the mouth, however, I cannot blame on anyone except myself. Everything from his dissertation to his latest article has influenced my thought and work. More importantly, while I was his student and through him began to grasp the concept of total consecration, I gained a desire to waste and wear myself out in this work.

2. For a general background on divine kingship, besides the works of Hugh Nibley, see the writings of S. H. Hooke, A. M. Hocart, and others. The work of such scholars is sadly neglected compared with others who avoided comparativist analyses. In his foreword to a reprinting of A. M. Hocart's *Kings and Councillors* (Chicago: University of Chicago Press, 1970), ix, the late E. E. Evans-Pritchard made quite pointed and cogent remarks about the deficiencies of the work of such men as Malinowski and Radcliffe-Brown when contrasted to someone such as Hocart who, along with a brilliant analytical mind, brought Greek, Sanskrit, and other language skills, together with a depth of understanding of many cultures, to the task of describing and interpreting other cultures. See also E. Washburn Hopkins's article, "The Divinity of Kings," *Journal of the American Oriental Society* 51 (December 1931): 309-16; A. Basu's "Hindu Doctrine of Divine Kingship," in *The Sacral Kingship* (Leiden: Brill, 1959), 167-71; and Jan Gonda's article, "The Sacred Character of Ancient Indian Kingship," in the same volume, 172-80.

3. For a brief survey see R. D. Milns, *Alexander the Great* (London: Robert Hale, 1968), 101.

4. *Pararaton*, ed. and tr. K. J. Padmapuspita (Jogjakarta: Penerbit Teman Siswa, 1966), contains the Kawi text and an Indonesian trans-

lation. *Pararaton*, tr. R. Pitono Hardjowardojo (Jakarta: Bhratara, 1965), contains only an Indonesian version. While Dutch translations have been published, the *Pararaton* is not available in English.

5. *Epigraphia Birmanica*, vol. 1, part 2, ed. Chas. Duroiselle (Rangoon: Supt., Govt. Printing and Stationery, Union of Burma, 1960), 1:141.

6. Than Tun in "Religion in Burma, A.D. 1000-1300," *Journal of Burma Research Society* 42/2 (1959): 50-51.

7. *Epigraphia Birmanica*, 1:146.

8. Perhaps the best discussion of the qualifications of a king is in the Mandean text of the 1,012 Questions. While it specifies the requirements for a priest, among the Mandeans every priest is a *malka br malkia* (a king, son of kings), and the means to union with the infinite. See especially E. S. Drower, *The Coronation of the Great Sislam* (Leiden: Brill, 1962).

9. George Coedès, *The Indianized States of Southeast Asia* (Honolulu: East-West Center Press, 1968), 75.

10. John Cady, *Thailand, Burma, Laos, and Cambodia* (Englewood Cliffs, NJ: Prentice-Hall, 1966), 50, cf. also 61, 73.

11. Gordon H. Luce, *Old Burma — Early Pagán*, 3 vols. (Locust Valley, NY: Augustin, 1969), 1:25.

12. *The Glass Palace Chronicle of the Kings of Burma*, tr. Pe Maung Tin and Gordon H. Luce (London: Oxford University Press, 1923), 30-33, contains a story of a hero, Sawhti/Minhti, who is supposed to have slain a number of monsters which had oppressed the kingdom and against which the king was powerless. Here we have an almost universal "mythic" theme — a youth of noble birthright entering the oppressed country, freeing the about-to-be sacrificed maidens from the monster, being recognized by the king as of a royal "bone and race," married to the king's daughter (Thirisandadevi), and proclaimed heir. I argue that historical information can be derived from *The Glass Palace Chronicle* and other such records because they are histories of the rituals of the realm.

13. Luce, *Old Burma — Early Pagán*, 1:186. While Luce speaks of the "spread" of Buddhist iconography, we can as easily say "diffusion." By "diffusion" this writer has no intention to imply that a succession of cultures can be traced around the globe from a single source, appearing to be cut with the same cookie cutter from the same dough, or copied by some xerox-type process. If that thesis is advanced, it raises more problems than it can possibly answer, and it has no more real explanatory power than either the quasi-mystical or biogenetically based depth-psychological models ad-

vanced by C. G. Jung and others for explaining similarities between cultures vastly separated in space and time.

We have good reason to suspect, on the other hand, the existence of multiple points in space/time (dispensations) that might have functioned as centers of diffusion, but even so, we must articulate our hypotheses and test them carefully, rather than simply asserting them. The best metaphor I can offer for explaining a modern general diffusionist hypothesis is by comparison with the plant world. Seeds, having a basic genetic pattern, are (in fact designed to be) dispersed—whether by the wind, by birds, on the fur or sometimes through the intestines of animals, on floodwaters or with a man's seed grain, etc. Similarly, certain ideas, culture patterns, technologies, and so forth (or human genetic traits, for that matter) can also be carried into or imported by a given group. But to suggest that a knowledge of origin and the means of importation answers or moots scholarly questions is not to follow the analogy far enough. The ecology of a seed's landing place is as important as the seed (cf. Matthew 13:3-8). What influences plant growth? Soil characteristics, rainfall, hours of sunshine per day, annual temperature variation—these are but a few of the factors that can not only determine germination and growth in a new locale, but can induce variation, selection, and ultimately, survival. How a seed of known genetic characteristics grows in a new environment tells us as much about the nature of the parent plant as it does about the offspring. The analogy goes further. Will our plant, once flowered, cross-pollinate with indigenous plants? Can it resist pests and diseases? Will it preserve essential characteristics or become an effectively new organism? And what if a crossbred or selection-adapted seed is somehow carried back to its point of origin or into still another environment? Will the parent plant predominate, or the new plant? This botanical analogy is offered as a model for a diffusionary hypothesis because it reflects the dynamics of the particular case, while not allowing us to neglect the broader historical context. Where diffusion has been used to end discussion it has been as surely misused as has the dogma of independent invention.

Diffusionism is not a panacea. Indeed, it will, if employed carefully, greatly complicate our picture of the past and invalidate many popularly held notions. The evidences available today of Chinese, Southeast Asian, and South Asian influence in Mesoamerica are a prime case in point. While some Americanists are now grudgingly examining evidences of transoceanic contacts, it has rightly been pointed out that the real question is not "Was there contact?" but rather "What was the significance of the contact which occurred?" "Were contacts repeated?" and "Did items diffuse in both directions?" and so forth.

Finally, those who would focus exclusively on Mesoamerica in their search for materials that might lend insight to an understanding of the Book of Mormon run the risk of neglecting any insights that might be gained from the growing body of literature which shows the interrelatedness of Andean and Mesoamerican civilizations. Those peoples had commerce, shared aspects of their calendar system, and in many other ways evidence almost continuous contact and mutual influence. The cultures of Mesoamerica and the Andes without question had at least as much contact with and influence on each other as either did with any Old World peoples and civilizations.

14. For a brief description of one kingdom in Central Africa which persisted almost into the twentieth century, see John Beattie, *Bunyoro: An African Kingdom* (New York: Holt, Rinehart, and Winston, 1964), 27-28. A number of the ex-ruling families of Central Africa claimed that their kingship had Egyptian roots. With the excellent evidence that exists of these peoples having migrated southward over the centuries and of conquering local peoples, Egyptologists would do well, in spite of the time gaps involved, to examine these peoples' claims *and* their institutions. On Southeast Asia see Robert Heine-Geldern, "Conceptions of State and Kingship in Southeast Asia," Data Paper: No. 18 (Ithaca, NY: Cornell University/Southeast Asia Program, 1956).

15. The rigidity of Western categories is manifest in more than scholarship. In administering the colonized kingdoms of the third world, Western powers, if they did not wholly dispossess or exterminate a ruling class, recognized and used the old regime for administrative purposes. The "rulers," whose power and legitimacy were undermined by military defeat and colonization, in turn exploited the Western view of their class. Thus, disputes of succession and attempted coups became cases of "sedition" and drew heavy reprisals from a colonial power. When the colonial powers were finally removed, many third-world peoples rose up (as in Central Africa) and massacred ruling groups whom they had not been able to remove in more traditional and often less violent ways because of their colonial status. The Meiji restoration in Japan replaced the Tokugawa *shogunate* because it had allowed Commodore Perry to pollute the sacred land and had demonstrated its loss of mandate in the process. The imposition of the treaty in 1854 and the resulting

loss of face both justified the Meiji takeover and brought to power a group committed to avenge the dishonor. That group led Japan into World War II. Such transfers of power were at least as common under divine kingship as in nation-states today, though not usually as violent.

16. Hugh Nibley, "Tenting, Toll, and Taxing," *Western Political Quarterly* 29 (1966): 599-630.

17. E. O. James, *The Tree of Life* (Leiden: Brill, 1966), esp. ch. 4.

18. Luce, *Old Burma—Early Pagán*, 2:14.

19. Ibid., 1:233. Coedès, *Indianized States*, 114-15, 175. See also C. J. Bleeker, "La Fonction Pontificale du Roi-Dieu," *The Sacred Bridge* (Leiden: Brill, 1963), 220-24.

20. See my informal discussion, "Righteousness as a Counter-culture," *New Era* 2 (April 1972): 46-49.

21. Nancy Falk, "Wilderness and Kingship in South Asia," *History of Religions* 13 (August 1973): 1-15.

22. Ibid., 11. Māra's threat and challenge is not an empty one. In his bestowal of "gifts" he buys up religionists and militarists and rules with blood and horror in this world of *saṃsara*.

23. Ibid., 12. See also Hugh Nibley, "Sparsiones," *Classical Journal* 40 (1945): 515-43.

24. Luce, *Old Burma—Early Pagán*, 1:130-31. In the more traditional version of this incident, rather than Māra having "wrent" upon the earth in frustration at the Buddha's refusing to worship him, it is the Buddha who seeks the earth's recognition and testimony as to his divinity—this by means of touching the earth with a particular ritual hand-position (*mudra*).

25. No society has a monopoly on this problem, of course. See Hugh Nibley, "The Unsolved Loyalty Problem: Our Western Heritage," *Western Political Quarterly* 6 (1953): 631-57.

26. See Hugh Nibley, "The Hierocentric State," *Western Political Quarterly* 4 (1951): 226-53.

27. Luce, *Old Burma—Early Pagán*, 1:72, 361.

28. Ibid., 72-73. After almost a millennium, of course, Burma still is not a united nation. It threatens to split along ethnic/religious lines in spite of Kyanzittha's best efforts.

29. Basically, the "Theravādin trap" involves accepting a philosophical definition of Buddhism that was articulated and perpetuated by a handful of highly literate monk/theologians, and using that definition to describe religion and societies of ancient and contemporary Sri Lanka and Buddhist Southeast Asia, even though the supposedly pure atheism of Theravāda has virtually no relationship

to popular religion as practiced either anciently or today. Popular, nominally Theravāda Buddhism is as syncretistic and polytheistic as the phenomenon described by Luce; cf. n. 27. Philosophers and theologians, when asked what people believe, all too often describe what they think the people should believe (and what is intellectually acceptable to themselves) rather than what actually exists.

30. Coedès, *Indianized States*, 369, n. 1.

31. See A. M. Hocart, *Memoirs of the Archaeological Survey of Ceylon*, vol. 4, *The Temple of the Tooth in Kandy* (London: Government of Ceylon, 1931). In the twentieth century, when Hocart visited the rites at Kandy, the Wednesday day service still included the participation of two old women whose "presence is said to be in imitation of the king's practice of retiring with dancing girls" in connection with the cult, p. 31. From 1828 until 1846, while the British government held control of the temple and its administration, as well as appointments to its priesthoods, this was taken by the people of Ceylon as a sign of the legitimacy of British rule, and the British governor in many ways took the ritual place of the king, p. 4. Of particular interest as well is Hocart's translation of "Temple Regulations, about A.D. 1300," to which he devotes an entire chapter. Thailand, which maneuvered through the period from the sixteenth century until the present without being formally colonized, still maintains the outward forms of divine kingship. King Birendra of Nepal's mud- and dung-smeared coronation a few years ago argues for the preservation of at least the forms there, in spite of a Harvard degree.

32. Coedès, *Indianized States*, 85.

33. Ibid., 135.

34. An important discussion of Gnosticism from a comparative viewpoint is Geo Widengren, *The Gnostic Attitude*, tr. Birger A. Pearson (Santa Barbara: University of California Institute of Religious Studies, 1973), cf. also *Le Origini Dello Gnosticismo* (Leiden: Brill, 1967).

35. To write about diffusion from India through Burma to Java (in whatever manner) is a modest task. The "spread" of Malayo-Polynesian languages from Madagascar to Hawaii is undisputable, for instance. And by some of the same means that the languages spread, the Indonesian *gamelan* (a percussion instrument) arrived in Madagascar, moved to and spread across Africa where it became known by, among other names, the *mdimba*, and was finally transplanted by escaped black slaves into the highlands of Guatemala, finally resulting in the *marimba*. Paddy rice (*O. sativa*) spread by the

same means to Africa. This process is well documented. See A. J. Carpenter, "The History of Rice in Africa," in I. Buddenhagen and G. Persley, eds., *Rice in Africa: Proceedings of a Conference: Held at the International Institute of Tropical Agriculture, Ibadan, Nigeria, 7-11 March 1977* (London: Academic Press, 1978), 3-10. Ideas themselves can move as freely as languages or material culture. A significant example of culture transfer (and feedback!) is found in the nonviolent philosophies that grow out of texts that deal with Christ and Krishna. In the eighteenth century, British colonial officers published English versions of the Gita. Western interest in Indian religions and texts grew quickly. Thoreau became involved with the subject, is known to have read the Gita, published other texts in the *Dial*, and translated at least eight chapters of the Harivamsa from French into English for publication. Thoreau's writings influenced Tolstoy, as did the Bible and the Gita. Gandhi was attracted to Tolstoy's ideas on pacifism, and his contacts with Tolstoy helped him to develop his philosophy of nonviolence. Martin Luther King brought Gandhi's ideas back to America and these were later adopted by Cesar Chavez. Such cases abound. Unfortunately, popular literature by Van Daniken and others has again compromised the "intellectual respectability" of the study of possible relationships between the high cultures of antiquity, but a great deal is being done. Some of the more important scholarly works include Robert Heine-Geldern's important essay in the *Handbook of Middle American Indians*, vol. 4, *Archaeological Frontiers and External Connections*, ed. Gordon F. Ekholm and Gordon R. Willey (Austin: University of Texas Press, 1966); the landmark *Man across the Sea: Problems in Pre-Columbian Contacts*, ed. C. L. Riley et al. (Austin: University of Texas Press, 1971); and the exhaustive forthcoming study (approximately 5,000 entries and 1,200 pages) by John L. Sorenson and Martin H. Raish, *Transoceanic Culture Contacts between the Old and New World in Pre-Columbian Times: A Comprehensive Annotated Bibliography*. A problem which may merit further exploration is the relative place given to trees of the genus Ficus in the Javanese *Nagara-Kertagama* (8.1.3) in comparison to other cultures, such as in F. J. Neumann's discussion of the place of *Ficus* trees in Aztec religion, "Paper: A Sacred Material in Aztec Religion," *History of Religions* 13 (November 1973): 151-59. Whatever the implications of this topic, enough evidence exists as to the relationship between Southeast Asia and the Americas to jeopardize both antidiffusionist views and the beliefs of those who hold that the pre-Columbian Americas were populated by *no more than three migrations* from the ancient Near East.

36. W. F. Albright and P. E. Dumont, "A Parallel between Indic and Babylonian Sacrificial Ritual," *Journal of the American Oriental Society* 54 (June 1934): 107-28.

37. Hugh Nibley, "Tenting, Toll and Taxing," 610.

38. Jan Gonda, *Ancient Indian Kingship from the Religious Point of View* (Leiden: Brill, 1966), 114. Contrast to this Charles Drekmeier, *Kingship and Community in Early India* (Stanford, CA: Stanford University Press, 1962), and, of course, A. L. Basham, *The Wonder That Was India* (New York: Grove Press, 1959). P. E. Dumont, *L'Asvamedha* (Paris: Paul Geuthner, 1927), though difficult to obtain, is still unsurpassed on this topic. While the Aśvamedha is best known through its inclusion in the *Mahabharata*, other sources are available and should be consulted. It should be noted that ostensibly the most scholarly translation to date, *Mahabharata* (Chicago: University of Chicago Press, 1973 and following), has been done by J. A. B. van Buitenen, an admitted historicist who sees "religion" being restricted to rituals and claims to be amazed at how little religion there is in the Mahabharata. Given the expense and enormity of the task, it is doubtful that many other scholars or presses will attempt a translation which is more sympathetic to the text. That is felt to be unfortunate, especially since the historicist systematically neglects certain perspectives. One topic in particular which I have found of special interest is an examination of the eighteen major books of the *Mahabharata* as a whole—comparing their structure to that of ancient year rites. What emerges from this attempt is best explained by defining the text as a super year rite which was effected to insure the transition from one cycle of years (*yuga*) to another. In other words, it might be called a *yuga* rite. The transition to the current (*Kali*) *yuga* was, of course, supposed to have occurred in the year of the Mahabharata war. Seen as a *yuga* rite in comparison with year rites, the Mahabharata exhibits a coherency completely contrary to the picture usually painted of it—a pastiche, the elements of which van Buitenen calls "disappointing," "inept," "silly," "inane," "needlessly presented," and "foolish," and, one suspects, he translates accordingly. See van Buitenen, *Mahabharata*, Book 1, xx-xxi. I must admit that few books can boast introductions which so clearly highlight the author's biases—or the insights which a comparative stance might have provided.

39. Gordon H. Luce, "Old Kyauksè and the Coming of the Burmans," *Journal of Burma Research Society* 42/1 (1959): 83; cf. also 101, and Luce, *Old Burma—Early Pagán*, 1:13.

40. Maung Htin Aung, *Burmese History Before 1287: A Defense of*

the Chronicles (Oxford: The Asoka Society, 1970), 14-15. In conversation, a prominent anthropologist conceded that the case for Old World-New World diffusion was indisputable, but that it was a taboo subject for anyone to write about who wanted to be invited to do research in a given country more than once. His feeling is that many nationalistic scholars in emerging nations feel a great burden to prove the value of the national culture and justify pride in indigenous institutions, and thus are either absolutely irrational or politically hamstrung on the topic of diffusion.

41. Pe Maung Tin, *Glass Palace Chronicle*, 91-92. Viewed in isolation, this narrative would probably be, indeed has been, dismissed as purely mythical. From a comparative perspective it becomes quite clear what is going on, and the probability of a historical basis for the story is highlighted.

42. The most complete example is probably still illustrated in Hugh Nibley, *An Approach to the Book of Mormon*, vol. 6, *The Collected Works of Hugh Nibley*, 3rd ed. (Salt Lake City: Deseret Book and F.A.R.M.S., 1988), 295-310. If anyone still wonders at the preoccupation with year rites in ancient texts, it might be well to recall that on or around the day elsewhere described as the birthday of the King, at a place perhaps coincidentally called the "Crossroads of the West," we fill vacancies in the line of succession, are instructed in the law, raise our hands in token of our acceptance of leadership for another year, and so forth.

43. Th. Pigeaud, *Java in the 14th Century: A Study in Cultural History*, 5 vols. (Hague: Martinus Nijhoff, 1960). This is a model of editing and scholarship. The five volumes, consisting of a transcription, notes on the text, translation, commentary, glossary and index, are a joy to work with. Also useful is Th. Pigeaud, *Literature of Java*, 3 vols. (Hague: Martinus Nijhoff, 1967). The text has not, however, been immune to an obstinately ahistorical reading by Clifford Geertz.

44. Pigeaud, *Java in the 14th Century*, 3:xii.

45. Ibid., 4:42.

46. After the spread of Islam, Java adopted the Moslem lunar calendar while retaining the *Saka* and *wuku* systems for some purposes. With the colonization of Java by the Dutch, the Christian calendar also came into use and is used in Indonesia today. On some topics, however, one is likely to encounter A.D., a.h., *Saka*, and *wuku* dates, though this is not as great a problem as is faced by the Chinese minority on Java. Also, the older systems contain a great deal of uncertainty and potential for error. Compared with Bali, on the other hand, Java's calendars are a model of simplicity.

47. For a basic description see Coedès, *Indianized States*, 239, and D. G. E. Hall, *A History of South-East Asia* (New York: Macmillan, 1970), 84. It will be seen from these sources that many positions taken in this paper go against the majority consensus regarding a number of issues.

48. Pigeaud, *Java in the 14th Century*, 3:3. All translations given are from Pigeaud. All citations given in the text will follow his system for numbering: canto, stanza number, line.

49. Ibid., 4:267.

50. On the persistence and spread of a calendar system, see the important article by Paul Kirchoff, "The Diffusion of a Great Religious [Calendar] System from India to Mexico," *XXXV Congreso Internacional de Americanistas*, vol. 1 (Mexico, D. F.: Editorial Libros de Mexico, 1964).

51. Pigeaud, *Java in the 14th Century*, 4:117, and P. J. Zoetmulder in his valuable *Kalangwan: A Survey of Old Javanese Literature* (Hague: Martinus Nijhoff, 1974), 352, both use the word "intermezzo" in their discussions. To my knowledge there is not a single scholar of Javanese literature who follows my point of view. All look at the text strictly from an isolated viewpoint, excluding the insights of comparative data.

52. Hugh Nibley, "The Arrow, the Hunter, and the State," *Western Political Quarterly* 2 (1949): 328-44; and "Man's Dominion," *New Era* (October 1972): 24.

53. For all the emphasis that has been placed on the existence of "Tantric" practices in Java, scholars have been careful to avoid the problem of what might happen to either "right-" or "left-handed" Tantra when it diffused into areas such as Java where meat and drink were not prohibited in the first place. Scholars would do well to overcome their distaste for Tantric studies, not only because of its probable origin as a popularization of divine kingship and sacred marriage rituals, but because it is doubtful that any Asian religions escaped its influence, and our view is severely distorted by pretending Tantra isn't there.

54. A. M. Hocart, *Kings and Councillors* (Chicago: University of Chicago Press, 1970).

55. The danger of a minority religion seeking allies in such a compromising context is highlighted in F. W. Grupp and W. M. Newman, "Political Ideology and Religious Preference," *Journal for the Scientific Study of Religion* 12 (December 1973): 404, table 1.

56. *Brigham Young Manuscript History*, 20 July 1849, 105. This letter was from Brigham Young, Heber C. Kimball, and Willard Richards, with copies going to Orson Hyde and others in Iowa.

22

Heroic Legitimation in Traditional Nomadic Societies

David B. Honey
Brigham Young University, Provo, Utah

It is a privilege to participate in the scholarly rite of *Festschrift* production. It is even more of an honor when this participation contributes to the celebration of the life and scholarship of one who has been an object of personal veneration since young adulthood.

Of all the scholarly publications of Dr. Nibley, the ones that I enjoyed the most were his contributions on questions of steppe nomadism. After concentrated study on Chinese historiography concerning the nomads both during and since graduate school, I find that his works continue to be not only relevant, but indeed unique, in their scope. For none has attempted, let alone succeeded, in setting the steppe cultures in the context of ancient worldwide practices as Nibley has; nor has anyone else who has delved into the origins of practices as varied as royal hunts, taxing, and charitable contributions been able to trace such practices with comparable energy and erudition to Inner Asian rituals.

Nibley's most extended treatment of nomadism came as part of his effort to elucidate the old world settings for the Book of Mormon travels of Lehi and the Jaredites in his *Lehi in the Desert and the World of the Jaredites*.[1] *The World of the Jaredites* sets the wanderings of the Jaredites in both ecological and social environments. Ecologically, we see the vast movements of hordes and herds across the steppes

562

in great wagons as now hunting, now herding, and again, now farming, the Jaredites seek a new home in true steppe style. The terrain, the weather, the type and pattern of the daily round of activities—it is all familiar to the student of nomadism. Socially, we view the blood relations and blood oaths, the contention between heroic khans, the sudden gathering and swift dispersal of the hosts, the oriental intrigues and opulent largess that lay behind the rise of the great men, and the more martial aspects of the "logistics of depredation" (borrowing a phrase from Professor John Smith at the University of California at Berkeley).

An earlier and more narrowly focused work is "The Hierocentric State."[2] Here Nibley sets the nomadic custom of the *quriltai,* or election *cum* elevation ceremony, in the framework of worldwide royal New Year assemblies. Although not dealing exclusively with the steppe variations of this ritual theme, Nibley's great contribution to nomadic studies in this article, even above his exhaustive examination of universal kingship and the role played by the king and his ritual hunts, progresses, and palaces, is his identification of the origin of this concept and these rituals as Central Asiatic. Only recently has the same provenance, by way of the Aryans, been tentatively posited as a "working hypothesis" by Joseph Fletcher, an historian of the steppes.[3]

Nibley again uncovers the steppe origin of widespread religiopolitical practices in his "Tenting, Toll, and Taxing."[4] Again we see vast movements across broad steppes, with the tent as holy center and the royal progression taking center stage. The interrelationship between the toll and tax on the one hand, and rite of passage and ritual combat on the other, is ingeniously and convincingly portrayed.

The earliest of the Nibley nomadic contributions is his study of the role played by the marked arrow in the formation of the state. His "The Arrow, The Hunter, and the State"[5] examines various religious, political, logistic, and social functions of this ubiquitous instrument. The importance of this study lies in the illumination it sheds on the manifold uses of the arrow on the steppes. For it was not only the supreme symbol of authority, but, as with the famous "Parthian shot," or terrifying whistling arrow of the Hsiung-nu, the chief means of enforcing a khan's commands or accomplishing his martial schemes.

About the only category of primary sources that Nibley did not delve into directly was the Chinese historical documents (although he did make good use of studies based on them, such as those by McGovern or Wittfogel and Feng).[6] The present notes are based directly on these documents and their portrayal of nomadic legitimation through the rise of great heroes. Heroic legitimation seems an appropriate subject for a *Festschrift* dedicated to one who has been many a Mormon scholar's hero. It is offered as a small token of appreciation for many years of instructive and pleasurable reading.

Heroic Legitimation in Traditional Nomadic Societies

The concept of legitimation among the nomads is inseparable from the personal charisma and martial qualities of great heroes.[7] Many factors go into defining a hero in nomadic terms: aristocratic lineage, sagacious leadership, military prowess, loyalty-inspiring charisma, wealth or the promise of it and attendant largess, and the sanction of divine approval or appointment. Since the economic basis of nomadic society is almost entirely grounded on the personal participation and productivity of every member of the society, it follows that leadership roles in such a society are naturally assumed by those most successful in the everyday logistics of nomadism. That is, legitimacy is earned; if it is inherited, it must be maintained through personal performance, lost through default, or shored up by a nonnomadic value system which happens under acculturation such as islamicization or sinification.

Since personal performance is at the heart of the maintenance, if not always the initial acquisition, of legitimation in traditional nomadic societies, our discussion will proceed by examining the various factors that constitute a legitimate leader in nomadic terms. We will then examine the importance of these factors as exhibited—and exploited—by traditional nomadic heroes in the formation and maintenance of intertribal confederacies, states, and empires. This discussion will focus on the patterns of succession followed by the Hsiung-nu, T'u-chüeh and Mongols.[8]

Personal Prowess

"Individualism" was the basis of the ruling class in traditional Mongolian society; that is, individual effort and achievement earned the respect of one's fellows.[9] It also garnered a sufficiency of material goods which enabled a nomad ambitious for power to point to himself as exemplar: following him would insure successful nomadizing, provide a share in his personal fortune, and could even lead to opportunities for pillaging. However, the test of performance was the key. No matter what, the leader or potential leader had to be able "to acquire charisma through successful activity."[10] The activity in question usually involved warfare. Several examples follow.

Mo-tu, the founder of the Hsiung-nu confederacy and its first famous Shan-yü (analogous to Khan; r. 209-174 B.C.), gained his position through his prowess as a field commander.[11] Another Hsiung-nu Shan-yü, An-kuo (r. A.D. 93-94), was not respected because he had earned no reputation while he was still Worthy King of the Left (the heir to the Shan-yü's see); he only survived one year as Shan-yü until he was killed by one of his own "brave" generals.[12]

After T'u-men (r. ca. A.D. 545-552) assumed the throne

of the T'u-chüeh, his state and position were both expanded through victorious warfare.[13] The Orkhon inscriptions are full of the martial exploits of Bilgä Khagan, Ïlteriš
Khagan, Prince Kül, and Bilgä Tonyukuk that substantiate
their right to rule.[14] The Mongols also prized martial valor
as one prerequisite for leadership. We need not cite specific
instances here.[15]

Even more basic than military prowess and renown
was the ability to insure the economic survival of the group.
The early history of the T'u-chüeh provides an instructive
instance of this: The leader of the first horde, A-pang-pa,
was stupid and ignorant; his state was hence extinguished.
His desolate descendants were saved by his grandnephew,
who gave them fire. Since he had saved them, they nom-
inated him ruler.[16] Another T'u-chüeh, A-shih-na, was
elected ruler by his brethren, even though he was the son
of a concubine, because he jumped the highest at the side
of a tree![17] Bilgä Khagan boasted, "I gathered all the poor
and destitute people together. I made the poor people
wealthy and the few people numerous."[18]

Aristocratic Heritage and Legitimate Lineages

Privileged clans appear among the early Scythians. The
"Royal" Scythians dominated the other Scythians, and
considered them as slaves.[19] John H. Kautsky defines the
aristocracy as members of society who live off the surplus
produced by peasants. In the case of nomads, they must
control a number of villages in order to be aristocrats. For
him, the origin of nomadic empires was traceable to the
founding of nomadic aristocracies by the "superimposi-
tion" of a conquering ruling class on the peasantry.[20] But
this interpretation does not account for the presence of
aristocracies among native nomadic states that had not
conquered sizeable sedentary populations. A. M. Khazanov has posited the provenance of aristocracies from other
than economic processes, in particular sociopolitical pro-

cesses.[21] These sociopolitical planes were most likely structured on the basis of differing degrees of prestige inherited from august ancestors, if the case of the creation of a noble line out of the lineage of Chinggis Khan is any indication of general historical processes.

Chinggis was the fountainhead of Mongol blue blood. William of Rubruck defined a member of the Mongol nobility as being of the family of Chinggis, "who was their first father and lord."[22] Later manifestations of Mongolian political entities found their basis of nobility in the imperial lineage. The Kalmucks, for instance, considered their most honored noble clan as descended from the Chinggisid line.[23] Hence it would seem that nobility was the residual honor inherited from ancestors who had earned great distinction. High birth was then a matter of genealogical record or manipulation.[24]

Regardless of the origin of noble clans, all nomadic societies seemed to have them.[25] Among the Hsiung-nu, the Hu-yen, Lan, and Hsü-pu families constituted the aristocracy, and the Hsiung-nu bureaucracy was staffed only by members of these families.[26] The clan of A-shih-na, derived from its eponymous founder, was the most honored one of the early T'u-chüeh.[27] And the Mongols had hereditary nobility even before the rise of Chinggis Khan.[28]

The importance of noble birth to support claims of legitimacy among nomads can be seen in the experience of Nurhachi, the founder of Manchu power. The great persecution he endured at the hands of other clan leaders during his rise has been interpreted by one scholar as having been due to their jealousy that he was not of an orthodox line.[29] Not only was noble lineage crucial, but usually an essential element was filiation with the one royal or legitimate line. In the case of the Hsiung-nu, the line that produced the Shan-yü was the Luan-t'i clan.[30] The T'u-chüeh's royal line was A-shih-na.[31] The Mongol royal clan was Borjigin; it was termed the "golden lineage" (*altan urugh*).[32] The Mongol royal line later on was further narrowed to include only the issue of Tolui, Chinggis's fourth and youngest son by his principal wife.[33]

The Sanction of Heaven and the Legitimation of Religion

Among the Mongols, "the ideological device for consolidating a khan's control was belief in Tenggeri or Tengri (scribally, Tngri), the universal victory-granting sky-god," writes Joseph Fletcher. He believes that this concept was derived from the early Aryans.[34] Even though the Hsiung-nu included the worship of heaven/sky among their pantheon, the appearance of the term "Son of Heaven" as part of the official title of the Shan-yü was a later borrowing and elaboration of the Chinese custom.[35] Direct descent from heaven, then, was not necessarily part of the earliest manifestations of the Eurasian steppe belief in Tenggeri, although belief in heaven-sanctioned power was.[36]

The belief in the legitimizing power and conquering might of heaven is most clearly seen among the T'u-chüeh and Mongols. The Orkhon inscriptions record the following on the debt owed by the early Turkish nation to heaven:

> I, the Heaven-like and Heaven-born Turkish Bilgä Kagan . . . since Heaven was gracious, and since I was granted with fortune, I succeeded to the throne. . . . By the grace of Heaven, he took the realm of those who had a realm, and captured the Kagan of those who had had a Kagan. . . . Due to the fact that Heaven granted strength, the soldiers of my father, the Kagan, were like wolves, and his enemies were like sheep.[37]

The sources on the Mongols are just as explicit, and much more numerous. A prayer offered to heaven by Chinggis himself at an early stage in his career has been preserved by Rashīd al-Dīn. Temujin sought heaven's aid in the following words: "If you know that my intention is just, send me power and victory from above and order that your angels, men, peris and spirits above give me their aid."[38] An angel, in fact, did appear in the guise of an eagle and revealed the *yasa* or Mongol legal code to Chinggis, according to the account of Grigor of Akanc'.[39] It was the will of God that this *yasa* be imposed upon the people of the world so that order could be maintained.[40]

It was crucial to Chinggis's plans that his fellow tribesmen recognize him as the recipient of heaven's mandate. Numerous portents and signs served to signify this fact.[41] The fact that Chinggis was miraculously protected from arrows and endured severe wounds without succumbing was proof enough of heaven's favor to the less spiritually attuned of his fellows; and his unfailing success in battle virtually guaranteed it.[42] They were thenceforth determined to carry out heaven's will and assist Chinggis in gaining sway over the whole world.

This, then, was the great ideological element behind the Mongols' grand scheme of conquest; it sustained the drive for conquest in the face of innumerable foes stretched over vast distances of the Asian continent. Neither were the Mongols ashamed to proclaim their sacred calling to the world. Indeed, it formed the cornerstone of their foreign policy: ambassadors were dispatched with the proclamation to submit to heaven's will or be swept away.[43] From the point of view of states vulnerable to the Mongol might, this ideology provided a welcome rationale for submitting. It also helped to rationalize the victory of the "barbarian" Mongols over the superior civilization of the Islamic East.[44]

Often the legitimacy that communication with heaven can confer was claimed by a nomadic ruler through alliance with a powerful shaman, or by his assumption of the role of shaman himself. The election of A-shih-na as ruler of the T'u-chüeh because he jumped the highest at a tree must be seen in this light, for when "a shaman climbs up a tree . . . he ascends symbolically to the highest heaven."[45] His physical prowess at the sacred spot, then, exhibited his spiritual fitness. Chinggis himself deposed the shaman Teb Tenggeri because he was a rival for the instructions — and hence the favor — of heaven.[46] The religious role exercised by Chinggis Khan, including his function as a shaman, was so powerful that after his death he was made to continue in it as the head of a cult.[47] The presence of an assisting shaman, or the exercise of this role by the leader himself, then, was an important element in obtaining legitimacy among the nomads.[48]

On a broader social level, organized religion also had a role to play in the legitimizing effort of nomad conquerors. The Mongols, for instance, made use of each of the religions they encountered to buttress their claims of legitimate rule.[49] But organized religion, as opposed to shamanistic beliefs and practices, was usually only politically useful after the initial conquest of a sedentary people had occurred; its adoption was therefore part of the process of acculturation (e.g., islamicization or sinification) even if the initial motivation for doing so was to assist in the consolidation of authority. This subject, then, is best treated in the context of acculturation, not legitimation.[50]

The Rise of Nomadic Supratribal Leaders

One important characteristic of nomadic empires is their ephemeral existence. The main factor in this ephemerality lay in the element of personal leadership, the foundation of such empires. Joseph Fletcher has succinctly explained this in the following manner:

> Steppe empires came into existence only through the efforts of individual aspirants for the office of supratribal ruler. . . . Being the ruler's creation, a steppe empire — as opposed to a confederation — depended for its existence upon his person. When he died, it ran a risk of collapse. . . . The continuation of an empire

therefore depended heavily upon the ruler's person, much less upon his office.[51]

The rise of a nomadic leader to the supratribal level seems to have been a series of stages in the process of acquiring renown through successful depredation. The experience of Temujin's rise as narrated in the "Secret History" is the best example.[52] But as it is a drawn-out, detailed account, the experience of the Turkish Khagan Ïlteriš cited *in medias res* from the Orkhon Inscriptions will reveal more than any individual passage from the Mongol history:

> My father, the kagan, went off with seventeen men. Having heard the news that [Ïlteriš] was marching off, those who were in towns went up mountains and those who were on mountains came down [from there]; thus they gathered and numbered to seventy men. . . . Having gone on campaigns forward and backward, he gathered together and collected men; they all numbered seven hundred men, [my father the kagan] organized and ordered the people who had lost their state and their kagan . . . in accordance with the rules of my ancestors. He [also organized there] the Tolis and the Tardus [peoples], and gave them a *yabgu* and a *šad*.[53]

The fact that Ïlteriš was already a Khagan certainly helped in his recruitment. But this prestige only garnered seventy men (up from an initial seventeen). It was his campaigns that gained him an increasing amount of followers. He later organized his people and those he had absorbed according to the prescribed procedures, probably out of the desire to legitimize his actions through hoary precedent more than any need for organizational efficiency.

After an aspirant for the position of supratribal leader had demonstrated his success as a battle commander, he was able to offer himself as *the* leader to follow in ever-ambitious exploits that needed the concerted effort of the tribes. As "ecologically, no social organization was needed above the level of the tribe,"[54] these supratribal exploits transcended the mundane humdrum of mere ecological existence and entered the realm in which the stuff of epics was formed and heroes forged. Indeed, the desire to duplicate the great deeds recited of the heroes of the traditional epics must be one of the most important factors for aspiring to the position of supratribal leader, whether Hsiung-nu Shan-yü, Turkish Šad, or Mongol Khan, and leading his hordes to glorious conquest.[55]

Just as the supratribal organization came into being for other than solely ecological reasons, such as warfare on a large scale, so it was that only through such activities were both the rationale and raw materials for the continuation of the supratribal organization maintained. Thomas Allsen explains that external war was an essential counterweight to the "centrifugal tendencies" of nomadic life and offered the possibilities of booty, grants of land, increased annual stipends, and advancement in rank for the princes and commanders who participated along with the supreme leader.[56] Indeed, warfare was such an essential element in the *raison d'être* of nomadic confederacies and empires that Joseph Fletcher considered the decimal organization of military command as one of the two devices, one structural and one ideological, for unifying and expanding such political entities.[57]

Let us now conclude our discussion of nomadic legitimation by examining the process of succession to the highest office, that of steppe emperor, among the Hsiung-nu, the T'u-chüeh, and the Mongols.

Nomadic Succession

The question of succession lies at the heart of the problem of legitimation in nomadic societies. This is because the many factors that impact on the success of an individual's claim to legitimacy—personal prowess, aristocratic birth and legitimate lineage, the ideological role of Tenggeri and the function of shamans, and the rise of supratribal leaders—combine into a showdown of power politics in which ideological arguments must face the threat of having to be backed up with military might. This is also true because the continuance of a particular political body depends upon the successful legitimation of the new ruler. For nomadic successions were often the occasion for bloody outbreaks of civil war; opportunities for actual combat and demonstrations of field generalship are, it is true, good tests for determining the fitness among rival claimants for rulership.[58] But if in these internecine struggles the winning faction fails to persuade the followers of the loser of the legitimacy of its victory, then the latter will often go elsewhere and found a separate political entity.[59] The process of succession, then, must legitimize the new ruler in order to insure the political and social survival of a nomadic supratribal entity.

There were two traditions of succession in nomadic societies, patrilineal and lineal, both based upon hereditary ties of kinship. All qualifying factors such as personal prowess and birthright being equal, the decisive element in choosing between patrilineal (father-to-son) and lineal (brother-to-brother) succession was the principle of tanistry, which principle, explains Joseph Fletcher, "held that the tribe should be led by the best qualified member of the chiefly house. At the chief's death, in other words, the succession did not pass automatically, in accordance with any principle of seniority such as primogeniture, but rather was supposed to go to the most competent of the eligible heirs."[60] The same was true of succession on the supratribal level.

Sometimes a particular strain of nomads utilized either patrilineal or lineal modes of succession, with tanistry again deciding who among the preferred generation should succeed. The early Hsiung-nu, on principle, opted for patrilineal, especially primogenital, succession.[61] The aberrations from the mode of patrilineal/primogenital succession occur chiefly toward the end of the Hsiung-nu empire. With the split into Northern and Southern empires (caused by a succession dispute),[62] lineal succession occurred almost exclusively, perhaps due to the immense influence of Hu-han-hsieh, for at his deathbed he made his sons promise to transmit the throne lineally among themselves.[63] After Shan-yü Hsiu-li (r. 128-140), various families vied in setting up their own candidates; it was not until seven years later that Chu-chu again established a line that maintained itself through regular succession, mostly through primogeniture, until the office of Shan-yü was done away with by Ts'ao Ts'ao in 216.[64]

The same tension that existed among the Hsiung-nu between the competing modes of lineal and patrilineal succession was present among the T'u-chüeh, as the following extended quotation will reveal:

> When T'a-pa (d. 580) was about to die he spoke to his son An-lo, saying: "I have heard that in terms of intimacy of relationship nothing exceeds that of father and son. [However], my elder brother was not close to his son and hence entrusted the throne to me. When I die, you must yield to Ta-lo-pien [An-lo's older brother; he eventually founded the Western T'u-chüeh]." After he expired, all [the great ones] within the state were about to set up Ta-lo-pien, but the masses would not agree since his mother was of low birth. An-lo was veritably of the nobility, and had been all along venerated by the T'u-chüeh. Sheh-t'u was the last to arrive; he spoke to all within the state, saying: "If you establish An-lo, then I will lead my brothers in serving him; if you establish Ta-lo-pien, I will surely remain on guard within my own territory and await you with sharp swords and long spears." Sheh-t'u was the eldest and was furthermore heroic; none within the state dared resist him. In the end they then set up An-lo as the successor.[65]

Besides showing that patrilineal succession was the preferred method among the T'u-chüeh,[66] the above story also illustrates the importance of both personal prowess and high birth to qualify one for an office that is obtained by inheritance.[67]

Among the early Mongols, both patrilineal and lineal succession took place, because, as pointed out by Thomas Allsen, the Mongols made an attempt through "bloody tanistry" (called "common consent" by Marco Polo) at succession through nomination of the best qualified candidate.[68] These elections took place at general gatherings of nobility called *quriltai*, especially convened for such a purpose.[69] Temujin received the epithet of Chinggis to go along with his newly bestowed title of Khan at a *quriltai* convened on the Onon river in 1206.[70] The best-known Mongolian succession assembly was, however, the one of 1245 that elected Güyüg; Plano Carpini was in attendance and left as detailed a description as could be expected from an outside observer.[71] Notwithstanding this nod toward democratic participation, the *quriltai* ceremony seemed to have been a *pro forma* procedure that merely confirmed the candidate who had emerged as the consensus choice either through behind-the-scenes maneuvering or open conflict. Again, the crucial factors were the personal qualities of the candidates themselves and how these qualities translated into influence. As H. Desmond Martin explains, even "if able to voice their opinions in open council, the amount of influence the imperial family and aristocracy were able to exert varied greatly according to circumstances and the personality of the reigning khagan."[72] In most nomadic cases, the personality and prowess of the candidates were, finally, even more important than the wishes of a late leader.

Notes

1. Reprinted in Hugh Nibley, *Lehi in the Desert, the World of the Jaredites, There Were Jaredites*, vol. 5, *The Collected Works of Hugh Nibley* (Salt Lake City: Deseret Book and F.A.R.M.S., 1988).

2. Hugh Nibley, "The Hierocentric State," *Western Political Quarterly* 4 (1951): 226-53.

3. Joseph Fletcher, "The Mongols: Ecological and Social Perspectives," *Harvard Journal of Asiatic Studies* 46 (1980): 11-50; see also discussion at n. 34 below.

4. Hugh Nibley, "Tenting, Toll, and Taxing," *Western Political Quarterly* 19 (1966): 599-630.

5. Hugh Nibley, "The Arrow, The Hunter, and the State," *Western Political Quarterly* 2 (1949): 328-44.

6. Karl A. Wittfogel and Feng Chia-sheng, *History of Chinese Society: Liao (907-1125)*. Transactions of the American Philosophical Society, n.s. vol. 36. (Philadelphia: American Philosophical Society, 1949); and W. M. McGovern, *The Early Empires of Central Asia* (Chapel Hill: University of North Carolina Press, 1939).

7. The term "hero" is used in the sense of an actual exemplar, living or dead, of cultural values, not as a mythical embodiment of national ethos who performs a ritual function. On the nomadic hero as living exemplar of steppe cultural norms, see Fletcher, "The Mongols," 14.

8. The Hsiung-nu first confronted China ca. A.D. 210; they remained formidable enemies for much of the Han dynasty (206 B.C.-A.D. 220); the T'u-chüeh were an early Turkish kingdom, ca. 552-651; the Mongols conquered during the thirteenth century.

9. Lawrence Krader, "The Origin of the State among the Nomads of Asia," in *Pastoral Production and Society* (Cambridge: Cambridge University Press, 1979), 229. It was also the basis of one's standing in the community, however low. For example, the Hsiung-nu, the T'u-chüeh, and the Mongols all were said by the Chinese to "abase the old and weak and value the young and strong." Composite translation based on Han shu 94a.3743 [Peking punctuated edition of the twenty-four dynastic histories (Peking: Chung-hua shu-chü, 1959-77); hereafter, all references to the dynastic histories will be to this edition] [parallel text of the *Shi chi*, tr. Burton Watson, *Records of the Grand Historian*, 2 vols. (New York: Columbia University Press, 1961), 2:156]; *Chou shu* 50.909 [tr. Liu Mau-tsai, *Die chinesischen Nachrichten aus Geschichte der Ost-Turken (T'u-kue)*, 2 vols. (Wiesbaden: Harrassowitz, 1958), 1:8]; and Chao Hung (1195-1246), *Meng Ta pei lu* 15a [in Wang Kuo-wei, ed., *Meng-ku shih-liao ssu-chung chiao-chu* (Peking: Ch'ing-hua hsüeh-hsiao yen-chiu so, 1926)]. The connection between health/age and performance is obvious. With regard to individual achievement as a leadership quality, compare the observations of Nikolai Muravev, a nineteenth-century

Russian traveler among the Turkmen, cited in A. M. Khazanov, *Nomads and the Outside World*, tr. Julia Crookenden (Cambridge: Cambridge University Press, 1984), 175; and Marco Polo, *The Description of the World*, tr. A. C. Moule and Paul Pelliot (London: George Routledge and Sons, 1938), par. 77 on p. 193. Cf. also Ammianus Marcellinus, XXXI, 2, 25.

10. Khazanov, *Nomads*, 167.

11. *Han shu* 94a.3753; Watson, tr., *Grand Historian*, 2:165.

12. *Hou Han shu* 89.2954.

13. *Chou shu* 50.908; Liu, *Die chinesischen Nachrichten*, 1:6.

14. For instance, Talat Tekin, *A Grammar of Orkhon Turkic* (Bloomington: Indiana University Press, 1968), 275-77, translates an early inscription that records in chronological order the campaigns of Bilgä Khagan when he was 17, 18, 20, 22, 26, 31, 33, and 40 years old.

15. For instance, in his *History of the Mongols*, in Christopher Dawson, ed., *Mission to Asia* (Toronto: University of Toronto Press, 1980), 19, John of Plano Carpini records that Chinggis, "a mighty hunter before the Lord . . . went into other territories and any men he could capture and get to join his band he did not let go again. He drew men to himself of his own nation and they followed him as their leader in all kinds of wrong-doing." The wrong-doings which Carpini lists after this all have to do with warring and plundering.

16. Summarizing *Chou shu* 50.908; Liu, *Die chinesischen Nachrichten*, 1:5; and *Pei shih* 99.3286 (tr. Uchida Gimpu et al., *Kiba minzoku shi—seishi Hokuteki den*, 3 vols. [Tokyo: Heibonsha, 1971-73], 2:66).

17. *Chou shu* 50.908; Liu, *Die chinesischen Nachrichten*, 1:6. See text on pp. 569-70 of the present study for the religious significance of this deed.

18. Tekin, *Orkhon Turkic*, 262.

19. Herodotus, IV, 20. John H. Kautsky, *The Politics of Aristocratic Empires* (Chapel Hill: University of North Carolina Press, 1982), 54, suggests that the Scythian people themselves were but "a semi-nomadic aristocracy which dominated the settled and agricultural masses." This view had been put forward much earlier by W. W. How and J. Wells, *A Commentary on Herodotus*, 2 vols. (Oxford: Oxford University Press, 1912), 2:427.

20. Kautsky, *Aristocratic Empires*, 63, 49. See 52-56 for his discussion of the origins of the aristocratic class among conquest states of nomads; chapter 4 of his work treats in general the theme of the origin and development of aristocracies.

21. Khazanov, *Nomads*, 148. Philip C. Salzman, "Inequality and

Oppression in Nomadic Society," in *Pastoral Production and Society*, 429-46, discusses the nonpastoral (i.e., nonnomadic) sources of social inequality.

22. William of Rubruck, *The Journey of William of Rubruck*, in Dawson, ed., *Mission to Asia*, 105.

23. Lawrence Krader, *Social Organization of the Mongol-Turkic Pastoral Nomads* (Hague: Mouton, 1963), 134.

24. The function of genealogies among nomadic societies, according to Khazanov, was to "legitimize social inequality" (Khazanov, *Nomads*, 142). See also Caroline Humphrey in *Pastoral Production and Society*, 235-59.

25. Even the Huns had them, despite Ammianus Marcellinus' comments to the contrary, Otto Maenchen-Helfen, *The World of the Huns* (Berkeley: University of California Press, 1973), 198-99. For the existence and general outlines of nomadic aristocracies, consult Eberhard, *China und seine westlichen Nachbarn* (Darmstadt: Wissenschaftliche Buchgesellschaft, 1978), 269-70; Khazanov, *Nomads*, 148-52; and Fletcher, "The Mongols," 16-17. For a detailed treatment of the Mongol aristocracy, see B. Ya. Vladimirtsov, *Le régime social des Mongols*, tr. Michel Carsow (Paris: Adrien-Maisonneuve, 1948), 89-100.

26. *Han shu* 94a.3751; Watson, *Grand Historian*, 2:163; for aristocratic office holders among the Hsiung-nu, see Yamada Nobuo, "Formation of the Hsiung-nu Nomadic State," *Acta Orientalia Hungarica* 36 (1982): 575-81.

27. *Pei shih* 99.3285; Uchida et al., *Kiba minzoku shi*, 2:65.

28. *Meng Ta pei lu* 2b (in Wang, ed., *Meng-ku shih-liao*); Krader, "Origin of the State," 227; Michael Prawdin, *The Mongol Empire: Its Rise and Legacy* (London: Allen and Unwin, 1952), 43.

29. Wada Sei, *Taashi kenkyū—Manshu hen* (Tokyo: Tōyō Bunko, 1955), 603-12.

30. *Han shu* 94a.3751. By the third century A.D., the Tu-ku clan produced the royal line of Hsiung-nu Shan-yüs (*Chin shu* 97.2550).

31. See n. 27 above.

32. Fletcher, "The Mongols," 19. On this lineage see Igor de Rachewiltz, tr., "The Secret History of the Mongols," *Papers on Far Eastern History* 5-18 (1971-84), commentary on par. 42; Paul Ratchnevsky, *Činggis-khan: sein Leben und Wirken*, Münchener Ostasiatische Studien Bd. 32 (Munich: F. Steiner Verlag, 1983), 13, n. 56; Paul Pelliot and Louis Hambis, eds. and trs., *Histoire des campagnes de Gengis Khan*, Tome I (Leiden: Brill, 1951), 118-20; and Sechin Jagchid and Paul Hyer, *Mongolia's Culture and Society* (Folkstone, England: Dawson, 1979), 247.

33. Thomas T. Allsen, *Mongol Imperialism* (Berkeley: University of California Press, 1987), 37-41; and Herbert Franke, *From Tribal Chieftain to Universal Emperor and God: The Legitimation of the Yüan Dynasty* (Munich: Bayerische Akademie der Wissenschaften, 1978), 22-24.

34. Fletcher, "The Mongols," 30. Nibley, "The Hierocentric State," should be consulted for confirmation of Fletcher's hypothesis. For Chinese and Christian contributions to the concept of universal empire, see Berthold Spuler, *The Muslim World, Part II: The Mongol Period*, tr. F. R. C. Bagley (Leiden: Brill, 1969), 5; and H. Franke, *From Tribal Chieftain to Universal Emperor*, 18. For references to modern scholarship on the nomadic belief in Tenggeri see Fletcher, "The Mongols," 31, n. 13; and for this ancient name (Tenggeri), see Sir Gerard Clauson, *An Etymological Dictionary of Pre-Thirteenth Century Turkish* (Oxford: Clarendon Press, 1972), 523b-24a.

35. See Hsieh Chien, "Hsiung-nu tsung-chiao hsin-yang chi ch'i liu-pien," *Bulletin of the Institute of History and Philology* 42/4 (1971): 571-614, for the Hsiung-nu religion. *Han shu* 94a.3751 indicates the Hsiung-nu borrowing of the Chinese title "Son of Heaven." For another Chinese influence on the title of the Hsiung-nu see David B. Honey, "Sinification and Legitimation: Liu Yüan, Shih Le, and the Founding of Han and Chao," Ph.D. diss., University of California, Berkeley, 1988, 43-44, n. 26.

36. Khazanov, *Nomads*, 239, n. 2.

37. Tekin, *Orkhon Turkic*, 261-62, 265-66. Cf. Mori Masao, "The T'u-chüeh Concept of Heaven," *Acta Asiatica* 24 (1981): 55.

38. Quoted in V. A. Riasanovsky, *Fundamental Principles of Mongolian Law* (Tientsin, 1937), 89. Compare the prayer recorded in de Rachewiltz, "Secret History," 103; and John Andrew Boyle, *The History of the World Conqueror by 'Ala-ad-Din 'Ata-Malik Juvaini*, 2 vols. (Manchester: Manchester University Press, 1958), 1:80-81.

39. Robert P. Blake and Richard N. Frye, "History of the Nation of Archers (the Mongols), By Grigor of Akanc'," *Harvard Journal of Asiatic Studies* 12 (1949): 333 (11:5-14).

40. Blake and Frye, "History of the Nation," 301 (4:40). On the *yasa* of Chinggis, see Boyle, *History of the World Conqueror*, 1:23-26; Dawson, *Mission to Asia*, 25; and Riasanovsky, *Mongolian Law*, 25-35 for discussion, and 83-86 for a collation of thirty-six extant articles from the code.

41. Cf. de Rachewiltz, "Secret History," 121. The "Secret History" is full of references to the power of heaven as aiding Chinggis or his lineage; as a sampling, consult paragraphs 80, 187, 199, 201, 203, 206, 208, 224, 240, 256, 267, and 275.

42. Riasanovsky, *Mongolian Law,* 27-28; Fletcher, "The Mongols," 31; and Franke, *From Tribal Chieftain to Universal Emperor,* 15-16.

43. On the political aims of the Mongols consult Dawson, *Mission to Asia,* 43-44. On the Mongol letters demanding submission, see E. Voeglin, "The Mongol Orders of Submission to European Powers 1245-1255," *Byzantion* 15 (1940-41): 378-413. For the place of heaven's will in the ideology of the Mongols and as a motivation for conquest, see Igor de Rachewiltz, "Some Remarks on the Ideological Foundation of Chingis Khan's Empire," *Papers on Far Eastern History* 7 (1973): 21-36; Fletcher, "The Mongols," 30-31, 34; and Franke, *From Tribal Chieftain to Universal Emperor,* 14-18. For heaven as the same motivating factor in the Ch'i-tan goal of world conquest, see Wittfogel and Feng, *History of Chinese Society,* 112. For general background consult Nibley, "Hierocentric State," 244-47.

44. Juvaini did ascribe the invasion and investment of Islamic civilization to divine will. On this consult Boyle, *History of the World Conqueror,* 1:xxxiii, xxxv; and Juvaini's expressions in ibid., 1:23-24, 39, and 144. Juvaini, of course, was not the only Islamic apologist to voice these sentiments. See, *inter alia,* the *Zij-i-Ilkhani* of Nasirad-Din Tusi, cited in Boyle, *The Mongol World Empire 1206-1370* (London: Variorum Reprints, 1977), 27:245-46. Cf. also Constantin D'Ohsson, *Histoire des Mongols, depuis Tchinguiz-Khan jusqu'a Timour Bey, ou Tamerlan,* 4 vols. (Le Haye et Amsterdam: Les Frères Van Cleef, 1834-35), 1:392-93.

45. Manabu Waida, "Notes on Sacred Kingship in Central Asia," *Numen* 23 (1976): 179-90; 181. The Mongols also included trees as part of their shamanistic rites of kingship; see Paul Pelliot, *Notes on Marco Polo,* 3 vols. (Paris: Imprimerie National, 1959-73), 2:627-37.

46. See the discussion in Fletcher, "The Mongols," 18, 34-35.

47. On Chinggis as shaman, the *Tabaqāt-i Nāsirī* of Jūzjanī Minhāj al-Dīn records, "Every now and again he used to fall into a trance . . . and that state of trance used to be similar to that which had happened to him at the outset of his rise" (quoted in Boyle, *Mongol World Empire,* 22:181); cf. William of Rubruck, *The Journey of William of Rubruck,* 121. The fundamental study on Chinggis as shaman remains Iwai Hirosato, "Chingisu Kan no sokui to fugeki ni tsuite," in *Tōyōshi ronsō* (Kyoto: Tōyōshi Kenkyūkwai, 1950), 107-30. For the cult of Chinggis, see N. Pallisen, "Die alte Religion der Mongolen unter der Kultus Tchingis-Chans," *Numen* 3 (1956): 178-229; and Sechin Jagchid, *Essays in Mongolian Studies,* Monograph 3 (Provo: David M. Kennedy Center for International Studies, Brigham Young University, 1988), 299-321; cf. also Tšy Žamtsarono,

"Kul't Chingisa v Ordose iz puteshestvia v iuzhnuiv Mongoliiv v 1919," *Central Asiatic Journal* 6 (1961): 194-234.

48. On the "shamanistic structure" of kingship in Inner Asia, see Manabu, "Sacred Kingship," and Iwai Hirosato, "Chingisu Kan no sokui."

49. Franke, *From Tribal Chieftain to Universal Emperor*, 7.

50. In China, acculturation translates into the process of sinification. For an analysis and historical survey of this process, see Honey, "Sinification and Legitimation," chap. 3. For a parallel process, see Speros Vryonis, Jr., *The Decline of Medieval Hellenism in Asia Minor and the Process of Islamization from the Eleventh through the Fifteenth Century* (Berkeley: University of California Press, 1971).

51. Fletcher, "The Mongols," 21, 22; cf. Douglas L. Johnson, *The Nature of Nomadism*, Department of Geography Research Paper No. 118 (Chicago: University of Chicago, 1969), 13. The same is true of modern autocracies; see, for instance, Andrew E. Janos, "Charismatics and Constitutions: The Politics of Succession in Non-Western Societies," *Journal of International and Area Studies* 1 (1986): 115-33.

52. For other primary sources on the rise of Chinggis more concise than the "Secret History," see *Meng Ta pei lu* 3a-b (in Wang, ed., *Meng-ku shih-liao*); Dawson, *Mission to Asia*, 5:18-22; Polo, *Description of the World*, par. 65-66 (pp. 162-65); and Boyle, *History of the World Conqueror*, 1:34-39.

53. Tekin, *Orkhon Turkic*, 265. The seventeen original men of Ilteriš, it should be pointed out, possibly played the role of a personal retinue of a leader. Sometimes they became *anda* or sworn brothers, which custom, according to Owen Lattimore, extended the principle of blood kinship among these adopted brethren and hence strengthened their bonds of loyalty; Owen Lattimore, *Studies in Frontier History, Collected Papers 1929-58* (London: Oxford University Press, 1962), 533. On this personal following of chiefs and aspirants for supratribal office, see Vladimirtsov, *Le régime social des Mongols*, 95ff; Beatrice F. Manz, "The Ulus Chagatay before and after Temur's Rise to Power: The Transformation from Tribal Confederation to Army of Conquest," *Central Asiatic Journal* 27 (1983): 88; and Fletcher, "The Mongols," 20.

54. Fletcher, "The Mongols," 14.

55. Oral epics constituted the chief means of preservation and transmittal of traditional lore among the nomads as well as the primary sources for sedentary historians. For instance, both Hsiung-nu and Hsien-pi epics were incorporated into Chinese historical accounts, with expected retouching (Owen Lattimore, *Inner Asian*

Frontiers of China [New York: Capitol Publishing and American Geographical Society, 1951], 464-65; and K. H. J. Gardiner and R. R. C. de Crespigny, "T'an-Shih Huai and the Hsien-pi Tribes of the Second Century," *Papers on Far Eastern History* 15 [1977]: 14). For an evaluation of traditional Turkish epics, see Nora K. Chadwick and Victor Zhirmunsky, *Oral Epics of Central Asia* (Cambridge: Cambridge University Press, 1969), esp. 79-95, for "individualism" in the heroic poems; and Faruk Sümer et al., *The Book of Dede Korkut: A Turkish Epic* (Austin: University of Texas Press, 1972). A very complete introduction to Mongolian heroic epics, including an extensive bibliography, is Walther Heissig, *Die mongolischen Heldenepen — Structur und Motiv*, Reinisch-Westfälische Akademie der Wissenschaften, Vorträge G 237 (Düsseldorf: Westdeutscher Verlag, 1978). For the six traditional theories on what set the nomadic empires, particularly the Mongols, in motion, see Fletcher, "The Mongols," 32-39; and Uchida Gimpu, *Hokku Ajiashi Kenkyū*, 2 vols. (Kyoto: Dobosha, 1975), 1:1-27, with emphasis on the Hsiung-nu.

56. Allsen, *Mongol Imperialism*, 78.

57. Fletcher, "The Mongols," 29-30; the ideological device was the belief in Tenggeri.

58. On this point see Fletcher, "The Mongols," 28.

59. As two prominent examples, wars of succession were responsible for splitting both the Hsiung-nu empire (into northern and southern halves ca. 55 B.C.) and T'u-chüeh (into eastern and western sections ca. A.D. 582). Theophylactus Simocatta, *History* VII, 8, 8-10, records a typical attempt at a coup among the Avars. Jack Goody, ed., *Succession to High Office* (Cambridge: Cambridge University Press, 1966), 5, includes such a partitioning of territory and duplication of the supreme office among the possible solutions to the problem of succession.

60. Fletcher, "The Mongols," 17.

61. Uchida Gimpu, *Kyodo-shi kenkyū* (Kyoto: Sogensha, 1953), 12, 14.

62. The split into northern and southern halves has been discussed in McGovern, *The Early Empires of Central Asia*, 169-70; and H. H. Dubs, *History of the Former Han Dynasty*, 3 vols. (Baltimore: Waverly Press, 1933-55), 2:190-96. See further Lin Kan, *Hsiung-nu shih*, rev. ed. (Huhhot: Inner Mongolia People's Publishing House, 1979), 100-119; and Uchida, *Hokku Ajiashi kenkyū*, 2:210-19.

63. According to the medieval commentator Hu San-hsing, cited in *Hou Han shu chi chieh* (reprinted Peking: Chung-hua shu-chü, 1984), 89.3a.

64. Treated by McGovern, *Early Empires of Central Asia*, 169-71; Honey, "Sinification and Legitimation," 18-22, recounts the decline of the office of Shan-yü among the Southern Hsiung-nu until A.D.216.

65. *Sui shu* 84.1865; Liu, *Die chinesischen Nachrichten*, 1:43. The same incident, with minor variants, is recorded in *Pei shih* 99.3290; tr. Uchida et al., *Kiba minzoku shi*, 2:74-75.

66. Among the first eight T'u-chüeh rulers (until the split into eastern and western hordes), succession passed from father to son three times, from brother to younger brother twice, and once from granduncle to grandnephew (according to the Chinese accounts). Among the eighth/ninth-century Uighurs, primogenital succession was preferred; Colin Mackerass, *The Uighur Empire According to the T'ang Dynastic Histories* (Columbia: University of South Carolina Press, 1972), 192-93.

67. For the interplay of birthright versus tanistry among another group of nomads, the Hsien-pi, consult T'ang Ch'ang-ju, *Wei Chin Nan-pei Ch'ao shih lun-ts'ung hsü-pien* (1959; reprinted Beijing: San-lien shu-tien, 1978), 138.

68. Allsen, *Mongol Imperialism*, 218-19, n. 4; Polo, *Description of the World*, par. 65 (162). Plano Carpini stated that formal election by the *quriltai* was written into the *yasa* by Chinggis (Dawson, *Mission to Asia*, 25).

69. There is little concrete evidence that earlier nomads had formal assemblies like the Mongolian *quriltai* other than passing references such as "they unitedly set him up" and the like.

70. On this famous occasion, consult the following: Ratchnevsky, *Činggis-khan*, 82-87; Pelliot, *Notes on Marco Polo*, 1:295-96; René Grousset, *Conqueror of the World*, tr. Marian McKellar and Denis Sinor (New York: Orion Press, 1966), 166-70; and B. Ya. Vladimirtsov, *The Life of Chingis Khan*, tr. Prince D. S. Mirsky (1930; reprinted New York and London: Benjamin Blom, 1969), 63-66.

71. Plano Carpini, in Dawson, *Mission to Asia*, 61-64; and summarized in Spuler, *The Mongol Period*, 15.

72. Martin, *Rise of Chingis Khan*, 314. In the case of the *quriltai* convened to name Chinggis' successor, it had no choice but to confirm the heir he had already chosen before his death, his third son Ögödei. For the succession to Chinggis, see the extended discussion in D'Ohsson, *Histoire des Mongols*, 2:8-13; cf. Vladimirtsov, *Life of Chingis Khan*, 149-51; and Allsen, *Mongol Imperialism*, 18-19, 37-38, 46.

23

Does the Qur'an Teach Creation *Ex Nihilo*?

Daniel C. Peterson
Brigham Young University, Provo, Utah

The canonical scriptures of the Judeo-Christian and Islamic tradition are content to affirm that God is the sovereign of creation, without giving a precise description of the creation and without offering a full account of where matter came from. On the doctrine of creation, however, mainstream theology in the three great monotheistic religions has gone considerably beyond the mandate of their respective scriptures.

The Judeo-Christian Matrix

"Traditional Christian doctrine," as W. R. Inge terms it, is "that the world was created out of nothing by an act of the Divine will, and in time."[1] "Believing Jews and Christians," writes J. A. Goldstein, "have long been convinced that their religion teaches that God created the world *ex nihilo*, from absolutely nothing. Yet medieval Jewish thinkers still held that the account of creation in Genesis could be interpreted to mean that God created from preexisting formless matter, and ancient Jewish texts state that he did so."[2] "It would be wrong," the editors of the New Jerusalem Bible say of Genesis 1:1, "to read the metaphysical concept of 'creation from nothingness' into the text." This notion, they say, was not to be formulated earlier than 2 Maccabees 7:28, which is to say in the period between the close of the Hebrew scriptures and the rise

584

of Christianity.[3] "The Hebrew words conventionally rendered 'create,' " notes T. H. Gaster, "though they came eventually to be used in an extended, metaphorical sense, are derived from handicrafts and plastic arts, and refer primarily to the mechanical fashioning of shapes, not to biological processes or metaphysical bringing into existence." They originally denoted actions such as to cut out or pare leather, to mold something into shape, or to fabricate something.[4] Thus, it is hardly surprising that the Bible can describe creation as "the work of [God's] hands."[5] (And it scarcely needs to be pointed out that the presupposition underlying such terms and such a description is anthropomorphic in the extreme.)[6] "Throughout the Old Testament," writes Keith Norman, "the image is that of the craftsman fashioning a work of art and skill, the potter shaping the vessel out of clay, or the weaver at his loom."[7] With that modifying fact in mind, we can proceed to Theodore Gaster's recognition that, in the Bible, "All things are represented as coming into being solely by the fiat of God. [But] it is nowhere stated out of what substances they were composed, for the central theme is not the physical origin of phenomena but their role in human existence and the orchestration of their several functions, what John Donne called 'the concinnity of parts.' " (Nonetheless, water and wind, because of their inchoate and apparently ungenerated nature, seem to have been granted some kind of priority.)[8]

In the intertestamental period, Gaster finds "a certain amount of ambivalence regarding the doctrine of *creatio ex nihilo*."[9] As noted above, 2 Maccabees 7:28 seems to affirm it—a fact which had been noted as early as Origen of Alexandria.[10] Was Origen correct in his interpretation? The Syriac recension of 2 Maccabees as well as some Greek manuscripts describe rather an organization of inchoate matter, which is the explicit position of *Wisdom of Solomon* 11:17.[11] And this latter notion seems, indeed, to fit the

argument of 2 Maccabees 7 considerably better than does
a notion of creation out of nothing. In that argument, a
zealous Jewish matriarch exhorts her sons to die rather
than submit to the unrighteous demands of Antiochus: Do
not fear, she tells them. God created the heavens and the
earth out of nothing, and created man in the same way
within the mother's womb. So, also in the same way, will
he raise you up to life after death. But of course, as Jews
of the Maccabean period well knew, human conception
does not occur *ex nihilo*. Not surprisingly, therefore, recent
scholarship on 2 Maccabees has denied that that work
teaches an origination out of nothing, noting along the
way that the Greek words often translated as "out of nothing" are ambiguous.[12]

Still, the connection between an expectation of physical
resurrection and faith in God's creative power, so clearly
enunciated in 2 Maccabees 7, is of considerable interest for
Qur'anic studies. "In essence," says Jonathan Goldstein,
who nevertheless denies that 2 Maccabees teaches it, "creation *ex nihilo* is a polemical doctrine, invoked to defend
the belief in bodily resurrection!"[13] When critics of resur-
rection-faith pointed out the difficulties posed by the corruption of corpses, by the ingestion of human bodies by
cannibals and predators and scavengers, and by other easily imagined cases, the concept of *ex nihilo* creation suggested a direct, effective, and essentially irrefutable re-
joinder.[14]

However, David Winston meets Goldstein's argument
head on. "Christian theologians," he declares, "did not
feel the need to invoke the concept of creation *ex nihilo* in
order to demonstrate the possibility of the resurrection of
the flesh."[15] And as we shall see below, Winston's position
is probably to be preferred. Certainly it accounts for the
Qur'anic passages on the subject.

By the time of the New Testament, Gaster sees an
increasing dominance of the doctrine, believing it to be

affirmed at Romans 4:17 and Hebrews 11:3.[16] However, even in the latter two passages creation *ex nihilo* is at most ambiguously attested; the standard work on the subject of *ex nihilo* creation denies that any such doctrine is to be found in the Greek New Testament at all.[17] It would seem, in fact, that the notion is not clearly taught by anybody until well past the period of primitive Christianity, that it was a non-issue for the earliest Christians, that it does not come to dominate theological thinking and writing even for some period beyond that, and that it must be read into early Jewish and Christian texts if it is to be found there at all.[18] (This is exactly the thesis that I shall advance with regard to the Qur'an.)

Winston notes that "there is no evidence that the [early] rabbis were especially attached to a doctrine of creation *ex nihilo*. Indeed, there is prima facie evidence that such a doctrine was far from being commonly accepted by them." He cites one ancient rabbinic text which, in order to establish the uniqueness of divine acts as opposed to human ones, gives ten examples which notably fail to include the most obvious one — namely the ability to make something from nothing. (In fact, one of the examples assumes the preexistence of water!)[19]

It may be that Tatian, a Christian writer and student of Justin Martyr who flourished at about A.D. 160, teaches the doctrine unclearly.[20] If he does, he seems to have developed it out of a confrontation with Valentinian Gnosticism, or, possibly, in response to the dualism of Marcion.[21] And, indeed, it is striking that the first Christian thinker to advance a clear doctrine of *ex nihilo* creation was not an adherent of the "main church" at all. This was Basilides, the great Gnostic teacher who, along with Valentinus and Marcion, actively taught during the reigns of Hadrian and Antoninus Pius (A.D. 130-160).[22] (The most sophisticated, most significant, and best educated Gnostics all seem to have denied the eternity of matter, although only he developed a true theory of *ex nihilo* creation.)[23] Basilides, who seemed put off by any notion that the supreme God might act directly in history, advanced a rather sophisticated negative theology — prior even to the more famous forms of negative theology which would come to dominate the philosophical schools some decades later.[24] It seems that it was precisely this negative theology, with its intense preoccupation with the absolute transcendence of the supreme being, which led to his promulgation of a doctrine of *ex nihilo* creation. If God transcended this world utterly, then his mode of creation — and Basilides, contrary to many Gnostic thinkers, thought of the supreme God as the creator of this world — must also transcend worldly analogies and models like the demiurgic "potter" of the *Timaeus*. Indeed, as God was to be incomprehensible, so also must his creative act be.[25] Even to describe the creation as occurring through the "will" of God was to speak too anthropomorphically, since God has no "will" — although Basilides would allow such talk as the most appropriate way to discuss the ineffable.[26] But the anthropomorphism of God-as-potter was simply more than Basilides could allow, and, besides, it seemed to limit God's omnipotence in the same way that the craftsman's power is constrained by the resistance and quirks of his materials.[27]

Educationally, the leading Gnostic thinkers of the first half of the second century were far better trained and equipped than the representatives of what would become the "orthodox" tradition or "main church."[28] This may go some distance toward explaining why it was that the notion of creation from absolutely nothing took hold among the Gnostics so much earlier than among mainstream Christians, who seem simply not even to have thought about it.[29] "Some Christian writers of the middle of the second century write of God's creative acts as if they were performed upon pre-existent matter," writes J. A. Goldstein, "as if the doctrine of creation *ex nihilo* never entered the author's mind."[30] And indeed, the idea probably had not, and would not until the third century.[31] Athenagoras, for example, who addressed his *Plea for the Christians* to Marcus Aurelius and Commodus about A.D. 177, taught a creation by God from preexisting matter, on the analogy of a potter and his clay.[32] Justin Martyr, too, affirmed God's creative role to be that of a giver of forms and shapes to matter already present.[33] So natural to him was the idea of creation from matter already present that he seems not to have regarded it as a problem at all.[34] Indeed, Gerhard May seems clearly irritated with him because he did not realize that creation *ex nihilo* was the allegedly logical implication of the biblical creation narrative.[35] It is worthy of note that, as I have mentioned previously, Justin had been a Platonist before his conversion, and he was the first Christian to equate the Genesis narrative with the account of the Demiurge in Plato's *Timaeus*. On this particular point, dealing with cosmogony, he evidently saw no distinction between Christian doctrine and Platonism.[36] Further, creation *ex nihilo* is at most ambiguously attested in the writings of Philo and Clement of Alexandria.[37] (Gerhard May denies it to both of them. He is again rather dismayed to note that Philo saw no contradiction between the Bible's account of creation and the notion of creation as an organizing of preexistent matter.)[38] However, as I have alluded to above, it is clearly taught in the works of Clement's successor at the Alexandrian catechetical school, Origen (who cannot, he says, understand how so many distinguished earlier thinkers had been able to think of matter as uncreated).[39]

By the early third century, creation *ex nihilo* had become a fundamental doctrine of orthodox Christianity.[40] Probably, it entered Christianity through Theophilus of Antioch, who is generally linked with Tatian as the first non-Gnostic Christian to have a clearly stated doctrine of *ex nihilo* creation (and for whom the case is considerably clearer than for the latter). His position in this regard was vastly influential in later Christian history, and most of the arguments used by later polemicists in this connection find their first expression from his pen.[41] (Basilides, like Theophilus, was from Syria, and this may point either to influence by the Gnostic thinker upon the catholic bishop, or, more likely, to their having drawn from a common Syrian source or tradition.)[42] For Theophilus, the idea of creation *ex nihilo* is necessary to safeguard the absolute freedom of God the Creator, whose omnipotence, he feels, cannot admissibly be constrained, as is that of the Timaean Demiurge, by the resistance of self-existent matter.[43] This is the argument picked up by the first great Latin Father, Tertullian (d. ca. A.D. 220), as well. Eternally existing matter, he contended, would subject God to limitations and would destroy the divine liberty. Even though the positing of a resistant and independently existing material realm would allow a fairly powerful theodicy or explanation of evil, it would do so at the expense of God's unutterable omnipotence, and this Tertullian was unwilling to countenance. It would be more worthy to believe that God freely creates evil than to view him as a slave — that is, to see him as limited in any way whatsoever by the presence of coexistent matter.[44]

Both W. R. Inge and Gerhard May have maintained that the notion of a temporally specifiable creation out of nothing was developed and accepted by Christian theologians of (what would become) the mainstream in response to Gnosticism — and to a philosophy which was manifestly related to Gnostic ideas — during the latter half of the second century.[45] This may well be true, since the theory to which many of the earlier Judeo-Christian Platonists leaned was, rather, that of emanation — a theory shared by the Gnostics. In Philo, for example, the "cause of the creation is the divine bounty, an ungrudging overflow of benevolent giving in which the Giver remains unaffected and undiminished, like a torch from which

other torches are lit, like the sun in giving out sunlight,
like a spring of water."[46] (The same metaphor, of one torch
lighting another, was used by Justin Martyr and by Nu-
menius of Apamea.)[47] Certainly the Christian insistence on
ex nihilo creation crystallized in the writings of Irenaeus
(d. ca. A.D. 202), the bishop of Lyon, from whom it received, in many ways, its lasting form.[48] And the literary
production of Irenaeus was dominated by his confrontation
with the Gnostics.[49] According to this understanding, as-
cription of the creation of the cosmos to the Supreme God
was a way of undercutting the devaluation of the physical
world by the Gnostics, who by and large — Basilides himself
is the obvious exception — attributed its origin to a rebellious lesser deity. "Ironically," Keith Norman observes,
"the reaction against the Marcionite and Gnostic views put
the orthodox Christian God up to compete for superlatives
with the Supreme Hidden God of Gnosticism, until finally
the biblical Father was pushed into a transcendent alien-
ness beyond comprehensible reality. Obviously this super-
Being could be no mere craftsman or artificer."[50]

The Qur'an

The Qur'an, on the other hand, seems in this regard
to reflect no influence from the intellectual currents agi-
tating Alexandria and other centers of late Hellenism. Instead, its themes are much closer to those of the biblical
canon. It is insistent that God is the creator of everything
(e.g., at Q 13:16; 39:62; 40:62). He is the "creator [*badī*] of
the heavens and the earth" (Q 2:117; 6:101). Indeed, this
is a major theme of the book, which likewise insists that
God's creative role and power are among the things which
distinguish him from false deities (Q 34:49; cf. 6:102; 7:191;
10:3, 34; 13:16; 14:32; 16:17, 20; 22:73; 25:3; 30:40; 31:11; 32:4;
35:40; 46:4; 52:36). Yet a survey of the words used in the
Qur'an in connection with "creation," and an examination
of the way in which they are used, reveals little or no

reason to suppose that any of them involve a creation from nothing. Ibn Rushd's contention has much to recommend it, when he alleges that the theologians' adherence to creation from nothing rests upon — of all things — an allegorical interpretation of the Qur'an, whose literal sense rather teaches a preexistent matter which simply received the form given it in God's creative act.[51] (Conceivably, the Qur'an's innocence of emanationist speculation is simply the flip side of its failure to assert creation *ex nihilo*; as Goldstein points out, not only 2 Maccabees but also "the other earliest Jewish and Christian texts which might seem to assert the [latter] doctrine are all in Greek.")[52]

The most common relevant Qur'anic root is *khalaqa*. Significantly, its original meaning seems to have been associated, much like the creation-related vocabulary of the Hebrew Bible, with such things as working leather. It expressed, too, "the idea of determining parts, and . . . the idea of polishing, equalising."[53] "What then," R. Arnaldez asks rather plaintively in the light of this and certain other aspects of the word, "can be said about the doctrine of creation *ex nihilo* in the Ḳur'an? Quite simply that Arabic, like all other languages, has had to use a word which originally signified something concrete and material for an ineffable reality."[54] But to assume from the start that Qur'anic creation was "ineffable" rather than "concrete and material" is to beg the question at issue.

Let us examine the evidence. We are told that God created the heavens and the earth in six days (Q 7:54; 10:3; 11:7; 25:59; 32:4; 50:38; 57:4),[55] and that mankind is also among his creations (as at 2:21; 6:94; 7:11; 26:184; 37:96; 41:21; cf. 5:18; 50:16; 51:56; 55:3; 56:57). What does this mean? An examination of the occurrences of the verb virtually rules out creation *ex nihilo*: Thus, Iblīs in particular (Q 7:12; 38:76) and the *jinn* in general (Q 15:27; 55:15) are created of fire [*min nār*]. Man, on the other hand, is said to have been created "from dust" [*min turāb*] (Q 30:20; this is specifically stated of Adam and Jesus at Q 3:59), from the "earth" [*arḍ*] (Q 20:55), "from clay" [*min ṭīn*] (Q 6:2; 7:12; 32:7; 38:71, 76; cf. 17:61), "from sounding clay, from mud" [*min ṣalṣāl min ḥamā'*] (Q 15:26, 15:28, 33), "from an extraction of clay" [*min sulālat ṭīn*] (Q 23:12), "from sticky clay" [*min ṭīn lāzib*] (37:11), and "from sounding clay like earthenware" [*min ṣalṣāl ka-al-fakhkhār*] (Q 55:14).[56] God created man with his hands [*khalaqtu bi-yadayya*] (Q 38:75)—recalling Jesus' "creation" of a bird from clay at Q 3:49 and 5:110—but was not at all wearied with the labor (Q 46:33; 50:38). R. Arnaldez, whose article on "*Khalḳ*" in the second edition of the *Encyclopedia of Islam* seeks to maintain the idea of *ex nihilo* creation, is forced to admit that "True, many Ḳur'anic verses call to mind a demiurgic action when the verb *khalaḳa* is followed by the preposition *min*." He therefore offers a suggestion which has, to my view, utterly nothing to recommend it: The various examples which can be cited, he says, "indicate clearly that the preposition denotes the matter with which these created beings are created, and not a pre-existent matter from which they would be created."[57] However, this is not to let the Qur'an speak for itself, but rather to impose upon it a previously held theological view. It is not even certain that such a position is intelligible.

Thomas O'Shaughnessy, commenting upon the *mu-khallaqa* of Q 22:5—rendered variously as "formed" (A. Y. Ali, Zafrulla Khan, Arberry, Bell), "shapely" (Pickthall), and "(wohl)gestaltet" (Paret)—notes that the association of *khalaqa* with "proportion" or "symmetry" would tend to "suggest that it is closer in meaning to 'form' or 'shape' than it is to 'create' in the strict sense of that word."[58] This is precisely the sense in which, according to Theodore Gaster as cited above, we are to take most if not all elements of the biblical vocabulary of creation. (We might perhaps recall here certain German words signifying creation, like "Schöpfung," "schöpfen," "schaffen," and "erschaffen" — clearly cognate as they are with the English verb "to shape.")[59]

The Qur'an also names yet other materials out of which man was created. He was produced from a single soul [*nafs*] (Q 4:1; 7:189; 39:6), or from a male and a female (Q 49:13). He was created from a kind of water (Q 25:54; 77:20-22; 86:5-7), as were all animals (Q 24:45). In other words, he was created from a drop of sperm [*min nutfa*] (Q 16:4; 36:77; 76:2; 80:18-19; cf. 53:45-46; 86:5-7).[60] But he was also created "from a blood clot" [*min ʿalaq*] (Q 96:2). How are we to reconcile these various statements? It would seem that there is really no contradiction, for the Qur'an affirms that human beings are created "by stages" [*aṭwāran*] (Q 71:14).[61] "He creates you in the wombs of your mothers, creation after creation" [*khalqan baʿda khalqin*] (Q 39:6). Man, the Qur'an says, was created from flesh and bones, which were created from "a lump of flesh [*muḍgha*] formed and unformed," which was created from a blood clot, which was created from a drop of semen, which was created from dust or clay (cf. Q 18:37; 22:5; 23:12-14; 35:11; 40:67; 75:37-38).[62]

Of course, the precise physiological conceptions which underlie such statements as those above do not concern us here. It suffices to notice that, in every case, the "creation" spoken of occurs from preexisting materials. (Can it be doubted that, when Q 78:8 describes God as having created mankind in "pairs" [*azwāj*], it intends thereby simply the divine role in normal human reproduction?) As Arnaldez puts it, with considerable understatement, "creation *ex nihilo* is not the incontestable deduction from the root <u>khalaka</u> in these Ḳur'anic contexts."[63] Only two passages would seem to be susceptible of an *ex nihilo* interpretation. Both occur in Sūra 19, "Maryam." When Zachariah expresses some doubt that he and Elizabeth should have a child at their age, the Lord replies, "Easy is that for Me, seeing that I created thee aforetime, when thou wast nothing [*wa-lam taku shay'*]" (Q 19:9, Arberry). Later, it is the unbelievers who express doubt, and this time they are doubting the possibility of fleshly resurrection. "Man says, 'What, when I am dead shall I then be brought forth alive? Will not man remember that We created him aforetime, when he was nothing? [*wa-lam yaku shay'*]" (Q 19:67). As O'Shaughnessy points out, if these two passages teach creation *ex nihilo*, they stand alone in the Qur'an in so doing.[64] This fact by itself is reason to suspect that they teach nothing of the sort.[65] And, indeed, we learn from Aristotle that the Platonists called preexistent matter "the non-existent," *to mē on*.[66] (Gerhard May notes that the earliest occurrences of the formula *ex nihilo*, "out of nothing," invariably refer to relative nonbeing, rather than to an absolute and ontologically understood nothingness. The formula existed, in fact, many decades before the doctrine, and was only pressed into service to support the notion of absolute creation out of utter nonbeing—as happened with *Mandate* 1:1 of the *Shepherd of Hermas*—when its original meaning was no longer comprehensible.)[67] Furthermore, the Syrian monastic writer Aphraates (d. A.D. 345)—whose connection with the Qur'an has been asserted by others in other contexts[68]—uses a similar argument to make precisely the same point as does the latter of the two passages in Q 19—and he clearly does not intend creation *ex nihilo*: "About this resurrection of the dead I shall instruct you, most dear one, to the best of my ability. God in the beginning created man; He molded him from dust and He raised him up. If, then, when man did not exist, He made him from nothing, how much easier is it for Him now to raise him up like a seed sown in the earth."[69] What is involved here is, as O'Shaughnessy rightly says, creation from, not absolute, but relative nonexistence, "when man did not exist *as man*, but existed only as dust or clay."[70] It is God's ability to give life to inanimate matter, both at birth and at the resurrection, which is the ultimate proof of his power. Creation *ex nihilo* is not the point at issue. Thus, the Qur'an follows not only Aphraates but other Syriac fathers, including St. Ephrem and Babai the Great, in taking Deuteronomy 32:39 as a resurrection text, when it seems to have referred wholly to the affairs of Israel and its enemies in this world alone. "See now that I, even I, am he, and there is no god with me: I kill, and I make alive; I wound, and I heal: neither is there any that can deliver out of my hand." So reads the pentateuchal text, and the Qur'an agrees with Aphraates not only in its eschatological application but in its attribution to Moses: "Has [the unbeliever] not been told of what is in the scrolls of Moses . . . that it is He [God] who makes to die, and that makes to live?" (Q 53:36, 44, Arberry).

If *khalaqa* is associated with preexisting material, the same is true of other words used Qur'anically in connection with God's creative activity. The root *jaᶜala*, for example, is used to describe God's creation of earth and sky (Q 40:64), of the constellations or zodiacal signs (Q 25:61), of darkness and light (Q 6:1; 10:67; 40:61), of the night, the sun, and the moon (Q 6:96). Indeed, it is very often used in precisely the same sense as *khalaqa*—as, for instance, when we are told that every living thing, including particularly the posterity of Adam, has been made from a kind of water (Q 21:30; 32:8; cf. also 23:12-14, in which, when it is taken with other similar passages, *jaᶜala* seems synonymous with *khalaqa*). But it is also used to refer to God's transforming of Sabbath-breakers into apes (Q 5:60), to the transformation of what is on the earth into barren sterility (Q 18:8), to the laying out of gardens (Q 36:34), to the production of fire from a green tree (Q 36:80), and to the building of ships and the reproduction of cattle (Q 43:12). It is a form of this root which is used when the children of Israel demand of Moses that he "make" them a god like the gods of the idolators (Q 7:138)—where presumably what is meant is the fashioning of a material idol. Likewise, it is the verb used by pharaoh when he orders Hāmān and his servants to build him a tower out of fired clay bricks, so that he may climb up to the god of Moses (Q 28:38).

Other verbs used in the Qur'an seem similarly to imply a preexistent material, an *Urstoff*, out of which the universe was made. At the very least, there is nothing in them which would necessitate reading the Qur'an as advocating creation *ex nihilo*. Heaven, for example, of which we are repeatedly told that God is the creator (using the root *khalaqa*, as at Q 65:12; 67:3; 71:15, and throughout the book), is said to have been "built," as an "edifice" [in both cases, the root is *bny*] (Q 2:22; 40:64; 50:6; 51:47; 78:12; 79:27; 91:5). In another version of pharaoh's order to Hāmān to build him a tower, *bny* is used as a synonym of *jaᶜala* (Q 40:36).

In the case of *bada'a*, too — which is used as a synonym of *khalaqa* at Q 7:29 — there is no reason in the text as it stands to infer a creation out of nothing. In the passages relevant to our present concern, the root *bada'a* invariably serves as an inceptive helping verb, with the actual content relating to the creation being supplied by another root. (See, for example, Q 10:4, 34; 21:104; 27:64; 29:19-20; 30:11, 27; 32:7; 85:13 [by implication].)

So much for *bada'a*. But the ammunition of those who would argue for an ex nihilo creation in the Qur'an is by no means yet exhausted. "While the root *bd'* suggests the idea of a 'beginning' which involves a continuation," Louis Gardet asserts, "the root *bdᶜ* implies, strictly, not a 'first time', but a radical innovation, an absolute bringing into existence."[71] Is this so? The root *badaᶜa* occurs only four times in the Qur'an — and never in the fourth form of the verb, which will prove so significant in the writings of Ḥamīd al-Dīn al-Kirmānī and the other Ismāᶜīlī Neoplatonists, as well as in Pseudo-Aristotle. The verbal noun of that fourth form is quite rightly rendered by M. Gardet as "absolute creation, primordial innovation." This is a good translation of its use in later philosophers and theologians (although it is apparently not the sense in which it is used in the *Theology of Aristotle*). "The commentators emphasize," remarks M. Gardet, "that God is called *Badīᶜ* by virtue of His absolute creation of the heavens and the earth, and *Khālik̠* by virtue of His creation (*k̠halk̠*) of man ('made of clay', LV, 14)." However, it is a grave and obvious methodological error to use the later commentary literature uncritically as a guide to the meaning of the Qur'an itself. Only factors external to the Qur'anic text would impel us to see in *badaᶜa* an indication of "absolute origination" in its pages; on its own, it offers no inducements to such a reading. In two of the four occurrences of the root, as mentioned above, God is simply declared to be the "creator of the heavens and the earth." Neither requires us to infer a creation *ex nihilo*.[72] The third instance of the root is as a Form VIII verb describing the allegedly unauthorized "invention" of monasticism by Christians (Q 57:27). The fourth occurrence is of the noun *bidᶜ*, "innovation." Admittedly, the latter two cases might be interpreted favorably to the concept of creation *ex nihilo*, but there is nothing in the context to suggest that they should be so taken.[73] (One might speculate that it is M. Gardet's immersion in the works of later theologians, or perhaps even his own theological background, which leads him to see in *badaᶜa* what is, quite simply, not Qur'anically there.)

The root *bara'a*, cognate with the verb *bārā'* of Genesis 1:1, occurs almost solely (in the contexts which concern us) in the neutral meanings of "creator" (Q 2:54; 59:24) or "creature" (Q 98:6-7). The one exception to this is Q 57:22, which speaks of misfortunes as being foreordained before God brings them about. But it is evident that misfortunes in this life, whether earthquakes or diseases or war, are "brought about" out of preexisting matter or circumstances. Thus, again, nothing in the Qur'anic use of *bara'a* compels one to assume *ex nihilo* creation — as we have seen, its biblical cognate *bārā'* was taken for centuries to mean an organization of preexistent matter—and, indeed, what evidence the book does furnish would seem to militate against such an assumption.

Much the same thing can be said of the root *nasha'a*, which in its Qur'anic incarnation means, basically, "to cause something to grow." God produces gardens, for example (Q 6:141; 23:19), and he makes trees grow (Q 56:72). He also causes clouds to swell up, heavy with rain [*yunshi'u al-sahāb al-thiqāl*] (Q 13:12). Significantly the root occasionally seems to be used as a synonym for *khalaqa*, as at Q 36:77-79 and 29:19-20. God created mankind from a single soul (Q 6:98) or from the earth (Q 11:61; 53:32). Verbs derived from this root are also used to describe the raising up of a new human generation (Q 6:6, 133; 21:11; 23:31, 42; 28:45), the birth of a child (Q 23:14), and the development of sensory apparatus (Q 23:78).

The most dramatic assertion of God's creative power in the Qur'an is the repeated declaration that he has merely to say to a thing " 'Be!' and it is" [*kun fa-yakūn*] (at Q 6:73; 36:82; and elsewhere).[74] This would seem, at first glance, to be promising material for the construction of a theory of *ex nihilo* creation and, indeed, the verses which fall into this category are the ones most commonly used to support such a theory.[75] But first glances can be deceptive. In several of the passages where this phrase occurs, creation *ex nihilo* is excluded by the context; in no passages is it required. As O'Shaughnessy puts it, these passages are "non-committal."[76] Thus, the subject of Q 3:47, 3:59, and 19:35 is the virginal conception of Jesus, of whom the second passage affirms that God first created him from dust, *then* said to him *kun fa-yakūn*.[77] This points up a rather odd characteristic of these passages: Q 2:117 is typical of them in stating that God "decrees a matter [*amr*]" and *then* "says to it [*lahu*] 'Be,' and it is" (cf. 3:47; 40:68). Q 16:40 actually speaks of a "thing" [*shay'*] to which God says *kun fa-yakūn*.[78] There seems, thus, to be an underlying and preexisting substrate to which the divine imperative is addressed, as clearly is the case in the story of the sabbath-breakers who are told "Be ye apes!" [*kūnū qirdatan*] (Q 2:65; 7:166). The command *kun!* would therefore seem to be more determinative or constitutive than productive of something out of utter nothingness.[79]

A further clue to the Qur'anic doctrine of creation occurs in certain polemical passages which might seem at first only marginally relevant. In accordance with the ancient notion of history as cyclical, almost every element of the traditional creation myths was taken up again in Judeo-Christian apocalyptic, which taught that God would renew the world in a new creation [*palingenesia; hadosh ha-ᶜolam*].[80] Not surprisingly, the same doctrine is abundantly attested in the Qur'an (as at Q 10:34; 21:104; 27:64; 29:19-20; 30:27). God creates once, and then he repeats the process to bring men before his tribunal at the judgment day (Q 10:4; 30:11; 32:10; 46:33-34). For we are dealing here, particularly, with the resurrection of the dead. Men will be "created" again when they are but bones and dust (Q 13:5; 17:49-51, 98-99; 32:10; 34:7; 36:77-82).[81] "Were we wearied in the first creation, that they should be in doubt about a new creation?" (Q 50:15). "Do they not see that God, who created the heavens and the earth and was not wearied thereby, is able to give life to the dead?" (Q 46:33).

The nature of resurrection as a revivification of once animate, now inanimate, matter, and the pointed comparisons to the initial creation (emphatically so at Q 22:5-6; 36:77-82; 75:37-40; 86:5-8), are significant in many ways. They sustain my contention that creation, for the Qur'an, was most likely conceived as the determination of preexistent matter. They are reminiscent of the argument of 2 Maccabees 7 and are precisely parallel to the concern for the resurrection of the dead which, according to Jonathan Goldstein, drove Jewish and Christian speculation on the origins of the world. Yet they support David Winston's denial that such a connection involves argument for *ex nihilo* creation.

"What," exclaim Muhammad's Makkan critics, "when we are dust shall we indeed then be raised up again in new creation?" (Q 13:5, Arberry; cf. 32:10; 34:7). "They say, 'What, when we are bones and broken bits, shall we really be raised up again in a new creation?'" To this, Muhammad is instructed to reply, " 'Let you be stones, or iron, or some creation yet more monstrous in your minds!' Then they will say, 'Who will bring us back?' Say: 'He who originated you the first time' " (Q 17:49-51, Arberry). "Have they not seen that God, who created the heavens and the earth, is powerful to create the like of them?" (Q 17:99; cf. 17:98, Arberry).

The argumentation of the Qur'an is remarkably similar to that of several earlier patristic writers. Justin Martyr wrote in his first *Apology,*

> We expect that our own bodies, even though they should be dead and buried in the earth, will be revived; for we claim that nothing is impossible with God. And what would seem more incredible to a thinking person than if we were not in a body and someone were to affirm that from a little drop of the human seed it were possible to shape bones, muscles and flesh into the human form we now see? . . . But as in the beginning you would not have believed it possible that from a little sperm such persons could be produced, and yet you actually see that they are, so now realize that it is not impossible that human bodies, after they are dead and disseminated in the earth like seeds, should at the appointed time, at God's command [*prostagma*], arise and assume immortality."[82]

We have seen Justin did not believe in creation from nothing. Similarly, Theophilus of Antioch, later in the same century, while he seems to have accepted a notion of *ex nihilo* cosmogony, nevertheless argues for resurrection from God's ability to form man "out of a small moist matter and a tiny drop."[83] Even Tatian, who has been adduced by some writers as a believer in *ex nihilo* origination, seems rather to imply creation from preexistent stuff in the very passage which is cited to prove such belief: "Before I was born," he writes, "I did not exist; I did not know who I was and was only latent in the substance of physical matter; it was through my birth that I, previously non-existent, came to believe that I did exist. In the same way, when I who was born, cease to exist through death and am no more seen, I shall once more be as in my previous state of non-existence followed by birth"[84] — i.e., latently present in physical matter. "If fire consumes my bit of flesh, the vaporized matter is still contained in the world. If I am annihilated in rivers and seas, or torn to pieces by wild beasts, I am still stored in a rich lord's treasuries. The poor, impious man does not know what is stored up, but God the ruler, when he wishes, will restore to its original state the substance [*hypostasin*] that is visible only to him."[85]

Amidst all his disagreements with the philosophers, al-Ghazālī found only three issues upon which to call them infidels. These were, as he lists them in his *Tahāfut al-Falāsifa*, "i) the problem of the eternity of the world, where they [the philosophers] maintained that all the substances are eternal, ii) their assertion that Divine knowledge does not encompass individual objects, iii) their denial of the resurrection of bodies. All these three theories are in violent opposition to Islam. To believe in them is to accuse the prophets of falsehood."[86] It is perhaps not coincidental that the same thinkers who denied *ex nihilo* creation denied also the resurrection of the body, and that an al-Ghazālī would insist on both, and on giving both equal weight. Nevertheless, despite the insistence of al-Ghazālī and others on the centrality of the dogma of creation out of absolute nothingness for Islamic belief, I must agree with Thomas O'Shaughnessy and Oliver Leaman that "it is questionable . . . whether the Qur'an itself gives any valid foundation for this teaching."[87] "For," as Ibn Rushd quite correctly points out, "it is not stated in Scripture that God was existing with absolutely nothing else: a text to this effect is nowhere to be found."[88] It is true that al-Ghazālī has the vast majority if not all of the commentators on his side, and that normative Islam, then as now, is decisive in its view of the issue. "But in abstract matters of this kind," as O'Shaughnessy notes, "the opinions of important commentators like Zamakhsharī, Rāzī, and Baydāwī reflect a later stage of the development of religious and philosophical thought in Islam, when this faith of desert tribesmen had come into closer contact with Christianity and with Hellenistic philosophy. The refinements of thought presupposed in an understanding of absolute nonexistence were foreign to those who first heard Muhammad's preaching at Mecca and Medina."[89] Ironically, al-Ghazālī, concerned at what he saw as an uncritical acceptance of Hellenistic presuppositions by Muslim intellectuals, seems clearly in this case to advance as essential to Islam a doctrine whose roots are not only extra-Qur'anic but, indeed, Greek.

Notes

1. William R. Inge, *The Philosophy of Plotinus*, 2nd ed., 2 vols. (London: Longmans, Green, 1923), 1:145.

2. Jonathan A. Goldstein, "The Origins of the Doctrine of Creation Ex Nihilo," *Journal of Jewish Studies* 35 (Autumn 1984): 127. Gerhard May, *Schöpfung aus dem Nichts: Die Entstehung der Lehre von der Creatio Ex Nihilo*, Arbeiten zur Kirchengeschichte, 48 (Berlin: Walter de Gruyter, 1978), vii, contends that a concept of *ex nihilo* creation is the most natural expression of the biblical view of the origins of the cosmos, and that it was logically inevitable that such a doctrine should arise. Creation by "forming" or "shaping" preexistent matter was, he contends, ultimately incompatible with Genesis 1, properly viewed (cf. also 75, 135, 153, et passim). But even May admits that his doctrine is simply not present in the text. His is a strange position, in view not only of the etymologies of the

words used for "creation" in the Bible, but also in the face of the fact that the Hebrews of the biblical period, as well as the rabbis and the early Christian Fathers, saw no difficulty in holding to precisely the idea of creation as the organization of preexistent matter.

3. New Jerusalem Bible, 17, n. "a" (on Genesis 1:1). We shall see below that even 2 Maccabees 7:28 is not beyond question as a proof text for *ex nihilo* creation.

4. T. H. Gaster, "Cosmogony," in George A. Buttrick et al., eds., *The Interpreter's Dictionary of the Bible*, 5 vols. (Nashville: Abingdon, 1962), 1:702.

5. Psalm 102:25; cf. Psalm 8:3.

6. Keith Norman, "Ex Nihilo: The Development of the Doctrines of God and Creation in Early Christianity," *BYU Studies* 17 (Spring 1977): 295.

7. Ibid. Among the passages cited by Norman are Isaiah 29:16; 40:22; 45:9; 51:13, 15-16; Psalms 74:13-17; 89:11; 90:2; Romans 9:20-23. We might also think of the ram-headed Egyptian god Khnum, of Elephantine, who formed the souls of men and women upon his potter's wheel, or of Ptah, the artificer-god of Memphis. Cf. Alan W. Shorter, *The Egyptian Gods* (London: Routledge and Kegan Paul, 1983), 8, 10.

8. Gaster, "Cosmogony," 702-4. 2 Peter 3:5 may reflect the notion of the priority of water.

9. Ibid., 706.

10. Origen, *De Principiis* II, 1, 5.

11. On the alternate readings of 2 Maccabees 7:28, see the remarks on that passage in the New Jerusalem Bible, 731, n. "e." For a discussion of *Wisdom of Solomon* 11:7, consult May, *Schöpfung aus dem Nichts*, 6.

12. Goldstein, "The Origins of the Doctrine of Creation Ex Nihilo," 127, 130; May, *Schöpfung aus dem Nichts*, 6-8.

13. Goldstein, "The Origins of the Doctrine of Creation Ex Nihilo," 134.

14. Ibid., 129-30.

15. David Winston, "Creation Ex Nihilo Revisited: A Reply to Jonathan Goldstein," *Journal of Jewish Studies* 37 (Spring 1986): 88.

16. Gaster, "Cosmogony," 706.

17. Winston, "Creation Ex Nihilo Revisited," 90-91, doubts that Romans 4:17 clearly asserts the idea, as does May, *Schöpfung aus dem Nichts*, 27 (where such an interpretation of Hebrews 11:3 is likewise contested). The standard work is certainly the aforemen-

tioned treatise by May, which at ibid., 26, categorically denies the presence of *ex nihilo* creation anywhere in the New Testament.

18. On the lack of interest the question held for earliest Christian thinking, see May, ibid., 183.

19. Winston, "Creation Ex Nihilo Revisited," 91; cf. May, *Schöpfung aus dem Nichts*, 23.

20. Winston, "Creation Ex Nihilo Revisited," 88, n. 1. Goldstein, "The Origins of the Doctrine of Creation Ex Nihilo," 132, and May, *Schöpfung aus dem Nichts*, 121, would have it that Tatian taught the doctrine "unambiguously," and that he is the first Christian to do so. Winston has, I think, effectively disposed of that claim. The so-called "Shepherd of Hermas," who wrote no later, probably, than A.D. 148, might have taught *ex nihilo* creation. See *Vision* 1.6 and *Mandate* 1.1. But, again, the relevant Greek phrase is not definite in positing absolute, rather than relative, nonbeing. Indeed, there seems good reason to prefer the latter.

21. May, *Schöpfung aus dem Nichts*, 62, 154-55.

22. Ibid., 71, 121, 183-84.

23. Ibid., 41, 42 n. 2, 184.

24. Ibid., 68, 69 n. 26. On his dislike of a God active in history, see ibid., p. 82. McKim's contention will be recalled: "Whereas the scriptural accounts spoke of the actions of God in history, Greek philosophy centered attention on the question of metaphysical being," Donald K. McKim, *Theological Turning Points: Major Issues in Christian Thought* (Atlanta: John Knox Press, 1988), 8. It has been suggested that Valentinian Gnosticism is a predecessor of Neoplatonism; in its concept of emanation as well as in its positing a God higher than the Intellect, it appears to foreshadow Plotinus. See May, *Schöpfung aus dem Nichts*, 110, n. 233.

25. May, *Schöpfung aus dem Nichts*, 76, 85.

26. Ibid., 71-72, 75.

27. Ibid., 75.

28. Ibid., 85.

29. Ibid., 84.

30. Goldstein, "The Origins of the Doctrine of Creation Ex Nihilo," 132; cf. May, *Schöpfung aus dem Nichts*, 139. Inge, *The Philosophy of Plotinus*, 1:145: "Christian orthodoxy denies . . . the theory that Matter is uncreated, and that creation consists in shaping it." This was almost certainly not always so, and it is difficult anyway to see what necessary connection might exist between absolutely fundamental constitutive Christian beliefs and this particular doctrine.

31. May, *Schöpfung aus dem Nichts,* 149. Norman, "Ex Nihilo," 307: "In fact, the rash of arguments in favor of *ex nihilo* creation at the end of the second century points to the newness of the concept. Tertullian's tract [*Against Hermogenes*] especially adds to the evidence that the argument was against an established belief within the Church, since it was directed against a fellow Christian rather than against Platonism."

32. See May, *Schöpfung aus dem Nichts,* 141.

33. See Justin Martyr, *Apology* 10: "And we have been taught that He in the beginning did of His goodness, for man's sake, create all things out of unformed matter." (See, too, his *Hortatory Address to the Greeks* XX, 29-33.) H. Chadwick, "Philo and the Beginnings of Christian Thought," in A. H. Armstrong, ed., *The Cambridge History of Later Greek and Early Medieval Philosophy* (Cambridge: Cambridge University Press, 1967), 161, declares rather weakly that "Justin does not insist on creation *ex nihilo*." (He evidently sees an ambivalence in Justin's mind, when the passages just cited are juxtaposed to *Dialogue* 5.) Gerhard May, on the other hand, argues — convincingly, in my opinion — that Justin absolutely does not teach creation *ex nihilo*. See May, *Schöpfung aus dem Nichts,* 121, 127, 134.

34. May, *Schöpfung aus dem Nichts,* 126.

35. Ibid., 135.

36. Ibid., 124-125, 183.

37. Chadwick, "Philo and the Beginnings of Christian Thought," 171.

38. See, for example, May, *Schöpfung aus dem Nichts,* 9-20; cf. 126, n. 33. Norman, "Ex Nihilo," 308, contends that Clement was aware of the concept of *ex nihilo* creation, but that "he does not view it as crucial to orthodoxy."

39. See Origen, *De Principiis* II, 1, 4. See also Chadwick, "Philo and the Beginnings of Christian Thought," 189.

40. May, *Schöpfung aus dem Nichts,* 183; Norman, "Ex Nihilo," 316. Although even then, Origen, for instance, could relegate it in his *Against Celsus* to the secondary sphere of "physics" rather than "theology," cf. ibid., 309.

41. May, *Schöpfung aus dem Nichts,* 75, 121, 149, 151, 159, 162, 169.

42. Ibid., 78, 160, 183-84.

43. Ibid., 164.

44. Norman, "Ex Nihilo," 307. Tertullian does not care to insist on *ex nihilo* creation, although it is clear that he personally believes in it. See his *De Resurrectione Carnis* 11, and Winston, "Creation Ex

Nihilo Revisited," 89-90. The dilemma of theodicy, basically stated, is that it seems impossible to reconcile the existence of a wholly good and all-powerful deity with the existence of evil. Why has he not eliminated it? Two clear and extreme alternatives immediately present themselves: Perhaps he is not truly good, or perhaps he is not able. Tertullian seemingly preferred the former option to the latter, although I am sure that he would have protested such an unnuanced statement of the dilemma.

45. Inge, *The Philosophy of Plotinus*, 1:145; May, *Schöpfung aus dem Nichts*, viii, ix, 119, 151, 153, 183, 184. It was around the middle of the second century that the confrontation between Christianity and philosophy began to grow serious. The two leading philosophies of the day were Stoicism and (Middle) Platonism—peripatetic philosophy was too much a school tradition during this period to be much of a practical challenge. For Middle Platonism, which reigned supreme from roughly 50 B.C. to A.D. 250, Plato's *Timaeus* was by far the preeminent text. See May, *Schöpfung aus dem Nichts*, 1-4.

46. Chadwick, "Philo and the Beginnings of Christian Thought," 142.

47. Ibid., 164; Phillip Merlan, "Greek Philosophy from Plato to Plotinus," in A. H. Armstrong, ed., *The Cambridge History of Later Greek and Early Medieval Philosophy* (Cambridge: Cambridge University Press, 1967), 102.

48. On the pivotal role of Irenaeus, see May, *Schöpfung aus dem Nichts*, x, 151; Norman, "Ex Nihilo," 303.

49. May, *Schöpfung aus dem Nichts*, 167-68.

50. Norman, "Ex Nihilo," 303; cf. the discussion on 303-4.

51. Ibn Rushd, "Decisive Treatise," in George F. Hourani, ed. and tr., *Averroes: On the Harmony of Religion and Philosophy* (London: Luzac, 1961), 56-57.

52. Goldstein, "The Origins of the Doctrine of Creation Ex Nihilo," 127.

53. R. Arnaldez, "Khalk," in E. van Donzel, B. Lewis, and Ch. Pellat, *The Encyclopaedia of Islam* (Leiden: Brill, 1960-), 4:980-88.

54. Ibid., 981.

55. Q 41:9 speaks of two days of creation.

56. The idea of man's creation from dust or clay is very old. For ancient Mesopotamian and Egyptian parallels, see Gaster, "Cosmogony," 705.

57. Arnaldez, "Khalk," 981.

58. Thomas O'Shaughnessy, "Creation from Nothing and the Teaching of the Qur'an," *Zeitschrift der Deutschen Morgenländischen Gesellschaft* 120 (1970): 279.

59. Suggested by O'Shaughnessy, ibid., 279, n. 17. See the relevant entries in *Der Grosse Duden: Herkunftswörterbuch;* also the *Oxford English Dictionary*.

60. This is reminiscent of the Mishnaic injunction (TB *Avot* 3:1) to "know whence thou art come." The answer to this question, obviously designed to promote humility in humankind, is "from a putrid drop [*tippah serukhah*]." I am indebted to David P. Wright for bringing this passage to my attention.

61. Compare Q 71:17: *wa Allāh anbatakum min al-arḍ nabātan*. See also Q 3:37.

62. Obviously, there exists a third possible mode of cosmogony, distinct both from creation *ex nihilo* and from creation as organization of preexisting material, that being creation as biological or sexual generation. This mode occurs in many ancient mythologies, as well as in a number of Gnostic systems. (See May, *Schöpfung aus dem Nichts*, 97-98, 102, for Valentinian Gnosticism). However, since such a position does not seem to occur among Muslims, and since no passage in the Qur'an—emphatically including those cited here—seems to teach such a concept, I shall omit discussion of it in this study. With Islam's explicit denial of the fatherhood of God, it is far less susceptible to such an interpretation than is Christianity.

63. Arnaldez, "Khalk," 982.

64. O'Shaughnessy, "Creation from Nothing," 277.

65. I do not, of course, mean to suggest that the Qur'an is a monolithic, totally consistent text, on this or any other matter. However, I see no *a priori* reason to take the opposite position, assuming that the Qur'an is inconsistent and self-contradictory. The situation must be weighed on a case-by-case basis, and, as I hope is clear from the argument that follows, the evidence of these two particular passages simply does not compel us to see the Qur'an as self-contradictory at this point. In the absence of compelling evidence, my inclination is to take the book as internally consistent.

66. Aristotle, *Physics* I, 9, 192a 6-7.

67. See May, *Schöpfung aus dem Nichts*, vii, 21, 78, 121, 155. For the case of the *Shepherd*, see 27.

68. O'Shaughnessy, "Creation from Nothing," 277-78, 280.

69. Cited in ibid., 278.

70. Ibid., 278 (emphasis in original).

71. All quotations from L. Gardet in this paragraph come from his article, "Ibdāʿ," in *The Encyclopedia of Islam*, 3:663-65.

72. I will, however, return below to Q 2:117, which is interesting for its use of another important and relevant Arabic form.

73. Innovation and invention are perfectly comprehensible as new insights based upon, or new utilizations of, preexisting ideas. Probably most intellectual historians and historians of science would insist on understanding them in this way.

74. According to one Egyptian myth, Ptah created the other gods by no act, but by spoken command. See the translation of the so-called "Memphite Theology" at Miriam Lichtheim, *Ancient Egyptian Literature, Volume 1: The Old and Middle Kingdoms* (Berkeley: University of California Press, 1975): 51-57.

75. Arnaldez, "Khalḳ," 982.

76. O'Shaughnessy, "Creation from Nothing," 274.

77. Ibid., 275, says that this verse refers to Adam, which is also true. The point remains the same.

78. The situation here is analogous to what Werner Foerster calls the evident "logical impossibility" expressed in Romans 4:17, where Paul represents God as "calling forth those things which are not as though they were" [*kalountos ta mē onta hos onta*]: "One can call forth only that which already exists. But God calls forth that which does not yet exist. He commands it, and in obedience to this command creation takes place. We must not try to evade the logical inconceivability of this statement by taking the *mē onta* [i.e., 'non-existent things'] as though in some sense they were *onta* [i.e., 'existent things']." See Werner Foerster, "Ktizō," in Gerhard Kittel, ed., *Theological Dictionary of the New Testament*, tr. Geoffrey W. Bromiley, 10 vols. (Grand Rapids: Eerdmans, 1965), 3:1010. Foerster is perhaps more tolerant of logical inconceivability than I am. In any case, whatever the merits of his position with regard to the Pauline position, it seems clear that we ought precisely to take the *mē onta* of the Qur'anic passages under discussion as though in some sense they were *onta*.

79. Presumably, when the Ikhwān al-Ṣafā' promise the righteous a power like God's, to say to a thing "Be!" and have it be, they were not pledging to human beings, even in Paradise, the capacity to produce *ex nihilo*. See *Rasā'il Ikhwān al-Ṣafā'* 1:158. I discuss this passage elsewhere, in a related but as yet unpublished paper.

80. Gaster, "Cosmogony," 708.

81. The point of Q 31:28 may be to affirm the complete identity of the person in both his mortal and resurrected state.

82. Justin Martyr, *Apology* I, 18-19. The translation is that of Thomas B. Falls. Compare Athenagoras, *On the Resurrection* 17, and the resurrection proceeding from preexistent materials portrayed in Pseudo-Justinian, *On the Resurrection* 6. See, too, May, *Schöpfung aus dem Nichts*, 137, 139.

83. Theophilus, *Ad Autolycam* I, 8. Cf. Winston, "Creation Ex Nihilo Revisited," 89.

84. Tatian, *Oratio ad Graecos* 6.

85. The translation and edition is that of Molly Whittaker. For human conception as a creation from relative nothingness, see Justin Martyr, *Apology* 10: "He created us when we were nothing." Tertullian (d. ca. A.D. 220) is apparently the first Christian writer to argue for the probability of resurrection from the alleged fact of God's *ex nihilo* creation of the cosmos generally. See May, *Schöpfung aus dem Nichts*, 139.

86. Al-Ghazālī, *Tahāfut al-Falāsifah*, tr. Sabih Ahmad Kamali, Pakistan Philosophical Congress Publication No. 3 (Lahore: Pakistan Philosophical Congress, 1963), 249.

87. O'Shaughnessy, "Creation from Nothing," 274; cf. Oliver Leaman, *An Introduction to Medieval Islamic Philosophy* (Cambridge: Cambridge University Press, 1985), 25-26.

88. Ibn Rushd, *Decisive Treatise*, 57.

89. O'Shaughnessy, "Creation from Nothing," 276-77.

24

The Handclasp and Embrace as Tokens of Recognition

Todd M. Compton
Los Angeles, California

The Symbolon: Unity, Separation, Unity

The present paper is excerpted from a much longer paper published in *Epoché*, the UCLA graduate journal of history of religions.[1] The paper began in a seminar examining Greek recognition drama, a type of play in which a child is separated from its (aristocratic) parents at birth (often it is stolen, or saved by strangers after a shipwreck), and so grows up as a slave or prostitute; but later, when it becomes an adult, it finds or is found by its parents (the recognition scene) through the help of tokens left with the child, often insignia or jewelry on a necklace, sometimes a ring; sometimes a peculiar scar. Often the tokens are kept in boxes and are dramatically extracted from the boxes, one by one, in the recognition scene. Critics, I found, have usually looked at recognition drama with contempt; however, all Greek drama is bathed in religion, sometimes very alien, and I wondered if the structure of recognition was not linked with religion in some way; and if the critics were not doing these plays an injustice because of their modern, secular bias and insensitivity to the nuances of ancient Greek religion and ritual. The climaxes of these recognition dramas seemed to have great meaning for the Greek playwrights and audiences; surely the recognition drama with tokens was not just a rickety, mechanistic plot device used as a crutch by playwrights of the stature of Aeschylus and

611

Euripides. As my research progressed, I found that the Greek/Hellenistic mystery cults involved tokens revealed at the high point of the secret rituals. These tokens were always kept in a box/basket called the *cista mystica*; and as they were brought out, the initiate had to speak certain passwords (also called tokens). After the experience, the initiate enjoyed a new intimacy with the central god or gods of the mystery and was prepared for a better state in the next life. Not much more was known about this token experience in the mysteries, but I thought the parallel was close enough to warrant a comparison of the climax of the recognition scene, with its crucial tokens, and the climax of the mystery ritual, with its tokens. As there are many continuities between the mystery religions and early Christianity, and since I was writing the paper for a history of religions seminar, I allowed myself to examine evidence in late antiquity, especially in Gnostic Christianity. I used three recognition plays in particular: Euripides' *Ion*, Menander's *Epitrepontes* (*Arbitrants*), and Plautus's *Rudens*.

There are a number of words in Greek and Latin that mean "token" in recognition drama — e.g., *anagnōrismata* ("things for making known again"), *spargana* (the swaddling wrappings of the lost child, often figured), *sēmeia* ("signs, marks, signals"). But one of the most interesting token-words is the basis for our word "symbol": *symbolon* (singular; plural: *symbola*), found as a name for tokens both in recognition and mystery.[2] This word means "things thrown together" (i.e., something thrown together after it has been once broken apart, from *ballo*, "thrown," and *sun-*, "with or together"). Liddell, Scott, and Jones, in their *Greek-English Lexicon*, define it thus: "tally, i.e., each of two halves or corresponding pieces of an *astragalos* [knucklebone] or other object, which two *xenoi* [guest-friends], or any two contracting parties, broke between them, each party keeping one piece, in order to have proof of the identity of the presenter of the other."[3] Both halves represent their two owners, and each is a symbol of identity, the individual, parted; the halves "thrown together," unified, are the symbol of two separate identities merging into one. So the *symbolon* is a precise image both for absolutely unique individuality and perfectly joined unity. No other parts would fit the two *symbolon* halves; paradoxically, their unique identity is what creates their complete unity as represented by the unified token. It is also significant that the perfect fitting together is dependent on a previous breaking.[4]

Later in the semantic development of the word, it came to be applied to "any token serving as proof of identity" — in which category we find the dramatic recognition token — and then developed on to other abstract and technical ideas: treaty, symbol, allegory, warrant, ticket. In the recognition *symbolon*, there is no longer the actual two-part, physically broken token,[5] but the token remains a symbol of dual identity, "thrown together" after a parting. Palaestra, the foundling of *Rudens*, owns her tokens; they define the most important part of her identity; but they were given to her by her father and mother and are inscribed with their names. When Palaestra and her father, Daemones, are "thrown together" again, her knowledge, through the tokens, unites with his knowledge through the tokens — the two realizations create a united, new (or rather, renewed) knowledge, and they are united. This is a recognition: a "knowing again," as the English word means exactly, just as does the Greek *anagnōrismos* (*ana-*, "again"; *gnōrizō*, "to make known").

Thus the contract *symbolon* (unity, separation into two, renewed unity of two) serves as a model for the whole recognition drama: as in *Rudens*, there is, at first, a unity of parent and child; there is a separation, by kidnapping; finally there is a reunion (through the knowledge-combining tokens). The recognition *symbolon* brings about the human *symbolon*.

Fig. 1. A Greek *symbolon* (guest-token) in the form of two clasped hands. Gabriel Herman, *Ritualised Friendship and the Greek City* (Cambridge: Cambridge University Press, 1988), 64

The handclasp and the embrace perfectly express this concept of two separate halves coming together to create a unity; and one of the tokens in the *Rudens* is a handclasp. Herman shows us an ivory *symbolon* carved in the likeness of two clasped hands (fig. 1).[6] Even more evocative is the embrace, for when the parent and child embrace, in a moment of high emotion after the recognition scene with token telling (identifying tokens one by one), they are renewing an embrace they had shared years earlier. The parent-child *symbolon*, broken by fate, violent nature, or human greed and malevolence, has been renewed.

The Handclasp

Among the *Rudens* tokens are "a tiny pair of clasped hands" ("*duae conexae maniculae*," 1169). I was originally interested in this token because it is such a perfect *symbolon* image on a human, physical level: two separate hands, symbols of the separate identities of their possessors, are joined, and fingers intertwine to make a new unity, complex yet simple. Though its "secular" use—as a widespread token of recognition, friendship, and agreement—is obvious,[7] it was also co-opted by the mystery religions for use as an emblem for many things: Love, initiation, arrival, salvation, union with the god, apotheosis.

I have found no solid evidence for the ritual hand-clasp — the *dexiōsis, dextrarum iunctio* — at Eleusis. However, in the culminating initiation scene in the Eleusis-influenced Lovatelli urn,[8] there is perhaps a hint of the *dexiōsis*. As the initiate approaches Demeter sitting on the *cista*, the goddess's snake rises from her lap to greet the initiate; he extends his right hand for the snake to touch. If, as I have argued, this scene reflects a high point of the mysteries, and if the touching of the snake and the right hand of the initiate is related to the *dextrarum iunctio*, we may conjecture that a handclasp as token (the snake represents the contents of the *cista*, the *symbola*, as well as the presence of the god) took place as part of the initiate's union with the god at Eleusis.

This, however, must remain conjectural. A remarkable piece of iconography from the Sabazian mysteries, on the other hand, supplies valuable evidence for the ritual hand-clasp in a mystery environment. A series of paintings in the tomb of Vincentius, a priest of Sabazius, near Rome and dating from the second century A.D.,[9] show the otherworld experiences of Vincentius' wife, Vibia. After death and judgment in the underworld, the final scene in the series, showing the heavenly banquet of the blessed, shows Vibia, standing on the threshold of a doorway, being led through it by a "good messenger" (so labeled by the artist), already inside the "heaven." The messenger brings her inside by means of a *dextrarum iunctio*. The whole act is labeled an *"inductio,"* a leading in. The *bonus angelus* has been variously interpreted, some authors ascribing him to Jewish or Christian influence (the Sabazian cult had earlier syncretized with Jewish inhabitants of Asia Minor); however, Leclerq regards him as Sabazius himself (cf. fig. 2).[10]

Though this representation is comparatively late, funeral iconography of the Attic Greeks[11] shows that the concept of the handclasp representing eschatological union was extremely common in classical Greece; there are eleven

Fig. 2. Painting from a Sabazian tomb near Rome; a good messenger brings the deceased, Vibia, to the banquet of the blessed. Johannes Leipoldt, *Die Religionen der Umwelt des Urchristentums* (Leipzig: Deichert, 1926), no. 166

examples of the motif in the Getty funerary collection alone. This handclasp's meaning is somewhat ambiguous; Brilliant, after summarizing some interpretations (an excerpt from life [which would seem unlikely, on a funerary monument], a farewell, a desired reunion), concludes thus: "Most probably the handshake expresses that continued community of the dead and the living within the bounds of the familiar society which in itself constitutes immortality."[12] There are representations of Hermes the psychopomp leading the soul of the dead by the hand,[13] which parallels the psychopomp in the Sabazian painting.

Another fairly late piece of evidence shows that in Plutarch's day the *dexiōsis* was used among the Pythagoreans as a symbol of love, brotherhood, and reconciliation. "We should pattern ourselves after the Pythagoreans, who, though related not at all by birth, yet sharing a common discipline, if ever they were led by anger into recrimination, never let the sun go down before they joined right hands, embraced each other, and were reconciled," wrote Plutarch in his essay on brotherly love.[14] We have already seen that Orphism and Pythagoreanism were a nearly inseparable phenomenon.[15]

In classical Greek iconography, there are also representations of Heracles clasping hands with various mythical figures.[16] One sixth-century vase shows him sharing the *dexiōsis* with Pholos, the centaur; another with Hermes; another with Athena; and yet another with a mythical king, possibly Zeus himself.[17]

In the Hellenistic period, Heracles became allegorized as the soul; his myth served to illustrate the trials and victories of the soul.[18] In the Igel monument, a remarkable piece of funerary art with Mithraic motifs,[19] Heracles as soul is combined with the *dexiōsis* motif; the handclasp is used to draw Heracles into heaven. The hero is in the *quadriga* (chariot), ascending into heaven; Athena emerges from a cloud and extends to him "a hand of succor,"[20] which Heracles grasps. This apotheosis scene "portrays the Heroisation of the personage laid in the tomb, or, in a more general fashion, the destiny of the soul, which, with the help of heavenly powers, reaches the abode of the blessed,"[21] according to Cumont. While the handclasp often expresses complete equality (as in the marriage handclasp, one of the most unvarying of Roman marriage rituals, and as in the handclasp used for treaty),[22] here it expresses salvation, the saving and the saved. It is diagonal, not level; Heracles reaches up, Athena reaches down. The goddess will draw the mortal up into heaven (cf. figs. 3 and 4). However, the sense of equality is not entirely gone: Heracles enters heaven by having a goddess descend to his level; he has come up to her level, almost. The clasp here symbolizes entrance, liminality, as it did in the *inductio* of Vibia, but it also emphasizes apotheosis, the entrance into the divine type of life, as it simultaneously suggests the condescension of the god that makes the apotheosis possible. This *dexiōsis* of salvation is suggested in a prayer to Isis: "Thou stretchest forth thy right hand of salvation," speaks the worshipper to the goddess.[23] The human must return the right hand to complete the manual *symbolon*.

Fig. 3. Abel and Melchizedek (mosaic) in St. Vital, Ravenna, Italy (sixth century A.D.). Courtesy of John W. Welch

The frescoes of the underground basilica on the Via Praenestina show "Apollo, the God of Light . . . holding out his hand graciously to receive the soul after passing through the last ordeal, and Victory is proffering the crown."[24]

The marriage handclasp—which represents uniting, love, equality, sexuality, and treaty between husband and wife as marriage begins[25]—is seen on a mythological and allegorical level in a Roman funerary urn portraying the marriage of Dionysos and Ariadne. The god and his wife clasp hands, standing side by side, while, above them, two overshadowing grapevines intertwine their leaves, a charming parallel expression of the *symbolon* theme. Beside them, Hypnos ("Sleep") approaches "to permit them to attain Olympus."[26] In Hellenistic times, Ariadne came to symbolize the soul who is united to deity; the central scene of the Villa of the Mysteries is a portrayal of Ariadne with Dionysos.[27]

Fig. 4. Melchizedek
(mosaic) in St.
Apollonaire, in Classe,
Ravenna, Italy (sixth
century A.D.). Courtesy
of John W. Welch

The handclasp was an important initiatory gesture in
the Mithraic mysteries. Iconography shows Mithras (himself often equated with the sun) clasping hands with Sol,
the Sun, in a gesture of agreement, friendship, and reconciliation (at one time there was an antagonism between
the two).[28] In one relief,[29] Mithra and Sol clasp hands over
an altar, while a spit of meat pecked at by a raven is directly
above the union of the hands. Vermaseren interprets this
as a treaty before "the divine meal which itself took place
before their ascent to heaven in the chariot of the sun."[30]
This is the paradigm for the initiate so he "himself can
devoutly hope for his own return to the eternal sunlight."[31]
Here the *dextrarum iunctio* represents precisely reunion and
reconciliation, as well as unity, equality, friendship between gods. However, now there is no environment of
threshold or entrance; it rather precedes the road to the
desired entrance as a preliminary rite.[32] Still, in actual Mith-

raic rite, there is some evidence that the handclasp came at the end of the initiation. According to Vermaseren,

> At a given moment, after the novice had been submitted to certain purification rites and had gone through a time of fasting and abstinence, he reached the end of his ordeals. He had sworn the oath, been branded on hands or forehead and had pressed the Father's right hand. . . . The joining of the right hands (*dexiōsis*) promoted the initiates to *sundexioi* with the Father.[33]

A builder of a Mithraeum writes that he made the temple so that "the *syndexi* might celebrate their vows with joy for eternity (*ut possint syndexi hilares celebrare vota per aevum*)."[34] A verbal *symbolon* of Firmicus uses the word: "Novice of the bull-theft, initiate (*sundexie*) of the proud Father."[35] *Sundexios* is a common word on the walls of the Dura Mithraeum.[36] In a Mithraeum at Capus, Eros (love) holds Psyche (soul) by the left hand.[37]

The handclasp continued in early Christian ritual, both gnostic and "orthodox." According to Galatians 2:9, "the right hand of fellowship" (*dexias koinōnias didonai tini*) is given "as a sign of friendship and trust,"[38] though this does not necessarily suggest ritual practice, such as we found in the Sabazian and Mithraic mysteries. The handclasp as marriage rite, however, continued in Christian surroundings.[39] The salvific handclasp is nearly the trademark of the iconography of Christ's postcrucifixion descent into Hades.[40] One of the most frequent scenes in this tradition is that of Christ grasping the hands of Adam and Eve to lift them up out of hell and to resurrect them. While sometimes he grasps their wrists, which emphasizes even more than the diagonal *dexiōsis* their helplessness and lack of equality,[41] in other depictions he lifts them with a true *dextrarum iunctio*.[42] The fifth-century *Gospel of Nicodemus*[43] describes a true handclasp: "And the Lord . . . took the right hand of Adam and went up out of hell (*tenens dexteram Adae ascendit ab inferis*), and all the saints followed him. . . . He went therefore into paradise holding our forefather by the hand, and delivered him, and all the righteous, unto Michael the archangel."[44] Here the *dexiōsis* starts the ascent, continues it, and ends it on the threshold of paradise. A similar handclasp is used in the apocalyptic *1 Enoch*: "And the angel Michael, . . . seizing me by my right hand and lifting me up, led me out into all the secrets of mercy; and he showed me all the secrets of righteousness."[45]

In some early Christian depictions of the Ascension of Christ, Christ himself, approaching heaven, clasps the hand of God, which descends from a stylized upper corner of the composition.[46] This symbolism is arresting: Christ, the Savior, reaches up to be saved, and must be drawn, or at least helped, up into heaven. Perhaps there is a residual emphasis on the unity and equality of the saving handclasp here, but it is nevertheless a saving, diagonal clasp.

All these examples come from "orthodox" Christianity;[47] on an iconographic level at least they are clear continuations of motifs such as we have seen in mystery religions. We may assume that there were some ritual continuities too; we know there were in the use of the *dexiōsis* in marriage rite.[48] The handclasp was also used in Gnostic ritual, and is especially prominent in Manichaean myth and rite. In the myth of the fall and return of the Primeval Man, he is sent forth from the Father of Greatness and the Mother of Life to do battle with the Prince of Darkness (matter); temporarily overcome by darkness, he sends up a prayer to his former home. The Father creates and sends forth the Living Spirit to rescue him:

> The Living Spirit, who was accompanied by the Mother of Life, extended his right hand to Primeval Man. The latter seized it and thus was drawn up out of the depths of the world of darkness. Together with the

Mother of Life and the Living Spirit he rose up and up, soared like victorious light out of darkness, till he was returned to the paradise of light, his celestial home, where his kin awaited him.[49]

As in the Mithraic scenario and the *Gospel of Nicodemus*, the handclasp is the beginning of salvation and ascent. However, Manichaeism adds a new touch to the picture, a protological *dexiōsis*: "The first 'right hand' is that which the Mother of Life gave to Primal Man when he was about to go forth to the war. . . . The second 'right hand' is that which the Living Spirit gave to Primal Man when he led him up out of the war," according to the *Kephalaia*. This second 'right hand' is the *aition* for the Manichaean ritual handclasp: "In the image of the mystery of that right hand originated the right hand that is in use among men in giving it to one another."[50] "On that account the Manichaeans when meeting one another grasp right hands in sign that they themselves are of those saved from the Darkness," says the *Acta Archelai*.[51] According to Jonas, the handclasp as a form of salutation spread through Europe as a result of Christian or Manichaean influences; previously it had been used only for conclusion of contracts.[52]

Other Gnostics also used the handclasp ritually. According to Lidzbarski, the central concept of Mandaean religion is "truth," *kusta*; this word is also used to refer to the bond which unites the faithful, and the handshake of brotherhood. In Mandaean baptism, the priest gives the *kusta* to the initiate standing in water, then crowns him with a wreath of myrtle. Afterwards, the *kusta* is repeated twice. This is similar in function to the Mithraic handclasp that made one an initiate.[53]

Thus the ritual handclasp in the mysteries and early Christianity[54] was linked with concepts of equality, friendship, agreement, liminality, entrance, marriage, sexuality, salvation, starting the path of initiation, ending the path of initiation, resurrection, forgiveness, reconciliation, communion of man with man, of human with god, of god with god,[55] and apotheosis.

The Ritual Embrace

In *Rudens* and *Ion*, the correct telling of the tokens, bringing about the recognition, is followed by the physical reunion of the two long-separated parties. There is a loving paternal or maternal embrace. This embrace is not left to the discretion of the actors, for the dramatist is careful to insert clear markers of the act in his dialogue. This is the final *symbolon* of the drama, the complete human token; like the handclasp—which is, as it were, a preparatory embrace, a symbol of this reunion [56]—it is the final fusion of identity in the drama, two long separate beings forming a renewed unity, re-creating an identity that had been fragmented and lost. It would seem to be overtly sexual but for the powerful filial maternal/paternal feelings it expresses. The lost child, who until this moment had been a cast-off foundling of low social status, discovers that he (in the case of *Ion*) is the son of a queen and the god of light; that she (in the case of Palaestra) is an authentic Athenian citizen and need no longer be a slave-prostitute.[57] The parents, on the other hand, are no longer childless, without heir. There is an emotional exaltation resulting from these factors that is found even in the fragmented ending of the *Epitrepontes*. The embrace is the primary emblem of this exaltation, and the sign of the child's new status, his re-adoption by his parent.

The first embrace in *Ion* takes place when Creusa recognizes Ion's ark. She rushes from the altar to embrace Ion and the tokens; as Ion does not trust her, this embrace is entirely maternal, and is not reciprocated. *Creusa*: "Slay me, slay me. But I will cling [*anthexomai*] to this ark and to you and to those things of yours that are hidden in it"

(1404). The reciprocal embrace takes place after the telling
of the tokens:

> *Ion*: My own dear mother! O the joy of seeing you,
> the joy of kissing your joyous face! [lit., "gladly I have
> fallen toward your glad cheeks": *asmenos . . . pros as-
> menas peptōka sas parēidas.*]
>
> *Creusa*: O my child, O light brighter than the sun to
> your mother (the god will understand), I hold you in
> my arms. My treasure, I never hoped for this. I thought
> you had gone to your long home with Persephone and
> the shades below.
>
> *Ion*: Ah, dearest mother, your arms are around me
> (*en kheroin sethen . . . phantazomai*)! You see me alive that
> was dead.
>
> *Creusa*: Ah, ye expanses of brilliant ether! What
> words, what cry shall I utter? Whence came this joy, this
> unexpected joy? How did I attain this rapture? . . . My
> child, not without tears was your birth; with lamenta-
> tions were you separated from your mother's arms.
> Now, cheek to cheek [*geneiasin para sethen*, lit., by your
> cheeks], I breathe again; happiness, blissful happiness
> has come to me (1437-60).

In the *Rudens*, there are separate embraces with both
the father and mother (though she is offstage). After Palaestra correctly identifies the last token, her father embraces her:

> *Daemones*: She is, she certainly is! I can't keep from
> hugging her any longer! (*contineri quin complectar non
> queo!*) Ah, my own daughter! I am the father that reared
> you! I am Daemones myself, and look, inside here is
> your mother, Daedalis!
>
> *Palaestra*: Ah, dear father, father unhoped for!
>
> *Daemones*: Ah, the joy of having you in my arms [*ut
> te amplector libens* — lit., "how gladly I embrace you"]. . . .
> Come, let's go to your mother, my child. She can make
> further inquiries and test you better, having had more
> to do with you and knowing more about those tokens

of yours (1172-80). [Later:] What's this I see? My wife, arms around her daughter's neck, clinging to her! (*uxor complexa collo retinet filiam!*) Comes precious near being a silly nuisance, all her fondling! Wife! Better call a halt on that kissing (*osculando*—the kiss is naturally closely associated with the embrace)[58] some time (1202-5).

There is some evidence for the presence of a ritual embrace in mystery cult. The return of Persephone from the underworld and her reunion with her mother is obviously the emotional climax of the *Hymn to Demeter*. Unfortunately, the reunion scene is fragmentary, but enough survives to be suggestive: "And when Demeter saw them, she rushed forth as does a Maenad down some thick-wooded mountain, while Persephone on the other side . . . of her mother, . . . and leaped down to run . . . " (damaged from 387-400). However, that an embrace took place is made certain by a following passage: "So did they then, with hearts at one [*homophrona thumon ekhousai*—lit., "having a one-minded soul"; the embrace is merely the outward token of the inward meshing of souls] greatly cheer each the other's soul and spirit with many an embrace [*amphagapazomenai*]: their hearts had relief from the griefs while each took and gave back joyousness [*gēthosunas d' edekhonto par' allēlōn edidon te*]" (434-37). Now Demeter causes crops to grow, teaches her mysteries to the Eleusinians, and she and her daughter ascend to heaven. "But when the bright goddess had taught them all, they went to Olympus to the gathering of the other gods. And there they dwell beside Zeus who delights in thunder, awful and reverend goddesses" (483-85).

How much of this was reflected in Eleusinian ritual is uncertain and debated. However, there seems to be good evidence that the drama of Demeter and Persephone was performed in the mysteries. Mylonas writes,

> There can be little doubt that at least part of the *drōmena* [the "things done," the ritual performance] was

a sacred pageant, the presentation of the story of Demeter and Persephone. Such a pageant, accompanied
with music, singing, and measured steps . . . could
have been very impressive and conducive of those feelings of awe, sorrow, despair, and joy which could, as
in tragedy, bring about a katharsis.[59]

"The initiates probably took a certain part in the *drō-
mena* . . . unlike the people in the theater . . . and thus
could share more fully the experiences of the Goddess."[60]
The best evidence for this, which also isolates the reunion
of Persephone and Demeter as the high point of the mysteries, is from Lactantius: "In the Mysteries of Demeter all
night long with torches kindled they seek for Persephone
and when she is found, the whole ritual closes with thanksgiving and the tossing of torches."[61] According to Clement,
"Demeter and Kore have come to be the subject of a mystic
drama (*drama*), and Eleusis celebrates with torches the ab-
duction of the daughter and the sorrowful wanderings of
the mother."[62] Nilsson writes:

> The reuniting of the Mother and the Maid was the
> kernel of the myth. Judging from the nature of the fes-
> tival, it must likewise have been the kernel of the Eleu-
> sinian Mysteries. . . . Demeter is rightly called the *mater
> dolorosa* of Greek religion. To this heartbreaking sorrow,
> the reunion of mother and daughter provided a joyful
> contrast, rousing the *mystae* to exultation and moving
> their minds with the deepest emotions.[63]

A late piece of evidence, questionable by itself, adds probability to the idea of ritual embrace at Eleusis. Lucian writes
that when the charlatan Alexander carried out rites somewhat modeled on the Eleusinian mysteries, a culminating
act was an embrace and a kiss. Lucian satirizes Alexander's
weakness for young, beautiful initiates; still, this may have
been a plausible reflection of Eleusinian practices.[64]
    There is some evidence for a mystic embrace in the

Orphic and Dionysiac mysteries. Guthrie thinks it probable
that a dramatic presentation of Demeter and Persephone
took place in Orphic rite, as at Eleusis.[65] As "Orphism" is
closely connected to the Pythagoreans, we may also recall
the Pythagorean custom of combining the handclasp and
embrace to accompany reconciliation, brotherly love.[66] In
the fourth "Orphic" gold plate, the soul, listing his qualifications, says, "I have sunk beneath the bosom of the
Mistress, the Queen of the Underworld"[67] (*despoinas d' hupo
kolpon edun*). This phrase has been variously interpreted;
according to one of the more likely interpretations it refers
to an adoption by the god. "It finds a close parallel in a
certain form of adoption-ritual, practised both on secular
occasions and in mystery-religions," writes Guthrie.[68]
Rohde writes that the phrase means, "I seek (as *hiketēs*
[suppliant]) the protection of her maternal bosom (or lap)."

> It would certainly be attractive to take this . . . as
> referring to a symbolical act, corresponding to the cer-
> emony in which . . . the adoption of a boy, his reception
> into a new *genos* [clan] was symbolically repre-
> sented. . . . But such a symbolical proceeding, if it was
> to bring about the association of the *mystēs* [initiate] with
> the goddess, must have taken place already in the *orgia*
> [rites] once held on earth. . . . Thus the fully initiated is
> *gennētēs* [kinsman] of the divine family, *kata tēn poiēsin*
> [according to adoption].[69]

The goddess embracing an infant, holding him to her
bosom, plays an important part in the *Hymn to Demeter*,
as Demeter becomes the nurse of Demophoon and tries to
make him immortal. "Gladly will I take the boy to my
breast (*hupodexomai*),[70] as you bid me, and will nurse him,"
says Demeter to Metaneira, the mother (226). "She took
the child in her fragrant bosom (*thuōdeï dexato kolpōi*) with
her divine hands. . . . So the goddess nursed in the palace
Demophoon" (231-35). Richardson, at line 232, concludes
that the whole sequence with Demophoon is "an adoption

ritual." "These similarities may be explained by the character of the mystic initiation as a rite of adoption, with which the idea of purification is also associated."[71] The initiate stands in the same relationship to the Eleusinian goddesses as Demophoon to Demeter, as is suggested by Sophocles: "The torch-lit shores, where the Potniai are nurses (tithēnountai) of the dread rites for mortals."[72] Richardson judges this rite to be connected with the "central significance of the Mysteries" and not merely part of a preliminary purification rite.[73] Thus in the "Orphic" gold plates, and in the Eleusinian cult, being drawn to the breast of the goddess, being adopted by her, is probably a rite of great importance. The relevance of this sort of adoptive ritual—defined by the specific act of embracing—to recognition drama should be clear. In recognition drama, the embrace is the immediate seal of recognition and love when the identity of the tested party has been proved. This is not exactly the same as adoption; it is more a re-adoption.

Just as we have seen Dionysos and Ariadne united by the *dextrarum iunctio*, there is also a pictorial tradition that portrays them embracing. A famous depiction of this embrace in the Villa of the Mysteries seems to be the focal point of whatever ritual acts are portrayed on those walls: "Occupying the center of the rear wall and directly opposite the main entrance, is the scene that is the culminating point of the whole series, the union of Dionysos and Ariadne."[74] "The central figure on this wall, and therewith of the whole fresco, was Ariadne. She is seated, erect and high, in its very center, the loving god in her lap. Dionysus, the woman's god, in the arms of the mortal woman whom his love made into a goddess."[75] A vase-painting of Ariadne and Dionysos also shows the embrace.[76] Again the embrace may seem overtly sexual, but Hellenistic allegory made the sexuality merely an image for divine-human union: "The myth of the god rescuing Ariadne, who had been cruelly abandoned on the island of Naxos, was understood to mean that the human soul, like the Cretan princess, could find immortal life and happiness in loving arms of the divine."[77] (And as we saw Eros and Psyche ["love" and "soul"] bound by the *dextrarum iunctio*, so we often see them bound by the embrace and kiss.[78] Thus the marriage of Dionysos and Ariadne, represented by the embrace, expressed many nuances of emotion and meaning: the *unio mystica*, human with god, which was the goal of initiation; the joy of the divine life; love; love creating apotheosis.

The kiss of peace of the New Testament apparently always included the embrace.[79] Sometimes the kiss and the embrace were both specified: Cyprian writes, "Holding to this faith, and meditating thereon day and night, let us too aspire to God with all our heart, disdaining the present and thinking only on the things that are to be, the fruition of the eternal kingdom, the embrace and the kiss of the Lord [*complexum et osculum Domini*], the vision of God."[80] A specific example appears in Luke 15:20: "And he arose, and came to his father. But when he was yet a great way off, his father saw him, and had compassion, and ran, and fell on his neck, and kissed him." Sometimes the kiss disappeared, leaving only the embrace: "The kiss or *pax* was eventually reduced to a mild embrace occasionally accompanied by a touching of the cheeks."[81] John Chrysostom writes of the holy kiss (1 Corinthians 16:20) exchanged by Christians that it "unites and makes one body."[82] He tells us that when we exchange the kiss as a symbol of love with our neighbors the Lord wants our souls to kiss and our hearts to embrace.[83] The kiss was used in baptismal initiation and in the mass (cf. fig. 5).[84]

As we move from mystery religion to Christianity to Gnostic Christianity, we again find strong parallels to the sacral paternal/maternal embrace in Manichaeism. When the Primeval Man returns to the heavenly world after his sojourn and combat in darkness, "The mother caught and

Fig. 5. Peter and Paul embrace and exchange the kiss of peace; mosaic in Palatin Chapel, Palermo, Italy. Nicholas J. Perella, *The Kiss Sacred and Profane* (Berkeley: University of California Press, 1969), fig. 10

kissed him: 'Thou art come again, exiled son. Hurry and pass into the light, for thy kind for thee greatly are longing.' " Widengren remarks on the vividness of this scene, "when the mother embraces and kisses him, the only son, whom she thought lost forever."[85] Since before his descent to darkness, matter, and the world, the Primeval Man (lit., the First Man) lived in the presence of the divine father and mother, this event is a true *re*cognition — an only son thought lost forever (cf. *Ion*) has unexpectedly returned from seeming death. And to make the embrace exactly symmetrical (as was the Manichaean handclasp, though in that case different parties, the Mother and the Spirit, deliver it), another Manichaean text portrays the mother embracing the son as he departs from the heavenly home: "The first embrace (*aspasmos*: greeting, embrace;

Böhlig translates "Kuß") is that which the Mother of Life gave to the First Man as he separated himself from her in order to come down to earth to the testing (*agōn*). Also, all the gods and angels . . . embraced him on that occasion. . . . Also, all who were to be of the Church . . . embraced (*aspazein*) him with love."[86] Thus the eschatological embrace is the reuniting of the protological embrace, after the painful parting, which is, from the point of view of the mother, a death. But the divine-human *symbolon* regains its original identity; there is an *anagnōrisis*, a recognition, a knowing again. The embrace is the renewed outward token reflecting the renewed inward token of knowledge and love.[87]

Notes

1. Todd M. Compton, "The Whole Token: Mystery Symbolism in Classical Recognition Drama," *Epoché* 13 (1985): 1-81.

2. For *symbola* in recognition, see *Ion* 1386; for *symbola* in mystery cult, see Clement of Alexandria, *Protrepticus* II, 15, 19, in *PG* 8:80, 88; cf. Liddell, Scott, and Jones, *Greek-English Lexicon*, s.v. *symbolon*, III, 5.

3. Ibid. Cf. also Gabriel Herman, *Ritualised Friendship and the Greek City* (Cambridge: Cambridge University Press, 1988), 62-67; Philippe Gauthier, *Symbola, Le étrangers et la justice dans les cités grecques* (Nancy: Université de Nancy, 1972), 62-66.

4. Yeats writes, in "Crazy Jane Talks with the Bishop," "Nothing can be sole or whole / That has not been rent." Ann Bergren writes, "What the *symbolon* symbolizes is a liason between two parts, a 'wholeness' or 'identity' constituted by the 'fault' of difference, like James' 'golden bowl'," "Allegorizing Winged Words: Simile and Symbolization in *Odyssey* V," *Classical World* 74 (1980): 109-23 (112).

5. Cf., however, Aeschylus' *Choephori*, in which Electra sees a cut-off piece of hair on Agamemnon's tomb (167), then later compares it with the shorn spot on Orestes' head (205-10).

6. Herman, *Ritualised Friendship*, 64.

7. An early example is Homer, *Odyssey* 3.36; cf. Livy, I, 58, 7; I, 21, 4; I, 41, 2. For the handclasp generally: Gerhard Neumann, *Gesten und Gebärden in der griechischen Kunst* (Berlin: de Gruyter, 1965), 49-58, cf. 59-65; Karl Sittl, *Die Gebärden der Griechen und Römer* (Leipzig: Teubner, 1890), 27-32, 290, 335-36, cf. 329; Louis Reekmans,

"La '*dextrarum iunctio*' dans l'iconographie," *Bulletin de l'Institut historique belge de Rome* 31 (1958): 23-95; B. Kötting, "*Dextrarum iunctio*," in Theodor Klauser et al., eds., *Reallexikon für Antike und Christentum* (Stuttgart: Hiersemann, 1950-88), 3:881-88; Richard Brilliant, *Gesture and Rank in Roman Art* (New Haven, CT: The Academy, 1963), 18-21; Franz Cumont, "The Dura Mithraeum," in John R. Hinnells, ed., *Mithraic Studies*, 2 vols. (Manchester: Manchester University Press, 1975), 1:196-98; Herman, *Ritualised Friendship*, 50-54, 64.

8. Walter Burkert, *Homo Necans* (Berkeley: University of California Press, 1983), 269, figs. 8-9; George Mylonas, *Eleusis and the Eleusinian Mysteries* (Princeton, NJ: Princeton University Press, 1961), 205-7, 243-44, fig. 83 (cf. fig. 84, the Torre Nova Sarcophagus); Carl Kerényi, *Eleusis, Archetypal Image of Mother and Daughter* (New York: Bollingen/Pantheon, 1967), 54-59.

9. See Erwin R. Goodenough, *Jewish Symbols in the Greco-Roman Period*, 13 vols. (New York: Bollingen/Pantheon, 1953-58), vol. 3, figs. 839, 842; 2:45-50; Franz Cumont, *Recherches sur la symbolisme funéraire des Romains* (Paris: Geuthner, 1942), 418, n. 1.

10. Henri Leclerq, "Sabazios," in *Dictionnaire d'archéologie chrétienne et de liturgie*, 15 vols. (Paris: Libraire Letouzey, 1924-53), 15:213. As to whether this can be used as evidence for earlier mystery, cf. Richard Seaford, "Dionysiac Drama and the Dionysiac Mysteries," *Classical Quarterly* 31 (1981): 252, on the essential conservatism of the mysteries.

11. For one example among, I believe, thousands, see Brilliant, *Gesture and Rank*, 19, figs. 1.16, 1.19.

12. Ibid., 20-21.

13. Donna Kurtz and John Boardman, *Greek Burial Customs* (London: Thames and Hudson, 1971), 129.

14. Plutarch, *De Fraterno Amore* XVII, 488b-c, tr. Helmbold: "*prin ē ton hēlion dunai tas dexias embalontes allēlois kai aspasamenoi dieluonto.*" Cf. Nicholas J. Perella, *The Kiss Sacred and Profane* (Berkeley: University of California Press, 1969), 16, who draws a parallel with Paul's, "Let not the sun go down on your wrath" (Ephesians 4:26), because we are members of one body.

15. See Compton, "The Whole Token," 7, n. 25, for the close relationship of Orphics and Pythagoreans.

16. Neumann, *Gesten und Gebärden*, 54, fig. 25; 55, fig. 26 a-b.

17. Ibid., 50-51.

18. Eugénie Strong, *Apotheosis and After Life* (London: Constable, 1915), 201.

19. Cumont, *Symbolisme funéraire des Romains*, fig. 1.

20. Ibid., 174. Cf. Strong, *Apotheosis and After Life*, 222-32.

21. Cumont, *Symbolisme funéraire des Romains*, 174.

22. See, e.g., Kötting, "Dextrarum iunctio," passim, and Reekmans, "La 'dextrarum iunctio' dans l'iconographie romaine et paleochretienne," passim.

23. Samuel Angus, *The Mystery Religions and Christianity* (New York: University Books, 1966), 119. Cf. Hans P. L'Orange, *Studies on the Iconography of Cosmic Kingship in the Ancient World* (New Rochelle, NY: Caratzas, 1982), 139-41, on the "saving right hand." Julian the Apostate, *Contra Galilaeos* I, 200B, says that Aesculapius "extended his right hand of salvation [*sōtērion heautou dexian*] to all the earth." Procopius, *De Bello Persico* II, 13, 8-9, calls the right hand the "token of salvation," *sōtērias symbolon*. See n. 46 below.

24. Angus, *Mystery Religions*, 141-42.

25. Reekmans, "La 'dextrarum iunctio' dans l'iconographie romaine et paleochrétienne," figs. 34-37, 32-33, 4-10. Cf. Ernest Crawley, *The Mystic Rose*, revised and enlarged by Theodore Besterman, 2 vols. in one (London: Methuen, 1927), 2:118-19.

26. Cumont, *Symbolisme funéraire des Romains*, 412, fig. 84.

27. Martin P. Nilsson, *The Dionysiac Mysteries of the Hellenistic and Roman Age* (New York: Arno, 1975), 71, fig. 10d; John Ferguson, "The Mystery Religions," in Richard Cavendish, ed., *Myth: An Illustrated Encyclopedia* (New York: Marshall Cavendish, 1980), 144-59 (149). K. Kerényi, *Dionysos: Archetypal Image of an Indestructible Life*, tr. R. Manheim (Princeton, NJ: Princeton University Press, 1976), 124-25. Cf. Burkert, *Homo Necans*, 233, n. 12, for Dionysos and Ariadne; 271, n. 22. Cf. n. 74 below.

28. M. J. Vermaseren, *Mithras: The Secret God*, tr. Therese and Vincent Megaw (London: Chatto and Windus, 1963), 98; figs. 32-33.

29. Ibid., 97, fig. 33.

30. Ibid.; cf. Leroy A. Campbell, *Mithraic Iconography and Ideology* (Leiden: Brill, 1968), 389. In the Mithraic mysteries, "pieces of the bull's flesh are pierced by spits and held above an altar to suggest the piercing of the bodies of the contracting parties likewise if they break the pledge."

31. Vermaseren, *Mithras: The Secret God*, 98.

32. Ibid.

33. This is, however, problematical. To become a *sundexios* was both a final step of initiation, and the beginning of it. Cf. Vermaseren, *Mithras: The Secret God*, 136-37, and E. D. Francis, "Mithraic Graffiti from Dura-Europos," in Hinnells, *Mithraic Studies*, 2:438-39:

"The term *sundexios* does not appear, as some have suggested, to be restricted to a specific grade. The *iunctio dextrarum* may have constituted the particular act by which one became *sundexios* or the one through which members continued to affirm their corporate bond."

34. Vermaseren, *Mithras: The Secret God*, 136-37.

35. Ibid.; Cumont, *Symbolisme funéraire des Romains*, 196.

36. Ibid.

37. Angus, *The Mystery Religions and Christianity*, 142.

38. Walter Bauer, *A Greek-English Lexicon of the New Testament*, tr. and adapted by William Arndt and F. Gingrich (Chicago/London: University of Chicago Press, 1979), s.v. *dexios*: 2a, 174, and s.v. *koinōnia*, ibid., 439. Cf. n. 14 above.

39. Reekmans, "La 'dextrarum iunctio' dans l'iconographie," figs. 32-37.

40. P. Verdier, "Descent of Christ into Hell," *New Catholic Encyclopedia* (New York: McGraw-Hill, 1967-79), 4:788-93, esp. 791, fig. 2-6.

41. See Neumann, *Gesten und Gebärden*, 59-65.

42. P. Verdier, "Descent of Christ into Hell," 791, fig. 5. See also F. Cabrol, "Descente du Christ aux enfers d'apres la liturgie," and A. De Meester, "Descente du Christ aux enfers dans les liturgies orientales," in *Dictionnaire d'archéologie chrétienne et de liturgie*, 682-96, and Friedrich Loofs, "Descent to Hades (Christ's)," in James Hastings, ed., *Encyclopedia of Religion and Ethics*, 13 vols. (New York: Scribners, 1928), 4:654-63.

43. M. R. James, *The Apocryphal New Testament* (Oxford: Clarendon, 1955), 95.

44. *Evangelium Nicodemi* (*Gospel of Nicodemus*) II, VII (XXIV), 1-2 (Tischendorf). There is much emphasis on Christ's saving hand: "And the Lord stretching forth his hand, said: Come unto me, all ye my saints which bear mine image and my likeness. . . . And the Lord holding the right hand of Adam, said unto him: Peace be unto thee with all thy children that are my righteous ones. . . . And the Lord stretched forth his hand and made the sign of the cross over Adam and over his saints, and he took the right hand of Adam and went up out of hell. . . . Then did holy David cry aloud and say: Sing unto the Lord a new song, for he hath done marvellous things. His right hand hath wrought salvation for him and his holy arm," James, *The Apocryphal New Testament*, 137-39. Cf. n. 23 above.

45. *1 Enoch* 71:3, in James H. Charlesworth, ed., *The Old Testament Pseudepigrapha*, 2 vols. (New York: Doubleday, 1983), 1:49.

46. See *Dictionnaire d'archéologie chrétienne et de liturgie* 1:2929-30, A (988) and B (989); cf. Cumont, *Symbolisme funéraire des Romains*, figs. 1, 2; also Gertrud Schiller, *Ikonographie der christlichen Kunst*, 4 vols. (Gütersloh: Gütersloher Verlagshaus, 1971), 3:140-65, figs. 443-521. For the hand of God alone extending from the cloud, see *Dictionnaire d'archéologie chrétienne et de liturgie* 10:1208. David Seely, "The Winged Sun Disk, the Hand of God and the Cloud: Symbols of the Presence of God and the Transfiguration," unpublished paper, 1983, 14-17. Goodenough, *Jewish Symbols in the Greco-Roman Period*, 1:247, n. 481.

47. By which I simply mean non-Gnostic; this does not do justice to the complexity of early Christianity. Cf. bibliography in my foreword to Hugh Nibley, *Mormonism and Early Christianity*, vol. 4, *The Collected Works of Hugh Nibley* (Salt Lake City: Deseret Book and F.A.R.M.S., 1987), xii, n. 8.

48. It is difficult to assess a statement such as is found in Minucius Felix, *Octavius* 9 (of Christians): "They know themselves by hidden *notae* [i.e., tokens, marks, signs; C. T. Lewis and C. Short, *A Latin Dictionary* (Oxford: Clarendon, 1890), s.v.] and *insignia* [i.e., signals, tokens, badges, insignia; Lewis and Short, *A Latin Dictionary*, s.v.] and love [those whom] they have scarcely known previously. . . . They call themselves brother and sister without distinction." Minucius (a Christian writer, fl. ca. 200 A.D.) has these words spoken by an anti-Christian, and a very unreliable interpreter of Christianity. Cf. E. R. Dodds, *Pagan and Christian in an Age of Anxiety* (New York: Norton, 1965), 111, on reasons for Christian unpopularity: "They appeared, moreover, to constitute a secret society, whose members recognized each other by private signs, as gypsies do today, and were bound together by some mysterious intimacy." Cf. Origen, *Contra Celsum* I, 1, in *PG* 11:652. Dodds draws the parallel between Minucius's *notae et insignia* and Dionysiac secret signs (Plautus, *Miles* 10-16: "Give me the *signum* [i.e., sign, mark, token, password; Lewis and Short, *A Latin Dictionary*, s.v.], if you are of these Bacchantes"; Apuleius, *Apology* 56).

49. Geo Widengren, *Mani and Manichaeism*, tr. Charles Kessler (New York: Holt, Rinehart, and Winston, 1965), 52.

50. A. Böhlig and H. J. Polotsky, trs. and eds., *Kephalaia* I (Stuttgart: Kohlhammer, 1940), 38, lines 20-21; 40, lines 5-7, 16-19; Hans Jonas, *The Gnostic Religion* (Boston: Beacon Press, 1963), 223.

51. Ibid., 222-23.

52. Ibid., 223, n. 25.

53. Cumont, "The Dura Mithraeum," 198. In a Mandaean ac-

count of the ultimate reunion of God and man, Ayar (Ether, equated with the Father in the Mandaean Father/Mother dyad — "The Mother is 'the Left,' the Father 'the Right': the Mother, Earth, the Father, Sky," Ethel S. Drower, *The Secret Adam* [Oxford: Clarendon, 1960], 13, 14) greets the approaching spirits. "And when he said 'The Place of Safe-keeping which is set apart for the company of the Great [Life],' they all rose to their feet. And as they grasped Ayar's hand in covenant [*kusta*] he said, 'The Great Life hath stretched forth His right hand to thee! Put away passion from thy thought! Thy thought shall be filled with Ours and thy garment and our Garment shall be One." Ibid., 55; cf. 24, n. 2. Here the *dexiōsis* is used in the context of arrival, covenant, and the final mystic communion. The handclasp is also found in the round dance of apostles in the Gnostic *Acts of John* 94: "He bade us therefore make as it were a ring, holding one another's hands, and himself standing in the midst." James, *The Apocryphal New Testament*, 253. See also Ethel S. Drower, *Water into Wine* (London: Murray, 1956), 102-11, the most extensive analysis of the *kusta*. Cf. the *Second Apocalypse of James* 57:10-11, in James Robinson, ed., *The Nag Hammadi Library* (New York: Harper & Row, 1977), 253, with Christ speaking at a gate: "But now, stretch out your [hand]. Now, take hold of me."

54. Following is a brief overview of extraclassical examples: for the handclasp in an Indian marriage rite, see *Ramayana of Valmiki*, tr. Robert Goldman (Princeton, NJ: Princeton University Press, 1984), vol. I, Sarga 72, lines 17-22, p. 262; J. A. B. Van Buitenen, ed. and tr., *The Mahabharata* I (Chicago: University of Chicago Press, 1973), 106, 444, n. 43.1. Arnold Van Gennep, *The Rites of Passage* (Chicago: University of Chicago Press, 1960), 105, describes a Brahmanic initiation culminating in a ritual death, which involves a bath, a change of clothing, a change of name, and the handclasp. Van Gennep defines the handclasp as one of the rites of incorporation ("a formal entrance, a meal in common, an exchange of handclasps" [28] — almost a point-by-point description of the portrayal of Vibia's entrance into paradise. Cf. marriage rites of incorporation, 132: "tying parts of each other's clothing together; touching each other reciprocally some way, . . . joining hands, intertwining the fingers, kissing, embracing"); he further cites examples of its use in Africa (28) and in Slavic brotherhoods (29). The rite of incorporation is the uniting of the token, of course. One of the more curious examples of the handclasp I have found was used in a Finnish folk song; cf. *The Kalevala*, tr. Francis P. Magoun, Jr. (Cambridge, MA: Harvard University Press, 1963), 380-81, 374-75: this was always performed

in pairs, and the two singers (one of whom starts a verse, while the other completes it) sit, facing each other, and hold the other's hands. This is called "hand in hand" (*kasi kateen*), a deux, or "singing in turn" (380). So the verbal token and the manual token are used simultaneously. For more on the handclasp as a marriage rite, see Crawley, *The Mystic Rose*, 118-19. For the handclasp in ancient Mesopotamia, see S. Mayassis, *Mystères et initiations dans la préhistoire et protohistoire* (Athens: Bibliotheque d'archéologie orientale d'Athènes, 1961), 49-51. It is "the expression of familiarity, of equality, of sympathy, of love, of protection. 'You are compassionate (oh! Marduk). . . . I am weak. . . . You grasp the hand.' 'Oh, you who save he who is captive, who take by the hand he who has fallen.' " The dead man prays to be resurrected, to grasp the hand of god in the presence of the great gods (50). This is the same salvific resurrecting handclasp we have noted earlier. Mayassis should be balanced by Svend A. Pallis, *The Babylonian Akitu Festival* (Copenhagen: A. F. Host, 1926), 174-83. See also Angel Gonzales, "El Rito de la Alianza," *Estudios Biblicos* 24 (1965): 217-38 (222); Mircea Eliade, *The Myth of the Eternal Return*, tr. W. Trask (New York: Bollingen/Pantheon, 1954), 23; Geo Widengren, "Reflections on the Origin of the Mithraic Mysteries," 645-68 of *Perennitas: Studi in onore di Angelo Brelich* (Rome: Edizioni dell' Ateneo, 1980), 662; E. O. James, *Christian Myth and Ritual* (Gloucester, MA: P. Smith, 1973), 162-63. I am indebted to Esther Gilman for the following two references. Frank Waters, *The Book of the Hopi* (New York: Viking Press, 1963), 252, writes that Hopi tradition records the original meeting of Hopis and Spaniards, saying "that Tovar and his men were conducted to Oraibi. They were met by all the clan chiefs at Tawtoma, as prescribed by prophecy, where four lines of sacred meal were drawn. The Bear Clan leader stepped up to the barrier and extended his hand, palm up, to the leader of the white men. If he was indeed the true Pahana, the Hopis knew he would extend his own hand, palm down, and clasp the Bear Clan leader's hand to form the *nakwach*, the ancient symbol of brotherhood. Tovar instead curtly commanded one of his men to drop a gift into the Bear chief's hand, believing that the Indian wanted a present of some kind. Instantly all the Hopi chiefs knew that Pahana had forgotten the ancient agreement made between their peoples at the time of their separation. Nevertheless, the Spaniards were escorted up to Oraibi, fed and quartered, and the agreement explained to them. It was understood that when the two were finally reconciled, each would correct the other's laws and faults; they would live side by side and share in common all the riches of the land and join their faiths in one religion that would establish the truth of life in a spirit of universal brotherhood. The Spaniards did not understand, and having found no gold, they soon departed." [Cf. 151, 344: *nakwa* is a mark of identification; *nakwach* is a symbol of brotherhood.]

This story is particularly interesting to me because it illustrates vividly the theme, so important in both *Epitrepontes* and *Rudens*, of the token as a sacred sign of recognition versus the token merely as something to be sold for money. I also find evocative the idea of white and red man forming a primeval token that was to be reunited in an exchange of culture and peace.

For the handclasp in Masonry and in Masonry-influenced Mormon iconography, see Richard Poulsen, *The Pure Experience of Order* (Albuquerque: University of New Mexico Press, 1982), 45-55; and Allen D. Roberts, "Where Are the All-Seeing Eyes?" *Sunstone* (May-June 1979): 22-37.

55. See Brilliant, *Gesture and Rank*, 20, n. 68; Neumann, *Gesten und Gebärden*, 52.

56. Cf. Cumont, *Symbolisme funéraire des Romains*, 412, fig. 84; Cumont, "The Dura Mithraeum," 197, calls the *dexiōsis* a "mutual embrace." The handclasp often shaded into an embrace (as in Mithraic iconography, Vermaseren, *Mithras: The Secret God*, fig. 32), or was combined with an embrace—numerous references in Sittl, *Die Gebärden der Griechen und Römer*, 32-33. E.g., Apollonius Rhodius, *Argonautica* III, 258: "They clasped the hand [*dexioōnto-dexioomai*, "greet with the right hand, welcome," cf. Liddell, Scott, and Jones, *Greek-English Lexicon*, s.v.] and embraced (*amphagapason*) their mother when they saw her."

57. She is also enabled to marry her lover, Plesidippus, an Athenian, who had tried to save her from Labrax, a "procurer."

58. Numerous references in Sittl, *Die Gebärden der Griechen und Römer*, 37. There was often a combination of the *dexiōsis*, embrace, and kiss. Sophocles, *Oedipus at Colonus* (1130-31), "And stretch to me your right hand, lord, so that I may touch and kiss, if it is lawful, your head."

59. Mylonas, *Eleusis and the Eleusinian Mysteries*, 261-62.

60. Ibid.

61. Lactantius, *Divinae Institutiones, Epitome*, 23 (*Corpus Scriptorum Ecclesiasticorum Latinorum* 19:689).

62. Clement of Alexandria, *Protreptica* II, 12. Cf. Psellus of late antiquity, *De Operatione Daemonum*, 3, according to whom the Eleusinian mysteries enacted the story of Demeter and Persephone;

Aphrodite rising from the sea; the ritual marriage of Persephone; Demeter's birth-pangs; a "goat-legged mime" of Zeus raping Demeter; then rites of Dionysos; the cista with cakes; a "sounding cauldron" and a gong; something done by Baubo" — text and translation in Jane Harrison, *Prolegomena to the Study of Greek Religion* (Cambridge: Cambridge University Press, 1922), 568-69; cf. Psellos, *De Operatione Daemonum*, ed. J. Boissonade (Amsterdam: Hakkert, 1964), 39. This seems garbled and overly inclusive, but at the least it suggests a ritual drama; that general idea must have been plausible to the writer's audience. Despite these references, there is a school of Eleusinian interpretation that denies a drama there (e.g., Kerényi, *Dionysos: Archetypal Image of an Indestructible Life*, 26, 116-17). One of the complications of the Eleusinian mysteries is that there was a version of them that took place at Alexandria; a technique used to disallow evidence for Eleusis is to ascribe a text to Alexandria, as Kerényi does here. N. J. Richardson, *The Homeric Hymn to Demeter* (Oxford: Clarendon, 1974), 25, is not convinced that initiates participated in the drama, though he believes one took place. Cf. Burkert, *Homo Necans*, 275, 286.

63. Martin P. Nilsson, *Greek Folk Religion* (New York: Harper, 1961), 54. Cf. Ugo Bianchi, *The Greek Mysteries* (Leiden: Brill, 1976), pls. 20-22; Mylonas, *Eleusis and the Eleusinian Mysteries*, pl. 88.

64. Lucian, *Alexander the False Prophet*, 39. Cf. Perella, *The Kiss Sacred and Profane*, 22.

65. W. K. C. Guthrie, *Orpheus and Greek Religion*, 2nd rev. ed. (London: Methuen, 1952), 204.

66. See n. 14 above.

67. Guthrie, *Orpheus and Greek Religion*, 172-74.

68. Ibid., 182.

69. Edwin Rohde, *Psyche*, tr. W. B. Hillis (London: K. Paul, Trench, Trubner, 1925), 601-3; cf. also Hugo Hepding, *Attis* (Giessen: Ricker, 1903), 178-89; George Thomson, *Aeschylus and Athens*, 2nd ed. (London: Lawrence and Wishart, 1946), 438, n. 35; Albrecht Dieterich, *Eine Mithrasliturgie* (Stuttgart: Teubner, 1966), 134-35. Contra, for Eleusis, cf. Mylonas, *Eleusis and the Eleusinian Mysteries*, 296.

70. Notice the force of *hupo* ("beneath," cf. the fourth Orphic plate) and *dekhomai*, "receive"; cf. Seaford, "Dionysiac Drama and the Dionysiac Mysteries," 247, n. 146, on *dekhomai* as a ritual term.

71. Richardson, *The Homeric Hymn to Demeter*, 232.

72. Sophocles, *Oedipus at Colonus*, 1050-51. Cf. Pausanias, *Graeciae Descriptio* IX, 35, 5, where Demeter is the nurse (*trophon*) of Trophonius.

73. Richardson, *The Homeric Hymn to Demeter*, 236; cf. 231-36.

74. Nilsson, *The Dionysiac Mysteries* 75 and fig. 10d.

75. Gunther Zuntz, *Persephone* (Oxford: Clarendon, 1971), 178. See 178, n. 3, for other versions of this scene. Cf. G. Van Hoorn, "Dionysus et Ariadne," *Mnemosyne*, series 4, 12 (1959): 193-97; Strong, *Apotheosis and After Life*, 200, for Dionysos as parabolic; cf. n. 27 above.

76. Ferguson, "The Mystery Religions," 149.

77. Ibid.

78. Perella, *The Kiss Sacred and Profane*, figs. 7, 62.

79. Ibid., fig. 10.

80. *Epistula* VI, 4 (*Corpus Scriptorum Ecclesiasticorum Latinorum* 3:484); cf. Perella, *The Kiss Sacred and Profane*, 31. Cyprian also wrote, "Fully blessed are they, who among you, having walked by this path of glory, have departed from the world and . . . have already attained the embrace and the kiss of the Lord," *Epistula* XXXVII, 3 (*Corpus Scriptorum Ecclesiasticorum Latinorum* 3:578); cf. Perella, *The Kiss Sacred and Profane*, 34.

81. Perella, *The Kiss Sacred and Profane*, 278.

82. John Chrysostom, *Homily on the First Epistle to the Corinthians*, XLIV, 2, in *PG* 61:376.

83. John Chrysostom, *De Compunctione* I, 3, in *PG* 47:398: *ton apo tēs kardias aspasmon*.

84. Perella, *The Kiss Sacred and Profane*, 18, 278.

85. Widengren, *Mani and Manichaeism*, 53.

86. Böhlig and Polotsky, *Kephalaia* I, 38, lines 22-30. Cf. Perella, *The Kiss Sacred and Profane*, 20-21.

87. As with the handclasp, the ritual embrace has an important parallel in the ancient Near East, this time in Egypt. Since there was a direct close dependence of the Isaic mysteries on Egyptian ritual, we may even make the hypothesis that such an embrace may have been as important to the Isaic mysteries as it was to Egyptian ritual. See Franz Cumont, *Oriental Religions in Roman Paganism* (New York: Dover, 1956), 94: "Even under the Caesars the ancient ceremonies dating back to the first ages of Egypt were scrupulously performed. . . . This ritual and the attitude toward it found their way for the most part into the Latin temples of Isis and Serapis. This fact has long been ignored, but there can be no doubt about it." Cf. ibid., 74, "One fact remains, namely, that Serapis and Osiris were either immediately identified or else were identical from the beginning." See ibid., 79, for the diffusion of this mystery in Greece. It was, of course, very prevalent in Rome.

In Egypt the embrace was closely tied to kingship succession: it was a paternal, father/son interchange, and also a means of transferring divine power. The King and son were assimilated to the theological paradigm of Horus and Osiris, whose embrace of reunion after the death of Osiris they copied. However, in Egypt, the kingship aspect of the rite always seems dominant. In the Memphis Theology, whose original text dates from before 2,700 B.C., near the beginning of Egyptian history (cf. James Pritchard, ed., *Ancient Near Eastern Texts Relating to the Old Testament* [Princeton, NJ: Princeton University Press, 1955], 4), the text ends in an embrace. Osiris "entered the mysterious portals in the glory of the lords of eternity" following the sun. "He joined with the court and associated with the gods. . . . His son Horus appeared as King of Upper Egypt and appeared as King of Lower Egypt, in the embrace of [cf. Henri Frankfort, *Kingship and the Gods* (Chicago: University of Chicago Press, 1948), 32: "in the arms of"] his father Osiris, together with [ibid., "in the presence of"] the gods." Frankfort, ibid., 35, calls this a " 'mystic communion' between father and son at the moment of succession, a unity and continuity of divine power." In a *Pyramid Text*, an embrace with Atum is mentioned: "Thou art cool in the embrace of thy father, in the embrace of Atum. Atum, let this Unas ascend to thee; embrace him. He is thy son, of thy body, throughout eternity" (ibid., 122). Earlier in the same text, there is the maternal embrace: "The embrace of thy mother Nut receives thee" (ibid., 121, cf. 135). This text is also full of purification, apotheosis, and perfect tense of accomplishments, but, unlike the Orphic plates, it is expressed in the second person. "Thou hast 'become,' thou art high, thou hast been transfigured."

These texts, according to Frankfort, are mythological, with occasional references to ritual (ibid., 123). But in what he calls "the Mystery Play of the Succession," the whole drama (dating from 2,000 B.C., the "actual script of a play") is overtly ritualistic. An important element of the "mystery" is the embrace between the new king (assimilated to Horus) and Osiris (represented by a bronze 'stomacher' fitting over the chest and back). "The immortal parts of Osiris seem immanent in it, and the mutual embrace of Horus and Osiris is effected." This act is reciprocal: divine power flows from the old king to his successor and son; but the son strengthens the father as he prepares for the arduous journey in the after life. "The 'embrace' is no mere sign of affection, but a true fusion, a communion between two living spirits, *unio mystica*" (ibid., 134). When Ramses I is embraced by Ptah, the god endows him with the

splendor of divine life, symbolized by gold, "the flesh of the gods."
Ptah spoke: "When I see thee my heart rejoices and I receive thee
in an embrace of gold, I enfold thee with permanence, stability, and
satisfaction; I endow thee with health and joy of heart; I immerse
thee in rejoicing, joy, gladness of heart, and delights—forever"
(ibid., 135). For two more examples of the Egyptian embrace, see
ibid., 135.

There are hints of the ritual embrace in Mesopotamia, see Mayassis, *Mystères et initiations dans la préhistoire et protohistoire*, 447-48.
Gilgamesh says, "I have embraced [Enkidu] as one embraces a wife,
I have raised him and I have placed him on his feet." Mayassis
notes the presence of the embrace in the ritual nursing the king
receives from the representative of a goddess.

The embrace is one of the most common of Van Gennep's "rites
of incorporation," *Rites of Passage*, 29, 132, 133. For the embrace in
the Hellenistic novel, with its possible relevance to mystery there,
see Reinhold Merkelbach, *Roman und Mysterium in der Antike* (Munich: Beck, 1962), 85-86, and 345, s.v. *Umarmung*. Philo interestingly
gives the kiss/embrace a cosmological significance. In *Questions on
Exodus* II, 78, and II, 169, he writes that the things of creation meet
in "an embrace and kiss of concord." The divine Logos is "the
mediator and bond of all things, weaving together the parts of the
universe, including contrarieties." His force (love) causes inimical,
irreconcilable things to unite in an embrace and kiss of love (Perella,
The Kiss Sacred and Profane, 15).

25

Mars and Anna Perenna: March Gods and the Etruscan New Year in Archaic Rome

John Franklin Hall
Brigham Young University, Provo, Utah

In historical times, the Roman New Year began on January 1. It was a time for celebration, the first day of the month of Janus, whose function as a god of beginnings and endings was depicted in the iconography of two faces, one directed forward, the other to the rear.[1] Roman consuls and other government officials regularly took office on this first day of the year, and their inauguration, a detailed and complicated act of religious ritual, comprised an integral part of the ceremonies of the day.[2] Since our modern calendar has developed from that of ancient Rome, the day has not entirely lost its significance even in our time. Indeed, the festive spirit, the departure of the aged old year, and the advent of the infant New Year are reminiscent of the Roman celebration. Some of these customs, however, are not to be found in the celebration of January 1, but rather as a part of the ritual activities associated with March 15, a day more familiar to modern society as a time of foreboding and caution. This aura of doom derives, of course, from the occurrence on that day of what was to the ancient Romans a catastrophic event, the assassination of Julius Caesar.

Caesar's Julian calendar perpetuated the civil year of the late republic with its January commencement. This first-century B.C. calendar was far more complex than the modern calendar. A solar-based twelve-month calendar, it nevertheless recalled its lunar origins through the scheduling of religious ceremonies and festivals on special days, the Kalends, Nones, and Ides, which were established to correlate with phases of the moon. Moreover, the individual days of the year were designated in accordance with religious practice as *dies fasti, nefasti,* or *comitiales* (i.e., days without religious restriction, days with religious restriction, and days for holding public meetings). Accordingly, the celebration of religious rites, the conduct of public or private business, and the functioning of the daily life of the entire state, were required to accord with the prescriptions and prohibitions of the calendar.[3]

Of course, Caesar's calendar was not the first Roman calendar. As noted above, it was preceded at some time by an antique lunar calendar. Another calendar in use during most of the period of the Roman republic, like the later Julian calendar, seems to have been solar-based.[4] However, "the history of the Roman calendar prior to Caesar's reform is, due to confusion in the tradition, one of the most contested areas of ancient chronology."[5] Modern scholarship agrees on a single point: the year had not always begun with January! Ancient *testimonia* is precise in this matter. Macrobius, in his work on religious festivals, and Ovid, in a fanciful mythological commentary on the calendar year, both identify March as the first month of the ancient Roman year.[6] Moreover, the nomenclature of the numerically named Roman months — Quinctilis, Sextilis, September, October, November, December — confirms March as the first in the order of months.[7]

The great Roman historian Theodor Mommsen presumed that the change of the New Year from March to January was initiated by Caesar as a part of his calendar reform and took effect in the year 46 B.C.[8] However, with the 1929 discovery of the *Fasti Antiates Minores,* a January New Year is shown rather to belong to the pre-Julian calendar of the republic, the so-called calendar of Numa.[9] The implementation of the January New Year is dated by most scholars to 153 B.C., when consuls are known to have begun to assume office on the first day of January. Previously, consular inaugurations were conducted on March 15. Michels views the transposition to January 1 as merely an accommodation to a civil calendar long in place.[10] This makes sense especially when we remember that the consular inauguration was a religious ceremony and, as with religious rites in general, would have persisted in a format and with a date whose change would not necessarily have coincided with calendar reform. Accordingly, acceptance should be accorded Michels' hypothesis that the republican calendar, or calendar of Numa, was established by the *decemviri* of 450 B.C., who by a recorded *lex de intercalandis* transformed the lunar calendar of the Etruscan monarchy to the lunisolar calendar of the republic.[11] Whereas the Etruscan calendar comprised a year of twelve lunar months beginning in March and ending either with February or with an added intercalary period, the decemviral calendar began in January and ended in December.[12]

In turn, the Etruscan lunar calendar had replaced at Rome a primitive agricultural calendar of sorts, the so-called calendar of Romulus. While ancient literary tradition complicates matters by an entirely false association of Numa with the calendar, it was to Tarquin and the Etruscans that Roman antiquarians linked the inclusion of the months of January and February, as well as the organization of the monthly system of the Ides, the Etruscan high holy day of the month, which always occurred when the moon was full.[13] Similarly, the regularization of religious festivals and ceremonies on the calendar is to be attributed to Rome's Etruscan rulers and not to Numa. Rome's intricate system of religious festivals, accordingly, took its origin from the Etruscans, as did many of the city's individual religious festivals.[14]

The Etruscan year began with the first full moon after the spring equinox, the *itus Velcitna* or the Ides of the Etruscan month of Velcitanus, an important Etruscan underworld deity.[15] With Etruscan reformation of calendar and cult at Rome, the Roman year, reorganized after Etruscan models and patterns, commenced on the Ides of March. But why the Ides and not the Kalends? If the year began with March, would not March 1 be its initial day? This logic may appear obvious to us and even to the Romans of a later era, but not to an inhabitant of archaic Rome, Etruscan or Latin, for whom the forces of nature and their association with particular gods counted more than the numbering of days.

It must be remembered that in Etruscan Rome, as in Etruria, the Ides were particularly sacred days, which were holy to Juppiter every month. Further, the Ides were also sacred to the most important gods of that month, whose ceremonies were performed at the full moon, which in the lunar calendar of the Etruscans would consistently occur on the Ides. Thus, the day of greatest religious significance was the Ides, which occurred in the middle of the month, and not the Kalends, which occurred at the beginning. In the Etruscan lunar calendar, moreover, the length of the month itself was determined by counting forward and backward from the day of the full moon, the Ides. In a real sense, a month was simply a period of days before and after the full moon, that is, it was calculated from the Ides, which was the holiest day of the twenty-eight day period. The first day of the month was thus unimportant. It was merely the furthest day from the Ides, counting backwards. The Ides was the important day of the month and, through the process of intercalation, the Ides of March was arranged to fall on the first full moon following the vernal equinox. In this fashion it served as the New Year's Day.

It is not only the inauguration of consuls on March 15, a vestigial reminder of Etruscan office-taking at the year's beginning, but, more importantly, the particular religious ceremony connected to the Ides of March that reveals the day's prominence in the old calendar. The several epigraphic survivals of ancient *fasti* as well as Ovid's literary piece of the same name, both provide a clear record of the festivals of March.[16]

The first day of the month was best known for the celebration of the *Matronalia*, a major state festival honoring Juno Lucina. A *feria Martis* was also recorded as being celebrated to pay homage to the month's eponymous god by way of affixing fresh laurel wreaths to the *sacrarium*, a shrine of Mars in the courtyard of the official residence of Rome's ancient kings, the *regia*. Accompanying this rite was a performance of the leaping dance and sacred hymn of Mars's Salian priests, in connection with which the divinely wrought figure-eight shields, or *ancile* were displayed.[17] Neither ceremony seems to pertain in any fashion to the celebration of a New Year.[18]

March 14 provides the date for the next festival of the month. Some calendars describe it as the *Equirria* of Mars, others as the *Mamuralia*.[19] In his *Fasti*, Ovid mentions under the notation for this day only the *Equirria*, observing that horse races were run in the Campus Martius in honor of Mars.[20] On calendars of later date, however, the *Mamuralia* is regularly listed in place of the *Equirria*, leading some modern scholars to suppose it to be an alternate name for the same festival. According to one view, an informal but popular name made acceptable by long usage among the common people supplanted the less familiar term *Equirria* as the name of the ceremony. A contrasting view suggests that *Mamuralia* was itself the archaic and proper name for the festival, while *Equirria* was a colloquial usage. Those who assert the latter follow the testimony of a sixth-century A.D. scholar of Roman government, Laurentius Lydus, who defines the *Mamuralia* as the festival of a separate cult of Mamurius Veturius.[21] In either instance the term *Ma-*

muralia is believed to derive from the archaic name of Mars preserved in the Salian hymn — *Mamor* or *Marmar*.[22]

Ovid preserves the tradition that the name of this legendary figure was included in the Salian hymn, explaining that when the original *ancile* of Mars fell from the heavens, then king Numa Pompilius commissioned a smith by the name of Mamurius Veturius to make copies of the shield lest the original be stolen, thereby bringing a disaster on the state which could be averted only by the sacrificial death of citizens. Mamurius accomplished the task and asked as his only recompense that his name be included in the sacred hymn of Mars's Salian priests.[23] A different depiction of Mamurius Veturius is preserved by Servius and Festus, who note that Varro identified Mamurius as an old man driven from the city, not as might be expected on March 14, but rather the following day on the Ides of March when the Salian priests went throughout the city beating the sacred *ancile* with wooden rods and shouting *"mamure, mamure."*[24] Both traditions link Mamurius to the *ancile* and the Salii. In Ovid's tale, Mamurius, by the exercise of his metallic craft, prevented the death of citizens as atonement for a slight to the gods. His tale may also connect to the Varronian account in which Mamurius is seen as a scapegoat, driven out in order to carry with him the sins of the populace, thereby averting the gods' retribution upon the city and its inhabitants. Modern scholarship generally accepts Mamurius as an agent of expiation and as a personification of Mars in his guise as a seasonal agricultural deity. Mamurius is taken as the Latin adaptation of the archaic Italic *Marmar*, and Veturius as a proper name derives from the adjective *vetus*. The cult is linked to the New Year with literally "Old Man Mars" expelled on the first day of the year.[25]

The traditional March 14 date for the *Mamuralia* is discrepant with Varro's placing the expulsion of Mamurius on the Ides. As Wissowa observed, to celebrate any major festival on an even-numbered day violates Roman tradition. He suggested that the *Mamuralia* may have originally occurred on the Ides and later been moved to avoid conflict with the other events of the day, religious rites of both Juppiter and Anna Perenna, as well as the inauguration of magistrates and officials.[26]

On the Ides of March, Juppiter was honored with the customary rites and sacrifices performed in his honor on the Ides of each and every month. The major event of the day, however, was celebrated in honor of Anna Perenna. Ovid notes that in a grove just north of the Campus Martius, Rome's populace would retire, drain a cup of wine for each year they wished to live, and ultimately engage in amorous pursuits.[27] The poet confesses confusion at properly identifying the goddess whose cult was thus celebrated. In desperation Ovid turned to Greek mythology, with the usual disastrous result when attempts are made to define Roman religion as if it were synonymous with Greek mythology, falsely linking the Roman goddess to Anna, in Greek myth a sister to the ill-fated Carthaginian queen Dido.[28] Greater credence can be given Ovid's perpetuation of an antique Etrusco-Italic legend of Anna as an old hag of a goddess who intervened to protect the chastity of Minerva pursued by an aroused Mars, by disguising herself as the object of his desire and tricking the god into marrying her.[29] Several Roman antiquarians attest further connection between Minerva and Anna. The goddesses are said to have shared shrines and temples, especially that of Minerva on the Campus Martius. In a recent monograph Torelli demonstrates the *Quinquatrus* of Minerva, a four-day female puberty rite, commenced in the festival of Anna Perenna and terminated with rites to Minerva on March 19.[30] Martial similarly emphasized the role of Anna as a fertility goddess, remarking that Anna's grove took delight in virgin blood.[31] Macrobius, following Varro, records that offerings were presented to Anna Perenna *ut annare perennareque commode liceat.*[32] In this statement is revealed the true identity of Anna Perenna. She was a female personification of the year, *anna* a feminization of the common Latin masculine noun *annus*, and yet her divine function also extended to provide for the continuation of years—*perennare*. Anna Perenna, then, was the goddess of the continuing year cycle, presumably with power to extend or curtail the continuation of that cycle, and in that sense a goddess with power over life, and so ultimately a goddess of life force or fertility. Her cult was celebrated on the first day of the New Year, and for obvious reasons. The association of Anna Perenna with beginnings explains the introduction of Roman maidens on the first day of the year into a new cycle of life as women, as well as the particular form her rites of worship took.

It is important to remember that March 15 was the New Year's day of the Etruscans, introduced at Rome with the Etruscan calendar during the two centuries of Etruscan overlordship at Rome. Accordingly, it is in examining Etruscan religious practices and beliefs that the interconnection of the several March festivals may be best understood.

Recently discovered epigraphic evidence and other archaeological material from Veii and Caere (the Etruscan cities closest in geographical proximity to Rome and with which Rome was most frequently associated historically) reveal in those places the cult of an Etruscan Anna Thannr. *Thannr* aproximates in Etruscan the Latin term *Perenna*. In Etruria, Thannr (just as was Anna Perenna at Rome) was the goddess associated with the beginning of life and procreative force. Anna Perenna was often associated with or identified as the Etruscan goddess and also as Menrvra, the Etruscan Minerva who is a fertility mother-goddess figure linked to the netherworld in her role of having powers over life and death. Here is further indication that in Etruria, as later in Rome, the goddesses were very much associated. Indeed, it is likely that the March rites of Anna Perenna and Minerva celebrated at Rome derived from earlier Etruscan rites upon which they were patterned by Rome's Etruscan rulers.[33]

Several well-known and important Etruscan bronze mirrors are engraven with the figures of this Thannr Menrvra. In each case she is depicted presiding over a ceremony of gods and goddesses who are standing around an oversized funeral urn from which Menrvra is raising a baby labeled *Maris husrnana*, signifying in Etruscan—the young Maris.

A *cista* from Etruscan Praeneste is even more remarkable. Not an infant Maris, but a decrepit and aged Maris is portrayed as entering a cauldron of boiling water, only to emerge from it as a youthful Maris. Again, Menrvra is present as if assisting or overseeing the process.[34] A remarkable tale that is told by Aelian, himself a citizen of Praeneste, describes a chthonic centaur by the name of Maris who died thrice and was reborn thrice. Although the figure of Maris on the *cista* is clearly not that of a centaur (though the horse was, of course, nevertheless associated with both the Roman Mars and the Etruscan Maris as a sacred animal), the theme of the legend represented on the *cista* is the same as that of Aelian's story—rebirth and rejuvenation. A youthful Maris, the Etruscan god of time, and in Etruria a netherdivinity like Menrvra, is brought back to life, reclaimed to the upper world by Menrvra or Thannr, both of whom are at various times identified as the god's consort. All three of these Etruscan underworld deities possessed fertility functions and were associated with life, death, and time.[35]

In Etruria their rites would clearly have been linked to the ending and the beginning of the year. When the Etruscan calendar and religious year was introduced in the early sixth century at Rome, festivals of the Etruscan Maris and Thannr were celebrated on the Ides of March. Maris was later syncretically linked to the archaic Latin Mamors or Marmar due to the shared fertility functions of the gods and, no doubt, the similarity of their names. From the syncretism of the old Italic god and the Etruscan god emerged a Roman Mars whose March cult was celebrated under the Etruscanized name of the Latin Mamors – Mamurius. The cult of Mamurius was closely linked to that of Etruscan Maris and particularly emphasized Maris's function as a god of time.[36]

The name Veturius may have been added, not in fact because of any connection with the Latin *vetus*, but rather because an Etruscan family at Rome, the Veturii, performed priestly rites at the underground altar of Mars in the Campus Martius. It was here that the horse races which comprised the *Equirria* were presented.[37] This Etruscan chthonic Mars is further connected to the Campus Martius by its ancient function as a cemetery of honor for the most worthy of Romans and as an entrance to the underworld. A joint shrine to two of Maris's sometime consorts, Anna Perenna and Minerva, was also to be found in the Campus Martius, and Anna's grove of delights was immediately adjacent.[38]

The ritual observances offered to these Etruscan divinities on the first day of the New Year clearly associates that date with the Etruscan religious calendar. Moreover, the institution of the March New Year at Rome coincided with the establishment of the Etruscan monarchy in the sixth century and endured through the period of Etruscan overlordship at Rome, and beyond.

A final mention should be made of the irony of the assassination of Julius Caesar on the Ides of March, at one time Rome's holiest day. Caesar was, of course, not only sole head of the Roman state in 44 B.C. by virtue of his office of *dictator perpetuus*, but he was and had been since the year 63 *pontifex maximus*, chief priest of the state and titular head of the Roman religion. More significantly, he possessed many Etruscan associations and had modeled his ritual and propaganda as dictator on that of the early Etruscan kings of Rome. Some maintain that his assassination was a preventive measure lest the old Etruscan-style monarchy be reestablished.[39] The day, and Caesar's personal connection to it, make all the more credible the depiction of his murder in terms of ritual sacrifice.[40]

Notes

1. Though a relatively minor god in classical times, in earliest Rome Janus was one of the most important gods of the fledgling settlement. A thorough treatment of his cult is offered in L. A. Holland, *Janus and the Bridge* (Rome: American Academy in Rome, 1961).

2. The inauguration to magisterial office was a rite in which the gods were consulted through the taking of auspices to approve appointment to office and bestowal of the religious powers which comprised the authority of public office in the sacral society that was archaic Rome. See P. Catalano, *Contributi allo studio del diritto augurale, Università di Torino, Memorie del Instituto Giuridico,* ser. 2:107 (1960): 15, 65, 91, 94, 214, 220-25, 240-45, 280, 289, 330-55, 423, 437, 550-60.

3. A thorough and comprehensive treatment of the Roman calendar, before and after the time of Caesar, is A. K. Michels, *The Calendar of the Roman Republic* (Princeton: Princeton University Press, 1967). For basic calendric organization, see 31-83.

4. The pre-Julian calendars are reviewed in Michels, *Calendar of the Roman Republic,* 3-30; also see H. H. Scullard, *Festivals and Ceremonies of the Roman Republic* (Ithaca, NY: Cornell University Press, 1981), 41-49; H. Hauben, "Some Observations on the Early Roman Calendar," *Ancient Society* 11-12 (1980-81): 241-55.

5. Hauben, "Some Observations on the Early Roman Calendar," 241.

6. Macrobius, *Saturnalia* I, 12, 6; Ovid, *Fasti* III, 135-36. No epigraphic evidence survives to corroborate the literary testimony. Though a number of *fasti,* official state calendars, survive in inscriptional form, all postdate the time of the calendar reform which established January as the year's first month. See W. W. Fowler, *The Roman Festivals of the Period of the Republic* (London: Macmillan, 1916), 11-13, and A. E. Samuel, *Greek and Roman Chronology: Calendars and Years in Classical Antiquity* (Munich: Beck, 1972), 153-54.

7. Fowler, *Roman Festivals of the Period of the Republic*, 5-7, provides a brief summary of evidence for March as the beginning of the Roman year in pre-Julian calendars.

8. Mommsen's discussion of the matter is found in his commentary on the passage in *CIL* I, 337. See also his *Die römische Chronologie bis auf Caesar*, 2nd ed. (Berlin: Weidmannsche Buchhandlung, 1859). A modern defense of Mommsen's position is made by W. Sontheimer, *Kleine Pauly*, 5 vols. (Stuttgart: Drückenmüller, 1967), 2:527, s.v. *Februarius* and col. 2:1311, s.v. *Ianuarius*. See also Hauben, "Some Observations on the Early Roman Calendar," 245, though Michels's Appendix 4 in *The Calendar of the Roman Republic* (207-32) is the most complete recent discussion of the problem.

9. Michels, *Calendar of the Roman Republic*, 25, 97, and n. 10; Samuel, *Greek and Roman Chronology*, 164; Hauben, "Some Observations on the Early Roman Calendar," 245.

10. Michels, *Calendar of the Roman Republic*, 97-99; Hauben, "Some Observations on the Early Roman Calendar," 45; for March 15 consular inaugurations up until 153 B.C. see T. R. S. Broughton, *The Magistrates of the Roman Republic*, 3 vols. (New York: American Philological Association, 1952), 2:637-39.

11. Cicero, *Atticus* VI, 1, 8, notes the involvement of the *decemviri* in calendar reform, but the account of Macrobius, *Saturnalia* I, 13, 21, citing as sources the early historians Sempronius Tuditanus and Cassius Hemina, provides more complete information in ascribing the origin of the first republican calendar to a decemviral law.

12. Michels, *Calendar of the Roman Republic*, 119-44, offers a detailed discussion of the problem with careful analysis of existing primary sources.

13. The Latin *idus* derives from the Etruscan *itus*, thus revealing the Etruscan origin not only of the term Ides, but also of the organizational system of the Roman calendar, according to Varro, *De Lingua Latina* VI, 4, and Macrobius, *Saturnalia* I, 15, 14-17. The occasion of each and every Ides was sacred to the Roman Juppiter and his Etruscan counterpart, Tinia. For such gods of light, the day of the month when the heavens were illuminated not only during the day but also at night by the brilliance of the full moon, seemed appropriately sacred. Varro, *De Lingua Latina* V, 47, and *Festus* 372 L, inform us that the Ides' sheep, or *ovis idulis*, was sacrificed to Juppiter by his own priest, the flamen Dialis, in the sacred precinct of Juppiter erected by the Etruscans on the *arx* of the Capitoline Hill. See also Macrobius, *Saturnalia* I, 15, 16. For Etruscan involvement in the calendar's development, see the note which follows.

14. The traditional legend of Numa as the author of Rome's religious and calendric system must be reconsidered in light of historical and archaeological evidence of the sort alluded to above, evidence which continues to appear as more is learned of the Etruscans and their important role in archaic Rome. Their involvement in the formulation of Rome's religious system was, however, not completely unknown in antiquity. Censorinus, *De Die Natali* 18, rejected the Numa fable and asserted that the origin of the twelve-month calendar was later, citing as his authority Junius Gracchanus who attributed the creation of January and February to the Etruscan Tarquin, and the development of intercalation to Servius Tullius, whose Etruscan background has recently been confirmed in R. Thomsen, *King Servius Tullius: A Historical Synthesis* (Copenhagen: Gyldendal, 1980). On the larger question of the so-called calendar of Numa as an Etruscan borrowing, see Michels, *Calendar of the Roman Republic*, 121-24 and 132-34.

15. Epigraphic evidence confirms that the Etruscan month of *Velcitna* began the Etruscan year and corresponded to the first month on the Roman calendar, March. See M. Pallottino, *Testimonia Linguae Etruscae*, 2nd ed. (Florence: Leo Olschki Editore, 1954), #856. For a discussion of the Etruscan calendar, see A. J. Pfiffig, *Religio Etrusca* (Graz: Akademische Druck- und Verlagsanstalt, 1975), 91-94.

16. Numerous *fasti* attest the religious events of March in general and the Ides in particular. The best summary of this information is to be found in H. H. Scullard, *Festivals and Ceremonies of the Roman Republic* (Ithaca, NY: Cornell University Press, 1981), 84-95, 258, 260. See also Fowler, *Roman Festivals of the Period of the Republic*, 33-65.

17. The rites of both ceremonies are detailed in Ovid, *Fasti* III, 351-94; Dionysius Halicarnassus, *Antiquitates Romanae* II, 71; Plutarch, *Numa* 13. See also Scullard, *Festivals and Ceremonies of the Roman Republic*, 84-87. The particular use of the laurel in connection with New Year rites of expiation, an important role of the Mars worshipped in earliest Rome (see below), is discussed in Hugh W. Nibley, "Sparsiones," *Classical Journal* 40 (1945): 517.

18. Contra Fowler, *Roman Festivals of the Period of the Republic*, 38-42, who argues that March 1 was the first day of the year, since it was the first day of the first month of the year. Other than the premise that the New Year's day must be the first day of the first month of the year, a premise that does not necessarily follow if the New Year's day was determined by considerations of religious ritual, the only evidence Fowler can adduce to substantiate his contention is the information that the sacred *ancile* were twelve in number, and

so must represent the twelve months of the year, thus symbolizing the advent of the New Year.

19. Fowler, *Roman Festivals of the Period of the Republic*, 44; Scullard, *Festivals and Ceremonies of the Roman Republic*, 89.

20. Ovid, *Fasti* III, 517-22.

21. The problem arises in the conflicting evidence of three surviving calendars which mention on March 14 a festival of Mars associated with horse races, a late imperial almanac of Philocalus (*CIL* I, 254), and rustic calendars (*menologia rustica* in *CIL* I, 281-82) also of late date which note for March 14 a festival of Mamurius, but make no mention of an *Equirria*. Mommsen, *CIL* I, 311, opines that the *Equirria* was the proper ceremony, and he is followed by Fowler, *Roman Festivals of the Period of the Republic*, 45-46. That the *Mamuralia* was actually the original festival of March 14 is held by H. Usener, "Italische Mythen," *Rheinisches Museum für Philologie* 30 (1875): 182-229, especially 209-13; and by J. G. Frazer, *The Golden Bough*, 2 vols. (London: Macmillan, 1890), 2:208. The latter view is based on acceptance of the testimony of Lydus, *De Mensibus* IV, 49, as well as that of earlier and more reliable authors who associate Mamurius Veturius with the events of March 14 and 15 (see below). A thorough presentation of the controversy is found in Fowler, *Roman Festivals of the Period of the Republic*, 44-50. See also Scullard, *Festivals and Ceremonies of the Roman Republic*, 89.

22. A. Illuminati, "Mamurius Veturius," *Studi e materiali di storia delle religioni* 32 (1961): 48 and n. 18. The most complete discussion on the derivation and development of the nomenclature of Mars is H. Wagenvoort, "The Origin of the Ludi Saeculares," *Studies in Roman Literature, Culture, and Religion* (Leiden: Brill, 1956), 207-12.

23. Ovid, *Fasti* III, 259-398. See also Illuminati, "Mamurius Veturius," 41-43; Scullard, *Festivals and Ceremonies of the Roman Republic*, 89.

24. Varro, *Festus* 117 L; Servius, *Commentarius in Aeneidem* VII, 188. Both accounts probably derive from work on the subject by the noted antiquarian Varro (Scullard, *Festivals and Ceremonies of the Roman Republic*, 89). Other sources also seem to follow Varro's version of Mamurius' activities; see Plutarch, *Numa* 4, 8, 15, 17; Pliny, *Naturalis Historia* XXXIV, 1. See also the treatment accorded Mamurius in Propertius IV, 2, 61; and Minucius Felix, *Octavius* XXIV, 3. The most complete accounting of references to Mamurius by ancient sources is Illuminati, "Mamurius Veturius," 41-64.

25. The true function of the god Mars in Etruscan and pre-Etruscan Rome is best explained in connection with his chthonic and

secular role, examined in considerable detail in Wagenvoort, "The Origin of the Ludi Saeculares," 193-232. See also John F. Hall, "The Saeculum Novum of Augustus and Its Etruscan Antecedents," in *Aufstieg und Niedergang der römischen Welt* (Berlin: de Gruyter, 1986), 2564-89. Much useful information is also found throughout Illuminati, "Mamurius Veturius," 41-80.

26. G. Wissowa, "De Feriis," 9-13, in W. H. Roscher, *Ausführliches Lexikon der griechischen und römischen Mythologie* (Berlin: Weidmannsche Buchhandlung, 1902). A discussion of Wissowa's contention is found in both Scullard, *Festivals and Ceremonies of the Roman Republic*, 89; and Fowler, *Roman Festivals of the Period of the Republic*, 44-48.

27. Ovid, *Fasti*, III, 523-42. The grove sacred to Anna Perenna and the site of her "bawdy fertility festival" has been shown to have been located in Via Flaminia ad lapidem primum, near the present site of Porta del Popolo. See R. E. A. Palmer, *Roman Religion and Roman Empire* (Philadelphia: University of Pennsylvania Press, 1973), 200; and Scullard, *Festivals and Ceremonies of the Roman Republic*, 90.

28. Ovid, *Fasti* III, 543-656. See also Scullard, *Festivals and Ceremonies of the Roman Republic*, 90.

29. Ovid, *Fasti* III, 660-96.

30. The role of Minerva as a goddess entrusted with overseeing the coming of age of Roman maidens and her association in this regard with Anna Perenna, a fertility goddess connected with the consummation of sexual activity for young women, even to the "duplicazioni di culti, di feste, e di santuari di Minerva e di Anna Perenna," is clearly demonstrated in M. Torelli, *Lavinio e Roma: riti iniziatici e matrimonio tra archeologia e storia* (Rome: Quasar, 1984), 62-74. Torelli also indicates that Mars, interestingly, fills a corresponding role in his guise as fertility god for young men at Rome (111-14). The connection of the three in the Etrusco-Italic legend referred to by Ovid is thus explained.

31. Martial, *Epigrammata* IV, 6, 16, makes clear allusion here to the fertility rites linked to the coming of age of Roman maidens.

32. Macrobius, *Saturnalia* I, 12, 6. Torelli, *Lavinio e Roma*, 57, argues that the usually reliable Varro is the source of Macrobius in these matters. For a summary of primary evidence and scholarly opinion on Anna Perenna, see R. Lamacchia, "Annae Festum Geniale Perennae," *Parola del Passato* 16 (1958): 381-404.

33. The evidence for the cult of Anna Thannr is summarized in Pfiffig, *Religio Etrusca*, 304-6.

34. Wagenvoort, "The Origin of the Ludi Saeculares," 213-22, offers a detailed explication of this evidence.

35. Aelian, *Varia Historia* IX, 16. See Wagenvoort, "The Origin of the Ludi Saeculares," 220-26. See also G. Hermansen, "Mares, Maris, Mars, and the Archaic Gods," *Studi Etruschi* 54 (1986): 147-64.

36. On the fertility and funereal function of the Mars cult and its association with the time and the beginning of the year, see Wagenvoort, "The Origin of the Ludi Saeculares," passim; Hermansen, "Mares, Maris, Mars, and the Archaic Gods," passim; Nibley, "Sparsiones," 516, 519-20; Hall, "The Saeculum Novum of Augustus and Its Etruscan Antecedents," 2569-74.

37. The rites of Mamurius Veturius, their specific conduct and their administration by the Veturii is explained in Illuminati, "Mamurius Veturius," 51-80.

38. Wagenvoort, "The Origin of the Ludi Saeculares," 210-13; Hall, "The Saeculum Novum of Augustus and Its Etruscan Antecedents," 2569-74.

39. John F. Hall, "The Municipal Aristocracy of Etruria and their Participation in Politics at Rome, B.C. 91 - A.D. 14," Ph.D. diss., University of Pennsylvania, 1984, 101-27; S. Weinstock, *Divus Julius* (Oxford: Oxford University Press, 1971), 175-79, 270-364.

40. Nibley, "Sparsiones," 525.

26

The Honey and the Smoke: Achilles and *Atē* in the *Iliad*

R. Douglas Phillips
Brigham Young University, Provo, Utah

In the ninth book of the *Iliad*, in a speech intended to persuade Achilles to return to the war, Phoenix warns his young friend, who has just reiterated his denunciation of Agamemnon and his blindness (*Iliad* 9.377, *ek gar eu phrenas heileto mētieta Zeus*: "For Zeus the counsellor has taken away his wits"), that he, Achilles himself, is in danger of succumbing to the same state of mind if he refuses Agamemnon's offer of reconciliation and rejects the embassy. Phoenix's warning takes the form of an allegory or parable in which a man who commits an offense may gain pardon if he allows the *Litai* (Prayers), the daughters of Zeus, to intercede in his behalf; but if he refuses, then *Atē* (which we here translate as "delusion") visits the unrepentant transgressor and punishes him:

> For there also the Prayers (*Litai*), the daughters of Zeus,
> and they are lame of their feet, and wrinkled, and cast
>   their eyes sidelong,
> who toil on their way left far behind by *Atē*;
> but she, *Atē*, strong and sound on her feet, and therefore
> far outruns all Prayers, and wins into every country
> to force men astray; and the Prayers follow as healers
>   after her.
> If a man venerates these daughters of Zeus as they draw
>   near,
> such a man they bring great advantage, and hear his
>   entreaty;

but if a man shall deny them, and stubbornly with a
    harsh word
refuse, they go to Zeus, son of Kronos, in supplication
that *Até* may overtake this man, that he be hurt, and
    punished.
So Achilleus: grant, you also, that Zeus' daughters be
    given
their honour, which, lordly though they be, curbs the
    will of others.

Iliad 9.502-14

This is the first hint we find in the epic that Achilles, who
as the wronged party in the quarrel has been blameless to
this point, as Phoenix himself points out, may fall victim
to *até*. The question whether he does in fact succumb to it
arises since he does reject Agamemnon's offer.

Some, like Cedric Whitman, reject the idea that Achilles
is a victim of *até*: "The highest heroes," he writes, "are not
men of delusion."[1] And although he does discuss other
parts of Phoenix's speech, such as the Meleager story,
which ironically has exactly the opposite effect on Achilles
to that which Phoenix intended, he does not mention the
allegory of *Até* and the *Litai* at all. For Whitman, the members of the embassy—Odysseus, Aias, and Phoenix—are
bound to the "simple assumptions" of the conventional
heroic code, and cannot therefore understand Achilles'
conception of his own honor, for which, according to Whitman, he wills his own death to maintain his integrity.
Phoenix offers an easy answer, says Whitman, which
Achilles cannot accept. The idea, therefore, that Achilles,
like some of the other major heroes in the story (e.g.,
Hector, Agamemnon, Patroclus, and so forth), might have
become a victim to delusion, as Phoenix implies he will if
he spurns Agamemnon's offer, would be fatal to his interpretation.

Martin Mueller, on the other hand, sees in Achilles the
blinded and deluded hero. Indeed, from the moment when
he asks Thetis for Zeus's help in Book 1, to his disillu-

sionment through the death of Patroclus, delusion is the essential part of his tragedy. But Mueller does not discuss the source or nature of his delusion, nor does he refer to him as a victim of *atē*. For this reason he does not refer to Phoenix's parable. Doyle, in his recent book on *atē*, does deal with the language of Phoenix's parable, but he does not discuss the implications for Achilles.[2]

Assuming that Phoenix's parable and its implied warning were intended by Homer to be taken seriously, we should like to see whether Achilles did in fact fall victim to *atē* and what form his delusion took. If, however, we follow those like J. Bremer, in his work *Hamartia*, and others who maintain that *atē* is a blindness or delusion caused by malicious divine interference, then it is easy to show that Achilles does not fit this pattern, and Bremer himself acknowledges the difficulty: "In Achilles' case, too, the element of divine intervention and malicious interference is there, though less marked and prominent than in, e.g., the case of Patroclus,"[3] although the only evidence that Bremer can produce is Phoenix's speech (which is, as we have seen, thoroughly allegorical, that is, *atē* is not to be seen as a real "goddess"), a problematical statement of Aias, also in Book 9, which we shall examine presently, and Achilles' words at Book 19.270-74, where he refers to Zeus's having deluded Agamemnon. These words supposedly apply also to Achilles, since he in turn was indirectly a victim of the *atē* or delusion that befell Agamemnon.

Aias's remarks in Book 9 on Achilles' mental state, referred to above, are significant since they provide a good example of the complex motivation of the heroes in the *Iliad* that Albin Lesky describes in his study of divine and human motivation in the Homeric epic.[4] At verses 628-32 Aias, who feels that Achilles is beyond persuasion, says:

> Achilleus
> has made savage the proud-hearted spirit (*thymos*)
>   within his body.
> He is hard and does not remember that friends'
>   affection
> wherein we honored him by the ships, far beyond all
>   others.
> Pitiless.
>
> *Iliad* 9.628-32

But at verse 636, he says:

> But *the gods* put in your breast a spirit (*thymos*)
> not to be placated, bad, for the sake of a single
> girl.
>
> *Iliad* 9.636-38

In the next verse, however, it is Achilles himself who is responsible:

> Now make gracious the spirit (*thymos*) within you.
>
> *Iliad* 9.639

One is reminded here of the passages from the book of Exodus, where, on the one hand, the Lord says to Moses: "See that thou do all those wonders before Pharaoh, which I have put in thine hand; but I will harden his heart that he shall not let the people go" (Exodus 4:21), but elsewhere we read: "And when Pharaoh saw that the rain and hail and the thunders were ceased, he sinned yet more, and hardened his heart, he and his servants" (Exodus 9:34-35).

But Achilles' reply to Aias is perhaps more to the point when he says, without any reference to the gods:

> All that you have said seems spoken after my own
>   mind.
> Yet still the heart in me swells up in anger (*cholos*),
>   when I remember
> the disgrace that he wrought upon me before the
>   Argives,

> the Son of Atreus, as if I were some dishonored
> vagabond.
>
> *Iliad* 9.645-48

We shall have occasion to return to this idea of the heart swelling with anger.

Since there are clear intimations of tragedy in Phoenix's and Aias's words to Achilles, if Homer means for us to take them seriously, as I believe he does, it would be surprising, I think, if Homer did not compose some part in his epic to correspond to and balance the speeches in Book 9, especially Phoenix's warning regarding *atē*. It would be dramatically effective to see his words fulfilled. We do witness, in Achilles' sending Patroclus to Nestor's tent in Book 11, a chain of events that begins to operate on Patroclus's own feelings, events that have nothing at all to do with divine influence or intervention, but which become an essential part of Patroclus's *atē*, and we see in Achilles' allowing him to go into battle in his stead and with his armor in Book 16, a man making fatal decisions without foreseeing the consequences. We can agree with Mueller that what characterizes Achilles in these decisions and acts is the unreality of his thinking, which Mueller calls "the rhetoric of the unreal." He writes, for example:

> When Patroclus asks for the arms of Achilles and for permission to defend the Achaeans, Achilles at first does not answer his request but instead indulges in the memory of the injustice that he has suffered at the hands of Agamemnon. The present situation would not seem so bleak, he argues, if Agamemnon had treated him kindly (16.72). From his rehearsal of past injuries his mind moves on to an imagined future. He will allow Patroclus to help the Achaeans, and as a result of this partial change of mind he expects that the Achaeans will honor him and bring him presents. It has always baffled critics how Achilles at this stage could not only omit any mention of Agamemnon's previous offer, but could ex-

press a desire for "gifts" when he had so violently rejected the treasures that Agamemnon had promised him.
The rhetoric of the unreal provides the solution to this
difficulty. The significance of Achilles' speech lies not in
its psychological continuity with the past but in the violent contrast it establishes between his indulgence in
an imaginary future and the actual reality that awaits
him.[5]

We see this unreality and delusion in Achilles' thinking
reach its climax in his prayer at Book 16 that he and Patroclus alone may sack Troy, a delusion underscored by
the irony that these two heroes will *not* be present on that
occasion:

> Father Zeus, Athene and Apollo, if only
> not one of all the Trojans could escape destruction,
>   not one
> of the Argives, but you and I could emerge from the
>   slaughter
> so that we two alone could break Troy's hallowed
>   coronal.
>
> Iliad 16.97-100

Thereupon, "at the deepest point of delusion," to use
Mueller's words, he sends his friend into battle and to his
death.[6]

We expect, then, after the death of Patroclus, some
statement on the part of Achilles expressing his disillu-
sionment and recognizing the mental state which has
caused him to commit his fatal error, a recognition such
as we have in the case of Hector, for example, or Agamemnon. Nor are we disappointed. In Book 18, after the
news of Patroclus's death is brought to him, Achilles, in
his long conversation with his mother, experiences a kind
of *anagnorisis* or recognition. When Thetis reveals to her
son that if he kills Hector in avenging Patroclus's death,
he must then lose his own life, Achilles delivers what
Malcolm Willcock calls "a very powerful and psychologi-

cally motivated speech comparable to Achilles' great speech of Book 9.308-409.'' [7] Totally disillusioned, Achilles says:

> May I die soon then; since I was not to stand by my
>   companion
> when he was killed. And now, far away from the land
>   of his fathers,
> he has perished, and lacked my fighting strength to
>   defend him.
>
> *Iliad* 18.98-100

> Now I shall go, to overtake that killer of a dear life,
> Hektor; then I will accept my own death at whatever
> time Zeus wishes to bring it about, and the other
>   immortals.
>
> *Iliad* 18.114-16

Placed at the center of this speech and forming the emotional climax is an outburst, a hopeless and anguished wish, by Achilles, which must apply to him especially and which provides the best insight into the true nature of his wrath and the blindness that it has produced, and which may be regarded as that *atē*, which Phoenix in Book 9 had warned would befall him:

> Why, I wish that strife would vanish from gods and
>   mortals
> and gall (*cholos*), which makes a man grow angry for
>   all his great mind,
> that gall of anger that swarms like smoke inside a
>   man's heart
> and becomes a thing sweeter to him by far than the
>   dripping of honey.
> So it was here that the lord of men Agamemnon
>   angered me.
>
> *Iliad* 18.107-11

In using the figures of the smoke and the honey in this striking double simile to describe Achilles' mental and emotional state, Homer shows himself not only a sensitive poet but a sound psychologist. The gradual and imperceptible darkening of the mind suggested by the image of the "smoke from a very small smouldering fire that fills all the house," as Leaf puts it in his comment on this passage,[8] recalls Achilles' words to Aias in Book 9.644-48, quoted above: "Yet still the heart in me swells up in anger (*cholos*)." Although some commentators see in the figure of the dripping honey the idea that anger slips easily like honey down the throat, it is more likely that Homer uses it to suggest how Achilles' anger and the hurt which produced it have become so delicious to him as he indulged himself, that he could not bring himself to give it up until it was too late, and now he curses it. The image of the sweet honey used in connection with *cholos* may be a little surprising and paradoxical since it literally means "gall" or "bile" and when used metaphorically refers to a "bitter anger." But Homer surely knew human nature well enough to know how sweet anger and resentment can be to one who sulks, and it is most important to note that it is Achilles himself who uses the simile, showing that he himself is eminently aware of the consequences of his anger.

When we consider the significance of this passage, that it constitutes Achilles' own statement on his mental and emotional state when he made the most disastrous decision of his life, that it is found in one of his most important speeches in the *Iliad*, and, as I believe, in a passage which Homer intended as a recognition, then it is safe to say that he is here referring to his blindness or delusion or *atē*, which destroyed his judgment, as Phoenix had warned that it would. This can be seen particularly in the words at verse 108, which in spite of the gnomic aorist must refer to Achilles' own case:

kai cholos, hos t' epheēke polyphrona per chalepēnai
and gall, which makes a man grow angry for all his
   great mind.

Iliad 18.108

It is significant that there is no mention here of any malicious interfering deity or god. So far as any outside agency inciting Achilles' *atē* is concerned, it is to be found in Agamemnon.

It is clear, then, that the source for Achilles' blindness or *atē* is to be found in his own being. Yet it appears to be an article of faith among some critics that Homer could not possibly have conceived of any delusion or *atē* that was not caused by an external divine agency, and that he could not have imagined a delusion that came from a man's own personality. This view takes its extreme form in the words of Bremer: "The Homeric conception of *atē* relates the error to an arbitrary and malicious interference of the gods with human action, causing infatuation in man and resulting in disaster."[9]

It may be objected that since Homer does not use the word *atē* in this passage, or, more correctly, that he does not have Achilles use it of himself, specifically of his state of mind, he cannot be thinking of it. Yet there is one other nearly equally important instance in the *Iliad* in which a hero is deluded and may properly be said to have become a victim of *atē*, without the word actually being used in his case. It seems to me that one cannot read the *Iliad* without believing that Homer expects us to see Hector as much blinded or deluded as was Agamemnon or Patroclus or Paris, who are specifically described as victims of *atē*. After he shows us Hector in his disturbing scenes with Poulydamas earlier, in his dangerous overconfidence at the end of Book 8, in his taunting of the dying Patroclus in Book 16, Homer says of him in Book 18 as Hector makes *his* disastrous mistake when he rejects the wise counsel of Poulydamas to lead the Trojan forces into the citadel of Troy and not remain that night on the battlefield:

> So spoke Hektor, and the Trojans thundered to hear him;

fools, since Pallas Athene had taken away the wits
   from them.
They gave their applause to Hektor in his counsel of
   evil,
but none to Poulydamas, who had spoken good sense
   before them.

Iliad 18.310-13

And yet when Hector has his moment of recognition in
Book 22, before the gates of Troy, shackled by his fate
(*moira*), as Homer says, where he refers to this very incident
and his fatal mistake in rejecting the warning of Poulydamas, he does not ascribe his error and delusion to Athene
or any other god, but to his *atasthaliai*, his own recklessness.
In his case, then, we cannot take the phrase that "Pallas
Athene took away the wits" in Book 18 as the whole or
even the most important element in his delusion. I suspect
that a careful examination of other examples of delusion
or *atē* in the *Iliad* from the standpoint of Homer's imaginative use of poetic language — for example, in the so-called
apology of Agamemnon, and from his dramatic technique
as found in his portrayal of Patroclus's career — would, as
in the case of the simile of the honey and the smoke, reveal
a much less rigid conception of *atē* and a greater appreciation of Homer's use of motivation in the *Iliad*.

In conclusion, I think that Homer intended us to see
Achilles as a victim of *atē* in fulfillment of Phoenix's warning in Book 9, but that this delusion had its source in his
own nature and being, as Homer's magnificent simile suggests, and was not due to the external operation of some
malignant god.

Notes

1. Cedric Whitman, *Homer and the Heroic Tradition* (New York:
Norton, 1965), 189.

2. Richard E. Doyle, "*Atē, Its Use and Meaning: A Study in the
Greek Poetic Tradition from Homer to Euripides* (New York: Fordham
University Press, 1984), 9-11.

3. J. M. Bremer, *Hamartia: Tragic Error in the Poetics of Aristotle and in Greek Tragedy* (Amsterdam: Hakkert, 1969), 110.

4. Albin Lesky, *Göttliche und menschliche Motivation in homerischen Epos* (Heidelberg: Winter Verlag, 1961).

5. Martin Mueller, "Knowledge and Delusion in the *Iliad*," in John Wright, ed., *Essays on the Iliad* (Bloomington: Indiana University Press, 1978), 118.

6. Martin Mueller, *The Iliad*, Unwin Critical Library (London: George Allen and Unwin, 1984), 50.

7. Malcolm Willcock, *A Companion to the Iliad* (Chicago: University of Chicago Press, 1976), 204.

8. Walter Leaf, *The Iliad*, 2nd ed. (London: Macmillan, 1902), 2:277.

9. Bremer, *Hamartia*, 111-12.

Index of Passages

671

Index of Names and Subjects

691